INTERPRETING JESUS

INTERPRETING JESUS

DALE C. ALLISON JR.

WILLIAM B. EERDMANS PUBLISHING COMPANY
GRAND RAPIDS, MICHIGAN

Wm. B. Eerdmans Publishing Co.
2006 44th Street SE, Grand Rapids, MI 49508
www.eerdmans.com

Published 2025

Book design by Lydia Hall

Printed in the United States of America

31 30 29 28 27 26 25 2 3 4 5 6 7

ISBN 978-0-8028-7919-6

Library of Congress Cataloging-in-Publication Data

A catalog record for this book is available from the Library of Congress.

Translations of Scripture and other ancient sources are the author's own unless otherwise noted.

For Clifton and Father George

ἔνθεν δὲ προτέρω πλέομεν ἀκαχήμενοι ἦτορ
. . . φίλους ὀλέσαντες ἑταίρους

—*Odyssey* 9.565–66

Contents

Preface

> The only apology that I can offer for writing so incompletely and inconclusively is that it is preferable to writing conclusively and mistakenly.
>
> —Alasdair MacIntyre[1]

After completing *Constructing Jesus* (2010), which I firmly believed would be my last book on the historical Jesus, I said to my wife, "Honey, I'm done with Jesus." Her immediate response was: "He'll be glad to hear that." But I was wrong. I have been unable to stay away. What he thinks now I do not know.

The proximate cause of this book is chapter 3, which I conceived shortly after Jeff Kripal asked me to write an essay on Jesus for an introductory handbook on religion.[2] That essay, aimed at undergraduates, remained on a popular level, and I wanted to develop its argument for an academic audience. So I wrote what was, in retrospect, an earlier version of chapter 3 and submitted it to a mainline journal. It was not accepted. One reviewer thought I was naïve and credulous regarding multiple matters. The other took me to be too skeptical regarding the Gospels yet too generous regarding extraordinary claims outside the Bible. Though irked, I was not surprised. Peer review typically represents, for understandable reasons, the status quo, and my submission was not the status quo.

In trying to come to terms with my reviewers' objections, which to my

1. MacIntyre, *Difficulties in Christian Belief*, 50.
2. Allison, "Paranormal Jesus."

mind stemmed more from our differing worldviews than from my reasoning, I contemplated the editor's kind offer to rewrite the piece. But I finally declined. It occurred that publication in a book would allow me the freedom to say exactly what I wished without bending sentences to please shadowy, anonymous figures looking over my shoulder. It also occurred that one more book on Jesus—who after all my years of study remains such a "strange figure"[3]—would allow me to unfold additional ideas that I had not previously found the time to develop for publication.

Chapters 2, 3, and 6 incorporate portions of the Kent Shaffer Lectures, which I gave at Yale Divinity School in April 2023. I am grateful to Harry Attridge, Adela Yarbro Collins, John Collins, Judy Gundry, Teresa Morgan, Lynn Haversat, Laura Nasrallah, Gregory Sterling, and Miroslav Volf for their hospitality on that pleasant occasion. I also read portions of chapter 3 for "The Archives of the Impossible" conference at Rice University in 2023. Chapter 1 greatly expands an essay published in a Festschrift honoring Craig Evans,[4] an essay that was in turn based on the Kennedy-Wright Lecture for the Centre for the Study of Christian Origins, University of Edinburgh (2019), and the Roland E. Murphy Memorial Lecture at the Catholic University of America (2020). A few pages in chapter 6 integrate portions of yet another lecture, this one delivered at a conference on the Bible and Cyprus and subsequently published in a volume of the proceedings.[5]

I wish to emphasize that my goals in the following pages are, as in my previous books on Jesus, strictly limited. *Interpreting Jesus* is a book of pensées, an anthology of miscellaneous pieces. It addresses a handful of topics that interest me, topics to which I believe I have my two mites to contribute. My ambition reaches no further. I hope the volume is not criticized for failing to meet larger ends to which it does not aspire.

I have tried, while writing these chapters, to read as many relevant books and articles as I could. But the appearance of proficiency can be only an illusory facade. The ever-growing number of new publications is not daunting: it is overwhelming. The pages are as the sands of the sea. They long ago surpassed anyone's ability to count them, much less read them. I am accordingly left in the slough of despond. Although I read as much now as ever and so continue to learn more and more, it often feels like less and less because the

3. So Nietzsche, *Antichrist*, 95. The German is *fremde Gestalt*. Cf. Schweitzer, *Quest of the Historical Jesus*, 478: "The historical Jesus is to our time a stranger [*Fremdling*]."

4. Allison, "Contingent Eschatology."

5. Allison, "Cyprus and Early Christianity."

percentage of published pages I am able to peruse keeps shrinking. The miserable upshot is that, despite my best efforts, I must at many points herein fail to cite or interact with germane contributions, many of them undoubtedly of real import. I lament the neglect, confess my failing, anticipate embarrassment, and apologize in advance to their authors.

Over the many years that enduring curiosity has kept me pondering the historical Jesus, my conversation partners have been many. I forgo a futile attempt to recall and recite all their names. I cannot, however, let this book go without thanking my student assistants—Carlos Acosta and Jackson Reynolds—and mentioning those who have commented on parts of this manuscript, conversed with me about its contents, or of late offered sincerely appreciated encouragement: Kristine Allison, Eric Barreto, Clifton Black, Lisa Bowens, John Burgess, James Ernest, Tucker Ferda, Mike Grosso, Jones Otisi Kalu, Ed Kelly, Chris Kettler, Jeff Kripal, Amy-Jill Levine, Robert Lipscomb, Joseph Luigs, Joel Marcus, Bertrand Méheust, Kaitlynn Merckling, Michael Murphy, James Neumann, David Neville, Elaine Pagels, George Parsenios, Heiner Schwenke, and John Wilson. Ὀφειλέτης εἰμί.

Abbreviations

All abbreviations used for ancient sources follow section 8.3 of *The SBL Handbook of Style*. 2nd ed. Atlanta: SBL Press, 2014.

AB	Anchor Bible
ABG	Arbeiten zur Bible und Ihrer Geschichte
AGJU	Arbeiten zur Geschichte des antiken Judentums und des Urchristentums
AGSU	Arbeiten zur Geschichte des Spätjudentums und Urchristentums
AnBib	Analecta Biblica
ANTJ	Arbeiten zum Neuen Testament und Judentum
AsJT	*Asia Journal of Theology*
ASNU	Acta Seminarii Neotestamentici Upsaliensis
ATR	*Australasian Theological Review*
AUSS	*Andrews University Seminary Studies*
AYRL	Anchor Yale Bible Reference Library
BBB	Bonner biblische Beiträge
BBR	*Bulletin for Biblical Research*
BDAG	Danker, Frederick W., Walter Bauer, William F. Arndt, and F. Wilbur Gingrich. *Greek-English Lexicon of the New Testament and Other Early Christian Literature*. 3rd ed. Chicago: University of Chicago Press, 2000
BeO	*Bibbia e oriente*
BETL	Bibliotheca Ephemeridum Theologicarum Lovaniensium
BGBE	Beiträge zur Geschichte der biblischen Exegese
BI	*Biblical Illustrator*
Bib	*Biblica*
BibAn	*The Biblical Annals*

BibInt	*Biblical Interpretation*
BibInt	Biblical Interpretation Series
BJS	Brown Judaic Studies
BR	*Biblical Research*
BRev	*Bible Review*
BTB	*Biblical Theology Bulletin*
BThSt	Biblisch-Theologische Studien
BTS	Biblical Tools and Studies
BWANT	Beiträge zur Wissenschaft vom Alten (und Neuen) Testament
BZ	*Biblische Zeitschrift*
BZAW	Beihefte zur Zeitschrift für die alttestamentliche Wissenschaft
BZNW	Beihefte zur Zeitschrift für die neutestamentliche Wissenschaft
CAP	Cowley, Arthur E. *Aramaic Papyri of the Fifth Century B.C.* Oxford: Clarendon, 1923
CBQ	*Catholic Biblical Quarterly*
CBQMS	Catholic Biblical Quarterly Monograph Series
CBR	*Currents in Biblical Research*
CEJL	Commentaries on Early Jewish Literature
CGTC	Cambridge Greek Testament Commentary
ConBNT	Coniectanea Biblica: New Testament
CSCO	Corpus Scriptorum Christianorum Orientalium. Edited by Jean Baptiste Chabot et al. Paris, 1903
DCLS	Deuterocanonical and Cognate Literature Studies
DJD	Discoveries in the Judaean Desert
DSD	*Dead Sea Discoveries*
EBib	Études bibliques
EC	*Early Christianity*
EHS.T	Europäische Hochschulschriften. Theologie
EJL	Early Judaism and Its Literature
EKKNT	Evangelisch-katholischer Kommentar zum Neuen Testament
ETL	*Ephemerides Theologicae Lovanienses*
ETS	Erfurter theologische Studien
EvQ	*Evangelical Quarterly*
ExpTim	*Expository Times*
FB	Forschung zur Bibel
FRLANT	Forschungen zur Religion und Literatur des Alten und Neuen Testaments
HBS	Herder's Biblical Studies
HBT	*Horizons in Biblical Theology*

HeyJ	*Heythrop Journal*
HibJ	*Hibbert Journal*
HThKNT	Herders Theologischer Kommentar zum Neuen Testament
HTR	*Harvard Theological Review*
HTS	Harvard Theological Studies
IBS	*Irish Biblical Studies*
ICC	International Critical Commentary
Int	*Interpretation*
JAJ	*Journal of Ancient Judaism*
JAOS	*Journal of the American Oriental Society*
JBL	*Journal of Biblical Literature*
JECS	*Journal of Early Christian Studies*
JETS	*Journal of the Evangelical Theological Society*
JFSR	*Journal of Feminist Studies in Religion*
JHebS	*Journal of Hebrew Scriptures*
JQR	*Jewish Quarterly Review*
JSHJ	*Journal for the Study of the Historical Jesus*
JSJ	*Journal for the Study of Judaism in the Persian, Hellenistic, and Roman Periods*
JSJSup	Journal for the Study of Judaism Supplement Series
JSNT	*Journal for the Study of the New Testament*
JSNTSup	Journal for the Study of the New Testament Supplement Series
JSOT	*Journal for the Study of the Old Testament*
JSOTSup	Journal for the Study of the Old Testament Supplement Series
JSP	*Journal for the Study of the Pseudepigrapha*
JSQ	*Jewish Studies Quarterly*
JSSM	Journal of Semitic Studies Monograph
JTS	*Journal of Theological Studies*
KEK	Kritisch-exegetischer Kommentar über das Neue Testament (Meyer-Kommentar)
LCL	Loeb Classical Library
LD	Lectio Divina
LNTS	Library of New Testament Studies
LSJ	Liddell, Henry George, Robert Scott, and Henry Stuart Jones. *A Greek-English Lexicon*. 9th ed. Oxford: Clarendon, 1996
LUÅ	Lunds universitets årsskrift
MTSR	*Method and Theory in the Study of Religion*
Neot	*Neotestamentica*
NHMS	Nag Hammadi and Manichaean Studies

NICNT	New International Commentary on the New Testament
NIGTC	New International Greek Testament Commentary
NovT	*Novum Testamentum*
NovTSup	Novum Testamentum Supplement
NRSVue	New Revised Standard Version updated edition
NTAbh	Neutestamentliche Abhandlungen
NTL	New Testament Library
NTM	New Testament Message
NTOA	Novum Testamentum et Orbis Antiquus
NTS	*New Testament Studies*
NTTS	New Testament Tools and Studies
ÖBS	Österreichische biblische Studien
OLA	Orientalia Lovaniensia Analecta
OTL	Old Testament Library
PEQ	*Palestine Exploration Quarterly*
PG	Patrologia Graeca [= *Patrologiae Cursus Completus*: Series Graeca]. Edited by Jacques-Paul Migne. 162 vols. Paris, 1857–86
PL	Patrologia Latina [= *Patrologiae Cursus Completus:* Series Latina]. Edited by Jacques-Paul Migne. 217 vols. Paris, 1844–64
PO	Patrologia Orientalis
QD	Quaestiones Disputatae
RB	*Revue Biblique*
RBS	Resources for Biblical Study
REJ	*Revue des études juives*
RevQ	*Revue de Qumran*
RHPR	*Revue d'histoire et de philosophie religieuses*
RTP	*Revue de théologie et de philosophie*
SAC	Studies in Antiquity and Christianity
SANT	Studien zum Alten und Neuen Testaments
SBAB	Stuttgarter biblische Aufsatzbände
SBLDS	Society of Biblical Literature Dissertation Series
SBLMS	Society of Biblical Literature Monograph Series
SBS	Stuttgarter Bibelstudien
SC	Sources chrétiennes
SCS	Septuagint and Cognate Studies
SemeiaSt	Semeia Studies
SemeiaSup	Semeia Supplements
SHR	Studies in the History of Religions
SJLA	Studies in Judaism in Late Antiquity

SNTSMS	Society for New Testament Studies Monograph Series
SP	Sacra Pagina
SR	*Studies in Religion*
STDJ	Studies on the Texts of the Desert of Judah
STNW	Studies of the New Testament and Its World
Str-B	Strack, H. L., and P. Billerbeck. *Kommentar zum Neuen Testament aus Talmud und Midrasch.* 6 vols. Munich, 1922–61
STRev	*Sewanee Theological Review*
SUNT	Studien zum Umwelt des Neuen Testament
SVTP	Studia in Veteris Testamenti Pseudepigraphica
SymS	Symposium Series
TDNT	*Theological Dictionary of the New Testament.* Edited by Gerhard Kittel and Gerhard Friedrich. Translated by Geoffrey W. Bromiley. 10 vols. Grand Rapids: Eerdmans, 1964–76
TF	*Theologische Forschung*
TGST	Tesi Gregoriana, Serie Teologia
ThH	Théologie historique
ThKNT	Theologischer Handkommentar zum Neuen Testament
TRev	*Theologische Revue*
TSAJ	Texte und Studien zum antiken Judentum
TU	Texte und Untersuchungen
TynBul	*Tyndale Bulletin*
VC	*Vigiliae Christianae*
VCSup	Vigiliae Christianae Supplements
VT	*Vetus Testamentum*
WBC	Word Biblical Commentary
WUNT	Wissenschaftliche Untersuchungen zum Neuen Testament
ZAW	*Zeitschrift für die alttestamentliche Wissenschaft*
ZNT	*Zeitschrift für Neues Testament*
ZNW	*Zeitschrift für die neutestamentliche Wissenschaft*

1

Contingent Eschatology

Imminence and Delay

> New Testament studies is a discipline which has to move forward gropingly. We are forced to work with many learned conjectures. . . . We have to form a total picture of Jesus which is largely hypothetical. In a sense which is not exactly comfortable our discipline is a study of "things not seen."
>
> —Birger Gerhardsson[1]

> He [Jesus] evidently attempted and expected a national repentance. If this was so, he failed; and those who recorded his life shrank from thinking that he did not do all he sought to do, and so the evidence has had to come through an antagonistic medium, and the part that this failure must be given in a true estimate of his life and death was very largely passed over by the early Church.
>
> —A. T. Cadoux[2]

The eschatological events—the final crisis, the coming of the Son of Man, the resurrection of the dead, the last judgment, the renewal of the world—were, for Jesus, not far off but near.[3] Indeed, the latter days had begun. Or so I have argued in previous publications.[4]

1. Gerhardsson, *Reliability*, 59.

2. A. T. Cadoux, *Essays*, 122.

3. By this I do not mean that Jesus expected "the end of the space-time universe." In this I agree with N. T. Wright even as I disagree with him in other respects about the nature of Jesus's eschatology; see my essay "Jesus and the Victory of Apocalyptic."

4. See esp. Allison, *Jesus of Nazareth*, and Allison, *Constructing Jesus*, 30–220. On the question of imminence, see also below, p. 73 n. 293.

My defense of this position makes me, in important respects, an ally of Albert Schweitzer.[5] I dissent, however, from his opinion that belief in a near end informed everything Jesus said and did. I do not promote what Schweitzer labeled "consistent eschatology" (*Konsequent Eschatologie*). I disbelieve, for instance, that Jesus's moral teaching was "oriented entirely by the expected supernatural consummation."[6] I instead envisage him as being more like the figure who inhabits the Synoptics. While eschatology is a major theme in Matthew, Mark, and Luke, it is not the exclusive focus or sole driver. Other things likewise matter, some greatly.

I will not, in the following pages, rehearse my reasons for holding these convictions. Nor, I should emphasize, will I dissent from my previous verdicts. I do, nonetheless, wish to add a significant qualification.[7] While I remain persuaded that Jesus took the end to be near, so near that the tribulation of the latter days—the "great tribulation" in Matthew and Revelation, "the birth pangs of the Messiah" in rabbinic literature[8]—had, for him, already overtaken the present,[9] I will urge that, near the end of his ministry, he foresaw an interim period, a time of brief duration between his death and the eschatological denouement.

Two circumstances, I will suggest, occasioned this change in outlook. The first was disappointment or disillusionment with his contemporaries' response to his mission.[10] The second was this: the prospect of suffering and death ceased to be, at some point, a hypothetical possibility and instead became a

5. Schweitzer, *Quest of the Historical Jesus.*

6. Schweitzer, *Mystery of the Kingdom of God*, 100.

7. I already introduced this qualification in an unpublished excursus in my doctoral dissertation (1982) and then in Davies and Allison, *Matthew*, 2:270–71. That I subsequently neglected what I wrote in those places until recently is likely due to my engagement with John Dominic Crossan and other members of the Jesus Seminar, an engagement that led me, through overreaction, to a one-sided emphasis. Reading Hays et al., *When the Son of Man Didn't Come*, was the occasion for returning to and developing my earlier thoughts.

8. Matt 24:21 (θλῖψις μεγάλη); Rev 7:14 (τῆς θλίψεως τῆς μεγάλης); b. Pesaḥ 118a; b. Sanh. 98b (חבלו של משיח). The Greek expressions go back to Dan 12:1: "There will be a time of tribulation [Theodotion: καιρὸς θλίψεως; LXX: ἡμέρα θλίψεως; MT: עת צרה], tribulation such as has not occurred from when a nation (first) appeared on the earth until that time."

9. On this, see Allison, "Q 12.51–53 and Mk 9:11–13."Cf. Cullmann, *Salvation in History*, 229–30; Luz, "Warum zog Jesus nach Jerusalem?"; Pitre, *Tribulation*, 381–507; and Ferda, *Galilean Crisis*, 182–85. (Pitre, following Mark 13, distinguishes between the preliminary "birth pangs" and "the great tribulation" proper. I do not.) For the present as the time of eschatological testing and trial in Jewish sources, see Allison, *End of the Ages*, 7–14; cf. from the Pauline corpus 1 Cor 7:26 ("the present distress") and 2 Thess 2:7 ("the mystery of lawlessness is already at work").

10. I do not, however, hew to the once popular notion that an initial, successful mission

near certainty. This meant that his followers, or at least some of them, would be, for a time, bereft of his presence.[11]

Tensions in the Tradition

Those of us who maintain that Jesus held an imminent eschatology must explain why some words attributed to him suggest or entail the passing of time between his end and the end of routine history. Here are the most obvious examples:

- Mark 2:20: "The days will come when the bridegroom will be taken from them, and then they will fast in that day."
- Mark 13:3–27: This discourse in its entirety envisages a span of time between the speaker's present and his future appearance as the Son of Man.
- Mark 13:34–35: "It is like a man going on a journey, when he leaves home and puts his servants in charge, each with his work, and commands the doorkeeper to be on the watch. Watch therefore, for you do not know when the master of the house will come."[12]
- Mark 14:7: "For you always have the poor with you . . . but me you do not always have."
- Mark 14:25: "Truly I tell you, I will never again drink of the fruit of the vine until that day when I drink it new in the kingdom of God" (cf. Luke 22:18).
- Matt 23:39 // Luke 13:35 (Q): "You will not see me from now on until you say, 'Blessed is he who comes in the name of the Lord.'"
- Matt 25:1–12: when the bridegroom—in Matthew he represents Jesus—is delayed, the wise take oil for their lamps; the foolish do not and instead sleep and are thereby shut out of the wedding banquet.
- Luke 17:22: "The days are coming when you will long to see one of the days of the Son of Man and you will not see it."
- Luke 19:11: Jesus deploys the parable of the pounds (19:12–27) "because he was near to Jerusalem, and because they [the disciples] supposed that the

was trailed by an unsuccessful period that led to disillusionment. On the history of this conception and critical analysis of it, see the important work of Ferda, *Galilean Crisis*.

11. Pitre, *Last Supper*, 20, wonders how the words of institution can be harmonized with my view that, for Jesus, the end was imminent. The following pages are my response.

12. Cf. the parable of the servant entrusted with supervision (Matt 24:45–51 // Luke 12:41–46). Here too an absent owner returns, and exegetes recurrently identify him as Jesus.

kingdom of God was to appear immediately." The parable counters their false belief.

- John 14:25–30: "I have said these things to you while I am still with you. But the Advocate, the Holy Spirit, whom the Father will send in my name, will teach you everything, and remind you of all that I have said to you. . . . You heard me say to you: 'I am going away, and I am coming to you.' If you loved me, you would rejoice that I am going to the Father, because the Father is greater than I. And now I have told you this before it occurs, so that when it does occur, you may believe. I will no longer talk much with you."
- John 16:16: "A little while, you will no longer see me."
- 1 Cor 11:24–25: "This is my body that is for you. Do this in remembrance of me. . . . This cup is the new covenant in my blood. Do this, as often as you drink it, in remembrance of me."[13]

The tradition, as I read it, contains two sorts of sayings that do not obviously cohere. Some reveal that Jesus looked for the final redemption in the very near future. Others put space between his personal, historical presence and the final events.

It is customary to resolve this tension either by reinterpreting one set of data—the texts that seem to entail genuine imminence do not really do so—or by arguing that the other set—that which implies delay—derives not from Jesus but from the church. According to proponents of the former option, we have no firm evidence that Jesus ever expected the kingdom to come in its fullness in the immediate future.[14] For partisans of the second alternative, none of the material that envisions delay goes back to Jesus: it all stems from Christian tradents.[15] The end was always, for Jesus, near in the same way.

13. Cf. Luke 22:19: "This is my body, which is given for you. Do this in remembrance of me."

14. The classic presentation of this position is Kümmel, *Promise and Fulfilment*. Cf. Cullmann, *Salvation in History*, 188–236. Ferda, *Second Coming*, also affirms that Jesus expected the end to come in his generation yet not immediately. For my rejoinder, see below, n. 293. Unlike Kümmel, however, Ferda thinks that Jesus did not distinguish between his own resurrection and the general resurrection. From a very different point of view, N. T. Wright, "Hope Deferred?," also denies that Jesus took the final consummation to be imminent.

15. The best known and still most detailed argument for this remains Grässer, *Parusieverzögerung*. Cf. also Grässer's *Naherwartung Jesu*. More recently, Fredriksen, *When Christians Were Jews*, doubts that Jesus envisaged an interim period; rather, "after several years of announcing the coming of the Kingdom . . . Jesus may have shifted the time frame of his prophecy, from *soon* to *now*" (68). Cf. her *Jesus of Nazareth*, 235–59: Jesus may have expected the kingdom to come during what turned out to be his last Passover.

What should we think? My list of texts does not, taken by itself, instill stout confidence that Jesus anticipated an interim period. It would have been natural for Christ adherents to read their own situation—they lived between Jesus's death and the general resurrection—into their teacher's words and to modify them accordingly. Many scholars, furthermore, think that some of the relevant passages, such as Mark 2:19–20 and John 14:25–30, are obviously post-Easter constructions.[16]

Nonetheless, the notion of an interim stage or temporal absence occurs in all strands of the tradition. This includes the earliest strands—Paul, Mark, and (for those of us who accept its existence) the Sayings Source Q.[17] Beyond that, even less conservative scholars often suppose that at least Mark 14:25 preserves something Jesus said;[18] and, for what it is worth, John Meier, who attributes only four parables to Jesus, includes the parable of the pounds/talents (Matt 25:14–20 // Luke 19:11–27) in his privileged group,[19] and that parable features an owner who goes on a journey, an owner who is, at least in Matthew and Luke, a cipher for Jesus.

Johannes Weiss and C. J. Cadoux

Were I forced to choose between the two views just introduced, I would steamroll the data. I would strive to assign to the nascent church all the texts that imply an interim period, or I would strive to interpret them so that they fail to suggest such. I do not, however, feel compelled to pursue either strategy. Rather, and without being dogmatic, I incline to another option.

Johannes Weiss urged that Jesus proclaimed repentance in the face of the imminent messianic kingdom. When, however, that proclamation did not meet the response hoped for, Jesus altered his outlook. In Weiss's words:

> Jesus became convinced that the end had been postponed. That which was so eagerly awaited was not yet happening, and to one who looked more

16. Bultmann, *History of the Synoptic Tradition*, 92, already observed that Mark 2:19b–20 "has for a long time been considered secondary." See further Grässer, *Parusieverzögerung*, 44–49.

17. Recent attempts to dispense with Q—e.g., Mosse, *Three Gospels*; Poirier and Peterson, *Marcan Priority without Q*; and Eve, *Relating the Gospels*—fail to persuade me; see my "Luke Rewriting Matthew?" Other recent defenders of Q include Kloppenborg, *Synoptic Problems*, and A. Kirk, *Jesus Tradition*, 203–97.

18. For the usual reasons, see Meier, *Marginal Jew*, 2:302–9.

19. Meier, *Marginal Jew*, 5:278–310.

> deeply, it was apparent that the Kingdom *could* not come. To date, the people had not yet brought forth in their ethical behavior the mature fruit of a genuine [repentance]. . . . In general . . . things had remained pretty much as they were. The people still wandered about like sheep without a shepherd. . . . What was worse, the leaders of the people explicitly rejected the purpose of God (Luke 7:30); they opposed Jesus and blasphemed the Spirit which was working in him. . . . Jesus concluded that the establishment by God of the messianic Kingdom could not yet take place; that an enormous obstacle, the guilt of the people, had to be removed; and that he would not live to see this happen, but first must fall victim to the hatred of his opponents.[20]

In brief, Jesus understood his proclamation of the kingdom to have a precondition, and when that precondition was not met to his satisfaction, he embraced an alternative.[21] This explains why one can find more than one point of view in the canonical Gospels.

Five decades later, in a book that never received the attention it deserved, C. J. Cadoux similarly urged that Jesus's thought concerning the future underwent a change.[22] Jesus initially hoped that his activity would stir up his contemporaries, that they would, in large numbers, discard the thought of rebellion against Rome, and that after—and because of—their repentance, and following a preliminary time of suffering, God would establish the eschatological kingdom: the peacemakers would inherit the earth.[23] Yet "this generation" did not repent to Jesus's satisfaction. It did not, as a body, embrace his message. It rather steered its own course. The consummation was, accordingly, postponed. Jesus, however, went to his death hoping that, despite initial rejection, his martyrdom would occasion a far-flung movement of repentance in Israel,

20. Weiss, *Jesus' Proclamation*, 86–87. The later reconstructions of Pesch, *Abendmahl*, 103–11, and Hampel, *Menschensohn*, are similar.

21. Beginning with John Nelson Darby (1800–1882), dispensationalist theologians have often made similar claims. Note, e.g., Chafer, *Kingdom in History and Prophecy*, 52–62: only after "the nation began to reject her King" did Jesus begin "to anticipate His sacrificial death" (61). I do not know the historical connection between this idea's appearance in dispensationalism and in critical scholarship, but there must be one; see further Ferda, *Galilean Crisis*, 86–88.

22. Cadoux, *Historic Mission*. To the best of my recall, the only significant scholar to engage Cadoux's work seriously in the first decades after its publication was Kümmel, in *Promise and Fulfilment*. One guesses that publication during World War II and Cadoux's status as a prominent pacifist contributed to its neglect.

23. Cadoux, *Historic Mission*, 218, 246.

and thence in the world at large, after which the kingdom would arrive in its fullness.[24] According to Cadoux, then, the Synoptics imagine more than one future because Jesus imagined more than one future.

It is no longer popular, in the wake of form criticism, to discern developmental stages in Jesus's thought. Because of the nature of our sources, most scholars now dismiss as fanciful attempts to divine such stages.[25] Yet the scenarios of Weiss and Cadoux raise a question that one should not summarily dismiss through appeal to the imperfect character of the extant documents. Both scholars assumed, as did so many older exponents of a "Galilean crisis," that Jesus could have revised his expectations because he took for granted, or eventually came to believe, that they were in some respect contingent.[26] He may, that is, have announced the nearness of the kingdom and yet believed that the outcome of affairs hinged, at least in part, on how people responded. Although full of eschatological hope, that hope was not so fixed as to prohibit him from entertaining, at some juncture, the possibility of a short postponement, a brief interlude. Can it be that Weiss and Cadoux were, in this matter, onto something? Even if they were not wholly right, perhaps they were not wholly wrong.

Rabbinic Evidence

I begin my attempt at an answer with a catena of rabbinic texts. These reveal that contingent eschatology was well known in later Jewish circles:[27]

24. Cadoux, *Historic Mission*, 262–65.

25. For Grässer, *Parusieverzögerung*, 5–6, 10–11, this is almost a necessary consequence of modern scholarship. But for important dissenting voices, see Ferda, *Galilean Crisis*, esp. 113–24.

26. Those who argue for an element of contingency in Jesus's eschatology include Schweitzer, *Mystery of the Kingdom*, 112–16, 233–34, 245, 255–56 (Jesus, at least initially, thought that the kingdom's coming required not the repentance of all Israel but solely his followers: the latter were "the violent" of Matt 11:12 who would take the kingdom by force); Dewick, *Eschatology*, 135–37, 141–42; A. T. Cadoux, *Essays*, 118–25, 134–37; Wilder, *Eschatology*, 73–77, 84 (Jesus "felt that the Kingdom could be hastened by repentance"); Greig, "Eschatological Ministry"; Gaston, *No Stone on Another*, 426–28; Jeremias, *New Testament Theology*, 139–41; Jeremias, "Naherwartung"; O'Neill, *Messiah*, 20–26; B. Smith, *Jesus' Twofold Teaching*; and Hays et al., *When the Son of Man Didn't Come*.

27. Nothing in what follows is from the Mishnah. Whether the Mishnah is antimessianic, as Jacob Neusner argued in *Messiah in Context*, it represents only one current within Judaism. Its tractates, furthermore, cannot represent everything its authors took to be important.

- y. Taʿan. 1:1 (63d): "R. Eliezer said: 'If the Israelites do not repent, they will never be redeemed,[28] as it says: "In repentance and rest you will be redeemed"' (Isa 30:15). R. Joshua said to him: 'So if the Israelites stand and do not repent, will they never be redeemed?' R. Eliezer said to him: 'The Holy One, blessed be he, will appoint over them a king as severe as Haman, and immediately they will repent and be redeemed.' What is the scriptural basis for this? 'And it is a time of distress for Jacob, yet he will be rescued from it' (Jer 30:7). R. Joshua said to him: 'But it is written: You were sold for nothing, and you will be redeemed without money' (Isa 52:3). How did R. Eliezer respond to this (verse)? '(The verse presupposes) repentance, as we read in Scripture: "He took a bag of money in his hand, etc."' (Prov 7:20). R. Joshua said to him: 'And behold it is written: "I am the Lord. In its time I will hasten it"' (Isa 60:22). How did R. Eliezer respond to this (verse)? '(The verse presupposes) repentance, as you say: "And now Israel, what does the Lord your God ask of you? That you fear, etc."' (Deut 10:12). R. ʾAḥa in the name of R. Joshua b. Levi: 'If you have merit, I will hasten it. And if you do not (have merit), at its appointed time.'"[29]
- y. Taʿan. 1:1 (64a): R. Simeon b. Yoḥai taught: "Isaiah said: 'There will be morning for the righteous, and night for the wicked, morning for Israel, and night for the idolaters' (cf. Isa 21:12). They [the Israelites] said to him: 'When?' He said to them: 'Whenever you want, so will he also; whenever you want it, he will also.' They asked him: 'What delays it?' He said to them: 'Repentance. "Come back again"' (Isa 21:12). R. ʾAḥa (said) in the name of R. Tanḥum by R. Ḥiyya: 'If Israel repents for one day, the Son of David will come immediately.' What is the scriptural basis for this? 'O that today you would hearken to his voice!' (Ps 95:7).[30] R. Levi said: 'If Israel were to keep a single Sabbath as prescribed, the Son of David would come immediately.'[31]

28. Pirqe R. El. 43 attributes the same remark to R. Jehudah.

29. For discussion of this text and its variants in b. Sanh. 97b and Tanḥ. Buber Beḥuqqotay 10:5, see Neusner, *Eliezer ben Hyrcanus*, 1:479; Schäfer, "Messianischen Hoffnungen," 238; Urbach, *Sages*, 668–71; and Landman, "Introduction," xix–xxiii. B. Sanh. 97b assigns two different views to Joshua. One is that God will move Israel to repent. The other is that the redemption will come even without repentance. In Midrash Tanḥuma, Joshua teaches that the end will come "whether they repent or not," whereas Eliezer holds that they will repent after God inflicts great distress on them.

30. Cf. R. Levi in Pesiq. Rab Kah. 24:12 (= Cant. Rab. 5:2:2): "Were Israel to vow repentance for but one day, they would be immediately redeemed." The prooftext is again Ps 95:7. Cf. Heb 4:5–11, where the "today" of Ps 95:7 becomes the present time of decision, with eschatological consequences for the author and his audience.

31. Exod. Rab. 6:7 also attributes this line to R. Levi. Both Lev. Rab. 3:1 and Eccles.

What is the scriptural basis? . . . 'In returning and rest you will be saved' (Isa 30:15). By means of returning and rest [Sabbath] you will be redeemed."

- Sipre Deut. 41: "If you keep the Torah, you may hope for (the coming of) Elijah."[32]
- Sipre Deut. 43: "The Holy One, blessed be he, said to Israel: 'Consider the ways that you had followed, and repent, whereupon you will immediately return to your cities, as it is said: "Return, O virgin of Israel, return to these your cities"' (Jer 31:21)."
- b. Yoma 86b: R. Jonathan said: "Great is repentance, because it brings about redemption, as it is said: 'And a redeemer will come to Zion, and to them who turn from transgression in Jacob' (Isa 59:20); that is, why will a redeemer come to Zion? Because of those who turn from transgression in Jacob."
- b. Sanh. 97b: Rab said: "All the predestined dates have passed, and the mat ter now depends on repentance and good deeds."
- b. Sanh. 98a: Ze'iri declared in the name of R. Ḥanina: "The Son of David will not come until there are no conceited people in Israel."
- b. Sanh. 98a: 'Ulla said: "Jerusalem will not be redeemed except by righteousness (*or* charity). As it is written: 'Zion will be redeemed with justice, and those who repent by righteousness (*or* charity) (Isa 1:27).'"[33]
- b. Sanh. 98a: R. Alexandri said: "R. Joshua b. Levi pointed out a contradiction. It is written: 'In its time [will the Messiah come]' while it is also written: 'I [the Lord] will hasten it' (Isa 60:22). If they are worthy, I will hasten it. If not, [he will come] at the due time."[34]
- b. Sanh. 98a: R. Joshua b. Levi asked the Messiah: "When will you come, master?" He said: "Today." When the rabbi returned to Elijah, the latter asked: "What did he say to you?" The rabbi said: "He spoke falsely to me, stating that he would come today, but he has not." Elijah responded: "This is what he said to you: 'Today, if you will hear his voice' (Ps 95:7)."
- b. Sanh. 99b: R. Levi said that the one who studies Torah "hastens the redemption."

Rab. 4:6 ascribe a similar sentiment to R. Ḥiyya b. Abba: "Israel will be redeemed only through the merit of the Sabbath."

32. Cf. Tg. Ezek 2:10: "If they observe the Torah, he will remove lamentation, weariness, and groaning from them."

33. Cf. Tg. Isa 1:28a: "Zion will be redeemed when justice is performed in her."

34. Cf. y. Ta'an. 1:1 (63d) and Mek. Pisḥa 14 on Exod 12:40. The latter explains conflicting dates for the exodus with this: "If they repent I will redeem them after the number of generations, and if not I will redeem them after the number of years."

- b. Šabb. 118b: R. Joḥanan said in the name of R. Simeon b. Yoḥai: "If Israel were to keep two Sabbaths according to the laws, they would be redeemed immediately."
- b. B. Bat. 10a: R. Judah said: "Great is charity, for it brings the redemption nearer, as it says: 'Thus says the Lord: Maintain justice and do what is right, for soon my salvation will come and my deliverance be revealed' (Isa 56:1)."
- b. ʿAbod. Zar. 9a: A sage of Eliyahu's school taught: "The world is to exist six thousand years. . . . Two thousand years are the period of the Messiah. Because of our sins a number of these years have already passed [without the Messiah coming]"; cf. b. Sanh. 97b.
- Gen. Rab. 2:4: R. Simeon b. Laqish said: "'And the Spirit of God hovered' (Gen 1:2). This alludes to the spirit of the Messiah, as you read: 'And the Spirit of the Lord will rest on him' (Isa 11:2). Through what merit will this [Spirit] finally come? 'Hovered over the face of the waters' (Gen 1:2) [symbolizes] the merit of repentance, which is likened to water, as it is written: 'Pour out your heart like water' (Lam 2:19)."[35]
- Exod. Rab. 25:12: R. Joḥanan said: "The Holy One, blessed be he, told Israel: 'Though I have set a definite term for the millennium that will come at the appointed time whether Israel returns in penitence or not, still if they repent even for one day, I will bring it before its appointed time.'"[36]
- Deut. Rab. 3:2: R. Simeon b. Ḥalafta said: "God said: 'When everything is ready [for Israel's] repentance, then I will tread with the heel of my foot on the winepress of Edom.' When will this be? 'And it will come to pass, because you hearken.'"
- Deut. Rab. 6:7: "If you fulfil this precept (Deut 22:6–7) you will hasten thereby the coming of King Messiah."
- Esth. Rab. 1:13: R. Isaac said: "Tomorrow when Israel repents God will take it [sovereignty] from the idolaters and restore it to them [the Israelites].[37] When will this be? 'When saviors will come up on Mount Zion' (Obad 21)."
- Cant. Rab. 2:5:3: "R. Judan said in the name of R. Ze'ira and R. Joḥanan in the name of R. Simeon b. Yoḥai: 'Great is the merit of maintaining the needy, since it causes the resurrection of the dead to come before its time.'"

35. Cf. Pesiq. Rab. 33:33: "When will the Spirit of God move on the face of the water [to bring about your redemption]? When you pour out your heart like water before the Lord, I, even I, will comfort you."

36. The text continues: "Just as we find that the Son of David will come as a reward for the observance of all commandments, so also will he come for the observance of one Sabbath day, because the Sabbath is equivalent to all the commandments."

37. Cf. Sipre Deut. 323: "If Israel would look closely at the words of Torah that I have given them, no nation or kingdom could dominate them."

- Cant. Rab. 4:8:3: "R. Joshua b. Levi said: 'Had Hezekiah chanted a paean over the fall of Sennacherib, he would have become the Messiah and Sennacherib would have been Gog and Magog. He, however, did not do so.'"[38]

Three observations are in order. First, the rabbis were not of one mind on the matter at hand. While R. Eliezer's view—the eschatological redemption will occur when Israel repents—appears to have been dominant among the Amoraim,[39] this was not the sole opinion. Some, such as R. Samuel in b. Sanh. 97b and R. Joshua in y. Taʿan. 1:1 (63d), held that God would redeem Israel even without repentance.[40] The disagreement mirrors Scripture and later Jewish ruminations on it. Sometimes the biblical sources make divine intervention contingent on Israel's repentance. Other times they do not, and there is a sort of compassionate determinism: God will see to it that things will work out no matter what the people do.[41]

Second, those who deemed repentance to be required could, in accord with multiple biblical passages, think of God as the proximate cause of that repentance.[42] According to R. Eliezer in y. Taʿan. 1:1 (63d) and Tanḥ. Buber Beḥuqqotay 10:5, and according to R. Joshua in b. Sanh. 97b, God will force the Israelites to repent by appointing for them "a king as severe as Haman."[43] This is a variant of the well-attested biblical notion that, when

38. Contrast b. Sanh. 98b: "There will be no Messiah for Israel because they have already enjoyed him during the reign of Hezekiah."

39. So Landman, "Introduction," xx. For repentance as the precondition or precursor of the end in later Jewish materials, see Patai, *Messiah Texts*, 65–80.

40. This matches the tradition that the final generation will be altogether unrepentant; see m. Soṭah 9:15 and the collection of opinions in b. Sanh. 97a.

41. See Raitt, *Theology of Exile*, and Unterman, *From Repentance to Redemption*. Raitt and Unterman document that conflicting beliefs already appear within Jeremiah and Ezekiel. Ideas vary from prophet to prophet, too; see Unterman, *Justice for All*, 141–77. The Dead Sea Scrolls also witness to more than one view; see Kugler, "Continuing Exile."

42. Cf. Ps 85; Isa 26:16; 44:22; Jer 24:4–7; 31:33; Lam 5:21; Ezek 11:19; 36:22–36. For this idea in the Dead Sea Scrolls, see Jason, *Repentance at Qumran*, 105–43 (on "predestined repentance").

43. Schäfer, "Messianischen Hoffnungen," 217, labels this a "synthesis" of the extremes: it lies between no redemption without repentance and redemption come what may. Cf. the harmonizing strategy of Saadia Gaon, *Book of Beliefs*, 294–95, 301: if Israel repents, Israel will be redeemed; but if the people fail to repent and the divinely appointed date for the end arrives, God will afflict them on such a scale that they will repent, and then the Messiah will come. Pirqe R. El. 43 offers another mediating proposal: "Israel does not repent quite sincerely until Elijah comes, as it is said: 'Lo, I will send you Elijah the prophet before the great and terrible day of the Lord comes. He will turn the hearts of parents to their children, and the hearts of the children to their parents' (Mal 4:5–6)." Here Israel repents, but it is an inadequate penitence until Elijah returns to help.

circumstances require, God will bring such distress on Israel that the people will amend their ways.[44] In short, although Israel must repent, God will make sure it happens.[45]

Third, while many of the texts cited represent solemn theological convictions, others seem to be purely rhetorical and may even border on the playful. To affirm, for instance, that one can hasten the coming of the messianic king by not killing a mother bird along with her fledglings is not really eschatological doctrine. It is instead a memorable way of emphasizing the importance of obeying Deut 22:6–7. The point is not to reveal what will move God to redeem Israel. The point rather appears to be: Obey this commandment as though its observance will bring the Messiah.

Earlier Jewish and Christian Texts

Although contingent eschatology was an option for many rabbis, this need not have much to do with Jesus. Rabbinic sources, given their dates, do not obviously supply immediate background for what a Galilean Jew of the first century might have thought. Reflections on the contingency of prophecy could, in theory, have arisen in response to, or at least have been intensified by, the disasters of 70 and 135. Did any before rabbinic times regard eschatological predictions as contingent?

Too few have probed this question.[46] Perhaps some assume that, although biblical prophecy often presents divine promises and judgments as contingent on the conduct of God's people, many postbiblical texts rather presuppose a predetermined scheme that human beings can in no way affect. Gerhard von Rad wrote that apocalyptic literature preserves "a philosophy which has dis-

44. Note, e.g., Deut 4:27–31; 1 Kgs 8:35–36; Ps 78:33–34; Hos 5:15; Prayer of Manasseh; 2 Bar. 13:10. For discussion, see Heschel, *Prophets*, 2:59–86. Cf. Pirqe R. El. 43: "Israel repents only because of distress, and because of oppression, and owing to exile, and because they have no sustenance."

45. Cf. Lam. Rab. 5:21: "'Return us to yourself, O Lord, that we may be returned' (Lam 5:21). The community of Israel said before the Holy One, blessed be he: 'Lord of the universe, it depends on you, so return us to yourself.' He said to them: 'It depends on you, as it is said: "Return to me, and I will return to you, says the Lord of hosts"' (Mal 3:7). The community said before him: 'Lord of the universe, it depends on you, as it is said: "Restore us, O God of our salvation"' (Ps 85:5)."

46. Exceptions include Zehnle, *Peter's Pentecost Discourse*, 71–73; Allison, "Rom. 11:11–15"; Ferda, "John the Baptist"; and Keener, *Acts*, 2:1106–8.

pensed with the phenomenon of the contingent."[47] Walter Schmithals agreed. In writings from what he dubbed "the apocalyptic movement," God no longer intervenes "in order to move men and nations to remorse and repentance" or makes any "contingent historical decisions." Rather, "history is surrendered into the hands of deterministic chronological speculation."[48]

One understands why von Rad and Schmithals made these large claims. The eschatological turning point is, in some sources, not just near but, as in Dan 9:24–27, proximate according to a revealed timetable.[49] In line with this, some Dead Sea Scrolls refer to the "appointed" eschatological date,[50] and 1QpHab VII, 13–14 prophesies that "all the times of God will come to their appointed end, as he determined for them." Such texts appear to cancel all contingency. Nonetheless, the stark—and implicitly deprecating—simplifications of von Rad and Schmithals are not helpful for our purposes. Even if their generalizations are true of some writings, they are not of others. Despite the apparent pessimism of certain prerabbinic texts and the chronological calculations in others, the rabbinic debates over eschatological redemption and repentance carry forward and amplify ideas that were already in the air before the Mishnah appeared. This appears from the following.

(1) The seer of 4 Ezra, perplexed over Israel's suffering and impatient for relief, wonders at one point: "O sovereign Lord . . . it is perhaps on account of us that the time of threshing is held back [*prohibeatur*] for the righteous—on account of the sins of those who dwell on earth." An angel responds: "Go and ask a woman who is with child if, when her nine months have been completed, her womb can keep the child within her any longer. . . . In Hades the chambers of the souls are like the womb. For just as a woman who is in travail makes haste to escape the pangs of birth, so also do these places hasten to give back those things that were committed to them from the beginning. Then the things that you desire to see will be disclosed to you" (4:39–43). Here a heavenly authority rebuts the thought that sin accounts for eschatological delay. The rejected opinion reminds one of R. Samuel b. Naḥmani in b. Sanh. 97b: a lack of justice delays the redemption.[51] The exchange, furthermore, is a bit like that between

47. Von Rad, *Old Testament Theology*, 2:306.

48. Schmithals, *Apocalyptic Movement*, 82.

49. See, e.g., Dan 12:5–12; 1 En. 93:1–10; 91:12–17; T. Mos. 10:12; 4 Ezra 11–12; 2 Bar. 53–74; and Apoc. Abr. 29. On chronological calculations of the end, see Beckwith, *Calendar and Chronology*, 217–75, and Beckwith, *Calendar, Chronology, and Worship*, 134–43.

50. See, e.g., the use of יעד and מועד in 1QS IV, 18; 1QM I, 10; III, 7. Cf. from a later time Tg. Neof. I Exod 12:42: "When the world reaches its appointed time to be redeemed."

51. Cf. Tg. Mic 4:8: "And you, O Messiah of Israel, who have been hidden away because

R. Eliezer and R. Joshua in y. Taʿan. 1:1 (63d). Ezra's proposal resembles that of Eliezer: without repentance, redemption does not come. The angel's counter is akin to Joshua's dissent: redemption comes even without repentance.

Fourth Ezra overtly rejects a contingent eschatology. Whether the vetoed thought occurred to the author of 4 Ezra for the first time as he wrote or—far more likely given the texts to be considered below—he heard someone propound it, his apocalypse establishes that linking eschatological deferral to deficient repentance was not a rabbinic novum.

(2) In Acts 3:19–21, the apostle Peter appeals to Jerusalem: "Repent, then, and turn again, that your sins may be blotted out, so that [ὅπως] times of refreshing may come from the presence of the Lord and that he may send the one appointed for you, Messiah Jesus, whom heaven must receive until the times of the establishment of all that God formerly spoke of through the mouth of his holy prophets."

These words, which likely conserve pre-Lukan sentiments,[52] set forth a contingent eschatology: were Israel to repent and turn from sin, God would send times of refreshing,[53] that is, would send Jesus the Messiah, and all that the prophets spoke of concerning the redemption would come to pass. As some have observed, this is, apart from the christological element, basically the same conception known from rabbinic literature.[54] Acts 3:19–21 appears to be proof that the view attributed to multiple rabbis was not, before them, just a

---

of the sins of the congregation of Zion, the kingdom will come to you, and the former dominion will be restored to the kingdom of the congregation of Jerusalem."

52. Cf. Maddox, *Purpose of Luke-Acts*, 129 (Luke preserves "an ancient tradition of Christian mission-preaching, marked by eschatological expressions almost obsolete in the rest of the New Testament"), and Pesch, *Apostelgeschichte*, 156 (the text reflects the beliefs of earliest Jewish Christianity). Contrast Jervell, *Apostelgeschichte*, 168, who takes the passage to be Lukan, and Lüdemann, *Acts of the Apostles*, 65, 111 n. 98, who finds only two traditional elements here: ἀνάψυξις ("refreshing") and ἀποκατάστασις ("restoration"). Against all this, see the detailed arguments of Zehnle, *Peter's Pentecost Discourse*, 44–60, 71–94, and Hahn, *Bekenntnisbildung und Theologie*, 113–38. Zehnle and Hahn demonstrate that, as compared with the rest of Luke-Acts, Peter's speech in Acts 3 contains some non-Lukan terminology as well as unusual titles for God, Jesus, and the audience. Cf. Barrett, *Acts*, 1:188–91.

53. Although some deny that "times of refreshing" refers to the eschatological restoration, the context discourages any other interpretation; cf. Hahn, *Bekenntnisbildung und Theologie*, 128–29; and see further Bauckham, "Restoration of Israel," 477–79. The "times of refreshing" and the "times of the establishment of all that God spoke" are two ways of referring to the same eschatological future.

54. So, e.g., Barrett, *Acts*, 1:203; Keener, *Acts*, 1:1106–8; Talbert, *Reading Acts*, 39–40; Haacker, *Apostelgeschichte*, 82; and Zwiep, "Haggadic Motifs," 330. Contrast, however, Zmijewski, *Apostelgeschichte*, 195: repentance will result in sharing the present Christian salvation.

hypothetical possibility that occurred to the author of 4 Ezra. Some follower or followers of Jesus already promulgated the idea, and probably early on given the seemingly primitive character of the surrounding speech. Indeed, Acts 3:19–21 might preserve, as F. F. Bruce conjectured, "the most primitive eschatology of all."[55]

(3) Eschatology is scarcely a major theme in Philo's extant writings. Yet in *Rewards* 87–98, 162–70, he looks forward to the fulfillment of Isa 11:6–9 ("the wolf will lie with the lamb"), the coming of a man who will subdue many nations,[56] and the sudden reversal of everything (πάντων). The realization of these dreams, he is clear, waits on people becoming worthy of salvation, taming their souls, cleaving to the commandments, and becoming virtuous. He thinks, furthermore, of these meritorious qualities, which will move God to return the scattered Jews to their homeland,[57] as induced by a suffering that will become "a medicine to save them": when those cast abroad accept the chastisements that have fallen on them "as a warning rather than as intending their perdition," and when they are "shamed into whole-heart conversion" (ὅλῃ ψυχῇ μεταβάλωσι), then they will win God's favor and pass from exile to their home. Grief will be "a medicine to save them from perdition."

In all this Philo anticipates the later rabbis who teach that punishment will occasion the repentance that will usher in the end.[58] Also reminiscent of the rabbis is his assertion that, once reformation has taken place, "everything will be reversed all of a sudden" (μεταβολὴ δὲ πάντων ἐξαπιναίως ἔσται). His ἐξαπιναίως ("all of a sudden") has its parallel in the rabbinic sources about repentance and the end:

55. Bruce, "Speeches in Acts," 68 (italics removed).

56. Philo's "there will come forth a man" (ἐξελεύσεται γὰρ ἄνθρωπος) draws on Num 24:7 LXX: "A man will come forth [ἐξελεύσεται ἄνθρωπος] from his seed and will rule many nations." Whether the allusion is properly messianic is debated; see Novenson, *Grammar of Messianism*, 126–28. For messianic application of lines from Balaam's oracle in Num 24, see CD VII, 18–21 and Tg. Neof. I and Tg. Ps.-J. ad loc. The messianic figure Simon bar Kosiba was known as "bar Kokhba," that is, "son of the star," with reference to Num 24:17: "A star will come out of Jacob, and a scepter will rise out of Israel"; see Justin, *1 Apol.* 31.6; y. Ta'an. 4:6 (68d); Eusebius, *Hist. eccl.* 4.6.2.

57. Against Fuller, *Restoration of Israel*, 94–101, and others, Philo's expectation of return to the land retains a literal sense, even if his usual emphasis lies elsewhere: the language is not merely allegorical. See Amir, *Hellenistische Gestalt*, 31–37, and Staples, "Reconstructing Israel," 303–35.

58. E.g., y. Ta'an. 1:1 (63d); b. Sanh. 97b; Tanḥ. Buber Beḥuqqotay 10:5. Cf. Lev 26:34–45, where confessing iniquity follows the miseries of exile; also Deut 4:25–31; 30:1–10; Neh 9:26–27.

- y. Taʿan. 1:1 (63d): "*Immediately* [מיד] they will repent and be redeemed."
- y. Taʿan. 1:1 (64a): "The Son of David will come *immediately* [מיד]"; "the Son of David would come *immediately* [מיד]."
- Sipre Deut. 43: "You will *immediately* [מיד] return to your cities."
- b. Šabb. 118b: "They would be redeemed *immediately* [מיד]."[59]

These parallels between the rabbis and Philo are signs of a long-standing tradition.

(4) The book of Tobit looks ahead, on three occasions, to the regathering of scattered Israel (Tob 13:5–6, 13; 14:5). The first instance joins this hope to Israel's repentance: "He will gather you from all the nations among whom you have been scattered. If you turn back [ἐὰν ἐπιστρέψετε] to him with all your heart and with all your soul, to do what is true before him, then he will turn to you and will no longer hide his face from you. . . . Turn back [ἐπιστρέψετε], you sinners, and do what is right before him; who knows whether he will look with favor on you and show you mercy?" (13:5–6). This seems to be the same belief that appears in Acts 3 and Philo: "if you turn" marks a condition that may or may not be met,[60] and it is attached directly to the promise of redemption.[61]

(5) When Moses entrusts sacred writings to Joshua in T. Mos. 1:18, he makes multiple demands.[62] These demands are designed to ensure that God's "name be invoked until the day of repentance [*diem paenitentiae*], in the visitation with which the Lord will visit them [the Israelites] in the fulfilment of the end of days." This line does not, in so many words, make the redemption hinge on Israel's repentance. Yet the two things coincide in time, and in the light of chapters 3–4, where repentance (3:4–10) leads to Israel's return to the land (4:5)—events of the past from the author's standpoint—it almost certainly assumes such a notion.[63] If so, the Testament of Moses becomes yet one more forerunner of the rabbinic sources collected above.[64]

59. Cf. also b. Sanh. 98a, where Elijah says that the Messiah will come "today, if you will hear his voice" (Ps 95:7), and T. Dan 6:4: "He (Satan) knows that *in the day* that Israel believes/trusts [πιστεύσει], the kingdom of the enemy (Satan) will come to an end."

60. So Vaticanus and Alexandrinus. Sinaiticus has instead ὅταν ἐπιστρέψητε: "whenever you turn."

61. Cf. Rabenau, *Studien zum Buch Tobit*, 81, and Ego, *Tobit*, 296.

62. The book in its present form is from the first century CE. Israeli, "'Taxo' and the Origin," is almost alone in classifying it as Christian.

63. So also Charles, *Apocrypha and Pseudepigrapha*, 2:415: "A great national repentance was to usher in the new kingdom of God, and was a necessary condition to its coming."

64. I do not presume that all Jewish sources understand "repentance" in precisely the same way. Different texts from different periods reflect differing emphases. See esp. Lam-

A related notion may lie to hand in T. Mos. 9:1–10:2. These verses tell the story of Taxo, the mysterious Levite whose martyrdom immediately precedes the advent of God's kingdom throughout the world. Jacob Licht urged that the deaths of Taxo and his sons—deaths that are actively sought—force the end.[65] Similarly, according to John Collins, the text embodies the notion that "the way to bring about a change in the course of history is not by violent rebellion but by moving God to action."[66] God, in other words, ushers in the eschaton in response to martyrdom. One is put in mind of Rev 6:9–11, wherein martyrs plead with God to avenge their blood and judge the earth's inhabitants, as well as Schweitzer's thesis that Jesus sought, through his suffering, to usher in the eschaton.[67]

(6) The Testaments of the Twelve Patriarchs contain the following sentences:[68]

- T. Sim. 6:2–4: "If [ἐάν] you (the descendants of the patriarch Simeon) remove from yourselves envy and all hardness of heart . . . then the whole earth will rest from trouble and all under heaven (will rest) from war."
- T. Jud. 23:3–5: "The Lord will bring you famine and plague, death and the vengeful sword, siege and scattering by enemies like dogs, the reproach of friends . . . consumption of God's sanctuary by fire, a desolate land, and yourselves enslaved by Gentiles. And they will castrate some of you as eunuchs for their wives. And as you return [ἐπιστρέψητε] to the Lord in entire

---

bert, *How Repentance Became Biblical*. Nonetheless, many sources, including the canonical Gospels, narrate calls to repentance as though they need no clarification. This suggests some broad, taken-for-granted agreement, such as repentance involving a change of practice and a turning from sin and evil toward God and the good.

65. Licht, "Taxo"; cf. Dodd, *Parables*, 56 ("the death of the martyrs is the condition precedent to the appearance of the Kingdom of God"); Carlson, "Vengeance and Angelic Mediation"; Tromp, *Assumption of Moses*, 228 (divine intervention is "set in motion by the death of the innocent Taxo and his sons"); and Lincicum, *Paul and the Early Jewish Encounter*, 96 (Taxo "forces God's hand to act to redeem his people and rout Israel's enemies"). Contrast Sprinkle, *Paul and Judaism Revisited*, 232–37: the testament seems to emphasize divine agency more than the Deuteronomic paradigm of repentance and restoration.

66. J. J. Collins, *Apocalyptic Imagination*, 134.

67. Given that the testament had been translated into German and English before Schweitzer wrote the *Quest of the Historical Jesus* (1906) and that he refers to the book elsewhere—*Mysticism of Paul the Apostle*, 55; the first draft goes back to 1906—one wonders to what degree, if any, his ideas about Jesus's death were stimulated by Taxo's story.

68. I sidestep the ongoing debate as to the origin of the Testaments. Although I believe that Jewish originals lie behind the current Christian collection, all that matters here is that they are prerabbinic and exhibit a contingent eschatology.

heart, penitent and going in all the commandments of God, the Lord will be concerned for you in mercy and will bring you back from the captivity of your enemies."[69]

- T. Iss. 6:1–4: "In the last times your sons will abandon sincerity and align themselves with insatiable desire. . . . Abandoning the commands of the Lord, they ally themselves with Beliar. . . . You then tell these things to your children, that if they sin, they might quickly return [ἐπιστρέψουσι] to the Lord. Because he is merciful, and he will bring them back, to return to their land."
- T. Zeb. 9:7–8: "Thereafter you will remember the Lord and repent [μετανοήσετε], and he will turn you around [ἐπιστρέψει] because he is merciful and compassionate. . . . And thereafter the Lord himself will arise on you, the light of righteousness with healing and compassion in his wings. He will liberate every captive of the sons of men from Beliar."[70]
- T. Dan 5:9–12: "When you turn back [ἐπιστρέψαντες] to the Lord, you will receive mercy, and he will lead you into his holy place, proclaiming peace to you. And there will arise for you from the tribe of Judah and (the tribe of Levi) the Lord's salvation. . . . The saints will refresh themselves in Eden; the righteous will dwell in the New Jerusalem."
- T. Dan 6:4: "He [Satan] knows that in the day that Israel trusts [*or* believes: πιστεύσει], the kingdom of the enemy [Satan] will come to an end."
- T. Benj. 10:8–11: "Then all will rise, some destined for glory, others for dishonor, for the Lord first judges Israel for the wrong she has committed and then he will do the same for all the nations. . . . If [ἐάν] you walk in holiness before the face of God, you will again dwell in me in hope. And all Israel will be gathered to the Lord."

Perhaps the most straightforward of these passages for our purposes is T. Dan 6:4: when Israel trusts or believes in God, the kingdom of Satan will pass away. This is the rough equivalent of what R. Jonathan says in b. Yoma 86b ("great is repentance, because it brings about redemption"), what Rab says in b. Sanh. 97b ("the matter now depends on repentance and good deeds"), and

69. Although these words could refer to the historical return of Israel from the Babylonian exile, it is more likely that they imagine the future, for ch. 24 (which is mostly or exclusively Christian) and ch. 25 are eschatological.

70. That human repentance is followed by "he will turn you around because he is merciful and compassionate" reminds one of those rabbinic texts in which God seeks to move Israel to repentance; see above, p. 11.

what the targumist adds to Isa 8:18: "If they see and repent, the decree that was decreed against them, that they go into exile . . . will be void."[71] As Hollander and de Jonge, commenting on T. Dan 6:4, write: "It is necessary for Israel to come to faith before the kingdom of the enemy is finally destroyed."[72]

Of the passages quoted above, several belong to those parts of the Testaments that display a sin-exile-return pattern.[73] The pattern derives from Deuteronomy, which in more than one place prophesies that Israel will sin greatly and that, as a consequence, God will send the people into exile; yet if or when, in response to their distress, they repent, God will bring them back to the land (see further below, pp. 30–34).

(7) In 2 Bar. 78:6–7, Baruch exhorts the exiles of Israel with these words:

> If [ܐܢ] you reckon that you have now suffered these things for your good so that you may not be condemned at the end and be tormented, then you will receive eternal hope—if, above all, you purge from your heart the idle error for which you were sent away from here. For if [ܐܢ] you do these things, in this way he [God] will continually remember you. He has always promised on our behalf to those who were more excellent than we that he will not forget or forsake our seed, but with much mercy he will assemble again those who were dispersed.

The promise that God will assemble the scattered tribes is conditional: "If you do these things." Although the regathering of Israel is God's gracious act—"with much mercy he will assemble again those who were dispersed"—and although other parts of 2 Baruch clearly teach that the end is near,[74] redemption remains contingent on the people forsaking the errors that caused exile in the first place: "The possibility of regathering is based on the moral proviso that

71. Cf. Tg. Isa 28:25: "If the house of Israel set their face to perform the law, would he not repent and gather them from among the Gentiles among whom they are scattered?"

72. Hollander and de Jonge, *Testaments of the Twelve Patriarchs*, 292.

73. T. Jud. 23:3–5; T. Iss. 6:1–4; T. Zeb. 9:7–8; and T. Dan 5:9–12. See the remarks of Hollander and de Jonge, *Testaments of the Twelve Patriarchs*, 51–56.

74. Note, e.g., 85:10: "The youth of this world has passed away, and the strength of the creation is already exhausted. And the coming of the times is very short and has passed by. And the pitcher is near to the cistern, and the ship to the port, and the course of the journey to the city, and life to its end."

they [scattered Israel] obey the law of Moses."[75] Other passages in 2 Baruch offer more of the same:

- 84:5–6: "Moses spoke to you before they [the pains of exile] happened to you, and behold, it has happened to you because you have forsaken the law. Behold, I also said to you after you suffered, that if [ܐܢ] you obey those things that I have said to you, you will receive from the Mighty One everything that has been stored up and preserved for you."
- 85:4–5: "If [ܐܢ] then we direct and dispose our hearts, we will receive everything that we lost with much gain. For whatever we lost was subject to corruption, and whatever we will receive will not be corruptible."

The repair of hearts is associated with what the exiles have suffered while abroad: "If you reckon that you have now suffered these things for your good so that you . . ." (78:6). This recalls Philo as well as those rabbinic passages in which the suffering of exile moves scattered Israel to repent, which in turn induces God to bring them home.[76]

(8) The eschatological reversal in Jub. 23 is not, according to Todd Hanneken, "determined by a pattern of history outside of human control. Contrary to what one might expect from an apocalypse, there is no indication of a determined time or auspicious dates for the events in Jub. 23. The responsibility is purely human. God had predicted that Israel would sin and require chastisement before repenting, but it could have been another generation. The events were foreseen by God, but the exact timing was not predetermined."[77] This interpretation, which makes the arrival of the latter days contingent on Israel's condition, tallies with 23:26, where ordinary history gives way to eschatological renewal when Israel returns to the commandments and seeks "the right way."[78]

Hanneken's exposition also lines up with Jub. 1:15, 22–23:

75. So Aune and Stewart, "From the Idealized Past," 162. At the same time, 2 Baruch is confident this will happen because divine sovereignty will see to it; cf. Crabbe, *Luke/Acts*, 222–25.

76. y. Taʿan. 1:1 (63d); b. Sanh. 97b; and Tanḥ. Buber Beḥuqqotay 10:5. On 2 Baruch's expectations, see further Bauckham, "Delay of the Parousia," 18–19.

77. Hanneken, *Subversion of the Apocalypses*, 126–27.

78. So also Nickelsburg, "Torah," 223–24. Contrast Lambert, "Did Israel Believe?" Lambert contends that, in Jubilees, the divine initiative is primary while human obedience and agency are relativized. For criticism, see VanderKam, "Recent Scholarship," 424–25; Sprinkle, *Paul and Judaism*, 210–14; and esp. Wells, *Grace and Agency*, 147–63.

> After this they will return to me from among the nations with all their minds, all their souls, and all their strength. Then I will gather them from among all the nations, and they will search for me so that I may be found by them when they searched for me with all their minds and with all their souls. . . . Then the Lord said to Moses: "I know their contrary nature, their way of thinking, and their stubbornness. They will not listen until they acknowledge their sins and the sins of their ancestors. After this they will return to me in a fully upright manner and with all (their) minds and all (their) souls. . . . I will create a holy spirit for them and will purify them in order that they may not turn away from me from that time forever."[79]

This prophecy indicates, in the words of James VanderKam, that "Israel will remain in its apostate condition until they become aware of it; that is, they must acknowledge or confess their and their ancestors' sins." Once they do "return with integrity" and fulfill their "covenantal responsibilities," God will respond by bringing Israel home from the diaspora and establishing a "permanent" state of affairs in the land.[80] Repentance will summon and win rescue.[81]

(9) In Bar 4:27–29, the promise that God will bring everlasting joy to Israel is prefaced by a call to return and seek God: "Take courage, my children, and cry to God, for you will be remembered by the one who brought this upon you. For just as you were disposed to go astray from God, return with tenfold zeal to seek him. For the one who brought these calamities upon you will bring you everlasting joy with your salvation." The causal connection between Israel returning to God and redemption also appears earlier, in 2:27–35: God will return the exiles to the land and establish an everlasting covenant with them after they, with divine aid, come to themselves and turn from (ἀποστρέψουσιν) wickedness. Just as the Lord brought calamity when the people went astray (2:29–30), so God will bring salvation when Israel repents.

Baruch does not explicitly declare "that returning to God is conditional for obtaining a reversal of destiny."[82] Yet what is not explicit can be implicit, and that appears to be the case here.[83] Given, moreover, that Baruch was likely

79. Translation of VanderKam, *Jubilees*, 1:131–32.

80. VanderKam, *Jubilees*, 1:159–60.

81. Jub. 50:5 may also assume this idea: "The jubilees will pass by until Israel is pure of every sexual evil, impurity, contamination, sin, and error. Then they will live confidently in the entire land. They will no longer have any satan or any evil one. The land will be pure from that time until eternity."

82. So Wacker, *Baruch*, 82.

83. See further Kiefer, *Exil*, 164–65; Nickelsburg, "Torah," 229; and Floyd, "Glimpse of the Emerging Synagogue," 32.

written in the second or first century BCE, any direct application for readers would have been not to the Babylonian exile of long ago but to the people's current, postexilic situation.

(10) G. H. Box translated the Old Church Slavonic of Apoc. Abr. 29:17–19 with these words: "And then shall righteous men of thy seed be left in the number which is kept secret by me, hastening in the glory of My Name to the place prepared beforehand for them, which thou sawest devastated in the picture [in the preceding vision], and they shall live and be established through sacrifices and gifts of righteousness and truth in the Age of the righteous."[84] Ryszard Rubinkiewicz rendered the same passage this way: "And then from your seed will be left the righteous men in their number, protected by me, who strive in the glory of my name toward the place prepared beforehand for them, which you saw deserted in the picture. And they will live, being affirmed by the sacrifices and the gifts of justice and truth in the age of justice."[85]

The crucial difference for our purposes is that whereas Box has the righteous "hastening" events on, in Rubinkiewicz's version they rather "strive in the glory" of God's name. Yet Rubinkiewicz attaches a footnote: "Or 'hastening,' Gk. *spoudazontes*."[86]

We face the same problem here as do commentators on 2 Pet 3:12: προσδοκῶντας καὶ σπεύδοντας τὴν παρουσίαν τῆς τοῦ θεοῦ ἡμέρας. Does this mean "waiting for and hastening the coming of the day of God" (so NRSVue), or is the better translation "looking for and earnestly desiring the coming of the day of God" (American Standard Version)? More likely the former. The reason is that other texts speak about the latter days being hastened:[87]

- Isa 60:22: "In its time I [the Lord] will hasten it [אחישנה]."[88]
- Sir 36:10 LXX: "Hasten the time" (σπεῦσον καιρόν) of deliverance for Israel.
- 4Q385 3 3–4: "The days will pass rapidly, until [all the children of] man will say: 'Are not the days hastening [ממהרים] on so that the children of

84. Box, *Apocalypse of Abraham*, 81.

85. Rubinkiewicz, "Apocalypse of Abraham," 1:705.

86. The translation in his *L'Apocalypse d'Abraham*, 195, is "qui se hâteront."

87. So too Bauckham, *Jude, 2 Peter*, 325, who cites most of the texts in my list. For the transitive use of σπεύδω with the meaning "to accelerate" or "to hasten," see LXX Esth 5:5; Isa 16:5; Sir 36:10; and Herm. Sim. 9.3.2 (80.2). For interpretative comments, see esp. von Allmen, "L'apocalyptique juive."

88. This verse is explicitly related to the final redemption in y. Taʿan. 1:1 (63d); b. Sanh. 98a; Tanḥ. Buber Beḥuqqotay 10:5; ʾAbot R. Nat. A 21; and Cant. Rab. 8:14:1.

Israel can inherit [the land]? . . . I measure [time and shorten] the days and the years.'"[89]

- Ps. Sol. 17:45(51): "May the Lord hasten [ταχύναι] his mercy on Israel."
- LAB 19:13: "When the time draws near to visit the world, I will command the years and order the times and they will be shortened, and the stars will hasten [*accelerabuntur*] and the light of the sun will hurry to fall . . . for I will hurry to raise you who are sleeping."
- 2 Bar. 20:1–2: "The days will come and the times will hasten, more than the former, and the periods will hasten more than those that are gone, and the years will pass more quickly than the present ones."
- 2 Bar. 54:1: "You hasten the beginnings of the (last) times."
- 2 Bar. 83:1: "The Most High will surely hasten the times."
- Barn. 4.3: "The Master has cut the seasons and the days short,[90] that his beloved might hasten [ταχύνῃ] and come."
- y. Taʿan. 1:1 (63d): "R. ʾAḥa in the name of R. Joshua b. Levi: 'If you have merit, "I will hasten [אחישנה] it."'"

The hastening of the end is, in y. Taʿan. 1:1 (63d), a direct response to Israel's merit. Second Peter 3:12 is similar: the faithful can speed on the advent of the last day by living holy and godly lives, because this will move God to act. In other words, human behavior affects divine behavior, as also in 2 Clement 12:6: "When you do these things [good works], he [the Lord] says, the kingdom of my Father will come." The matter is likely the same in Apoc. Abr. 29:17–19.

(11) Although it is riddled with gaps, much of 4Q398 (4QHalakhic Letter [4QMMT[e]]) is fairly clear, including this section:

It is written that you will [stray] from the pa[t]h and evil will encounter you. And it is written: [and] it will happen when al[l these] thing[s will befa]ll [you at the e]nd of days, the blessing [and] the curse, [then you will take it] to your he[art] and you will return to him with all your heart and with a[ll

89. Cf. the use of מהר in the Eighteen Benedictions: "Speedily [מהרה] cause the offspring of your servant David to flourish."

90. For cutting short seasons or days, see also LAB 19:13 ("and when the time draws near to visit the world, I will command the years and order the times and they will be shortened"); Mark 13:20 ("if the Lord had not cut short those days, no one would be saved"; cf. Matt 24:22); Apoc. Abr. 29:13 ("the curtailing of the age of impiety"); 5 Ezra 2:10 ("pray that your days may be few, that they may be shortened"); Three Forms 44:16 ("the times are cut short and the days have shortened and our time has been fulfilled").

your] soul at the end of time . . . in the book of Moses and in the b[ooks of the prophet]s, that they/there will come. (4Q398 14–17)[91]

These lines borrow from Deut 30:1–3 and 31:29:[92]

DEUT 30:1–2; 31:29	**4Q398 14–17**
30:1–2: When all these things have happened to you [והיה כי־יבאו עליך כל־הדברים האלה], the blessing and the curse [הברכה והקללה] that I have set before you, if you call them to mind among all the nations where the LORD your God has driven you, and return [ושבת] to the LORD your God, and you and your children obey him with all your heart and with all your soul [בכל־לבבך ובכל־נפשך]. 31:29: For I know that after my death you will surely act corruptly, turning aside from the path [וסרתם מן־הדרך] that I have commanded you. In the latter days [באחרית הימים] trouble will befall you [וקראת אתכם הרעה], because you will do what is evil in the sight of the LORD, provoking him to anger through the work of your hands.	It is written that you will stray from the path [שתסור מהדרך] and evil will encounter you [וקרתך הרעה]. And it is written: and it will happen when all these things will befall you [כי יבוא עליכה כול הדברים האלה] at the end of days [באחרית הימים], the blessing and the curse [הברכה והקללה], then you will take it to your heart and you will return [ושבתה] to him with all your heart and with all your soul [בכל לבבכה ובכל נפשכה] at the end of time.

Deuteronomy 30:3 immediately goes on to promise that Israel's return to the Lord will issue in their return to the land: "Then the LORD your God will . . . gather you again from all the people among whom the LORD your God has scattered you." Given its interaction with Deuteronomy, 4QMMT likely did the same. We do not, however, know for sure. The damaged fragments leave us

91. I follow the reconstruction of von Weissenberg, *4QMMT*, 103.

92. See further Bernstein, "Employment and Interpretation," 47–49. There are also links to Deut 4:29–30; see von Weissenberg, *4QMMT*, 189–91.

unsure about much.[93] What is clear is the document's eschatological reading of Deut 30. The events envisioned are for "the end of days" (באחרית הימים) and "the end of time" (באחרית העת).[94] 4Q398, then, envisages end-time repentance—"you will take it to your heart and you will return [ושבתה] to him with all your heart and with all your soul"—as does another line in 4QMMT: "This is the end of days when they will return [שישובו] in Israel" (4Q398 11–13).

In most of the scrolls, the Qumran sectarians are the penitents of the latter days. They are the elect who, through their repentance, usher in "the totality of the promised age."[95] By contrast, in 4QMMT, which likely represents an early stage in the community's history, repentance is an opportunity for outsiders, so that for them, in the words of John Collins, "the time of decision is now. It is time to usher in the end of days by returning to the covenant."[96]

(12) The promise of redemption in Ps. Sol. 17 occurs within a context of moral exhortation. Sigmund Mowinckel inferred that "the author certainly means to say that it is because of her sins that Israel has still to wait for the day of grace when the Anointed One can come. Therefore the hour may be hastened by penitence and the fulfilling of the Law, by study of the Scriptures and good works; but it may also be delayed by sin and impenitence."[97] This verdict accords with 18:3–5: "And your love is on the seed Abraham, the son of Israel. Your chastisement is on us as on a firstborn, an only son, so as to turn [ἀποστρέψαι] the obedient soul away from ignorant stupidity. May God

93. The DJD edition places 4Q398 14–17 I + 11–13 right after 4Q397 14–21 but takes 4Q398 21 to mean "at the end of days when they will return to Israel." See Qimron and Strugnell, *Miqṣat Maʿaśe Ha-Torah*, 58–61. The sequence, however, is far from certain; see von Weissenberg, *4QMMT*, 85–89. Furthermore, 4Q398 21, which has בישראל, likely refers to those who turn (i.e., "repent") "in Israel."

94. The phrase באחרית הימים appears several times in the MT, where it originally meant something like "in future days." In the Dead Sea Scrolls it has eschatological sense; see Steudel, "אחרית הימים." Steudel takes the meaning to be "the final period of history." For another view, see von Weissenberg, *4QMMT*, 190–91.

95. So Jason, *Repentance at Qumran*, 203. Cf. 248: "Only an ongoing penitential life would bring about this [eschatological] age in all its completeness." Note 4QpPs^a 1–10 II: those who return to the law and do God's bidding during the time of affliction will be delivered from Belial and delight in the land.

96. J. J. Collins, "Expectation of the End," 81. Nickelsburg, *Jewish Literature*, 148, offers a related assessment: "Now that 'the end of days' has come, or is imminent, it is time to repent and return to God, so that the blessings of the covenant may come on Israel (C 13–16; cf. Deut 30:1–3)." Nickelsburg's citation of C 13–16 here refers to 4Q396 13–16 (4QMMTc).

97. Mowinckel, *He That Cometh*, 297.

purify Israel for the day of mercy and blessing, for the day of election, at the manifestation of his anointed one [χριστοῦ]." Before the coming of the day of the messianic Son of David, Israel will be cleansed and become obedient. We seem to have here a forerunner of the idea R. Eliezer upholds in y. Taʿan. 1:1 (63d) (see above, p. 8), for it is in response to "chastisement" (παιδεία) that Israel repents (ἀποστρέψαι) and so sets the scene for God to bring redemption. Although the people must change for events to unfold, God, by afflicting the people, will see to it that they do so.

Contingency in the Jewish Bible

Although the preceding pages do not exhaust the evidence,[98] they establish that, long before the rabbis, some reckoned the eschatological redemption to be contingent on Israel's repentance.[99] Later ruminations about the Son of David not coming until this or that happens descend from earlier speculation.

This should not surprise. All the texts I have cited interact with the Jewish Bible, and again and again the latter makes God's promises and judgments

98. I have, e.g., not discussed 4Q398 11–13 4–5, which includes the line "this is the end of days, when they will return in Israel to the Torah." This may reflect a contingent eschatology; so Ferda, "John the Baptist," 161. Nor have I engaged the claim of Wacholder, *Dawn of Qumran*, 21 (cf. 13), that, in 11QTemple, "the ultimate acceptance" of the document's Torah will "redeem Israel unto eternity." I have additionally said nothing about Rom 11:11–15, which might reflect Paul's reworking of the idea that Israel's repentance will augur the end; see Allison, "Rom. 11:11–15," and cf. Moo, *Romans*, 696–97.

99. According to Lambert, "Repentance," 1134, "contrary to certain scholarly accounts, there was no apparent expectation of a nationwide repentance that would usher in redemption." His reason is that before "later Judaism and Christianity . . . only divine transformation of the world order can secure a significant change in national circumstance." I see things differently. A Jeremian pessimism does not rule all the sources, nor does the idea of unmerited, overriding grace—which certainly does occur; cf. Jer 24:4–7; 33:1–9; Lam 5:21 (see the discussion of this in Lam. Rab. ad loc); Ezek 11:16–21; 36:16–38; Mic 7:18–20; 4Q504 1–2 (esp. ll. 5–6)—appear everywhere. Further, divine mercy and human merit are not always two distinct ideas in the sources, nor are they everywhere antagonistic, competitive, or mutually exclusive. See esp. Wells, *Grace and Agency*. Perhaps most importantly, the idea of overriding grace is not front and center in most of the texts I gathered above on pp. 13–26. This includes Acts 3, Philo's *Rewards and Punishments*, Tobit, the Testaments of the Twelve Patriarchs, 2 Baruch, and the Apocalypse of Abraham. God does, in some of these sources, send suffering in order to goad Israel, but it is still up to the nation to respond rightly.

contingent on human behavior.[100] Jeremiah 18:5–11, for instance, offers these generalizations, which appear to be programmatic:[101]

> Then the word of the LORD came to me: Can I not do with you, O house of Israel, just as this potter has done? says the LORD. Just like the clay in the potter's hand, so are you in my hand, O house of Israel. At one moment I may declare concerning a nation or a kingdom, that I will pluck up and break down and destroy it, but if that nation, concerning which I have spoken, turns from its evil, I will change my mind about the disaster that I intended to bring on it. And at another moment I may declare concerning a nation or a kingdom that I will build and plant it, but if it does evil in my sight, not listening to my voice, then I will change my mind about the good that I had intended to do to it. Now, therefore, say to the people of Judah and the inhabitants of Jerusalem: Thus says the LORD: Look, I am a potter shaping evil against you and devising a plan against you. Turn now, all of you from your evil way, and amend your ways and your doings.

According to Jack Lundbom: "Yahweh does not use his divine power in any way that he wishes."[102] Rather, as William Holladay writes: "Yahweh has a 'plan' . . . which he 'intends' . . . ; but whether he puts it into operation or not depends upon whether or not the people turn from their evil way: if they will, he will not. Yahweh is capable of both uprooting and demolishing on the one

100. The same is true of ancient Near Eastern prophecy generally; see Tiemeyer, "Prophecy as a Way," and Carver, "Biblical Prophecy." Tiemeyer writes of the possible "cancellation of a prediction" (331), of a divine decision that indicates not "what *infallibly* will happen" but "informs about the likely outcome" (332), and of how "prayer, repentance and supplication might bring about a revised prediction" (341). According to Carver, "when a prophecy (or other divinatory 'message') was received but did not come to pass, an ancient Mesopotamian or Judean would assume that there had been a change of mind on the part of the deity, thereby canceling the prophecy, whether for the deity's own reasons or because of human response" (276). Further, "all forms of divination in Mesopotamia and the Bible are, unless otherwise indicated, expected to be contingent" (278). Cf. de Jong, "Fallacy of True and False," 4: "When prophets announced a disaster, they . . . functioned as guardians of the collective well-being; such predictions were revealed in order to be averted. If the threatening disaster foretold by a prophet was successfully averted, this did not make the prophecy 'false.' Instead, the prophet had done a good job protecting the well-being of society."

101. The question of how this passage relates to the rest of canonical Jeremiah is of no consequence for my purposes; so too the issue of what comes from the prophet himself as opposed to later redaction.

102. Lundbom, *Jeremiah*, 1:812.

hand, and of building and planting on the other. He may intend the one, but if the response of the people demands it, he will do the other."[103] Jeremiah's oracle is not an oracle of doom. Nor is it an oracle of salvation. It is instead an oracle of doom and salvation, with the outcome pending what people do. It is a bit like those prophecies prefaced by אולי, "perhaps" (e.g., Jer 21:2; 26:3; 36:3; Ezek 12:3).

The book of Jonah supplies a narrative counterpart.[104] God commanded Jonah to go to Nineveh and cry out against the people: "Yet forty days and Nineveh will be destroyed" (3:4). The prophecy was never fulfilled. The reason is that "the people of Nineveh believed God, proclaimed a fast, and put on sackcloth, from the greatest of them unto the least" (3:5). The king himself arose from his throne, tore his robes, covered himself with sackcloth, sat in ashes, and issued a decree that all should fast and turn from evil and violence (3:6–8). As Matt 12:41 // Luke 11:32 observes, the people repented—and "God saw their deeds, that they turned from their evil ways, and God repented of the evil that he had said he would do against them, and he did it not" (Jonah 3:10). Although Jonah's prophecy was spoken without condition (3:4), the course of the story reveals that it was contingent all along.[105]

Here—as Aquinas observes[106]—the principle of Jer 18:7–8 has taken narrative form: "At one moment I may declare concerning a nation or a kingdom, that I will pluck up and break down and destroy it, but if that nation, concerning which I have spoken, turns from its evil, I will change my mind about the disaster that I intended to bring on it." A seventh-century Christian reader of the Bible got it right: "God often seems to say one thing and then does another. For example . . . he (God) said: 'Three more days and Nineveh will be destroyed,' and yet is was not destroyed. . . . In response to what people do, even

103. Holladay, *Jeremiah*, 1:515. Conditional prophecies also appear in Jer 4:1–4; 7:5–7; 12:14–17; 17:24–27; 22:4–5; 26:1–6; 27:18; 38:17–18; 42:10. The form is common throughout Scripture: Exod 19:5–6; Deut 28:1–15; Josh 24:20–21; 1 Sam 7:3; 12:14–17; 1 Kgs 2:4; 6:11–13; 9:3–9; Ps 132:11–12; Isa 1:18–20; Ezek 33:1–15; Zech 3:7. It presumably originated in moral exhortation—do this and X will happen; do that and X will not happen—and was reinforced by experience: not all accredited prophecies came to pass. For instance, whereas Huldah prophesied that Josiah would be gathered to his grave in peace (2 Kgs 22:20), he was murdered (in battle?) by Pharaoh Neco (23:28–30). Helpful here is R. P. Carroll, *When Prophecy Failed*.

104. Cf. H. W. Wolff, *Studien zum Jonabuch*, 16–18.

105. Cf. Poole, *Annotations*, 2:931: "The threat is express and peremptory in its form and words; though there be a reserve with God on condition of repentance, which operated in due time."

106. Aquinas, *Summa Theologica* 2.2:171 art. 6 obj. 2: Jer 18:7–8 is illustrated by "the example of the Ninevites, according to Jonah 3:10: 'The Lord had mercy with regard to the evil that he had said that he would do to them, and he did it not.'"

the divine oracles can be changed and adapted for the sake of utility."[107] Or, as Abraham Heschel puts it: "Prophetic predictions are seldom final. No word is God's final word. Judgment, far from being absolute, is conditional."[108]

This is certainly the case in 2 Kgs 20:1–6. King Hezekiah is sick and on the point of death. The prophet Isaiah instructs him to set his house in order, for he will soon die: he will not recover (20:1). The vaticination is unqualified. Yet the Lord's word to Hezekiah by way of Isaiah does not come to pass. After Hezekiah prays and weeps bitterly, God gives the prophet a new word: the king will live, fifteen years will be added to his life. Repentance suffices to alter the declared word of God (cf. Isa 38:1–6). It is the same in Jer 26:18–19:

> Micah of Moresheth, who prophesied during the days of King Hezekiah of Judah, said to all the people of Judah: "Thus says the Lord of hosts, Zion shall be ploughed as a field; Jerusalem shall become a heap of ruins, and the mountain of the house a wooded height" (Mic 3:12). Did King Hezekiah of Judah and all Judah actually put him to death? Did he not fear the Lord and entreat the favor of the Lord, and did not the Lord change his mind about the disaster that he had pronounced against them?[109]

If, in some sources, repentance cancels predictions of judgment, in Judg 2:1–3 human sin cancels a divine promise of aid:

> Now the angel of the Lord went up from Gilgal to Bochim, and said: "I brought you up from Egypt, and brought you into the land that I had promised to your ancestors. I said: 'I will never break my covenant with you. For your part, do not make a covenant with the inhabitants of this land; tear down their altars.' But you have not obeyed my command. See what you have done! So now I say, I will not drive them out before you; but they shall become adversaries to you, and their gods shall be a snare to you."

In this story, God says: "I will never break my covenant with you." God nevertheless does just that. The reason is Israel's disobedience. The irrevocable

107. Bardy, *Trophées de Damas*, 221–22.

108. Heschel, *Prophets*, 2:194.

109. See further Hibbard, "True and False Prophecy," 353: "By the standard of Deuteronomy [18:22], Micah is a false prophet. His prediction about Jerusalem's destruction was factually incorrect: Jerusalem did not fall to the Assyrians in the eighth century. However, that is not how Jeremiah 26 . . . remembers this prophet. The point made by the defenders of Jeremiah in ch. 26, and by extension the editors of the book, is that Micah's message was the catalyst for change in royal and religious policy."

is not, then, the unconditional.[110] One recalls the cancelation of a promise in Deut 28:68: "The LORD will bring you back in ships to Egypt, by a route that I promised you would never see again."

First Samuel 2:27–36 illustrates the same principle. Here "a man of God" comes to Eli and, having recounted the favors of God and the rebellion of the priests, proclaims: "Thus says the LORD, the God of Israel: 'I promised that your house and your father's house would walk before me forever.' But now, says the LORD: 'Far be it from me, because those honoring me I will honor, and those despising me will be lightly esteemed'" (2:30). "The man of God" goes on to announce that, despite the Lord's promise, the house of Eli will be cut off; God will raise up another line of priests. As one commentator puts it: "Though Yahweh has to admit that he once made the promise that Eli would function as priest before him, he now reverses that promise in a new oracle and underscores it with an oath."[111] The initial promise was, in retrospect, contingent.

Repentance, Eschatology, and Scripture

The Tanak contains additional passages that illustrate the often conditional nature of prophecy.[112] For our purposes, however, what matters above all is that contingency appears in prophetic passages that many in Jesus's day regarded as eschatological. Joel's depiction of the terrible day of the Lord (1:1–2:27) is punctuated by calls to repent, fast, and put on sackcloth (1:8–9; 2:12–17). The prophet declares that if Israel repents, the dreaded day of the Lord will turn

110. Note also Ezek 20:15–17: "I swore to them in the wilderness that I would not bring them into the land that I had given them, a land flowing with milk and honey, the most glorious of all lands, because they rejected my ordinances and did not observe my statutes, and profaned my Sabbaths; for their heart went after their idols. Nevertheless, my eye spared them, and I did not destroy them or make an end of them in the wilderness." Cf. 20:18–22.

111. Klein, *1 Samuel*, 27.

112. E.g., Gen 20:1–7 (the unqualified prediction in 20:3—which does not come to pass—is revealed to be conditional by the continuation of the narrative); Exod 32:9–14 (Moses's intercession thwarts God's intention to consume disobedient Israel; cf. Num 14:11–25; Deut 9:15–29; Ps 106:19–23); Judg 2:19–22 (Israel's disobedience undoes God's promise that the people will occupy the whole land); 1 Sam 23:6–29 (the prophecy that the citizens of Keilah will hand David over serves as a warning that allows him to evade capture; cf. the interpretation in Josephus, *Ant.* 6.274); 2 Chr 12:1–8 (God repents of destroying Israel by the hands of the Egyptians when Israel humbly confesses "the LORD is in the right"); and Amos 7:1–6 (Amos's intercession cancels two visions of divine judgment that he has been given).

into a day of blessing: "'Yet even now,' says the LORD, 'return to me with all your hearts, with fasting, weeping, and mourning, and rend your hearts, not your garments.' Return to the LORD your God, for he is gracious and merciful, slow to anger, abounding in kindness, and repents of evil. Who knows whether he will not turn and repent and leave a blessing behind?" (2:12–14). Israel's fate, whether a blessing or a curse, hinges on whether or not the people repent.

Zephaniah 2:1–3 is similar: "Gather together, gather, O shameless nation, before you are driven away like the drifting chaff, before there comes on you the fierce anger of the LORD, before there comes on you the day of the LORD's wrath. Seek the LORD, all you humble of the land, who do his commands; seek righteousness, seek humility; perhaps you may be hidden on the day of the LORD's wrath." The possibility—not assurance—of being "hidden" from divine wrath depends on seeking humility and righteousness and doing the commandments.

God's acceptance of Israel is also contingent in Zechariah: "'Return to me,' says the LORD of hosts, 'and I will return to you'" (1:3). Malachi 3:7 repeats the refrain: "Return to me, and I will return to you, says the LORD of hosts."[113] Paul Hanson took Zechariah to teach that "the human endeavor of rebuilding the temple" is "the condition for the arrival of the messianic Kingdom." The prophet, that is, offers "the wonders of the eschaton now, if only the people" would rally "behind the hierocratic program."[114]

Of special importance for my topic are those texts that make the return from exile contingent on Israel's return to God. Deuteronomy 30:1–10—which "contains many of the elements that appear in prophetic descriptions of the eschatological age"[115]—is perhaps here preeminent:[116]

113. Cf. Isa 45:22 ("turn to me and be saved"); 55:7 ("let them return to the LORD, that he may have mercy on them"); Jer 15:19 ("if you turn back, I will take you back").

114. Hanson, *Dawn of Apocalyptic*, 245–46, 448. He urged the same for Haggai. Cf. G. F. Moore, *Judaism in the First Centuries*, 2:350: "The burden of the prophets from first to last" appears in those "utterances which make the coming of the Messiah conditional on repentance, we might say, on a complete reformation."

115. So Unterman, *Justice for All*, 159.

116. The passage appears to have been well known; note, beyond the texts cited below, 4Q504 4 10–13; Philo, *Conf.* 197; *Praem.* 115; Rom 2:29; and the use of Deut 30:1–10 in the Letter of Aristeas, on which see Matusova, *Letter of Aristeas*, 12–34. Recall also that the phrase "the curses written in Deuteronomy" is a refrain on Jewish inscriptions; see Trebilco, *Jewish Communities*, 60–69.

> When all these things have happened to you, the blessings and the curses that I have set before you, if you call them to mind among all the nations where the LORD your God has driven you, and return to the LORD your God, and you and your children obey him with all your heart and with all your soul, just as I am commanding you today, then the LORD your God will restore your fortunes and have compassion on you, gathering you again from all the peoples among whom the LORD your God has scattered you. Even if you are exiled to the ends of the world, from there the LORD your God will gather you, and from there he will bring you back. The LORD your God will bring you into the land that your ancestors possessed, and you will possess it; he will make you more prosperous and numerous than your ancestors.
>
> Moreover, the LORD your God will circumcise your heart and the heart of your descendants, so that you will love the LORD your God with all your heart and with all your soul, in order that you may live. The LORD your God will put all these curses on your enemies and on the adversaries who took advantage of you. Then you shall again obey the LORD, observing all his commandments that I am commanding you today, and the LORD your God will make you abundantly prosperous in all your undertakings, in the fruit of your body, in the fruit of your livestock, and in the fruit of your soil. For the LORD will again take delight in prospering you, just as he delighted in prospering your ancestors, when you obey the LORD your God by observing his commandments and decrees that are written in this book of the law, because you turn to the LORD your God with all your heart and with all your soul.[117]

Many believed, long after the return from the Babylonian exile, that the scattered tribes still existed in some faraway place or places and would return in the latter days.[118] Indeed, Israel as a whole was often thought of as still be-

117. This passage strongly recalls Jer 18:5–11 (see above) and is closely related in important ways to traditions in Jeremiah; see H. W. Wolff, "Kerygma."

118. See, e.g., Jub. 1:15; Ps. Sol. 8:28; 11:2–3; 17:4, 21, 26–28, 44; 1 En. 57:1; 90:33; 11QTemple LVII, 5–6; 4QpsEzek[b] 1 II; 4Q504 1–2, 6 12–14; 4Q509 3; 4Q528; Philo, *Praem.* 164–65, 168; 4 Ezra 13:32–50; 2 Bar. 78; Sib. Or. 2:170–73; T. Iss. 6:2–4; T. Dan 5:8–9; T. Naph. 4:2–5; T. Ash. 7:3; T. Benj. 9:2; 10:11; T. Jos. 19:3–8 (Armenian); Mek. Beshallaḥ 7; m. Sanh. 10:3; t. Sanh. 13:12; y. Sanh. 10:6 (29c); b. Sanh. 110b; Tg. Neof. I Num 24:7; Tg. Isa 6:13; 53:8; Tg. Hos 2:2; Tg. Mic 5:6; Commodian, *Instructions* 42 (2.1); *Carmen apologeticum* 941–46. Relevant biblical texts include 1 Chr 16:35; Neh 1:8–9; Pss 106:47; 147:2; Isa 11:11–13; 27:12–13;

ing in exile, despite many Jews being in the land.[119] From this point of view, Deuteronomy's prophecies about exiles repenting would have been about all Israel repenting.[120] This is exactly what we find in Tg. Ps.-J. Deut 30:2–4: Israel's repentance will lead not just to return from exile but to the return of Elijah, the advent of King Messiah, the abolition of the evil inclination, and the prolongation of life forever. In other words, when Israel repents, the end will come. Associating the end of exile with the people's repentance would have meshed with the far-flung conviction that the ongoing exile was a punishment for sin.[121] If sin caused the exile, then turning from sin should undo it.[122]

The targumist did not originate the eschatological reading of Deut 30. He rather inherited it, for it is also attested in rabbinic texts,[123] Philo,[124] the Testaments of the Twelve Patriarchs,[125] Tobit,[126] Jubilees,[127] 4Q396

43:5–6, 14–21; 49:6; 56:8; 60:3–7; 66:18–24; Jer 23:8; 29:10–14; 31:1, 8, 10; 32:37–41; Ezek 11:17–20; 20:33–44; 28:25; 34:11–16; 36:24; 37:11–28; 39:26–27; Hos 11:11; Zeph 3:20; Zech 8:7; 10:6–12; 2 Macc 1:27; 2:7, 18; Sir 36:13; 48:10; Tob 13:5, 13; 14:5; Bar 2:27–35; 4:37; 5:5. See further Kiefer, *Exil*, 287–306, 564–90, 611–42, and Fuller, *Restoration of Israel*.

119. Here I agree with N. T. Wright, *Paul and the Faithfulness of God*, 139–63. But for criticism of Wright, see Bryan, *Jesus and Israel's Traditions*, 12–20. For a helpful overview of the debate on this subject, see Piotrowski, "Concept of Exile."

120. Cf. the exhortation in 2 Chr 30:9: "As you return to the LORD, your kindred and your children will find compassion with their captors and return to this land." The Deuteronomist's eschatological expectation was doubtless encouraged by the belief of some that the Babylonian exiles who returned to the land did so only after they repented; cf. Neh 1:8–9; Jer 29:12–14; 4 Bar. 6:13–14, 21–22; 7:20–22.

121. Note, e.g., Deut 4:29–30; 30:1–3; 31:29; 1 Kgs 8:46–50; Isa 5:11–13; Dan 9:24–27; Amos 5:25–27; Bar 3:8; Jub. 1:7–14; 4Q504 1–2, 6; 11QTemple LIX; T. Levi 16; Philo, *Conf.* 118–21; m. ʾAbot 5:9. On this motif, see esp. Steck, *Israel*; also Kiefer, *Exil*, 245–61.

122. Cf. Jer 3:14 ("return, O faithless children . . . and I will bring you to Zion"); Bar 2:32–34 ("they will . . . turn from their stubbornness and their wicked deeds. . . . I will bring them again into the land"); Liv. Pro. Ezek 18 (the people will be in Media "until the completion of their error"); and note Piotrowski, "Concept of Exile," 217.

123. E.g., Mek. Pisḥa 14 on Exod 12:40 and Num. Rab. 7:10.

124. See Philo, *Praem.* 87–98, 162–70 (discussed above) and the notes in F. H. Colson's Loeb edition, which document borrowing from Deut 30 in more than one place.

125. T. Jud. 23:3–5; T. Iss. 6:1–4; and T. Benj. 10:8–11; see above, pp. 17–19.

126. See above, p. 16. According to Nickelsburg, "Torah," 227, Tobit alludes to Deut 30:2 and reproduces the "Deuteronomic scheme." So too Fitzmyer, *Tobit*, 310. See further Steck, *Israel*, 147–49, and DiLella, "Deuteronomistic Background."

127. For points of contact between Jub. 1 (see above, p. 20) and Deut 30:1–10, see Steck, *Israel*, 159, and VanderKam, *Jubilees*, 1:145–47, 159–60.

(4QMMTc) 10–15,[128] and (arguably) 11QTemple[129] and Bar 4:5–5:9.[130] It was obviously well known. Furthermore, the idea that Israel's repentance will initiate the end was, at some point, read into additional biblical texts, among them:

- Deut 4:30–31: "In your distress, when all these things have happened to you in time to come, you will return to the LORD your God and heed him. Because the LORD your God is a merciful God, he will neither abandon

128. This clearly quotes Deut 30:1–2; see above, p. 24.

129. The parallels between 11QTemple LIX, 9–13 and Deut 30:1–10 are not only thematic but at points verbal:

11QTEMPLE LIX, 9–13	**DEUT 30:1–10**
Afterward they will return [ישובו] to me with all their heart and with all their soul [בכול לבבמה ובכול נפשמה],	When all these things have happened to you . . . if you . . . return [ושבת] to the LORD . . . with all your heart and with all your soul [בכל־לבבך ובכל־נפשך],
according to all the words of this Torah [התורה הזואת]	just as I am commanding you today // when you obey the LORD . . . God by observing his commandments and decrees that are written in this book of the Torah [בספר התורה הזה],
and I will save them from the hand of their enemies and redeem them from the hand of those who hate them and bring them into the land of their fathers [והביאותים לארץ אבותיהמה].	then the LORD . . . will restore your fortunes and have compassion on you, gathering you again from all the peoples among whom the LORD your God has scattered you. Even if you are exiled to the ends of the world, from there the LORD your God will gather you, and from there he will bring you back. The LORD your God will bring you into the land that your fathers possessed [והביאך יהוה אלהיך אל־הארץ אשר־ירשו אבתיך];
I will redeem them and increase them and rejoice over them. I will be their God and they will be my people.	he will make you more prosperous and numerous than your ancestors, and the LORD your God will make you abundantly prosperous in all your undertakings.

130. Dependence on or allusion to Deuteronomy appears likely in Bar 4:7 (cf. Deut 32:16–17), 8 (cf. 32:18), 15 (cf. 28:49–50), 25 (cf. 33:29). Note also the echoes of Deut 28 and 30 in Bar 2:27–35, which foresees that God will return the exiles to the land once they come to themselves and turn from wickedness. See further Lincicum, *Paul*, 93–95.

you nor destroy you; he will not forget the covenant with your ancestors that he swore to them."[131]

- Isa 59:20: "And he will come to Zion as redeemer, to those in Jacob who turn from transgression, says the Lord."[132]
- Hos 3:5: "Afterward the Israelites will return and seek the Lord their God and David their king. They will come in awe to the Lord and to his goodness in the latter days."[133]
- Hos 14:1–8: "Return, O Israel, to the Lord your God, for you have stumbled because of your iniquity. Take words with you and return to the Lord; say to him: 'Take away all guilt; accept that which is good, and we will offer the fruit of our lips. Assyria shall not save us; we will not ride upon horses; we will say no more: "Our God," to the work of our hands. In you the orphan finds mercy.' I will heal their disloyalty; I will love them freely, for my anger has turned from them. . . . They will again live beneath my shadow. . . . O Ephraim, what have I to do with idols? It is I who answer and look after you."[134]
- Zech 10:8–10: "I will signal for them and gather them in, for I have redeemed them, and they shall be as numerous as they were before. Though I scattered them among the nations, yet in far countries they shall remember me, and they shall rear their children and return. I will bring them home from the land of Egypt, and gather them from Assyria; I will bring them to the land of Gilead and to Lebanon, until there is no room for them."[135]

131. The LXX turns באחרית הימים ("in time to come") into ἐπ᾽ ἐσχάτῳ τῶν ἡμερῶν ("at the end of days"). Tg. Neof. I Deut. 4:30 has this: "At the time you are in trouble and all these troubles meet you at the very end of days [בסוף עקב יומיא], you will return before the Lord your God and listen to the voice of the Memra of the Lord." Deut. Rab. 2:23, commenting on Deut 4:30, includes repentance as one of the reasons Israel will be redeemed in the time to come.

132. b. Yoma 86b cites Isa 59:20 as the prooftext for R. Jonathan's claim that "great is repentance, because it brings about redemption." On the conflicting interpretations of this verse, see Urbach, "Redemption and Repentance," 191–93. Rom 11:26–27, which anticipates a time when Israel will no longer be "hardened," cites Isa 59:20–21 as proof that "all Israel will be saved."

133. The targum turns this into: "After that, the people of Israel will return and seek the worship of the Lord their God and will obey the anointed one Son of David their king. And they will follow eagerly the worship of the Lord, and great will be his goodness that will come to them in the end of days."

134. T. Sim. 6:1–4 borrows from Hos 14:5–7 in prophesying the era when "the whole earth will be at rest from trouble and everything under heaven will be free from war." The targum expands Hos 14:8 with these words: "They will be gathered from among their exiles, they will dwell in the shade of their anointed one. The dead will be resurrected."

135. In the targum this becomes: "I will call to assemble their exiles and I will bring them

- Mal 3:7 (// Zech 1:3): "Return to me and I will return to you, says the LORD of hosts."[136]

CONTINGENCY IN THE SYNOPTIC TRADITION?

The preceding pages are all preamble. They establish that, before and after Jesus's day, some did not take the date of the eschatological redemption to be inexorably fixed.[137] They rather thought or assumed that the end could be or had been delayed, or that it might be hastened by collective repentance. The upshot is that scholars who ask us to envisage Jesus modifying his expectations according to this or that circumstance are not asking us to imagine something utterly out of accord with his religious tradition.

This is in their favor. But there is a difference between bare possibility and probability. In order to gain a sense of the latter, exegesis is required. So the question now becomes, Do any texts attributed to Jesus suggest that his expectations were, like the expectations of at least some others, in any sense contingent? I begin by reviewing the texts that seem most relevant and leave aside for now the issue of origin.[138]

(1) The Lord's Prayer contains the words "your kingdom come" (Matt 6:10 // Luke 11:2; Did. 8.2). This petition presumes that the coming of God's kingdom is, like bread, forgiveness, and deliverance, a proper object of petition. Since,

near, for I have delivered them, and they shall multiply, as it was promised concerning them they shall multiply. As I scattered them among the nations, and they were remembering my fear in a distant land, so shall they prolong the years of their life with their children and shall return. And as I brought them back from the land of Egypt so shall I bring their exiles near from Assyria and shall bring them into the land of Gilead and the Sanctuary, and it will not be sufficient for them."

136. Rabbi Eliezer in b. Sanh. 97b quotes Mal 3:7 as a prooftext for his view that if Israel repents, they will be redeemed. Note that Malachi ends with the promise that God, as part of the end-time scenario, will send Elijah, who will reconcile families.

137. According to A. E. Harvey, *Jesus and the Constraints of History*, 70, to the question "what is holding back the great restoration? . . . the answer which (by the time of Jesus) was usually given was that God could hardly be expected to act until there was evidence of greater faithfulness, and greater readiness to repent, among his chosen people." In view of our vast ignorance, I prefer the more cautious "sometimes given" over Harvey's "usually given."

138. The remainder of this chapter offers proposals and suggestions that, in almost every case, require expansion and additional defense, especially in view of the ever-proliferating secondary literature; but as doing so would have resulted in a long book rather than a long chapter, I content myself with undeveloped outlines of arguments.

moreover, people typically pray in the hope that doing so will make a difference, to pray sincerely "your kingdom come" is seemingly to hope that God will hearken and so hasten the day.[139] This, then, is eschatological optimism. The end will come soon,[140] and one may pray for it to come even sooner. Dietrich Bonhoeffer got it right: the Our Father calls upon God to "hasten the end of the kingdoms of this world, and establish his own kingdom in power and glory!"[141]

The Parables of Enoch, which were composed close to the time of Jesus,[142] supply a close conceptual parallel. According to 1 En. 47:1–2,

> In those days, there had arisen the prayer of the righteous, and the blood of the righteous one, from the earth into the presence of the Lord of Spirits. In those days, the holy ones [angels] who dwell in the heights of heaven were uniting with one voice, . . . and were interceding and praying on behalf of the blood of the righteous that had been shed, and [on behalf of] the prayer of the righteous, that it might not be vain in the presence of the Lord of Spirits; that judgment might be executed for them.

The verses immediately following depict the Head of Days taking his seat so that the judgment can begin. He does so in large measure because, as the text explains, "the prayer of the righteous has been heard" (47:3–4). Here the final judgment arrives when God heeds the supplication of both the angels and the righteous, so that the suffering saints will be delivered from their present plight.

139. Cf. Asting, *Heiligkeit*, 81–84; Wilder, *Eschatology*, 75; Cadoux, *Historic Mission*, 201; B. Smith, *Jesus' Twofold Teaching*, 122 ("the prayers of the disciples actually contribute to the future realization of the Kingdom, its culmination"); Hays, "Delay of the Parousia," 84–85; Tiwald, *Sayings Source*, 101. I take for granted the eschatological nature of "your kingdom come."

140. Cf. the Kaddish prayer: "Exalted and hallowed be his great name in the world that he created according to his will. May he let his kingdom rule in your lifetime and in your days and in the lifetime of the whole house of Israel, *speedily and in a near time* [בעגלא ובזמן קריב]." If this prayer was known to Jesus, the Lord's Prayer might echo it; so, among others, Jeremias, *New Testament Theology*, 198.

141. Bonhoeffer, *Cost of Discipleship*, 185. Cf. Cyprian, *Mort.* 18: "With frequently repeated prayers we entreat and beg that the day of his kingdom may be hastened [*acceleret*]." This understanding of "your kingdom come" occurs even to exegetes who are allergic to it. Luther, "Small Catechism," 153, wrote: "The kingdom of God comes indeed without our prayer, of itself; but we pray in this petition that it may come unto us also."

142. For the reasons, see Nickelsburg and VanderKam, *1 Enoch*, 2:58–63.

John Meier, who attributes the Lord's Prayer to Jesus, writes that, in Jesus's proclamation, people "can either wisely prepare for" the coming of the kingdom "or foolishly ignore its imminent arrival. But they can do nothing to stop it, alter its timetable, or change its nature."[143] Yet why then enjoin followers to pray for the kingdom to come? We can hardly elucidate "your kingdom come" through later perfunctory Christian practice, as though the words are an expression of a nebulous piety. Nor can we sensibly imagine that Jesus was like one of those old Calvinists who taught that nothing human beings do, including prayer, has any influence on God.[144] Jesus was remembered as asserting that prayer could move mountains (Mark 11:23; cf. Luke 17:6), and he evidently shared the pious passion of Daniel, who prayed: "O Lord, hear; O Lord, forgive; O Lord, listen and act and do not delay! For your own sake, O my God, because your city and your people bear your name!" (Dan 9:19).[145]

"Your kingdom come" was not tepid emotivism or theoretical hope. It was not an expression of desire alone but rather a real prayer, a heartfelt cry for God to act, to establish the divine will on earth among human beings as that will is now observed in heaven among the angels. Tertullian wrote:

> How do some pray for some protraction of the age? . . . Our wish is that our reign be hastened, not our servitude protracted. Even if it had not been prescribed in the prayer that we should ask for the advent of the kingdom, we should, unbidden, have sent forth that cry, hastening toward the realization of our hope. The souls of the martyrs beneath the altar cry in jealousy to the Lord: "How long Lord, will you not avenge our blood on the inhabitants of the earth?" (Rev 6:10). . . . Lord, may your kingdom come with all speed. (*Or.* 5)

This is decent exegesis.[146]

143. Meier, *Marginal Jew*, 5:307. He adds: "So too, despite endless homiletical nonsense spouted from pulpits, humans can do nothing to 'hasten the coming of the kingdom of God.'"

144. Cf. Calvin, *Institutes* 3.20.3: prayer "is not so much for his [God's] sake as for ours."

145. Cf. 2 Bar. 21:25 ("show quickly your glory, and do not put off what you have promised") and recall the heartfelt "maranatha" of 1 Cor 16:22 and Did. 10.5–6; cf. Rev 22:20. According to Fiedler, *Matthäusevangelium*, 169, Jesus's prayer for the coming of the kingdom means "that God will not extend the delay too long."

146. A few wonder whether or how a prayer for the coming of the kingdom coheres with certainty of its imminence; see, e.g., Grässer, *Parusieverzögerung*, 95–103. This, however, asks too much of non-Vulcan authors and their writings. Note that, in Rev 22:20, "I am

(2) The parable of the persistent widow appears in Luke 18:1–8:

> Then Jesus told them a parable about their need to pray always and not to lose heart. He said: "In a certain city there was a judge who neither feared God nor had respect for people. In that city there was a widow who kept coming to him and saying: 'Grant me justice against my opponent.' For a while he refused; but later he said to himself: 'Though I have no fear of God and no respect for anyone, yet because this widow keeps bothering me, I will grant her justice, so that she may not wear me out by continually coming.'" And the Lord said: "Listen to what the unjust judge says. And will not God grant justice to his chosen ones who cry to him day and night? Will he delay long [μακροθυμεῖ] in helping them? I tell you, he will quickly [ἐν τάχει][147] grant justice to them. And yet, when the Son of Man comes, will he find faith on earth?"

Whatever the tradition history of this parable,[148] it reminds one of 1 En. 104:2–3: "Your cry will be heard. Cry for judgment and it will appear for you." It is also similar to Sir 35:16–22: God "will listen to the prayer of one who is wronged"; the prayer of those pleasing to the Lord "pierces the clouds and will not rest until it reaches its goal"; the Most High will respond to prayer without "delay" in performing "justice for the righteous" and executing judgment.[149] Luke's passage, which concerns "the end-time resolution of the problems of the present,"[150] teaches that God can,

---

coming soon" and the prayer "Come, Lord Jesus" stand side by side. Valuable here is Moule, "Influence of Circumstances."

147. I take ἐν τάχει to mean not "suddenly" but "quickly" or "without delay"; cf. Acts 12:7; 22:18; 25:4; Rev 3:11 (ἔρχομαι ταχύ); 22:7, 12, 20 (ἔρχομαι ταχύ); 1 Clem. 23.5 (ταχὺ ἥξει καὶ οὐ χρονιεῖ)—although just perhaps the two senses can merge for Luke; cf. 17:26–37.

148. Delling, "Gleichnis," and Catchpole, "Son of Man's Search," argue for its basic unity. Many, however, regard Luke 18:6–8 as secondary; so, e.g., Bovon, "Apocalyptic Traditions," and Curkpatrick, "Dissonance." For Freed, "Parable of the Judge," the parable is Lukan from beginning to end. My view is that 18:2–8a likely represents Luke's source, to which he added an introduction (18:1) and a concluding question (18:8b). Perhaps 18:7b is also redactional. The extent and nature of pre-Lukan expansions, if any, are unclear to me. One can reconstruct an original parable whose sense has been negated by Christian revision; so, e.g., Merz, "How a Woman." That, however, is highly hypothetical, and I remain unpersuaded that the parable in 18:1–8 as it stands fundamentally misrepresents Jesus's intention, if he composed it; cf. Snodgrass, *Stories with Intent*, 455–58. The message in Luke is in any case thoroughly eschatological.

149. For the question of direct dependence on Sir 35:16–22, see Kartzow, "Rewritten Stereotypes."

150. Nolland, *Luke*, 2:871.

for the sake of the elect who cry out day and night, shorten the time of distress; that is, God can usher in the eschatological redemption ahead of schedule. In the words of Jörg Jeremias: "God's will to preserve his own is stronger than his will to destroy: so he 'changes' his will because of the cry of affliction and intercession."[151] To those who ask it will be given (cf. Matt 7:7–11 // Luke 11:9–13). Persistence in prayer will not be without effect.[152] This holds even for the eschatological drama. We have here the same mentality on display in the prayer "your kingdom come." God, who heeds earnest prayer, will not long delay.[153]

According to b. B. Meṣ. 85b, "Elijah used to frequent Rabbi's academy. One day—it was New Moon—he [Rabbi] was waiting for him [Elijah], but he failed to come. He said to him [the next day]: 'Why did you delay?' He replied: '[I had to wait] until I awoke Abraham, washed his hands, and he prayed and I put him to rest again. Likewise to Isaac and Jacob.' [Rabbi said:] 'But why not wake them together?' [Elijah said:] 'I feared that they would wax strong in prayer and bring the Messiah before his time.'" Here it is the prayer of the great patriarchs that, working together, would hasten the end.[154] In Luke 18, it is Jesus's followers, the "chosen who cry to him day and night," who can move God to bring redemption.

(3) The mournful Jesus of Luke 13:34–35 (// Matt 23:37–39 [Q]) prophesies: "Jerusalem, Jerusalem, the city that kills the prophets and stones those who are sent to it! How often have I desired to gather your children together as a hen gathers her brood under her wings, and you were not willing! See, your house is left to you. And I tell you, you will not see me until [ἕως] the time comes when you say: 'Blessed is the one who comes in the name of the Lord.'"[155] Interpreters, whether with reference to Matthew or Luke, to Jesus or Q, commonly follow one of two very divergent paths. Either they find a declaration

151. Jörg Jeremias, *Reue Gottes*, 121. Cf. Wilder, *Eschatology*, 76; Jeremias, *New Testament Theology*, 140; Weder, *Gleichnisse Jesu*, 271–72; and Blomberg, *Interpreting the Parables*, 274.

152. Cf. Luke 11:5–8 and see Grässer, *Parusieverzögerung*, 36. What Marshall, *Luke*, 462, writes regarding Luke 11:5–8 also suits 18:1–8: "Any encouragement to go on praying must necessarily be based on an assurance that God answers prayer. The point of the parable . . . is: Go on praying because God responds graciously to the needs of his children." Cf. Matt 7:7–11 // Luke 11:9–13 (Q).

153. For Montefiore, *Synoptic Gospels*, 554–55, Luke 18:1–8 could be taken "to imply that the cause for the delay of the Parousia is the lack of faith among Christians and of that joyousness and constancy in prayer which spring from it."

154. Cf. b. Ketub. 111a v.l.: "That they [the people Israel] will not force the end through excessive prayer."

155. Luke does not have Matthew's "from now on" (ἀπ᾽ ἄρτι), which is presumably redactional; cf. Matt 26:29, 64. Matthew does not have Luke's "the time comes when" (ἥξει ὅτε), but that may not have stood in the earliest copy of Luke. For the reconstruction of Q, see S. R. Johnson, Steinhauser, and Jolliffe, *Q 13:34–35*.

of unqualified judgment or, less frequently, they have thought the words to mean that Israel might one day welcome Jesus.

My view is instead that of Origen and Jerome: the sentence is conditional.[156] It indeed conveys a contingent eschatology.[157] On this reading, the passage means not, when the Messiah comes, his people will bless him, but rather, when his people bless him, the Messiah will come: redemption waits on Israel recognizing Jesus's messianic status.

Ἕως can, especially after a negation, function to express contingency: the state depicted in the first half of a sentence lasts only until the state depicted in the second half is realized.[158] In such cases, the meaning of ἕως is often not purely temporal ("until") but properly conditional and so close to "unless."[159]

156. Cf. Origen, *Comm. Matt.* ad loc ("Until they understand their own desertion and say in repentance: 'Blessed is he who comes in the name of the Lord,' they will not see the Son of God") and Jerome, *Comm. Matt.* ad loc ("Unless you repent and confess that I am he of whom the prophets sang . . . you will not see my face. Let them confess as blessed he who comes in the name of the Lord and they will see the face of Christ").

157. I first argued this in "Matt. 23:39 = Luke 13:35b," which later appeared in revised form in Allison, *Jesus Tradition in Q*, 192–204. Those favorable to my proposal, or of similar mind, include Van Der Kwaak, "Klage über Jerusalem"; Borg, *Conflict*, 182–84; Harrington, *Matthew*, 330; K. H. Tan, *Zion Traditions*, 115–18; Subramanian, *Synoptic Gospels*, 115–18; France, *Matthew*, 884–85; Fisk, "*See My Tears*," 168–69; Talbert, *Matthew*, 260; D. Turner, *Israel's Last Prophet*, 326–29; Runesson, *Divine Wrath*, 245–46; Tiwald, "Hat Gott sein Haus verlassen," 75–76. For dissent, see Luz, *Matthew*, 3:163–64, and Konradt, *Israel*, 236–37. (Luz's objection from the wider Matthean context does not apply to my case, which concerns the sense the saying might have had if uttered by Jesus, who never abandoned hope for Israel.)

158. Cf. Goodwin, *Syntax of the Moods and Tenses*, 235–37.

159. Cf. van Der Kwaak, "Klage über Jerusalem," 169–70. Illustrations include:

- Plato, *Phaed.* 101D: "You would not reply to him until [ἕως] you had examined the consequences."
- Xenophon, *Cyr.* 5.5.37: "These must always make trouble until [ἕως] they are put in order."
- Matt 5:26 // Luke 12:59: "You will not get out until [ἕως] you have paid the last penny."
- Matt 17:9: "Tell no one about the vision until [ἕως] the Son of Man has been raised from the dead."
- Luke 22:18: "I will not drink of the fruit of the vine until [ἕως] the kingdom of God comes" (cf. 22:16).
- Acts 23:12: "The Jews joined in a conspiracy and bound themselves by an oath neither to eat nor to drink until [ἕως] they had killed Paul" (cf. 23:14, 21).
- 2 Thess 2:7: "Only he who now restrains (will do so) until [ἕως] he is out of the way."
- Did. 14.2: "Everyone having a dispute with a fellow should not be allowed to assemble with you, until [ἕως] they have reconciled."

Moreover, given that Luke 13:34–35 is attributed to Jesus, one should add that the Hebrew or Aramaic עד—which the LXX so often renders with ἕως—sometimes signifies more than the inevitable passing of a temporal span: it can, just like ἕως, state a precondition that may or may not be met.[160]

This holds for a number of rabbinic sentences that express, in a stereotyped form, the conditions that will precede the eschatological redemption:

- b. Sanh. 97a: R. Isaac said: "The Son of David will not come until [עד] the whole world is converted to the belief of the heretics."[161]
- b. Sanh. 98a: Ze'iri said in R. Ḥanina's name: "The Son of David will not come until [עד] there are no conceited men in Israel."
- b. Sanh. 98a: R. Ḥama b. Ḥanina said: "The Son of David will not come until [עד] even the pettiest kingdom ceases to hold power over Israel."
- b. Sanh. 98a: R. Simlai said in the name of R. Elezar b. Simeon: "The Son of David will not come until [עד] all judges and officers are gone from Israel."
- b. Sanh. 98a: R. Ḥanina said: "The Son of David will not come until [עד] a fish is sought for an invalid and cannot be procured."
- b. Sanh. 98b: Rab said: "The Son of David will not come until [עד] the [Roman] power enfolds Israel for nine months."
- b. Nid. 13b: "The Son of David will not come until [עד] all the souls in the

160. Note the following:

- Gen 28:15: "I will not leave you until [עד; LXX: ἕως] I have done that of which I have spoken to you."
- Gen 19:22: "I can do nothing until [עד; LXX: ἕως] you arrive there."
- Gen 29:8: "We cannot water the sheep until [עד; LXX: ἕως] all the flocks are gathered and the stone is rolled away from the mouth of the well."
- Deut 22:2: "It shall be with you until [עד; LXX: ἕως] your brother seeks it" (cf. 11QTemple LXIV, 15).
- Ezra 4:21: "Make a decree . . . that this city not be built again until [עד] a decree is made by me."
- Ahiqar 130–31 no. 43 (Lindenberger): "Rest for your soul do not take until [עד] you have paid back the loan."
- CAP 2:17: "Ours you have a right to seize until [עד] you are indemnified in full."
- 1QS VIII, 16–18: "No member of the covenant who blatantly takes away a word from all that is commanded shall touch the sacred meal . . . until [עד] his deeds are cleansed from all error."
- m. Ber. 7:5: "The blessing over wine may not be said until [עד] water be added to it."

161. This is followed by additional conditions introduced by עד: "until denunciators are in abundance," "until scholars are few," "until the (last) *peruṭah* has gone from the purse," "until the redemption is despaired of."

storehouse of souls have been disposed of" (cf. b. ʿAbod. Zar. 5a; b. Yeb. 62a, 63b; Lev. Rab. 15:1).

- b. Yoma 10a: "The Son of David will not come until [עד] the wicked kingdom of Rome will have spread over the whole world for nine months."

All these rabbinic texts have the same structure:

(a) statement about the messianic advent with adverbial particle of negation ("the Son of David/King Messiah will not come")
(b) conditional particle (עד)
(c) condition to be met (in Israel) for fulfillment of the messianic advent (e.g., "no conceited men in Israel")[162]

Luke 13:35b // Matt 23:39 is formally similar:

(a) statement about the messianic advent with adverbial particle of negation ("you will not see me," "me" being Jesus the Messiah)
(b) conditional particle (ἕως)
(c) condition to be met (in Israel) for fulfillment of the messianic advent (the people bless Jesus and so acknowledge his messianic status)

No one knows how old the formula in the Babylonian Talmud might be, so I do not claim that the saying attributed to Jesus echoes that formula. The parallelism nevertheless remains suggestive. My proposal is that, whether or not there is a tradition-historical connection between the rabbinic formulations and Luke 13:34–35 // Matt 23:37–39, the latter functions as do the statements in the Talmud: the lamentation expresses the condition of the arrival of the future age. That is, the end waits on Jerusalem.[163] Luke 13:34–35 // Matt 23:37–39 is, then, very close to Acts 3:19–21, where Peter declares that Jerusalem's repentance will move God to send the Messiah.

(4) Following delineation of some of the messianic woes, Mark 13:10 stipulates that "the good news must first be proclaimed to all nations."[164] This means, to quote Joel Marcus, that "the worldwide proclamation of the gospel

162. Note also b. ʿAbod. Zar. 5a: R. Jose said: "'The Son of David will not come until [עד] all the souls destined for bodies are exhausted."

163. Cf. b. Sanh. 98a: "'Ulla said: 'Jerusalem will not be redeemed except by righteousness (*or* charity). As it is written: "Zion will be redeemed with justice, and those who repent by righteousness (*or* charity).""'

164. I take 13:10 to be a single sentence and associate "to all nations" with "proclaimed." See Yarbro Collins, *Mark*, 591–92.

has to happen before the final end can come (cf. Matt 24:14)."[165] Mark 13:10 is then, again to cite Marcus, "part of the Markan Jesus' answer to the disciples' question as to the timing of the end (13:4)."[166] Perhaps the verse represents a revisionary expansion of the Jewish idea that, in the latter days, Israel will repent. If so, the nations must repent before the end, too. They cannot do so, however, without being missionized, which is why "the good news must first be proclaimed to all nations." Yet whatever the theological genealogy,[167] the end has a precondition in Mark 13:10: it arrives only after a particular task is finished; its coming depends "on the actions of the disciples."[168] One is put in mind of the old argument that Paul took the successful completion of the Gentile mission to be a precondition for Jesus's return, so that the apostle could indeed hasten the Lord's day through missionizing.[169] One further recalls the significant role that Mark 13:10 and its Matthean parallel have played for many Protestant Christian missionaries: by proclaiming the gospel to the ends of the earth they have hoped to hasten on the end.[170]

(5) The Jesus of Mark 13:20 says: "If God had not shortened [ἐκολόβωσεν]

165. Marcus, *Mark*, 2:883. Cf. Matt 24:14: "And this good news of the kingdom will be proclaimed throughout the world, as a testimony to all the nations; and then the end will come." Some interpreters would demur: Mark 13:10 refers not to the consummation but to the temple's destruction. From Mark's first-century point of view, however, those two events were not neatly divided; the one was rather the harbinger of the other. Cf. Verheyden, "Persecution and Eschatology," 1157–58: Mark's πρῶτον does not (against some exegetes) mark "a first step in a long history"; the sense is rather eschatological.

166. Marcus, *Mark*, 2:883. Cf. Marxsen, *Mark the Evangelist*, 177 ("the proclamation [of the gospel] helps to hasten the coming of the Parousia"), and Hays, "Delay of the Parousia," 85. I assume that Mark 13:10 has to do, and had to do in any preredactional form (if one existed), with the worldwide Gentile mission; see Bird, "Mission as an Apocalyptic Event," 130–31.

167. The eschatological sense is in any case clear; see Pitre, *Tribulation*, 256–64.

168. Pitre, *Tribulation*, 268.

169. Cf. Rom 11:25 ("until the fullness of the Gentiles comes") and see Cullmann, "Eschatology and Missions," 417–20; Munck, *Paul and the Salvation of Mankind*, 36–68; Hengel, *Between Jesus and Paul*, 51; and Stuhlmacher, *Biblical Theology*, 490–92. In their discussions of Paul, all four scholars cite Mark 13:10. A few also urge that Luke the Evangelist believed that the end might be hastened by Christian activities; see, e.g., Mattill, *Luke and the Last Things*, 226–35. Mattill writes: "If Luke did not think of his literary efforts and prayers as causing the *Parousia* to come more quickly he at least intended to do his best to help fulfill those conditions without which it could not come and without which those prayers could not be answered" (234).

170. See C. J. Moore, "Can We Hasten the Parousia?" Against Stein, *Jesus, the Temple*, 83, I find no good reason to suppose that "by the time Mark wrote his Gospel there was a sense that the gospel had been made known to all these nations," that is, "the Roman world and its neighbors."

the days, no flesh would have been saved. But because of the elect whom he chose, he shortened [ἐκολόβωσεν] the days."[171] Here the time of the eschatological crisis is imagined as lasting for a preordained period of time,[172] and yet it is a period of time God can—indeed seemingly will—cut short.[173] For the sake of the elect, God will mercifully alter the timing of the latter days. The fixed time, in other words, is not fixed.[174] Comparable are texts in which the end is "hastened" (see above, pp. 22–23) and rabbinic passages in which the end comes "before its time."[175] Canticles Rabbah 2:8:1 also supplies a conceptual parallel. This reconciles Gen 15:13, which foresees Israel spending four hundred years in Egypt, with the shorter period entailed by other biblical passages. When Moses

> said to Israel: "In this month you will be redeemed," they said to him: "Our teacher, Moses, how can we be delivered? Did not the Holy One, blessed be he, say to Abraham: 'And they will serve them, and they will afflict them four hundred years,' and so far only two hundred and ten have passed?" He said to them: "Since God desires to deliver you, he takes no heed of your reckonings but 'leaps over the mountains' (Cant 2:8). The 'mountains' and 'hills' mentioned here refer to the calculations and periods. He leaps over calculations, periods, and terminations, and in this month you are to be delivered."

171. Cf. the parallel in Matt 24:22: "If those days had not been cut short, no one would be saved; but for the sake of the elect those days will be cut short." Luke has no corresponding line.

172. On the notion of a prescribed measure in eschatological expectation, see esp. Stuhlmann, *Eschatologische Mass*. Note 4 Ezra 4:36–37: "He has measured the age in the balance, and measured the times by measure, and numbered the times by number; and he will not move or arouse them until that measure is fulfilled." Dan 9:24–27 played a crucial role here.

173. Cf. Jeremias, *New Testament Theology*, 140. For parallels, see above, p. 23 n. 90. Although some cite 1 En. 80:2 as comparable, this likely means not "in the days of the sinners the years will grow shorter" but rather "in the days of the sinners the rainy season will grow shorter." See Nickelsburg and VanderKam, *1 Enoch*, 2:523–24.

174. Cf. Pitre, *Tribulation*, 322: "The duration of the tribulation will somehow be shorter than either (a) the length originally intended by God or (b) the duration that the wicked among human beings deserve, or both." For me, (a) is far more likely, but Pitre holds that (a) and (b) are likely true at the same time.

175. E.g., b. B. Meṣ. 85b (were Abraham, Isaac, and Jacob to pray together, Messiah would come "before his time"); Cant. Rab. 2:5:3 ("great is the merit of maintaining the needy, since it causes the resurrection of the dead to come before its time"); and 2:7:1 ("by making their yoke [the yoke of the nations] too heavy on Israel they would cause the end to come before it was due").

Divine benevolence can flout the calendar.

(6) Mark 13:17–18 is a hortatory woe about the latter days: "Woe to those who are pregnant and to those who are nursing infants in those days! Pray that it may not be in winter."[176] This, to quote Anthony Giambrone, "hints that a ray of mercy (if only a ray) might intervene to adjust the timescale." The prophecy is a "wedge in the door. The hour is not foreordained. It is subject to adjustment through prayer."[177] On this view, 13:17–18 is kin to 13:20: one can hope for merciful adjustment in the eschatological schedule.

The Motif of Delay

(7) The Synoptic sayings so far introduced either anticipate that the latter days will be cut short—so Mark 13:20—or presume that certain behaviors—prayer in the case of Matt 6:10 // Luke 11:2; Luke 18:1–8; and perhaps Mark 13:17–18; recognition of Jesus's identity in Matt 23:37–39 // Luke 13:34–35; proclamation of the gospel in Mark 13:10—may help effect the same welcome end. Luke 13:6–9, the parable of the barren fig tree, is different. Here God "intervenes not to shorten the days, but to give the unrepentant still another chance."[178] The parable contemplates not hastening but delay:

> A man had a fig tree planted in his vineyard; and he came looking for fruit on it and found none. So he said to the gardener: "See here! For three years I have come looking for fruit on this fig tree, and still I find none. Cut it down! Why should it be wasting the soil?" He replied: "Sir, let it alone for one more year, until I dig round it and put manure on it. If it bears fruit next year, well and good; but if not, you can cut it down."

This fable, found in Luke alone, and presumably from his special tradition,[179] communicates both God's merciful patience and the need for human repentance. The request of the gardener is, on the level of theological application,

176. The comparable prayer in Matt 24:20 is that flight be neither in winter nor on the Sabbath. Luke has no parallel.

177. Giambrone, *Quest for the Historical Christ*, 373–75.

178. So Cadbury, *Making of Luke-Acts*, 295.

179. The parable contains only a few obviously Lukan characteristics; see Jeremias, *Sprache des Lukasevangeliums*, 227–28, and Harmansa, *Zeit der Entscheidung*, 87–97, 146.

a plea for divine mercy.[180] Although the tree is unfruitful, and although it has been so for some time, the gardener seeks to win it an additional year: "Sir, let it alone for one more year, until I dig around it and put manure on it." Even so, the owner will not abide a lack of productivity forever: "If it bears fruit next year, well and good; but if not, you can cut it down."

The fig tree probably stands for Israel or some noteworthy portion of it, as in multiple biblical and extrabiblical texts, including Mark 11:12–14, 20–21.[181] As with the fig tree, so with the people: both have been unfruitful. It is possible, however, that God will refrain from judgment and instead forbearingly tender a period of respite. Judgment may be withheld even when due, in which case people will gain another chance to "bear fruit worthy of repentance" (Matt 3:8 // Luke 3:8).

The evangelist interpreted Luke 13:6–9 in terms of corporate repentance, for the parable is subjoined to the words "unless you repent, you will all perish" (13:5). Most exegetes, whether writing about Jesus or Luke, have followed suit. T. W. Manson wrote: "The central point . . . is the need for repentance," and "the conversation between the owner of the vineyard and his workman is reminiscent of Rabbinical passages in which the attributes of God debate, the attribute of justice with the attribute of mercy. If God dealt with Israel by strict justice, Israel would perish. But He does not. He gives another chance."[182]

180. One is reminded of Old Testament stories in which a pious hero prays for others to be spared; recall, e.g., Abraham in Gen 18 and Moses in Exod 32. Cf. Bovon, *Luke*, 2:272.

181. For the association of Israel or some part of it with the fig or fig tree, see Isa 28:4; Jer 8:13; 24:1–10; 29:17; Hos 9:10; Joel 1:7; Mic 7:1; Mark 11:12–14. For the association of Israel with a vineyard, see Isa 5:1–7; 27:2–6; Jer 2:21; 12:10–11; Ps 80:8–18; Ezek 15; Hos 10:1. For "fruit(s)" in ethico-religious speech as a symbol of good works, repentance, or reformation, see Ps 1:3; Prov 1:31; Isa 3:10; Hos 10:1; Sir 23:25; Matt 3:10; 7:16–20; 12:33; Luke 3:9; John 15:2, 4, 5, 8, 16; Rom 6:22; Jas 3:17–18; Josephus, *Ant.* 20.48; 2 Bar. 32:1; 4 Bar. 9:14; Apoc. Adam 6:1; b. Qidd. 40a; etc. For cutting down trees in warnings of judgment, see Isa 10:33–34; Jer 22:7; Ezek 31:2–14; 4Q302; Matt 7:19; CMC 98:8–99:8; etc. On the prevalence of plant metaphors in connection with God's people, see esp. Elliott, *Survivors of Israel*, 329–44. The equation of the fig tree with humanity (e.g., Augustine) or sinners (so Questions of James to John 5:7–11) derives from the need to universalize the text for Christian exhortation. The parallel in Apoc. Pet. 2—which is, for Bauckham, "Two Fig Tree Parables," independent of Luke—makes the equation unequivocal by opening and closing the parable with "the fig tree is the house of Israel." Cf. Cyril of Alexandria, *Comm. Lk.* 96; Ephraem, *Comm. Diat.* 14:26–27; Trench, *Parables*, 271; Godet, *Luke*, 2:118; Snodgrass, *Stories with Intent*, 255–64; etc. In my view, an allegorical reading is inevitable; cf. Boucher, *Mysterious Parable*, 35: "If the discursive effect of the barren fig tree is to state that Israel has been unrighteous but will be spared destruction for a time, then it follows the owner stands for God, the tree for Israel, the fruit for righteousness, the destruction for the final punishment."

182. T. W. Manson, *Sayings of Jesus*, 275. See further Harmansa, *Zeit der Entscheidung*, 116–24.

Within its larger Lukan context, 13:6–9 calls to mind the proclamation of John the Baptist: "Bear fruits worthy of repentance. . . . Already the axe is laid at the root of the trees. So every tree that does not bear good fruit is cut down and thrown into the fire" (3:8–9). Perhaps our evangelist discerned in the parable of the barren fig tree partial explanation for the failure of the Baptist's apocalypse to materialize: divine grace had postponed things.[183] Elsewhere in Luke-Acts one detects anxiety over the apparent failure of eschatological events to unfold as many had expected. The parable of the ten pounds in 19:11–17, for instance, makes the apologetical point that Jesus, unlike his disciples, did not believe that the kingdom was to appear immediately (cf. Acts 1:6–7).

Even without the Lukan setting, the parable, with its repeated references to time—"three years I have come looking"; "let it alone for one more year"; "if it bears fruit next year"—prods one to contemplate the eschatological judgment and whether or not its date has been irrevocably fixed. If the time for judgment has come but not been executed, it would seem that God can "grant a reprieve from the sentence already pronounced"[184] and "may rescind his own holy will."[185]

The closing sentence further underlines contingency: "And if [κἄν] it bears fruit next year, well and good; but if [εἰ] not, you can cut it down." The future, according to these words, is unsettled. The fig tree may be cut down. But then again, maybe not. It has no predestined fate.[186] In like manner, Israel's future is open. If the people do not repent, judgment will overtake them. What will

183. Cf. Hiers, *Jesus and the Future*, 35: "Perhaps the saying here is related to Luke's concern to explain the delay of the parousia." Luke 13:7 D adds "bring the axe" (φέρε τὴν ἀξίνην), thereby strengthening the link with 3:9, which also features an axe (ἀξίνη). Commentators often link Luke 13:6–9 with Matt 3:10 // Luke 3:9; so, e.g., Origen, *Hom. Jer.* 18:5; Cyril of Alexandria, *Comm. Lk.* 96; Peter of Alexandria, *Can. Ep.* 3:23; Albert Magnus, *Ennarationes in primam partem Evangelium Lucae*, 282 (ed. Borgnet); Henry, *Matthew to John*, 721; Lapide, *Great Commentary*, 1:121; Nevin, *Popular Expositor*, 856; Tannehill, *Luke*, 275; Böhlemann, *Jesus und der Täfer*, 163–64; and Gruber, "Gerichtskonsequenz," 584.

184. So Jeremias, *Parables*, 170. The accent on mercy is highlighted the more if Luke 13:6–9 rewrites or alludes to a parable preserved in Ahiqar: "O my boy! thou art like the tree which was fruitless beside the water, and its master was fain to cut it down, and it said to him, 'Remove me to another place, and if I do not bear fruit, cut me down.' And its master said to it, 'Thou being beside the water hast not borne fruit, how shalt thou bear fruit when thou art in another place?'" (8:30 Arabic; trans. from Charles, *Apocrypha and Pseudepigrapha*, 2:775). In this tale (which occurs also in the Syriac and Armenian versions), the tree is cut down. In Luke, by contrast, destruction is deferred.

185. Jeremias, *New Testament Theology*, 140.

186. That the owner's response to the gardener's request is not narrated adds to the open-ended nature of the parable.

happen if, to the contrary, they repent—as in the adaptation of our parable in Apocalypse of Peter 2—goes unsaid. Presumably, however, it will be good fortune of some sort.

Luke 13:6–9, then, contains both an element of contingency and an element of uncertainty. The contingency is the date of judgment, which God's mercy may disregard. The uncertainty is the fate of Israel as represented by the fig tree: the future is undecided.[187] The final events, it appears, neither hew to a fixed schedule nor have a predetermined outcome.

It is, I should add, perhaps only from one point of view that Luke 13:6–9, with its request for a merciful delay, conflicts with those Synoptic passages that yearn for the end to come sooner rather than later. The rule in our sources seems to be this. When the future is envisaged as rescue, it is natural to long for its acceleration. When judgment is to the fore, one may hope for postponement, as in these texts:[188]

- Sib. Or. 4:162–70: "Ah, wretched mortals, change these things, and do not lead the great God to all sorts of anger, but abandon daggers and groanings, murders and outrages, and wash your whole bodies in perennial rivers. Stretch out your hands to heaven and ask forgiveness for your previous deeds and make propitiation for bitter impiety with words of praise; God will grant repentance and will not destroy. He will stop his wrath again if you all practice honorable piety in your hearts."[189]
- Sib. Or. 5:357–59: "Let law, wisdom, and glory rule over the righteous, lest one day the imperishable God in anger destroy the livelihood of men with every race and a shameless tribe."
- Gk. Apoc. Ezra 3:5–6: "If I see that the justice of the world has become abundant, I will be longsuffering toward them. If not, I will stretch out my hand and I will grasp the inhabited world from its four corners and I will gather them all together to the valley of Jehoshaphat and I will wipe out the human race and the world will be no more."[190]

187. Cf. Luke 13:5: "Unless you repent [ἐὰν μή], you will all likewise perish." This envisages two possible futures—perishing without repentance and repentance without perishing.

188. As well as in certain millenarian movements that seek to defer catastrophe; on this phenomenon, see Wojcik, "Avertive Apocalypticism."

189. The text continues: "If you do not obey me, evil-minded ones, but love impiety, and receive all these things with evil ears, there will be fire throughout the whole world" (4:171–73).

190. Cf. also Mek. Shirata 5. This gives several illustrations of God offering an "extension of time" for repentance. Rom 2:4 seems related: "Or do you despise the riches of his

The source of hope for both a speedy end and delayed judgment is divine mercy, which hastens the good and procrastinates the bad. That mercy, of course, cannot at the same time accelerate and put off the consummation. The relevant texts, however, appear to have served chiefly to warn or comfort, to challenge or encourage. Their conflict with hope for a near end lies only within a prosaic, literally minded logic. This is why both sorts of materials appear in Luke-Acts. Similarly, if in one place Tertullian counsels praying for the end to come now, in another he advises Christians to pray "for the delay of the final consummation."[191] Consistency is not the hallmark of eschatological hope or exhortation.

Delay in Jewish Sources

The thought of eschatological delay was, I should stress before moving forward, at home in Jesus's religious tradition. The most important text is Hab 2:3: "If it [the end] delays [יתמהמה; LXX: ὑστερήσῃ], wait for it; it will surely come, it will not be late [LXX: χρονίσῃ]."[192] These words counter the impatient thought, whether of the prophet or someone else, that God has been unexpectedly slow to act. Later interpreters found eschatology here.[193]

This includes the author of the Qumran pesher on Habakkuk. The commentary on Hab 2:3 in 1QpHab VII, 7 asserts that "the last time will be prolonged [יארוך] and will be greater than anything of which the prophets spoke, for the mysteries of God are awesome."[194] The line clearly implies, in Collins's

kindness and forbearance and patience? Do you not realize that God's kindness is meant to lead you to repentance?"

191. For the latter, see *Apol.* 39. For the former, see *Or.* 5.

192. Note also Isa 13:22 LXX (ταχὺ ἔρχεται καὶ οὐ χρονιεῖ: "it comes soon and will not delay"; quoted in 1 Clem. 23.5) and Isa 51:14 LXX (ἐν γὰρ τῷ σῴζεσθαί σε οὐ στήσεται οὐδὲ χρονιεῖ: "for when you are saved he will not stand still nor delay").

193. See esp. Strobel, *Verzögerungsproblem*—although many of his proposals are quite tenuous. The prophet himself might have had in view "the day of the Lord"; so Andersen, *Habakkuk*, 205.

194. For additional instances of "mystery" in connection with eschatological delay in the Dead Sea Scrolls and the New Testament, see Ruzer, "Eschatological Failure." 4Q521, the so-called Messianic Apocalypse, includes the phrase "not be delayed [לוא יתאחר]" (2 II). The words that follow, which draw on Isa 61 and prophesy resurrection, are properly eschatological, so "not be delayed" must concern the end. As a lacuna, however, precedes "not be delayed," we can infer no more than that—although one wonders about an echo of Dan 9:19: "O Lord . . . do not delay [אל־תאחר]!"

words, "that the end . . . had not come when initially expected."[195] Indeed, the prophets themselves appear to have been mistaken or uninformed on the matter: "God told Habakkuk to write down the things that are going to come upon the last generation, but the fulfillment of the time of the end he did not make known to him" (7:1–2).

This interpretation of Hab 2:3 may advert to a change in the divine plan due to some unspecified circumstance. Perhaps, however, the delay is, if I may so put it, not objective but subjective: although God has set a date, it remains unrevealed, and people in their ignorance have expected the end prematurely.[196]

Whatever the resolution of that issue, the later targum on the Minor Prophets is more theoretical than 1QpHab VII, 7–13. This rewrites Hab 2:3 so that there may or may not be delay: "The prophecy is ready for a time and the end is fixed, nor will it fail; if there is delay [אם יהי ארכא] in the matter, wait for it, for it will come in its time and will not be deferred." The hypothetical אם ("if, supposing that") leaves the matter open. In the targum, then, the prophet does not know one way or the other. Delay is a possibility, not a certainty.

By contrast, 4 Ezra 4:38–43 rebuts altogether the thought of delay. The seer may wonder whether "the time of threshing" has been "delayed" or "held back" (*prohibeatur*) because of "the sins of those who dwell on earth." An angel, however, authoritatively disabuses him of this notion.

Whereas 4 Ezra offers a reason, if only to withdraw it, for eschatological delay—the cause is sin—no explanation is hazarded in Hab 2:3, 1QpHab VII, 7–13, or Tg. Hab 2:3.[197] The same is true in Ezekiel. In countering the proverb "the days are prolonged [יארכו; LXX: μακράν], and every vision comes to nothing" (12:22), Ezekiel does not excuse or explain apparent postponement. The prophet instead confidently avers that "the fulfillment of every vision" (12:23)

195. J. J. Collins, *Apocalyptic Imagination*, 159. The sectarians may have expected the end to come forty years or so after the death of the Teacher of Righteousness; see J. J. Collins, "Expectation of the End," 82–85.

196. So Lim, *Earliest Commentary*, 103–4: "The implication is that the prophetic predictions are wrong, or at least inaccurate as regards the chronology of the end. The error is a consequence of the nature of the mysteries of God that are the objects of wonder. The pesher is anchored on the principle of *mysterium dei*, which explains that the perceived delay is predicated on human . . . inability to fathom the divine will." Cf. the interpretation of Matt 25:5—"the bridegroom was delayed"—in *Opus Imperfectum* ad loc: "In truth, he is not delaying, but he seems to delay as far as our fickleness is concerned." The continuation in 1QpHab VII, 10–14 refers to a "fixed end," but the precise connotations of this are unclear.

197. Rev 6:10 belongs here too if the sense is "there will be no more delay." This, however, is uncertain; see Aune, *Revelation*, 2:568. Heb 10:37 also quotes Hab 2:3 without accounting for the delay.

"will no longer be delayed" (12:25), that none of the Lord's "words will be delayed any longer" (12:28; cf. Tg. Isa 46:13: "My salvation will not be delayed [יתעכב]"). Here reaffirmation counters disillusionment.

There is also no explicit explanation for delay in the so-called Songs of David preserved in the Cairo Genizah (which may well go back to Second Temple or early rabbinic times).[198] At one point we read: "I (God) have brought the end [קץ] near, and you will no longer delay [ועוד לא תאחר] it" (CšD 1:14). Despite the silence, however, one wonders whether Israel's sin is here implicit: God is bringing the end near and will not allow the sin of the people to delay it any longer.[199] However precisely understood, the subject is delay, and an allusion to Hab 2:3 seems, given the common theme and vocabulary—עוד, קץ, אחר—likely.[200]

Other sources are clearer. According to b. Nid. 13b, "Our rabbis taught: Proselytes and those that play with children delay [מעכבין] the advent of the Messiah." While the precise nature of this offense may elude us—the Talmud suggests more than one possibility—the words offer at least a partial rationalization for the Messiah's delay, a rationalization involving immoral human behavior.[201] Human failing also is to the fore in y. Taʿan. 1:1 (64a) ("What delays [מעכב] it? . . . [The lack of] repentance") and b. Ketub. 111a ("so that they [the people] not [through misdeeds] delay [ירחקו] the end"). In these sources, redemption waits until the people are worthy.

The same idea is to hand in additional rabbinic passages that tacitly explain eschatological delay. To claim, for example, that some years of the messianic age have, because of sin, passed without the Messiah coming (b. ʿAbod. Zar. 9a; b. Sanh. 97b), or to assert that, had Hezekiah acted properly, he would have become the Messiah (Cant. Rab. 4:8:3), is to explain why the arrival of redemption lies in the future rather than the past: had things been better, hopes and dreams would have been realized. The strategy in these traditions is

198. Cf. Stec, *Genizah Psalms*, 22: "My own view is that all the evidence is consistent with an origin of the Genizah Psalms in about the 1st century CE, and that there are no linguistic features that would suggest or require a date later than the 2nd century. It seems likely to me that our psalms were composed in Palestine at about the same time as, or slightly later than, the literature of Qumran."

199. My interpretation takes the second half of 1:14 to contain a quotation: "You (God) prophesied by your spirit through the mouth of your servant, for (God said) 'I have brought nigh the end and you (Israel) will no longer delay it.'" But there are difficult interpretive issues here; see Stec, *Genizah Psalms*, 63–64.

200. Cf. Stec, *Genizah Psalms*, 63: "The whole hemistich may be a loose allusion to Hab. 2:23."

201. See further Klausner, *Messianic Idea*, 430–32.

implied in some of the nonrabbinic texts introduced above.[202] In Acts 3:19–21 and T. Dan 6:4, for instance, eschatological redemption could seemingly come at any moment because the people might repent at any moment. If the end has not come, it must be because the people have not yet properly prepared themselves.[203] Until they do, the redemption tarries.

Further Texts of Delay

(8) Returning to the Synoptics, the motif of delay is not confined to Luke 13:6–9. It also appears in the parable of the servant entrusted with supervision, found in Matt 24:45–51 and Luke 12:42–46. It is regularly assigned to the Sayings Source. *The Critical Edition of Q* proposes this reconstruction:

> Who then is the faithful [[and]] wise slave whom the master put over his household to give [[them]] food on time? Blessed is that slave whose master, on coming, will find so doing. [[Amen]], I tell you, he will appoint him over all his possessions. But if that slave says in his heart: My master is delayed [χρονίζει], and begins to beat [[his fellow slaves]], and eats and drinks [[with the]] drunk[[ards]], the master of that slave will come on a day he does not expect and at an hour he does not know, and will cut him to pieces and give him an inheritance with the faithless.[204]

The first three sentences borrow language from the famous encounter of Joseph and Potiphar's wife, which (in the words of James Kugel) "came to be seen by ancient interpreters as *the* central episode in his life."[205] According to Genesis, "Joseph found favor in his [Potiphar's] sight and was pleasing to him, and he appointed him over his house, and all that he had he gave into Joseph's

202. For the argument that parts of Deutero-Isaiah already attribute delay to Israel's guilt, see A. Labahn, "Delay of Salvation."

203. Cf. 2 Pet 3:1–10, which addresses scoffers who ask, "Where is the promise of his coming?" The writer moves on to assert that "the Lord is not slow about his promise, as some think of slowness, but is patient with you, not wanting any to perish, but all to come to repentance" (3:9). This seems to anticipate Tertullian, *Apol.* 39: "We pray for the delay of the final consummation"—presumably so that more will be redeemed and fewer suffer perdition. Cf. also perhaps Cant. Rab. 2:7:1: "God adjured Israel . . . that they should not seek to hasten the end."

204. Robinson, Hoffmann, and Kloppenborg, *Critical Edition of Q*, 366–75.

205. So Kugel, *Traditions of the Bible*, 442.

hand. And it happened that after he appointed him over his house and over all that was his, the Lord blessed the house of the Egyptian" (39:4–5 LXX).[206] As exegetes have often observed,[207] the rhetorical question, "Who then is the faithful and wise slave whom the master put over his household to give them food on time?," mimics Gen 39:4–5:

Q 12:42:	κατ(έ)στησε(ν)	. . . ἐπὶ τῆς (οἰκετ)είας	αὐτοῦ
Gen 39:4 LXX:	κατέστησεν	. . . ἐπὶ τοῦ οἴκου	αὐτοῦ
Gen 39:5 LXX:	κατασταθῆναι	. . . ἐπὶ τοῦ οἴκου	αὐτοῦ

Only in these places in the Greek Bible does καθίστημι immediately precede ἐπί + οἰκ-. Beyond that, multiple texts reveal that the language of Gen 39:4–5 and closely related verses from the story of Joseph became a refrain in retellings of what happened to the patriarch.[208]

That the resemblance just noted is not coincidence follows from the long list of additional analogies between Q 12:42–44 and Joseph's saga:

- If Joseph's "lord" (κύριος: Gen 39:3–4 LXX; etc.) hands him his assignment, in our parable the slave or servant's "lord" (κύριος: Q 12:42–43) leaves him in charge.

206. MT: "And Joseph found favor in his [lord's] sight and he served him, and he appointed him over his house, and all that was his he gave into his hand. And it happened from the time that he appointed him over his house and over all that was his, that the Lord blessed the house of the Egyptian." The targums do not introduce major changes.

207. Note, e.g., Albertus Magnus, *Super Mt cap. xv–xxviii* (Opera Omnia 21/1, ed. B. Schmidt), 581; Grotius, *Operum theologicarum*, 2:1:235; Calmet, *Commentarium literale*, 7:299; Wettstein, *Novum Testamentum Graecum*, 1:506; Lapide, *Great Commentary*, 2:462; Luz, *Matthew*, 3:223; Fiedler, *Matthäusevangeilum*, 370; Howes, *Formative Stratum*, 112–13; and W. T. Wilson, *Matthew*, 2:302.

208. Gen 41:40 ("you shall be over my house"), 41 ("I have set you over all the land of Egypt"), 33 ("set him over the land of Egypt"), 43 ("he set him over all the land of Egypt"); 45:8 ("he has made me . . . lord of all his house); Ps 104:21 LXX (the king "appointed him lord over his house"); Jub. 39:3 (Potiphar "appointed Joseph over all of his house"); 40:7 (Pharaoh made Joseph "ruler over all of his house"); Philo, *Ios.* 37 (Joseph "received authority over his fellow servants and the charge of the whole household"), 38 ("appointed him steward of his household"), 117 ("take charge of my house and the superintendence of all Egypt"); T. Jos. 2:1 ("this chief officer of Pharaoh entrusted to me his household"); 11:6 ("he entrusted me with his household"); Josephus, *Ant.* 2.39 (Potiphar "committed the charge of his household into his hands"); Jos. Asen. 4:7 ("Pharaoh appointed him ruler of all our land"); 20:9 (Pharaoh "appointed me chief over the whole land of Egypt"); Acts 7:9–10 (Pharaoh "appointed him ruler over Egypt and over all his household").

- If Joseph is especially "wise" in Gen 41:33, 39 (LXX: φρόνιμος), Jesus asks: "Who then is the faithful [[and]] wise [φρόνιμος] slave?"[209]
- If Potiphar sets Joseph "over all his possessions" (Gen 39:5; LXX: ἐν πᾶσιν τοῖς ὑπάρχουσιν αὐτῷ), the master in Q sets the wise servant "over all his possessions" (ἐπὶ πᾶσιν τοῖς ὑπάρχουσιν αὐτοῦ).[210]
- If Joseph is a "servant" (Gen 39:17, 19; 41:12), the figure in the Synoptic story is a "slave" or "servant" (δοῦλος); and while the LXX uses παῖς in this connection, other sources characterize Joseph as a δοῦλος.[211]
- If Joseph supplies the rations of grain for Egypt (Gen 41:53–57), the faithful servant in the Gospels is ordered "to give [[them]] their food in its season."[212]
- If Joseph is a servant who becomes an overseer, the wise servant in Matthew and Luke likewise becomes an overseer.
- If Joseph faces temptation while his lord is away from home (cf. LXX 39:16: ἕως ἦλθεν ὁ κύριος), the situation is the same in Q 12:42–46 (cf. 12:43: ἐλθὼν ὁ κύριος).

While the wise servant in Jesus's parable is like the famous patriarch, the wicked servant may be modeled on another famous figure, Nadan. The latter, in the tale of Ahiqar, despises his lord, beats his fellow servants, and eats and

209. Joseph's wisdom became proverbial; see Ps 105:22; Artapanus frag. 2 = Eusebius, *Praep. ev.* 9:23:1 (φρονήσει); Jub. 40:5; Philo, *Ios.* 117 (φρόνιμος); Josephus, *Ant.* 2.9 (φρονήσει); Acts 7:10; Tg. Onq. Gen 37:3 ("he was a wise son"). See further Feldman, *Josephus's Interpretation*, 346–51. Feldman documents that Josephus "uses [of Joseph] no fewer than six different synonyms—σοφία, σύνεσις, δεξιότης, φρόνησις, φρόνημα, and λογισμός. It is the quality of φρόνησις, with its connotations of intelligence, sagacity, practical wisdom, and understanding, that Josephus ascribes to Joseph over and over again" (347).

210. The phrase πᾶσιν τοῖς ὑπάρχουσιν occurs only one other time in the LXX, that being Jdt 8:10, where, unlike Gen 39:5 and Q 12:44, it is not prefaced by a preposition, not succeeded by a masculine pronoun, and not preceded by two occurrences of καθίστημι.

211. E.g., T. Jos. repeatedly: 1:5; 11:2, 3; 13:6, 7, 8; 15:2, 3. Cf. Philo, *Ios.* 37, 47, 51, 66.

212. While Matt 24:45 has τὴν τροφὴν ἐν καιρῷ ("food in its time"), Luke 12:42 has ἐν καιρῷ τὸ σιτομέτριον ("measure of grain in its time"). Although the *Critical Edition of Q* prints Luke's text, it laconically observes in a note: "Luke's τὸ σιτομέτριον or Matthew's τὴν τροφήν." If, as I argued in *Intertextual Jesus*, 238–39, Luke here reproduces Q, this is one more point of contact with Joseph, for σῖτος ("grain") is one of the key words in his story (LXX of Gen 41:35, 49; 42:2; etc.), and the related verb σιτομετρέω ("deal out rations of grain") appears in Gen 47:12 and 14 LXX. See further—all in connection with Joseph—Gen 42:19 LXX (σιτοδοσίας), 33 (σιτοδοσίας); Jos. Asen. 4:8 (σιτοδοτεῖ); 25:6 (σιτοδότης); 26:3 (σιτοδοσίαν, δώσω σῖτον); 26:4 (σιτοδοσίαν); Josephus, *Ant.* 2.124 (σῖτον . . . δοῦναι μεμετρημένον), 189 (σῖτον . . . διδόντος).

drinks with dissolute individuals (Ahiqar 3:2; 4:15).[213] R. H. Charles thought that Ahiqar's language "coloured one of our Lord's parables."[214]

Whatever one makes of the parallel with Ahiqar, the story of the servant entrusted with supervision trails and illustrates, in both Matthew and Luke, the imperative: "You must be ready, for the Son of Man is coming at an unexpected hour" (Matt 24:44; Luke 12:40). This makes "my master is delayed [χρονίζει]"—a possible echo of Hab 2:3[215]—an eschatological circumstance. Furthermore, as it is the master's unexpectedly prolonged and unexplained absence that enables misbehavior, the line is not an infelicitous, secondary addition. On the contrary, the master's delay—which belongs to the intertext, to Genesis's story of Joseph[216]—is crucial for interpretation. How one should behave in his absence is in fact the main point.[217]

Modern exegetes typically decipher Matt 24:45–51 and Luke 12:42–46 with several equations: the lord is Jesus; the servant stands for his followers (or their leaders); the delay of the master is the unexpectedly prolonged time between the first and second advents; and the lord's return is the parousia. The authors of Q, Matthew, and Luke, like so many commentators after them, already probably thought in these terms.[218] We have no sound cause to posit a primitive version that did little more than pillory the religious elite or warn that the final reckoning was to hand.[219] The motif of eschatological delay likely belonged to the parable from the beginning.

213. For the germane Syriac, Arabic, and Armenian passages, see Charles, *Apocrypha and Pseudepigrapha*, 2:740–41, 749.

214. Charles, *Apocrypha and Pseudepigrapha*, 2:719. See further von Gemünden, *Vegetationsmetaphorik*, 135–38.

215. See Allison, *Intertextual Jesus*, 131–32; also Strobel, *Verzögerungsproblem*, 215–22.

216. According to Gen 39:11, 16, Potiphar was away from home when his wife caught Joseph's garment and implored him to lie with her; cf. Josephus, *Ant.* 2.45 (everyone else was at a public festival); b. Soṭah 36b (everyone had gone to a pagan festival); and Gen. Rab. 87:5 (Potiphar's wife said, "But he is not here").

217. Cf. Dodd, *Parables*, 126 ("the responsibility [that] must be borne in the absence of the master is clearly essential"); Weiser, *Knechtsgleichnisse*, 191–93; and Roth, *Parables in Q*, 90 ("the key issue for the advancement of the plot in the second half of the parable is . . . that the return of the master is delayed"). Other parables in the Jesus tradition employ the motif of a master or authority figure absent for some time, and it is sensible to see the same situation here; cf. Mark 12:1–12 (parable of the wicked tenants); 13:34–37 (parable of the waiting slaves); Matt 25:14–30 (parable of the talents); and Luke 19:12–27 (parable of the pounds).

218. Cf. Roth, *Parables in Q*, 92–106. Earlier ecclesiastical exegetes often think instead in terms of the death and judgment of individuals; cf. Lapide, *Great Commentary*, 2:461–65.

219. Contrast Dodd, *Parables*, 125–27, and Jeremias, *Parables*, 55–58.

In Hab 2:3–4, the injunction to wait for the end if it seems to tarry is immediately trailed by this: "Look at the proud! Their spirit is not right in them, but the righteous live by their faith." The Qumran pesher on Habakkuk elaborates this ethical dualism: those who patiently wait are "the men of truth" who "observe the law, whose hands do not grow slack in the service of the truth, when the last end-time is drawn out for them" (1QpHab VII, 10–12). By contrast, those without right spirit "will not find favor at the judgment" (VII, 14–16). The targum is similar. It turns Hab 2:4 into this: "Behold, the wicked think that all these things are not so, but the righteous will live by the truth of them." Perception of eschatological delay naturally led to reflections on proper and improper responses to it. In this respect, Q 12:42–46 belongs to an exegetical tradition.

(9) The parable in Matt 25:1–12 features ten bridesmaids. Five are foolish, five prudent. When they go out to meet the bridegroom, only five have oil. As the bridegroom tarries (χρονίζοντος), sleep overcomes all. When the bridegroom finally approaches, the wise wake up and trim their lamps. The foolish leave to buy oil and so miss the bridegroom's arrival. The moral of the story is to "keep awake," for one does not know the day or the hour (cf. Matt 24:36–44).

In its present context, the parable is an allegory. The bridegroom is Jesus. The bridesmaids—or at least the five wise bridesmaids—are the faithful community. The bridegroom's delay is the delay of the parousia.[220] The return of the bridegroom is the second advent. The exclusion of the foolish is eschatological judgment.

As with the parable of the servant entrusted with supervision, no motive is offered for the bridegroom's apparent delay.[221] The procrastination, which is an essential element of the story,[222] is unexplained here, too. There is, however, a difference. In Matt 24:45–51 // Luke 12:42–46, awareness of delay becomes the

220. This is the dominant interpretation in exegetical history; cf. Jerome, *Comm. Matt.* ad loc; Augustine, *Serm.* 43.8, Chrysostom, *Hom. Matt.* 78:1; *Opus Imperfectum* 52 ad loc; Trench, *Parables*, 199 (the bridegroom's delay hints "that the time of his return might possibly be delayed very far beyond the expectation of the first disciples"); Balabanski, *Eschatology*, 24–54; etc. See further Wailes, *Medieval Allegories*, 177–84. Contrast Kümmel, *Promise and Fulfilment*, 58: "The problem of the delayed parousia is in no way suggested in the parable, since the trait 'while the bridegroom tarried' (25:5) belongs only to the vivid embellishment of the picture half."

221. Cf. again Hab 2:3 LXX: "If it should tarry, wait for it, for when it comes it will come and not delay [χρονίσῃ]."

222. Cf. Snodgrass, *Stories with Intent*, 516: "We cannot delete the delay as a secondary or unimportant factor. The parable is framed on the fact of the delay."

occasion for misbehavior. In Matt 25:1–12, there is neither awareness of delay nor misbehavior. It is simply a question of eschatological vigilance: "Keep awake therefore, for you know neither the day nor the hour" (25:13).[223]

Contingency and the Historical Jesus

What, if anything, might the texts just reviewed tell us about Jesus? One could seek an answer by running each unit through the gauntlet of the criteria of authenticity and then drawing inferences from what survives the ordeal. I do not adopt that tactic. I am unable to determine, to my satisfaction, the origin of most of the sayings and parables just introduced. I am, to be sure, persuaded that Mark 13:10 derives from Mark or a post-Easter predecessor and tells us directly nothing about the historical Jesus.[224] I am also fairly confident that Jesus composed the Lord's Prayer, with its petition for the coming of the kingdom.[225] For the rest, however, uncertainty inhabits me. The case can go either way, as it does in the secondary literature.[226] Nevertheless, even if I do not

223. Although the comparable rabbinic parables in b. Šabb. 153a and Eccles. Rab. 9:8 are about death rather than the last day, the lesson is the same: be prepared for what you cannot predict.

224. Cf. Sundkler, "Jesus et les païens"; Kümmel, *Promise and Fulfilment*, 84–86; and Dunn, *Jesus Remembered*, 435–36.

225. Cf. Meier, *Marginal Jew*, 2:293–94.

226. Regarding the relevant parables, Meier, *Marginal Jew*, 3:230 judges that none belong among the "happy few" that, in his judgment, merit "the coveted accolade of going back to the historical Jesus." It is easy, however, to find dissenting voices. For Jesus as the author of Luke 18:1–8 (the widow and the unjust judge), see Catchpole, "Son of Man's Search." For the dominical origin of Luke 13:6–9 (the unfruitful fig tree), see Heininger, *Metaphorik*, 129–31. Harmansa, *Zeit der Entscheidung*, 149–50, inclines to an origin with Jesus but does not exclude the possibility of a post-Easter genesis. For the authenticity of Matt 24:45–51 // Luke 12:42–46 (the parable of the servant entrusted with supervision), see Weiser, *Knechtsgleichnisse*, 204–14, and Luz, *Matthew*, 3:222–23. But Fleddermann, Q, 637, attributes the parable to "the author of Q." For the partial authenticity of Matt 25:1–12 (the ten bridesmaids), see Puig i Tàrrech, *Parabole des dix vierges*, 123–262; Riniker, *Gerichtsverkündigung Jesu*, 258; and Luz, *Matthew*, 3:227–28. Contrast Bornkamm, "Verzögerung." Donfried, "Allegory of the Ten Virgins," argues for a redactional origin. Kümmel, *Promise and Fulfilment*, 79–82, favors tracing Matt 23:37–39 // Luke 13:34–35 to Jesus. So too Aune, *Prophecy in Early Christianity*, 175–76. Schulz, Q, 348–60, and Fleddermann, Q, 704–7, are on the other side. Regarding Mark 13:10, 17–18, 20, discussions of their genesis are few and far between; but for an attempt to authenticate the unit to which 13:17–18 and 13:20 belong—Mark 13:14–23—see Pitre, *Tribulation*, 348–77.

know the pedigree of most of the individual units, I doubt, given my general evaluation of the tradition, that all are purely post-Easter, devoid of input from Jesus. I am rather persuaded that, while there is no surfeit of evidence, the several sayings and parables—which come from Q, Mark, M, and L—taken in the aggregate make it likely—not overwhelmingly likely but more likely than not—that Jesus, at some point or on occasion, conceived of the arrival of the end as in some sense contingent. This inference has the advantage of helping us to account for why he promulgates acute near expectation in some sayings, an interim period in others. It is, furthermore, consistent with his hope that all the tribes of Israel would return to the land at the end.[227] For that hope was recurrently, as we have seen, coupled with the prospect of a far-flung eschatological repentance, something Jesus called for but, to judge from any number of texts, did not (to his way of seeing) observe.[228]

Suggestions

What more might be hazarded? Here I can do no more than briefly outline a few tentative proposals.

(1) Jesus not only submitted to John's baptism but praised him (Mark 1:9–11; 11:27–33; Matt 11:7–19 // Luke 7:24–35 [Q]). It follows that he embraced the chief contents of the Baptist's proclamation. Among these was the proximity of the end.[229] The Baptist, however, was arrested and executed without the eschaton arriving, and those who had taken his urgent message to heart might well have wondered, as the time after his unhappy and likely unexpected exit wore on, how to fathom the delay.[230] Millenarian movements regularly face the

227. See Allison, *Jesus Tradition in Q*, 176–91; Allison, *Jesus of Nazareth*, 141–45; Allison, *Constructing Jesus*, 67–76; and Meier, "Jesus, the Twelve."

228. See Ferda, *Galilean Crisis*, 219–55, and recall especially the various derogatory remarks about "this generation" (e.g., Mark 8:12; Matt 11:16 // Luke 7:31; Matt 12:41–42 // Luke 11:31–32) as well as the woes in Matt 11:20–24 // Luke 10:12–15. Note further Mark 6:4; Gos. Thom. 31; Matt 23:37–39 // Luke 13:34–35; and the multiple warnings of judgment in all strands of the tradition. On the sayings about "this generation," see below, pp. 102–3. I know of no strong reason to suppose that Jesus contributed nothing to this group of sayings. See further Ferda, *Galilean Crisis*, 238–42.

229. Note especially the ἤδη of Matt 3:10 // Luke 3:9 (Q)—"*already* the axe is laid to the root of the trees"—and see J. Taylor, *Immerser*, 132–54, and Bilde, *Originality of Jesus*, 198–216.

230. For suggestive remarks about how Jesus may have coped with John's death, see further Syreeni, "John's Ministry."

task of accounting for delay in the eschatological proceedings.[231] So it would have made sense, and might even have been incumbent, for Jesus, as a sort of successor to the Baptist, to have theorized perceived postponement—and all the more if, as appears probable, his public ministry lasted, as the Gospel of John has it, for more than a single year.[232] The longer his ministry, the more likely a sense of delay.

In such a context, Luke 13:6–9 would have made good sense: the judgment John declared had been put off for a bit. The axe laid at the root of the tree (Matt 3:10 // Luke 3:9) had not yet been picked up to strike its target (Luke 13:7). God had graciously given Israel more time in order to "make fruit" (Luke 13:9), that is, to "bear fruit worthy of repentance" (Matt 3:8 // Luke 3:8).[233] If, then—this is for me a genuine if—Jesus composed something close to Luke 13:6–9, then, given his eschatological outlook, it is plausible that the parable was a sort of rationalization, an explanation of why, despite expectation, the end had seemingly tarried.[234] The same may hold for Matt 24:45–51 // Luke 12:42–46 (the parable of the servant entrusted with supervision) and Matt 25:1–12 (the parable of the bridesmaids), if they go back to things Jesus said.[235]

(2) The parable of the widow and the unjust judge (Luke 18:1–8) does not explain delay. It rather, like "your kingdom come" (Matt 6:10 // Luke 11:2), encourages the faithful to hope that they might speed on the consummation through

231. See Allison, *Jesus of Nazareth*, 94, 167–69, and *Constructing Jesus*, 148–53; also below, pp. 65–66.

232. For reasons to prefer John's chronology over that in the Synoptics, see D. M. Smith, *John among the Gospels*, 203–4, and Frey, *Theology and History*, 125–27.

233. I am hardly the first to suggest an interpretation of Luke 13:6–9 along these lines; note, e.g., Heininger, *Metaphorik*, 130; von Gemünden, *Vegetationsmetaphorik*, 139–41; Böhlemann, *Jesus und der Täufer*, 163–64; and Theissen and Merz, "Gerichtsverzögerung," 233–34. According to Theissen and Merz, Jesus construed his ministry as the merciful period of prolongation after John's death. See further Theissen and Merz, "Zeichen Jona." Exegetical tradition has often read Luke 13:6–9 over against the Baptist's proclamation; see above, p. 48 n. 183. Occasionally an interpreter, appealing to Johannine chronology, has thought of the "three years I have come looking for fruit" as referring to Jesus's public ministry; so, e.g., Riesner, *Messias Jesus*, 88, 314.

234. This understanding of Luke 13:6–9 is consistent with one reading of the sign of Jonah. Theissen and Merz, "Gerichtsverzögerung," argue at length that, for Jesus, that sign (Matt 12:39 // Luke 11:29 [Q]) was repentance, specifically John's call to repentance in the face of imminent, wrathful judgment, and that Jesus believed that judgment had been delayed, as happened with Nineveh in Jonah's day. Cf. also Theissen and Merz, "Delay of the Parousia."

235. It is, however, possible that, even if Jesus authored some form of Matt 25:1–12, the motif of delay was added by a later contributor to the tradition. E.g., Balabanski, *Eschatology*, 29–54, regards 25:5–7a as secondary.

prayer. There is no inexorable contradiction with the texts that highlight delay. One can rationalize apparent delay and impatiently hope for the end at the same time.[236] Such tension is in fact common in millenarian movements.[237] The different emphases do not, by themselves, require multiple authors.

Hope, Disappointment, Parables

(3) Tucker Ferda, after observing that "the tradition is rife with attempts to theologize [the] rejection [of Jesus]," persuasively argues that, while "the early church is doubtless responsible for some of this," it is quite "likely that Jesus adopted similar explanatory strategies. These include labeling critics ('this generation'), self-description (as a rejected prophet), and claims about the epistemology of his opponents (blindness and ignorance)."[238]

Ferda cautiously refrains, however, from periodizing Jesus's public career. His sensible argument is that popularity and rejection need not characterize distinct stages. One can be admired and scorned at the same time because various groups or different individuals own differing evaluations. Ferda draws an analogy with the Baptist. We have good evidence that some disregarded or even disdained John. According to Matt 11:16–20 // Luke 7:31–35 (Q), for instance, some said he had a demon. We also know that the Baptist was popular. Both Josephus (*Ant.* 18.116–18) and the Synoptics report that he attracted large crowds. Ferda writes: "It would be foolish to take the impression of popularity as one 'fact' of the tradition and pit it against the other 'fact' of rejection, concluding that we must either choose one impression as more reliable than the other, or decide that we should starkly periodize John's career. A much more reasonable explanation is that John encountered different people during his ministry, and some liked him and listened to him, while others did not."[239] Might it not have been the same with Jesus? Might he not have met with a mixed reception from the beginning and throughout his ministry? I agree with Ferda that the answer is yes. I nonetheless wish to go in another direction.

236. Cf. Tuckett, *Q and the History*, 141: it is "wrong to assume that an awareness of a delay in the Parousia ('Parusieverzögerung') and an expectation of imminent eschatological events ('Naherwartung') are mutually exclusive options." For the argument that, in Luke-Acts, "delay does not oppose but undergirds expectation of an imminent End," see J. T. Carroll, *Response to the End*.

237. See Allison, *Constructing Jesus*, 148–53.

238. Ferda, *Galilean Crisis*, 234.

239. Ferda, *Galilean Crisis*, 255.

The so-called parables of growth—the parable of the sower (Mark 4:3–8), the parable of the seed growing secretly (Mark 4:26–29), the parable of the mustard seed (Mark 4:30–32; Matt 13:31–32 // Luke 13:18–19 [Q]), and the parable of the leaven (Matt 13:33 // Luke 13:20–21 [Q])—have to do with the contrast between messianic expectation and what Jesus saw around him.[240] Although his reality could hardly be identified with the eschaton, these parables recount how much can spring from little, and further how, once the small seed is sown, the harvest will follow: the process that has begun will come to abundant fruition. Comparable is 1 Clem. 23.3–5, which appeals to the growth of trees and vines in countering eschatological cynicism: "In a brief time the fruit of the tree reaches maturity. Truly his [God's] purpose will be accomplished quickly and suddenly."

There is, however, more to the parables of growth than this. We cannot convincingly reduce them to illustrations of the contrast or discontinuity between beginning and end. According to Ulrich Luz,

> An absolutely understood contrast obviously destroys the possibility of discovering a relation between beginning and end in our parables. Yet that is precisely what is important in the images. The small mustard seed becomes the large tree. The little leaven becomes the entire mass of dough. At the same time, the relationship means that the kingdom of God is not simply something that is totally different from the present reality. At some point Jesus' own experiences . . . must be inserted into this relation.[241]

If the small beginning in the parables of growth represents Jesus's ministry, then these same parables imply that, before the coming climax, that ministry will increase in its scope and impact: "The seed sprouts and grows . . . first the stalk, then the head, then the full grain in the head" (Mark 4:27–28). In other words, the parables seem to reflect an optimistic estimate of what will happen before the kingdom arrives in its fullness. The mustard seed "grows up" (ἀναβαίνει, Mark 4:32).

What precisely will happen? In view of the popular topos that repentance will augur the end, my proposal is that the parables of growth mirror Jesus's

240. Still helpful is Dahl, *Memory of the Early Church*. Cf. Hultgren, *Parables*, 396–97: "How could the ministry of Jesus and his disciples have anything to do with the kingdom? The glorious kingdom of Israel's expectation has not arrived." I leave open the question of authenticity here, although I doubt that all four parables are exclusively post-Easter compositions. For an argument that Jesus authored at least the parable of the mustard seed, see Meier, *Marginal Jew*, 5:231–40.

241. Luz, *Matthew*, 2:260–61.

initial hope that more and more people would align with his cause. "We cannot but believe that what he asked for he thought possible."[242] And since Jesus almost certainly did not operate with a clear distinction between God's kingdom and its inhabitants[243]—"it would be meaningless to speak of a 'King' or a 'Kingdom' unless one implied the existence, beside the King, of subjects"[244]—he could, in Madeleine Boucher's words, "speak of the growth of the eschatological community as though it were the growth of the kingdom itself."[245] One recalls the enigmatic Matt 11:12, where the kingdom suffers violence. This, whatever the precise sense, refers by metonymy to those who belong to the kingdom: its members suffer violence.

The parables of growth are, in my estimation, not unlike Jub. 23, where the divine utopia arrives gradually or in stages;[246] and not unlike Apoc. Abr. 29:14, where "the age of justice starts to grow"; and not unlike y. Ber. 1:1 (2c) and y. Yoma 3:2 (40b), where R. Ḥiyya the Great states that the redemption, like the dawn, comes at the beginning little by little but then grows greater and greater.[247]

The disparity between the fulfillment of eschatological dreams and their inauguration in Jesus's controversial movement will, according to the para-

242. So A. T. Cadoux, *Essays*, 123. Cf. Raitt, "Prophetic Summons," 31–32, on the Old Testament prophetic passages "in which the people's failure to repent is given as an explanation to justify their approaching doom": "At some earlier point . . . repentance was not yet a failure, not yet surrendered as an impossibility. The people can be judged for failure to repent only if they were earlier clearly called to repentance" (italics deleted).

243. See Allison, *Constructing Jesus*, 202–3. Cf. R. Zimmermann, *Puzzling the Parables*, 255: in Mark 4:30–32 "the kingdom becomes a metaphor for a new community." It is important to recall in this connection how often in extant texts trees and plants stand for Israel; see above n. 181.

244. So Cadoux, *Historic Mission*, 111.

245. Boucher, *Mysterious Parable*, 55. Cf. Cadoux, *Historic Mission*, 113–14; Flusser, *Sage from Galilee*, 81 (the kingdom is "an expanding realm embracing ever more and more people"); and Roth, *Parables in Q*, 324 ("at present the [Q] group is insignificant and hidden, but it will grow and be marvelously revealed").

246. Jub. 23:26–27: "In those days the children will begin to study the laws, to seek out the commands, and to return to the right way. The days will begin to become numerous and increase." Cf. VanderKam, *Jubilees*, 2:694: "That change is not instantaneous."

247. Cf. Theissen and Merz, "Delay of the Parousia," 60: "In the case of the metaphors of sowing and harvest, the Baptist concentrates on the short period during which the wheat and the chaff are separated and the wheat is being gathered into the granary (Luke 3:17), whereas Jesus describes a much longer period of sowing and reaping in his parables of growth." On eschatological redemption as a process, see Allison, *Constructing Jesus*, 98–116, and Ferda, *Second Coming*, 388–401.

bles of growth, not persist indefinitely. Before the culmination, the number of inhabitants of the kingdom will increase dramatically: "And other seeds fell into good soil and brought forth grain, growing up and increasing and yielding thirtyfold and sixtyfold and a hundredfold" (Mark 4:8). A flourishing movement of repentance will—as in so many of the Jewish texts introduced above—herald the arrival of God's eschatological kingdom.[248]

Now if Jesus associated the coming kingdom with Israel's repentance, and if repentance involved embracing his message, then an overwhelmingly positive response would, in theory, have betokened the kingdom's coming, might indeed have sped it on.[249] What, then, might he have thought if, as the sayings about "this generation" imply (see above, n. 228), there had been, to his mind, repentance on an insufficient scale? What if his initial hope or expectation was not matched by what came to pass? What if, in particular, as the conflict stories and the passion narratives suggest, few leaders had thrown in with his cause? If Jesus ever hoped, to borrow the words of Luke 1:17, "to make ready a people prepared for the Lord," one doubts that he ever looked about and thought to himself, Yes, that has been achieved.

I am not here positing a disjunction between an early period of success and a later period of failure, as did the old theorists of a Galilean crisis. Here I

248. Cf. Boucher, *Mysterious Parable*, 46: "If the statement in vss. 10–12 [of Mark 4] emphasizes the absolute control of God over man's destiny, the parable of the sower and its explanation stress the need for man to respond to the proclamation of the kingdom. The success of the proclamation depends as much on the hearer as on the speaker. It is incumbent on man to resist the attacks of Satan, 'tribulation or persecution,' 'the cares of the world, and the delight in riches, and the desire for other things'; and to 'hear the word and accept it and bear fruit' (vss. 15–20). The statement on the purpose of parables treats of God's sovereignty and predestination, the parable and its explanation treat of man's role and responsibility."

249. Here I recall Cadoux, *Historic Mission*, 206: "Some modern expositors have been misled by Jesus' undoubted disapproval of the violence of the Zealots into hastily concluding that he assigned no part at all to human responsibility in the matter [of the Kingdom's coming]. His Parable of the Seed growing secretly (Mk. iv.26–29) has often been explained as if its purpose was to bring out the insignificance or almost the irrelevance of any human activity in regard to the coming of the Kingdom, and the sole dependence of this latter on the sovereign act of God. But if so, the Parable—with its allusions to the farmer's sowing and reaping, and his dependence on the clock-like succession of the seasons—is singularly ill-adapted to its purpose. It brings out, indeed, the mystery of the Divine workings, and (by implication) the impotence of man without them; but so far from 'excluding the thought of human agency,' or emphasizing the incalculability of the time at which God will act, it does the exact opposite. The farmer's strenuous co-operation with God and his confident reliance on a harvest at a particular time are integral parts of the truth which the Parable conveys." Is there not some truth in all this?

agree with Ferda. But I do detect a contrast between initial, enthusiastic optimism and subsequent disappointment. Despite a warm welcome from some, a welcome that lasted throughout his ministry, many others were, from start to finish, indifferent at best or hostile at worst; and their number and status were such that Jesus at no time could have reckoned that the people as a whole had repented. If, then, his eschatological scenario included the well-attested idea of Israel's corporate repentance, he might, as time moved on, and in the light of the mixed reception he had received, have found himself less optimistic and entertaining the possibility that the kingdom had been or would be deferred for a bit. His thought would then be that which 4 Ezra 4:38–43 rejects: human failure has delayed the time of threshing. Such a possibility is consistent with Matt 23:37–39 // Luke 13:34–35: the consummation is contingent on positive response to Jesus, and so far the response has fallen short.[250]

Parallels from the History of Religions

The movement surrounding Sabbatai Ṣevi supplies a parallel. Baruch of Arezzo, writing soon after Sabbatai's death, wrote that the "redemption had not arrived when he [Sabbatai] said it would." Baruch's explanation was this: "At the time of our messiah's first appearance, there indeed sprang up a penitential movement encompassing the entire Jewish people. But it is essential to grasp that this repentance was incomplete. For people repented only of their sins against God; of sins against their fellow humans . . . they did not repent at all." Here sin of a particular sort accounts for eschatological delay. Sabbatai Ṣevi, however, will come again, and so there will be another opportunity to repent: "The Lord, whose hand is always stretched out to welcome the penitent, will then accept our repentance. This, God willing, will be the ultimate Redemption."[251]

In the same century, another messianic apologist, Yehudah Leib of Zelechow, was convinced that an unprecedented "great repentance" had indeed been "effected in all of Israel." But then he had to offer a different rationalization for the failure of the end to appear: while the redemption had come

250. Snodgrass, *Stories with Intent*, 264, believes that there is a difference in tone between "the language of laments over Jerusalem (13:34–35; 19:41–44)" and the parable in Luke 13:6–9, and that this "suggests the parable belongs to the beginning or middle of Jesus' ministry." In other words, one passage is more optimistic than the other. This suggestion appeals to me.

251. Baruch of Arezzo, "Memorial to the Children of Israel," in Halperin, *Sabbatai Zevi*, 96–96. Baruch appeals to Deut 30:3–4, 8 for support.

up to the brink of arrival, it did not arrive because the pious had committed liturgical errors.[252]

It is human to explain and excuse disappointment. The Unarians, a modern UFO cult, blamed the nonarrival of otherworldly saviors on their own failings: they needed to evolve further spiritually.[253] When Rabbi Schneerson passed in 1994 and was not revealed as the Messiah, many faithful followers blamed themselves: had they been worthy, Moshiach would have come.[254] Christian tradition supplies similar apologetical rationalizations. For instance, the nineteenth-century Catholic saint Don Bosco, when explaining prophetic dreams that failed to come to pass, remarked: "If one does not follow the revelation which has been received, then it is clear that the things prophesied will not take place."[255]

If Jesus sensed eschatological delay, he would presumably have looked for a reason. In this he will not have been altogether unlike Paul. Israel's failure to embrace what the apostle took to be "God's gospel" (Rom 1:1) led to studied reflection (Rom 9–11).

Repentance

(4) As we have seen, Israel's repentance is, in multiple rabbinic and intertestamental sources, a condition of eschatological redemption. It is likely not coincidence that Mark's summary of Jesus's message relates the kingdom's coming to repentance: "The kingdom of God has come near; repent, and believe in the good news" (Mark 1:15; cf. Matt 4:17).[256] I concur with N. T. Wright: Jesus "sum-

252. Carlebach, "Two Amens," 250–51.

253. Tumminia, *When Prophecy Never Fails*, 37.

254. Shaffir, "When Prophecy Is Not Validated," 127–28.

255. See Phelan, *Don Bosco*, 277.

256. The words either go back to Jesus or are someone's impression of what he was all about. In either case, Mark 1:15 likely catches an important part of his proclamation. My view, as opposed to Lambert, *How Repentance Became Biblical*, 144–47, is that Jesus, who played the role of prophet, appealed to both individuals and the nation to repent. See Merklein, "Umkehrpredigt"; Chilton, "Jesus and the Repentance"; N. T. Wright, *Victory of God*, 246–58; Crossley, "Semitic Background"; and Crossley, *Jesus and the Chaos of History*, 106–11. Calling Israel to repentance was characteristic of prophets; cf. 2 Kgs 17:13: "The LORD warned Israel and Judah by every prophet and every seer, saying: 'Turn from your evil ways and keep my commandments'"; and "it would be very surprising for a herald of the eschaton not to invoke the mighty theme of the nation's need to turn to God"; so Sanders, *Jesus and Judaism*, 108. Furthermore, Jesus's predecessor, the Baptist, preached repentance

moned Israel to a once-for-all national repentance, such as would be necessary for the exile to end at last."[257] In this there was almost certainly continuity with the Baptist, to whose baptism he submitted: John's task was the same.[258]

Jesus's call to repent in the face of the kingdom's nearness might mean simply: the kingdom is coming no matter what you do, and if you are not ready, watch out! Most interpreters construe the text this way, apparently with scant reflection. Yet given that so many texts make repentance the necessary prelude to redemption, they could be wrong. The sense of Mark 1:15 could instead be: the kingdom of God is at hand, and if you repent, it will arrive in its fullness posthaste.[259] E. C. Dewick took Mark 1:15 to mean that the connection between repentance and the kingdom's advent "is most intimate; indeed, we might almost say that they express the human and Divine aspects of the same thing. Human repentance is a necessary prelude to the coming of God's Kingdom; God's Kingdom is the certain sequel to human repentance."[260] On this view—which was also perhaps that of the Baptist[261]—Jesus's proclamation

(Mark 1:4; Matt 3:8 // Luke 3:8; cf. Josephus, *Ant.* 18.117), and early Christian missionaries did the same (Acts 2:38; 3:19; 5:31; 8:22; Rom 2:4; 1 Thess 1:9). We have no good reason to posit discontinuity in this matter. This is all the more so if John 4:1 preserves the memory that Jesus at some point baptized, for "we can only think of a variation of John's baptism with a similar meaning of repentance or forgiveness in face of a coming judgment"; so Frey, *Theology and History*, 122. See further Syreeni, "John's Ministry," 84–87. Additionally, "Jesus' repeated invitation to the public to enter the kingdom of God makes much better sense in the context of the call to repent . . . than outside of such a context"; so rightly C. A. Evans, "Baptism of John," 63. That the verb μετανοέω ("repent") and the noun μετάνοια ("repentance") are infrequent in the Gospels is hardly a decisive objection: Jesus preferred the figurative, the picturesque, the parabolic over the abstract; cf. Schlosser, *Règne de Dieu*, 1:103. And as N. T. Wright, *Victory of God*, 251–53, correctly insists, the idea of repentance can be present even when μετάνοια and μετανοέω are not.

257. N. T. Wright, *Victory of God*, 251. On 252–53 he appeals to Matt 11:20–24 // Luke 10:13–15; Matt 12:38–41 // Luke 11:29–32; and Luke 13:1–5 as illustrating the idea of corporate repentance.

258. See esp. Ferda, "John the Baptist." Cf. the summary of the Baptist's purpose in Luke 1:16–17: "He will turn many of the people of Israel to the Lord their God. With the spirit and power of Elijah he will go before him, to turn the hearts of parents to their children, and the disobedient to the wisdom of the righteous, to make ready a people prepared for the Lord."

259. Cf. the thought of Yehudah Leib (see p. 65 above): salvation is near, for we are now in "a period of grace in which the Creator will redeem his sons from among the nations and restore the crown to its former glory. [Yet] this will come about only on condition that we rectify the wrong stated above and other unseemly matters." See Carlebach, "Two Amens," 248.

260. Dewick, *Eschatology*, 141.

261. Our sources are too fragmentary to judge the matter, however.

was akin to Zech 1, where God's acceptance of Israel is contingent on Israel's acceptance of God: "'Return to me,' says the LORD of hosts, 'and I will return to you'" (1:3). Josef Klausner thought that Jesus's "one idea was to implant within his nation the idea of the coming of the Messiah and, by repentance and good works, hasten the 'end.'"[262] Although this is overstatement, I doubt that it is wholly off the mark.[263]

The Death of the Baptist

(5) Mark 9:11–13 is a notoriously perplexing passage. F. C. Burkitt characterized it as "abrupt," "unliterary," and "obscure."[264] Having been asked, "Why do the scribes say that Elijah must come first?," Jesus replies with two questions of his own plus an assertion:

- Question 1 (9:12a): "Is Elijah indeed coming first to restore all things?"[265]
- Question 2 (9:12b): "How then is it written about the Son of Man that he is to suffer and be treated with contempt?"
- Assertion (9:13): "Elijah has come, and they did to him whatever they pleased, as it is written about him."

Bultmann argued that 9:12b is a post-Markan gloss.[266] Others have taken it to be an awkward Markan insertion (as I once did).[267] Still others have surmised that the half-verse is displaced (maybe it followed 9:10).[268] Joel Marcus, however, has urged that Mark's sequence, while difficult, is intelligible as it stands. His case, supported by parallels from the Mekilta, is that Mark 9:11–13 is an example of the sort of juxtaposition of scriptural contradictions one often

262. Klausner, *Jesus of Nazareth*, 368; cf. 399 and 403. The idea is not uncommon in older scholarship; see n. 26 above.

263. Dodd, *Parables*, 30, urged that Jesus cannot have made the kingdom's coming conditional on repentance because the kingdom had already come. The objection is cogent only if one sets the presence of the kingdom against its futurity. For Jesus, however, the kingdom was present yet still to come because its arrival was not a point in time but a series of events extending over time; see Allison, *Constructing Jesus*, 98–116.

264. Burkitt, *Christian Beginnings*, 33.

265. On the reasons for punctuating this as a question, see Marcus, "Mark 9,11–13," 47–48.

266. Bultmann, *History of the Synoptic Tradition*, 124–25, 332.

267. See Davies and Allison, *Matthew*, 2:711.

268. See Oke, "Rearrangement and Transmission."

finds in the rabbis. According to Malachi, Elijah is to heal human relations before the last day: "I will send you the prophet Elijah before the great and terrible day of the Lord comes. He will turn the hearts of parents to their children and the hearts of children to their parents, so that I will not come and strike the land with a curse" (Mal 4:5–6).[269] This stands in tension with the scriptural prophecy that the Son of Man (= Messiah Jesus) is to suffer. Mark's laconic text is an attempt to reconcile the conflict through an "implicit syllogism." Because Jesus is a suffering Messiah, his forerunner (the Baptist) must be a suffering Elijah.[270] I favor this analysis.[271]

What I wish to stress here is the contradiction between the Baptist's execution and Malachi's job for Elijah. The prophet was expected to effect reconciliation and, as Mark has it, "restore all things." That, however, had not happened. "All things" had not been restored. John's ministry issued not in eschatological peace but a violent death. If, then, Jesus spoke something like Mark 9:12–13,[272] he directly faced the failure of John's mission as Elijah,[273] that is, he wrestled with an unexpected interruption in the eschatological script; and if he confronted that challenge, reflections about contingency would almost certainly have arisen.

Jesus and Martyrdom

(6) According to the old theories of a Galilean crisis, Jesus did not initially expect to die. Only later, after adversity and disillusionment in the north, did he resolve that his fate would be martyrdom in the south. I prefer a slightly different scenario.

269. Cf. Sir 48:10; Luke 1:16–17; 4 Ezra 6:26; m. 'Ed. 8:7. While the idea must also have been known at Qumran, the evidence is sparse; see 4Q521 2 3 (an allusion to Mal 4:6) and 4Q558 1 II, 4 ("I will send Elijah be[fore] . . .").

270. For all this, see Marcus, "Mark 9,11–13." I am unpersuaded by those, such as Casey, *Aramaic Sources*, 111–37, and Rothschild, *Baptist Traditions*, 189–91, who argue that "the Son of Man" here originally referred to the Baptist. See Allison, "Q 12.51–53 and Mk 9:11–13," for the possibility that "Son of Man" here carries collective sense and signifies not Jesus alone but the saints of the Most High who are persecuted before the consummation.

271. But for another view, see Bryan, *Israel's Traditions of Judgement*, 88–129. For Bryan, the task of returning Israel to covenant faithfulness had been, in Jesus's mind, accomplished through John.

272. For this possibility, see Allison, "Q 12.51–53 and Mk 9:11–13." Contrast Öhler, "Expectation of Elijah," 474–75. Öhler discerns Mark's hand throughout 9:9–13.

273. Jesus probably thought of John as Elijah because John probably already did so; see Trumbower, "Role of Malachi," and Marcus, *John the Baptist*, 46–61.

As Jesus believed, from the commencement of his ministry, that the end was near, the possibility of distress, persecution, and an untimely death was there from the start. This is because his tradition was steeped in the expectation that, before the redemption, the eschatological woes would "wear out the saints of the Most High" (Dan 7:25).[274] Text after text looks into the future and foresees terror and tribulation, including death for the righteous.[275] If Jewish eschatology was optimistic, it was equally catastrophic.[276]

The possibility of travail and death did not, then, require disappointment with his contemporaries. Indeed, Jesus could, I think, have uttered something like Mark 9:1 at the outset of his ministry: "There are some standing here who will not taste death until they see that the kingdom of God has come with power." "Some" signifies not all, which means that some will taste death. The speaker drops no hint as to which group he belongs to.

We do not, to be sure, know that Jesus uttered something resembling Mark 9:1. Yet we equally do not know that he did not.[277] Mark 9:1 is intelligible coming from Jesus, who interpreted his present in terms of the eschatological tribulation. If the end was to hand, so too inevitably were misfortune and even the possibility of martyrdom. Death was at first, however, no more than a possibility. In no text, Jewish or Christian, do all the righteous perish before the turning point. The sources typically envisage some or many persevering to the end and being saved.[278] Jesus might well have initially hoped to survive "the period of affliction" (4Q171 II, 10), to avoid tasting death until the kingdom of God had come with power.

274. Schweitzer, *Mystery of the Kingdom*, 219–23, had this part right.

275. See further Allison, *End of the Ages*, 5–25, and Pitre, *Tribulation*, 41–130.

276. Cf. Scholem, *Messianic Idea*, 7: "Messianic apocalypticism" always has "two aspects," these being "the catastrophic and destructive nature of the redemption on the one hand and the utopianism of realized Messianism on the other. Jewish Messianism is in its origins and by its nature—this cannot be sufficiently emphasized—a theory of catastrophe."

277. For arguments against authenticity, see Meier, *Marginal Jew*, 2:341–44, and Niemand, *Jesus und sein Weg*, 182–83. For the other side, see Pesch, *Markusevangelium*, 2:66–67, and Allison, *Jesus of Nazareth*, 148–50. Against Mark 9:1 being a redactional creation, see Yarbro Collins, *Mark*, 412–13.

278. Cf. Mark 13:13 and Mek. Vayassaʿ 5. The latter promises that those who keep the Sabbath will escape the suffering that augurs the advent of the messiah. Against Meier, *Marginal Jew*, 2:342–43, Mark 9:1 need not suggest "an interval of some years" or "hint that decades might well intervene before" the kingdom's arrival. This reads in what is not there. It presupposes the normal course of history, where people die as they grow old. Jesus, however, lived inside an eschatological scenario in which tribulation "such as has never occurred since nations first came into existence" (Dan 12:1) had begun to fall upon the world.

If at one time Jesus harbored such hope, later on he let it go.[279] The evidence that he eventually expected to die an untimely death is substantial,[280] and it harmonizes with those traditions where he foresees being absent from his disciples.[281] Exactly why—and precisely when[282]—he became persuaded that suffering violence and death were almost certainly his lot remains opaque. Perhaps it was his perception of adverse circumstances: he could see whither things were tending. Or perhaps he was informed by a sixth sense, which allowed him truly to anticipate the future.[283] Or perhaps disappointment and opposition moved him to live into the tradition of the martyred prophet.[284] Or perhaps all three were true at the same time. Whatever the cause or causes may have been, we have insufficient reason to connect his change of mind directly with a Galilean crisis.[285]

279. Positing that Jesus did not originally or always expect to die before the consummation may help account for the motif of followers resisting his presentiment of martyrdom: Mark 8:27–33; 9:30–32; 10:32–40.

280. See Allison, *Constructing Jesus*, 387–433; Allison, *Resurrection of Jesus*, 183–206. Mark has no formal passion predictions until chapter 8. Might this reflect a memory that Jesus became convinced of his own death only near the end? But a caveat is necessary. Maybe, even at the end, he was, so to speak, 95% sure that he would die but 5% hopeful that he would not. It is human nature to have two minds sometimes and to hesitate in the face of misfortune and pain. Maybe he expected to die yet hoped against hope that he might not, that the redemption would come before death. Cf. Mark 14:32–42, and see Allison, *Resurrection of Jesus*, 191.

281. See esp. Cadoux, *Historic Mission*, 311–15, and Ferda, *Second Coming*. On the assumption that Jesus authored some of the relevant materials—Matt 24:45–51 // Luke 12:42–46; Matt 25:14–30 // Luke 19:12–27; Mark 13:33–37; Luke 12:35–38, 47–48; 21:34–36—the former wrote: "If Jesus intended by these descriptions to teach only the duty of alertness in a crisis, it is surely very extraordinary that he should have felt it necessary to throw on to the screen so often the same scene of servants whose absent master has left them in charge, who do not know when he will return, but do know that, when he returns, he will expect to find not only that they are ready to receive him, but that they have been loyally doing their duty in his absence" (*Historical Mission*, 314).

282. I incline to think this happened not long before his final days. C. A. Evans, *Mark*, 2:11, even urges that Jesus may not have spoken clearly of his death until after he had come to Jerusalem.

283. For the possibility of precognition, which I take seriously, see chapter 3.

284. On the common link between martyrdom and the prophetic vocation, see esp. Steck, *Israel*. Relevant texts include 1 Kgs 18:4, 13; 19:10, 14; 2 Chr 24:20–21; 36:15–21; Neh 9:26; Jer 2:30; 26:20–24; Jub. 1:12; 4QpHos[a] II, 3–6; Acts 7:51–52; Rom 11:3; 1 Thess 2:14–16; Heb 11:32–38; Jas 5:10–11; Rev 11:6–7; 16:6; 18:24; Josephus, *Ant*. 10.38; As. Isa. 2:16; 5:1–14; Lives of the Prophets; 4 Bar. 9:21–32; Tg. Isa 28:1. The topos recurs in the Gospels: Matt 5:11–12 // Luke 6:22–23; Matt 23:29–32 // Luke 11:47–51; Matt 22:6; Mark 6:4; 12:2–5; Luke 4:24; 13:33–34; John 4:44.

285. And also no reason to endorse Schweitzer, *Mystery of the Kingdom*, 125, for whom Jesus decided that his death would complete the unachieved penitence of the faithful.

There is, for me, a parallel here with Paul. Like other scholars, I detect change or development in the apostle's expectation of the end. When writing 1 Thessalonians, he was fully persuaded that he would live to see Jesus return. A few years later, when writing Philippians, he had begun to entertain another possibility, that he might die before the parousia. In Ed Sanders's words: "As the Lord delayed, it seemed increasingly unsatisfactory—not only to Paul's converts, but finally to Paul himself—to think of the dead in Christ as lying in the grave, decaying, for month after month, year after year until the resurrection. When thinking of his own death, Paul himself wanted there to be an inner true self that could be with the Lord immediately after death."[286] If this is correct, then in one sense Paul recapitulated Jesus's experience. Both had hoped at one time not to taste death. They later recognized that another future awaited them.

Delay, Imminence, and Interim

(7) Many have surmised that, if Jesus authored the parable of the servant entrusted with supervision (Matt 24:45–51 // Luke 12:42–46), the master of the household stood for God, not Jesus.[287] In rabbinic parables, the authority figure typically represents the deity,[288] and the same is unambiguously true in Mark 12:1–12, the parable of the wicked tenants: the absent owner of a vineyard is a transparent cipher for God. When contemplated apart from its Synoptic contexts, moreover, nothing in the parable of the servant entrusted with supervision requires that the "lord" be Jesus.

One can make a like case for the parable of the bridesmaids (Matt 25:1–12).[289] While Jewish tradition, including the Old Testament, sometimes likens God to a bridegroom, it seemingly does not, before very late sources, do the same

286. Sanders, *Comparing Judaism and Christianity*, 256. Cf. Schnelle, *Theology of the New Testament*, 367: "While in 1 Thess. 4:17 and 1 Cor. 15:51 he [Paul] expected to be transformed and taken up to the heavenly world before he died, it is clear that by the time he wrote 2 Cor. 5:1–10 and esp. Phil. 1:21–23, he reckoned with the possibility of his own death before the parousia."

287. So, e.g., Jeremias, *Parables*, 56–58, and Gregg, *Historical Jesus*, 218–19. For the other side, see Wenham, *Parables*, 76–80, and Snodgrass, *Stories with Intent*, 513–15. Perhaps it is relevant that, in Jewish sources, the lines between God's activity and the actions of a divine intermediary can be all but indistinguishable. On this topic, see J. R. Kirk, *Man Attested by God*, 44–176, and Ferda, *Second Coming*, 308–17.

288. For a helpful collection, see Notley and Safrai, *Parables of the Sages*.

289. See Weder, *Gleichnisse Jesu*, 244–49.

for the Messiah.[290] G. R. Beasley-Murray wrote: "We do not feel compelled to view Jesus as the burglar in the parable of the Burglar, nor a capitalist in the parable of the Talents (Matt. 25:14ff.), nor a vulture on account of what he says in Luke 17:37. Why then should we feel compelled to identify him with the bridegroom in the parable of the Ten Maidens, as though it gives a description of his wedding night?"[291]

If the parable of the servant entrusted with supervision or the parable of the bridesmaids originated in Jesus's speech, and if he did not tacitly identify himself with either the master of the household or the groom, how might those parables have functioned for him? They probably summoned readiness for a near end despite perceived delay. Millenarian movements can cope with deferral and disappointment by reaffirming nearness and emphasizing preparedness for the pending denouement.[292] We see this, for instance, in 1QpHab VII, 5–17. Although this acknowledges that the end time has been prolonged against all expectation, the pesher quotes Hab 2:3 ("it will come in its time and will not be deferred") and affirms that the end time "will surely come and it will not be late." The upshot is that "the men of truth who observe the law" should not "grow slack in the service of the truth" when the redemption tarries.

There is, however, yet another albeit closely related possibility for the Synoptic parables. If Jesus, as it seems, came to believe that he would die before the denouement, he must have anticipated an interim period, however brief.[293] That is, he must have foreseen a space between his earthly ministry

290. Note, e.g., Isa 62:5; Jer 2:2; Ezek 16:7–8; Hos 2:16, 19–20; 4Q434a; and Mek. Shirata 3. See further Jeremias, "νύμφη," 1101–2.

291. Beasley-Murray, *Jesus and the Kingdom of God*, 213–14.

292. Cf. Melton, "Spiritualization and Reaffirmation."

293. See esp. Ferda, *Second Coming*. His main argument convinces. We disagree, however, on two points. First, Ferda doubts, or at least regards the data as insufficient to establish, that Jesus held a contingent eschatology or revised his eschatological scenario in any significant way. Second, he urges, as did Kümmel and Cullmann, that Jesus expected the consummation sometime in his generation but not necessarily in the immediate future: "We search in vain for evidence of an eschatology that is more imminent than the view that the generation then living is the last." Regarding the latter point. (a) both Mark 1.15 and Matt 10:7 // Luke 10:9 (Q) use ἤγγικεν of the kingdom's arrival. If this fairly represents an Aramaic verb Jesus employed (cf. קרב), it is worth noting that, while there has been much dispute as to whether in the Synoptics the perfect means "has arrived" or "is just about to arrive," no one opts for "may or may not be really close." Cf. the use of ἤγγικεν in Rom 13:12 ("the day is near"); Jas 5:8 ("the coming of the Lord is near"); and 1 Pet 4:7 ("the end of all things is near"). (b) Luke 19:11 represents Jesus's followers as "supposing that the kingdom of God would appear immediately [παραχρῆμα μέλλει]." See below, p. 77. (c) The passion narratives parade correlations between Jesus's end and eschatological expectations; see Allison, *End of*

and his vindication as the Son of Man, a period when he, following martyrdom, would be absent from his supporters. This opens the possibility that, if either Matt 24:45–51 // Luke 12:42–46 or Matt 25:1–12 fairly reflects a narrative he composed, the absent master and tarrying bridegroom were ciphers for a departed Jesus, the return of that master and the arrival of the bridegroom ciphers for his reappearance at the eschatological climax.[294] The parenetical

---

the Ages, 26–61. I know of no real parallel in antiquity to this exceedingly peculiar interpretive move. The best explanation is that it reflects the struggle to fathom why Jesus's death was not soon followed by the consummation. But there would have been no issue had Jesus's circle not believed the redemption to be truly imminent. (d) The end is typically quite close for messianic movements, and it was near for others in the first century CE; cf. Matt 3:10 // Luke 3:9 ("already [ἤδη] the axe is laid at the root of the tree"); Rom 13:12 ("the night is far gone [προέκοψεν], the day is near"); 1 Cor 7:29 ("the appointed time has grown short [συνεσταλμένος ἐστίν]"), 31 ("the present form of this world is passing away [παράγει]"); Phil 4:5 ("the Lord is near" [ἔγγυς]); 4 Ezra 4:26 ("the world is hastening swiftly to its end"); 8:61 ("my judgment is now drawing near"); 2 Bar. 82:2 ("the fulfillment of his judgment is not far"); 85:10 ("the youth of this world has passed away, and the power of creation is already exhausted, and the coming of the times is very near"). One thinks of Paul and the Thessalonians. Had he preached that Jesus would return some time in the next twenty to forty years or so, the death of some converts would not have surprised. Yet it did surprise. The end was close enough that, when a couple of people passed on, believers were taken aback. Note also ἔρχομαι ταχύ ("I come quickly") in Rev 2:16; 3:11; 11:14; 22:7, 12, 20 and δεῖ γενέσθαι ἐν τάχει ("what must soon take place") in Rev 1:1 and 22:6. (e) The traditions about the disciples' pre-Easter mission make most sense if the end was imminent. Not only does Jesus instruct disciples to proclaim the nearness of the kingdom (Matt 10:7 // Luke 9:2), but a sense of urgency would explain why they go out in the first place: there is not enough time for Jesus to do everything himself. Imminent expectation would also account for Luke 10:4: "Greet no one on the road." Cf. the interpretation in Jeremias, *New Testament Theology*, 133: "In no circumstances . . . may the messengers involve themselves in any loss of time. Their duty, to proclaim the nearness of the reign of God, must be fulfilled with the utmost speed. Every minute is precious." Matt 10:23 may also belong here. (f) The phrase "after three days" (Mark 8:31; 9:31; 10:34), which corresponds neither to Hos 6:2 ("after two days he will revive us; on the third day he will raise us up") nor to the chronology in Mark 14–16, likely goes back to Jesus's speech. Moreover, the passion predictions, in my view, descend from predictions about the latter days: although the saints will suffer and die, "after three days" they will rise. Following the crucifixion, the scope of the prediction was naturally narrowed to Jesus alone. See Allison, *Resurrection of Jesus*, 187–90. Now "after three days" is an idiom meaning "pretty soon" or "after a short indefinite interval"; see J. B. Bauer, "Drei Tage," and Gradwohl, "Drei Tage und der dritte Tag." The expression might signify a few days or perhaps be stretched to even a few weeks. It is not so pliant as to come from someone who envisioned the end to be perhaps years or decades ahead.

294. The same holds for the journeying master in Mark 13:34–37 and Luke 12:35–38 if those texts conserve dominical tradition.

effect, however, would be the same as if the master of the household and the groom stood for God. Stay awake. Be prepared. Do not lose heart. "The one who endures to the end will be saved" (Mark 13:13).

Return to Schweitzer and Matthew 10:23

(8) Schweitzer famously argued that Jesus, as Matt 10:23 has it, sent forth his disciples with these words: "When they persecute you in one town, flee to the next;[295] for truly I tell you, you will not have gone through all the towns of Israel before the Son of Man comes." When the disciples returned and the redemption had not arrived, Jesus changed strategies. He decided to usher in the kingdom by suffering the eschatological ordeal in his own person. This is what moved him to go to Jerusalem and court death. In short, Jesus began with one eschatological scenario and, when it dissolved, ended with another.[296]

Few seriously entertain Schweitzer's reconstruction today.[297] Not only are many doubtful that Jesus authored 10:23,[298] but there is no parallel in Mark 6 or Luke 9 or 10, so it is possible that Matthew inserted 10:23 into its present context.[299] In such a case, we cannot recover the pre-Matthean setting, much less the *Sitz im Leben Jesu*, if any.

Schweitzer, however, may not have been entirely mistaken. Nothing in Matt 10:23 necessitates a post-Easter setting, although of course that hardly establishes a pre-Easter origin.[300] Furthermore, despite the lack of a Lukan

295. Flight was an eschatological topos; cf. Zech 14:5; Ps. Sol. 17:25; Matt 3:7 // Luke 3:7; Mark 13:14; Rev 6:15–16; 12:6; Liv. Pro. Jer 12; Apoc. El. 4:21; etc.

296. For all this, see Schweitzer, *Mystery of the Kingdom*, and Schweitzer, *Quest of the Historical Jesus*, 327–29 (Matt 10:23 marks "the first postponement of the parousia").

297. Perhaps closest is Luz, "Warum zog Jesus nach Jerusalem?" See also Luz, *Matthew*, 2:91. While N. T. Wright, *Victory of God*, 577–79, and Pitre, *Tribulation*, 381–507, concur that Jesus thought of himself as enduring, as a sacrifice, the eschatological woes in his own person, they do not associate this with Matt 10:23 or a change in strategy due to disappointment.

298. Note, e.g., Sanders and Davies, *Synoptic Gospels*, 310–12 (the sentence is probably from "early Christians opposed to the Gentile mission"), and Meier, *Marginal Jew*, 2:339–41.

299. A few even assign the verse to the evangelist; so Frankemölle, *Jahwe-Bund und Kirche Christi*, 130–33, and Gundry, *Matthew*, 194.

300. See further Allison, *Jesus of Nazareth*, 148–50. Lindars, *Jesus Son of Man*, 122–23, argues for the authenticity of a form of Matt 10:23 with "kingdom of God" instead of "Son of Man." According to Luz, *Matthew*, 2:91, "if our logion does go back to Jesus it must belong to the last period of time before his death, when the resistance against the proclamation of the kingdom of God in Israel was already public."

parallel, the verse is unlikely to be a redactional creation. One can indeed make a case that the saying stood in Q's missionary discourse.[301] Certainly if Luke found it in that source, his exclusion would be altogether understandable.

Religions sometimes preserve, against what one might expect, failed forecasts.[302] According to Dan 12:11, "from the time that the regular burnt offering is taken away and the abomination that desolates is set up, there shall be one thousand two hundred and ninety days." Yet the beatitude in the next verse contains a different number, which modern exegetes typically construe as a correction of the erroneous calculation in 12:11: "Happy are those who persevere and attain the thousand three hundred and thirty-five days" (12:12).[303] In like fashion, "there are a large number of dateable apocalyptic predictions still extant in the early Muslim religious literature indicating that the proto-Muslims expected the world to come to an end either during the year 70/689–90 or during the year 100/717. The fact that these predictions are still available in such quantities long after the obvious disconfirmation discrediting the original prediction demonstrates the belief in this date and its power within the community."[304] Again, when William Miller (1782–1849) predicted that Jesus would return on October 22, 1844, his faithful followers did not, as one might have expected, conveniently forget his forecast. They instead fundamentally reinterpreted his words: the second coming had indeed occurred, but spiritually in heaven, not physically on earth.[305]

Matthew 10:23 might similarly preserve the memory that Jesus and his disciples lived with a hope that disappointed them: they had expected the Son of Man to come in circumstances that failed to materialize. Such a thesis harmonizes not only with the near expectation in other parts of the tradition but has the advantage of accounting for Matt 10:23. As perusal of recent commentaries reveals, the verse remains otherwise exceedingly hard to account for.[306]

301. See Davies and Allison, *Matthew*, 2:188. But Schürmann, *Traditionsgeschichtliche Untersuchungen*, 150–56, contends instead that 10:23 originally followed Q 12:11–12 (cf. Matt 10:19–20). On the unity of 10:23, see Davies and Allison, *Matthew* 2:189.

302. Most of the essays in Stone, *Expecting Armageddon*, are here relevant.

303. See J. J. Collins, *Daniel*, 400–401. One also recalls the contradiction between Huldah's prophecy that Josiah will die in peace and not see calamity (2 Kgs 22:20) and the king's death in battle (23:29–30).

304. So Cook, "Beginnings of Islam," 64. See further Bashear, "Muslim Apocalypses."

305. Loughborough, *Great Second Advent Movement*, 185–97.

306. See Künzi, *Naherwartungslogien*. He shows that, before Reimarus, it was common to divine in Matt 10:23 a prophecy of the resurrection or the sending of the Spirit or the destruction of Jerusalem. The usual strategy today is to assign the word to a Christian prophet; so Meier, *Marginal Jew*, 2:340–41. He holds that "the setting presupposed by the saying is

To be sure, even if one decides that Matt 10:23 might come from Jesus, that scarcely corroborates Schweitzer's idea that disappointed expectation moved Jesus to decide heroically that he alone would suffer the affliction of the latter days. I do not espouse that idea. Matthew 10:23 is, however, perhaps one more bit of evidence that an unexpected protraction of the consummation was not foreign to Jesus. For if he did articulate something close to that sentence, it is hard to see, given what we otherwise know about him, that he could ever have regarded it as having been fulfilled. And a prophecy unfulfilled would surely have occasioned reflection.[307]

Closing Remarks

According to Luke 19:11, when Jesus neared Jerusalem, his disciples "supposed that the kingdom of God was to appear immediately." This editorial remark introduces the parable of the absentee nobleman, which discloses that Jesus did not share his followers' expectation of an imminent parousia (19:12–27). This is apologetics. Luke wants readers to know that Jesus did not share a hope that, in retrospect, had come undone: he knew better than others.[308]

Apologetics, however, need not be utterly devoid of memory, and it is plausible that Luke was aware that Jesus's followers had, while he was with them, expected a near end. Had the evangelist not known this, it is far from clear why he would have invented it from scratch.[309] Given, then, the main argument of the previous pages, one may at least ask whether 19:11 preserves another memory, this being that, when nearing his end, Jesus's *Naherwartung* was not

---

not the very brief, programmatic mission of the twelve during the ministry of the historical Jesus, but a thoroughgoing mission to each and every town (*poleis*, 'cities' in the Greek, actually signifying 'towns' of any size) in Israel—presumably all of the Jewish-inhabited towns of both Galilee and Judea." Our sources, however, say nothing about the intended scope of the disciples' pre-Easter mission. Beyond that, even if the present formulation in Matt 10:23 reflects post-Easter circumstances, it could still rewrite or develop a word of Jesus; see Allison, *Jesus of Nazareth*, 149–50.

307. Luz, *Matthew*, 2:93, entertains another possibility: if Matt 10:23 is dominical—he leaves the question open—it could come from "a farewell statement of Jesus that would speak of the continuing proclamation of the kingdom of God after his execution." It would, in other words, have been exhortation and encouragement for an ongoing mission during his absence.

308. See further Allison, *Constructing Jesus*, 65–67. The parable, I take it, is about the parousia, not Jesus's resurrection or ascension; see Fusco, "Point of View."

309. See further Bilde, *Originality of Jesus*, 33, 150–52.

precisely what it had been before, that he had come to contemplate eschatological delay, and that his martyrdom meant a gap, however brief, between his suffering and the consummation.[310]

Whatever the truth about Luke 19:11—we can do no more than wonder—the thesis that Jesus perceived delay in the eschatological proceedings is both sensible and consonant with the data. While his original and dominant expectation was of imminent judgment and impending redemption, some texts imply the passage of time between his death and the eschatological finale, and those texts likely remember rightly. Or so I have argued. Jesus at some point recognized that the ongoing course of events did not hew to his initial high hopes. And the idea of contingency, which was part of his tradition and which appears in prophetic books he was doubtless familiar with,[311] helped him to make sense of this. He may even, in line with Mark 13:32, have at some point expressed a certain agnosticism regarding the date of the eschatological day of reckoning.[312]

Yet holding that no one knows the day or hour is wholly different from asserting that no one knows the decade or century.[313] We have no good reason to suppose that Jesus ever let go of his near expectation.[314] We equally have no good reason to imagine that he ever gave up the thought that the eschatological drama had begun, or that the end-time ordeal was present, or that the coming

310. Although Erlemann, *Naherwartung und Parusieverzögerung*, 403 n. 127, doubts that Luke 19:12–27, in current form, goes back to Jesus, he judges that the structure—appointment // absence // return // reckoning—may do so.

311. E.g., Jeremiah and Jonah; see above, pp. 26–28. Matt 12:38–40 // Luke 11:29–30 (Q) and Matt 12:41–42 // Luke 11:31–32 (Q) refer to Jonah; Mark's Jesus quotes Jer 7:11 in Mark 11:17 and alludes to Jer 5:21 in Mark 8:18; and Matt 23:38 // Luke 13:35 (Q) alludes to Jer 12:7; see Allison, *Intertextual Jesus*, 126–28.

312. The debate over the authenticity of Mark 13:32 instructs us about the limitations of our tools. Some, appealing to the criterion of embarrassment, are convinced that the church did not invent a saying that restricts Jesus's knowledge. Others, persuaded that Jesus can hardly have referred to himself as "the Son" without qualification, are just as confident on the other side. See further Barrett, *Jesus and the Gospel Tradition*, 25–26, and Meier, *Marginal Jew*, 2:347.

313. Cf. Colwell, *Approach to the Teaching*, 93: Mark 13:32 says "no more than, 'No one knows *exactly* when it will come.' A modern preacher would say, 'No man knows the minute and the second,' but Jesus' watch had neither a minute nor a second hand. The hour was the small exact unit of time for Jesus and his friends."

314. Here I depart from Weiss, *Jesus' Proclamation*, 91, who held that, near the end of his life, Jesus's revised expectation was that the end would "occur sometime within the important period of the next ten, twenty, or thirty years."

of the Son of Man and the resurrection of the dead were proximate.[315] On the contrary, his consistent *Naherwartung* explains why, after Easter, his closest followers maintained their imminent expectation[316] and colored their passion narratives with eschatological hues (see further n. 293).

Eschatological impatience, however, cannot long endure without birthing a sense of delay, and I have argued that this probably happened in Jesus's case. He came to believe that the redemption would tarry a bit, that it would arrive a little later than initially hoped, and that he would likely die before the redemption, so that his followers would have to soldier on for a short time without him.[317] Adopting a contingent eschatology did not mean a change of plan or moving the end down the road, much less putting it off indefinitely. It rather meant taking into account likely martyrdom[318] and so, in turn, anticipating a parenthetical period between his end in particular and the end in general. Far from the delay of the consummation being, in the words of Luise Schottroff, "a pure invention of scholarship," it was a problem Jesus himself already confronted.[319] Moreover, while he did not imagine that human exertion could bring the kingdom, Jesus evidently believed that circumstances could affect the time of its arrival, and that they had in fact done so.[320]

315. In my view, Jesus did not anticipate his personal vindication before the general resurrection; cf. Schweitzer, *Mystery of the Kingdom*, 201–14; Cadoux, *Historic Mission*, 293–98; Jeremias, *New Testament Theology*, 285–86; Jeremias, "Drei-Tage-Worte"; Allison, *Resurrection of Jesus*, 183–206; and Ferda, *Second Coming*, 349–56.

316. See further my article, "Ist die Apokalyptik?"

317. This is how I understand Mark 14:25: "Truly I tell you, I will never again drink of the fruit of the vine until that day when I drink it new in the kingdom of God" (cf. Luke 22:18). Although this implies, especially when read within the context of the Last Supper, Jesus's absence, it does not suggest a long absence. See Schlosser, *Règne de Dieu*, 395–98.

318. Which in turn implied taking part in the general resurrection of the dead. This is one reason for thinking that the formal predictions of death and resurrection in Mark 8:31; 9:31; 10:33–34 may descend from prophecies of Jesus.

319. The quotation is from Schottroff, "Conceptions of the History," 216. I decline her proposal that "the linear understanding of time" is an imposition by "the winners in history" on the first-century Christian sources.

320. The rabbis, as we have seen, disagreed on whether God would guarantee Israel's repentance. As to what Jesus thought of the matter, or whether he gave it any thought at all, I am unsure. The sources let us down here. Yet it remains possible that, as Weiss and Cadoux hold, Jesus thought his death might play its part in the eschatological turning of Israel; cf. Jer 31:34; 33:8; Ezek 37:23; Zech 3:9. If Jesus found himself in Isa 61, he may likewise have read himself into earlier chapters that feature a suffering servant who dies for others; see below, pp. 134–35. Mark 10:45 ("give his life as a ransom for many") and 14:24 ("poured out for many") seem to echo Isa 53:11–12 ("poured out himself to death," "bore the sin of many").

EXCURSUS

JOACHIM JEREMIAS AND ESCHATOLOGICAL ERROR

The previous pages are not theological. Nor are they theology in disguise. I have done my best, despite my personal religious interests, to pursue the evidence as a historian, mustering arguments accessible to all. I am, however, keenly aware that some of my readers will, because of their personal commitments, have trouble taking a tranquil tour of the arguments: a Jesus who expected what did not come to pass troubles them. Perhaps, then, it is not out of line to say a few words about this issue, or rather to review, if briefly, how one famous New Testament scholar, Joachim Jeremias, attended to this subject.[1]

Jeremias was a practicing Lutheran who professed Jesus to be the decisive revelation of God: "The life, acts, and death of Jesus, the authoritative word of him who dared to say *'Abba'*, the one who with divine authority invited sinners to this table, and as the servant of God went to the cross—all this is the call of God."[2] Indeed, "the good news of Jesus in word and deed is the origin of Christianity," and "there is no other revelation of God but the incarnate Word."[3]

And yet, according to Jeremias, Jesus held a *Naherwartung*: the kingdom of God was nigh, the night was far gone, the day was at hand, the radical transformation of the world was near.[4] And he was wrong. "Must we not concede that Jesus' expectation of an imminent end was one that remained unfulfilled? Honesty and the demand for truthfulness compel us to the answer 'Yes.' Jesus expected that the end would come soon."[5] But how can the definitive divine revelation be coupled with prophetic error?

In dealing with this question, Jeremias adopted four different but complementary strategies. (1) Jesus's belief in the nearness of the end was the outer dress of "spiritual judgments" (*geistliche Urteile*) regarding God's active grace in the present. We must, so to speak, demythologize Jesus's culturally learned and so culturally relative language about the latter days

1. Readers interested in my own reflections on this topic may look at *End of the Ages*, 172–79, and *Resurrecting Jesus*, 111–48. The latter includes an overview of theological responses to the proposition that Jesus took the end to be near.

2. Jeremias, *Jesus and the Message*, 13.

3. Jeremias, *Jesus and the Message*, 12–13.

4. See esp. Jeremias, "Naherwartung."

5. Jeremias, *New Testament Theology*, 139.

in order to discover what it may mean for us: "The near expectation is only the clothing for the spiritual knowledge that all earthly existence lives out of God's gracious reprieve."[6] More fully:

> The hour of fulfillment has broken in, the royal rule of God is manifesting itself in the here and now; soon comes the catastrophe, which will introduce its definitive arrival. Use the time before it is too late! It is a matter of life or death. If one wishes to put these spiritual judgments into a single sentence, then it is this, that God has given a gracious reprieve. It is not for Jesus to satisfy the curiosity of his hearers, but what matters to him is the concern to awaken and maintain in them, through the tireless reference to the impending catastrophe, the knowledge of the gift of the gracious reprieve.[7]

This is perhaps a bit like the old exegetical distinction between the literal and the allegorical, or the later liberal distinction between the husk and the kernel: the language of eschatology communicates the presence of divine grace. Jeremias's words also remind one of Rudolf Bultmann's demythologizing existentialism: what matters is the decision that eschatological expectation forces one to make between life and death, between God and the world.[8]

(2) Jeremias's second strategy was to adopt a particular view of the incarnation, according to which the Son of God laid aside certain divine attributes in order to become truly human (cf. Phil 2:7). This *kenosis* or self-emptying accounts for Jesus, in his incarnate state, not knowing everything: he voluntarily let go of his omniscience, temporarily setting it to the side. Taking the form of a servant, he subjected himself to the vicissitudes of human existence. And because no human being unerringly knows the future, the incarnate Jesus did not unerringly know the future. The New

6. Jeremias, "Naherwartung," 144.

7. Jeremias, "Naherwartung," 143.

8. Cf. Bultmann, *Theology of the New Testament*, 1.22–23. "Prophetic consciousness always expects the judgment of God, and likewise the time of salvation to be brought in by God, in the immediate future, as may be clearly seen in the great prophets of the Old Testament. And the reason this is so is that to the prophetic consciousness the sovereignty of God, the absoluteness of His will, is so overpowering that before it the world sinks away and seems to be at its end. The consciousness that man's relation toward God decides his fate and that the hour of decision is of limited duration clothes itself in the consciousness that the hour of decision is for the world, too. The word which the prophet is conscious of having to speak by God's commission takes the form of the final word by which God summons men to definitive decision."

Testament has no place for infallibility. Jesus's eschatological error, then, is "an expression of *vere homo*," that is, "it belongs to the incarnation."[9]

(3) Jesus believed, according to Jeremias, in a God whose will is not fixed and unalterable but in a gracious deity who, in response to human need, can alter the eschatological timetable:

> God can *shorten* the time of distress for the sake of the elect who cry out to him day and night (Luke 18.7f.); he can hear the cry "Thy kingdom come." And not only can God do that, he will do it. If he were to keep to the length of the time of distress originally appointed, no-one would be able to survive, "but for the sake of the elect, whom he chose, he shortened the days" (Mark 13.20 par.). On the other hand, however, God can also hear the request, "Let it alone this year also," and *lengthen* the period of grace (Luke 13.6–9). Thus Jesus takes into account the possibility that God may rescind his own holy will.[10]

While God may have "ordered the course of history and appointed the hour of judgment," the Father "is not the immovable, unchangeable God who in the end can only be described in negations. He is not a God to whom it is pointless to pray. He is a gracious God, who hears prayers and intercessions (Luke 13.8f.; 22.31f.), and is capable in his mercy of rescinding his own holy will."[11]

Jeremias is not, in these words, only a historian. His personal theology is also on display.[12] This includes the contrast he draws between Jesus and Jer 18:7–10. In the latter, human repentance can cancel predicted judgment and human evil can cancel salvific acts. Ever the Lutheran, Jeremias fashions a Jesus who "knows only of a *gracious* action on the part of God." More particularly, "whereas according to Jer. 18, God's gracious repentance is his answer to penitence (v. 8), Jesus makes no mention of previous human contributions as the basis of the correction of the appointed time; it happens as a result of pure mercy"—an idea that, in Jeremias's view, has no parallel "anywhere else in the world of Jesus."[13]

Jesus did, then, have a contingent eschatology. Yet it was unlike that of the rabbis or the Jesus of this chapter, for whom Israel's conduct had a central role to play in what would or would not come to pass. For Jeremias, there is nothing but "pure mercy."

9. Jeremias, "Naherwartung," 144.
10. Jeremias, *New Testament Theology*, 140.
11. Jeremias, *New Testament Theology*, 140.
12. This is obvious in the parallel paragraphs in "Naherwartung," 143–44.
13. Jeremias, *New Testament Theology*, 140–41.

(4) Jeremias made one more hermeneutical proposal about Jesus's eschatological expectations. It comes to expression in the final pages of his *New Testament Theology*:

> It is a common Christian view that the resurrection of Jesus was bound up with his taking a place at the right hand of God and the beginning of the kingly reign of Christ. But because Christ's reign had not yet taken visible form and the old age continued on its way, a distinction was soon made between the present sitting of Christ at God's right hand and his final entry into glory, i.e. between a provisional and a definitive enthronement. Now the conception of a provisional enthronement arrived at in this way is a contradiction in itself and a forced solution, which suggests that originally Easter must have seemed to the disciples to be the definitive turning point, the beginning of the new age, the hour of Christ's entry into reign.[14]

Jeremias found a trace of this earliest idea, that the resurrection was Jesus's entry into reign, in Matt 28:18: "All authority in heaven and earth has been given to me." Like so many exegetes, Jeremias discerned here an implicit claim to the fulfillment of Dan 7:14, where the Son of Man receives dominion, glory, and kingdom, that all peoples, nations, and languages should serve him. This suggests that "the prophecy that the Son of man would be enthroned as ruler of the world was fulfilled in the resurrection."[15] Indeed,

> the disciples' immediate experience of the resurrection of Jesus [was] not as a unique mighty act of God *in the course of* history hastening towards its end (though this is what it must have seemed to them after a short interval), but as the dawn of the eschaton. They saw Jesus in shining light. They were witnesses of his entry into glory. In other words, *they experienced the parousia*. . . .
>
> For the earliest community, to believe meant to live here and now in the consummation of the world. . . . The believer stands in the Easter of the time of salvation; he has been snatched out of a corrupt generation, doomed to destruction (Gal. 1.4; Acts 2.40); he has been saved through the waves of the flood (I Peter 3.20) and the Red Sea (I Cor. 10.1ff.); he is a new creation. These eschatological indicatives, and many like them, presuppose that a real experience of the dawning of God's new world stood at the beginning of the history of the church.[16]

14. Jeremias, *New Testament Theology*, 310.
15. Jeremias, *New Testament Theology*, 310.
16. Jeremias, *New Testament Theology*, 310–11 (emphasis original).

Those who know the history of New Testament scholarship will recognize at once that Jeremias has here become a sort of late-in-life convert to C. H. Dodd's realized eschatology. When Jeremias argues that the resurrection was the parousia, that is, the fulfillment of what Jesus prophesied, or when he contends that the church turned Jesus's Easter vindication into a provisional enthronement and so came to project an additional victory—the second coming—onto the future, he echoes Dodd.[17]

There remains, however, a significant distinction between the two scholars. For Dodd, Jesus never intended eschatological language to be taken literally, as it so often has been. Rather, Jesus looked forward, in figurative language, to his vindication and exaltation in a way that corresponds to what actually happened.[18]

For Jeremias, however, what took place did not seamlessly line up with what Jesus had anticipated. Jesus remains, on Jeremias's view, a Schweitzerian prophet whose expectations, taken in their natural and intended sense, did not come to pass, because the end, as he conceived it, did not materialize. Although Jesus proclaimed that the end would come soon, it did not. The mismatch between expectation and fulfillment is ineradicable.

Yet that was not, for Jeremias, the last word theologically. For Easter, while it may not have been what Jesus concretely had in mind, was nonetheless God's vindication and authorization of him and his cause. It meant for Jesus exaltation, and it meant for his followers a new creation. The parousia, Jeremias avers, occurred, and all was fulfilled—just not in the way that Jesus anticipated.[19] If I may so put it, Jeremias's view comes down to this: while the historical Jesus thought like Schweitzer's Jesus, God thought like C. H. Dodd.

17. See, e.g., Dodd, *Apostolic Preaching*, esp. 135–67. Dodd persuaded others in this matter, most notably Glasson, *Second Advent*, and J. A. T. Robinson, *Jesus and His Coming*. One can already see Jeremias, in his *Parables*, 230 n. 3, endeavoring to harmonize his own work with Dodd's. Whether Jeremias, in equating the parousia with the resurrection, was also influenced by Bartsch, *Auferstehungszeugnis*, I have been unable to learn.

18. In this regard both George Caird and N. T. Wright are Dodd's descendants; see Caird, *Language and Imagery*, 243–71, and N. T. Wright, *Victory of Jesus*.

19. Here one recalls prophetic and millenarian movements that, via retrospective reasoning, hold their expectations to have been fulfilled, although in an unanticipated fashion; see Melton, "Spiritualization and Reaffirmation."

2

Enacting Moses

Jesus and Simeon Stylites

> The pattern of prophecy and fulfillment was not merely a scribal exercise among the literate few. It had a direct impact on Jewish history in the Roman period.
>
> —John J. Collins[1]

> It was not only Matthew, Mark and Luke who saw Jesus's true context as being the saving history of Israel, nor was Paul the only first-century Jew who thought in terms of "types" and fulfilment; others, quite possibly including Jesus, thought in the same way.
>
> —E. P. Sanders[2]

Early Christians remembered Jesus as being, in certain respects, like Moses. The fact is prominently on display in Matthew, especially the first five chapters. In these, when Israel's savior is born, a wicked king rules. That king—Herod the Great—slaughters Jewish infants.[3] After the deliverer miraculously escapes, his years growing up go unrecounted. He then passes through the waters, after which he enters the desert, where he remains for forty days, hungry and tempted to worship a false god. After all that, he ascends a mountain, where he sets his demands beside those of the lawgiver.

If the course of events suffices to recall Moses, so do additional facts. Matthew 2:15 quotes, as fulfilled in Jesus's life, Hos 11:1: "Out of Egypt have I called

1. J. J. Collins, *Scepter and Star*, 219.
2. Sanders, *Historical Figure of Jesus*, 84.
3. Herod is also like Pharaoh in T. Mos. 6:2–6: he kills young as well as old and imposes judgments "as did the Egyptians."

my son." If one knows Hosea, one knows that the original context has to do with the exodus: "When Israel was a child, I loved him, and out of Egypt have I called my son." My inference is that, for Matthew, Jesus's history is a typological replay of the old history. The same thought will occur to any who recognize that Matt 2:19–20—"when Herod died, the angel of the Lord appeared in a dream to Joseph in Egypt, saying: 'Rise, take the child and his mother and go to the land of Israel, for those seeking the life of the child have died'"—is largely cut and pasted from Exod 4:19–20: "After these many days, the king of Egypt died. The LORD said to Moses in Midian: 'Go back to Egypt, for all those seeking your life have died.'"

I will stop there, although not for a lack of material, either in Matthew or elsewhere.[4] My concern in this chapter is not the First Gospel but the historical Jesus. What I wish to argue is that the parallels between Jesus and Moses in Matthew were not, one and all, post-Easter inventions. They rather owe something to Jesus himself and his self-conception. In presenting Jesus as a new Moses, Matthew was enlarging an already-existing typology, and that typology was in his tradition ultimately because Jesus presented himself in Mosaic terms. Indeed, my conviction is that Jesus stepped into the prophecy in Deut 18:15–18: "The LORD your God will raise up for you a prophet like me from among your own people; you will heed such a prophet. . . . I will put my words in the mouth of the prophet, who will speak everything that I command."

This is not the usual story. The critical literature is full of arguments claiming that Jesus associated himself with Daniel's one like a Son of Man, or that he read himself into portions of Isaiah, or that he thought he was the Davidic Messiah, or that he did none of those things because, in the words of Robert Funk, Jesus "had nothing to say about himself, other than that he had no permanent address."[5] The proposition that Jesus took himself to be the Mosaic eschatological prophet has only a few supporters.[6] Here, however, the minority is correct.

4. See further Allison, *New Moses*. For Jesus as Mosaic or as the prophet like Moses of Deut 18:15–18 in Luke-Acts, see Moessner, *Lord of the Banquet*; Moessner, *Luke the Historian*, 205–37; G. F. Woods, *Finger of God*; Butticaz and Marguerat, "Figure de Moïse"; Schiffner, *Lukas liest Exodus*; and Lear, "Luke's Use." For Mosaic echoes and the new exodus theme in Mark, see S. W. Kim, *Jesus and the Missional Movement*, 161–231. For John, see Glasson, *Moses in the Fourth Gospel*; P. N. Anderson, "Having-Sent-Me Father"; and Lierman, "Mosaic Pattern."

5. Funk, *Honest to Jesus*, 320.

6. Those who infer that Deut 18:15–18 was operative for Jesus, or that he saw himself in Mosaic terms, include Jeremias, "Μωυσῆς," 867–68; Jeremias, *New Testament Theology*, 83–85; Marshall, *New Testament Christology*, 53–54; B. F. Meyer, "Appointed Deed," 173 (although Meyer dramatically underestimates the evidence for his conclusion); McKnight,

Before making my case, however, I wish to make another. I begin with a very long detour through the early biographies of Simeon Stylites (ca. 390–459). These biographies, like Matthew's Gospel, contain Moses typologies. And these typologies are not solely literary. They rather grew out of the memory that the flesh-and-blood Simeon sought to assimilate himself to the lawgiver. In other words, the literary typologies are not artificial impositions. They rather enlarge a semblance that the famous celebrity himself fashioned.

Simeon's Story

Comparisons between the canonical writings and ancient biographies typically focus on non-Christian biographies.[7] Scant attention has been paid to how we might profit from looking into later Christian hagiobiography.[8] This is understandable. Christian lives have usually been fenced off from the general study of Greco-Roman biographies. The two groups traditionally constitute their own areas of specialization. Moreover, if our goal is to understand the Gospels in their original contexts, it seems prudent to learn what biography was before Christian Gospels appeared. Nonetheless, putting the Gospels and later hagiobiography side by side has some things to teach us, or so I will now argue.

"Jesus and Prophetic Actions"; McKnight, *Jesus and His Death*, 197–200; Haacker, *Was Jesus lehrte*, 88–89; and Pitre, *Last Supper*.

7. The thesis that the canonical Gospels are specimens of Greco-Roman biography has won wide support of late. Especially influential has been Burridge, *What Are the Gospels?* See also Frickenschmidt, *Evangelium als Biographie*; Keener and Wright, *Biographies and Jesus*; and Keener, *Christobiography*. But for questions, see the essays by Kelber, Dinkler, Shively, and Breytenbach in Calhoun, Moessner, and Nicklas, *Modern and Ancient Literary Criticism*. While the form of the New Testament Gospels reflects the influence of the Greco-Roman biography, the substance of the Gospels aligns them more closely, in my judgment, with certain sections of the Jewish Bible, especially the narratives about Moses, Elijah, and Elisha. Cf. Hengel, *Acts and the History*, 30–31; Luz, "Matthew's Interpretive 'Tendencies'"; and Baum, "Biographies of Jesus." Baum's conclusion is: "The four New Testament Gospels are biographies of Jesus in Old Testament and rabbinic style with comparatively slight Graeco-Roman influences" (58). Cf. Baum, "Biographien." Note also the conclusion of L. Alexander, "What Is a Gospel?," 29: while the "external shape" of the Gospels is "strongly reminiscent of the Greek *bios*," their "narrative mode and the theological framework (connectives, narrative structure, use of direct speech, intertextuality) owe much more to the Bible."

8. Although note Keener, *Christobiography*, 96–98. I borrow the term "hagiobiography" from A. Wilson, "Biographical Models," 107.

It may be helpful to begin with a summary of Simeon's story as related in our earliest source.[9] He was born in northern Syria, in the little village of Sisa, and grew up shepherding sheep. One Sunday in church, after hearing the passage that blesses those who weep and mourn (Luke 6:20–26), the youngster determined to become a monk.

Simeon eventually joined a group of ascetics. He surpassed them all in severity. While they fasted every other day, he went without food and water for a week at a time. Eventually Simeon was expelled. His self-tortures, which included tying a coarse cord around his waist so tightly that it bled, were deemed excessive. He was an unsuitable example for other monks.

After leaving the monastery, Simeon retreated to the solitude of a tiny cottage, where one day it entered his head to undertake a great fast of forty days and forty nights. He urged a friend to seal the door to his cell with mud and not to return for forty days. Unwilling to abet a death, the friend insisted that he would help only if he could leave ten rolls and a jar of water. Simeon consented. The priest sealed the door.

After forty days passed, the seal was broken, the door opened. The rolls were still there. So too the water. Simeon himself was prostrate, unable to speak or move. Yet after the priest rinsed his mouth and gave him communion, he stirred, opened his eyes, and began to recover.

Following this success, Simeon made every Lenten fast a complete fast from both food and water. The first few times he tried this, he stood for several days, then carried on while sitting, then finished while lying down. After years of practice, however, Simeon, the sources report to our incredulity, learned to stand the whole time. Initially, he had a wooden support to aid him. Later, he was able to stand on his own the entire time.

After passing three years in his tiny dwelling, Simeon moved to a nearby hilltop above a village near Antioch. There, over several decades, he passed the remainder of his years. Initially he chained himself to a rock, like a dog on a leash, within a circular enclosure. But as his fame grew, as people came to him for counsel, prayer, healing, and blessing, as the crowds swelled and the roads to his pillar became like rivers with pilgrims from throughout the Roman Empire and beyond, the saint invented the notion of standing on a pillar, on which he eventu-

9. This and the following paragraphs summarize Theodoret of Cyrrhus, *R.H.* 26. For the Greek text—which appears, with the exception of two or three long interpolations, to have been transmitted in fairly stable fashion—see Theodoret of Cyrrus, *Histoire des moines de Syrie*, ed. Canivet and Leroy-Molinghen (SC 234, 257). For an English translation, see Richard Price, *History of the Monks of Syria*, 160–72.

ally set a square platform—six feet by six feet—open to the elements. The column was at first only a few feet high. By his death, however, it stood over sixty feet.

Raised on his pillar, Simeon became a public spectacle, "the great wonder of the world" (so Theodoret, *R.H.* 26.1). He ate just once a week. He forsook sleep. He stood night and day, moving only to bend his waist in worship. (He had others bind his feet in such a way that he could never recline.) One understands why someone reportedly asked Simeon: "Are you a man or of a bodiless nature? . . . I hear everyone repeating that you neither eat nor lie down, both of which are proper to human beings—for no one with a human nature could live without sleep and food" (*R.H.* 26.23).

The Sources

Three biographies of Simeon survive. The earliest, on which the previous paragraphs draw, is chapter 26 of Theodoret of Cyrrhus's *Historia Religiosa*. It was written in 440–44,[10] while Simeon was at the height of his fame. The bishop conversed with him as well as with individuals who knew him well, including two of Simeon's abbots. So although hagiographical and designed, in good Greek fashion, to parade "a life of true philosophy by means of physical discipline, in pursuit of the higher virtue of the soul,"[11] Theodoret's account is a valuable source for the historical Simeon.[12]

A much longer life is extant in Syriac and appears to be independent of Theodoret's narrative.[13] It overflows with wonders—with Simeon's visions, miraculous healings, effective curses, and the saint's power over the natural world. Most of the Syriac Life is in fact a catena of miracle stories and revelations. Yet this is not because the *Vita* is late and nothing but legend. On the contrary, it was composed within fourteen years of Simeon's death, by a monk or monks at Simeon's monastery or one nearby.[14] The biography preserves

10. See Richard Price, *History of the Monks of Syria*, xiii–xv.

11. S. A. Harvey, "Sense of a Stylite," 379.

12. Vööbus, *Early Monasticism*, 208–9, regards it as "unparalleled for quality" and "of inestimable value." Cf. Canivet, *Monachisme*, 109. More cautious is Frankfurter, "Stylites and Phallobatēs," 193 n. 33: "While he can be trusted to a certain degree as a *witness* to some of Symeon's *deeds*, Theodoret wields no authority on Symeon's *motivations*."

13. See Delehaye, *Saints stylites*, vii–ix, xxx.

14. See Vööbus, *Early Monasticism*, 209–10. A note at the end of one manuscript attributes the Syriac Life to two monks: Simeon bar-Eupolemos/Apollo and Bar-Ḥaṭar bar Udan; see Lietzmann, *Leben des heiligen Symeon Stylites*, 187–88, and Doran, *Simeon Stylites*,

traditions close to Simeon and, despite its panegyrical nature, comes from a milieu in which authentic memories of the saint lived on.[15]

The Syriac Life is extant in three recensions. It is unclear whether we can establish a simple genealogy and reconstruct an Ur-text.[16] Despite this, the three recensions are much more alike than unalike, and their wonder-filled world reflects the wonder-filled life of Simeon.

The third major source for Simeon is a shorter life of uncertain date.[17] It is extant (with much textual variation) in Greek, Latin, and Coptic.[18] The work categorizes itself as a biography (βίος), and the opening words attribute the whole to a certain Antonius, a figure otherwise unknown. As the narrator approaches the end of his story, he relates several episodes in the first-person singular, representing himself as Simeon's friend and disciple. Whether this is the truth or a fiction remains opaque.[19] Whatever the author's real name

---

197. There is no sound reason to doubt the claim. Occasionally the narrative uses the first person; note, e.g., Syriac Life 12: "The saint told us these things." (All quotations of the Syriac Life herein are from Doran.)

15. So Peeters, *Tréfonds oriental*, 114. Cf. 112: in the Syriac Life we must often be "sur le terrain de la vérité historique."

16. See Vööbus, "Discovery of New Manuscript Sources," and Doran, *Simeon Stylites*, 45–65. One recension is represented by Vatican ms. syr. 160, a fifth-century manuscript published in Assemani, *Acta sanctorum*, 2:273–394. Doran, *Simeon Stylites*, 101–98, offers an English translation of this. For the argument that Simeon of Marimîn, a priest, along with an archdeacon, Cyrus—two individuals named in the colophon of Vatican ms. syr. 160—directed the production of this manuscript, see Boero, "Context of Production." Boero further contends that the Vatican manuscript may be the autograph. A second recension appears in two manuscripts, Brit. Mus. Add. 14484 (sixth century) and Brit. Mus. Add. 12174 (twelfth century). The former was printed, with corrections and emendations, in Bedjan, *Acta martyrum*, 4:507–644, and was translated into English by Lent, "Life of Simeon Stylites." The latter is reprinted in Lent, *Life of Saint Simeon Stylites*. A third recension is represented by manuscripts discovered by Vööbus; see his "Discovery of New Manuscript Sources." An edition based on two of those manuscripts, along with a French translation, is to appear in Sources Chrétiennes.

17. Some raise the possibility of a date in the sixth or seventh century; see Caseau, "Syméon l'Ancien," 82–83, and Mayer and Allen, *Churches of Syrian Antioch*, 106–7.

18. For a critical edition of the text, see Lietzmann, *Leben des heiligen Symeon Stylites*, 20–78. Doran, *Simeon Stylites*, 87–100, supplies an English translation.

19. See further Lane-Fox, "*Life of Daniel*," 182–85. Barnes, *Early Christian Hagiography*, 259, ascribes it to a disciple of Simeon. S. A. Harvey, "Stylite's Liturgy," 527, regards Antonius as "a disciple in the monastic community that served Simeon." For a largely skeptical evaluation of Antonius, see Peeters, *Tréfonds oriental*, 107–12, and Lane-Fox, "*Life of Daniel*." For a more positive take, in response to Peeters, see Festugière, *Antioche païenne et chrètienne*, 376–87. For a more recent and more nuanced approach, see Flusin, "Syméon et les philologues."

and identity, his work draws in part on oral sources, probably not all late and unreliable.[20]

Simeon and Moses

The long Syriac Life parades numerous parallels between Simeon and Moses. It is usually up to biblically informed readers to spot them.[21] At several points, however, the author of the Life assists us by explicitly remarking on certain resemblances:

1. In one of his many visions, Simeon sees Moses and hears a heavenly voice say: "This is Moses, the great prophet who received the law from God on Mount Sinai. Mighty signs and works were done by him, he became great before God and was glorified before all humanity. No prophet equal to him arose after him in Israel. You [Simeon] too if you succeed will be exalted above all the men of your generation. As I was with my servant Moses so I will be with you and I will do whatever you wish" (41).
2. A few chapters after this we are told that Simeon, being entranced by the fasts of Moses and Elijah, inquired of "experts in Scripture" what they could tell him about those two ancient worthies: "Who truly will tell me and teach and show me how and by what means these two men pleased God their Lord and deserved all this excellent portion? Was it by fasting that they truly pleased God? or by prayer and faith? or by zeal for their Lord?" (44).
3. The author likens Simeon's heroic fasting to that of Moses, who "did not eat bread or drink water while he was on the mountain with his Lord. . . . Moses was refreshed: his food was the divine vision, his drink the heavenly glory" (108). Simeon, however, outperformed Moses, who "fasted for forty days and forty nights only twice." The Stylite did this many times.
4. In accounting for Simeon's fame, the Syriac Life claims that "whoever obeys and keeps and does" God's "will is kept and magnified and becomes famous." There follow, as illustration, the names Abraham, Moses, and Elijah (111).
5. The Syriac Life likens Simeon's departure from the earth to Moses's depar-

20. Cf. Vööbus, *Early Monasticism*, 211. Antonius is independent of the Syriac Life but may reflect a knowledge of Theodoret.

21. Cf. Krueger, "Typological Figuration," 399: "In the majority of late ancient saints' lives the typological construction of the narrative remains implicit. The author assumed that the audience was familiar with a great number of biblical stories and appealed to specific biblical figures by name only occasionally."

ture: "For God aroused the whole world to greet and worship his friend [Simeon] and manifest his glory in his lifetime, as he did to holy Mar Moses when he brought him up the mountain and showed him the land of promise and then led him away. The blessed Mar Simeon summoned all humankind. . . . He commanded and admonished them to keep the laws and commandments of our Lord" (115).[22]

6. A late chapter includes a list of several figures Simeon resembles: Abraham who believed, Moses who was humble and holy, Joshua and Elijah who were companions of Moses, Elisha who did miracles, Job who suffered so much, and Simon Cephas, foundation of the church (130).

These overt comparisons do not stand alone. There are also implicit comparisons. Chapter 108, for example, offers this extravagant characterization of the lawgiver: he was "the great prophet, the clear-seeing eye of all Israel, the victorious athlete, the wise master builder, the diligent servant, the watchful sailor, the famous pilot, the trained scribe, the faithful servant." In the Syriac Life, all these attributes equally characterize Simeon:

MOSES	SIMEON
great prophet	seer of future events (3, 38, 68–69, 105)
victorious athlete	winning athlete (120; cf. 1, 38, 45, 47, 54, 65, 74, 124)
wise master builder	wise master builder (120, 124; cf. 119: reliable master builder)
diligent servant	genuine servant (118)
watchful sailor	vigilant sailor (118), skillful sailor (124)
famous pilot	wise pilot, helmsman of the world's ship (118), skillful pilot (120), watchful pilot (124)
trained scribe	practiced scribe (120)
faithful steward	faithful steward (191)

For those paying attention, Moses is very much like Simeon, and Simeon is very much like Moses.

Given the shared characteristics and the unequivocal comparisons, it is natural to see a Moses typology in additional places throughout the Syriac Life, even where it is not overt:

22. Cf. Jacob of Serug's homily on Simeon: "When his end approached and his blessing arrived, his Lord revealed to him the day of his death just as to Moses" (cf. Deut 31:14, 16; 32:49–50); see S. A. Harvey, "Homily on Simeon Stylite," 24.

1. The first sentence dubs Simeon "the friend of God." Because of Exod 33:11—"the Lord used to speak to Moses face to face, as a man speaks to his friend"—the appellation was regularly associated with Moses.[23] Later in the book we read that Simeon "spoke familiarly with his Lord" (130).
2. Simeon, before his call, is a shepherd (1–2). The Bible reports the same of Moses, and notwithstanding all his achievements, he was always remembered as a shepherd.[24] Beyond that, Simeon's first vision occurs precisely while he is with his flock, as also happened with Moses.[25]
3. In his inaugural vision, Simeon is taken to a mountain, where he is shown stones and told, "Take and build," and he famously spends the latter decades of his ministry on a mountain. The chief image of Moses in Jewish and Christian lore is, of course, of him receiving the law on the top of a mountain (Syriac Life 4; Exod 19–40). Moreover, just as Moses died on a mountain (Deut 32:48–50), so too Simeon.
4. Moses, in the words of Exod 24:3, "told the people all the words of the Lord and all the ordinances; and all the people answered with one voice, and said: 'All the words that the Lord has spoken we will do.'" In like fashion, Simeon establishes "the laws and ordinance of the holy church," and an angel tells him that all will submit to his authority and obey his "word and ordinance" (Syriac Life 3).
5. As the Syriac Life observes, recalling Exod 34:29–30, 35, Moses "glowed." It reports the same of Simeon. Once "much light shone inside" a cave when Simeon was in it (24).[26] On another occasion "his face was radiant and shone" (52–53). On a third occasion a man in desperate need had a vision in which Simeon's face was "like lightning" (68). Yet another time, when he straightened himself after praying, onlookers saw that "his face was like the rays of the sun" (75).

23. Cf. 115, where the comparison is between Moses and God's "friend" (i.e., Simeon). For Moses as God's "friend," see Philo, *Sacr.* 130; *Mos.* 1.156–57; *Leg.* 3:204; Sib. Or. 2:245; LAB 24:3; 25:3, 5; Clement of Alexandria, *Strom.* 2.5.20–21; 4.399; Origen, *Princ.* 3.2.5; *Hom. Luc.* (PG 17:353); Apos. Con. 6.19.4; Aphrahat, *Dem.* 17.3; etc.

24. Exod 3:1–12; Ps 77:20; Philo, *Mos.* 1.60–66; Josephus, *Ant.* 2.263–64; LAB 19:3, 9; Mek. Beshallaḥ 7; Clement of Alexandria, *Strom.* 1.23; Jerome, *Vit. Malch.* 5; etc. Note also that both Moses and Simeon come to "shepherd" the people of God: Num 27:16–17; Ps 77:20; Syriac Life 5 ("you will shepherd the flock of Christ").

25. Syriac Life 2–5 ("this is the first vision that appeared to the blessed man as he shepherded the flock"); Exod 3:1–12.

26. Simeon's cave might recall the cleft or cave Moses hides in on Sinai (Exod 33:22), as does the cave Elijah enters in 1 Kgs 19:13; cf. b. Meg. 19b ("the cave in which Moses and Elijah stood"); b. Pesaḥ. 54a; Pesiq. Rab. 4:2 ("Moses hid in a cave . . . and Elijah hid in a cave").

6. One of Simeon's opponents is characterized, without elaboration, as "a second Pharaoh" (60), a phrase that presumes hearers' acquaintance with the first part of Exodus.
7. Twice in the Syriac Life (64, 85), Simeon is asked to supply water for people exhausted by thirst. In both instances his intercession makes a dry spring gush water. Moses also famously brought forth water for the thirsty in a miraculous manner (Exod 17:6; Num 20:2–13; 21:16–18).[27]

Moses and the Historical Simeon

What might we make of all these parallels, which together constitute a substantial typology? One major function is undoubtedly apologetical. Simeon's behavior was both extreme and, in certain respects, unprecedented. So he had critics.[28] The Syriac Life comes to his defense by constructing parallels with figures everyone admired, most prominently Moses.

My aim here, however, is not to decipher the literary functions of the *Vita*'s Moses typology. It is rather to uncover the origin of the typology.

The author of the Syriac Life was not the first to discern parallels between Simeon and Moses. We know this because Simeon is also like Moses in an earlier biography, that of Theodoret.[29] After relating, near the beginning of his account, that Simeon grew up shepherding animals, Theodoret observes that this made him like Jacob, Joseph, Moses, David, and Micah (*R.H.* 26.2).[30] More importantly, when he discusses the matter of Simeon's fasting, he reports that the ascetic "longed to fast forty days without food, like the men of God Moses and Elijah" (*R.H.* 26.7). Moses is the one name common to both assertions. Theodoret, moreover, asserts that it was Simeon himself who wanted to be like Moses and the Moses-like Elijah.

Those are the only explicit comparisons. But there is more. The remark about Moses and Elijah fasting directly follows a sentence that refers to "the summit where he [Simeon] now stands." The Greek is τῇ κορυφῇ ἐφ' ἧς νῦν

27. Note also the story that appears only in manuscripts B and M; see Doran, *Simeon Stylites*, 210–11.

28. Theodoret, *R.H.* 26.14, speaks of "the pillar mocked by lovers of mockery." He also asks "fault-finders to curb their tongues" (26.12).

29. The short work of Antonius has nothing to contribute here. It compares Simeon to David, Job, and Christ, not Moses. It does, however, depict his face shining as the sun (28, 29).

30. Cf. Basil of Caesarea, *Homily 33 on the Martyr Mamas* (PG 31:593b), where being a shepherd makes the martyr Mamas like Moses.

ἕστηκεν (*R.H.* 26.7). Mountains appear at several dramatic points in Moses's story (above all Exod 3, 19–34 and Deut 4–5, 9–10, 32–33), and in Exod 17:9–10 LXX, we find the same combination of ἵστημι and κορυφή with Moses as the subject: ἕστηκα ἐπὶ τῆς κορυφῆς τοῦ βουνοῦ ("I [Moses] stand on the summit of the hill").[31] When one adds that Moses's fast of forty days—in contrast to Elijah's—took place precisely while he was on a mountain,[32] it is hard to doubt that the text deliberately echoes the Pentateuch.

An intertextually savvy reader might, when perusing Theodoret's work, espy additional parallels between its hero and the lawgiver.[33] My point, however, is made. The developed Moses typology in the Syriac Life was not the creation, *ex nihilo*, of its author. Whoever composed that life took up a conventional comparison, one also on display, if much less prominently, in Theodoret's account.

Who first ventured the typology? One could posit that one of Simeon's supporters first thought of the analogy and that, once made, it caught on. It was, that is, Simeon's devotees who first found meaning in the circumstance that he was once a shepherd, as Moses had been. It was they who invented the tale that Simeon's first vision occurred while he was tending his flock, as happened to Moses. And it was they who would spread the rumor that people saw the stylite shine like the sun, as did Moses.

But the evidence resists this account. Although it would be foolish to discount the contributions of those who passed on and inscribed the traditions about Simeon—we have after all biographies, not an autobiography—I am confident that the typology originated with Simeon. That is, the monk was remembered as being like Moses because he set out to be like him. Multiple points converge to compel this conclusion.

1. Given that Theodoret composed his history fifteen or more years before Simeon's death, we know that the association with Moses was made while

31. The combination appears elsewhere in the LXX only in Judg 9:7 and 1 Sam 26:13.

32. Exod 34:28; Deut 9:9, 18, 25; 10:10. Contrast 1 Kgs 19:4–9: Elijah fasts on his way to Horeb, not after he arrives there.

33. For example, Simeon is "a man of God" (7, 15, 20), a designation the Old Testament uses repeatedly (although not exclusively) of Moses: Deut 33:1; Josh 14:6; 1 Chr 23:14; 2 Chr 30:16; Ezra 3:2; Ps 90 superscription; 1 Esdr 5:49; cf. 4Q377 1 II, 10. The term is part of a Moses typology in Pesiq. Rab. 4:2: "Moses was called man of God (Deut 33:1), and Elijah was called man of God (1 Kgs 17:18)." Simeon, furthermore, issues commandments (8: ἐντολαί) and laws (13: νόμοι), and at one point he shines (13; cf. Exod 34:29–35)—although this appears to be a metaphor, not an ocular event.

the stylite was yet alive. Theodoret's work further establishes that someone who knew Simeon face to face thought the correlation apt.

2. Both Theodoret and the Syriac Life explicitly assert that Simeon aspired to be like Moses. According to the former: "Endeavoring always to be increasing his wealth of virtue, he longed, like the men of God Moses and Elijah, to pass forty days without food."[34] According to the latter, Simeon was preoccupied with Moses and Elijah and pondered their conduct:

   > He was constantly meditating and marveling on those two men set for a sign, Mar Moses and Mar Elijah, saying: "Who truly will tell me and teach and show me how and by what means these two men pleased God their Lord and deserved all this excellent portion? Was it by fasting that they truly pleased God? or by prayer and faith? or by love? or by humility? or by bodily chastity? or by zeal for their Lord?" For he was greatly amazed by their wonderful appearance and the dignity given to them by God their Creator. He was always quizzing experts in the scriptures to learn from them about the lifestyles of these two powerful athletes, Moses and Elijah. (44)

   These words agree with Theodoret in locating the birth of our typology in Simeon's own mind.

3. Simeon spent the last decades of his life on a mountain and, as one later source has it, his pillar stood "at the very peak of the mountain" (Evagrius Scholasticus, *E.H.* 1.14). This is so much a part of his story that to doubt it would be to doubt Simeon's existence. To my knowledge, however, no one doubts that Simeon was a historical figure or disputes that multitudes made pilgrimage to see him standing on a pillar on a mountain.[35] Now of course mountains play important roles in worldwide religion and mythology, and one could offer several reasons why Simeon determined to live where he did. Yet the sources, which draw multiple parallels between Moses and Simeon, supply a straightforward and sufficient answer. If Simeon wished to be literally like Moses, living on a mountain would have been one way to do it.

4. Another motif in the sources guarantees this is the right inference. Theo-

34. Theodoret, *R.H.* 26.7: αὔξειν δὲ ἀεὶ τῆς ἀρετῆς τὸν πλοῦτον φιλονεικῶν ἐπεθύμησε Μωϋσῇ καὶ Ἠλίᾳ τοῖς θείοις ἀνθρώποις παραπλησίως τεσσαράκοντα ἡμέρας ἄσιτος διαμεῖναι.

35. The ruins of Simeon's enclosure remain to this day. Multiple photos appear if one Googles "Simeon Stylites remains of pillar."

doret and the Syriac Life affirm that Simeon sought to go without food and water for forty days and nights.[36] He indeed tried to do this every Lent. Although we are inevitably incredulous and may wonder whether he cheated,[37] we should, I submit, keep an open mind.[38] But however the circumstance is explained, we cannot doubt that already, during his lifetime, Simeon was famed for achieving his aspiration, namely, a death-defying fast of forty days and nights while on a mountain. And whereas Scripture knows of three biblical worthies who undertook such a long fast—Moses, Elijah, and Jesus—only one of them—Moses—was remembered as doing so on a mountain. That makes him the chief object of Simeon's imitation. So too does the circumstance that Simeon abstained from water as well as food. That circumstance is not reported of Elijah or Jesus, only Moses.[39]

36. Theodoret, *R.H.* 26.9; Syriac Life 44, 46. Theodoret's Greek is: Ἐξ ἐκείνου τοίνυν μέχρις καὶ τήμερον—ὀκτὼ δὲ καὶ εἴκοσι διελήλυθεν ἔτη—τὰς τετταράκοντα ἄσιτος διαμένει ἡμέρας. That ἄσιτος ("without food, fasting") includes giving up water as well as solid food is clear from the immediate context, as the words just cited immediately trail an account of Simeon's first Lenten fast, when the saint refused to drink the water left for him. This event was, for Theodoret, the first in a series.

37. The possibility of cheating is broached in one version of the Syriac Life: "When the brethren saw his [Simeon's] severe toil, and desired to conduct themselves in like manner but were not able, they planned how they might bring false accusation against him. So they said to a certain simple-minded brother of the covenant: 'Take a dish and put into it morsels of bread and bits of cooked food; then go and show it to the abbot and say to him: "This food I took from Simeon as he was partaking of it. This mode of life which he keeps up is mere dissimulation"'" (5). But the plot fails and the investigating abbot finds Simeon innocent. Beyond that, if Simeon cheated, he would have required, given his permanent habitation on a pillar, the help of one or more confederates, and their dissimulation would have had to go on for years, and for most of the time out in the open. Cf. Theodoret, *R.H.* 26.22: "Night and day he is standing within view of all; for having removed the doors and demolished a sizeable part of the enclosing wall, he is exposed to all as a new and extraordinary spectacle."

38. Comparisons enlarge the possibilities. In 1901, the well-known Jain, Shrimad Rajchandra, took the vow of *sallekhana*, or *samadhi-maran*, and fasted to death. He lasted thirty-six days, the last twenty-four without water. See Laidlaw, "Life Worth Living," 180. In like manner, in 1955, another celebrated Jain, Shantisagar, when in his early eighties, also took the vow to fast to the end. For twenty-five days he sipped only water. Without water, he lasted another eleven days. See Jani, *Jaina Path of Purification*, 1. Beyond such parallels, Theodoret, *R.H.* 26.7, reports that the first time Simeon tried to fast for forty days, he ended up unconscious and near death. His account also indicates that Simeon accomplished his astonishing feat only after years of effort, during which he repeatedly came up short. He was like a great athlete who learned, over the years, to push himself a little further each time out. And Syriac Life 10 recounts that, on one early occasion during Lent, Simeon had to take the eucharist "midway through the fast." That does not sound like pure fiction to me.

39. Exod 34:28; Deut 9:9. Contrast 1 Kgs 19:8; Matt 4:2; Luke 4:2. When the Syriac Life

5. Simeon endeavored not only to fast on a mountain for forty days: he aspired to do so while standing. This is a Mosaic trait.[40] Deuteronomy 10:10 has Moses recollect: "I stood up [עמדתי] on the mountain forty days and forty nights." This is a reprise of 9:9: "When I went up the mountain to receive the stone tablets, the tablets of the covenant that the LORD made with you, I stood up on the mountain for forty days and forty nights; I neither ate bread nor drank water." Now the Hebrew verb עמד can mean "stay" or "remain," but its first sense is "stand" or "stand up," and this is the sense multiple Jewish sources find in Deut 10:10.[41] Furthermore, Moses is depicted in other passages as standing on a hill or mountain.[42] So if Simeon determined to fast from food and water for forty days and nights and to do so precisely while standing on a mountain, his chief inspiration must have been Moses.[43]
6. The fasts of Jesus and Elijah, it is worth noting, are themselves imitations of

---

affirms that Elijah and Jesus went without water (108–9), it is not following Scripture but assimilating Elijah and Jesus to Simeon and Moses. Cf. Apoc. Abr. 12:1–3, where Abraham fasts from bread and water as he journeys to Sinai with an angel. The presence of an angel and the journey assimilate his experience to that of Elijah (cf. 1 Kgs 19:5–8) whereas his abstention from water as well as food makes him like Moses.

40. According to Epiphanius, *Pan.* 1:13, Dositheus, a would-be prophet like Moses in some sources (see n. 214), persisted in a fast from both food and water that led to his death. If true, one wonders whether he was imitating Moses, especially as Dositheus was known as "the standing one." See Isser, *Dositheans*, 138–40.

41. Cf., e.g., b. Meg. 21a: "One verse says: 'And I sat in the mountain' [Deut. 9:9], and another verse says: 'And I stood in the mountain' [Deut. 10:10]. Rab says: 'He [Moses] stood when he learned and sat while he went over [what he had learned].' R. Ḥanina said: 'He was neither sitting nor standing, but stooping.' R. Johanan said: '"Sitting" here means only "staying," as it says: "And you stayed in Kadesh many days"' [Deut. 1:46]. Rabba said: 'The easy things [he learned] standing and the hard ones sitting.'" Note also Tg. Neof. I Deut 10:10; Tg. Onq. Deut 10:10; and Exod. Rab. 43:4. In Deut 10:10, the LXX translates עמדתי with εἱστήκειν (a pluperfect form of ἵστημι), which can mean either "stood" or "remained."

42. Exod 3:5; 17:6; 33:21; Deut 5:31. For Moses as the subject of עמד, see also 1Q22 I, 2; 4Q158 7–8 5; 4Q377 1 II, 7–8 (on this, see Fletcher-Louis, *All the Glory of Adam*, 141–48); Mek. Beshallaḥ 4 on Exod 14:15; b. Šabb. 30a; etc. Note that Elijah stands on Horeb when he seeks to reprise Moses's experience there (1 Kgs 19:11, 13) and that Moses is "the standing one" in Memar Marqah 4:12.

43. Note also perhaps Deut 5:31: "But you [Moses], stand here by me, and I will tell you all the commandments." Sipre Deut. 357 takes this to mean: "Moses was spoken to by God only while he was standing." None of this, I concede, explains the pillar. That must have involved thoughts independent of Moses. For the discussion of possible precedents and motives, see G. R. H. Wright, "Simeon's Ancestors"; G. R. H. Wright, "Heritage of the Stylites"; Frankfurter, "Stylites and Phallobatēs"; Eastmond, "Body vs. Column"; and Stang, "Digging Holes."

Moses's fast. First Kings 19:8 (Elijah "ate and drank and went in the strength of that food forty days and forty nights") belongs to a string of parallels between the prophet and the lawgiver (see below, p. 143). As for Jesus's fast of forty days and nights, it too simulates Moses's feat. This follows from the context in Matt 4 and Luke 4. Both chapters feature a typological replay of the exodus: Jesus goes into the desert, he is tempted by hunger, he is tempted by idolatry, and he responds by quoting lines from Deuteronomy—lines that, in their original context, are about Israel's time in the wilderness under Moses's direction.[44] Jesus's fast is like Moses's fast, and Elijah's fast is like Moses's fast. So too Simeon's fast.

Typology and History

When Theodoret claims that Simeon tried to copy the actions of famous figures before him, above all Moses, we should believe him. Simeon sought and obtained an intertextual identity. While his body was on a pillar, his mind was in the Bible. Scripture was for him more than a source of theology. It was no less, or probably even more, a sourcebook for mimesis, an anthology of models to be imitated, models that were, for him, real beings, not just literary figures.[45] He longed to assimilate himself to Moses, to confirm to his πολιτεία, his conduct.[46] It bears remembering that the saint himself, in his turn, had his imitators, such as Daniel the Stylite, who ascended a pillar because Simeon had ascended a pillar.

We are accustomed to regard conspicuous parallels between two figures or two events as existing only on a literary or theological level. That Paul writes about Christ as the second Adam leads no one to wonder whether Jesus sought to emulate the protoplast, and that Abraham is modeled on Job in the Testament of Abraham[47] moves none of us to ask whether the patriarch, if he existed, could have been acquainted with the book of Job. Most typologies are either pure fiction or—like Eusebius's portrayal of Constantine as a new Moses[48]—

44. The most helpful work remains, over half a century after its appearance, Gerhardsson, *Testing of God's Son*.

45. Cf. Lane-Fox, "*Life of Daniel*," 213–15: Simeon motivated himself through biblical models.

46. Cf. Gregory Nazianzen, *Or.* 2.105: "The examples of the past serve as rules and models for our warning and imitation."

47. Allison, "Job in the *Testament of Abraham*."

48. On this, see A. Wilson, "Biographical Models," 112–20, and Damgaard, *Recasting*

impositions on the past.[49] Indeed, when typological elements are everywhere in a text, that is a good sign we are untethered to the real past as opposed to the imaginary past. For this reason, some of us find next to no history in Matt 1–2: the resemblances with the infancy legends about Moses are too good to be historically true.[50]

Some typologies, however, are different. Some incorporate genuine memories.[51] Some have grown out of what a historical actor had in mind. Some are not third-person and ex post facto but rather autobiographical and prospective.[52] That is, a literary typology can be the descendant of an enacted typology. This was the case with Simeon. The Moses typologies in the sources for him are not uninformed by his words, deeds, and self-conception. The *synkrisis* has certainly grown beyond its origins, but it was planted while Simeon yet lived.

This should not surprise. It is human to imitate others, and human to imitate heroes.

I wished to be like my father growing up. I still do, which is why I have never dropped the "Jr." after my name. My late father, of course, was not a celebrated religious hero, and my aspiration was, in the great scheme of things, relatively modest. But those with large ambitions sometimes imitate people of outsized achievement. Napoleon wanted to be like Julius Caesar, just as Caesar wanted to be like Alexander the Great. In similar fashion, religious individuals of large aspiration may seek to emulate famed religious heroes. Paul claimed to imitate Jesus Christ (1 Cor 11:1). What that entailed for him I am unsure, yet I doubt his words were empty.

Because Moses is my subject, I inexorably recall Martin Luther King Jr.'s famous 1968 speech at the Memphis Masonic Temple. King said that he had "been to the mountaintop." He said that he had "seen the Promised Land." And

---

Moses, 153–81. Damgaard urges that the idea of Constantine as another Moses may not have been Eusebius's invention but could have been suggested by Constantine's own propaganda. See further Damgaard, "Propaganda against Propaganda."

49. This is often the case in later Christian writings wherein bishops and spiritual worthies become like Moses; see Rapp, "Comparison, Paradigm"; Sterk, *Renouncing the World*; and Damgaard, *Recasting Moses*, 183–219.

50. See Allison, *New Moses*, 140–65, and Aus, *Matthew 1–2*.

51. See, in addition to what follows, the important work of Le Donne, *Historiographical Jesus*. He effectively demonstrates that divorcing history from typology can lead us astray.

52. The issue can be complex. When Josephus implicitly compared himself with scriptural heroes—Jeremiah, Daniel, maybe Joseph (see Daube, "Typology in Josephus," and Gray, *Prophetic Figures*, 70–79)—was the move wholly literary retrojection, or did he, decades earlier, sometimes think of himself as acting like others before him?

he added, with foreboding: "I may not get there with you." Here King is Moses on Mount Pisgah. The civil rights leader inserted himself into the old trope that likens the experience of African Americans to the experience of enslaved Israel in olden times. Whatever one makes of this provocative self-conception, the typology is indisputably first-person.

So too are these words, from Gregory Nazianzen: "I was running in order to lay hold of God, and so I went up on the mountain, and I rent the cloud, that I might become detached from matter and material things, and I gathered into myself as much as I could. And directing my gaze, I barely saw the back parts of God, and this while sheltering in the rock, in the word made flesh for us" (*Or.* 28.3). As with King, so with Gregory: Moses goes unnamed. Yet the implicit comparison—Gregory's experience is like Moses's experience in Exod 33—is incontestable.[53]

Moses and the Synoptic Jesus

I turn now at last to the New Testament. I have already observed that, in the Gospels, above all Matthew, Jesus has a Mosaic mien. At this point I argue that Moses and the exodus are forcefully present in sayings that circulated before the Gospels were put together. After that I will explore the implications. For the moment, then, I leave to the side the devilishly difficult and always contested problem of origin.

(1) When accused, in Luke 11:20, of casting out demons by Beelzebul, Jesus responds with several sharp, defensive sentences, among them this arresting claim: "If I by the finger of God [ἐν δακτύλῳ θεοῦ] cast out demons, then the kingdom of God has come upon you."[54]

The phrase "finger of God" occurs three times in the Tanak. Two concern the writing of the Ten Commandments (Exod 31:18; Deut 9:10). The other has to do with Moses's ability to perform miracles. When the magicians of Egypt fail to match his feats, they confess to Pharaoh: "This is the finger of God" (Exod 8:19 MT: אצבע אלהים; LXX: δάκτυλος θεοῦ). Jesus's saying al-

53. For additional instances of individuals likening themselves to Moses in one way or another, see Athanasius, *Narr. fug.* 10; Theodoret of Cyrrhus, *R.H.* 1.1; and Palladius, *Dial.* 7 (Theophilus of Alexandria dubbed himself "another Moses").

54. The parallel in Matt 12:28, however, has instead "Spirit of God." Those who attribute the saying to Q more often than not prefer Luke's version; cf. Robinson, Hoffmann, and Kloppenborg, *Critical Edition of Q*, 232. For the reasons, see Meier, *Marginal Jew*, 2:410–11. For the other side, see Wall, "Finger of God," and Fleddermann, *Q*, 483–84.

ludes to this confession—a conclusion all the surer as there are additional links between Luke's immediate context and traditions about Moses and Pharaoh's magicians.[55]

Norman Perrin paraphrased the sense of Luke 11:20 this way: "This is not the work of demons, but of God, and if God is at work in this manner, then you are even now experiencing the New Exodus: the Kingdom of God has come upon you."[56] This is true, but it is not the whole truth. There is not only a new exodus. There is also a new Moses. For if Jesus works his wonders by the finger of God, he is playing the part of the lawgiver. He is after all the emphatic subject: "If I [ἐγώ] cast out demons." John Meier is right: in Luke 11:20, Jesus "places himself alongside Moses and Aaron, genuine messengers from God who were empowered by him to perform symbolic miracles connected with Israel's liberation from slavery."[57]

(2) At the Last Supper, the Jesus of Mark 14:24 uses the phrase "my blood of the covenant" (τὸ αἷμά μου τῆς διαθήκης; so also Matt 26:28). This clearly alludes to Exod 24:8, where Moses takes blood and, dashing it on the people, declares: "This is the blood of the covenant [MT: דם־הברית; LXX: τὸ αἷμα τῆς διαθῆκης] that the Lord has made with you in accordance with all these words." Commentators through the centuries have regularly spotted the borrowing here, and they also (although less often) have recognized an implicit citation in the closely related formulation in Luke 22:20 and 1 Cor 11:25: "The new covenant in my blood."[58] In Mark's Last Supper, then, Jesus borrows the language of Exod 24:8 to elucidate his own situation, again enacting the part of Moses.[59]

(3) The Synoptic Jesus, on multiple occasions, employs the expression "this generation" (ἡ γενεὰ αὕτη).[60] It is typically if not invariably disparaging. This

55. For details, see Allison, *Intertextual Jesus*, 53–57; M. Labahn, "Jesu Exorzismen"; and E. J. Woods, *"Finger of God,"* 61–100. The latter sees an allusion to Deut 9:10 as well as Exod 8:19.

56. Perrin, *Rediscovering the Teaching of Jesus*, 67.

57. Meier, *Marginal Jew*, 2:411. Cf. McKnight, *Jesus and His Death*, 197–99. In Exod 8:16–19, God speaks to Moses who in turn instructs Aaron to stretch out his staff and strike the earth.

58. Cf. Chrysostom, *Hom. Matt.* 82.1; Theophylact, *Comm. Mk.* ad loc; Victorinus, *Comm. Rev.* 5.5; Remigius *apud* Aquinas, *Catena Aurea* ad loc; Maldonatus, *Commentarii Quattuor Evangelista*, 1:406; Lightfoot, *Commentary on the New Testament*, 2:353; Poole, *Annotations*, 3:127; Bengel, *Gnomon Novi Testamenti*, 1:151 ("Antitheton, Exod. 24,8"); Gundry, *Use of the Old Testament*, 57–58; Pesch, *Abendmahl*, 95–96; Puig i Tàrrech, "Jesus and Jewish Writings," 99–101; Culpepper, *Matthew*, 515; Gustafsson, *Aspects of Coherency*, 216; etc.

59. See further Pitre, *Last Supper*, 90–120.

60. Mark 8:12, 38; 9:19; 13:30; Matt 11:16 // Luke 7:31; Matt 12:39 // Luke 11:29;

is because the idiom derives from the Tanak, where it characterizes the wicked generation of Noah and, above all, that of Moses: Gen 7:1 ("you [Noah] alone are righteous before me in this generation [MT: בדור הזה; LXX: ἐν τῇ γενεᾷ ταύτῃ]") and Deut 1:35 ("not one of this evil generation [MT: הדור הרע הזה; LXX omits] will see the good land that I swore to give to your ancestors"). Beyond this, several of the Synoptic formulations clearly mirror pentateuchal phrases, so that Jesus's generation is like Moses's generation, whose misdeeds were proverbial:[61]

- Mark 9:19—"O faithless generation [γενεὰ ἄπιστος]"—echoes Deut 32:20: "A perverse generation [MT: דור; LXX: γενεά], children in whom there is no faithfulness [MT: אמן; LXX: πίστις]."
- Matt 12:39–42 // Luke 11:29–32 (Q)—"This generation is an evil generation [ἡ γενεὰ αὕτη γενεὰ πονηρά ἐστιν]"—recalls Num 32:13—"the generation doing evil [MT: הדור העשה הרע; LXX: ἡ γενεὰ οἱ ποιοῦντες τὰ πονηρά]"—as well as Deut 1:35—"this evil generation [MT: הדור הרע הזה]."
- Mark 8:38—"this adulterous and sinful generation [τῇ γενεᾷ ταύτῃ τῇ μοιχαλίδι καὶ ἁμαρτωλῷ]"—is similar to Deut 32:20 (see above) and in its structure resembles Deut 32:5: "A perverse and crooked generation [MT: דור עקש ופתלתל; LXX: γενεὰ σκολιὰ καὶ διεστραμμένη]."
- Matt 17:17 // Luke 9:41—"faithless and perverse generation [γενεὰ ἄπιστος καὶ διεστραμμένη]"—is likewise influenced by Deut 32:20 and 32:5 (see above).

The upshot is that, in these sayings, Jesus's experience is like that of Moses: he is enveloped by a faithless, evil, perverse generation.

(4) Multiple Synoptic sayings refer to entering the kingdom of God. A century ago, Hans Windisch observed that they are modeled on biblical lines about entering the land of promise.[62] The Synoptic idiom is εἰσελθεῖν εἰς τὴν

Matt 12:41–42 // Luke 11:31–32; Matt 17:17 // Luke 9:41; Matt 23:35–36 // Luke 11:50–51; Matt 12:45; Luke 16:8; 17:25. The standard treatment remains Lövestam, *Jesus and "This Generation."*

61. Cf. Pss 78:8 ("they should not be like their ancestors, a stubborn and rebellious generation, a generation whose heart was not steadfast"), 22 ("they had no faith in God and did not trust his saving power"), 32 ("in spite of all this they still sinned; they did not believe his wonders"); 95:10 ("for forty years I loathed that generation"); 106:24 ("they despised the pleasant land, having no faith in his promise"); Acts 7:39–43; etc.

62. Windisch, "Sprüche vom Eingehen." I followed Windisch on this subject in *Constructing Jesus*, 179–81. Since then I have greatly profited from Haacker, "Eternal Life." Note also Haacker, *Was Jesus lehrte*, 88–89, as well as Swartley, *Israel's Scripture Tradi-*

βασιλείαν.[63] The Old Testament idiom is εἰσελθεῖν εἰς τὴν γῆν (for בוא אל־הארץ).[64] And in the Synoptics, as in the Pentateuch, the tense is future: Israel will enter the land, and those winning eschatological salvation will enter the kingdom.

Particularly striking is the use of the similar idioms in warnings about moral failure:

Warnings about Not Entering the Land

- Num 20:24: "For he [Aaron] will not enter the land [MT: לא יבא אל־הארץ; LXX: οὐ μὴ εἰσέλθητε εἰς τὴν γῆν] that I have given to the Israelites, because you rebelled against my command at the waters of Meribah."
- Deut 4:21: "The LORD was angry with me [Moses] because of you, and he vowed that I should not . . . enter the good land [MT: ולבלתי־בא אל־הארץ; LXX: μὴ εἰσέλθω εἰς τὴν γῆν] that the LORD your God is giving for your possession."
- Ezek 13:9: "My hand will be against the prophets who see false visions and utter lying divinations; they will not be in the council of my people, nor be enrolled in the register of the house of Israel, nor will they enter the land [MT: ואל־אדמת ישראל לא יבוא; LXX: εἰς τὴν γῆν τοῦ Ἰσραηλ οὐκ εἰσελεύσονται]."
- Ezek 20:38: "I will purge out the rebels among you, and those who transgress against me; I will bring them out of the land where they reside as aliens, but they will not enter the land [MT: ואל־אדמת ישראל לא יבוא; LXX: εἰς τὴν γῆν τοῦ Ἰσραηλ οὐκ εἰσελεύσονται] of Israel."

Warnings about Not Entering the Kingdom

- Matt 5:20: "For I tell you, unless your righteousness exceeds that of the scribes and Pharisees, you will never enter the kingdom of heaven [οὐ μὴ εἰσέλθητε εἰς τὴν βασιλείαν τῶν οὐρανῶν]."
- Matt 7:21: "Not everyone who says to me, 'Lord, Lord,' will enter the kingdom of heaven [οὐ . . . εἰσελεύσεται εἰς τὴν βασιλείαν τῶν οὐρανῶν], but only the one who does the will of my Father in heaven."

---

tions, 104–5. Against the thesis of Berger, *Formgeschichte*, 182–84, that the background is rather Deut 23:1–7, which features lines about entrance into the assembly of Israel, see Horn, "Synoptischen Einlaßsprüche," 199–200.

63. Mark 9:47; 10:15, 24, 25; Matt 5:20; 7:21; 21:31; Luke 23:42; John 3:5; cf. Gos. Thom. 22, 99, 114.

64. Exod 12:25; Lev 19:23; Num 15:2; 20:24; Deut 4:21; 9:28; Ezek 13:9; cf. 11Q19 LVI, 12; LX, 16; T. Mos. 2:1; T. Levi 12:5. Variations of this formula occur in Deut 1:8; 4:1; 6:18; Judg 18:9.

- Matt 23:13: "But woe to you, scribes and Pharisees, hypocrites! For you lock people out of the kingdom of heaven. For you do not go in [οὐκ εἰσέρχεσθε] yourselves, and when others are going in, you stop them."
- Mark 10:15: "Truly I tell you, whoever does not receive the kingdom of God as a little child will never enter it [οὐ μὴ εἰσέλθῃ εἰς αὐτήν]."[65]
- John 3:5: "Unless one is born of water and Spirit, one will not be able to enter into the kingdom of God [οὐ δύναται εἰσελθεῖν εἰς τὴν βασιλείαν τοῦ θεοῦ]."

These formal similarities suggest the Jesus tradition's debt to Israel's wilderness traditions.[66] Such an inference is consistent with other kingdom sayings that feature key words belonging to refrains about the promised land:

- The kingdom is "inherited" or "obtained" (κληρονομέω): Matt 25:34;[67] cf. Matt 19:29; Mark 10:17; and Luke 10:25, where "inherit life" = "inherit the kingdom";[68] also Matt 5:5 ("inherit the earth/land").
- The land is "inherited" or "obtained" (נחל, ירש; LXX: κληρονομέω): Lev 20:24; Num 33:54; Deut 1:8, 39; 4:22; 6:18; 8:1; 9:5, 6; 10:11; 12:29; 16:20; Josh 18:3; Ps 37:9; etc.

- The kingdom is "given" (δίδωμι): Luke 12:32; Matt 21:43.
- The land is "given" (נתן; LXX: δίδωμι): Lev 20:24; Num 33:53; Deut 1:8, 39; 2:29; 9:6; 19:8; 26:9; 27:2; Josh 1:2, 11, 14, 15; 2:9; 24:13; Judg 6:9; Ps 136:21; Jer 16:15; etc.

- Some but not all will "see" the kingdom: Mark 9:1; Luke 9:27; John 3:3; cf. Matt 16:28.
- Some but not all will "see" the land: Num 14:22–24; 32:6–15; Deut 1:35–36; Josh 5:6.

To inherit the kingdom is like inheriting the land. To be given the kingdom is like being given the land. To see the kingdom is like seeing the land. I agree,

65. Haacker, "Eternal Life," 149–50, notes the possible parallel with Deut 1:39: "As for your little ones . . . your children, who today do not yet know right from wrong, they will enter there; to them I will give it, and they will take possession of it."

66. Cf. Ps 95:11, where "they will not enter my rest" is modeled on the warnings about not entering the land.

67. Cf. 1 Cor 6:9–10; 15:50; Gal 5:19–21; Ign. *Eph.* 16.1.

68. For the functional synonymity of "life" and "kingdom" see Allison, *Constructing Jesus*, 186–89.

then, with Karl Haacker (although I balk at his use of the word "certain"): "The large number of parallels from the Old Testament make it certain that the verbs used by Jesus in his sayings about participation in the kingdom or (eternal) life have been borrowed from the tradition concerning the land promised to the descendants of Abraham, Isaac, and Jacob and given to the people of Israel."[69] As with the sayings about "this generation," those about entering the kingdom project a situation similar to that of "the Israelites on their journey through the wilderness," that is, "a situation in which a whole generation, with but a few exceptions, failed to keep their trust in God with which they had started on the journey."[70]

The idea of an eschatological entrance into the land appears also in Matt 8:11 // Luke 13:28–29: "And many will come from east and west and will recline at table with Abraham, Isaac, and Jacob in the kingdom of God."[71] However precisely understood,[72] this prophecy takes up the traditional image of exiled Israel returning from east and west.[73] This tallies with the proposal that other sayings implicitly liken entering the kingdom to entering the land—and all the more as, in Isaiah and elsewhere, the return from exile is a new exodus.[74]

(5) While their wording is different, the versions of the Lord's Prayer in Matthew and Luke have Jesus teaching his followers to pray to be given each day their "daily bread":

69. Haacker, "Eternal Life," 148.

70. Haacker, "Eternal Life," 148–49.

71. I have translated the Q reconstruction in the *Critical Edition of Q*. The chief question is whether Q had "east and west" (so Matthew) or "east and west and north and south" (so Luke), the latter being a likely allusion to Ps 107:3. The question cannot be resolved and does not matter for our purposes.

72. My inclination is to associate the kingdom in this saying with the land of Israel. For relevant considerations, see Willitts, "Jesus, the Kingdom."

73. For this belief, see above, p. 32 n. 118. In *Jesus Tradition in Q*, 176–91, I argued that those who come from east and west are, for Q and (if dominical) for Jesus, Jews from the diaspora. I observed that, in prophecies about restoration from exile, "east" and "west" are directly tied only to Jews. I stand by my point that those from east and west cannot be Gentiles alone (as so many modern scholars suppose). Some critics have responded that the saying includes in its purview Gentiles as well as Jews because some of the relevant prophetic sayings link the return of exiles to the feast for all people; so, e.g., Yeung, *Faith in Jesus and Paul*, 277–78, and Pitre, *Tribulation*, 279–83. Even if they are right, that does not affect my point here.

74. While return from exile is eschatological hope in the Synoptics, the historical return in the sixth century BCE was also, as in 4 Baruch and the Coptic Jeremiah Apocryphon, sometimes construed as a new exodus; cf. Allison, *4 Baruch*, 21–22.

Matt 6:11: τὸν ἄρτον ἡμῶν τὸν ἐπιούσιον δὸς ἡμῖν σήμερον
Luke 11:3: τὸν ἄρτον ἡμῶν τὸν ἐπιούσιον δίδου ἡμῖν τὸ καθ᾽ ἡμέραν

While the experts continue to debate the precise meaning of ἐπιούσιος and the precise sense of the petition,[75] a host of commentators has, from early times, spied an allusion to the famous story of the manna in Exod 16.[76] Scripture speaks of manna as "bread" (לחם, ἄρτος)[77] and of it being "given" (נתן, δίδωμι) (Exod 16:8, 15, 29; Ps 78:24; cf. John 6:32; Rev 2:17). Exodus 16, furthermore, emphasizes that the manna was sent daily or day by day,[78] and Luke's τὸ καθ᾽ ἡμέραν has its exact counterpart in Exod 16:5 LXX (τὸ καθ᾽ ἡμέραν εἰς ἡμέραν for MT's דבר־יום ביומו).[79] So the Lord's Prayer, in its petition for bread, evokes the episode of the manna and suggests some parallel between the situation of Jesus's followers and the situation of Israel hungering in the desert.[80] We have here the same typology as in the sayings about "this generation" and entering the kingdom as though it were the land: Jesus's hearers are in a new exodus.

(6) Jesus admonishes his followers in Luke 12:35–38: "Fasten a belt around your waists and let your lamps be lit. And be like people waiting for their lord to return from the wedding banquet, so that as soon as he comes and knocks they open the door for him. Blessed are those servants whom the lord finds alert when he comes. Truly I say to you, he will gird himself and have them sit down to eat, and he will come and serve them. If he comes during the second or third watch of the night and finds them so (prepared), blessed are those (slaves)."[81] According to François Bovon, to be ready by fastening one's belt recalls

75. See Black, *Lord's Prayer*, 141–57. My view is that ἐπιούσιος likely renders the Aramaic פתגם יום or סכום יום, as in Tgs. Onq. and Neof. I Exod. 5:13; 16:4; Lev. 23:37; see Grelot, "Quatrième demande."

76. See the overview of reception history in Carmignac, *Recherches*, 200–210. For detailed discussion, see esp. Philonenko, *Notre Père*, 117–38, and Pitre, *Last Supper*, 159–93.

77. Exod 16:4, 8, 12, 15, 22, 29, 32; Deut 8:3; Neh 9:15; Pss 78:25; 105:40; Wis 16:20; cf. LAB 10:7; 19:5; John 6:31–34; 5 Ezra 1:19; Justin, *Dial.* 57.2; 131:3; b. Yoma 75b; etc.

78. Exod 16:4 (MT: דבר־יום ביומו; LXX: τὸ τῆς ἡμέρας εἰς ἡμέραν), 5, 22–30. Note additionally that, in John 6:34, the allusion to the first we-petition in the Our Father occurs in a discussion of Moses and the manna; cf. Lindars, "Discourse and Tradition," 88.

79. The Greek idiom appears only two other times in the LXX: Lev 23:37 and Tob 10:7.

80. Given Jesus's eschatological outlook, it is worth adding that some expected the return of the manna in the latter days or messianic times; cf. 4Q511 X, 9; 2 Bar. 29:3–8; Rev 2:17; Sib. Or. 2:347; 7:149; Mek. Vayassaʿ 5 on Exod 16:25; 6 on 16:32; Tanḥ. Buber Beshallaḥ 4:21; b. Ḥag. 12b; Num. Rab. 11:2; Ruth Rab. 5:6; Eccles. Rab. 1:9:1.

81. Although the *Critical Edition of Q* excludes Luke 12:35–38 from the Sayings Source,

> the precipitous departure from Egypt, the nocturnal exodus. Once the simultaneous . . . presence . . . of the belt and the lamp is noticed, the allusion to the Passover is undeniable. It was [furthermore] believed that Passover . . . took place at night. Jewish hope expected the Messiah at midnight.[82] Jesus' listeners, therefore, were the faithful who counted on the nocturnal arrival of the Messiah . . . [and] had their lamps lit in the night while the rest of the world was sleeping.[83]

Bovon's reading, which has strong support from the history of interpretation,[84] commends itself. In addition to his general observations, Luke's language is identical to LXX Exod 12:11 in all but the position of the pronoun:

Exod 12:11 LXX:	αἱ ὀσφύες ὑμῶν περιεζωσμέναι
Luke 12:35:	ὑμῶν αἱ ὀσφύες περιεζωσμέναι

Nestle-Aland editions of the Greek New Testament in fact italicize Luke's words, reflecting the editors' judgment that we have here a "direct quotation." Our two verses are alone in the Greek Bible in following αἱ ὀσφύες + ὑμῶν or ὑμῶν + ὀσφύες with the nominative plural feminine perfect passive participle of περιζώννυμι. Once more, then, the Synoptic Jesus moves language associated with the foundational story of Moses to his own story. Jesus, in the midst of the eschatological drama, repeats words that Moses, in preparation for the exodus from Egypt, addressed to Israel.

(7) The Sermon on the Mount contains six paragraphs in which Jesus sets his words beside and even, at points, over against Moses: "But I say to you" (ἐγὼ δὲ λέγω ὑμῖν).[85] Moses permitted swearing. Jesus prohibits taking an oath

---

some argue for its inclusion; so, e.g., Kohlmann, "Lk 12.35–38," and März, ". . . *Lasst eure Lampen Brennen!*" I incline to agree with them.

82. Cf. Mek. Pisḥa 14 on Exod 12:42; Frg. Tg. P Exod 15:18; Tg. Neof. I, Tg. Ps.-J., and Frg. Tg. V on Exod 12:42; Exod. Rab. 18:12; Jerome, *Comm. Matt ad* 25:6. Note also Jer 38(31):8 LXX: scattered Israel will return "at the feast of Passover." See further Pitre, *Last Supper*, 388–89.

83. Bovon, *Luke*, 2:231.

84. Note, e.g., Cyril of Alexandria, *Comm. Lk.* 92; Theodoret of Cyrrhus, *Quaest. Exod.* 24:3; Albertus Magnus, *Ex. sec. part. Luc. (x–xxiv)* ad loc; Lapide, *Great Commentary*, 3:494; Strobel, *Verzögerungsproblem*, 208–10, 223–25; Lövestam, *Spiritual Wakefulness*, 93–94; Schweizer, *Luke*, 213; Fitzmyer, *Luke*, 1:987; Green, *Luke*, 500; and Pao and Schnabel, "Luke," 331.

85. See Marcus, "Enigma of the Antitheses." Some of the so-called antitheses likely owe their form to the evangelist. Bultmann, *History of the Synoptic Tradition*, 134–36, however, argued that the form itself, in two or three cases, predates Matthew. His conclusion, despite

(5:34–37).[86] Moses prohibited adultery. Jesus, outdoing him, forbids looking at a woman in order to lust after her (5:27–30). Moses made provision for divorce. Jesus makes no such provision (5:31–32). And so on. In these paragraphs, Jesus does not just interpret Torah but, in this or that instance, amends it; and while Jewish sources sometimes reject the Torah's clear sense, so that in this particular the Sermon on the Mount is not unique, Matt 5:21–48's "striking feature is its emphatic, 'in-your-face' way" of making its claims: "You have heard . . . but I say to you."[87] Jesus here assumes a "Mosaic-like or 'prophet-like-Moses'-like authority,"[88] so the question of his relationship to the lawgiver is almost inevitably posed, as the history of reception reveals.

(8) The major themes of Luke 6:27–45 (Q) are vengeance, love, and judging others. All three are, in Jewish sources, closely associated with Lev 19, as is the golden rule, which appears in Luke 6:31. Indeed, the central part of the Sermon on the Plain consistently engages Lev 19 and attendant traditions.[89] In doing so, Jesus is not a conventional exegete. He is rather the provocateur—rewriting, qualifying, and even reversing Moses. If the latter mandates being holy because God is holy (Lev 19:2), Jesus mandates being merciful because God is merciful (Luke 6:36). If Moses instructs one to judge one's neighbor (Lev 19:15, 17), Jesus prohibits judging others (Luke 6:37). And if Moses enjoins love of and proper behavior toward one's own people and resident aliens (Lev 19:5–18, 33–34), Jesus demands doing good to enemies, to those who hate, curse, abuse, strike, and steal (Luke 6:27–35).[90] Assuming his own authority, Jesus, throughout Luke 6:27–45, unapologetically recasts, augments, inverts, and supersedes foundational words of Moses. By what authority does he do so? One might

dissent, still seems the best option; cf. Davies and Allison, *Matthew*, 1:504–5, and Luz, *Matthew*, 1:227–28. This opens the possibility that, before Matthew, Jesus was remembered as not just interpreting the Torah but, in this or that instance, modifying it, as though perhaps he were a new lawgiver.

86. For debate as to how to relate Jesus's prohibition of oaths to Torah, see Meier, "Did the Historical Jesus?"; Hagner, "Response"; Klawans, "Prohibition"; and Meier, "Historical Jesus and Oaths."

87. So Klawans, "Prohibition," 42.

88. Joseph, *Jesus, the Essenes*, 100.

89. See at length Allison, *Intertextual Jesus*, 29–38, and Allison, *Constructing Jesus*, 351–74. Without reference to my work, Goldstone, "Rebuke, Lending," comes to very similar conclusions. So too Goldstone, *Dangerous Duty of Rebuke*, 58–59.

90. Matt 5:43 makes the relationship to Leviticus explicit: "You have heard that it was said: 'You will love your neighbor [Lev 19:18] and hate your enemy.' But I say to you. . . ."

wonder whether his words "change the customs that Moses handed down to us" (Acts 6:14) or even if they "represent a new 'law.'"[91]

(9) Even more audacious than Luke 6:27–45 and the "but I say to you" of Matt 5:21–48 is the saying in Luke 14:26 (Q): "If anyone comes to me and does not hate his own father and mother . . . he cannot be my disciple." These words—which the Torah-observant Matthew softens[92]—have incessantly posed the problem of how they relate to the Decalogue's authoritative norm. Jesus seems to oppose the family piety of "honor your father and mother" (Exod 20:12; Deut 5:16).[93] Whatever the answer to that issue, the sole point here is that Luke 14:26, like other Synoptic passages, moves one to wonder why Jesus's words are, to borrow from Paul, "not like Moses" (2 Cor 3:13).

(10) The Jesus of Matt 11:25–27 and Luke 10:21–22 prays: "I thank you, Father, Lord of heaven and earth, that you hid these things from the wise and understanding and revealed them to children. Yes, Father, for so has it been pleasing to you." Jesus then dramatically adds: "All has been handed over to me by my Father, and no one knows the Son except the Father, nor (does anyone know) the Father except the Son and to whomever the Son decides to reveal him."[94] As I have argued at length in several places, the claim to be the exclusive revealer of divine knowledge is, within a Jewish context, and in a way reminiscent of the prologue to John's Gospel (1:1–18), naturally read over against traditions about Moses as the unique mediator of divine revelation, whom God knew face to face.[95]

91. Joseph, *Jesus, the Essenes*, 56.

92. Matt 10:37: "He who loves father or mother more than me is not worthy of me." But Gos. Thom. 55 agrees with Luke: "Whoever does not hate his father and his mother cannot become a disciple to me. And whoever does not hate his brothers and sisters and take up his cross in my way will not be worthy of me."

93. See Luz, *Matthew*, 2:112–13.

94. I pass over the slight differences between Matthew and Luke here and translate the Greek of *Critical Edition of Q*.

95. Cf. Eusebius, *Ecl. Proph.* 1.12 (PG 22:1064c–1065b); Bruno of Segni, *Comm. Matt.* ad loc (PL 165:173a); Levertoff, "Matthew," 156 ("what is said of Moses [Dt 34[10–12]] is true in a much higher degree of Him"); Dabeck, "Moses und Elias," 177; Grimm, *Jesus Einspruch*, 68–69; and W. T. Wilson, *Matthew*, 2:403. For my work on this passage, see Allison, "Two Notes"; Davies and Allison, *Matthew*, 2:283–87; Allison, *New Moses*, 218–33; and Allison, *Intertextual Jesus*, 43–51. Those in agreement or partial agreement with me include Garland, *Reading Matthew*, 132; R. Brown, *Introduction to the New Testament*, 184 n. 27; M. Talbot, *Heureux les doux*, 75–81; Nolland, *Matthew*, 474; F. Shaw, *Discernment of Revelation*, 214–19; C. A. Evans, *Matthew*, 246–47; and E. Talbot, "Rest, Eschatology." For dissent, see Grindheim, *God's Equal*, 179–80.

In Exod 33:12–13, Moses prays: "You [God] have said: 'I know you by name, and you have also found favor in my sight.' Now if I have found favor in your sight, show me your ways, so that I may know you and find favor in your sight." Here God knows Moses and Moses prays that he might in turn know God. The theme is mutual knowledge, and Jewish tradition made that knowledge exclusive—no one has known God as did Moses—and well-nigh universal.[96] In Matthew and Luke, however, it is not Moses but Jesus who receives all ("all things"), who alone knows God ("nor does anyone know the Father except the Son"), and who is God's chief mouthpiece and mediator ("to whomever the Son decides to reveal him").

Matthew's additions in 11:28–30 encourage such an approach to our text. When Jesus avows, "I am meek [πραΰς]" (11:29), he is claiming a Mosaic virtue, for the latter was, because of Num 12:3 ("the man Moses was very meek [LXX: πραΰς], more so than anyone on the face of the earth"), Judaism's exemplar in meekness. When Jesus promises "I will give you rest" (κἀγὼ ἀναπαύσω ὑμᾶς, Matt 11:28), his language is close to Exod 33:14 LXX (καὶ καταπαύσω σε). And when Jesus enjoins "take my yoke upon you" (ἄρατε τὸν

96. Regarding Moses's uniqueness, Num 12:7–8 (Moses "is entrusted with all my house. Face to face I speak with him and clearly, not in riddles, and the form of the Lord he beholds") and Deut 34:10 ("not since has there arisen a prophet in Israel like Moses, whom the Lord knew face to face") were the chief texts; cf. also Ps 103:7. For obvious reasons, Exod 33:11; Num 12:7–8; and Deut 34:10 were often contemplated together; cf. Sir 45:3–5; Philo, *Leg.* 3.100–103; *Her.* 262; Ps.-Clem. Hom. 17.18; Sipre Deut. 357; Tg. Ps.-J. Num 12:8; etc. "No one knows the Son" has a striking parallel in 4Q374 ii 2 if that text's "and though no one had known you" (line 9) refers to Moses, as argued by Fletcher-Louis, *All the Glory of Adam*, 136–39. For the scope of Moses's knowledge, note 4Q378 26 1 ("having knowledge of the Most High"); Ezek. Trag. 80 (Moses can count the number of stars, an ability otherwise associated only with the deity; cf. Ps 147:4; Isa 40:26; 1 En. 93:14; LAB 21:2; Gk. Apoc. Ezra 2:32–3:2; b. Sanh. 39a), 89 ("things present, past, and future you [Moses] will see"); Jub. 1:4 (God showed to Moses "what happened before as well as what was to come"); Let. Aris. 139 (God endowed Moses with "knowledge of all things"); LAB 19:10 ("He showed him the place from which the clouds draw up water to water the whole earth, and the place from which the river takes its water, and the land of Egypt, and the place in the firmament from which only the holy land drinks. And he showed him the place from which the manna rained on the people, even unto the paths of paradise"); 4 Ezra 14:4–6; 2 Bar. 59:4–11 (a catalogue of things heavenly and things future known to Moses); Sipre Deut. 357 ("he showed him the entire world, from the day of creation to the resurrection of the dead"); b. Meg. 19b ("the Holy One, blessed be he, showed Moses the minutiae of the Torah, the minutiae of the scribes, and the innovations that would be introduced by the scribes"); b. Ned. 38a ("fifty gates of understanding were created in the world, and all but one were given to Moses, for it is said: 'For you have made him [Moses] a little lower than God [Ps 8:5]'").

ζυγόν μου ἐφ᾽ ὑμᾶς, Matt 11:29), he deploys an idiom associated with Torah and its revelatory demands.[97]

(11) The Synoptics contain four different versions of what Jesus forbade his disciples to take when he sent them out for mission:

	MATT 10:9–10	**MARK 6:8–9**	**LUKE 9:3**	**LUKE 10:4**
PROHIBITED	gold	bread	staff	money bag
	silver	traveler's bag	traveler's bag	traveler's bag
	copper	copper	bread	sandals
	traveler's bag	two shirts	money	
	two tunics		two tunics	
	sandals			
	staff			
ALLOWED		staff		
		sandals		

As unraveling the tradition history behind these differing accounts may be beyond our ability,[98] we likely cannot, even presuming a historical nucleus, recover exactly what Jesus enjoined disciples to take or not take. Yet given that Exod 12:11—"This is how you shall eat it: your loins girded, your sandals on your feet, and your staff in your hand; and you shall eat it hurriedly. It is the Passover of the LORD"—is put to typological use in Jewish and Christian sources,[99] one wonders whether a related hermeneutical tactic—an escha-

97. Compare rabbinic formulations featuring verb + על ("on") + עול ("yoke") with reference to Torah or the commandments: m. ʾAbot 3:5 ("everyone who receives the yoke of Torah on himself"); t. Soṭah 14:4 ("they removed the yoke of heaven off themselves"); Tanḥ. Buber Huqqat 6:27 ("they never took on themselves the yoke of the Holy One"); y. Roš. Haš. 3:7 (59c) ("they took on themselves the yoke of Torah"); etc. Note also that Torah could be spoken of as "the law of Moses"; see n. 188.

98. Although it is a good bet that the allowance of staff and sandals reflects the situation in Mark's time and place; cf. Nineham, *Mark*, 169.

99. Namely Isa 52:11–12; Luke 12:35–38; and 1 Pet 1:13. On Luke 12:35 see above, pp. 107–8, and Allison, *Intertextual Jesus*, 60–61. On Isa 52:11–12 ("Depart, depart, go out thence . . . go out from the midst of her, purify yourselves, you who bear the vessels of the LORD. For you will not go out in haste, and you will not go in flight, for the LORD will go before you, and the God of Israel will be your rear guard"), see Willey, *Remember the Former Things*, 132–37; and note Blenkinsopp, *Isaiah 40–55*, 343: "The command to 'go (out) thence' (*ṣĕʾû miššām*)" belongs to an "Exodus theme. . . . The anticipated return from Babylon is given fuller resonance by the use of language associated with the departure from Egypt: unlike the people's ancestors leaving Egypt, they will not depart in haste (*bĕḥippāzôn*, only here

tological updating—lies behind Mark 6:8–9 and its parallels. This is all the more so given Josephus's report that Theudas persuaded many to gather their possessions and follow him into the wilderness (*Ant.* 20:97). Doubtless this leader sought to replay the exodus, when the people went into the desert with many goods (Exod 12:11, 34–36).

Joel Marcus has observed that "there are strong overlaps between the Markan description of" the disciples' "equipment and OT portrayals of the gear of the Israelites whom God led out of Egypt and sustained in the desert for forty years."[100] Just as the Israelites had no need to take bread (because they would be given bread from heaven; cf. Exod 16; Num 11), the Markan missionaries are commanded not to take bread; and just as the Israelites required only one set of clothes (because they would not wear out; cf. Deut 8:4; 29:5; Neh 9:21), so Jesus's followers require only one shirt. In addition,

> three of the items mentioned in Mark 6:8–9—clothes, bread, and sandals—also come together significantly in Deut 29:5–6, and sandals are again mentioned in the introductions for eating the Passover in Exod 12:11, along with a fourth item from Mark 6:8–9, the walking staff. . . . Thus, although some recent exegetes have stressed the overlaps between Jesus' missionary charge and the practice of the wandering Cynic philosophers . . . there are more extensive parallels with the Exodus tradition.[101]

Marcus's interpretation of all this—he confines himself to Mark's redactional layer—is that "the disciples' missionary journey will be a participation in the new exodus inaugurated by Jesus. . . . The twelve will not need to take along with them the usual travel kit, because they will be entering into this divine act of eschatological liberation, and the God of the exodus . . . will sustain them along the way."[102]

In linking Jesus's missionary instructions with the exodus from Egypt, Marcus stands in an interpretive tradition. Tertullian wrote:

---

and Exod 12:11; Deut 16:3), and they will not easily take to flight (*mĕnûsâ*, only here and Lev 26:36). And as on that first occasion, they will be protected both in front and behind by the numinous cloud and fire (Exod 13:21–22; 14:19–20)." On the exodus typology in 1 Peter, including a likely allusion to Exod 12:11 in 1 Pet 1:13 ("gird up the loins of your mind"), see Marcar, "Exodus in the General Letters," 169–78.

100. Marcus, *Mark*, 1:389.

101. Marcus, *Mark*, 1:389.

102. Marcus, *Mark*, 1:389–90. For criticism of Marcus (which I find unpersuasive), see Rogers, "Shaking the Dust," 176–77.

> When the children of Israel went out of Egypt, the creator brought them forth laden with their spoils of gold and silver vessels, and with loads besides of clothing and unleavened dough, whereas Christ commanded his disciples not to carry even a staff for the journey. . . . Consider the difference presented in the occasions and you will understand how it was one and the same power that arranged the mission of his people according to their poverty in the one case and their plenty in the other. . . . Even shoes he forbade them [the disciples] to carry. For it was he under whose protection the people wore out not even a shoe (Deut. 29:5), even in the wilderness for the space of so many years. (Tertullian, *Marc.* 4:24)

Tertullian, in explaining the dissimilarities in terms of the different occasions, was countering Marcion, who evidently leveraged the differences to stress the conflict between old and new. In line with this, the Marcionite Megethius is reported to have taught the following:

> The God of Genesis commanded Moses in the going up from Egypt saying: "Make ready with loins girded, having sandals on feet, staffs in your hands, and traveler's bags upon you. Carry away the gold and silver and all the other things of the Egyptians." But our good Lord, sending his disciples out into the world, says: "Neither sandals on your feet, nor traveler's bag, nor two cloaks, nor money in your belts. See how clearly the good one opposes the teachings of that one."[103]

For Megethius, the different directions reflect different divinities. Other commentators, of a more orthodox stripe, remark on the dissimilarities in order to make other points.[104]

My surmise is that, if the historical Jesus, when sending out disciples, adverted to Moses's instruction for the exodus, he drew a parallel in order to mark a difference. The exodus was remembered as undertaken in haste;[105] and whereas Isa 52:11–12 envisages a new exodus undertaken without hurry, Jesus rather thought of his moment, the moment of eschatological crisis, as demanding even more haste than did the flight from Egypt. If Moses permitted the

103. Adamantius, *Der Dialog des Adamantius*, ed. Sande Bakhuyzen, 22. Megethius seems here to conflate Luke 9:3 (which prohibits traveler's bag, money, and two tunics) with 10:4 (which prohibits travel bag, money bag, and sandals).

104. E.g., Ambrose, *Exp. Luc.* 7.57–60; Isho'dad of Merv, *Comm. Matt.* 7; Dionysius bar Salibi, *Comm. E. ad Matt.* 10:10; Paschasius Radbertus, *Exp. Matt. libri xii* on Matt 10:10.

105. Exod 12:11, 33–39 (prophesied in Gen 15:14); Deut 16:3; Jub. 49:23; Ezek. Trag. 182; Philo, *Her.* 255; etc.

escaping Israelites to take with them bread, money, sandals, and staff,[106] Jesus forbade such. In accord with this, Luke 10:4 directly subjoins to the list of prohibited objects this admonition: "Greet no one on the way."[107] The injunction, as startling as the directions before it, stresses urgency. In the words of Joachim Jeremias, "in no circumstances . . . may the messengers involve themselves in any loss of time. Their duty, to proclaim the nearness of the reign of God, must be fulfilled with the utmost speed. Every minute is precious."[108]

The Historical Jesus and Moses

The passages just introduced are of three kinds. In some, Jesus acts like Moses. In others, those around Jesus are implicitly compared to those around Moses. In still others, Jesus is Moses's authoritative counterpart, supplementing or amending Torah for the eschatological crisis.

Jesus Is Like Moses

- He casts out demons by "the finger of God" (Luke 11:20).
- He inaugurates a covenant through blood (Mark 14:24).
- He is the supreme mediator of divine revelation (Matt 11:25–27; Luke 10:21–22).

Those around Jesus Are Compared with Those around Moses

- His generation is like that of Moses (Mark 9:19; Matt 12:39–42 // Luke 11:29–32; etc.).
- His followers rely on God for bread for the coming day (Matt 6:11; Luke 11:3).
- His disciples are to be ready, just like Israel at the exodus (Luke 12:35–38).
- Some will enter and inherit the kingdom just as some in Israel entered and inherited the land (Matt 7:21; Mark 10:15; John 3:5; etc.)
- His disciples must make do with even less than fleeing Israel took (Matt 10:9–10 par.).

106. Exod 12:11, 34–39. Robinson, Hoffmann, and Kloppenborg, *Critical Edition of Q*, 164, regard the four items I have listed as representing Q's text (if πῆραν = "knapsack" was for food). Cf. Fleddermann, *Q*, 407.

107. This likely belonged to Q; so also Robinson, Hoffmann, and Kloppenborg, *Critical Edition of Q*, 164. Matthew presumably omitted the words because of the tension with 5:47 ("if you greet only your brothers, what more are you doing than others?").

108. Jeremias, *New Testament Theology*, 133. Cf. 2 Kgs 4:29, where urgency occasions Elisha's demand that Gehazi give no greeting on his way to save a life.

Jesus Rewrites or Sets His Words over against Words of Moses

- He employs the "you have heard . . . but I say to you" formula (Matt 5:21–48).
- He revises Lev 19 (Luke 6:27–45).
- He gainsays the Decalogue's imperative to love father and mother (Luke 14:26).

What, taken together, might all this tell us about Jesus of Nazareth? Few with a critical bent would be stoutly confident that all this material stems directly from Jesus. Many would, for instance, and without much hesitation, assign the christological self-revelation in Matt 11:25–27 and Luke 10:21–22 to the post-Easter period.[109]

Yet the matter is different regarding the logion about the finger of God, the sayings about "this generation," the sayings about entering and inheriting the kingdom, the Lord's Prayer, the central part of the Sermon on the Plain, and the command to hate parents. Indeed, were I so disposed, I might claim that the academic consensus deems these units—fully half of those examined—to rest on things Jesus said.

I am not, however, so disposed. Even if I knew how to undertake a head-count, adding up votes is no way to do history. Recourse to such would not be argument but a lethargic appeal to authority.

Alternatively, one could approach the problem by applying the traditional criteria of authenticity to particular sayings, thereby hoping to establish which really come from Jesus. I also eschew that maneuver.

I adopt another strategy.[110] Rather than analyzing the sayings individually, I prefer to contemplate them as a group. When I do so, I observe that the Mosaic and new exodus motifs run across the sources. They appear in so-called Q material, in Mark, in Markan/Q overlaps, and in traditions unique to Matthew and Luke:

The Sayings Source (Q)

- Luke 6:27–45 // Matt 5:38–48; 7:1–5, 15–20
- Luke 10:21–22 // Matt 11:25–27
- Luke 11:20 // Matt 12:28
- Luke 14:26 // Matt 10:37

109. For surveys of the discussion (and dissent from it), see Pitre, "Historical Jesus," and Pitre, "From Reimarus to Allison."

110. For the reasons see below in chapter 6.

The Sayings Source (Q) and Mark

- Mark 6:6–9; Matt 10:9–10 // Luke 10:4 (cf. Luke 9:3)
- Mark 9:19; Matt 12:39–42 // Luke 11:29–32; etc.

Mark

- Mark 10:15
- Mark 14:24

Luke alone

- Luke 12:35–38[111]

Matthew alone

- Matt 5:21, 27, 31, 33, 38, 43; 7:21

Now either all these materials mislead us about Jesus or at least some do not. Either the specified logia are one hundred percent distortion, or the ecclesiastical contribution is not thoroughgoing. To which alternative do the data beckon? In my judgment, positing a beginning with Jesus has more explanatory power. It helps explain why allusions to Moses are already in Q and Mark, our earliest sources: they were there from the start. It helps explain why some early Christ adherents had a Moses Christology, why—like Peter in Acts 3 and Stephen in Acts 7—they made Jesus out to be the prophet like Moses foretold in Deut 18:15–18:[112] the move was natural given that he likened himself to the lawgiver. It helps

111. Some, however, assign this unit to Q; see n. 81 above.

112. See Schoeps, *Theologie und Geschichte*, 87–116; Teeple, *Mosaic Eschatological Prophet*; Fuller, *Foundations*, 167–73; and Lierman, *New Testament Moses*, esp. 258–88. Cf. above all the quotations of Deut 18:15–18 in Acts 3:22 and 7:37 and the allusions to the same in Matt 17:5; Mark 9:7; and Luke 9:35. The episode of the transfiguration was, in my judgment, initially formulated with both Deut 18:15–18 and Moses's radiance in mind. For analysis see Marcus, *Way of the Lord*, 80–93. Not all, however, agree; see, e.g., D. Zeller, "Bedeutung." Recall further John 1:45 ("we have found the one Moses in the law and the prophets wrote about") and the definite article (ὁ) before "prophet" in Matt 21:11; Luke 7:39 v.l.; John 6:14; 7:40, 52 v.l. I wholeheartedly agree with Lierman, *New Testament Moses*, that New Testament scholars have, in general, insufficiently appreciated the relevance of traditions about Moses for the development of early Christology. Lindars, *New Testament Apologetic*, 204–10, denies that the interpretation of Jesus as Mosaic prophet goes back to the earliest times. My view is that it does, but that the tradition was sometimes ambivalent about a category associated with the so-called sign prophets, such as Theudas and the Egyptian; cf. Vermes, *Jesus the Jew*, 97–99, and recall the warnings against false Christs and false prophets in Matt 24:23–26; Mark 13:21–23; and Luke 17:23.

explain why some early Christ adherents conceived of their situation to be a new exodus:[113] they were prodded to do this because Jesus had done so before them. It helps explain why the parallels and contrasts between Jesus and the lawgiver appear in all four canonical Gospels: those contrasts and parallels are downstream in all currents because they were at the source. And it lines up with the fact that some of the relevant materials—hate mother and father, this generation is faithless, love your enemies—seem severe and potentially offensive: Jesus, as we know on other grounds, could be provocative and exceptionally challenging.

Objections

What might be said on the other side, for the view that Jesus donned Moses's mantle only after he departed this life? One objection I foresee is that my argument depends wholly on the implicit. Not once is Moses named in the materials to which I have drawn attention. Jesus says neither "a greater than Moses is here" nor "I am like Moses." The Mosaic subtexts are covert, and the meanings I uncover must be read in.

My response is this. First, none of the intertextual proposals I have made is mine, by which I mean mine alone. In every case the history of interpretation offers support, in most cases very strong support.

Second, the Hebrew Bible, the Apocrypha, the Dead Sea Scrolls, the Pseudepigrapha, Philo, Josephus, and the rabbis—that is, almost all the written evidence we have—show us that, before and after the turn of the era, practicing Jews lived in their foundational stories. Josephus boasted that Jews had a "thorough and accurate knowledge" of the law (τοῦ νόμου), by which he meant the Mosaic legislation.[114] And if they knew the legislation, they likewise must have known the stories in which that legislation is embedded. Josephus went on: "Should anyone of our nation be questioned about the laws, he would repeat them all more readily than his own name. The result, then, of our thorough grounding in the laws from the first dawn of intelligence is that we have them, as it were, engraved on our souls."[115] While this is braggadocio, it cannot be

113. For this theme, see Allison, "Son of God as Israel"; Marcus, *Way of the Lord*; Watts, *Isaiah's New Exodus*; and Davies, *Christian Engagements with Judaism*, 123–40.

114. Josephus, *C. Ap.* 2.175. Cf. Philo, *Legat.* 210: "Holding that the laws are oracles vouchsafed by God and having been trained in this doctrine from their earliest years, they carry the likeness of the commandments enshrined in their souls."

115. Josephus, *C. Ap.* 2.178. Cf. *Ant.* 4.210 ("it is good that these laws should be so graven on their hearts and stored in the memory that they can never be effaced"); Philo, *Hypoth.* 7.12

wholly tendentious, and it is safe to say, with E. P. Sanders, that "Jews were generally well educated in the Bible."[116] This includes even those who could not read, because they often heard texts read and expounded. To quote Josephus again: every week people "desert their occupations and assemble to listen to the law."[117]

Now Jesus was, if he was anything, a practicing Jew of some kind. So too those most attracted to him. This alone suggests that he was *homo biblicus*, that his world was the scriptural world, that the biblical characters were his contemporaries, that he attended to Moses and the prophets and so could allude to them in the expectation of being understood.

But we have far more than a loose inference. We rather have a mountain of evidence, namely, the sources for Jesus, including the sayings attributed to him. These are saturated with allusions to biblical texts.[118] Matthew, Mark, and Luke are indeed, as those acquainted with the secondary literature know, intertextual wonderlands.[119] What good reason moves us to suppose that, in this particular, they are wholly out of step with the individual they commemorate? One might hazard that we should be distrustful, that since early Christians preoccupied themselves with Scripture, we should suspect that its each and every appearance in the Gospels is overlay.[120] This, however, would be skepticism run amok. It would be to replace evidence with imagination. That his followers did something is no reason at all to surmise Jesus did not. More particularly, that they added scriptural allusions and quotations to the tradition hardly entails or even suggests that they started from scratch, that Jesus himself never quoted or alluded to the law and the prophets. On the contrary, those who first formulated the tradition, like those who passed it on later, took themselves to be Jesus's followers, and surely in many important

(Moses "required them to assemble in the same place on these seventh days, and sitting together in a respectful and orderly manner hear the laws read so that none should be ignorant of them").

116. Sanders, *Judaism*, 197.

117. Josephus, *C. Ap.* 2.175. Cf. *Ant.* 16.43 ("we give every seventh day over to the study of our customs and law . . . through which we can avoid sinning"); Luke 4:16; Acts 13:14–15.

118. This includes the so-called sapiential materials assigned to Q; see Allison, *Intertextual Jesus*, 5–9.

119. As is the Gospel of John. The exception here is the Gospel of Thomas. But in this regard, as in others, it represents a secondary development.

120. Cf. Bultmann in Bultmann and Kundsin, *Form Criticism*, 45: "Most of the words of Torah which cite the Old Testament are suspected of originating in the theological debates of the primitive community."

respects they were. Positing an unscriptural Jesus explains absolutely nothing. Positing an intertextual Jesus helps explain why the tradition is what it is.

Now Jesus and his hearers knew that Moses worked wonders by "the finger of God," so if he ever claimed to do the same, an analogy would have suggested itself. They likewise knew that Moses had commanded one to honor father and mother, so if Jesus ever told people to hate father and mother, questions about his understanding of and authority over against Moses would have been inevitable. Again, Jesus and his followers knew that the generation in the wilderness was faithless, sinful, evil, perverse, so if he ever characterized his own generation in the same terms, they would have taken him to be likening the present to the past. Similarly, Jesus and his hearers knew the story of the manna in the wilderness, so if he ever encouraged people to pray for bread for the coming day, they would have drawn a line from their circumstances to the days of Moses. In other words, the interpretations I have offered would not have been remote to Jesus or his followers. All they required were the social memories that were part of "popular Israelite culture."[121]

There is, however, another objection. My take on Jesus, some will think, gives him too high a self-conception. How can we believe that he took himself to be in a new exodus in which he was Moses's counterpart? According to an esteemed academic tradition, Jesus preached not himself but the kingdom.

This is a perfectly reasonable rebuttal. Yet it will work only if one hews to the old critical orthodoxy, if one holds that while Jesus may have thought of himself as an eschatological prophet, he did not suppose himself to be any particular eschatological prophet.[122] If one clings to that creed, then my arguments will not, I concede, compel. They have a chance of persuading only if one deems it plausible, on other grounds, that Jesus entertained exalted thoughts about himself.

I cannot here review this controversial issue or survey the complex evidence. All I can do is register my conviction that Jesus took himself to be the center of his own eschatological scenario and indeed Israel's king in waiting.[123]

121. I borrow the phrase from Horsley, "Study of the Historical Jesus," 291.

122. While this is a common trope in modern scholarship, was it a common trope in Jesus's world? Was not the expectation of an eschatological prophet typically more distinct? Was it not usually about a prophet like Moses or the returning Elijah or Jeremiah or some such? It is notable that early Christian sources are not content to dub John the Baptist a prophet; they rather characterize him as Elijah; see below, p. 142.

123. See Allison, *Constructing Jesus*, 221–304. See also the important contribution of Theissen and Merz, "From the Historical Jesus."

Once one allows that, the possibility that he identified himself with the prophet like Moses of Deut 18:15–18 ceases to be remote.

Rabbinic sources know the axiom: "As the first redeemer was, so will the last redeemer be."[124] Two scriptural roots are entwined in these words. The first is the expectation of a new exodus, well attested in Isaiah and elsewhere.[125] The second is the oracle in Deut 18:15–18: God will raise up a prophet like Moses. Once the latter was given eschatological sense, as already in 1QS IX, 11 and 4Q175,[126] the expectation of a prophet like Moses naturally merged, in some circles, with the expectation of a new exodus, as in the Gospels and the rabbis: the new exodus will have a new Moses.[127] This in turn led some to expect that Israel's eschatological king would be like Moses, another belief to which again the Gospels and the rabbis attest.[128] The mingling of motifs

124. Cf. Tanḥ. 'Eqev 7b (Str-B. 3:824); Num. Rab. 11:2; Ruth Rab. 5:6; Eccles. Rab. 1:9:1; Pesiq. Rab Kah. 5:1. The καθώς . . . οὕτως of John 3:14 ("just as Moses lifted up the serpent in the wilderness, thus is it necessary for the Son of Man to be lifted up") has its close parallels in these texts, which perhaps argues for the antiquity of this sort of formulation. Cf. also Ps.-Clem. Rec. 1.57: *ut fecit Moyses, ita fecit etiam Jesus* ("as Moses worked [signs and wonders], so also did Jesus").

125. Discussion in Sahlin, "New Exodus of Salvation"; Stuhlmueller, *Creative Redemption*, 59–98; Barstad, *Way in the Wilderness*; and Ninow, *Indicators of Typology*, 157–241. Illustrations include Isa 10:24–26; 11:11–16; 40:1–11; 41:17–20; 43:18–21; 48:20–21; 49:8–12; 51:10–11; 52:11–12; Jer 6:14–15; 23:7–8; 31:31–34; Ezek 20:33–44; Hos 2:14–15; Mic 7:12, 15; also 1QS VIII, 12–16; 1QM XI, 6–11; 2 Bar. 29:8; Sib. Or. 7:148–49; and Rev 15:2–4.

126. And also perhaps in 4Q375 I, 1–4: "[All that] your God commands you by the prophet's mouth, and you will keep [all] these [pre]cepts, and will return to the Lord your God with all [your heart and with al]l your soul, and your God will repent of the fury of his great wrath [or order to save y]ou from your trials." Samaritan sources are here relevant; cf. Ps.-Clem. Rec. 1:54 (the Samaritans "expect from the prophecies of Moses the one true prophet"); Origen, *Cels.* 1.57 ("after the times of Jesus, Dositheus the Samaritan wished to persuade the Samaritans that he was the Christ predicted by Moses"); Eusebius, *Theoph.* 4.35 ("the Samaritans were persuaded that Dositheus . . . was the prophet of whom Moses prophesied; and he so deceived them that they declared him to be the Christ"). On the Samaritan figure of Taheb, who will fulfill Deut 18:15–18, see Dexinger's *Taheb* and "Reflections on the Relationship."

127. Deutero-Isaiah likely already moves in this direction; see below, pp. 134–35.

128. Martyn, *History and Theology*, 102–28, remains helpful here. He infers from John not only that some followers of Jesus identified him as the Mosaic Messiah but that the evangelist knew Jews who held the Messiah to be Mosaic. One wonders about 4Q521 2 II, 1: "[For the heav]ens and the earth will heed [ישמעו] his anointed one [למשיחו]." If this alludes to Deut 18:15 ("him you will heed [תשמעון]"), it may identify the eschatological prophet like Moses with "his anointed one" or "Messiah." But J. J. Collins, "He Shall Not

was doubtless encouraged by the tradition that Moses was king and prophet,[129] for both prophets and kings were God's "messiahs," that is, "anointed ones."[130] Furthermore, that all this happened not just among Jesus's followers and later rabbis but also among first-century non-Christian Jews appears from the sign prophets we learn of from Josephus, for some of them aspired both to rule or be king and to be like Moses (see below, pp. 136–40). There was a tradition here. Jesus stood within it.

Additional Possibilities

If sayings attributed to Jesus reflect a Mosaic self-conception, what of his purported actions? There are at least four possibilities here.

(1) According to Matt 4:1–2 and Luke 4:1–2, Jesus once entered the wilderness, where he fasted forty days and (in Matthew) forty nights. Both Gospels go on to relate details of the affair, which features a dialogue between Jesus and the devil. A closely related tradition appears in the much briefer and indeed cryptic Mark 1:12–13: "And immediately the Spirit drove him out into the wilderness. And he was in the wilderness forty days, tempted by Satan, and he was with wild beasts. And the angels served him." Although Mark's laconic account fails to say that Jesus went without food, this appears to be implied in his conclusion: "The angels served [διηκόνουν] him." This almost certainly means they fed him.[131]

Judge," identifies the anointed figure in 4Q521 with Elijah; and Moses or the prophet like Moses are distinguished from the Messiah in 1QS IX, 11; 4Q175; and Fg. Tg. V Exod 12:42.

129. For Moses as a prophet, see Deut 18:15, 18; 34:10; Hos 12:13; Sir 46:1; Wis 11:1; Aristob. 2; Philo, *Det.* 135; *Mos.* 1.57; *QG* 1.86; 4:29; *Virt.* 51; Josephus, *Ant.* 2.327; 4.165, 329; T. Mos. 1:5; 3:11; 11:16; LAB 53:8; 2 Bar. 59:4–11; Asc. Isa. 3:8; 5:1–13; m. Soṭah 1:9; Tg. Neof. Deut 33:22; Tg. Cant 1:8; 1 Clem. 43.6; Barn. 6.8; etc. For Moses as king or ruler, see Num 12:7; Deut 33:5(?); Ezek. Trag. 74–79; Philo, *Mos.* 1.148–49, 158, 334; Sib. Or. 11:38–40; Sipre Num. 78; Sipre Deut. 357; etc. For discussion, see Meeks, *Prophet-King*; Meeks, "Moses as God and King"; Feldman, *Philo's Portrayal of Moses*, 280–91; and Lierman, *New Testament Moses*, 32–64, 79–123.

130. Note 4Q377 2 5: "Moses his anointed" (מושה משיחו). This may refer to Moses's status as anointed prophet; so Fabry, "Moses," and Joseph, *Jesus, the Essenes*, 83–84. For kings as anointed, see 1 Sam 9:16; 10:1; 16:1–13; 1 Kgs 1:32–40; 2 Kgs 9:1–13; 11:4–12; 23:30; etc. For prophets as anointed—not so common—see 1 Kgs 19:16; 1 Chr 16:22; Ps 105:15; Isa 61:1; 4Q521(?); 11QMelch II, 16–18(?), and the discussion in Jassen, *Mediating the Divine*, 85–103. Those anointed in CD II, 12; VI, 1; and 1QM XI, 7 may or may not be prophets; perhaps they are priests.

131. Cf. Mark 1:31, where Peter's mother-in-law "serves" (διηκόνει) Jesus and his disci-

Long ago I became persuaded of two things. First, the temptation story in Matthew and Luke is a haggadic tale fashioned via creative reflection on Deut 6–8.[132] Second, Mark's version of the temptation likely presents Jesus as a new Adam: by besting the devil, he recovers paradise.[133] I accordingly reckoned the stories to be fiction.[134] In view of the previous pages, however, I now confess to having second thoughts. I have begun to entertain the possibility that the matter is less cut and dry. If Jesus did sometimes deliberately speak like a new Moses, why might he not sometimes have sought to act like Moses? More particularly, might he not at some point, and like Simeon Stylites after him, have aspired to fast in the desert in imitation of the lawgiver?[135] If he did, a historical kernel would lie behind the Synoptic accounts of the temptation. The stories would then be like the baptismal narratives, which I take to be mythological elaborations of the historical fact that Jesus submitted to John's baptism. Maybe the temptation narratives similarly elaborate a circumstance from Jesus's life, in this case a retreat to the wilderness to repeat Moses's fast. I do not, I admit, know how to pass beyond speculation here. Yet pondering Simeon Stylites makes the possibility seem real rather than, as it was for me once, remote.

(2) That a group known as "the Twelve" accompanied Jesus appears to be a fact, although as with everything some doubt.[136] Only a little lower down on the scale of probability is the eschatological nature of that group: they functioned (among other things) as an eschatological sign, as a promise of the fulfillment of hope for Israel's return from exile and the gathering of all the tribes to the land.[137] Indeed, John Meier is likely right to contend that their constitution was a "prophetic act" intended to "set in motion the regathering of the twelve tribes, even before these twelve men actually did anything."[138]

ples. This must mean supplying the evening meal; cf. the sense of the verb in T. Job 12:1–2; Luke 12:37; 17:8; 22:26–27; John 12:2; Acts 6:2; Josephus, *Ant.* 11.163; etc.

132. See Gerhardsson, *Testing of God's Son*.

133. For the argument see Allison, "Behind the Temptations of Jesus." Cf. Klauck, *Vorspiel im Himmel?*, 55–60.

134. Even if they incorporate accurate memories of Jesus; see below, pp. 373–74.

135. The sources otherwise have him in the desert or wilderness (ἔρημος): Mark 1:35, 45; 6:31–35; Luke 5:16.

136. For persuasive arguments for historicity see Meye, *Jesus and the Twelve*, 192–209; Sanders, *Jesus and Judaism*, 98–106; Trilling, *Studien zur Jesusüberlieferung*, 185–208; Meier, "Circle of the Twelve"; Meier, "Jesus, the Twelve"; and Wenell, *Jesus and Land*, 116–21.

137. Allison, *Constructing Jesus*, 67–76. But for hesitation on the matter, see McKnight, "Jesus and the Twelve."

138. Meier, *Marginal Jew*, 3:153.

The Synoptics do not depict a group of twelve gradually or spontaneously forming around Jesus. They rather have him deliberately creating the Twelve or sending them forth at a particular moment. According to Mark 3:13–14, Jesus went up on a mountain "and called to him those whom he wanted, and they went to him. And he made them [*or* appointed: ἐποίησεν] twelve." Luke 6:12–13 is similar: after praying on a mountain through the evening, Jesus "called his disciples, choosing [ἐκλεξάμενος] from them twelve, whom he named apostles." Matthew is a bit different. He relates that Jesus, after imploring his hearers to "ask the Lord of the harvest to send out laborers into his harvest," then "summoned his twelve disciples"—here introduced abruptly and without explanation—"and gave them authority over unclean spirits," after which he sent them out (9:37–10:5). This, despite the differences, refers to a specific occasion.

What might we make of this memory, if that is what it is?[139] The number twelve, within a Jewish context, always called to mind, first and above all, the twelve tribes. It can be no different with Jesus's twelve disciples. There is more, however.

Moses is more than once associated with a group of twelve.[140] At the beginning of Numbers, the Lord directs him and Aaron to employ the aid of twelve men, who will be with them as they conduct the first census of Israel (1:1–46). A few chapters later, Moses arranges for "the leaders of Israel," of which there are twelve, to make offerings, which they do, one tribal representative each day for twelve days (Num 7:1–88). Then, according to Deut 1:23, Moses sent forth twelve men to scout out the land of promise. This last refers back to the much fuller account in Num 13, where God instructs Moses to select a leader from each of the twelve tribes and to send them forth to spy out the land of Canaan.

It is natural to identify the twelve men in Num 1 with the group of twelve in Num 7.[141] Beyond that, it is hard to generalize how ancient readers might

139. For the argument that Jesus sent out the Twelve for mission, see Meier, *Marginal Jew*, 3:154–63; cf. Theissen, *New Testament*, 23: "Favoring the historicity of the mission is that the disciples did not preach the parousia of the returning Kurios, but *metanoia* (Mark 6:12). They promised the coming of the reign of God (Luke 10:9). They did not baptize, but preached and healed. They didn't even demand 'belief'! All that points to a time before Easter."

140. In addition to what follows recall the western panel of the synagogue at Dura Europos, which has Moses striking a rock to produce water: he is surrounded by twelve men who represent the twelve tribes.

141. The twelve who make offerings in Num 7 are identified as "the leaders [נשיאי, ἄρχοντες] of Israel, heads [ראשי, ἄρχοντες] of their ancestral houses, the leaders [נשיאי, ἄρχοντες] of the tribes" (7:2). This harks back to 1:16: the Twelve "were those chosen from the congregation, the leaders [נשיאי, ἄρχοντες] of their ancestral tribes, the heads [ראשי, χιλίαρχοι] of the divisions of Israel."

have linked the texts just cited as well as those passages that speak, without the number twelve, of Israel's leaders or princes (נשיאים; ἄρχοντες).[142] Still, many hearers and readers have assumed, in part because of Num 1 and 7, that there were, in Moses's day, and at his instigation, twelve phylarchs or tribal leaders.[143] It is no wonder, then, that reflection on Matt 9:37–10:5; Mark 3:13–14; Luke 6:12–13 or on Jesus and the Twelve in general has spurred some to recollect Moses and the group(s) of twelve associated with him or, alternatively, that reflection on the group(s) of twelve around Moses has led some to think about the Twelve in the New Testament.[144] This has been all the more natural as:

a. The twelve disciples are with Jesus, share his responsibilities, and are rulers and judges to whom he gives authority.[145] All this mirrors the phylarchs and Moses.
b. Mark 3:13 introduces the calling of the Twelve with the notice that Jesus "went up into the mountain" (ἀναβαίνει εἰς τὸ ὄρος). This reproduces an idiom recurrently associated in the Pentateuch with Moses: ἀναβαίνω + εἰς τὸ ὄρος.[146] If not a coincidence, this reflects Mark's perception, or that of a predecessor, of a Mosaic aura in Jesus's election of the Twelve.

142. See, e.g., Exod 16:22; 18:13–26; 22:28; 34:30–32; 35:27; Lev 4:22–26; Num 10:4, 11–28; 21:18; 27:2; 31:13; 32:2; 34:16–29; 36:1; Deut 31:28. The most helpful contribution of which I am aware remains Horbury, "Twelve and the Phylarchs."

143. Tg. Ps.-J. Lev 4:15 turns "the elders of the congregation" into "the twelve elders of the congregation who have been appointed officers over the twelve tribes."

144. Cf. Origen, *Hom. Exod.* 11.6; *Hom. Josh.* 18.11; Ps.-Clem. Rec. 1:40; Eusebius, *Dem. ev.* 3.2 (94a) ("Moses sent out twelve men to spy out the land, and likewise . . . our savior sent out twelve apostles to visit all the Gentiles"); Lapide, *Commentaria in Scripturam Sacram*, 2:194 ("allegorically and figuratively, these twelve princes [in Num 1:1–16] represent the twelve apostles"); Hobbes, *Leviathan*, 303; Grotius, *Operum theologicarum*, 2:1:188; Bengel, *Gnomon Novi Testamenti*, 1:116; Gfrörer, *Jahrhundert des Heils*, 369–74 (Jesus's appointment of the Twelve "is very important evidence that Jesus Christ himself wanted to act as did Moses, that he thus applied the magisterial passage Deut. 18:15 to himself"); Chavasse, "Jesus: Christ and Moses," 248–49; Schoeps, *Theologie und Geschichte*, 96–97; Farrer, "Ministry in the New Testament," 120–24; Strobel, "Berg der Offenbarung," 143; Pesch, *Markusevangelium*, 1:204; Horbury, "Twelve and the Phylarchs"; Bauckham, "James and the Church," 430; Marcus, *Mark*, 1:266; Bovon, *Luke*, 1:344; Pitre, *Last Supper*, 54; and Porter and Dyer, *Origins of New Testament Christology*, 41.

145. Matt 19:28 // Luke 22:28–30 (Q); Mark 6:7; 10:35–40; Luke 10:19. Cf. Num 1:5: the leaders are "with" (LXX: μετά) Moses and Aaron.

146. Cf. Marcus, *Mark*, 1:266. Ἀναβαίνω + εἰς τὸ ὄρος occurs 24× in the LXX. Of these, eighteen occur in the Pentateuch and are mostly of Moses: Exod 19:3, 12, 13; 24:12, 13, 18; 34:1, 2, 4; Num 27:12; Deut 1:24, 41, 43; 5:5; 9:9; 10:1, 3; 32:49; cf. Philo, *Mos.* 2.161.

c. The appointment of the Twelve in Mark 3 and parallels is immediately trailed by a list of their names. This resembles Num 1:1–16, where the notice to enroll twelve men to help Moses and Aaron (cf. 1:44) introduces a list of their names.[147] The same pattern appears in 13:1–16: Moses selects twelve leaders—they are φυλάρχοι in Philo, *Mos.* 1.221—and their twelve names are given. The latter list includes this note: "Moses changed the name [LXX: ἐπωνόμασεν] of Hoshea son of Nun to Joshua" (Num 13:16). Occurring in a list of twelve leaders, the comment might call to mind Mark 3:16: ("Simon whom he named [ἐπέθηκεν ὄνομα] Peter") and Luke 6:14 ("Simon whom he named [ὠνόμασεν] Peter"). It did so for Eusebius (*Dem. ev.* 3:2 [93d]).
d. If Jesus, in Mark 6:7, sends out the Twelve "two by two" (δύο δύο), and if the list in Matt 10:2–4 is divided into six pairs,[148] Num 7:1–3 also divides its twelve leaders into pairs: there are two leaders in each of the six wagons carrying them. Josephus, *Ant.* 3.220, puts it this way: "The phylarchs came two by two [κατὰ δύο]."
e. The LXX employs ἀποστέλλω when it tells of Moses sending forth twelve men in Num 13:2, 3, 16, 17, 27; and Deut 1:22. The Synoptics use the same verb of Jesus sending forth the Twelve (Matt 10:5, 16, 40; Mark 3:14; 6:7; Luke 10:1, 3, 16).[149]
f. Moses, in Deut 1:23, sends twelve men to reconnoiter the land of promise. In the Synoptics, Jesus sends forth the Twelve into parts of Israel (cf. Matt 10:5–6; Mark 6:6–7; Luke 10:1).

In listing these items, my goal is not to insist on the historicity of each particular. I am, in fact, agnostic as to whether Jesus gathered the Twelve on a mountain or sent out messengers two by two. My point is instead this. The tradition about Jesus commissioning the Twelve includes several items that can be linked to a Moses typology. I suggest that this reflects somebody's conviction that, when Jesus selected and sent out the Twelve, he was playing a Mosaic part. My further suggestion is that someone held this conviction because Jesus intentionally implanted it.

147. Further, if "these are the names [τὰ ὀνόματα ἐστιν ταῦτα] of the twelve apostles" (Matt 10:2) introduces Matthew's list, "these are the names [ταῦτα τὰ ὀνόματα] of the men" introduces the list in Numbers (1:5).

148. The pattern is A καί B, C καί D, E καί F, G καί H, I καί J, K καί L. Cf. Origen, *Fr. Luc.* 158: "Matthew also shows that the apostles were ordered two by two, in his list of them, for he arranges them in pairs."

149. Note C. A. Evans, "Baptism of John," 69: "It is probable that the designation 'apostle,' meaning 'one sent,' derives from the story of Moses sending the twelve spies."

Where such a proposal lies on the scale of probability I am unsure. But I am emboldened to entertain the idea seriously because the phylarchs, far from being dead memories in Jesus's time and place, were familiar characters,[150] and because the Dead Sea Scrolls show us that they lived on as types for eschatological figures, which is what the Twelve were for Jesus.[151]

(In Luke 10:1, Jesus appoints not twelve but seventy-two [or seventy] and sends them out for mission. This likely belongs to the redactional level: Luke knew two missionary discourses, one from Mark, one from Q, and rather than conflating them as did Matthew, he kept them apart, designing one for the Twelve, the other for the larger group.[152] Be that as it may, whereas some commentators on Luke 10:1 recall the seventy nations of Gen 10, others—with better reason[153]—are put in mind of Exod 24:1, 9 and Num 11:16, 24, which refer to the seventy elders around Moses. As Cyril of Alexandria (*Hom. Lk.* 60 *ad* 10:2–3) wrote: the seventy Jesus sent forth were "prefigured in the words of Moses, for at God's command he also chose seventy."[154] Luke's number functions as does the seventy-two in the Epistle of Aristeas and m. Yad. 3:5–4:4 to "recall the deeds of Moses and the elders in the wilderness."[155] This take on the seventy or seventy-two in Luke 10:1 is akin to my suggestion about Jesus and the Twelve: the verse alludes to a group associated with Moses. As Ps.-Clem. Rec. 1.40 has it: Jesus chose twelve "whom he named apostles, after which he approved seventy-two other disciples, so that in this way the multitude, recognizing the pattern of Moses, would believe, for this is what the prophet Moses foretold would come.")

(3) All four canonical Gospels have Jesus, through miraculous means, feed a large crowd in a deserted locale.[156] One may, with David Friedrich Strauss,

150. Horbury, "Twelve and the Phylarchs," established this.

151. Cf. 1QS ("twelve men and three priests" rule the end-time community); 1QM V, 1–2 ("on the shield of the Prince of the whole congregation they will write his name . . . and the names of the twelve commanders [שרי] of their tribes"); 4Q164 1 7 ("the chiefs [ראשי] of the tribes of Israel in the last days").

152. Cf. Meier, *Marginal Jew*, 3:154, and Bovon, *Luke*, 2:22.

153. See Lear, "Luke's Use," 175.

154. Cf. Eusebius, *Dem. ev.* 3.2 (93d), Lapide, *Great Commentary*, 3:431; Lightfoot, *Commentary on the New Testament*, 3:94; Strack and Billerbeck, *Kommentar zum Neuen Testament*, 2:166; S. G. Wilson, *Gentiles and the Gentile Mission*, 46–47; Schürmann, *Lukasevangelium*, 2:1:54; Pitre, "Jesus, the New Temple," 80–81; Lear, "Luke's Use," 175; Riesner, *Messias Jesus*, 257; and Hengel and Schwemer, *Jesus and Judaism*, 382.

155. So Simon-Shoshan, "On That Day," 116.

156. Matt 14:13–21; 15:32–39; Mark 6:30–44; 8:1–10; Luke 9:10–17; John 6:1–15. All three

deem the story to be wholly mythical.[157] If that is the right view, then what I am about to suggest is off target. Others, however, believe, as did Albert Schweitzer, that a real "event has been distorted into a miracle."[158] Still others, of more orthodox conviction, hold that the episode occurred as recounted, multiplication and all.[159] Given our historical distance and the nature of the sources, I fail to see how anyone can divine what actually occurred.[160] I nonetheless incline to suppose that, whatever happened in the telling, at one point in his ministry Jesus sought, a bit like the sign prophets in Josephus, to replay in some way an event from the life of Moses.[161] The history of interpretation shows us that readers of the Gospels have often recalled Exod 16 and the miraculous provision of the manna.[162]

The evangelists themselves had such recall.[163] In John, the crowd responds to the miracle by inferring that Jesus is "the prophet who is to come into the world" (6:14). This means he is the eschatological Mosaic prophet of Deut 18:15–18, as subsequent words, which refer to the manna and juxtapose Jesus and Moses (John 6:22–51), confirm. In Mark, the people sit in groups of hundreds and fifties (6:40). The remark is otiose unless the intent is to recall arrangements Moses made in the wilderness.[164] The denizens at Khirbet Qum-

---

Synoptics use ἔρημος: Matt 14:13, 15; Mark 6:31, 32, 35; Luke 9:12. Throughout the Greek Pentateuch the word designates the place of Israel's desert wanderings.

157. Strauss, *Life of Jesus*, 507–19. Cf. MacDonald, *Mythologizing Jesus*, 27–32.

158. Schweitzer, *Mystery of the Kingdom*, 170. Cf. Eve, "Growth of the Nature Miracles," 78–81.

159. So, e.g., Cranfield, *Mark*, 220–21.

160. See further Meier, *Marginal Jew*, 2:965–66.

161. Here I can appeal to Pitre, *Last Supper*, 66–90, who argues for a historical nucleus and a Mosaic interpretation.

162. A sampling: Tertullian, *Marc.* 4.21; Eusebius, *Dem. ev.* 3.2 (92b–c); Cyril of Alexandria, *Comm. Lk.* 48; Strauss, *Life of Jesus*, 517; Gfrörer, *Jahrhundert des Heils*, 364–65; Keim, *History of Jesus*, 4:198–99; Schoeps, *Theologie und Geschichte*, 92; Cranfield, *Mark*, 222; Kertelge, *Wunder Jesu*, 133–34; Lane, *Mark*, 229–30 (the multitude "is characterized as the people of the new exodus"; "Mark portrays Jesus as the eschatological Savior, the second Moses who transforms a leaderless flock into the people of God"); Stegner, *Narrative Theology*, 53–81; Watts, *Isaiah's New Exodus*, 178–79; Lierman, *New Testament Moses*, 107–13; and C. A. Evans, *Matthew*, 294. Contrast Saito, *Mosevorstellungen*, 47–50.

163. There are also, as is well known, very strong links to the miracle of Elisha in 2 Kgs 4:42–44. But the latter does not have a wilderness setting, and allusion to one text does not exclude allusion to another.

164. Note Exod 18:21, 25–26; Deut 1:13–15; LAB 27:3, 5, 15 and cf. Montefiore, "Revolt in the Desert?," 137 (Mark's "combination of number and orderliness . . . carries overtones of the military divisions of the Jews during their wilderness wanderings"); Pesch, *Markus-*

ran, one recalls, sought to reproduce the organization of Israel in the desert.[165] Beyond this, the feeding occurs in the wilderness after Jesus has crossed a sea (Mark 6:32; cf. Exod 14–16); the crowd is fed in the evening (Mark 6:35), which is when the manna fell (Num 11:9); and the evangelist notes that Jesus's kindness prevents the people from being like sheep without a shepherd (Mark 6:34), a phrase that recalls Num 27:17: Moses appoints Joshua so that Israel will "not be like sheep without a shepherd."[166] In sum, if Jesus aimed to gather a crowd in the wilderness in order to conjure memories of Moses and the exodus, his intention lived on in the tradition.[167] Perhaps his hope or thought was akin to the expectation in Eccles. Rab. 1:9:1: "As the former redeemer caused manna to descend, as it is said: 'Behold, I will cause to rain bread from heaven for you' (Exod 16:4), so will the latter redeemer cause manna to descend."

(4) All four canonical Gospels depict Jesus being more than once on a "mountain" (ὄρος). Most of the relevant notices occur before the last week in Jerusalem and seemingly have him making a deliberate choice to ascend a high place:

- choosing the Twelve: Mark 3:13 // Luke 6:12
- going up on a mountain to pray: Mark 6:46 // Matt 14:23
- leading three disciples up a mountain: Mark 9:2 // Matt 17:1 // Luke 9:28
- preaching the Sermon on the Mount: Matt 5:1–2 (contrast Luke 6:17)
- sitting on a mount near the Sea of Galilee: Matt 15:29
- feeding of the five thousand: John 6:3
- withdrawing to be alone: John 6:15

The references to Jesus sitting on a mountain in Matt 5:1–2 and 15:29 are almost certainly redactional and belong to the evangelist's well-developed Moses typology.[168] Moreover, John 6:3 likely reflects Matthean influence.[169] Notwith-

evangelium, 1:352; Guelich, *Mark*, 1:341; Stegner, *Narrative Theology*, 57; Marcus, *Mark*, 1:419; Black, *Mark*, 159; Pitre, *Last Supper*, 72–75; Kollmann, "Brot und Fisch," 298; etc. For dissent, see Aus, *Feeding the Five Thousand*, 69–89.

165. Cf. 4Q378 3 II + 4 6–7; also the imitation of the exodus arrangements in 1QM IV, 1–5; VI, 10–11; 1QS II, 21–24; 1QSa I, 14–15; CD-A XIII, 1. Discussion in Pitre, *Last Supper*, 72–75.

166. For the Mosaic elements in Matthew's version of the same story see Allison, *New Moses*, 238–42.

167. See further, and at great length, the arguments of Pitre, *Last Supper*, 66–90, and J. R. Robinson, *Markan Typology*, 153–80.

168. See Allison, *New Moses*, 172–80, 238–42.

169. See Allison, "Reflections on Matthew," 55–57.

standing these likelihoods, it remains a fact that all four canonical Gospels associate Jesus with mountains,[170] and further that they need not have done so. Acts tells many stories about Peter and Paul. Not one is set on a mountain.

This raises the possibility that the multiple references in the tradition preserve the memory that, on occasion, Jesus deliberately withdrew to mountainous places. How one could ever go beyond that and establish that, in this regard, they remember rightly, I am unsure. Yet if he did so, it was not to preach to or meet people; and if one is otherwise persuaded, as am I, that Jesus thought of himself in Mosaic terms, one naturally wonders whether he was not, in this particular, a bit like Simeon Stylites, who climbed a mountain with Moses in mind.[171]

One can similarly ask whether the numerous references to the "desert" or "wilderness" (ἔρημος) in the Gospels hold memory and whether, if they do, they have something to do with Jesus's Mosaic self-conception (Mark 1:12 par.; 1:35 par.; 1:45 par.; 6:31–32, 35 par.; Luke 4:42; 5:16; John 11:54). Other Jews near his time withdrew to the wilderness for theological reasons,[172] and the evangelists associated the desert with new exodus themes.[173]

Further Observations

I subjoin three observations to the proposal that Jesus probably spoke and acted in ways designed to recall Moses and the exodus.

(1) Jesus was teacher, prophet, and miracle worker. All our evidence, moreover, presents him as entering those vocations deliberately and, if I may so put it, with gusto. He did not teach only when begged to do so. He rather, moving from place to place, looked for audiences. Similarly, he was not a reluctant prophet but a provocateur who uttered woes and warned of judgment.[174] Nor

170. So too the Gospel of the Hebrews as quoted by Origen, *Hom. Jer.* 15.4; *Comm. Jo.* 2.12.

171. Cf. Chavasse, "Jesus: Christ and Moses," 247–48.

172. For an overview, see Hengel, *Zealots*, 249–53. Cf. especially the use of Isa 40:1 in 1QS VIII, 12–16; also Josephus, *Bell.* 2.259 (deceivers led the multitudes "out into the desert, in the belief that God would there give tokens of deliverance"); 7.438 (on Cyrene, Jonathan the Weaver led people "forth into the desert, promising them a display of signs and apparitions"); and Matt 24:26 ("So, if they say to you: 'Look! He is in the wilderness,' do not go out. If they say: 'Look! He is in the inner rooms,' do not believe it").

173. Cf. Mauser, *Christ in the Wilderness*; Marcus, *Way of the Lord*, 23–26; Allison, *New Moses*, s.v. "New exodus" in Index of Subjects.

174. On this theme, see Reiser, *Jesus and Judgment*; Riniker, *Gerichtsverkündigung Jesu*; Zager, *Gottesherrschaft und Endgericht*; Wolter, "'Gericht' und 'Heil'"; and Frayer-Griggs, *Saved through Fire*, 145–98.

did he hide his wonder-working prowess under a bushel. He instead battled demons in public and helped those who begged for healing.

It is not enough, however, to observe that Jesus deliberately set out to be teacher, prophet, and miracle worker. The tradition depicts him as being, for each vocation, more than exceptional. It has him construe his miracles as the fulfilment of scriptural oracles and manifestations of the kingdom of God (Matt 11:4–6 // Luke 7:22–23 [Q]; Matt 12:27 // Luke 11:20 [Q]).[175] It recollects him as saying that John the Baptist was a prophet and more than a prophet (Matt 11:9 // Luke 7:26 [Q]),[176] with the clear implication that the same must hold for the speaker. And it has him teaching not as others but "with authority."[177]

We cannot enter the closet of Jesus's psyche, nor can we recover his primary personal motives. We nonetheless have good reason to infer that he had an "extraordinary sense of mission,"[178] and further that he was, in his own mind—not just in the minds of sympathizers—teacher, prophet, and miracle worker on a grand scale, perhaps even on an unprecedented scale.[179] Matthew and Luke found it fitting to attribute to him this eschatological beatitude: "Blessed are the eyes that see the things you see. For I say to you that many prophets and kings longed to see the things you see and did not see them, and to hear the things you hear and did not hear them" (Matt 13:16–17 // Luke 10:23–24 [Q]).[180] The gist of this enormous claim is, in the words of T. W. Manson, "that what for all former generations lay still in the future is now a present reality."[181]

175. More likely than not, both units fairly represent Jesus; see Meier, *Marginal Jew*, 2:130–37, 400–401, 404–23.

176. We can safely assign this saying to Jesus; see Meier, *Marginal Jew*, 2:138–40.

177. For Jesus teaching with "authority" (ἐξουσία) see Matt 7:29; Mark 1:22, 27; Luke 4:32, 36. On the problem of Jesus and Torah, the central work is now Meier, *Marginal Jew*, vol. 4. My view is that Jesus was less conservative regarding Torah than appears from Sanders, *Jesus and Judaism*, 245–69; see Allison, *Resurrection of Jesus*, 149–97. I believe that Jesus at points espoused something close to the idea in Sipre Deut. 175: "A prophet from among you—and not from outside the land—of your brothers—and not from foreigners—will the Lord your God raise up for you—and not for the nations. . . . To him you will hearken (Deut 18:15). Even if he tells you to disobey one of the commandments in the Torah, as did Elijah at Mount Carmel, yet according to the needs of the hour listen to [= obey] him"; cf. b. Yeb. 90b; b. Sanh. 90a.

178. The phrase is from W. Manson, *Jesus the Messiah*, 97.

179. My conviction is that early high Christology grew directly out of Jesus's large conception of himself; see Allison, *Constructing Jesus*, 221–304.

180. I have translated Luke's version.

181. T. W. Manson, *Sayings of Jesus*, 80.

If Jesus was capable of thinking along these lines,[182] to whom might he have likened himself? It is theoretically possible that he never compared himself to anyone. Yet this seems unlikely on its face. How could one function as a Jewish prophet without emulating particular Jewish prophets?

In Mark 8:27–30, the disciples report that some take Jesus to be John the Baptist, others Elijah or one of the prophets. As this is followed by Peter's confession of Jesus as the Messiah, many deem the entire scene to be a wholesale invention from the post-Easter period.[183] Yet Mark 6:14–16 raises the same three options, and given everything we know about Jesus—his affinity with John the Baptist,[184] his purported miracles, his prophetic demeanor—the popular estimations in Mark 6 and 8—which do not include Lord, Son of God, Son of Man, or even Messiah—do not pass beyond what is reasonably credible before Easter. And if, as seems likely, some were endeavoring, when Jesus was among them, to assess him via comparison with others, it beggars belief that he was altogether indifferent and gave the matter no thought—especially as multiple traditions depict him comparing himself with others or their situations.[185]

Now Scripture celebrates Moses as teacher as well as prophet and miracle worker. Indeed, it remembers him as the gold standard, the supreme instantiation of all three vocations. Deuteronomy ends with this fulsome praise: "Never since has there arisen a prophet in Israel like Moses, whom the LORD knew face to face. He was unequalled for all the signs and wonders that the LORD sent him to perform in the land of Egypt . . . and for all the mighty deeds and all the terrifying displays of power that Moses performed in the sight of all Israel" (34:10–12). Moses's miracles, according to these words, are without equal,[186] and he is likewise a prophet like none other.[187] In Num 12:6–8, he is even more than a prophet: "If there is a prophet among you, I the LORD

182. For the argument that he was, see Meier, *Marginal Jew*, 2:434–39.

183. E.g., Conzelmann, *Jesus*, 41–42; Gnilka, *Markus*, 2:18; and Casey, *Jesus of Nazareth*, 395.

184. Scholars often, in my judgment, underestimate the continuity between John and Jesus; see Allison, *Constructing Jesus*, 204–20.

185. Note, e.g., Matt 11:16–19 // Luke 7:31–35 (the Baptist); Matt 12:38–41 // Luke 11:29–30, 32 (Jonah); Matt 12:42 // Luke 11:31 (Solomon); Mark 2:23–28 (David).

186. Cf. the recollections of Moses' mighty miracles in Deut 6:22; Ps 105:26–42; Jub. 48:4–6; Wis 10:16; Sir 45:2–3; Artap. 3; LAB 9:7, 10; Acts 7:36; Ps.-Clem. Rec. 1:41; and Basil, *Spir.* 29 (74) ("by the superabundance of gifts, wrought in him [Gregory the Wonderworker] by the Spirit in all power and in signs and marvels, he was styled a second Moses"). Moses's power to work wonders is one reason many invoked his name to work magic; cf. Gager, *Moses in Greco-Roman Paganism*, 134–61.

187. Cf. Philo, *Mut.* 103, 125; *Somn.* 2.189 (Moses is "the chief prophet," ὁ ἀρχιπροφήτης);

make myself known to him in a vision, I speak with him in a dream. Not so with my servant Moses; he is entrusted with all my house. With him I speak mouth to mouth, clearly, and not in dark speech; and he beholds the form of the Lord." These words advert not to a single episode but to the whole of Moses's career as recipient of the Torah (which could be called "the law of my servant Moses").[188] Similar is Sir 45:5: God allowed Moses "to hear his voice, and led him into the dark clouds, and gave him the commandments face to face, the law of life and knowledge, so that he might teach [διδάξαι] Jacob the covenant, and Israel his decrees." Moses taught Israel divine statutes and ordinances and, in his unique capacity as mediator of the Torah, remains teacher without peer. That is why T. Mos. 11:16 characterizes him as "the perfect teacher in the world," and why the rabbis speak of "Moses our rabbi/teacher" (משה רבינו).[189]

Given all this, if a first-century Jew consulted his cultural encyclopedia in order to find precedent for a stupendous miracle worker who was also a prophet and a teacher of impressive authority, the obvious and seemingly only choice would have been Moses, who was revered as the superlative in all three offices.[190] And Jesus—who was not more modest than Gregory Nazianzen or Martin Luther King Jr.—was, I suggest, audacious enough to make that choice for himself.[191]

QG 1.86 (Moses is "the proto-prophet," ὁ πρωτοπροφήτης); and *Mos.* 2.187 (Moses is the prophet "most highly approved," προφήτης γέγονε δοκιμώτατος).

188. So Mal 4:4. "The Torah of Moses" became common: Josh 8:31–32; 1 Kgs 2:3; 2 Chr 23:18; Ezra 3:2; Neh 8:1; Dan 9:11; 1 Esdr 9:39; Bar 2:2; Sus 3; 1QS V, 8; 4Q256 IX, 7; CD-A XV, 2; Luke 2:22; John 7:23; 1 Cor 9:9; Heb 10:28; m. Yoma 3:8; etc. Cf. Tanḥ. Buber Shofetim 5:4 and Mek. R. Shimon bar Yoḥai Shirata 27:6: the Torah "is called by his name."

189. Mek. Beshallaḥ 3 on Exod 14:13; t. ʿAbod. Zar. 3:19; y. B. Bat. 8:3 (16a); b. Ber. 3b; Deut. Rab. 10:1; 3:17; etc. The LXX uses διδάσκω to translate למד with Moses as subject in Deut 4:1, 14; 6:1; 31:22; 32:44; cf. 4 Macc 18:18; Philo, *Mut.* 220. Note also LAB 12.2. "Moses will come and . . . will illumine the law for us and will explain from his own mouth the law of God and set up rules for our race."

190. Meier, *Marginal Jew*, 4:655–56, tentatively suggests that "Jesus' pronouncements on the Torah fit into his larger understanding of himself as the Elijah-like prophet of the end-time." The better fit is with his understanding of himself as the Mosaic prophet of the end time. I acknowledge, however, that in m. B. Meṣ. 1:8; 2:8; 3:4, 5; m. ʿEd. 8:7; b. Ber. 35b; b. Šabb. 108a; and elsewhere, Elijah is an interpreter of the law who settles disputes, and it is possible that some, in the prerabbinic period, understood the returning Elijah to be a teacher. For discussion see Xeravits, *King, Priest, Prophet*, 186–91.

191. Moses was also remembered as a king; see n. 129 above. There is, then, an additional parallel for those of us who believe Jesus thought of himself as destined to be king in Israel; cf. Allison, *Constructing Jesus*, 279–93.

In Luke 24:19, Cleopas styles Jesus a prophet "mighty in deed and word" (δυνατὸς ἐν ἔργῳ καὶ λόγῳ). In Acts 7:22, Stephen uses similar language to celebrate Moses: he was "powerful in his words and deeds" (δυνατὸς ἐν λόγοις καὶ ἔργοις αὐτοῦ). As this parallel belongs to a longer list of parallels between Jesus and Moses that runs throughout Luke-Acts,[192] and as Acts 7:22 is soon followed by 7:37 ("God will raise up a prophet like me from among your brothers"), which ties Jesus to Deut 18:18 ("I will raise up for them a prophet like you from among your brothers"), the correlation appears to be deliberate: the evangelist thought that Jesus was, in word and deed, like Moses.[193] Now perhaps the relevant clauses in Acts 7:22 and Luke 24:19 are redactional creations.[194] Yet even if they are, not all creations are *ex nihilo*, and in this case the parallel reflects a sensible interpretation of what Luke found in his tradition: Jesus was *novus Moses*. The evangelist was able to find the idea there, I submit, because Jesus put it there. The evangelist, that is, observed what Jesus had enacted.

(2) It was once common to affirm that Jesus saw himself as Isaiah's suffering servant.[195] It is much less common nowadays.[196] Still, the view retains informed proponents,[197] and in my opinion one can hardly exclude it with confidence—in part because it is highly likely (on other grounds) both that Jesus envisaged suffering for himself and that he paid heed to Second Isaiah.[198] For those who agree, it is relevant that Second Isaiah's servant has a Mosaic

192. See Zehnle, *Peter's Pentecost Discourse*, 79–82.

193. Cf. Lüdemann, *Acts of the Apostles*, 100: "Clearly the author is creating a parallel between the two figures, one that we see again in verses 35–36." Akagi, "Not the Prophet Like Moses," has not persuaded me to the contrary.

194. So Lüdemann, *Acts of the Apostles*, 100.

195. One-time influential statements include Fuller, *Mission and Achievement*, 86–95; V. Taylor, *Jesus and His Sacrifice*, 39–48; and Jeremias, *Servant of God*.

196. Important dissenting voices include Barrett, "Background of Mark 10.45," and Hooker, *Jesus and the Servant*. For an update of the latter's objections see her "Did the Use of Isaiah 53?"

197. E.g., N. T. Wright, *Victory of God*, 2:579–91; Betz, "Jesus and Isaiah 53"; and Stuhlmacher, *Biblical Theology*, 146–64.

198. See further Allison, *Constructing Jesus*, 263–67, 387–433, and Barber, "Did Jesus Anticipate Suffering?" I remain persuaded that Mark 10:45 is an ironic reversal of Dan 7 via Isa 53; cf. Davies and Allison, *Matthew*, 3:95–98, and see further Watts, *Isaiah's New Exodus*, 269–87. For other parts of the Jesus tradition that turn Scripture upside down or inside out see Allison, *Intertextual Jesus*, 192–97, 220–22, and cf. Marcus, "Sacred Subversion." In related fashion, the Parables of Enoch, when characterizing their central eschatological figure, fuse traditions from Second Isaiah with traditions from Dan 7; cf. Nickelsburg and VanderKam, *1 Enoch*, 2:44, 116–18.

cast,[199] so much so that b. Soṭah 14a reads Moses into Isa 53[200] and Gerhard von Rad took the servant to be "a prophet like Moses" à la Deut 18:15–18.[201] It does not, for our purposes, matter whom the authors of the so-called Servant Songs thought they were writing about. All that matters is that the servant displays Mosaic features.[202] If, then, Jesus associated himself, or himself and the group around him, with Isaiah's servant, this might have encouraged him to forge a link between himself and Moses. Alternatively, maybe a Mosaic self-conception prodded him to find himself in Isaiah's servant.[203]

(3) Jesus's name is, in Greek, the same as that of Joshua: Ἰησοῦς (for Hebrew יהושע). Given the shared name, it is surprising that the earliest Christian writings nowhere develop a Joshua typology.[204] This stands in marked contrast to later sources, which often draw parallels between Jesus and Joshua.[205] The Epistle of Barnabas, for instance, affirms that Moses renamed the son of Nun—from Hoshea to Joshua (Num 13:16)—in order to intimate that God would reveal all through his Son Jesus (Barn. 12.8–9). There is nothing like this in earlier Christian texts. Presumably part of the explanation is that Jesus's

199. See Bentzen, *King and Messiah*, 65–67; Coats, *Moses Tradition*, 186–88; Allison, *New Moses*, 68–71; Hugenberger, "Servant of the Lord"; Baltzer, *Deutero-Isaiah*, 18–22; Theophilos, *Jesus as New Moses*, 102–18; and Schöttler, ". . . Uns zum Heil."

200. With reference to Exod 32:32: Moses poured himself out to death and bore the sin of many.

201. Von Rad, *Old Testament Theology*, 2:261–62.

202. Like Moses, the figure in Isaiah brings Torah and teaches God's word (42:4), bears the title "servant," is meek (42:2–3; 50:5–6; 53:3–4), is a "prophet," has God's Spirit (42:1), has royal features (cf. n. 129 above), represents Israel, establishes justice (42:1–4), makes a covenant (42:6; 49:8), intercedes for his people (53:12; cf. Ps 99:6), guides them and leads them by streams of water (Isa 49:10), is an instrument of healing (53:5), suffers on behalf of others, is God's "elect" or "chosen one" (42:1; cf. Ps 106:23), conducts Israel out of exile (Isa 49:6), appears to be a leper (53:1–3), and is, beyond all this, the central figure of a new exodus.

203. Cf. Schoeps, *Theologie und Geschichte*, 95 (although he writes about the early church, not Jesus). The speech in Acts 3:13 clearly borrows from Isa 52:13 and 53:11 and at the same time features a Moses Christology; see Zehnle, *Peter's Pentecost Discourse*, 75–89. This integration of traditions is quite old; cf. Hurtado, *Lord Jesus Christ*, 194: the speech in Acts 3 "represents another case of the author of Acts showing knowledge of very early christological tradition."

204. Against Brown with Evans, *History of the Quest*, 2:590, I find no clear evidence, in the early tradition, of Jesus being like Joshua. The only real possibilities are, to my mind, in Hebrews (4:8) and Jude (1), and they are far from obvious; see Ounsworth, *Joshua Typology*, and McKay, "Is Joshua a Type of Christ?" The attempt of van Aarde, "Jesus als Joshua," to add more leaves me unpersuaded.

205. See Daniélou, *From Shadows to Reality*, 229–43, and Farber, *Images of Joshua*, 275–365.

first followers thought in eschatological terms, and there were no firm eschatological expectations associated with Joshua.

That, however, is unlikely to be the whole answer.[206] While there were no eschatological expectations associated with Elisha, early Christians nonetheless crafted stories about Jesus that inescapably recall tales about that prophet.[207] They could have done the same with Joshua. They could, for instance, have had the disciples declare to Jesus, as Israel declared to Joshua: "All that you have commanded us we will do, and wherever you send us we will go" (Josh 1:16). Or they could have likened the twelve disciples to the twelve men Joshua directed to set up twelve stones in the Jordan (4:1–9). Or they could have claimed that, when Jesus died, the sun stood still (10:1–14). They did not. I suggest that, in bypassing Joshua, they were following Jesus, who was instead focused on Moses. He did not aspire to be like Joshua, who was Moses's subordinate, but to be, at the least, Moses's equal.

C. H. Dodd once observed that "the New Testament itself avers that it was Jesus Christ Himself who first directed the minds of His followers to certain parts of the scriptures as those in which they might find illumination upon the meaning of His mission and destiny."[208] Dodd went on to urge that the New Testament does not here mislead us. Although qualifications are in order, there is some truth in his conviction, and my suggestion is that the converse may also hold. Maybe Jesus's followers neglected certain portions of the Old Testament because he neglected them.[209]

Historical Parallels

The sources for Jesus and Simeon Stylites exhibit multiple parallels between their heroes and Moses. We have no good reason, I contend, to imagine that those two men were altogether blind to what some of their followers saw. On the contrary, both Simeon and Jesus were remembered as being like Moses

206. For explanations as to why the New Testament pays so little attention to Joshua—who is not even on the list of heroes in Heb 11—see Vos, "Josua und Jesus." He entertains eight options but does not focus on the historical Jesus.

207. See R. Brown, "Jesus and Elisha."

208. Dodd, *According to the Scriptures*, 110.

209. Matt 5 and Luke 6, which enjoin love of enemies and turning the other cheek, might suggest that Jesus was ill at ease with a figure linked with as much violence as is Joshua. But then Moses unleashed ten plagues, including one that effected the death of all firstborn Egyptians.

because, in certain respects, they sought to be like him. They were not amorphous putty in the hands of inventive sculptors, not nebulous characters waiting for imaginative narrators to turn them into what they never were. It is not just authors who follow cultural scripts. Historical actors can do so, too.

Regarding Jesus in particular, I am emboldened in this conviction because we know of several figures in his century who tried to replay the salvific past, including the Mosaic past. These are the so-called sign prophets we read of in Josephus.[210] We sadly know far too little about them. Josephus's reviews are both succinct and unsympathetic. It seems clear, however, that several of them, to quote Richard Bauckham, worked "with a new Exodus typology—or, better, a new wilderness-conquest typology, since they seem to have expected not to repeat the exodus from Egypt itself but to repeat the events that followed it. They went into the desert in order to reconstitute themselves the people of God, becoming like Israel in the ideal period in the wilderness under Moses' leadership."[211]

Several of these individuals, presumably influenced by prophetic oracles,[212] drew large crowds into the desert.[213] Most or all claimed to be a prophet, some perhaps "the prophet" of Deut 18:15–18.[214] They promised to work "signs," that

210. In addition to what follows, see Hengel, *Zealots*, 229–33; Gray, *Prophetic Figures*; Allison, *New Moses*, 78–84; and Bauckham, "Messianism."

211. Bauckham, "Messianism," 44. Cf. Tg. Neof. I Exod. 12:42 and Fg. Tg. P Exod 15:18: when the redemption comes, "Moses will go up from the wilderness."

212. Note, e.g., Isa 40:3 ("in the wilderness prepare the way of the Lord, make straight in the desert a highway for our God"); 43:19 ("I will make a way in the desert"); and Hos 2:14–15 ("I will now persuade her, and bring her into the wilderness, and speak tenderly to her. . . . There she shall respond as in the days of her youth, as at the time when she came out of the land of Egypt").

213. Josephus, *Ant.* 20.168 // *Bell.* 2.259 ("imposters and deceivers"), 261–62 (the Egyptian); *Ant.* 20.188 ("a certain imposter"); *Bell.* 7.438 (Jonathan). Cf. Matt 24:23–26 ("If any one says to you. 'Behold, here is the Christ' or 'There he is' do not believe it. For false Christs and false prophets will arise and show great signs and wonders. . . . If they say to you: 'Behold, he is in the wilderness,' do not go out"); Rev 12:6 ("the woman fled into the wilderness"); Tg. Neof. I Exod 12:42 ("Moses will go up from the midst of the desert"); and Tanḥ. 'Eqev 7b (Str-B 3:824: "Akiba said: 'Just as Israel spent forty years in the wilderness, so will he [Messiah] draw them forth and cause them to go into the wilderness and will make them eat leaves and straw'").

214. See Josephus, *Ant.* 20.97 (Theudas), 169 // *Bell.* 2.261 (the Egyptian; cf. Acts 21:38); 6.285 (a certain "false prophet"); 7:437–41 (Jonathan). When Josephus designates others as "deceivers" (γόητες: *Ant.* 20.167, 188), he implies that they were false prophets, like those denounced in Deut 18:19–22; cf. *Bell.* 2:261: the Egyptian was a "false prophet" (ψευδοπροφήτης) and "deceiver" (γόης). Note also that he uses γοητεία of the magicians who sought to imitate

is, spectacular authenticating miracles.[215] The latter included the parting of the Jordan and the collapse of the walls of Jerusalem, both irresistibly reminiscent of earlier wonders.[216] One man, who sought to be king, was known as "the Egyptian."[217] He led a crowd of about thirty thousand from the desert to the

---

Moses: *Ant.* 2.286, 302. Theudas is also named in Acts 5:36, where he is said to have claimed to be somebody (λέγων εἶναι τινα ἑαυτόν). Perhaps it was already true in the first century that, as the Peter of Ps.-Clem. Rec. 1.43 has it, Jews often conversed about the prophet like Moses. Origen links Theudas and Judas the Galilean with a certain Dositheus (first century CE?) who purportedly "wished to persuade the Samaritans that he was the Christ predicted by Moses," a likely reference to Deut. 18:15–18 (*Cels.* 1.57); see above, n. 40; Isser, *Dositheans*; and cf. Origen, *Cels.* 6.11; *Comm. Jo.* 13:27; and Epiphanius, *Pan.* 1.13. From a later time, Socrates, *H.E.* 7.38, reports on "a certain Jewish imposter" from fifth-century Crete who "pretended that he was Moses, and had been sent from heaven to lead out the Jews inhabiting that island, and conduct them through the sea"; he pledged "to guide them through a dry sea into the land of promise."

215. Josephus, *Ant.* 18.85–87 (a Samaritan who promised to uncover sacred vessels buried by Moses; cf. Liv. Pro. Jer. 14–15 and see Dexinger, "Josephus Ant 18,85–87"); 20:97 (Theudas), 168 ("imposters and deceivers" promised "signs and wonders [τέρατα καὶ σημεῖα—a phrase used of Moses and false prophets: LXX of Exod 7:3, 9; 11:9–10; Deut 4:34; 6:22; 7:19; 34:11; Mark 13:22] wrought in harmony with God's design") // *Bell.* 2.259 ("signs of freedom," σημεῖα ἐλευθερίας; cf. *Ant.* 3.64: the ἐλευθερίας of the exodus), 169 (the Egyptian); *Ant.* 20.188 ("a certain deceiver" promised "salvation" [σωτηρίαν; cf. *Ant.* 3.64: the σωτηρίας of the exodus] and "rest from troubles" [παῦλαν κακῶν; the Pentateuch regularly associates "rest" with the land of Canaan: Deut 3:20; 12:9, 10; 25:19; Josh 1:13; etc.); *Bell.* 7.437–41 (Jonathan promised "signs and apparitions"). Barnett, "Jewish Sign Prophets," 682–83, observes that "signs of freedom" occurs in Josephus's version of the exodus (*Ant.* 2.327) and further that "marvels and signs wrought in harmony with God's design" is close to Josephus's description of what Moses did before Pharaoh (*Ant.* 2.286). The common vocabulary intimates that Josephus thought of the unnamed deceivers as trying to emulate the lawgiver.

216. Josephus, *Ant.* 20.97–99 (Theudas), 169–72 // *Bell.* 2.261–63 (the Egyptian). That Theudas sought, like Joshua, to split the Jordan and not, like Moses, the Red Sea, hardly cancels a Mosaic self-conception. Not only was the Red Sea nowhere in the vicinity, but Joshua's crossing was in imitation of Moses's crossing; cf. Dharamraj, *Prophet Like Moses?*, 200–205. To divide and cross the Jordan was to repeat the exodus again, and to be like Joshua was to be like Moses (cf. Josh 1:5, 17; 3:7). Josephus, it is worth noting, uses σχίζω of Theudas's scheme, and the verb occurs in Exod 14:21 LXX ("Moses stretched out his hand over the sea . . . and the water was divided") but not in Joshua's story. Cf. the imitation of the miracle at the Red Sea in Liv. Pro. Ezek 7–9: "Once when there was a multitude with him [Ezekiel] the Chaldeans were afraid that they would rebel, and came up against them to destroy them. And he made the water [of the river Chebar] stop so that they might escape by getting to the other side. And those of the enemies who dared to pursue were drowned." John the Baptist's ritual at the Jordan, some suggest, may have involved crossing the river and entering the land; see Webb, *John the Baptizer*, 361–65.

217. Josephus, *Bell.* 2.261–63 // *Ant.* 20.169–72. According to *Bell.* 2.262, he wished to set himself up as a tyrant, that is, rule (τυραννεῖν).

Mount of Olives by a circuitous route (περιαγαγών), a detail implying that he sought to relive the exodus, for Exod 13:18 has it that "God led the people by the roundabout way of the wilderness toward the Red Sea."[218] Another leader asked his followers to "take up their belongings and to follow him." This echoes Gen 15:14 ("they will come out with great possessions") and Exod 12:33–36, where the Israelites pack their goods for their wilderness sojourn (cf. Exod 11:2; Ps 105:37). One should further not overlook that these prophetic leaders had the authority to command sympathizers at risk of death. These people lived inside their typologies with dedicated fervor.

Whether or not "the first half of the first century CE witnessed a growing awareness of the fundamental relevance of Israel's wilderness traditions"[219]—perhaps we know too little about adjacent periods to draw the comparison—those traditions did not belong to the dead past; and more than one aspiring leader played the role of Moses. I am confident that, had any of the movements endured long enough to produce sympathetic biographies, some of them would have featured Moses typologies.

The appearance of new exodus and new Moses motifs in the Jesus tradition is, given all this, not so remarkable. If, for Jesus, his time was that of a new exodus, and if, for Jesus, he was his generation's Moses, neither interpretive move would have been unprecedented or obscure. Jesus belonged to a religious culture in which the sacred past of Moses, the first redeemer, could be reenacted.

What we see in Jesus and the sign prophets as well as Simeon Stylites is, I should perhaps add, rather different from what we find in many other sources. In 4 Macc 2:17, Moses is an exemplar of reason. In Heb 11:23–28, he is a model of faith. In 1 Clem. 17.5–6, he is a paradigm of humility, while in 53:2–54:1 he is a model of love. In Philo, Moses is the exemplar of multiple virtues: love of humanity, justice, goodness, hatred of evil (*Mos.* 1.9–10). He is indeed the "living impersonation of law" (1.162) who "displayed for all to see . . . a piece of work beautiful and godlike, a model for those who are willing

218. Josephus, *Bell.* 2.262. "There is," according to Hengel, *Zealots*, 230, "an obvious analogy here with the Exodus from Egypt of the Israelites, who also took all their movable possessions when they left their homes in Goshen and went with [Moses] into the desert." Cf. Amos 2:10 LXX ("I brought you out of the land of Egypt and led you around [περιήγαγον] in the wilderness for forty years"); Acts 21:38 ("are you [Paul] not the Egyptian, then, who recently stirred up a revolt and led the four thousand men of the Assassins out into the wilderness?"); and note Tg. Onq. Gen 49:11, where the Messiah leads his people around Jerusalem.

219. So Haacker, "Eternal Life," 152.

to copy it" (1.158). For these authors, the lawgiver is an example for everyone.[220] All should be humble as was Moses. All should be faithful as was Moses. All should love as did Moses. The *imitatio Mosi* does not mean walking about the desert or fasting for forty days or ascending a literal mountain.

It was otherwise with Simeon, Jesus, and the sign prophets. Their focus was not on Moses's exemplary excellence but his singular deeds, not on his ideal character but his distinctive acts and unique role. To be like Moses was, for them, not to embody this or that moral virtue. It was rather to assimilate the present to the sacred past. Moses was for them not the universal but the particular.[221]

And Elijah?

Jesus, I have argued, believed himself to be the eschatological prophet like Moses. John Meier has instead urged that Jesus "consciously took upon himself the role of the prophet Elijah, who was expected to return to restore Israel and prepare it for the coming of its God."[222] This, according to Meier, follows from the convergence of four facts: (1) Jesus worked in northern Israel, where Elijah worked; (2) the accounts of the calling of disciples show that Jesus acted as did Elijah when he called Elisha;[223] (3) if Elijah called Israel to religious renewal, Jesus set for himself the same task—a task that one can read out of Mal 4:6: Elijah "will turn the hearts of parents to their children and the hearts of children to their parents"; and (4) Jesus's miracles, which included raising the dead, resemble Elijah's miracles, which included raising the dead.[224]

In an earlier work I shared some second thoughts about Meier's case and ended up confessing that I was unsure what to think.[225] I do not, however,

220. Cf. Gregory of Nyssa, *Laud. Bas.* 125–26 (ed. W. Jaeger): "One would not go wrong by making the virtue of the lawgiver the goal of his life."

221. The same may be said of the historical Jeremiah, who likely understood himself to be a prophet like Moses; cf. Allison, *New Moses*, 53–62.

222. Meier, *Marginal Jew*, 3:623. J. J. Collins, "Jesus and the Messiahs," comes to the same conclusion.

223. The commentary tradition consistently recognizes the parallels between 1 Kgs 19:12–21 on the one hand and the call stories in Mark 1:16–20; Matt 8:18–22 // Luke 9:57–60 (Q); and Luke 9:61–62 on the other. See Allison, *Intertextual Jesus*, 142–45.

224. Relevant here are Matt 11:4–6 // Luke 7:22 (Q) and 4Q521, which share so many features: both should perhaps be associated with Elijah; see J. J. Collins, *Scepter and the Star*, 131–41. Also germane here is Poirier, "Jesus as an Elijianic Figure."

225. Allison, *Constructing Jesus*, 267–70. For additional criticism, see Hägerland, "Prophet like Elijah."

deny that there are some notable resemblances between the historical Jesus and Elijah. How, then, does this circumstance comport with my claims about Jesus and Moses?

In John 1:19–21, after the Baptist denies that he is "the Christ," he is asked, "Are you Elijah?" When he rejects that possibility as well, the question becomes: "Are you the prophet [ὁ προφήτης]?" Commentators, beginning with Origen, have regularly taken the definite article to refer to Deut 18:15, 18: John is being asked if he is the prophet like Moses.[226] If so, the text differentiates the latter from Elijah. The Synoptics presuppose the same distinction, for while they explicitly equate the Baptist with the prophecy in Mal 4:5 ("I will send you Elijah before the great and terrible day of the LORD comes"; Matt 11:10; 17:10–13; Mark 9:11–13; Luke 7:27), they tacitly associate Jesus with the prophecy in Deut 18:15 ("him you will heed").[227] Again the two figures are distinct. Is it plausible, then, that Jesus saw himself not only as the prophet like Moses but, as Meier thinks, the returning Elijah? Do we not have here two distinct eschatological roles, only one of which Jesus could have enacted?

If, as argued in the previous chapter, Jesus's eschatological expectations underwent some development, one might hazard that it was the same with his self-understanding. The assumption that, from beginning to end, Jesus held only one pellucid view of everything is a leftover from old ecclesiastical exegesis. Nothing prohibits the critical historian from wondering whether he might have set out to fulfill the mission of Elijah but later changed course and aspired to be the prophet like Moses.[228] Or vice versa. Or, to entertain a related option, maybe Jesus, as the Synoptics have it, regarded the Baptist as the returning Elijah and made himself out to be the prophet like Moses; but, after John's death, perhaps Jesus concluded that Elijah's task of unifying the people (Mal 4:5–6; Sir 48:10) remained to be completed. He then resolved to finish what the Baptist had started,[229] which meant picking up the mantle of

226. Origen, *Comm. Jo.* 6.8. Cf. Chrysostom, *Hom. Jo.* 16.2; Cyril of Alexandria, *Comm. Jo.* 10 ad loc; Bengel, *Gnomon Novi Testamenti*, 1:313; Godet, *John*, 1:304; Westcott, *John*, 34; Lindars, *John*, 104; Frey, *Theology and History*, 30–31; etc.

227. The voice at the transfiguration commands heeding Jesus: ἀκούετε αὐτοῦ or αὐτοῦ ἀκούετε. This adverts to Deut 18:15: "him you will heed/hear" (LXX: αὐτου ἀκουσεσθε). See Matt 17:5; Mark 9:7; Luke 9:35.

228. J. A. T. Robinson, "Elijah, John, and Jesus," maintained that Jesus took up the role of the eschatological Elijah early in his ministry but later abandoned it.

229. Cf. Witherington, *Jesus the Seer*, 250.

John's Elijah.[230] This could account for why some traditions about Jesus echo stories about Elisha.[231]

These are, however, little more than bare possibilities. They do not, unless I am missing something, have a firm foothold in the sources. They are likely roads to nowhere.

Another option is that Jesus equated the returning Elijah with the prophet like Moses, that for him Deut 18:15, 18 (understood eschatologically) and Mal 4:5–6 foretold one end-time figure.[232] He could then have played both Moses and Elijah at the same time. This would account for why the sources depict him as resembling both figures.

The difficulty here is twofold: (a) in Mark 8:27–30 Jesus passes over and so tacitly discards the identification with Elijah when he hears it and (b) in several places Jesus hails the Baptist as the returning Elijah:

- Matt 11:10 // Luke 7:27 (Q): John the Baptist "is the one concerning whom it has been written: 'Behold I send my messenger before you, who will prepare your way before you'" (Mal 3:1).
- Mark 9:9–13: In discussing why "the scribes say that Elijah must come first," Jesus says: "Elijah has come, and they did to him whatever they pleased, as it is written of him." This clearly refers to the Baptist.
- Matt 11:14: "If you are willing to accept it, he is Elijah who is about to come."

Perhaps these texts amount to false testimony. Yet if Jesus saw himself as Elijah, I fail to see what the tradition would have gained by contradicting him.

I lean toward another possibility, one that involves modifying Meier's verdict: while Jesus may at times—above all when calling disciples (cf. 1 Kgs 19:19–21)—

230. Marcus, "John the Baptist and Jesus," suggests that such an idea goes back to the Baptist. For an analogy see Life of Daniel the Stylite 22: Daniel received the leather tunic of Simeon after the latter's death "in order that the new Elisha might receive the mantle of Elijah."

231. See R. Brown, "Jesus and Elisha," and Sauerwein, *Elischa*, 201–6. Luke 4:24–27 has Jesus illustrate "no prophet is acceptable in his own country" by referring to Elisha: "There were many lepers in Israel in the time of the prophet Elisha, and none of them was cleansed, but only Naaman the Syrian." Elisha began his career at the Jordan by receiving a double portion of Elijah's spirit (2 Kgs 2:6–12), and he raised the dead (4:18–37; cf. 13:20–21), healed lepers (5:1–19), multiplied loaves (4:42–44), and assisted the poor and needy (4:1–7). In addition, the command to missionaries in Luke 10:4, not to greet anyone on the way, is modeled on 2 Kgs 4:29, where Elisha says to his servant: "If you meet anyone, give no greeting, and if anyone greets you, do not answer." See Allison, *Intertextual Jesus*, 145–47.

232. According to Bockmuehl, *This Jesus*, 46, some prior to Jesus may have identified the Elijah of Mal 4:5 with the prophet like Moses of Deut 18:15. Note that the promise of Elijah in Mal 4:5 is immediately preceded by a reference to "the teaching of my servant Moses" (4:4).

have acted the part of Elijah, as Meier thinks, yet he did so without finding himself in Malachi's oracle, which he rather associated with John. This would align Jesus with the Synoptic writers, who depict Jesus as being like Elijah in certain ways yet have him, at the same time, identifying the Baptist with Elijah.

Harmony with the tradition is not the only thing favoring this view. Joel Marcus has made a decent case that John regarded himself as Elijah.[233] If the Baptist did in fact do so, I think it likely that Jesus, given his high estimate of John, would have gone along. My supposition, then, is that Jesus read himself into Deut 18:15, 18 but not Mal 4:5–6.

This, however, scarcely entails that he was adverse to imitating or being compared with Elijah, for the latter resembles Moses in much Jewish tradition. There is a surfeit of parallels between the canonical stories of the two men: the one is quite like the other.[234] The correlations were as obvious to premodern readers as they are to us.[235] This is one reason the two are so closely related in so many texts. Elijah is mentioned right after Moses at the end of Malachi.[236] The pair appear beside Jesus in the story of the transfiguration (Matt 17:3–4; Mark 9:4–5; Luke 9:30–33). The two witnesses of Rev 11:1–13 are likely Moses and Elijah or their eschatological twins.[237] In Deut Rab 3:17, Joḥanan b. Zakkai prophesies: "Moses, I swear to you, as you devoted your life to their service in this world, so too in the time to come when I bring Elijah the prophet to them, the two of you will come together." One suspects that Moses escapes death in Jewish legend in part because Elijah had ascended to heaven, and it was unseemly for the imitator, in such an important matter, to outdo his model.[238]

If, then, Jesus held himself to be a new Moses, it would not have been peculiar for him to reckon himself as also being, in this or that respect, a bit like Elijah. The resemblances of the two figures were well known. To be like Moses was to be like Elijah. To be like Elijah was to be like Moses.

233. Marcus, *John the Baptist*, 46–61. Cf. Öhler, "Expectation of Elijah," and Vallançon, *Développement des traditions*, 421–22.

234. For details, see Allison, *New Moses*, 39–45; J. Walsh, *1 Kings*, 284–89 (Elijah "is in many ways, though not all, a Moses *redivivus*"); Roberts, "God, Prophet, and King"; and Dharamraj, *Prophet Like Moses*. Some have even hazarded that the historical Elijah may have set out to imitate the lawgiver; cf. Gray, *I and II Kings*, 376, 409.

235. Dozens of parallels are laid out in Pesiq. Rab. 4:2. Many of them reappear in modern treatments of 1–2 Kings; see previous note.

236. The LXX reverses Mal 4:4 and 4:5–6, so that Moses is mentioned last, after Elijah. I am unsure what to read into this.

237. See Aune, *Revelation 6–16*, 598–603.

238. For Moses avoiding death see Philo, *Sacr.* 8; *QG* 1.86; Josephus, *Ant.* 4.326; Sipre Deut. 357; b. Soṭah 13b. Josephus uses ἀφανίζω of both Moses and Elijah: *Ant.* 4.326; 9.28. Discussion in Loewenstamm, "Death of Moses," and Begg, "Josephus's Portrayal."

Typological thinking is not mathematical reasoning. A can be B and at the same time C. Jesus being like more than one figure is no stranger than Philo presenting Moses as king, legislator, high priest, and prophet (*Mos.* 2.8, 292), or than early Christian literature giving Jesus multiple titles—Son of God, Son of Man, Son of David, etc. Indeed, in some contexts, the more the better: multiple comparisons, like multiple titles, are ways of adding significance and augmenting importance. In Matthew, Jesus is not just like Moses: he is also like Jeremiah, Jonah, Elisha, and (especially in the passion narrative) David.[239] Similarly, in later sacred biography, saints are again and again favorably compared with multiple biblical worthies. The Life of Pachomius manages to liken Antony of the desert to three men in a single sentence: "The life of our truly virtuous and most ascetic Antony was like that of the great Elijah and Elisha and of John the Baptist."[240] Gregory of Nyssa, in his *Eulogy for Basil the Great*, explicitly compares his brother with a series of scriptural heroes: Moses, Samuel, Elijah, John the Baptist, Paul. Theodoret compares James of Nisibis with Moses, Phinehas, Elijah, Elisha, Jesus, and the apostles (*R.H.* 1.4–5, 9, 10, 13). The several relationships are not competing—like being the President of the United States and Supreme Court Justice at the same time—but rather complementary.[241]

Here I may usefully return to Simeon Stylites. He strove, as we saw earlier, to be like Moses, which means that the Moses typologies in our sources are amplifications of his own aspirations. His biographers, however, also compare him with Elijah, and they tell stories in which he is like the Tishbite. In this too they develop his self-conception.[242] Theodoret relates that Simeon, eager to grow in virtue, "ardently desired, like the divine men Moses and Elijah, to endure forty days without food" (*R.H.* 26.7). Here Elijah and Moses represent the same goal. The two also appear together in the Syriac Life, which has it that Simeon

239. For David see N. C. Johnson, *Suffering Son of David*. For Elisha see the commentaries on Matt 14:13–21 (the feeding of the five thousand). For Jonah see the commentaries on 8:23–27 (the stilling of the storm) and cf. 12:40: "Just as Jonah was three days and three nights in the belly of the sea-monster, so for three days and three nights the Son of Man will be in the heart of the earth." For Jeremiah see Knowles, *Jeremiah in Matthew's Gospel*.

240. Sancti Pachomii 2. Athanasius's *Life of Antony* likens Antony to Moses, David, Elijah, and Job.

241. Cf. Meier, "From Elijah-Like Prophet," 66, on the problem of Jesus being an Elijah-like eschatological prophet and also having Davidic sonship: "Popular religion is not as worried about mixing categories that are theoretically quite distinct as are academic theologians."

242. Simeon was scarcely the only monk to seek to emulate Elijah; see Frankfurter, *Elijah in Upper Egypt*, 71–73.

> was constantly meditating and marveling on those two men set for a sign, Mar Moses and Mar Elijah, saying: "Who truly will tell me and teach and show me how and by what means these two men pleased God their Lord and deserved all this excellent portion? Was it by fasting that they truly pleased God? or by prayer and faith? or by love? or by humility? or by bodily chastity? or by zeal for their Lord?" For he was greatly amazed by their wonderful appearance and the dignity given to them by God their creator. He was always quizzing experts in the scriptures to learn from them about the lifestyles of these two powerful athletes, Moses and Elijah.

The passage continues by recounting that Simeon's celebrated conduct was directly inspired by what he learned about the two scriptural worthies:

> One [expert in the scriptures] said [Moses and Elijah pleased God] by humility, another by love, another by zeal for God. . . . He asked everyone in order to learn from everyone. . . . When he had learned all these things from everybody and he had been instructed in the holy scriptures which were read before him, the saint began to fix them all in his own self: fasting without limit;[243] standing day and night (a thing whose very narration is beyond mortal man without God's help);[244] continual, uninterrupted prayer at all times; formidable supplication whose like had not been seen among men; zeal for God in the service of his Lord burning like a fire; chastity of body with pure limbs.

The Life additionally relates two visions in which Elijah appears to the monk and encourages him not to fear kings or judges (Syriac Life 42–43). In the second of these, Elijah says: "Once the Lord is someone's helper, how can anyone trouble or hurt him? For Ahab and Jezebel could not hurt or trouble me when I decreed their death and destruction. I gave their corpses as food to animals and I killed their priests and burnt their courtiers. In like manner no one can harm you as long as the Lord helps you." Again Simeon is like Elijah—as is also

243. See further the Syriac Life 108, where Simeon's fasting is explicitly compared with the forty-day fasts of Moses and Elijah.

244. For Moses standing, see above, p. 98. Scripture also depicts Elijah as standing: 1 Kgs 17:1 ("as the LORD the God of Israel lives, before whom I stand"); 18:15 ("as the LORD of hosts lives, before whom I stand"); 19:11 ("go out and stand on the mountain"), 13 (Elijah "stood at the entrance to the cave"). Note that Antony, according to Athanasius, *Vit. Ant.* 7, paid heed to 1 Kgs 18:15, and further that he exhorted himself: "It is incumbent on the ascetic always to examine his own life over against the conduct of the great Elijah, as in a mirror."

the case when Simeon, like the Tishbite, successfully prays for rain during a drought (Syriac Life 75; cf. 1 Kgs 17:1–7; 18:1, 41–46; also Liv. Pro. Elijah 4–5; 4 Ezra 7:109; Jas 5:17–18) and causes a vessel full of oil to remain miraculously full for an extended period of time (Syriac Life 29; cf. 1 Kgs 17:8–16).

There was, for both Simeon and his biographers, no tension between imitating Moses and imitating Elijah. The two saints were not, for them, unrelated or dissimilar. They rather resembled one another, so that one could be like both at the same time.[245] It was likely not so different with Jesus.[246]

Closing Remarks

My use of Simeon in this chapter, one might protest, overlooks the ways in which he and Jesus, who were from different times and places, were dissimilar. For Simeon, who reminded people of Job,[247] Moses and Elijah modeled an ascetical program. For Jesus, who in the early sources is nowhere compared with Job, the two ancient worthies were part of an eschatological scenario involving a new exodus.[248] Beyond this, the ministries and self-conceptions of Jesus and Simeon were very different. Jesus was an itinerant teacher whose words were collected into discourses.[249] Simeon stayed put, and we have no

245. Cf., from a much later time, Bonaventure's *Vita Francisci*: Francis was like both Moses and Elijah (7:13).

246. Jesus is also sometimes like Elisha; see n. 231 above. This should not surprise, for Elisha is Elijah's disciple and inherits his mantle, and in 1–2 Kings they appear together (cf. Sir 48:1–16; Luke 4:25–27) and are much alike. Both, for instance, cause the Jordan to part so they can cross (2 Kgs 2:8, 14); both provide oil for a poor widow (1 Kgs 17:8–16; 2 Kgs 4:1–7); and both bring a woman's son back to life (1 Kgs 17:17–24; 2 Kgs 4:8–37). Ancient readers noted the parallels and added to them; cf. Liv. Pro. Elisha 5 and see Ginzberg, *Legends of the Jews*, 2:1025–27. If pondering Moses could lead to pondering Elijah and vice versa, contemplating Elijah could lead to contemplating Elisha and vice versa. Thoughts naturally moved from one figure to another. I note that Syriac Life 130, after comparing Simeon to Moses and Elijah, immediately likens him to Elisha: he "exhibited signs and miracles like Elisha." Cf. Antonius, *Vit. Sim.* 22, where a barren woman conceives after Simeon's intercession; this recalls Elisha in 2 Kgs 4:11–17.

247. Syriac Life 48 contains an extended comparison with Job (cf. 7, 17, 130; also Mardin ms. 84 and British ms. 548). Antonius, *Vit. Sim.* 7, labels the ascetic "the new Job" (cf. 17).

248. There is no imminent eschatological expectation in the sources about Simeon.

249. Here again Jesus is like Moses. The Pentateuch is full of the latter's discourses, and he "wanders" (Num 32:13) with Israel for years and appears repeatedly in the wilderness and on mountains.

real discourses from him.[250] No less significantly, Simeon was not a messianic claimant. He did not expect to become the king of anything. He rather thought of himself as Jesus's loyal servant and follower.

One can, however, make too much of such differences. I for one do not think that the ascetical impulse was altogether foreign to Jesus.[251] Furthermore, Simeon's admirers exalted him in extreme terms, and I find no hint that Simeon deterred them. Theodoret wrote that his deeds "surpass human nature" (*R.H.* 26.1, 3), and the bishop fretted that Simeon's life "may seem to posterity to be a myth totally devoid of truth" (*R.H.* 26.1). The Syriac Life narrates a vision in which a man who "looked like lightning," a man with outer garments "like the sun" and a face "like rays of fire," declared to Simeon: "There will not be anyone, either among the ancients or the moderns, greater than you" (3). Then, in three different places, the biography quotes John 14:12—"the one who believes in me will also do the works that I do and, in fact, will do greater works than these"—and characterizes Simeon's miracles as grander than those of Peter and Paul.[252]

I do not, however, press those points here. I appeal to Simeon only as an aid to thinking about one aspect of Jesus and the Gospels. Simeon in all his strangeness is a memorable illustration that typologies are not confined to texts. They can also be embodied and lived into.

250. Even though, according to Theodoret, *R.H.* 26.25, Simeon exhorted audiences twice a day.

251. Allison, *Jesus of Nazareth*, 172–216, and Joseph, "Ascetic Jesus."

252. Syriac Life 12, 65 ("It is written about blessed Mar Simeon Cephas [Peter] that as he was passing by, his shadow fell on the sick and they were healed [Acts 5:15]; about the apostle Paul that they used to take his belt or his turban and go and place them on those injured by the enemy and they would be healed of their affliction [Acts 19:12]. So concerning the blessed Mar Simeon. He was very much in spirit their brother and their disciple. . . . Yet his measure was exalted more than anyone. For he did not walk on the ground so that his shadow would fall on anyone nor did he send any of his clothing anywhere to the sick, but only the word of prayer issued from his mouth and went to far-off regions and his Lord worked healing and relief"), 78. The same tradition appears in Theodoret, *R.H.* 26.17, who asserts that Simeon's miracles are "countless" (μυρία). According to Lohfink, *Jesus of Nazareth*, 137, "there was no miracle worker in antiquity besides Jesus from whom we have such a large number of plausibly attested miracles handed down to us." This may be true for an early time (although "plausibly" is a weasel word); but if antiquity includes late antiquity, it is false. According to Öhler, "Jesusforschung," 33, the canonical Gospels attribute six exorcisms, seventeen healings (including resurrections of the dead), and eight nature miracles to Jesus. By my count, the three biographies of Simeon attribute to him over twenty healings, four exorcisms, eight effective curses, and twenty-three nature miracles. The author of the Syriac Life, I note, cannot decide whether Simeon's miracles should be counted in the thousands or tens of thousands (78).

While the Gospels richly repay literary analysis, they also richly repay historical analysis. This is because, although they are not history in the modern sense, they are equally not fiction in the modern sense. And it would be a mistake to reduce them without remainder to their authors' theologies, narrative strategies, and compositional aims. For over and above embodying those things, they also preserve memories—even if often fuzzy—of things Jesus said and did. Among those memories is Jesus's perception of himself as a new Moses in a new exodus.

Earlier I recalled that Martin Luther King Jr. was able to liken himself to Moses. I would like to end with another American who entered a Moses typology. Harriet Tubman was, despite being a woman, known as "the Black Moses."[253] The appellation was not bestowed on her after she was dead and gone. She was rather already known by this honorific during her lifetime, and indeed while she was a conductor on the underground railroad. Who first gave her the title we do not know. It was in any case—and this is my point here—not attached to her against her will. She rather, despite her obvious humility, embraced it. In an interview after the Civil War, she said—clearly alluding to Exod 3—"I felt like Moses. De Lord tole me to do dis. I said, 'O Lord, I can't—don't ask me—take somebody else.' Den I could hear de Lord answer, 'It's you I want, Harriet Tubman'—jess as clar I heard him speak—an' den I'd go agen down South an' bring up my brudders and sisters."[254]

Because she freed slaves from bondage and led them to a supposed promised land, Tubman worked out in her own mind analogies between herself and Moses. This is not a literary fact but a historical fact.

As it was with Harriet Tubman, and as it was with Simeon Stylites, so too with Jesus: he thought of himself as being, in certain ways, like Moses. His reasons for so thinking were not their reasons—they were not eschatological prophets or messianic figures—but the basic hermeneutical move was similar. All three interpreted the present by recalling and reliving the Mosaic past.

253. On occasion, however, precision preferred "a black she Moses"; see McMahon, *Harriet Tubman*, 58.

254. As quoted in Sernett, *Harriet Tubman*, 42. For words to similar effect, see McMahon, *Tubman*, 151–52. According to Sernett, Tubman used the "coded language of songs and spirituals to communicate with potential passengers on her railroad, such as, 'Moses go down in Egypt, Till ole Pharo' let me go' . . . which she sang as a warning" (69). Sernett also refers to an occasion in 1859 when Tubman, before speaking, was introduced as "'Moses'—after that ancient leader, who took men and women into the Promised Land." Note also 57: Tubman was "universally known" among slaves that she rescued as "Moses the deliverer" (48).

3

Everywhere a Miracle

The Metanormal Jesus

> The idea that everything is in principle comprehensible to humans—and therefore that nothing can exist that is not comprehensible to humans—is unworthy of head space.
>
> —Bryan Magee[1]

> In so far as the Church did (chiefly during the corrupt and sceptical eighteenth century) urge miracles as a reason for belief, her fault is evident: but it is not what Mr. Blatchford supposes. It is not that she asked men to believe anything so incredible; it is that she asked men to be converted by anything so commonplace.
>
> —G. K. Chesterton[2]

> I have nothing to offer except a way of looking at things.
>
> —Erik Erikson[3]

The critical quest for the historical Jesus began during the Enlightenment. The instigators were European deists. Unlike the Protestant Reformers, who rejected all Roman Catholic miracles as unworthy of credence, the deists took the next step and deemed all miracles, of whatever provenance, as unworthy of credence. This included the miracles in the Gospels.[4] But then how does

1. Magee, *Ultimate Questions*, 15.
2. Chesterton, "Miracles and Modern Civilisation," 389.
3. Erikson, *Childhood and Society*, 403.
4. I do not here engage the issue of genre, i.e., how one might define an early Christian

one account for the many stories? That riddle eventually begat all the questions that instigated an academic discipline. Who wrote the Gospels? When did they first appear? What sources lie behind them? What is their relationship to one another? How much real memory do they contain?

Three strategies for explaining—or rather explaining away—the miracles appeared early on. In the eighteenth century, Hermann Samuel Reimarus, a German Lutheran and teacher of Semitic languages at the Hamburg Gymnasium, appealed to the passing of time and bad faith. The miracles appear in documents written decades after Jesus's departure, "when very few of those who had known Jesus were still alive. Nothing then was easier than to invent as many miracles" as the authors pleased "without fear of their writings being readily understood or refuted."[5] The evangelists told tall tales because promotion of their cause mattered more to them than devotion to the truth, and they could get away with it.[6]

In the early nineteenth century, the Heidelberg theologian H. E. G. Paulus was of another mind. While he agreed with Reimarus that miracles are impossible, he found much more history in Matthew, Mark, Luke, and John. His explanation for the miracles was this. The disciples were children of their age, and having been nurtured on the fantastic stories in the Jewish Scriptures, they had been primed to turn the mundane into the supernatural. On one occasion, Jesus prayed over a woman who was taken for dead; she was, however, only comatose, and when she subsequently, through wholly natural causes, climbed back to the land of the living, Jesus got the credit.[7] On another occasion, Jesus was walking along the shore of the Sea of Galilee while his disciples were on a boat some distance away, and through the mist they mistook him to be striding on the waves.[8] For Paulus, the Gospels relate real events over which supernatural explanations have been laid. Miracles are not facts. They are interpretations.[9]

---

miracle story. Interested readers may consult R. Zimmermann, "Frühchristlichen Wundererzählungen," and Kiffiak, "Zimmermann's Genre."

5. Reimarus, *Fragments*, 233.

6. This proposal goes back to antiquity. Eusebius, *Hier.* 2.2, attributes it to Sossianus Hierocles, who compared Jesus unfavorably to Apollonius of Tyana. Cf. Origen, *Cels.* 2:26: the stories in the Gospels are, according to one Jewish opponent, "inventions." A recent proponent of this view is MacDonald, *Mythologizing Jesus*. According to MacDonald, the Gospel writers, imitating primarily Homeric epics, "injected him [Jesus] with narrative steroids to let him compete with the mythological heroes of Greece and Rome" (10).

7. Paulus, *Leben Jesu*, 1:246–48.

8. Paulus, *Leben Jesu*, 1:357–65.

9. For a related and recent although far more nuanced approach to the miracle stories

Not long after Paulus, David Friedrich Strauss, whose free thinking cost him his professorship and turned him into a private scholar, essayed a third strategy. For him, the miracle stories were mythological representations of theological inferences. If Jesus was the Messiah, then, in line with Jewish expectation, he must have been like Moses; and if he was like Moses, then he must have been trailed by the sorts of wonders that attended his predecessor. So Christians fashioned a story of their lord being transfigured into light, as had happened to Moses.[10] In like manner, if Jesus had been the greatest of all prophets, then he must have been greater than Elisha; and if Elisha had managed, as the tale goes, to feed one hundred men with twenty loaves of barley and some fresh ears of grain, surely Jesus could have done the trick with even fewer provisions, and even more people, and that more than once.[11] In short, the religious imagination transformed theological ideas into mythical stories. Those stories are full of meaning. They are not full of history.[12]

When it comes to the matter of miracles, the descendants of Reimarus, Paulus, and Strauss rule the roost. Albert Schweitzer, one of my intellectual heroes, never once to my memory entertained the possibility that anything truly extraordinary took place during Jesus's ministry.[13] Neither did Rudolf Bultmann. Siding with Kant, Schleiermacher, Hegel, and his teacher, Adolf von Harnack,[14] he emphatically insisted: "Modern man acknowledges as reality only such phenomena or events as are comprehensible within the framework of the rational order of the universe. He does not acknowledge miracles because they do not

that does not name Paulus, see Eve, "Growth of the Nature Miracles." One recalls the repeated attempts to explain the ten plagues in naturalistic terms; see, e.g., Hort, "Plagues of Egypt."

10. Matt 17:1–8; Mark 9:2–8; Luke 9:28–36; Exod 34:29–35. See Strauss, *Life of Jesus*, 535–46.

11. 2 Kgs 4:42–44; Matt 14:13–21; 15:32–39; Mark 6:32–44; 8:1–10; Luke 9:10–17; John 6:1–13. See Strauss, *Life of Jesus*, 507–19.

12. In significant ways, Crossley, "Nature Miracles," reminds me of Strauss: what matters about the miracle stories is not their historicity—which Crossley like Strauss more than doubts—but "what they reveal about ideology, belief, historical change, and so on." For an earlier proponent of a related approach, see Woolston, *Discourse on the Miracles*. Woolston argued that the miracles "were never wrought" (3); they are "but Figure and Parable" (61).

13. Observations in Africa, however, later generated an interest in the paranormal; see Schweitzer, "Métapsychique."

14. Harnack, *What Is Christianity?*, 26: "What happens in space and time is subject to the general laws of motion, and . . . in this sense, as an interruption of the order of Nature, there can be no such things as 'miracles'"; they "belong only to the realm of fantasy and metaphor."

fit into this lawful order. When a strange or marvelous accident occurs, he does not rest until he has found a rational cause."[15] Ernst Käsemann concurred: "We may say that today the battle is over, not perhaps as yet in the arena of church life, but certainly in the field of theological science. It has ended in the defeat of the concept of miracle which has been traditional in the Church."[16]

Even less liberal scholars have joined the crowd here. Joachim Jeremias argued in influential publications that the first three Gospels are, for the most part, reliable guides to what Jesus said. The miracle stories were, for him, another matter. Some, he thought, sprouted from linguistic misunderstanding. Others, he held, were embellishments by people who "had great powers of imagination" and loved "unusual happenings." Jeremias did believe that Jesus was an effective healer, but he judged his successes restricted to "psychogenic suffering" that responded to his therapeutic ministrations.[17] In other words, nothing too much out of the ordinary.[18]

A Personal Confession

This is the academic tradition of incredulity into which I was baptized as a budding scholar. I studied Jeremias and Bultmann. I read and pondered Schweitzer and Strauss. And I learned from many other erudite authorities, including my teachers in the flesh, that if I aspired to be taken seriously, so-called miracles were out of bounds. Even when they were tactful and did not say this in so many words, their example spoke loudly: Do not go there.

They never won me to their side. There are two reasons. The first is this. If I was studying mainstream biblical scholars by day, I was reading the marginalized parapsychologists by night. I read William James's writings on psychical research, and I figured that if a man as intellectually gifted as he, and renowned

15. Bultmann, *Jesus Christ and Mythology*, 37–38. Cf. Bultmann, *Faith and Understanding*, 249: "The idea of miracles has . . . become untenable and it must be abandoned." In "Zur Frage des Wunders," in *Glauben und Verstehen*, 1:214, Bultmann speaks confidently of the "destruction of miracle thinking."

16. Käsemann, "Is the Gospel Objective?," in *Essays on New Testament Themes*, 48.

17. Jeremias, *New Testament Theology*, 86–92. Cf. Dodd, *Founder of Christianity*, 44: "It may be that if we had been there we might have found a 'scientific' explanation of what the early Christians regarded as miraculous."

18. Jeremias's view resembles that of Bousset, *Kyrios Christos*, 98–106: Jesus was a healer and exorcist, but beyond that the miracle stories in the Gospels, which are full of "migratory motifs," were borrowed from the environment.

for everything else he wrote about, took this subject seriously, then so could I.[19] I read the books of J. B. Rhine, who ran Duke's Parapsychology Laboratory, and I decided that if the only way for his critics to get around some of his experimental results was to accuse participants of cheating, then he may have been on to something.[20] And I read Arthur Koestler's *The Roots of Coincidence* and found his pairing of "the perversity of physics" with the oddities of parapsychology to be illuminating, liberating, and very un-Bultmannian.[21]

The second reason I did not servilely follow my teachers was purely personal. It is one thing to read books and articles, untangle their arguments, and to do one's best to decide, from a distance, who is right. It is quite another thing when real life intrudes and supplies evidence for one conclusion as opposed to another. This is what happened to me. Leaving aside the details here, all I will say is this. I believe that, among other experiences my secular education never anticipated, I have, on two occasions, foreseen in detail specific events before they came to pass, one time a few hours before, the other two weeks before.[22] I also firmly believe that I was once present when an object perversely, and in the twinkling of an eye, moved of its own accord from one side of a room to the other.[23] And I am inclined to believe that a woman, three days dead, once awakened me in the middle of the night to comfort me, and further that, one afternoon a few weeks later, she spoke to me out of the blue, telling me to do something immediately.[24]

Perhaps I should be reticent to confide all this. Maybe I will be academically ostracized and lose my accreditation in the guild. I am keenly aware that claims such as mine commonly evoke strong resistance or even ridicule in certain circles, including some circles in which I move. Many, sitting in the seat of scoffers, are reflexively and unnervingly self-confident that those with claims such as mine must be, even when we have academic credentials, self-deceived, less than rational, or in the thrall of some religious enthusiasm. Over a century ago, George Foster wrote: "An intelligent man who now affirms his

19. See Murphy and Ballou, *William James*. Especially important for me was James's "Final Impressions."

20. See esp. J. B. Rhine, *Reach of the Mind*. For criticism of the famed Pearce-Pratt experiment, which seems to establish clairvoyance beyond doubt, see Hansel, *ESP*. When I read Hansel in college, his critique backfired. I remember thinking: if this is the best he can do, he is probably wrong.

21. Koestler, *Roots of Coincidence*.

22. Brief accounts of these experiences are written up by Kripal, *Superhumanities*, 161–62.

23. For this story, see my *Encountering Mystery*, 165–69.

24. See Allison, *Resurrection of Jesus*, 215.

faith in such [miracle] stories as actual facts can hardly know what intellectual honesty means."[25] Even more extreme was Frederic Harrison: belief in miracles is "the commencement of insanity."[26] The attitude of those who believe that miracles or the paranormal have been splintered on the rocks of rationalism is the same as my serene confidence regarding the conspiracy theory that lizard people run the world: nothing to it.

But it would be dishonest to run from what I have seen. How can I agree with Bultmann that everything is "comprehensible within the framework of the rational order of the universe" when my own eyes contradict him? No less importantly, if one opens the right books, or gets enough people to be honest, one soon discovers that there is nothing peculiar about me. The unusual is not so unusual.[27]

My goal in this chapter, however, is not to persuade anyone that this or that really happened to me. It is rather to invite readers, whether they sympathize with my worldview or not, to ponder my predicament. What if a historian of the early Jesus movement decides—on empirical, not theological grounds[28]—that sometimes people see the future, that clairvoyance is not uncommon, that additional metanormal claims should be seriously entertained, and even that enigmatic capacities sometimes congregate in exceptional or charismatically gifted individuals, in what Max Weber termed "religious virtuosi"?[29]

The short answer is: It makes everything much more difficult. My open-mindedness about all sorts of things—an open-mindedness that is, I repeat,

25. Foster, *Finality of the Christian Religion*, 132 (italics removed).

26. As quoted by Eire, *They Flew*, 362.

27. See Greeley, *Sociology of the Paranormal*; Cardeña, Lynn, and Krippner, *Varieties of Anomalous Experience*; Castro, Burrows, and Wooffitt, "Paranormal Is (Still) Normal"; and Kripal, *Flip*.

28. I am emphatically not a postmaterialist because I am a Christian. I am a post-materialist for empirical reasons; see the collection of evidence in Kelly and Kelly et al., *Irreducible Mind*.

29. Weber, *Sociology of Religion*, 166–83. For three well-documented examples, see Méheust, *Un voyant prodigieux*; Barrington, Stevenson, and Weaver, *World in a Grain of Sand*; and Lugli, *Gustavo Rol*. For two less-critically investigated illustrations, see Phelan, *Don Bosco*, 266–301, and Narasimhaswamiji, *Life of Sai Baba*, 735–67. For reviews of the relevant experimental data, which are so often misrepresented by polemicists, see Radin, *Conscious Universe*; Radin, *Supernormal*; D. H. Powell, *ESP Enigma*; and Bem et al., "Feeling the Future." Even if one doubts the force of the evidence from the lab, one can nonetheless accept the reality of certain paranormal phenomena; see Dyson, *Scientist as Rebel*, 321–33. There is a mountain of anecdotal evidence in the old issues of *Journal of the Society of Psychical Research* (https://onlinebooks.library.upenn.edu/webbin/serial?id=jsocpsychicrsch). See also the materials collected in L. E. Rhine, *Hidden Channels*, and Prince, *Noted Witnesses*.

rooted not in my theology but in human experience—does not annul the fact that people can, for the sake of a cause, concoct stories out of next to nothing. Reimarus was right about that. People also can misperceive and turn things into what they were not. Paulus was right about that. And early Christians did create and embellish narratives by mixing together ingredients to hand in the Jewish Scriptures. Strauss was right about that. The skeptics, in other words, have taught us much. We cannot go around them. How, then, might one proceed?

Common Tactics

To prepare the way for my own proposal and its defense, I wish first to contemplate how others have conducted business.

Several years ago Robert Webb outlined three different strategies historians have adopted when assessing the so-called miracles of Jesus. The first he labels "naturalistic." This approach, which refuses to invoke divine causation at any point, regards all observable events as the effects of causes within a closed universe. On this view, history is, without exception, "subject to the scientific paradigm."[30] The second strategy Webb dubs "critical theistic." While it employs historical-critical tools and need not, in every instance, insist on adopting a supernatural interpretation, it is amenable to such because it accepts the possibility of divine intervention and "views history as having precedence over science."[31] The third approach, "methodological-naturalistic history," is the one Webb champions. This strategic demarcation holds that, "for the purposes of doing historical work, the historian is methodologically limited to causation within the physical, space-time universe, but this does not limit the historian's personal ontological worldview, just her/his historical method as a historian."[32] Webb reckons this to be the preferred via media. It sets ontological convictions aside and reconstructs the past by restricting itself to "description and explanation of cause and effect of human events within the natural sphere alone."[33]

In direct response to Webb, Michael Licona penned an article urging that historians are not, in principle, barred from investigating miracle claims.[34]

30. Webb, "Rules of the Game," 75.

31. Webb, "Rules of the Game," 75–76.

32. Webb, "Rules of the Game," 78.

33. Webb, "Rules of the Game," 79. Webb is here representative of many in the guild. E.g., Meier, *Marginal Jew*, vol. 2, defends substantially the same view.

34. Licona, "Historians and Miracle Claims."

Sounding a bit like Wolfhart Pannenberg,[35] he contends that it is not unreasonable to posit or infer a theoretical entity, such as God, when the data cannot be otherwise elucidated. And such data exist. In this connection he uses the word "miracle": "We may recognize that an event is a miracle when the event (a) is extremely unlikely to have occurred given the circumstances and/or natural law and (b) it occurs in an environment or context charged with religious significance. The stronger the context is charged in this manner, the stronger the evidence becomes that we have a miracle on our hands, if the historical evidence for the event itself is good."[36] The resurrection of Jesus, Licona urges, is a case in point. He concedes, however, that one's worldview inevitably plays a role in whatever explanation one posits. In theory, a historian could, he recognizes, concede that an anomalous event occurred yet refrain from offering any explanation, natural or supernatural.

Webb's piece on miracles also elicited a response from Robert Miller.[37] He insists that our knowledge of and confidence in "the laws of nature" should govern historical research. To illustrate: when evaluating the accounts of Jesus walking on the water, two generalizations should guide our thinking: first, "human beings do not walk on water," and second, Jesus was a human being. It inexorably follows that Jesus did not walk on water. Miller admits that "we do not know everything about how the world works," yet he affirms that "we do know a great deal," indeed enough to establish that the miracle attributed to Jesus cannot be historical.[38] Thus "methodological naturalists are under no . . . intellectual obligation to consider the possibility that Jesus walked on water."[39] The same is true, Miller affirms, of all the other miracle stories in the Gospels. History contains no divine interpolations.

I will, in what follows, offer reflections on both Licona and Miller, this because the views they defend represent many in today's guild. I will then propose another way of approaching some of the issues surrounding "the haunting problem of miracles."[40] My point of departure is the unassailable fact that extraordinary claims appear in both non-Christian and nonreligious contexts; and my position is that not all such claims should be dismissed as fiction, and further that, regarding stories about Jesus, one may reasonably adopt an ap-

35. Note esp. Pannenberg, *Jesus—God and Man*, and Pannenberg, *Theology and the Philosophy*.

36. Licona, "Historians and Miracle Claims," 119.

37. Miller, "Domain and Function."

38. Miller, "Domain and Function," 140.

39. Miller, "Domain and Function," 142.

40. The phrase is from Sanday, *Life of Christ*, 203.

proach that, independent of theistic or other religious beliefs, is nonreductive and open-minded. Traditional supernaturalism, skepticism of all extraordinary claims, and historical agnosticism do not exhaust our options.

Licona's Stance

(a) Before engaging Licona, I wish to confide that, while many regard his proposals as academically out of bounds, I am not among them. I see no reason to insist that historians be taken seriously only after they have, in effect, renounced their religious convictions.[41] Rejecting epistemic imperialism and totalizing ontologies, I do not slam the door on the possibility—remote as I regard it—of someone persuading me, on historical grounds, of a theological conclusion I do not already hold. I wish to keep my metaphysical options open and so am happy to follow anyone's line of argumentation, after which I can decide for myself.

(b) Licona claims that historians of early Christianity can appeal to the supernatural when the evidence pushes them in that direction. Yet apart from the resurrection of Jesus, which is a subject beyond the scope of this essay,[42] he offers no illustration. What might he have in mind, and how might he persuade us?

Jesus appears to have been, in his own mind and in the minds of others, a successful exorcist.[43] The Synoptics attribute this circumstance to the power of God (Matt 12:28; Luke 11:20). Modern critical scholars, however, do not find themselves flummoxed for a mundane explanation. Exorcisms are a well-known phenomenon in many times and places, and anthropologists and psychologists have little difficulty explaining most of the reports in terms of epilepsy, severe psychosis, dissociative identity disorder, cultural role playing, and so on.[44] Some modern accounts of exorcism, it is true, contain claims that, if factual, raise the specter of the metanormal. Some witnesses report, for

41. In this matter, and despite my disagreements with them and their disagreements with me, I have no problem with either Giambrone, *Quest for the Historical Christ*, or Rowlands, *Metaphysics of Historical Jesus Research*. Contrast Crook, "On the Treatment of Miracles." Crook, speaking for a multitude, urges that the study of Christian origins, if it wants to situate itself within the field of religion, must exclude the possibility of the miraculous. This view of course has been around for quite some time; cf. E. Zeller, "Tübinger historische Schule," 109: "Miracle and the historical view of things exclude each other; whoever wants the one cannot admit the other."

42. Licona argues his own position at length in *Resurrection of Jesus*.

43. For a review of the evidence, see esp. Witmer, *Jesus, the Galilean Exorcist*, 97–202.

44. See, e.g., Lewis, *Ecstatic Religion*; Davies, *Jesus the Healer*; Craffert, *Galilean Shaman*, 245–308; Casey, *Jesus of Nazareth*, 247–56; and Girgis, *On Satan, Demons, and Psychiatry*.

instance, that a possessed individual showed a detailed knowledge of things he or she could not have known by ordinary means, or that a victim rose up into the air and could not be pulled down even by several people.[45] Whatever one makes of such reports, the Gospels contain nothing so remarkable and so nothing clearly beyond conventional explanation.

One might, as rebuttal, respond that Mark 5:3–4 defies this generalization. The verses describe the Gerasene demoniac with these words: "No one could restrain him anymore, even with a chain; for he had often been restrained with shackles and chains, but the chains he wrenched apart, and the shackles he broke in pieces; and no one had the strength to subdue him." It would, however, be perilous to build much on this. Not only do the words sound like the vivid embellishment of an animated storyteller,[46] but we do not know the genealogy of this story with its "rambling complexities."[47] Nor do we know who first narrated it nor how reliable or credulous that narrator was. This is not to say the story is unadulterated fiction.[48] Perhaps "the cure of a hysteria sufferer was accompanied by a paroxysm which frightened the swine and so led to a stampede."[49] Yet how can a conscientious historian, in a case such as this, ever move beyond "perhaps," much less venture a positive verdict about supernatural agency?[50] The same holds for all the other reports of Jesus casting out demons.

It is not otherwise with the healing stories. Jesus was, as the global testimony establishes, a charismatic healer.[51] Yet even before the early Mesmerists,

45. This is true of several of the case studies in Naegeli-Osjord, *Possession and Exorcism*.

46. Cf. the over-the-top language in the Arabic Gospel of the Infancy 14, which borrows from Mark 5: "There was a demoniac woman whom Satan, accursed and rebellious, had beset. . . . She could neither bear clothes, nor live in a house; and as often as they tied her up with chains and thongs, she broke them, and fled naked into waste places; and standing in cross-roads and cemeteries, she kept throwing stones at people."

47. So Funk et al., *Acts of Jesus*, 78.

48. But note Sanders and Davies, *Synoptic Gospels*, 169: "The story is hard to reconcile with Jesus' probable history, and it conforms so completely to stories of exorcism, that it is usually recognized as a popular story, probably originally Jewish . . . which has simply been attached to Jesus."

49. So Nineham, *Mark*, 152. Cf. Marcus, *Mark*, 1:348: "There is probably some sort of historical event at the root of this story." Cf. Funk et al., *Acts of Jesus*, 78: "Some vague historical event might lie behind the present narrative."

50. Cf. Meier, *Marginal Jew*, 2:653: although inclined "to the view that an exorcism performed by Jesus near Gerasa lies at the basis of the Gospel narrative in Mark 5:1–20," Meier doubts "that much can be said about the historical event; too many layers of literary activity and theological imagination have been superimposed." Note also Sanders, *Historical Figure of Jesus*, 135: "I am at a loss to explain the story in the sense of finding a historical kernel."

51. For detailed argument, see Meier, *Marginal Jew*, 2:617–45; Blackburn, "Miracles of Je-

the ability of a patient's mind or imagination to ameliorate or heal various illnesses in surprising ways was established knowledge.[52] The dramatic successes of some faith healers should have ceased to surprise long ago.[53] Although we do not understand how this happens, the mind can, when in the right state, become its own drugstore and work wonders: a physician who heals himself. Sometimes the mind has beaten paralysis, arthritis, angina, migraines, and multiple sclerosis; and the recurrent link between healing and "faith" in the Gospels suggests, in many cases at least, a strong psychosomatic component, akin to what one often sees with modern miracle workers.[54] So too the texts that recall that Jesus healed not "all" but "many" (Mark 1:34; 3:10). One can then suppose, as did Martin Dibelius, that many who came to Jesus had "psychically conditioned maladies" that he "healed by means of an impact upon" their "psychical life";[55] and further that others, whose illnesses were not purely psychogenic or psychosomatic, were healed because Jesus called forth a potent placebo effect.[56] Is this not how most historians tame the healings documented on the Epidauros inscriptions and attributed to Asklepios? Barry Schwartz

sus"; Theissen, "Wunder Jesu"; and Öhler, "Jesusforschung," 33–34. Contrast Bousset, *Kyrios Christos*, 98: "The earliest tradition of Jesus's life was still relatively free from the miraculous."

52. See Vidal, "Modernizing the Miraculous Body."

53. Eye-opening with regard to the role of faith in healing is the documentary of magician Derren Brown, "Miracles for Sale."

54. Note, e.g., Matt 13:58; Mark 5:34; 10:52; Luke 7:50. On this motif see Theissen, *Miracle Stories*, 129–40.

55. Dibelius, *Jesus*, 82. Cf. Davies, *Jesus the Healer*, 69–77; Capps, *Jesus the Village Psychiatrist* (stressing the likelihood that some people Jesus healed suffered from conversion disorder); and Craffert, *Galilean Shaman*, 245–308 (emphasizing the "biopsychosocial" dimensions of disease and healing). Attempts to understand the Gospel miracles in psychosomatic terms go back at least to the nineteenth century; see Mullin, *Miracles and the Modern Imagination*, 149–51, and note Harnack, *Christianity and History*, 63 ("Much that was formerly rejected has been re-established on a close investigation, and in the light of comprehensive experience. Who in these days, for example, could make such short work of the miraculous cures in the Gospels as was the custom of scholars formerly?"); Schmiedel, "Gospels," 1885 ("It is quite permissible for us to regard as historical only those of the class which even at the present day physicians are able to effect by psychical methods. . . . It is not at all difficult to understand how the contemporaries of Jesus, after seeing some wonderful deed or deeds wrought by him which they regarded as miracles, should have credited him with every other kind of miraculous power without distinguishing, as the modern mind does, between those maladies which are amenable to psychical influence and those which are not"); and Mickelm, *Miracles and the New Psychology*.

56. See further the helpful article of Meggitt, "Historical Jesus and Healing." On the subject in general, see Benedetti, *Placebo Effects*. We should not forget, however, that the effectiveness of placebos (and nocebos) remains enigmatic; see Kelly, "Psychophysiological Influence."

opines that "so certain are we of the mind/body connection that it is difficult not to believe that the sick and possessed were healed when Jesus laid his hands on them."[57]

None of this of course eradicates the possibility of a supernatural intervention or metanormal dynamics from any of the stories. My point, however, is another: the sources do not *force* secular historians into a corner or leave them floundering for nonmetanormal explanations.

The healing stories in the Gospels are, as probative evidence for supernatural intervention, inadequate in three additional ways. First, there is always, as with Mark 5:1–20, the genealogical problem. While one may confidently maintain, given the tradition as a whole, that Jesus was a successful healer, it is difficult if not impossible to pin down the origin of any particular story or to establish the reliability of its details. This is scarcely to say that none of the relevant stories or their details are historical—I certainly am not so skeptical—only that, because our tools are so crude, we may be unable to confirm historicity even when it is there.[58]

The Christian apologist John Douglas (1721–1807) argued that, in order to merit belief, a miracle story must (1) be published not long after the time it was purportedly worked; (2) be published in the place where it happened or not far away; and (3) be critically examined in the time and place in which it occurred.[59] These are sensible demands. The problem is that he imagined that the miracles of the New Testament, as opposed to all non-Christian and pagan miracles, pass this test. He was mistaken.[60]

57. Schwartz, "Where There's Smoke," 29. See further Remus, *Jesus as Healer*, 104–18, and cf. Casey, *Jesus of Nazareth*, 246: "Jesus' healings generally fall within the parameters of what is perceived to be possible by traditional healers who operate within communities of people who accept their powers. He does not heal broken limbs, prevent illness or grant immortality. He enables people who have been classified as ill to return to normal life."

58. Instructive here are the restricted conclusions of Meier, *Marginal Jew*, 2:509–1038; cf. Meggitt, "Historical Jesus and Healing," 21. But for attempts to argue the contrary see Latourelle, *Miracles of Jesus*, and Twelftree, *Jesus the Miracle Worker*.

59. J. Douglas, *Criterion*, 46–47. Cf. Stephen, "Proof of Miracles," 340: "Whoever attempts to draw important inferences from the alleged occurrence of any detailed matter of fact which was not closely, impartially, and completely inquired into at the time, the result of the inquiry being authentically recorded for future reference, is trying to make a pyramid stand on its point."

60. One wonders if some New Testament scholars are shaped by this old prejudice, which was once a common feature of Christian apologetics. Note, e.g., Paley, *Evidences of Christianity*, 176–206, who recurrently dismisses "Popish" miracles as less well attested than New Testament miracles. Catholic apologists, while defending Catholic miracles, have also often privileged the biblical texts as especially strong witnesses; cf. J. H. Newman, *Two Essays*, 70–94.

Second, "the Gospels supply us with *symptoms* associated with ill-health and not *diagnoses*,"[61] and it is hazardous to infer much from a claim to healing that is unattached to a modern medical diagnosis and unattended by prolonged evaluation after the alleged fact.[62] What sent Peter's mother-in-law to bed with a fever (Mark 1:30)? Influenza? Tuberculosis? Malaria?[63] We do not even know, as Vincent Taylor observed, whether "the malady was incipient or grave."[64]

The Roman Catholic Church has stringent requirements for recognizing a miraculous healing at Lourdes. Those requirements include diagnosis, prognosis, and follow-up by qualified physicians. Without all this, the church will not officially declare that a miracle has taken place. It goes without saying that the Gospels, by contrast, offer nothing along these lines. We have no doctor's evaluation of the woman "with a flow of blood" (Mark 5:24–34).[65] We have no report of her condition before she touched Jesus, no report of her condition after that, nor confirmation that her malady thereafter failed to recur. The same holds for all our stories, even if one deems them to be utterly historical in every detail. Did the Gerasene demoniac, presuming he was a historical character, perhaps suffer from dissociative identity disorder?[66] How could anyone know? We furthermore have no idea what percentage of the blind, deaf, and paralyzed whom Jesus purportedly healed had ailments that were, in modern terms, psychosomatically conditioned and without organic cause. So-called hysterical paralysis is, at least in our world, far from rare.

Third, even if one could overcome the obstacles just introduced, there would remain the question of agency.[67] Being without an explanation does

61. Wallis, *Galilean Wonderworker*, 179.

62. A few who follow up claims to faith healing sometimes find that nothing much changed except a believer's perceptions; see, e.g., Rose, *Faith Healing*, 137–70, and Pattison, Lapins, and Doerr, "Faith Healing."

63. Luff, *Impact of Jesus*, 143, infers it was malaria from Luke's πυρετῷ μεγάλῳ ("high fever," 4:38). Whether she has that right, her survey of "health hazards in first-century Palestine" (114–44) is eye opening.

64. So V. Taylor, *Mark*, 179.

65. We do not even know for certain the nature of the affliction. While the commentary tradition thinks of a vaginal or uterine hemorrhage (cf. Lev 15:19, 25, 33; 20:18), Levine, "Discharging Responsibility," 384, observes that the matter is not perfectly clear. I note that the Syriac Life of Simeon Stylites tells of a male suffering "a flow of blood of many years' duration. This flow was a great trial to him as he could not put clothes on his prostrate body because of the flow of blood" (see Doran, *Simeon Stylites*, 215). This obviously was not a uterine hemorrhage.

66. For a diagnosis of multiple personality disorder see Hankoff, "Religious Healing."

67. I must here pass over a batch of difficult theological and philosophical questions, including the nature of an act of God. The question of agency is all the more abstruse because Christians historically have thought of the deity not only as the source of so-called miracles but also as being providentially involved in ordinary events, such as the production of food,

not force one to invoke a divine potentate. There are on record a large number of truly dramatic healings whose explanation appears to elude current scientific knowledge.[68] And perhaps, if we knew more about what happened with Jesus, we would find ourselves at points stumped to fit everything into a reductionistic template. Nonetheless, those who study placebos and the dramatic spontaneous remission of all sorts of ailments typically do so within a modern scientific framework, not a theological context. They do not, on the whole, take themselves to be documenting supernatural activity but rather to be seeking to understand the ill-understood potentials of human minds and bodies. So even if one were to grant the historicity of this or that healing story in the Gospels and deem the cure beyond present-day medical knowledge, that by itself would not, without further ado, establish the Christian God as the inevitable explanation (see further below, pp. 202–4).

But what, one might retort, does someone allergic to the supernatural do with the two reports that Jesus healed individuals from a distance, with the healing of a centurion's servant or son (Matt 8:5–13 // Luke 7:1–10; cf. John 4:46–54) and the healing of a Syrophoenician's daughter (Mark 7:24–30)? A placebo requires belief. What if a patient—the Syrophoenician's daughter or the centurion's son or servant—knows nothing? This might indeed take us beyond the normal and so be a forceful objection—but only if we knew more. We do not, however, know more. We certainly do not know enough to exclude the suggestion of Gerd Theissen: "In order to explain the distant healings of Jesus we must presuppose only that the Syrophoenician woman told her little daughter that she was looking for help from a famous Galilean healer, and the servant of the centurion of Capernaum had knowledge of his master's attempt to meet this healer in order to ask him for help. This may explain why the daughter and the servant felt better."[69] This may or may not be how things transpired. Yet we need to be able to pass beyond such an open-ended disjunction before asserting that the evidence nudges us into supernatural territory.

---

for which thanks is returned. Lohfink, *Jesus of Nazareth*, 139–43, even urges that God works miracles only in and through "nature" and its "autonomy."

68. For famous, well-documented, and truly remarkable healings at Lourdes, see Boissarie, *Healing at Lourdes*, and Carrel, *Voyage to Lourdes*. For examples from other shrines, see Leuret and Bon, *Documented Account of Miracles*. See further Gardner, *Healing Miracles*; O'Regan and Hirshberg, *Spontaneous Remission*; Hirshberg and Barasch, *Remarkable Recovery*; and Duffin, *Medical Miracles*. These books document many instances of diseases, including malignant cancers, disappearing rapidly, completely, and permanently without medical treatment.

69. Theissen, "Jesus and His Followers," 56.

One might complain that all this appears to be *ad hoc*: one explains miracle A this way, miracle B another way, miracle C yet another way, until they are all gone. Yet historians proceed in this fashion with the stories of other figures,[70] and what is the alternative? A simple appeal to quantity? Making divine intervention Ockham's razor in order to account for everything in one supernatural swoop would not qualify as a sensible historical method. We do not know, simply because there are so many stories about Martin of Tours,[71] Sāī Bābā,[72] and Oral Roberts, that those men indeed worked wonders beyond run-of-the-mill explanation. Appeal to an otherworldly power would indeed explain all the miracles stories about those three figures and so would be parsimonious, yet that cannot decide our thoughts.

One might further complain that I have made things too easy by leaving John 9 out of account. Here Jesus heals a man who is said to have been "blind from birth" (τυφλὸς ἐκ γενετῆς, 9:1; cf. 9:2, 19). Does this not demand divine intervention? I do not think so. Even were we to presume, for the sake of argument, that John 9 is unsullied history, "blind from birth" is not an up-to-date medical diagnosis. We know neither the cause of the affliction nor whether it was prenatal, perinatal, or postnatal.[73] Nor do we know the degree of visual impairment. Did the man see nothing at all, or could he rather make out hazy shapes or colors? Did he have retinitis pigmentosa as a child with the condition worsening over time? The possibilities are more than many. I grant that, if the man's optic nerves had never functioned at all but then, in an instant, began to work properly, and if his visual cortex effectively processed (without having done so before) the incoming signals, that would indeed beggar belief. So too

70. See, e.g., the treatment of Martin of Tours's miracles in Stancliffe, *St. Martin*, esp. 249–61, and of Sadhu Sundar Singh's miracles in Emmet, "Miracles of Sadhu Sundar Singh." The latter concludes: "There seems no reason to doubt that in most cases something remarkable, whether by way of coincidence or otherwise, really did happen; it is not a case of pure fiction or myth. It is, however, obvious to the careful reader that there is nothing which cannot be explained by human agency or on the lines of the principles of modern psychology, especially in its study of the phenomena of trance, intense concentration, and auto-suggestion" (317).

71. In his *Life of Saint Martin*, Sulpicius Severus, who knew Martin, recounts, among other wonders, resurrections (7–8), healings (16, 19), exorcisms (18), and conversations with angels and demons (19, 21–22, 24). See further Delehaye, "Saint Martin et Sulpice Sévère."

72. For many firsthand testimonies to Sāī Bābā's prodigious miracle working, see Haraldsson, *Modern Miracles*.

73. Nobody in first-century Galilee could have distinguished between blindness from birth and blindness acquired shortly after birth.

if the man's eye sockets were devoid of eyeballs[74]—although had that been true the evangelist would likely say so.[75] But who can insist, on the basis of John 9, that such conditions obtained? John Meier, who thinks "it more likely than not that Jesus healed a blind man in Jerusalem under the curious circumstances related in 9:6–7," also thinks

> whether the man was "blind from birth" (9:1) cannot be decided. It could be that the tendency of John's Gospel to heighten the miraculous element in miracle stories has given us the only healing [in the Gospels] of a man specifically said to be born blind. Then, too, a man blind from birth supplies a convenient symbol of a humanity born into a world of spiritual darkness. Granted these theological tendencies in the Fourth Gospel, no decision can be made on the historicity of the detail that the man was born blind.[76]

"No decision can be made" is a prudent verdict. This does not entail that John 9, if it contains memory, cannot derive from a truly extraordinary event, only that we have no way, via historical reasoning, to establish that it did.

But what then of the stories of Jesus bringing the dead back to life (e.g., Mark 5:35–43; Luke 7:11–17; John 11:38–44) and the so-called nature miracles, such as the feeding of the five thousand (Matt 14:13–21; Mark 6:32–44; Luke 9:10–17; John 6:1–15), the stilling of the storm (Matt 8:23–27; Mark 4:35–41; Luke 8:22–25), and the cursing of the fig tree (Matt 21:18–19; Mark 11:12–14, 20)?[77] These stories, one might insist, surpass all ordinary human ability.

The problem of genealogy, however, equally attends these episodes. As unwelcome as the fact may be, we cannot establish—or at least I do not know how to establish—which details reliably mirror what happened. It is symptomatic that John Meier, after analyzing at great length the reports of Jesus

74. Cf. Epidauros stele 1:9: "A man came as a suppliant to the god. He was so blind that one of his eyes had only the eyelids left—within them was nothing [ἐνεῖμεν δ᾽ ἐν αὐτοῖς μηθέν], but they were entirely empty [κενεὰ ὅλως]. Some of those in the sanctuary laughed at his silliness to think that he could recover his sight when one of his eyes had not even a trace of the ball, only the space alone. As he slept a vision appeared to him. It seemed to him that the god prepared some drug, then, opening his eyelids, poured it into them. When day came he departed with the sight of both eyes restored."

75. Cf. Wallis, *Galilean Wonderworker*, 149: "If Jesus had restored missing limbs, conjured up eyeballs for empty sockets, or mended fractured bones, we would surely have known about it; but we don't."

76. Meier, *Marginal Jew*, 2:698.

77. I leave aside here the question whether "nature miracles" is the most fitting term as well as the issue of whether they really constitute a type; see Theissen, *Miracle Stories*, 94–112.

raising Jairus's daughter and the widow of Nain and Lazarus, comes in each case to the same guarded, colorless, disappointing conclusion: they all reflect "some incident in the life of the historical Jesus" about which we can say next to nothing more.[78]

Even were it otherwise, how could a scrupulous historian ever exclude autoresuscitation in a case or two, that is, exclude as wholly destitute of possibility the notion that Jesus raised someone from apparent but not real death, someone yet harboring a spark of life?[79] In 1866 in Florence, Don Bosco, the Italian priest and educator, was asked to pray over a boy who had just died. The youngster returned to life. Years later the saint mused: "Perhaps he was not dead."[80] More recently, the Brazilian healer Thomaz Green Morton, while at the bedside of a woman thought to have just passed, said: "What do you mean she's dead? Don't grieve—that won't help her." When, a few minutes later, she revived, the family attributed her "resurrection" to Morton. Although he denied having anything to do with her recovery, the family was unpersuaded.[81]

Even in the twenty-first century, with our immeasurably improved medicine, autoresuscitations continue to occur: patients declared dead sometimes stir to life and rejoin family and friends.[82] Such events must have been far more common in an era bereft of stethoscopes and ECGs.

As for the nature miracles, consider the accounts of Jesus multiplying loaves and fishes for five thousand people (Matt 14:31–21; Mark 6:32–44; Luke 9:10–17; John 6:1–15). Many take the story to be ancient on the basis of multiple attestation. John, many suppose, is here independent of the Synoptics, and Mark and Matthew have an apparent doublet in the story of the feeding of the four thousand (Matt 15:32–39; Mark 8:1–10). Yet even if one concurs, what more can anyone say with assurance? We scarcely have enough evidence to eliminate with high confidence rationalizing explanations. Maybe, as many imagine, Jesus, seeing a large crowd without food, distributed his own provisions along

78. Meier, *Marginal Jew*, 2:773–873 at 831. Cf. the verdict of Fuller, *Interpreting the Miracles*, 32, 39: some of the healings "have some factual basis in them," but "we can never be certain of the authenticity of any actual miracle story in the Gospels. While a few of them may rest upon specific memory, most of them have probably been shaped out of generalized memories."

79. The theory of autoresuscitation has been around since at least Schleiermacher; see his *Life of Jesus*, 217–18. Note the story in Philostratus, *Vit. Apoll.* 4.45: Apollonius raised a girl from "seeming death" (τοῦ δοκοῦντος θανάτου).

80. See Phelan, *Don Bosco*, 286.

81. Pulos and Richman, *Miracles and Other Realities*, 56.

82. See Hornby, Hornby, and Shemie, "Systematic Review," and Wiese et al., "Lazarus-Phänomen."

with those of his disciples. Others, taking the hint and emulating his action, did likewise, and with this spontaneous outburst of contagious generosity there was enough for all.[83] Soon, however, Jesus's pious admirers construed the event as an astonishing wonder: Jesus had transmuted a few loaves and fishes into scores of loaves and fishes. There are of course other skeptical scenarios.[84] No one, admittedly, can credibly claim that any of them are more probable than not. Yet the same holds for the traditional, supernatural explanation (unless one's theology or a certain view of the Bible dictates otherwise). Although one may sensibly hold that Jesus congregated with a large crowd in a deserted place, no one can, given our distance from the event and the thin nature of our sources, establish exactly what induced the conviction that food had been miraculously provided and hunger assuaged.[85] We further know neither who first came to that conclusion nor exactly when. I can go no further than did Reginald Fuller: "We recognize here a factual nucleus" that is "no longer recoverable."[86]

Just how slight the information in the Gospels is may be illustrated further through comparison with evidence of a more substantial kind. During the beatification process for the Italian Carmelite, Father Angiolo Paoli (1642–1720), depositions were taken from multiple witnesses as to his deeds and character.[87] A significant number testified, under oath, that they had themselves seen him multiply food and drink for the poor and sick.[88] Their testimonies are firsthand

83. Cf. Paulus, *Leben Jesu*, 1:351–56.

84. See, e.g., Strauss, *Life of Jesus*, 516 ("if, in figurative discourses, Jesus had sometimes represented himself as him who was able to give the true bread of life to the wandering and hungering people, perhaps also placing in opposition to this, the leaven of the Pharisees," then legend "may have converted this into the fact of a miraculous feeding of the hungry multitude in the wilderness by Jesus"); Pesch, *Markusevangelium*, 1:355–56 (the parallels with the story of Elisha feeding a hundred men in 2 Kgs 4:42–44 are so extensive that the gospel story must be mostly derived from Scripture); and Eve, "Growth of the Nature Miracles," 78–81 ("the feeding story developed out of the memory of Jesus arranging for a crowd of people to be fed on one or more occasions by means that are now lost to us [perhaps even by the often-touted encouragement of sharing], but which were regarded as sufficiently striking at the time to suggest 2 Kings 4:42–44 as an appropriate frame for remembering and narrating the story").

85. See further Meier, *Marginal Jew*, 2:950–67. He concludes: "Our sources do not allow us to specify the details of the event" (966).

86. Fuller, *Critical Introduction*, 99.

87. For an introduction and overview, see Schamoni and Besler, *Charismatische Heilige*, 68–77.

88. See Cacciari, *Della Vita*, 291–319 (https://tinyurl.com/5x97354u). Cacciari was the Postulator of the Cause and had access to the original documents and testimonies. For

and full of concrete details, including dates, places, and names.[89] Now if I were a Roman Catholic of a particular stripe, I might find the evidence for Paoli's miracles to be compelling. As I am not, I confess to be at a loss. Some of the testimony is, in my judgment, truly puzzling. Yet if this is the situation with regard to a case where we have an abundance of firsthand testimony acquired under oath—that is, if it is hard to know what to make of the astounding claims of a sizable group of deposed, critically examined eyewitnesses[90]—how can the Gospels, which in every respect fail to rise to the evidential level of the statements about Saint Paoli, compel, on purely historical grounds, a theological conclusion?

Licona himself concedes that, when it comes to Jesus's miracles, "even those historians who are open to divine causation may admit there is usually insufficient data for determining whether a psychosomatic or supernatural cause was responsible for the improved states of those healed."[91] The word "usually" implies "not always." Although it is clear that, for Licona, the resurrection

a brief introduction in English to Paoli's multiplication miracles, see Thurston, *Physical Phenomena*, 391–94.

89. As a small sample of the relevant testimony, I cite the words of a certain Father Castelli, General of the Servite Order, as printed in Thurston, *Physical Phenomena*, 392–93: "Opening a cupboard in the wall where Father General's Socius used to put napkins and other table utensils, he discovered some scraps of bread (*tozzi di pane*) which all together did not amount to the volume of a small loaf (*pagnotta*) and a half, or two at the utmost, and these he stowed away in his left sleeve. Then the General, and Father Master Maggini who was also present, remarked smilingly: 'You haven't got much loot after all, Father Angiolo.' When they had talked awhile, he set off home, and the General and Father Maggini decided to accompany him. The three had got as far as the Torre de' Conti, when Father Angiolo began giving alms to various persons of both sexes, big and little, who begged from him, distributing the scraps of bread that he had taken from the General's room, but without breaking them up in any way. He continued to do this all the way to S. Pietro in Vincoli; at which Father Maggini was so astounded that he turned to him and said: 'Good gracious! Have you a basketful of bread in your sleeve? You have been giving alms to all the beggars in the city with the bread you got from Father General.' Father Angiolo made no answer, but the General, who had watched everything that had happened, made a sign to his companion to hold his tongue." Multiplication miracles are also associated with the nineteenth-century Roman Catholic Don Bosco; see Schamoni, *Wunder sind Tatsachen*, 206–8. For additional testimonies to the purported miraculous production of food, see Lapide, *Great Commentary*, 2:56–57; Thurston, *Physical Phenomena*, 385–95; Schamoni, *Wunder sind Tatsachen*, 206–28; Laurentin, *Miracles in El Paso?*, 49, 95–99; Haraldsson, *Modern Miracles*, 108, 117–18, 136–37, 220–22, 234–35; and Keener, *Miracles Today*, 181–82.

90. On the relatively critical nature of many eighteenth-century ecclesiastical investigations into miracle stories in the cause of beatification see Haynes, *Philosopher King*, 116–50.

91. Licona, "Historians and Miracle Claims," 122.

of Jesus is an exception, he does not indicate what additional exceptions he believes there might be. We are left to guess.[92]

(c) This leads to another issue. Historians who accept the traditional Christian claim that Jesus worked genuine miracles face the challenge of what to do with the similar claims for non-Christian miracle workers. It is hardly sensible, when looking at the stories of others, to see only legend, fraud, or credulous malobservation or to posit the placebo effect, and yet to adopt a wholly different tactic when dealing with one's own tradition. Licona, however, does not broach this crucial issue. What should we make of the comparative material, much of which comes with more abundant testimony than anything we find in the Gospels? In other words, how do we respond to Ernst Troeltsch's claim that "it is impossible for historical thought to believe the Christian miracles but deny the non-Christian"?[93]

In Licona's judgment, one may speak of a "miracle" when confronted with an "extremely unlikely" event that happens "in an environment or context charged with religious significance."[94] Does this assume a Christian context? What if the context is not Christian? The multiplication miracles of the Hindu holy man Sathya Sāī Bābā (1926–2011), however one accounts for them, are far better attested than those of Jesus. We not only have interviews with any number of twentieth-century eyewitnesses,[95] but also the testimony of a renowned magician—Doug Henning—that he did not know how to duplicate

92. See further Lowis, *Gospel Miracles*. Lowis reviews, one by one, in a nonprejudicial manner, each miracle in the canonical Gospels, asking which demand a supernatural explanation. His results are meager.

93. Troeltsch, *Absoluteness of Christianity*, 48.

94. Cf. Larmer, "Miracles and Criteria," 77: a miracle must have taken place "in a moral and religious context" and have "moral and religious significance." The extent to which post-Enlightenment ideas of miracles correspond to what anyone in the first-century thought is an important question, and Horsley, *Jesus and Magic*, raises it. We should beware of reading our ideas of "natural" and "supernatural" into ancient sources (even if I tend to see more continuity between pre- and post-Enlightenment thought than does Horsley). Biblical writers did believe that what is impossible for people is possible for God (Matt 19:26; Mark 10:27; Luke 18:27), and they believed in events that, "by a particular volition of God," violated "the ordinary course of things"; so Sabatier, *Outlines of a Philosophy*, 72. Still, the Gospels say nothing about natural law, nor do they reflect on what it means for something to be "contrary to nature" (παρὰ φύσιν; the expression is from Aristotle, *Gen. an.* 770b) or "beyond human nature" (ὑψηλότερα τῆς ἀνθρωπείας φύσεως; the expression is from Theodoret, *R.H.* 26.1). Horsley is, furthermore, right to stress the social and political aspects of the healings and exorcisms, matters which this chapter passes by.

95. See Haraldsson, *Modern Miracles*, 108, 117–18, 136–37, 220–22, 234–35.

all of Sāī Bābā's feats, if they happened as reported.[96] Would Licona speak in this instance of a miracle?[97] I presume not. But if he were to do so, would the Christian God be the agent?[98] We could skirt the issue if all non-Christian miracle stories were more poorly attested than the miracles of Jesus. The facts, however, are otherwise and so demand hard comparative work.[99] Indeed, other religions also appeal to their miracles as evidence of their truth; that is, miracles serve an apologetical function almost everywhere.[100] Moreover, experiences that many would consider "miraculous" if they were to occur within their own religious contexts are frequently attested outside any religious context at all, in everyday or secular circumstances.[101]

(d) Licona asserts that historians "should force themselves to confront data and arguments that are problematic to their preferred hypotheses."[102] I wholeheartedly agree. As an example of how this might work, consider the Marian apparitions that began in Zeitoun, Egypt, in April 1968. The story is long and complicated, but the gist is this.[103] Between 1968 and 1971, literally hundreds of thousands of people, Muslims, Orthodox, and others, reported seeing, above the dome of St. Mary's Coptic Orthodox Church, a glowing apparition. Popular opinion identified it with the Virgin Mary. The figure, which never spoke, was usually preceded by flashes of small circular lights and often ac-

96. Haraldsson, *Modern Miracles*, 212–14.

97. Many Christians traditionally appeal to the devil when explaining the miracles of outsiders, thus treating them the way Jesus's opponents reportedly treated him (Matt 12:24; Mark 3:22; Luke 11:15).

98. Although the fact is often neglected, so-called miracles are understood very differently in different religious and philosophical systems. For some Buddhist options see Fiordalis, "Wondrous Display." For a panentheistic approach unaligned with any religious tradition see Murphy, *Future of the Body*.

99. See Weddle, *Miracles*. Valuable here is the online journal, *Paranthropology: Journal of Anthropological Approaches to the Paranormal*, edited by Jack Hunter. Every issue contains articles discussing seemingly well-attested (and often firsthand) purported metanormal phenomena from around the world and a wide variety of cultural, personal, and religious contexts. See also Young and Goulet, *Being Changed by Cross-Cultural Encounters*.

100. For an illustration see Verellen, "'Evidential Miracles.'"

101. See further Kripal, *Comparing Religions*, esp. 226–69, 365–94. Much of Murphy, *Future of the Body*, is also relevant. One wonders how widespread is the misapprehension of Nichols, "Miracles in Science and Theology," 711, who writes that, were "putatively miraculous events" due "to an unknown law of nature, that law ought to be visible in secular contexts as well"; but as Nichols erroneously imagines that such events do not occur (at least very often) in such contexts, "the simplest explanation" is "divine action."

102. Licona, "Historians and Miracle Claims," 116.

103. For what follows see esp. Dumsday, *Marian Apparitions*.

companied by bright bird-shaped, gliding lights. The dome itself was also often luminous. The sight was seen by multitudes—reportedly over 200,000 some evenings—including skeptics, over a protracted period of time, and people took photographs.[104]

How does one explain the data? The photographs eliminate the possibility of hallucination or mass hysteria. One predisposed to believe in Marian apparitions can think the Blessed Virgin Mary truly appeared. A skeptic might hazard that observers interpreted an unexplained electromagnetic phenomenon in accord with their religious convictions (although I know of no natural phenomenon closely akin to what the pictures from Zeitoun depict).[105] Perhaps then it was all a hoax? Maybe someone in the dome, with motives unknown, put on a light show with electronic equipment. A Van de Graaff generator (which produces an electronic plasma by ionizing matter) could mimic some of the effects observed at St. Mary's. This would not, however, explain why the sightings persisted even after city authorities shut off the electrical grid that included the church; and unless the ecclesiastical authorities who investigated were either beyond incompetent or coconspirators—all the facts are against that—they would have found evidence of such a sophisticated trick on the occasions when they explored the church. Yet another suggestion, as unconventional to modern science as the straightforward interpretation of the pious, is that the apparition was the projection of a communal psychic force. Those who had visited St. Mary's Church over the years had focused their energy on the Virgin Mary, and this built up until it created a "psychic blueprint" of Mary, one so real that it manifested itself as a visible image. The collective imagination produced a collective vision.[106]

Whatever the reader may think, I freely admit I do not know what to think. After studying the wealth of testimony, I find no mundane explanation credible.[107] Here then is a case where the data, at least for me, mystify. This, however, is only because the evidence is so abundant—thousands of witnesses, detailed testimonies, striking photographs, conscientious investigation.

Returning to Licona: not a single miracle story in the canonical Gospels comes close to Zeitoun in terms of evidence. This leaves me with a question.

104. For photographs, see Palmer, *Our Lady Returns to Egypt*, and Zaki, *Our Lord's Mother Visits Egypt*.

105. Nickell, *Looking for a Miracle*, 186–87, unpersuasively suggests that the best explanation is "earthquake lights."

106. This is the thesis of Rogo, *Miracles*, 250–57.

107. Dumsday, *Marian Apparitions*, argues at length that the facts have no conventional explanation.

What sense would it make for a historian to come away from Zeitoun with no settled conclusion—this is what I have done—yet to suppose that the stories in the Gospels, which suffer greatly by evidential comparison, beckon us toward a particular theological conclusion?

Miller's Stance

I return now to Miller. His views epitomize far-flung sentiments.[108]

(a) Most contemporary historians deny the possibility of supernatural intervention. Their predilection, which is often dogmatic, derives in part from the humanistic impulse to liberate critical study from confessional captivity. As Carlos Eire puts it: "Supernatural phenomena are modernity's foil, significant foci for the articulation of the norms of 'modernity' itself."[109]

The skeptical turn is equally, however, the upshot of an incontestable and conspicuous fact: the historical-critical sword has mercilessly slain miracle after miracle. No historian believes that, when Catherine of Alexandria was tortured on the wheel, it splintered into pieces that skewered her tormentors. There may not even have been a Catherine of Alexandria. Nor does any historian hold that, after Saint Denis's head was cut off, he picked it up and, while the angels sang, walked two miles to his grave. Nor do any in the academy imagine that angels transported Mary's house in Nazareth to Dalmatia, after which they moved it to Italy.[110] The religious past is littered with countless discredited claims. When one contemplates what we have learned about folklore and human misperception, placebos and religious enthusiasm, and the laws of probability and our predisposition to wish fulfillment, it hardly surprises

108. For the classic statement of the skeptical tradition and its sense of probabilities, see Lecky, *Spirit of Rationalism*, 155–201. For the genealogy of modern skepticism see Mullin, *Miracles and the Modern Imagination* (this includes the progress of biblical studies), and Sommer, "Geisterglaube." One should not forget, however, that antiquity had its skeptics, too. Suffice it to recall Lucian's satirical writings, the fragments of Porphyry preserved in Macarius Magnes's *Apocriticus*, and Eusebius's *Reply to Hierocles* (with its scathing assessment of Philostratus's *Life of Apollonius*). Nor were the Middle Ages bereft of skepticism; cf. Caciola, *Discerning Spirits*, and Justice, "Did the Middle Ages Believe." Probably every religious tradition has developed criteria for separating true miracles from false; cf. J. A. C. Brown, "Faithful Dissenters."

109. Eire, "Incombustible Weber," 138.

110. On this see G. E. Phillips, *House of the Virgin Mary*, and Vélez, *Miraculous Flying House*. The former defends the tale as historical. The latter seeks to understand the legend.

that Conyers Middleton's once scandalous critique of miracles has become the commonsense norm.[111]

(b) Nonetheless, that people often lie or exaggerate, wittingly and unwittingly, does not mean they always lie or exaggerate, and the existence of false narratives does not entail the nonexistence of true narratives. Yet Miller is sure that, without exception, so-called miracles do not occur. His justification is "knowledge of the laws of nature."[112] He explains neither exactly what those laws are nor how we come to recognize them—issues that, at least for me, remain quite perplexing.[113] Perhaps he believes, as many seemingly do, that Hume, with his appeal to uniform experience, settled the issue.[114] If so, I would disagree.[115] The pertinent question, however, is whether any amount of evidence could sway someone with Miller's convictions.

Although he is confident that Jesus did not walk on the water, what would Miller say if the evidence to the contrary seemed overwhelming? The case is certainly not like that of a square circle, which is logically impossible. What if we had over a hundred depositions from sworn witnesses, taken during a formal process of inquiry, who claimed to have seen Jesus walk on the water? And what if their claims had to do not with a single incident but with hundreds,

111. Middleton, *Free Inquiry*. Although Middleton claimed to exclude biblical miracles from his criticism, this was a thinly disguised conceit, as John Wesley recognized.

112. Miller, "Domain and Function," 135.

113. For the broader discussion see J. W. Carroll, "Laws of Nature." For the argument that there are no scientific laws in the metaphysical sense but only models see van Fraassen, *Laws and Symmetry*. Perhaps it is worth remarking that the second law of thermodynamics, which is generally taken to be a foundational, fundamental fact about the cosmos, has recently been questioned on experimental grounds; see Sheehan et al., "Experimental Test."

114. Hume, *Enquiries*, 109–31. Cf. Strauss, *New Life of Jesus*, 1:199 ("Hume's Essay on Miracles . . . carries with it such general conviction, that the question may be regarded as having been by it virtually settled"), and Fales, "It Is Not Reasonable," 301 ("If causation is necessarily mediated by forces, and if Newton's third law obtains, necessarily, then miracles are impossible. I take the necessities in question to be metaphysical necessities, in which case the impossibility of miracles is a metaphysical impossibility. Not even God can do things impossible in that sense"). Although associated above all with Hume, the argument has a long pedigree; cf. Cicero, *Div.* 2.28.61: Chrysippus found an explanation for everything "in the laws of nature" and insisted that "nothing actually happens that cannot happen."

115. Critics of Hume include D. Johnson, *Hume, Holism*, and Earman, *Hume's Abject Failure*. For a redoubtable defense, see Fales, *Reading Sacred Texts*, 38–133 (with criticism of Earman). Like Augustine, many modern theologians, it should be noted, do not imagine that a miracle cancels nature's order or laws; it rather contradicts only our imperfect knowledge of that order or those laws; cf. Alston, "How to Think about Divine Action," and Pannenberg, *Systematic Theology*, 2:44–46.

even thousands of occasions over the course of many years? And what if the witnesses included well-educated religious leaders as well as authorities who rejected his message but, after seeing him walk on water, attributed his feat to the devil? And what if, furthermore, we had the records of interviews with Jesus himself, interviews that verified his own belief that he could walk on water? Would Miller know, without investigation, what investigation would yield?

Miller would no doubt respond that the question is beside the point, for in the real world no such pile of evidence exists for anything so outlandish. Yet we do have such evidence—if not for Jesus walking on the water, then for the Franciscan priest Joseph of Cupertino (1603–63) rising into the air.[116] During the canonization process for this Roman Catholic ascetic, who appears to have been a sort of simpleton, dozens and dozens deposed that they had seen the ecstatic, raptured Joseph levitate, sometimes a little bit off the ground, other times several feet into the air. The occasions could last for more than a few minutes, were spaced over a period of thirty-five years, took place in different cities, and occurred both inside and outside of churches, sometimes in broad daylight. Witnesses included popes, cardinals, politicians, military leaders, physicians, and Joseph's immediate superiors. One of the latter recorded seventy supposed instances of levitation while another said he had seen Joseph levitate a thousand times. Critical members of the Inquisition, suspicious of Joseph's "ostentatious sanctity," also observed the saint hanging in the air. There were, in addition to all this, a few Protestants—most prominently Johann Friedrich, Duke of Brunswick, the patron of G. W. Leibniz—who converted to Catholicism after seeing Joseph rise from the ground. At one point, Joseph—whom authorities moved from one place to another when crowds got out of hand—vainly prayed for the displays to stop. They never did. Or so the story goes.

The historical evidence for Joseph's metanormal ability is so overwhelming that, were nothing extraordinary involved, the matter would not be debated. But if we know, before pondering the testimony, that so-called miracles never occur, then evidential support such as that just summarized does not really matter, and in connection with Joseph of Cupertino one need not make a case for fraud or mass hysteria or any other reductionistic scenario.

116. For what follows see Pastrovicchi, *St. Joseph of Copertino*; Dingwall, *Some Human Oddities*, 9–37; Eire, "Good, the Bad, and the Airborne"; Eire, *They Flew*, 98–167; and Grosso, *Man Who Could Fly*. For a skeptical treatment of Joseph see R. D. Smith, *Comparative Miracles*, 45–50. Smith imagines, to my incredulity, that Joseph was a "gymnast," and that misperception and legendary exaggeration turned some of his leaps into levitations. This is skepticism that has flatlined.

Indeed, one need not offer any substitute narrative for the surviving sources. One just knows. Argument is otiose. Testimony is irrelevant. The conclusion is foregone.[117]

To contend that miracles are false because, by definition, they break the unbreakable laws of nature is—if that is all one is doing—to win by fiat, not empirical inquiry. Those so-called laws are inferences from experience, idealizations of current data, and they remain mysterious to me. On this point, T. H. Huxley seems prudent: "No one is entitled to say *a priori* that any given so-called miraculous event is impossible."[118] It is illogical to insist that all the data fall in line if one rejects, without further ado, all the data that are not in the line. Rules with exceptions cease to be rules. Outliers negate homogeneity. One black swan means that not all swans are white—and Joseph of Cupertino was, I am inclined to think, a black swan.

I wish to be clear here. Even if Mircea Eliade was right to suppose that "in certain circumstances the human body can escape the laws of gravity,"[119] and even if I have no rationalistic explanation for the reports about Joseph of Cupertino, I am not here making the case that Jesus levitated above the Sea of Galilee. I do not affirm that he did. This is not, however, because of an unshakable, dogmatic skepticism regarding the extraordinary. We should not be like the early Protestants who denied all Catholic miracles on ideological grounds, whatever the historical testimony. I doubt that Jesus walked on the water because the limited historical evidence does not move me to infer that he did.[120] It certainly amounts to little beside the evidence for Joseph of Copertino's levitations. Even if all things are possible, not all things are probable.

117. In this connection I cannot but recall what James Parton, a nineteenth-century Protestant journalist, wrote regarding the rapid disappearance of an inoperable tumor that Roman Catholics construed as a miracle: "No amount or quality of testimony could convince a Protestant mind that Mrs. Mattingly's tumor was cured miraculously. . . . For my part, if the President and Vice President [of the United States], if the whole cabinet, both houses of Congress, and the Judges of the Supreme Court, had all sworn that they saw this thing done, and I myself had seen it,—nay if the tumor had been on my own body, and had seemed to myself to be suddenly healed,—still, I should think it more probable that all those witnesses, including myself, were mistaken, than that such a miracle had been performed." See Parton, "Our Roman Catholic Brethren," 451. Such transcendent skepticism is intellectual nihilism.

118. Huxley, *Science and Christian Thought*, 133. See further Schwenke, *Transcendente Begegnungen*, esp. 170–91.

119. Eliade, "Folklore as an Instrument of Knowledge," 35. Part of his evidence was the documentation for Joseph of Cupertino.

120. The evidence is such that Meier, *Marginal Jew*, 2:923, can conclude: it is "likely that

(c) Although Miller refrains from defining "miracle," the task is relevant.[121] One person's miracle is another person's latent human ability. What if Jesus once prayed for a so-called leper, for an individual with a severe skin disorder, say someone covered with psoriasis,[122] and very soon thereafter, perhaps immediately, the patches began to fade, until they disappeared altogether? That would not of itself demand an act of God. In 1951, in Birmingham, England, a sixteen-year-old boy, suffering from congenital *ichthyosiform erythroderma*, shed, in response to hypnotic suggestion, his black, horny layer of skin and grew new, normal skin.[123] The case hardly stands alone. That hypnosis and placebos—the modern medical functional equivalents of faith—have speedily eradicated warts, eczema, psoriasis, allergic rashes, and other skin ailments is well documented.[124] That we do not understand how this works, that current scientific knowledge does not encompass everything,[125] scarcely compels us to invoke an interventionist deity.

When it comes to the metanormal, we need not operate with the stark, unimaginative antithesis: either human invention or divine intervention. There is a large space, full of possibilities, between skeptical dismissal on the one side and religious apologetics on the other side.

(d) Given the direction of my argument, it is instructive to contrast Miller's dismissal of the story of Jesus walking on the water with Rudolf Otto's treatment of the same episode in his once well-known book, *The Kingdom of God and the Son of Man*.[126] Otto did not contend that, since people do not walk on the water, Jesus did not walk on the water. He rather argued, after a critical comparison of Matt 14:22–33; Mark 6:45–52; and John 6:16–21, that, in a primitive version of the story, "Jesus had appeared and given reassurance,

---

the story of the walking on the water is a creation of the early church and does not go back to an incident in Jesus' public ministry."

121. For a summary of some of the issues see Twelftree, "Miraculous in the New Testament," 422–23.

122. The צרעת of the Hebrew Bible and the λέπρα of the New Testament are almost certainly not to be identified with, or at least not exclusively with, what we refer to as "leprosy," that is, Hansen's disease or Elephantiasis Graecorum. In the Bible, "leprosy" appears to cover a variety of skin diseases; cf. Philo, *Post.* 47; *Somn.* 1.202.

123. Mason, "Ichthyosiform Erythrodermia," 422–23.

124. See the survey of Kelly, "Psychophysiological Influence."

125. Cf. Bettley, "Ichthyosis and Hypnosis," 996, commenting on the case of the remission of *ichthyosiform erythroderma* referred to above: "It is surprising that it should respond to any kind of treatment; that it should respond to hypnotic suggestion demands a revision of current concepts of the relation between mind and body."

126. Otto, *Kingdom of God*, 368–74.

but had not entered bodily into the ship. After giving reassurance, he had 'passed them by' and vanished again. . . . Presumably, therefore, a phantom-like 'apparitio' was originally meant, which tradition materialized into a bodily walking on the water."[127]

Although Otto observed that one could offer a psychological account of the vision, he preferred another explanation:

> Perhaps the time is long since past when men believed that they must trace strange phenomena such as these back to purely subjective impressions, while they persistently passed over phenomena testified by the history of religion,[128] and by analogous phenomena in general psychic experience. In view of the investigations and scientific collections of materials by Myers and Podmore[129] it is no longer permissible for a serious investigator to pass over these things with the remark that "of course we cannot believe it." Real spiritual "operatio in distans" is now a subject for serious research. It is especially true of the kind of "operatio" where one person intends to affect another; this is perceived by the latter, possibly in a hallucinative visual way as a vision of the distant person. Circumstances, such as the moment of death or times of great affliction, are most prominent in this respect.[130]

Whether one concurs with Otto's tradition history (I find it no more than interesting)[131] or with his explanation of what happened (I am doubtful) or with his positive estimate of the work of Myers (I concur),[132] the lesson is this. Otto was a critical historian who posited a metanormal explanation for a

127. Otto, *Kingdom of God*, 370.

128. In his previous paragraphs, Otto refers to examples from both Islam and Christianity.

129. Here Otto cites Gurney, Myers, and Podmore, *Phantasms of the Living*.

130. Otto, *Kingdom of God*, 373. For a very similar evaluation that appears to be independent of Otto see Montefiore, *Miracles of Jesus*, 87–92. Montefiore uses the word "bilocation" and appeals to modern testimony regarding the Italian priest and stigmatist Padre Pio. Even closer are stories attributed to Simeon Stylites; see Doran, *Simeon Stylites*, 151–53, 226–27.

131. Here is his summary: "An original narrative, which at first, perhaps, told simply the strange phenomenon of an 'apparitio,' well known in the charismatic milieu; then came in John the addition that after the 'apparitio' the ship was quickly and suddenly saved and brought to land; in Mark the further addition that when Jesus appeared the disciples received him bodily into the boat; in Matthew the further heightening that Peter actually descended from the boat to go and meet Jesus who, in bodily form, was walking on the water" (Otto, *Kingdom of God*, 369).

132. In large measure, Kelly and Kelly et al., *Irreducible Mind*, is a successful vindication of Myers's work and his major conclusions about the human mind and consciousness.

seemingly miraculous event without having recourse to specifically Christian theological categories.

David Friedrich Strauss could make the same move. He is often regarded as an archcynic regarding all things miraculous. If by that one means that Strauss disbelieved in divine intervention in history, then he was indeed an unvarnished skeptic. If, however, one means that he believed in nothing beyond deistic reason, he was not.[133] In the wake of his own firsthand investigations, which included observation of both a Mesmerist and an exorcist, Strauss became convinced of the reality of clairvoyance, telepathy, precognition, and remarkable healings. In other words, jettisoning the Christian God did not require jettisoning the metanormal (which he sought to account for in terms of "animal magnetism," a then-popular concept). This fact is on display in the third edition of his *Life of Jesus*.[134] There Strauss acknowledged that some of Jesus's successful healings and exorcisms may have been manifestations of unusual or extraordinary human abilities.

This estimate reveals the plasticity of the word "miracle," and it raises the question of what exactly it is that Miller and others have meant when they have declared that miracles are impossible. What does this generalization exclude? Reading other people's minds? Seeing things at a distance? Knowing the future? Moving objects with the mind alone? Being healed swiftly in response to spoken words? Inexplicably glowing? Many well-informed modern individuals have believed, independently of their religious convictions or lack thereof, that some or even all of these things belong to the natural order of things. For them, these things are, even if occasional and beyond current scientific explanation, natural, not supernatural.[135]

(e) Apart from declaring miracles—undefined—to be unhistorical, Miller nowhere indicates what more we should say about them. Perhaps he deliberately leaves the issue to one side. I should like, however, to stress that, even if one discounts all miracles and pledges allegiance to the immutable laws of nature, this says nothing about where miracle stories come from. Disbelief in the metanormal certainly should not mean that stories featuring miracles must be late and legendary. Harnack was right: "We now know that it is not after they have been long dead, nor even after the lapse of many years, that miracles have been reported of eminent persons, but at once, often the very

133. For what follows see Fabisiak, *Nocturnal Side of Science*.

134. Strauss, *Leben Jesu*, 2:5–10. Cf. Hodgson, "Editor's Notes," xlii–xliii, 791–92.

135. See esp. Murphy, *Future of the Body*.

next day. The habit of condemning a narrative, or of ascribing it to a later age, only because it includes . . . miracles, is a piece of prejudice."[136]

People can and do experience events that they deem inexplicable or regard as supernatural. Indeed, countless people in all times and places have thought themselves to be witnesses of events resembling those recorded in the Gospels, including the so-called nature miracles.[137] So if a pericope recounts a miraculous event, that in and of itself is insufficient cause for deeming it pure fiction. Put simply, there is no reason, whatever one's philosophical or religious disposition, to deny that people could have perceived Jesus doing seemingly astounding things.[138]

Reports of divine intervention may be reports of historical events even if there is no such thing as divine intervention. One may, for instance, disbelieve that the Virgin Mary revealed herself at Fatima on October 13, 1917. But that many members of a crowd of around 70,000 and others some miles away thought that they saw the sun change color, spin, and then fall from the sky—the so-called solar miracle—is a fact.[139] That many attribute what they saw to supernatural intervention does not, even if Mary was uninvolved, annul the historicity of the event. Only insatiable skepticism can altogether deny the event.[140]

Preliminary Summation

Most New Testament scholarship operates with one of the three alternatives Webb delineates: (1) miracles, defined as acts of divine intervention, occur; or (2) miracles so defined never occur; or (3) miracles so defined may occur but are beyond the historian's ken. Yet, as have I shown, the third edition of Strauss's *Das Leben Jesu* reveals another option, one also on display in much

136. Harnack, *What Is Christianity?*, 26.

137. Keener, *Miracles*, should forever put this issue to rest. Yet why the lesson was not learned by everyone long ago is hard to fathom. Acquaintance with the twenty-second chapter of Augustine's *City of God* or Book 4 of Gregory the Great's *Dialogues* or any number of other well-known sources—including Roman Catholic canonization proceedings—should have sufficed. Cf. Hengel and Schwemer, *Jesus and Judaism*, 520–26.

138. I note, however, that Ehrman, *Jesus before the Gospels*, 220–25, seems to raise the possibility that all the stories of Jesus working wonders are exclusively post-Easter in origin.

139. See Marchi, *Fatima*, and McClure, *Evidence for Marian Apparitions*, 77–85.

140. Cf. Dawkins, *Magic of Reality*, 249: "Somebody told a lie in reporting that 70,000 people saw the sun move, and the lie got repeated and spread around, just like any of the popular urban legends that whizz around the internet."

more dramatic and consistent fashion in Otto's *Kingdom of God and the Son of Man*.[141] Otto seeks to apprehend Jesus as a charismatic akin to certain itinerant Sufis and the nineteenth-century Christian healer Johann Christoph Blumhardt. For Otto, Jesus, like a few others, showed "a capacity for spiritual and psychic talents of a distinctive kind," talents such as telepathy and second sight "which indeed far surpass the limits of normal psychic operation" but nevertheless "are not magic invasions into the life of nature."[142]

The belief that some people have exercised certain metanormal powers was for neither Strauss nor Otto a theological postulate. It was rather an empirical conclusion, an inference from the data—one that, in Strauss's case, was bolstered by personal observation. Of course many in our culture, including many biblical scholars, would disagree with them on this score. The reality of so-called paranormal experiences is often vigorously disputed by, among others, "educated secularizing elites" who feel it a duty to "combat the superstitions of ordinary people."[143]

What, however, of those of us who agree with Strauss and Otto, that "some things that are normally impossible do occasionally happen"?[144] What if we do not share the current physicalist orthodoxy and believe—prior to and apart from all theological considerations—that the world is not as tame as so many assume? What if we think that unmitigated rationalism and run-of-the-mill reductionism cannot adequately deal with all the peculiar events that fill not just the history of religions but ordinary life? What if Chesterton's assertion that "there is a choking cataract of human testimony" in favor of so-called miracles does not make us cringe?[145]

All worldviews are constricted, fragile, and imperfect. This includes explanatory frameworks that are unremittingly supernatural and social imaginaries that are reflexively reductionistic. I plight my troth to neither.

141. A sign of the unfortunate disregard of Otto's contribution is that neither Meier, in his discussion of miracles in the second volume of *Marginal Jew*, nor Keener, in his two-volume tome, *Miracles*, mentions Otto even once. He is also completely missing from the massive, two-volume tome edited by R. Zimmermann, *Kompendium der frühchristlichen Wundererzählungen*. Note, by contrast, the positive use of Otto by Dunn, *Jesus and the Spirit*, 72–74.

142. Otto, *Kingdom of God*, 340. Related approaches appear in T. H. Wright, "Miracles," and Montefiore, *Miracles of Jesus*. Many of the latter's suggestions and conclusions approach my own. Scholars, however, seem to have taken scant notice of Montefiore's book. Cf. also the treatments of Jesus's miracles by two writers outside the New Testament guild: Grosso, *Frontiers of the Soul*, 42–64, and Méheust, *Jésus thaumaturge*.

143. Taves, *Fits, Trances, and Visions*, 4.

144. Eire, *They Flew*, xiv.

145. Chesterton, *Orthodoxy*, 150.

We should be able to disentangle historical questions, including questions about supposed miracles, from theological or antitheological inclinations. I concede that, as a matter of historical fact, asking "Did Jesus do miracles?" has more often than not been an indirect way of asking "Is Christianity the true religion?"[146] Nothing, however, requires merging the two questions. They are not mutually imbricated.[147] Thinking otherwise is but a habit.

The Clairvoyant Jesus

Being open-minded about the possibility that Jesus had metanormal abilities is one thing. Making a historical argument for it is another. Standing in the way of the latter is the problem that comes up repeatedly in this volume: the sources are such that, more often than not, it is all but impossible to come to confident conclusions about the extent of the historicity of any particular story or saying. It is my contention, however, that this unhappy circumstance need not be the cul-de-sac of our endeavors. This is because, even when we cannot usually establish the authenticity of individual incidents and their details, patterns across the sources may tell us important things. Consider, as possible illustrations, the following texts:

1. Mark 2:1–12, healing a man who cannot walk. The story includes the comment that Jesus "perceived in his spirit" the things that others were "questioning in their hearts" (2:8).[148] Here Mark depicts Jesus as having been, on this occasion, telepathic. Henry Alford commented: "The knowledge is immediate and supernatural, as is most carefully and precisely here signified."[149]

146. Cf. C. J. Wright, *Miracle in History*, 12: "Miracles, being . . . regarded through Christian history as 'evidences' of the truths of Christianity, were held to be essentially one with those truths. Christianity stood or fell with them. Even to within a generation ago this position was confidently maintained by Protestant and Catholic apologetic alike, the only difference between the two types of miracle apology being that whereas the former regarded Christianity as born of miracle the latter in addition to this declared that miracle 'conserves and propagates Christianity.'"

147. Cf. Dusenbury, *I Judge No One*, 57: "The idea of prodigiousness is linked, conceptually and historically, to the idea of divinity, but the former by no means entails the latter."

148. The parallel in Matt 9:4 opens with: "But Jesus, knowing their thoughts." Luke 5:21, however, has simply: "Then the scribes and Pharisees began to question, saying."

149. Alford, *Greek Testament*, 1:320 (italics deleted). See further Bullard, *Thoughts of Many Hearts*, 82–99. Christian tradition often associates this circumstance with Jesus's deity; so, e.g., Ambrose, *Cain* 1.9.37; Maldonatus, *Commentary on the Holy Gospels*, 194 ("God

2. Mark 6:45–52, walking on the water. When it is evening and the disciples are on a boat far from shore, Jesus sees their plight (6:48). According to Adela Yarbro Collins, "because of the darkness and the distance, Jesus's ability to see the disciples, even if he were on a mountain, is extraordinary."[150]
3. Mark 7:24–30, the Syrophoenician woman. Jesus assures a woman who has asked him to heal her daughter, a woman who is away from her house, that "the demon has left your daughter." This in the event proves true (7:29–30). The commentaries hand us three options: Jesus knows the demon has gone because (a) he senses from afar what has happened, (b) he has perfect faith in God, or (c) he has himself worked the deed at a distance.
4. Mark 9:33–37, true greatness. When Jesus asks his disciples what they were arguing about on the way, they say nothing. The query is rhetorical, for the ensuing declaration, which commends humility, reveals that, as the parallel in Luke 9:47 puts it, Jesus "perceived the thought of their hearts" (εἰδὼς τὸν διαλογισμὸν τῆς καρδίας). D. E. Nineham observed: "Jesus knows by supernatural insight what had been going on in the disciples' minds."[151]
5. Mark 11:1–10, the triumphal entry. Jesus, according to 11:2, knew that there was a donkey in the village ahead that was his to borrow. The older commentaries tend to discern in this incident Jesus's supernatural knowledge and authority. As Matthew Poole remarked: Jesus's instructions "were an evident argument of Christ's Divine nature, who could tell all particular circumstances, and also which way the heart of man would incline."[152] By contrast, post-Enlightenment commentators, more rationalistic than their predecessors, often speculate that Jesus must have had a friend in Bethany.[153]
6. Mark 12:41–44, a poor widow's charity. Jesus inexplicably knows details about a woman he presumably has never met. Modern exegetes sometimes highlight the circumstance in order to urge that the story cannot be his-

alone knows the hearts and thoughts of men. Hence, from this passage, the ancient Fathers have rightly concluded the Godhead of Christ"); and Swete, *Mark*, 36. Post-Enlightenment commentaries, by contrast, often deny that anything extraordinary was involved; cf. V. Taylor, *Mark*, 196.

150. Yarbro Collins, *Mark*, 333. Cf. Pesch, *Markusevangelium*, 1:360 ("superior divine knowledge"); Guelich, *Mark*, 1:350 ("miraculous 'telescopic' vision"); and Marcus, *Mark*, 1:423 ("supernatural insight").

151. Nineham, *Mark*, 257. See further Bullard, *Thoughts of Many Hearts*, 114–19.

152. Poole, *Annotations*, 3:96.

153. So, e.g., C. A. Evans, *Mark*, 2:143. Some remain undecided; cf. Cranfield, *Mark*, 349: "It is possible that Mark thought of this as an instance of supernatural knowledge on the part of Jesus—but it is not necessary to infer this. His narrative does not exclude the possibility of a previous arrangement or of the owner of the foal actually being with Jesus."

torical. Joel Marcus conjectures that a parable lies behind this story, in part because "unless we presume that Jesus is exercising clairvoyance, which is not mentioned in the account, it is impossible to explain how he could know (a) that the woman is a widow, (b) the amount she is contributing, and (c) the percentage of her livelihood it represents."[154] Yet whatever the tradition history, 12:41–44 as it stands is not a parable: it presents itself as an event from Jesus's life.[155]

7. Mark 14:18–21, the vaticination of betrayal. Jesus knows that one of his disciples is contemplating betraying him to the authorities (cf. John 13:21–30). Leontius of Constantinople took this to be a sign of Jesus's "prescience as God" (*Hom.* 6:5). Minus the last two words, the point is obvious.
8. Matt 26:67–68, mocking Jesus. Some cruelly strike a blindfolded Jesus and ask him to "prophesy" and say who hit him (cf. Mark 14:65; Luke 22:63–64). They are mocking Jesus's purported ability to know things without seeing them. As Theophylact observed: "They mocked him in this manner because the people considered him to be a prophet" (*Comm. Matt.* ad loc).
9. Matt 12:22–30 // Luke 11:14–23, collusion with Satan. In a verse commonly assigned to Q, we read that Jesus knew what his opponents were thinking: "Knowing their thoughts [εἰδὼς δὲ τὰς ἐνθυμήσεις αὐτῶν], he said to them" (Matt 12:25; Luke 11:17). Premodern commentaries regularly found in this evidence of Jesus's deity: God alone knows human thoughts and hearts.[156]
10. Matt 8:5–13, healing a centurion's servant or son. The parallel in Luke 7:1–10 ends with the notice that "when those who had been sent [by the centurion] returned to the house, they found the servant well." Matthew's conclusion is different: "Jesus said to the centurion: 'Go. As you have believed may it be done for you.' And the servant was healed at that very hour." Although Jesus's *fiat* may stem from his faith in God or his own powers, Matt 8:13 also allows the inference that Jesus knows from afar what has transpired.[157]
11. Matt 12:15–21, healing multitudes. In his introduction to this story, with its parallel in Mark 3:7–12, the First Evangelist declares that Jesus departed from a synagogue because he was "aware" (γνούς) of what certain opponents were plotting against him (12:15).

154. Marcus, *Mark*, 2:859.

155. So too Luke 21:1–4. Note Marshall, *Luke*, 751: "Nor can we rule out the possibility that he [Jesus] had knowledge, natural or perhaps clairvoyant, of the nature of the woman's gift."

156. So, e.g., Cyril of Alexandria, *Hom. Lk.* 80; *Opus Imperfectum* ad loc; Chromatius of Aquileia, *Tract. Matt.* 49; Theophylact, *Comm. Matt.* ad loc. See further Bullard, *Thoughts of Many Hearts*, 120–30. Contrast T. W. Manson, *Sayings of Jesus*, 85: the passage "does not imply thought-reading."

157. Cf. Montefiore, *Miracles of Jesus*, 48–49.

12. Luke 5:1–11; John 21:1–11, a miraculous draught of fish. Despite the many significant differences between their accounts of what was probably at one point the same story,[158] both Luke and John write that Jesus knew where the disciples, who had labored in vain all night, could collect a large haul of fish. The commentaries split over whether Jesus causes the fish to gather in one place or instead, through extraordinary means, knows they are there.[159]
13. Luke 6:6–11, healing of a withered hand. A Lukan addition to Mark 3:1–6 claims that Jesus "knew the thoughts" (αὐτὸς δὲ ᾔδει τοὺς διαλογισμούς) of his opponents (Luke 6:8; cf. Matt 12:15). Cyril of Alexandria, in accord with his Christology, read Jesus's omniscience into the text (*Hom. Lk.* 23). Someone without Cyril's view might instead deem Jesus to be a "mind reader."[160]
14. Luke 7:36–50, Jesus is anointed. After a woman he has not met bathes Jesus's feet with her tears, his offended host says to himself: "If this man were a prophet, he would have known who and what kind of woman this is who is touching him—that she is a sinner" (7:39). The thought reflects the conviction that, were Jesus what people say he is, he should have extraordinary knowledge (cf. John 4:16–19). Ironically, as the story moves forward, he exhibits such. He not only reads his host's thoughts but knows all about the woman's many sins (Luke 7:40–48).[161]
15. John 1:35–51, the call of disciples. Jesus knows Nathanael's character prior to meeting him. Indeed, Jesus has, before their face-to-face encounter, seen him sitting under a fig tree. Nathanael, taking up Philip's claim in 1:45 ("we have found him about whom Moses in the law and also the prophets wrote"), reacts by professing that Jesus is Son of God and Israel's king (1:48–49). Jesus displays here, in Bultmann's phrase, "miraculous knowledge."[162]
16. John 2:23–25, Jesus's ministry in Jerusalem. The Fourth Evangelist expresses his general impression about Jesus's clairvoyant and telepathic abilities with these words: "When he was in Jerusalem during the Passover festival, many believed in his name because they saw the signs that he was doing. But Jesus on his part would not entrust himself to them, because he knew all people and needed no one to testify about anyone; for he himself knew

158. See Allison, *Resurrection of Jesus*, 68–72.

159. Cf. Godet, *Luke*, 1:257: "The miraculous draught may be only a miracle of knowledge; Jesus had a supernatural knowledge of a large shoal of fish to be found in this place. . . . Jesus may, however, have wrought by His own will what is frequently produced by physical circumstances."

160. See further Bullard, *Thoughts of Many Hearts*, 99–103.

161. See further Bullard, *Thoughts of Many Hearts*, 103–14.

162. Bultmann, *John*, 104.

what was in everyone."[163] Commentator after commentator finds here a sign of Jesus's deity.[164]

17. John 4:4–42, meeting a Samaritan woman. At one point in the conversation Jesus says: "Go, call your husband, and come back." She responds: "I have no husband." To this Jesus says: "You are right in saying 'I have no husband'; for you have had five husbands, and the one you have now is not your husband. What you have said is true" (4:16–18). The woman reacts with these words: "Sir, I see that you are a prophet" (4:19). She later tells the people of her city: "Come and see a man who told me everything I have ever done" (4:29).
18. John 6:60–70, knowledge of complaints and unbelief. In this passage, the evangelist relates that Jesus was "aware that his disciples were complaining" (6:61) and that he "knew from the first who were the ones who did not believe, and who was the one who would betray him" (6:64). According to Augustine, although the disciples kept their grumbling to themselves, Jesus knew "within himself" what they had said (*Tract. Ev. Jo.* 27.3). Chrysostom, commenting on 6:61, avows that "it is an attribute of his Godhead to bring secret things to light" (*Hom. Jo.* 47.2).[165]
19. John 6:70–71 and 13:11, awareness of coming betrayal. Already in John 6 Jesus knows what Judas is thinking.
20. John 11:1–44, raising Lazarus. Before he departs for Lazarus's village, Jesus announces, without having received any news, that Lazarus has died (11:11–14). "Jesus' knowledge of Lazarus' sleep must," to quote C. K. Barrett, "be supernatural."[166]
21. John 16:13–33, Jesus's parting discourse. The disciples say to one another: "What does he mean by saying to us: 'A little while, and you will no longer see me, and again a little while and you will see me'; and 'Because I am going to the Father'?" (16:17–18). The evangelist then observes: "Jesus knew that they wanted to ask him, so he said to them: 'Are you discussing among

163. According to McHugh, *John*, 219, "for greater clarity" the closing words of John 2 should "be interpretively rendered *because he knew by intuition what people were like*." Lindars, *John*, 145, remarks: "No doubt this is an apologetic motif rather than a direct personal reminiscence, though not without some basis in fact."

164. Note, e.g., Chrysostom, *Hom. Jo.* 24.1 ("to know what is in the heart of men belongs to God alone"); Cyril of Alexandria, *Comm. Jo.* 2.1 ad loc ("God alone understands what is in us, and Christ understands them, so is he not God by nature?"); Morris, *John*, 207 ("this is to be understood in the light of the Old Testament view that God alone knows what is in man").

165. Cf. Lapide, *Great Commentary*, 4:262.

166. Barrett, *John*, 392. Athanasius, *C. Ar.* 3.37, attributes Jesus's knowledge of Lazarus's condition to the unity of Father and Son (John 14:11).

> yourselves what I meant when I said,'" etc. (16:19). After Jesus continues and answers the disciples' questions, they confess: "Now we know that you know all things" (16:30).

It is unsurprising, given the quantity of material,[167] that Ps.-Clem. Rec. 5.10 summarizes Jesus's deeds with these words: "By command alone he made the blind see, the deaf hear, the demons flee, restored health to the sick, and gave life to the dead. And, because nothing was impossible for him, he even perceived people's thoughts."[168]

What might we make of the family of texts just introduced? One can dismiss them all on the ground that people gain knowledge of the world only through the customary senses. On this view, Christ followers, in order to magnify their hero, attributed to him an ability he did not have. Perhaps they felt emboldened to do so because they thought of him as a prophet and because, in a few biblical stories, prophets know things from afar.[169] The Pharisee of Luke 7:39 thinks that, were Jesus really a prophet, "he would have known who and what kind of woman this is who is touching him—that she is a sinner."[170] Or perhaps, more particularly, they thought of him as the prophet like Moses of Deut 18:15–18 (cf. Acts 3:22–26; 7:37), and as tradition had granted the lawgiver practical omniscience, it was natural to claim the same for Jesus.[171] Or perhaps some

167. For additional possibilities from Luke see Bullard, *Thoughts of Many Hearts*, 130–53. Note also Egerton Papyrus frag. 2 recto: "But Jesus, knowing their mind [εἰδὼς [τὴν δι]άνοιαν [αὐτ]ῶν], scolded them."

168. Cf. the generalization in Athanasius, *C. Ar.* 3.37: Jesus "foreknew the reasonings of the disciples and was aware of what was in the heart of each."

169. 1 Sam 9:20; 2 Kgs 5:26; 6:8–10, 32–33; Ezek 8:1–16; 24:1–2. Cf. Luke 3:16 D ("knowing their thoughts"—of the Baptist); Ps.-Clem. Hom. 3.11: ("he is a true prophet who always knows all things and even the thoughts of all men"); and Aquinas, *Summa Theologica* 2.2:171 art. 3 ("Elisha knew prophetically what his disciple Gehazi had done in his absence, and in like manner the secret thoughts of one man are manifested prophetically to another, according to 1 Cor 14:25"). B. Newman, *Permeable Self*, 71, notes that, in medieval hagiography, telepathy is a prophetic talent. Bultmann, whose worldview prevented him from entertaining the possibility that Jesus had metanormal abilities, cited parallel accounts from antiquity and thought the motif of extraordinary knowledge to be part of the so-called divine-man concept; see his commentary: *John*, 102. For criticism, see Bullard, *Thoughts of Many Hearts*, 28–45.

170. Cf. John 4:19: after Jesus tells the Samaritan woman that she has had five husbands, she responds: "I see that you are a prophet."

171. Moses was remembered not only as a prophet but as the author of the Pentateuch, which recounts the creation of the world, prophesies the future (at least in Jewish and Christian interpretation), and describes much in between. On Moses's unparalleled knowledge see p. 111 n. 96.

thought that the Messiah would be clairvoyant and so they made Jesus out to be such.[172] Or perhaps they imagined that, if Jesus was a divine intermediary, he should be prescient, as is Metatron in 3 Enoch.[173] Or perhaps they simply enjoyed enhancing Jesus's status by bestowing on him a marvelous ability found in entertaining stories from the Greco-Roman world, including Judaism.[174]

Such dogmatic incredulity is not, however, automatic for those who judge clairvoyance and telepathy to be authentic albeit sporadic, baffling human aptitudes. Morton Smith, who can hardly be accused of theological bias in this matter, opined: "The belief that Jesus knew the minds of people he met may be founded on fact. Some people are uncannily . . . able to read the minds of others."[175]

Unfortunately, even when one believes that people sometimes know things in puzzling ways, this hardly verifies the historicity of any particular Gospel episode. That would be a non sequitur. At the same time, it would not be unreasonable to infer, given the thudding regularity of the motif, that the traditions featuring a clairvoyant and telepathic Jesus preserve the impression

172. Cf. John 4:29: "Come and see a man who has told me everything I have ever done! He cannot be the Messiah, can he?" Isa 11:1–3 foresees that "a shoot shall come out from the stock of Jesse, and a branch shall grow out of his roots. The spirit of the Lord shall rest on him, the spirit of wisdom and understanding, the spirit of counsel and might, the spirit of knowledge and the fear of the Lord. His delight shall be in the fear of the Lord. He shall not judge by what his eyes see, or decide by what his ears hear." This was a messianic oracle in Judaism (Ps. Sol. 17:21–32; 1 En. 49:3–4; Tg. Isa 11:1–4), and early Christians found its fulfilment in Jesus (Rom 15:8–12; T. Levi 18:7). One could, moreover, conjecture that, when the blindfolded Jesus is hit and asked, "Who is it that struck you?" (Luke 22:64; cf. Mark 14:65; Matt 26:67–68), Isa 11:3 is in the background: were he truly the Messiah, he should be able to know without seeing. There would then be a parallel in b. Sanh. 93b, where a quotation of Isa 11:2–3 is followed by the claim that Bar Kochba was revealed to be a false Messiah and killed by the rabbis when he could not judge by scent alone. But the rabbinic parallel is presumably a late legend; 4QpIsa[a] 8–10 *ad* Isa 11:3 seemingly takes Isa 11:3 to mean that the Davidic Messiah will heed "the priests of renown"; the Synoptic scene makes perfect sense without the intertextual proposal; and no text in which Jesus is clairvoyant alludes to Isa 11:1–3. 4Q534 I, 8 ("he will know the secrets of man") is also potentially relevant if it concerns a messianic figure, yet this is debated; see Joseph, "His Wisdom Will Reach All Peoples."

173. On the exceptional knowledge of Metatron (cf. 3 En. 11:1–3; 48C:4) and its parallels in John, see Muñoa, "John, Jesus, and Metatron."

174. Cf. Herodotus, *Hist.* 1.47 (the Pythian priestess); Diogenes Laertius, *Vit. phil.* 8. 41 (Pythagoras); Josephus, *Ant.* 13.311–13 (Judas the Essene); 15:373–78 (Manaemus the Essene); Pliny, *Nat.* 7.174 (Hermotimus of Clazomenae); Dio Cassius, *Hist rom.* 67.18 (Apollonius); Philostratus, *Vit. Apoll.* 3.16.1–4 (Iarchas of India); 5.24.2 (Apollonius); t. Pesaḥ. 2:15 (Gamaliel); y. Šeb. 9:1 (38d) (Simeon b. Yoḥai); y. Soṭah 1:4 (16d) (R. Me'ir); Lev. Rab. 21:8 (Akiba). See further Bieler, *ΘΕΙΟΣ ΑΝΗΡ*, 87–90, and recall Peter's knowledge of the hidden deed of Ananias and Sapphira in Acts 5:1–11.

175. M. Smith, *Jesus the Magician*, 115.

of some who actually knew him.[176] For whatever one makes of the individual units, the pertinent notices appear in Q, Mark, M, L, and John and so constitute a pattern across the sources. It is my guess that, if something more mundane were this well attested, many scholars would, with little hesitation, deem it to be historical. To put the matter in perspective: the canonical sources recount six exorcisms (Mark 1:21–27 par.; 5:1–20 par.; 7:24–30 par.; 9:14–29 par.; Matt 12:22–23 // Luke 11:14–15; Matt 9:32–34). Apparent extrasensory perception appears in three times as many episodes as the casting out of demons, an activity that most of us confidently associate with Jesus.

Beyond that, the notices remain sporadic and scattered;[177] there are no allusions to the few Hebrew Bible texts in which a prophet shows second sight; and the references to the motif of Jesus's extraordinary knowledge are, at least in Matthew and Mark, "almost casual,"[178] while the summaries of Jesus's activities in all three Synoptics remain silent on the matter (Matt 4:23–25; Mark 1:32–34; etc.).[179] Additionally, the evangelists offer no explicit interpretation of the phenomenon,[180] and they narrate stories in which Jesus does not know what others are thinking or what has happened until he is told. In Mark 4–5, for instance, he asks after a man's name (5:9), inquires who touched his garment (5:30), and is caught unawares during a storm (4:35–41). Luke and John do show an interest in our theme. But they did not invent it, as the material in Q, Mark, and M reveals.[181] They were only emphasizing and amplifying what seems to have been there from the beginning.[182]

176. So too Otto, *Kingdom of God*, 351–56; Dunn, *Jesus and the Spirit*, 83; Hill, *New Testament Prophecy*, 60; Montefiore, *Miracles of Jesus*, 23–49; and Luff, *Impact of Jesus*, 68.

177. Cf. Otto, *Kingdom of God*, 353: "Jesus' charismatic gift is recorded only as it were in hidden corners of our tradition"; it is "incidental" in character.

178. So A. E. Harvey, *Jesus and the Constraints of History*, 106.

179. Contrast Ps.-Clem. Rec. 5.10 (quoted above).

180. Perhaps Mark or Matthew took it to indicate Jesus's prophetic status; see n. 169. Given John's Christology, in which Jesus and the Father are one (John 10:30–38), the Fourth Evangelist may have construed the ability as properly divine: God alone knows hearts; cf. 1 Kgs 8:39; 1 Cor 18:9; Pss 38:9; 44:21; 94:11; 139:2–4, 23; Prov 15:11; Jer 12:3; Wis 1:6; Sir 42:18; 4Q185 1–3 III, 11–12; Philo, *Cher.* 16–18; Rom 8:27; Josephus, *Bell.* 5.413; 2 Bar. 83:2–3; 4 Ezra 16:54; Sib. Or. 8:359–77; etc. See further Bullard, *Thoughts of Many Hearts*, 55–62. For Bullard, God's knowledge of inner thoughts is the key to Luke's deployment of the motif.

181. For Luke see Bullard, *Thoughts of Many Hearts*. He views Luke 2:34–35 ("so that the inner thoughts of many will be revealed") as programmatic (which it may or may not be: the verse is difficult), helpfully traces the theme throughout Luke, detects influence from Ps 94 (LXX 93), and (in accord with the old theological tradition) takes Jesus's knowledge of unspoken thoughts "to be a divine ability which he possesses by virtue of his identity as Lord" (178). For John see Tripp, "Jesus' Special Knowledge."

182. Cf. R. Brown, *Jesus: God and Man*, 49: "Probably as far back as one can trace the

If the impression that the tradition here leaves is correct, one need not, I wish to stress, seek an explanation in religious doctrine, even if Christian theologians and commentators typically have. Morton Smith is the proof. Furthermore, while many claims for extraordinary knowledge belong to a theological or religious context—"it is a real charism attested in ecclesial life"[183]—many do not,[184] and the modern debates over whether one should believe in those abilities have nothing to do with religion.[185]

Mark Twain wrote that once, after receiving a thick envelope in the post, he unaccountably felt moved, before opening it, to announce to a visiting relative:

> I will tell you everything this letter contains—date, signature, and all—without breaking the seal. It is from a Mr. Wright, of Virginia, Nevada, and is dated the 2d of March—seven days ago. Mr. Wright proposes to make a book about the silver mines and the Great Bonanza, and asks what I, as a friend, think of the idea. He says his subjects are to be so and so, their order and sequence so and so, and he will close with a history of the chief feature of the book, the Great Bonanza.

Every detail allegedly proved correct.[186] Had Twain been a religious hero, his admirers would doubtless have assigned his incredible feat—which is far more dramatic than anything in my list about Jesus—to God. Twain, however,

---

tradition, Jesus was presented as a man with more than ordinary knowledge and perception of other men."

183. So Giambrone, *Quest of the Historical Jesus*, 361. Many stories featuring telepathy and clairvoyance appear in the sources for the desert fathers, people who often engaged in practices that encouraged altered stages of consciousness and who likely did, from time to time, gain knowledge through extraordinary means.

184. Illustrations from antiquity include Plutarch, *Caes.* 47; Eunapius, *Liv. phil. soph.* 49; and Augustine, *Gen. litt.* 12.17. Contrast Philostratus, *Vit. Apoll.* 1.19: a certain individual, on being told that Apollonius "knows all that human beings keep unspoken," worships him and deems him to be a supernatural being (δαίμονα). See further Dodds, "Supernormal Phenomena."

185. Hegel, Schopenhauer, Henry Sidgwick, William James, Freud, C. D. Broad, E. R. Dodds, and Arthur Koestler all believed in telepathy and clairvoyance on empirical grounds, not for religious reasons. So too a number of academics of my personal acquaintance. In medieval sources, demoniacs as well as saints can read minds; cf. B. Newman, *Permeable Self*, 10–11.

186. See Twain, "Mental Telegraphy." Anyone who reads this will quickly realize that Twain was dead serious.

was a nonreligious man who was cynical about much, and he attributed what happened to an ill-understood human faculty.[187] Nothing prohibits historians of the Gospels from doing the same for the texts listed above. In other words, one need not be a Christian of a particular stripe to acknowledge that Jesus sometimes knew things through enigmatic means.

Jesus the Prophet

The sources for Jesus purport not only that he occasionally had uncanny knowledge about the present but also that he could sometimes divine the future. I forgo a complete listing of the relevant texts and note as representative the following:

1. All the canonical Gospels report that Jesus anticipated an untimely death, in particular an untimely death in Jerusalem (Matt 26:2; Mark 8:31–33; 9:9, 30–32; 10:33–34; 14:8, 22–25, 27–28; Luke 13:32–33; 22:37; John 8:21–30; 10:11, 17–18; 12:23–25, 32–33).
2. The Jesus of Mark 10:35–40 prophesies that two of the Twelve, James and John of Zebedee, will suffer martyrdom.[188]
3. In Mark 14:12–16, Jesus foresees that two of his disciples will shortly run into a man carrying a jar of water and that he and his followers will be welcomed in the house the man will enter.[189]
4. According to Mark 14:17–21 and John 13:10–11, 18–30, Jesus predicted that one of his disciples would betray him.
5. In both the Synoptics and John, Jesus expects that his disciples will flee from him (Mark 14:27, 30; John 16:32).
6. Our sources also have Jesus foretelling that Peter will deny him three times (Mark 14:30; Luke 22:31–34; John 13:36–38).
7. All four Gospels purport that Jesus anticipated persecution and tribulation for his immediate followers (e.g., Matt 10:19, 23–25; Mark 10:39; 13:9–13; Luke 12:11; John 15:18–25; 16:1–4).
8. A prophecy that Jesus will reunite with his disciples after his death appears in Mark 14:28; John 14:3; 16:16–22.

187. Cf. Augustine, *Gen. litt.* 12.13: some say "that the human soul has a natural power of divination within it."

188. The evidence is that only James so died; see Davies and Allison, *Matthew*, 3:90–92.

189. The abbreviated account in Matt 26:17–20 lacks the predictive element.

9. Several sources have Jesus forecasting that Jerusalem or its temple will be devastated (Mark 13:2; 14:58; 15:29; Luke 19:44; 21:20–24; 23:27–31; Acts 6:14).
10. Matt 17:24–27 has Jesus declaring that Peter will catch a fish with a coin in its mouth.
11. In John 14:15–31 and 15:26, Jesus consoles his followers by promising the coming of the Holy Spirit (cf. Mark 13:11).

Although this catalogue is incomplete, it shows that the topos of a premonitory Jesus is well attested. Given this, it is unsurprising that some deemed him to be a "prophet" (Matt 21:11; Mark 6:15; 8:28; Luke 7:16; 24:19; John 4:19; 6:14; 7:40, 52; 9:17; Acts 3:22–23; 7:37; Gos. Thom. 31) while others reckoned him to be a "false prophet,"[190] or that Mark portrays him as having uttered a long discourse that is predictive from beginning to end (13:5–37). Nor is it peculiar that prophets and prophecy were at home in the movement he inspired.[191] As he was, so were they.

We are better off here than with the texts in which Jesus exhibits telepathic and clairvoyant powers, for we can say with some assurance that at least numbers 1 and 9 likely recall rightly. We have good reason to hold that Jesus anticipated an untimely death and that he warned of the temple's destruction.[192] Both prognoses, furthermore, came to pass (even if, in his own mind, the two events were not cleanly and distantly separated).[193]

Beyond that, however, the texts I listed are difficult to evaluate. It is hardly possible to render a firm, confident judgment on the historicity of most of them. Still, the motif of Jesus as prophet is so widely attested that, even without a positive estimate of numbers 1 and 9, the motif is unlikely to be, in its entirety, a later accretion. The evidence for the historical Jesus having functioned as some sort of seer is good.

The skeptic can reasonably respond that while Jesus and those around him likely did imagine that he sometimes saw the future, nothing extraordinary

190. For the polemical tradition that Jesus was a false prophet see Stanton, "Jesus of Nazareth."

191. Note Acts 2:17–18; 11:27; 13:1; 19:6; 21:9–10; Rom 12:6; 1 Cor 11:4–5; 12:10, 28–29; 13:8–9; 14:1, 3–6, 22, 24, 29, 31, 32, 37, 39; Eph 3:5; 1 Thess 5:20; 1 John 4:1; Rev 2:20; 10:11; 11:3–6; Did. 11.3–12. See further Aune, *Prophecy in Early Christianity*.

192. See Allison, *Jesus of Nazareth*, 97–101; Allison, *Constructing Jesus*, 387–433; Ådna, *Jesu Stellung*; S. Petersen, "Mutmaßungen"; and Barber, *Historical Jesus*, 81–114. Cf. Sanders and Davies, *Synoptic Gospels*, 18: "The temple was destroyed by fire, and many of the stones remained standing—some can be seen to this day. Here [in Mark 13:2] we probably have a genuine prediction, not a fake one written after the fact, since it did not come true in a precise sense."

193. See Jeremias, "Drei-Tage-Worte," and Allison, *Resurrection of Jesus*, 184–92.

was involved. Perhaps he anticipated his death not because he had a true premonition but because he could see whither things were tending toward the end of his ministry.[194] And maybe his warnings about Jerusalem stemmed from a realistic estimate of the political situation: he sensed the way the winds were blowing, intuiting that a growing aspiration for Jewish independence would eventuate in Roman wrath. For the rest, one might hold, the relevant predictions are *ex eventu*. Tradents, aspiring to make Jesus look like Moses and other remarkable figures,[195] were guilty of hindsight bias. They remembered a few chance hits, added to their number,[196] and then overlooked all the misses.[197] On this account, the impression of a prescient Jesus would go back to nothing out of the ordinary.

This is not, however, the only alternative to a forthright supernatural account, even if the secondary literature usually assumes it is. When discussing how Jesus might have foreseen his death, Miller notes only two explanations: either Jesus was keenly aware of the danger he was in and made a good guess, or he spoke from divine revelation.[198] Yet the historical record is full of individuals who reportedly foresaw, through some opaque capacity, future events, including untimely death and disaster for themselves and people dear to them.[199] Swedenborg appears to have predicted the day of his death over a month before it happened.[200] Abraham Lincoln, three days before he was

194. Cf. the much-cited words of Dodd, *Parables*, 40: "It needed, not supernatural prescience, but the ordinary insight of an intelligent person, to see whither things were tending, at least during the later stages of the ministry."

195. Deut 34:5–6 was widely understood to imply that Moses prophesied his own death; cf. Philo, *Mos.* 2.291; Josephus, *Ant.* 4.326; and Sipre Deut. 357. Prophecies of one's own death are attributed to many, including Rebekah (Jub. 35:6), Socrates (Plato, *Apol.* 39c), Paul (Acts 20:22), Peter (Mart. Pet. Paul 55, 61), Pythagoras (Iamblichus, *Vit. Pyth.* 142), and Saint Cuthbert (Bede, *H.E.* 4.29). According to Josephus, *Bell.* 2.159, the Essenes could predict the future.

196. Cf. Celsus in Origen, *Cels.* 2.15: the disciples "devised the fiction that he [Jesus] knew everything before it happened."

197. Cf. these words by a former follower of the modern Hindu holy man Sathya Sāī Bābā: "The baktas [devotees] will only talk about predictions that Swami made and that came true, or of promises of healing when the patient recovered. They will not mention those instances when Swami made promises and nothing happened" (quoted in Haraldsson, *Modern Miracles*, 179).

198. Miller, "Domain and Function," 141–42.

199. I am fully aware of the standard objections, based on statistics, to the value of the anecdotal nature of the evidence in such cases; but discussion of that tangled topic would take us far beyond the scope of this essay. Interested readers may consult D. Evans, *Spirituality and Human Nature*, 132–46.

200. Prince, *Noted Witnesses*, 55.

murdered, reportedly dreamed of his body lying in state in the East Room, and he heard someone say, "He was killed by an assassin."[201] Such stories may not be legion, but they are there.[202] And they need not, as Aristotle recognized, have anything to do with God (*Div. somn.* 463b: οὐ θεοῦ πέμποντος). David Dusenbury is right: "There are grounds in secular literature, and in life, for believing that a premonition of one's death may be an integrally human form of cognition. To grant that this form of cognition is rare, or uncanny, is not to grant that it is mythic. Many forms of natural cognition are rare, and human cognition is *per se* uncanny."[203]

My best guess is that the motif of Jesus as prophet grew in part out of his indeed foreseeing, via a facility we do not understand—sometimes perhaps in a vision (cf. Luke 10:18; John 1:48)—a few things that did in fact happen to him and to those close to him, above all his death and their misfortunes. In line with this, over half of the entries in the list above involve death and trauma (nos. 1, 2, 4, 5, 6, 7, and 9), and those who study these things inform us that extreme duress often incubates the metanormal. In the words of Jeff Kripal: "Strong emotion (pathos), particularly around trauma and death, is the most common catalyst of robust paranormal events. Trauma, it seems, is what 'electrifies,' 'zaps,' or 'magnetizes,' and hence empowers the imagination."[204] Maybe

201. Lamon, *Recollections of Abraham Lincoln*, 116–17.

202. For a few random examples, see Aristotle frag. 1 (Ross); Flammarion, *Death and Its Mystery*, 1:312–14; 2:185–97; and Santos and Fenwick, "Death, End of Life Experiences," 175–76.

203. Dusenbury, *I Judge No One*, 55. He makes this point precisely in connection with Jesus's presentiment of his own death.

204. Kripal, *Comparing Religions*, 251. Cf. Dodds, "Supernormal Phenomena," 184 ("a disproportionate number of ancient 'precognitions' seem to concern death or . . . violent accidents, and the same is true today"); Stephenson, "Precognition of Disaster"; and Jawer and Micozzi, *Spiritual Anatomy of Emotion*, 198–231. That stories featuring clairvoyance and prediction recur in stories of gung-ho ascetics who traumatized their bodies and courted death is not, to my mind, simply another hagiographical motif. It rather has its roots in actual experiences. For possibilities from the Christian tradition see Palladius, *Hist. Laus.* 17.3–5; Hist. mon. Aeg. 1.2, 10; 6.1; 8.17–18, 48; 16.1; Apoph. Pat. (Systematic Collection) 18; Syriac Life of Simeon Stylites 38 (trans. Doran, 122); Vivian, Vivian, and Russell, *Life of the Jura Fathers*, 177–78; Benz, *Vision*, 189–207 (multiple examples); Vecoli, *Spirito soffia nel deserto*, 109–41 (Pachomian sources); B. Newman, *Permeable Self*, 59–106 (fourteen men and women from the thirteenth century plus Jean-Marie Vianney and Padre Pio); Moschos, *Spiritual Meadow*, 7; Isaac, *Saint Paisios*, 224, 577–97; and the stories of various Roman Catholic saints in Schamoni, *Wunder sind Tatsachen*, 252–308. Christians often associate such stories with 1 Cor 12:8 (λόγος γνώσεως, "word of knowledge") and 14:24–25 ("the secret of the unbeliever's heart are disclosed").

it was so for Jesus. There is, of course, a large element of conjecture here, but this is the case with every historical reconstruction.

Appealing to Experience

Ernst Troeltsch spoke for a multitude when he argued that, in pursuing "a genuinely modern history," we should always reason from analogy.[205] For him, the present displays a "fundamental homogeneity" with the past: "The key to historical criticism is analogy to what happens before our very eyes and within us." That is, "agreement with normal, customary, or at least frequently attested happenings or conditions as we have experienced them is the hallmark of probability for all the events that historical criticism will adjudge to have actually happened or will allow." For Troeltsch, this precluded, against "the old dogmatic method," positing supernatural intervention to explain any past event, because we do not espy supernatural intervention in any present event. No miracles now, no miracles then. While there are of course many reports of miracles, we should disbelieve them. Present experience and "the omnipotence of analogy" forbid finding in the past what does not occur in the present.[206]

This is a variation on David Hume's old argument against miracles. Hume asserted that "firm and unalterable experience" established the laws of nature, and since miracles break those laws, we should reject all testimony to them.[207] In his words: "The maxim, by which we commonly conduct ourselves in our reasonings, is, that the objects, of which we have no experience, resemble those, of which we have; that what we have found to be most usual is always most probable; and that when there is an opposition of arguments, we ought to give the preference to such as are founded on the greater number of observations."[208]

205. Troeltsch, "Über historische und dogmatische Methode in der Theologie," in *Gesammelte Schriften*, 2:729–53. This and the following quotations are from p. 732.

206. Note also Troeltsch, *Christian Thought*, 15: "The old miracle apologetic . . . has been rendered untenable, not by theories, but by documents, by discoveries, by the results of exploration. The force of such evidence cannot be resisted by anyone whose sense of truth has been educated by philology, or even by anyone possessing an average amount of ordinary 'common sense.'"

207. Hume, *Enquiries*, 114. Hume was not, strictly speaking, arguing that miracles cannot happen but that we do not and cannot have good reason to believe in them.

208. Hume, *Enquiries*, 117. In terms of the genealogy of ideas, Hume is an heir of Protestant cessationism, the view that miracles happened only in biblical times, not later. Hume

The problem with Hume is not his appeal to recurrent human experience, and the problem with Troeltsch is not his emphasis on the fundamental role of analogy in critical historical thinking. In these matters they seem sensible. How can we not navigate the past or reconstruct it without relying on the solid knowledge we have in and of the present?[209] How can we avoid projecting the present onto the past? We cannot but think analogically, from the known to the unknown, or from the better known to the lesser known. As it is now, so was it then, at least with regard to what is possible.

My objection is different. Both Hume and Troeltsch had, in my view, truncated ideas about the present, and this led them to defective ideas about what was possible in the past. They looked around and beheld a humdrum uniformity, a stage without strange incursions or mystifying events. They were sure that our world exhibits a lawful order, and that nothing in it ever rises above the level of today's rational or scientific understanding.

I live in another world, one in which puzzling and inexplicable affairs are not so rare.[210] To my mind, the reductionistic worldview of Troeltsch and like-opinioned others is an illusory construct that has been empirically falsified. It fails to match repeated human experience.[211] I rather agree with Augustine: "That a rational explanation cannot be given for something does not mean that it could not have happened in the past, or that it could not happen in the future, seeing that there are these things in the present that are equally insusceptible of rational explanation" (*Civ.* 21.5.1). The analogous includes the anomalous.

My convictions about this subject mean that, when the sources for Jesus often depict him as seemingly reading thoughts or knowing something from afar or before the fact, my instinctive response is not: That's impossible. It is rather: Well, maybe. Since claims for telepathy, clairvoyance, and foreknowledge exist cross-culturally and cross-temporally,[212] and since some of those claims are, at least in my judgment, credibly attested,[213] we have no reason

---

and the cessationists may not agree about the Bible, but they agree about postbiblical history and the present: there are no miracles. See D. Walker, "Cessation of Miracles."

209. For the issues here see esp. V. A. Harvey, *Historian and Believer*.

210. By "inexplicable" I mean "inexplicable" only in terms of current scientific knowledge. This does not exclude in principle the possibility of a "rational" explanation.

211. Particularly helpful here is Kelly and Kelly et al., *Irreducible Mind*.

212. See Dodds, "Supernormal Phenomena," and Targ, Schlitz, and Irwin, "Psi-Related Experiences," 222–23.

213. Cf. Mayer, *Extraordinary Knowing*; D. H. Powell, *ESP Enigma*, 25–72; and Barušs and Mossbridge, *Transcendent Mind*, 29–52.

to posit that similar claims from the first-century Mediterranean world must be, in every case, bogus. On the contrary: If something happens now, it likely happened then, too.

Whenever we study any text, we inevitably bring our presuppositions and experiences to it, and different experiences and presuppositions naturally lead to different readings. Today we admit the truth of this when we acknowledge the importance, for instance, of feminist hermeneutics. But for me there is also, for want of a better term, a Fortean way of seeing. (Charles Fort spent his time cataloguing reports of anomalous events damned by the science of his day.)[214] This approach recognizes the reality of the metanormal, but it is not theologically driven (although it need not be, as was Fort, antagonistic to theology). It is instead empirically grounded. To borrow from Hume, it is a species of reasoning that derives "from the testimony of men, and the reports of eyewitnesses and spectators."[215] It recognizes that, although numerous astounding claims do not endure critical scrutiny, a fair number, after judicious scrutiny, leave us still scratching our heads.[216]

One may object that I have here surreptitiously changed the subject. Hume and Troeltsch wrote first of miracles in the proper sense of the word—inexplicable events worked directly by God—whereas I am discussing clairvoyance and telepathy, phenomena that, if real, appear to be occasional, cryptic human potentials. But against this objection, the theological tradition has much more often than not construed Jesus's ability to read minds or see things from afar as manifestations of his deity and so as being miracles in the proper sense. I am not changing the subject, just how it is interpreted.

More importantly, the arguments of Hume and Troeltsch are essentially epistemological, not theological. Their subject is human knowledge, not the Supreme Being. They do not directly address the subject of agency. Their judgments are, to take them at their word, founded not in opinions about a divinity but rather inferred from human experience, from "what happens before our very eyes and within us" (so Troeltsch) or from "firm and unalterable experience" (so Hume).[217] It is the same for me and my historical inferences. I am happy to let experience be the arbiter of historical truth. I depart from Hume and Troeltsch only in this, that I have different ideas as to what human expe-

214. For an orientation to Fort, see Kripal, *Authors of the Impossible*, 92–143.

215. Hume, *Enquiries*, 111.

216. For illustrations, see Beloff, "Extreme Phenomena."

217. This is why Hume's arguments have been brought to bear on secular paranormal claims; note, e.g., Flew, "Problem of Evidencing." According to Fales, *Reading Sacred Texts*, 130, Hume's "argument is epistemological, not ontological."

rience discloses and so different ideas as to what counts as truth. Once more, then, I am not changing the subject.

A Luminous Jesus?

So far, I urged that, if clairvoyance, telepathy, and foreknowledge are real phenomena, it is not unreasonable, given the breadth of testimony, to suppose that Jesus may on occasion have known this or that via some yet-unexplained mechanism. The argument is an inference from a family of texts in the Gospels construed in the light of cross-cultural and cross-temporal testimony. But what might one make of a single story that reports something even more extraordinary?

The Synoptics recount that, on one occasion, Jesus was transfigured into light. Mark puts it this way: "And after six days, Jesus took with him Peter and James and John, and he led them up a high mountain apart by themselves; and he was transfigured before them. and his clothes became dazzling white, such as no one on earth could bleach them" (Mark 9:2–3).[218]

The critical literature has any number of explanations for these words. Maybe one of Jesus's disciples hallucinated the scene in a vision and the story grew in the telling. Or maybe someone had a dream that was taken to be revelatory and that became the seed from which everything grew. Or maybe the morning sun rose behind Jesus while he stood on a mountain and his sleepy, credulous followers awakened to behold the sight. Or maybe there was, à la Strauss, no historical basis at all: the episode, designed to make Jesus like or greater than Moses, was spun out of the legend of the lawgiver glowing on Sinai.

These are all rationalizing solutions, the usual suspects that the critical literature lines up for us, after which we get to pick one. But we are not, I submit, compelled to do so.

The reports, from numerous times and places, of people seeing glowing individuals are not at all hard to find. Of course many stories of luminous individuals are, beyond all doubt, legendary,[219] and others may or may not be so: we often have little more than bare claims in sources whose relationship

218. Cf. Matt 17:2 ("and he was transfigured before them, and his face shone like the sun, and his clothes became dazzling white") and Luke 9:29 ("and while he was praying, the appearance of his face changed, and his clothes became dazzling white").

219. E.g., the stories about a radiant Adam (Sir 49:16; LAE Gk. 20:2; Gen. Rab. 11:2; 12:6) or the Israelites at Sinai (LAB 12:7).

to history is opaque.[220] There are, however, numerous firsthand reports of somebody seemingly emitting or apparently surrounded by an inexplicable, unearthly light.[221] Indeed, the alleged phenomenon is "embarrassingly well documented."[222] Here in brief are seven illustrations:

- These are the words of a nun, Ana of the Incarnation, who reported (in a sworn deposition) that, while standing one evening at the cell door of St. Teresa of Ávila, she saw this: "Her face had a very clear light, and glimmers like golden rays emanated from her. It lasted and I saw it for an hour's time. . . . [Then] she lost the radiance, and seemed to be in darkness."[223]
- A certain Father Lemoyne, a Roman Catholic friend of Don Bosco, testified that, in 1888, "a wonderful occasion took place. Don Bosco's face seemed gradually to become radiant until it appeared to be luminously transparent. Startled, I went to the window to see whether there might be a light in the playground which reflected on his face. But there was no light. This happened on three consecutive nights. The refulgence would increase until his face became resplendent with a strong and beautiful light; then it would slowly diminish until it finally disappeared."[224]
- These words recall a man's encounter with Maximilian Kolbe, the Polish Franciscan and victim of Auschwitz, who was canonized in 1982: "He became, as I watched, transfigured in a diaphanous form, almost transparent, and surrounded by a halo of light, all of which lasted as he spoke. . . . I found myself trembling with a sort of fear, filled with confusion—so moved that tears came to my eyes."[225]
- The following report is catalogued in the Religious Experience Research Centre at the University of Wales, Trinity Saint David: "It was early summer

220. E.g., the claims for monks in the Apoph. Pat. (Alphabetical Collection): Arsenius the Great (Arsenius 27), Abba Pambo (Pambo 1, 12), Joseph of Panephysis (Joseph of Panephysis 7), Sisoes (Sisoes 14), and Silvanus (Silvanus 12); and the claims for the Baal Shem Tov in Shivḥei ha-Besht, see Ben-Amos and Mintz, *In Praise of the Baal Shem Tov*, 28, 50, 79, 136, 243.

221. Collections include Thurston, *Physical Phenomena*, 62–70; Schamoni, *Wunder sind Tatsachen*, 235–45; Alvarado, "Observations of Luminous Phenomena"; and Treece, *Sanctified Body*, 61–82. Sometimes reports have no religious context; see Russell, "Parapsychic Luminosities," and Corliss, *Rare Halos*, 82–91.

222. So Treece, *Sanctified Body*, 30.

223. As quoted in Silverio de Santa Teresa, *Obras de Sta. Teresa*, xiii n1. For additional firsthand reports concerning Teresa, see O. Leroy, "Visage resplendissant."

224. Phelan, *Don Bosco*, 336–37.

225. Treece, *Sanctified Body*, 29–30.

and it was cloudy and we all took our seats in the front room of the house. Sister Gemmel spoke to us about her work among the methylated spirit drinkers that she cared for. . . . Gradually as she spoke I became aware of the fact that she was bathed in light. It was as if the sun had come out and a shaft of light was falling on her. It was only when we emerged outside that I realized it was still cloudy. For the first and only time the 4 ladies in the car were silent with wonder on the journey home. I always regret that I did not share my experience with the 3 passengers in the car—perhaps they had seen it too."[226]

- According to the Hieromonk Maximos, the elder of a hermitage on Mount Athos, the Elder Paisios of Mount Athos was transfigured before him in 1977: "When I told him goodbye, [after a vigil] before the break of dawn, I actually saw his face shining with light. He was radiating a white light, like the high-beam headlights of a car in thick fog, except that it didn't blind us. . . . When they [two theologians who had escorted Paisios back to his hermitage] returned, I heard them saying between themselves, 'What was that light?' They asked me, 'Did you see something on Father Paisios?' . . . They told me how they had seen his face luminous and shining with an unusual light, unlike that of the sun, or starlight."[227]
- Three decades ago, a friend of mine sought initiation into an esoteric Sufi order. The process involved having an audience with an Iranian Sheikh who was then touring the United States. My friend and his teacher met in a small hotel room in New Mexico for a short period of time. They sat face-to-face in lotus position, the teacher on a small sheepskin rug, fingering his prayer beads. Neither spoke. The occasion became, however, more than memorable for my friend, for he claims that, after a bit, the Sufi master began to emit a light. That light became brighter and brighter until it lit up the entire room and my friend had to look away. After that, the luminescence faded away and the fifteen-minute encounter was over, leaving the startled observer to interpret what had happened.
- In January 2019, a member of my immediate family and three others had an audience with the late Vajrayana master Khenpo Karthar Rinpoche, a Tibetan holy man. Here, from an email to me, are his words: "The four of us sat down in front of him, and he poured us tea. As he did so, I discerned a soft white light radiating from him—like a halo around his seated figure.

226. Fox, *Spiritual Encounters*, 117.

227. Isaac, *Saint Paisios*, 616–17. Additional accounts of Paisios glowing by additional witnesses are quoted on pp. 617–21.

> And the longer I looked, the brighter the glow seemed. At first I thought it was some strange effect of the light coming through the window next to him where snow was sparkling as it fell. But within a few minutes more, I had no doubt: this man was actually glowing. And the glow only became clearer as the afternoon light turned to dusk. After our audience, during which Rinpoche answered our questions and gave teachings through a Tibetan translator, all four of us left in a state of wonderment and joy. We confirmed with each other: we had all seen his body glowing."

Now I am not naïve. I have no illusion that quoting such naked testimony amounts to argument. Many, without willful mendacity, have persuaded themselves that they have seen things with no better foundation than their own imagination or the will to believe. The countless sightings of Bigfoot do not exorcise my doubt. Testimony, including testimony to radiant figures, can do no more than inaugurate a discussion, which I cannot enter here. All I can do is share my conviction that study of the copious materials has left me with an open mind, and indeed (to be honest) inclined to think it more likely than not that, on occasion, and whatever the cause, some human beings have appeared anomalously radiant.

Having come to this conclusion—not via theological or apologetical reasoning but on the ground of repeated firsthand testimony—I think we should add to the usual explanations for the story of the transfiguration this possibility: an unusual historical event—a vision of a radiant Jesus—lies behind our accounts, an event that was subsequently narrated in such a way as to highlight the parallels with Moses on Sinai.[228] I unfortunately see no way to push this proposal over the line dividing the possible from the probable—although the same is true of its reductionistic rivals. The proportion of history to fiction in our story, as in so many episodes in the canonical Gospels, is beyond my ability to measure. I am convinced, however, that my proposal merits more than curt dismissal.

Craig Keener and Wilhelm Schamoni

My approach to the Gospels has partial precedent not only in the work of Strauss and Otto. Evangelical biblical scholar Craig Keener has produced two large volumes entitled *Miracles*. His subtitle is *The Credibility of the New Tes-*

228. On these parallels, which Strauss rightly highlighted, see Allison, *New Moses*, 243–48.

tament Accounts.[229] These volumes are very wide ranging. They introduce and discuss a host of topics: miracles in antiquity and Christian history; Hume's case against miracles; miracle stories from contemporary Asia, Africa, Latin America, and the Caribbean; recent reports of the supernatural in the Western world; proposed explanations for extraordinary claims; demons and exorcisms in antiquity; and spirit possession and exorcism today.

Keener has two main goals. The first is to show that miracle stories are not always second- or third- or fourthhand friend-of-a-friend tales. Frequently they come directly from eyewitnesses.[230] In this Keener is one hundred percent correct. Knowledge of the facts leaves no room for argument. His second aim is to dispute the "inflexibly antisupernaturalist paradigm," to establish that some firsthand accounts invite what he calls "supernatural" or "superhuman" explanations.[231] That is obviously a far more difficult task.[232]

Keener's volumes grew out of his earlier book on the historical Jesus.[233] He indeed regards *Miracles* as a companion or sequel.[234] In the earlier work he was unable, he tells us, to respond adequately to the charge that the large number of miracle stories in the canonical Gospels proves them to be more fiction than fact. *Miracles* is the counter to this. It argues by means of analogy: "The kinds of miracle claims most frequently attested in the Gospels . . . are also attested by many eyewitnesses today."[235] Keener collects a host of firsthand accounts that feature the blind being healed, the lame walking, the dead being raised, groups being fed with scant rations, and prayers calming storms. His aim is to use "analogies from human experience" to reduce incredulity toward what we find in the Gospels.[236] The upshot is that we need not "treat the miracles [in the Gospels] differently than, that is, less authentic than, the rest of the narratives in which they occur."[237]

Another partial parallel for my strategy is a 1979 book by the popular German author and Roman Catholic Wilhelm Schamoni. The title is *Wunder sind*

229. Keener, *Miracles*. See also his shorter volume, *Miracles Today*.

230. Cf. Keener, *Miracles*, 2:764: miracle reports "can belong even to the eyewitness level . . . and need not be attributed to a long process of oral development." See also Keener's *Christobiography*, 331–45.

231. Keener, *Miracles*, 1:10.

232. For doubt that he has succeeded here see Kahl, "Jesus als Wundertäter," 179–80.

233. Keener, *Historical Jesus*.

234. Keener, *Miracles*, 1:5.

235. Keener, *Miracles*, 1:7.

236. The quoted words appear in Keener, *Miracles*, 1:15.

237. Keener, *Miracles*, 1:16.

Tatsachen ("Miracles Are Facts"). An earlier edition appeared as *Parallelen zum Neuen Testament aus Heiligsprechungsakten übersetz* ("Parallels to the New Testament Translated from the Acts of Canonization"). The volume is overtly theological and apologetical. The main argument is this. God worked signs through Jesus, doing things only God could do, in order to help hearers to believe in him. After Jesus departed, the same thing happened with the apostles: God accredited their mission through signs and wonders. And ever since the apostolic age, God has continued to be active, validating the lives and teaching of the saints through miracles.

In order to show this, Schamoni appeals to Catholic records of canonization, summarizing and quoting firsthand, sworn testimony to countless miracles.[238] He knows full well that, in our secular age, miracles are passé for many. He also knows that modern doubt steers much modern study of the Gospels. But he is confident that, if one gives a fair hearing to independent affidavits received under oath, the truth is plain: miracles are public facts. And this in turn "throws new light on the gospel reports."[239] That is, the later stories add credibility to the earlier stories: "The reader who feels disturbed by so much corrosive criticism of the gospel miracles, in which strangely enough the theologians today can participate, . . . will observe the astonishing similarity between the succinct reports in the Gospels and that which is so abundantly documented in the acts of canonization."[240] "In the acts of canonization, one can find parallels, almost without exception, to every marvelous deed in the New Testament, and that mostly in abundance."[241]

238. The names of his chapters are mostly quotations from the Gospels: "the blind see" (Matt 11:5), "those who cannot walk walk" (11:5), "lepers are cleansed" (11:5), "those who cannot speak speak, those who cannot hear hear" (Mark 7:37), "the dead are raised" (Matt 11:5), "the fever left her" (Mark 1:31), a man who had a withered hand (3:1), "there was a man who had dropsy" (Luke 14:2), "he healed every disease and every infirmity" (Matt 9:35), "five loaves and two fishes" (Mark 6:38), "at your words I will throw out the nets" (Luke 5:5), "his face shown as the sun" (Matt 17:2), "there appeared to them Elijah with Moses" (Mark 9:4), "truly the prophet, who is to come into the world" (John 6:14), "he knew what was in people" (2:25).

239. Schamoni, *Wunder sind Tatsachen*, xv.

240. Schamoni, *Wunder sind Tatsachen*, xix.

241. Schamoni, *Wunder sind Tatsachen*, xxii. Cf. 344, with reference to the miraculous travel of Philip in Acts 8:39–40: "Since bilocation is not a rare phenomenon in the lives of the saints, one can ask whether what is reported about the 'deacon' Philip in Acts 8:26 and 8:39f. is not best understood in this context." Although one may object that 8:39–40 is ostensibly about transvection or teleportation, not bilocation, the general point is clear: parallels strengthen plausibility.

Now I am not, unlike Schamoni, a Roman Catholic apologist, and I am not, unlike Keener, a conservative evangelical. Moreover, I am less sanguine than they about how much history the Gospels preserve. I nonetheless regard their collections of materials as highly instructive, and I believe they are right to call attention to the similarities between the stories in the Gospels and the firsthand testimonies from later times and different places. The parallels merit exploration. We should compare like with like.

Provisos

I do, however, wish to distinguish my approach from theirs in four ways. First, Schamoni draws exclusively from stories of Roman Catholic saints, and Keener's testimonies come mostly from contemporary Christians.[242] If, however, we are to conduct ourselves as historians, we should seek to gather parallels from as many sources as possible. That will take us into the territory of other religions and beyond.[243] The ostensibly inexplicable is not the exclusive property of Christians. Claims about clairvoyance and telepathy, for example, are everywhere, and it is not only Christian saints who purportedly glow. If Schamoni finds parallels to the Gospels in the acts of canonization, and if Keener finds them in Christian reports from our age, one can equally find them, and in abundance, in narratives—not all of them self-evidently late or legendary—about Tibetan karmapas, Sufi masters, Hindu gurus, and individuals without religious affiliation. Our study, then, should have no boundaries. We should cast our nets wherever the out-of-the-ordinary can be caught.

Second, Schamoni believes that God worked the events he summarizes. Keener similarly thinks that God or "supernatural agents" are the best explanations for many of the stories he recounts. One can, however, embrace their analogical, historical reasoning without subscribing to any particular theological program. This follows from the fact that the same sorts of stories appear within different religious traditions, which interpret them in diverse ways. The events, in other words, are not self-interpreting.[244]

242. Unlike Schamoni, Keener does not altogether ignore claims outside Christian circles; see *Miracles* 1:242–49. He indeed contends that some of them "could be used to challenge Western Enlightenment skepticism about extranormal events."

243. Here I agree with Crossan, *Birth of Christianity*, 303–4: "It is not ethical for an *historian* to give special protection and privilege to Christian miracles." Yet it certainly happens. For me this is the Achilles' heel of some Christian apologetics: skepticism toward every miracle not their own.

244. See further Kripal, *Comparing Religions*, 226–35.

If, to illustrate, we decide that, now and then, a human being appears to shine, and further that the explanation is not always hallucination or a trick of optical diffraction, should we think of the work of the Holy Spirit, a rare species of bioluminescence, a cryptic human potential, a manifestation of what the Tibetans call the rainbow body, or something else? Or might it be prudent to confess that the explanation escapes us, at least for now? There is no compulsory connection between the metanormal and any single theology.[245] If a Hindu were to levitate, that would not prove the truth of that Hindu's theology, and if Jesus sometimes saw the future, that does not establish the reality of the God of Israel.

It is useful in this connection to invoke the old theological distinction between a miracle and a wonder. The former is an inexplicable event occasioned by God (the supernatural). The latter is an inexplicable event occasioned by some unknown cause or cryptic agent (the preternatural).[246] To call something a miracle is to stake a claim about the agent. To dub something a wonder or marvel is to acknowledge the reality of a circumstance without attributing it directly to God or perhaps any agent or offering any explanation at all.[247]

For me, there are many wonders or, as Harnack puts it, "of the marvelous and the inexplicable there is plenty."[248] Miracles in the proper sense are an-

245. Cf. the various explanations for the famous miracle of the rain that saved Roman troops in 172 CE: it was Jupiter; it was the Christian God answering the prayers of Christian soldiers; it was Hermas at the instigation of an Egyptian magos; or it was Julian the Chaldean Theurgis through some secret wisdom. See Fowden, "Pagan Versions."

246. See Ward, *Miracles and the Medieval Mind*, 3–32, and Bartlett, *Natural and the Supernatural*, 1–33. In some writers, wonders or preternatural events include the works of Satan or demons who (unlike God) work exclusively through secondary causes; cf. Aquinas, *Summa contra Gentiles* book 3, part 2, chs. 101–3.

247. Cf. the distinction in Spinoza, *Theologico-Political Treatise*, 85: "miracle" can be "interpreted in two senses: either as that which has natural causes, but cannot be examined by the human intellect; or as that which has no cause save God and God's will." There is a hard problem here. What we think we know of the natural order cannot, as Augustine, *Civ.* 21.8, observes, be identified with the natural order as such, which implies that we may not know enough to distinguish between what is nature and what, if anything, might be beyond nature. Cf. G. F. Woods, "Evidential Value," 24 ("we do not know enough about the limits of the natural order either to deny the possibility of miracles or to identify one if it takes place"), and Crossan, *Birth of Christianity*, 303–4. One's understanding of "miracle" depends on one's understanding of "nature"; and any identification of a "miracle" involves deciding what is impossible for human beings, a subject on which there is no agreement. Is levitation, if it occurs, a rarely exhibited human ability, or does it require a special act of God, who alone can do the trick? The same may be asked of the spontaneous remission of severe maladies and much else. Rahner, *Visions and Prophecies*, 92–94, attributes many prophecies and instances of clairvoyance to "natural faculties." One recalls here Augustine's perplexity over some cases of clairvoyance and prophecy known to him; see *Gen. litt.* 12.17–18.

248. Harnack, *What Is Christianity?*, 28.

other story. Identifying an unseen agent, whether God or some other, is, in my judgment, a near-Herculean task. One can of course produce explanations by slotting events into one's religious tradition, and I hardly oppose such attempts. Indeed, I offer a few theological musings below (pp. 208–10). Yet for me that move takes one beyond the realm of the historian. It instead seems prudent, when I am fashioning public arguments, to acknowledge the reality of certain offbeat phenomena while leaving their explanations truly open. And I see no reason why someone who does not share my religious convictions, including an atheist, cannot join me in this.

One can have a gap without a god of the gap. A fact and its explanation are not the same thing. One can acknowledge a circumstance while not knowing its cause. Moreover, that some inexplicable things have, in the course of human history, attracted religious interpretations, or been used to authenticate religious ideas or figures, scarcely requires that they must do so, that they cannot receive other interpretations or be used in other ways or indeed be awarded no interpretation at all. Although Jacalyn Duffin, the well-known medical historian, candidly acknowledges that some healings in the Catholic records of canonization are startling and without current explanation, she remains an atheist. It causes her no anxiety to join "that really happened" with "I cannot explain it."[249]

We can have an empiricism of high strangeness that, for historical purposes, brackets religious assessments and ontological politics. So-called miracles are in and of themselves equivocal. To think otherwise is to fail to see that only a worldview collapses their indeterminacy and gives them meaning, thus domesticating the inexplicable within a system of belief.[250]

249. Cf. Duffin, *Medical Saints*, 175–77. The metanormal is so often construed in exclusively religious terms because, among other reasons, (1) certain metanormal phenomena are abetted by severe asceticism, and that has been primarily the province of religious adepts, and (2) many have reflexively attributed the inexplicable to God, gods, angels, or demons.

250. Much of the problem here is that Christian apologists have long employed biblical miracles to authenticate doctrine. One recalls, e.g., John Locke's "A Discourse on Miracles" (1706), and Joseph Butler's *Analogy of Religion* (1736), 208–19. But to make the argument work, one has to deny miracles to outsiders. This explains Locke's words: miracles are "the basis on which divine mission is always established, and consequently that foundation on which the believers of any divine revelation must ultimately bottom their faith"; yet "what the Persees say of their Zoroaster, or the Indians of their Brama (not to mention all the wild stories of the religions further east) is so obscure, or so manifestly fabulous, that no account can be made of it"; see Locke, *Reasonableness of Christianity*, 86 and 81 respectively. Cf., from a Roman Catholic point of view, Lessius, *Consultation* (1621), 36–37 ("That Religion, in which very many miracles have byn wrought throughout all ages, is to be preferred before those which be destitute of miracles.

My third qualification has to do with the limits of my strategy when it comes to Jesus and the Gospels. The analogies that Keener and Schamoni compile teach us—no matter what worldview we inhabit—that the stories in the Gospels *could* derive from people who observed Jesus. People do, as a matter of fact, perceive what they think are miracles, whether they are right or not. In addition, the more puzzling accounts enhance, in my opinion, the possibility that at least some of the parallel events in the Gospels would, if we knew more about them, still stump us.

I do not, however, see how to pass beyond that. For example, that some carefully examined modern healings defy conventional explanation does not entail that the same holds for all, most, or some of the healing stories in the Gospels. Parallels cannot establish historicity, only open possibilities. Fabrication, exaggeration, and naïveté we always have with us, and historians cannot do everything. The frustrating and humbling truth is that often all we can do is assemble the possibilities and move on.

The Nature Miracles

My final caveat has to do specifically with the so-called nature miracles. The Gospels purport that Jesus turned water into wine (John 2:1–11), calmed the sea (Mark 4:35–41), fed thousands with a few scraps (6:30–44), walked on the water (6:45–52), made a fig tree wither with a word (11:12–20), and so on. Such stories are, for me, far more difficult to credit than metanormal knowledge. This is in part because the reports are of singular events. I have much more confidence in themes and motifs that are characteristic because they recur in multiple forms and across sources. The less data we have to work with, the less robust our conclusions. Furthermore, neither Jesus's sayings nor the evangelists' summaries of his activities refer to the nature miracles.

For that miracles are as it were certayne diuine seales and Testifmonyes, whereby Religion is confirmed. . . . But only Catholic Religion doth shine with true miracles, and therefore is it the true Religion, and to be preferred before all other Religions, as having testimony thereof only from God") and 46 ("We neuer read that dead were raysed to life by heretikes, the blind made to see, the lame straightened, the palsy cured, Diuells cast out of men. Such miracles as these were never wrought by Luther, Calvin, or any of their followers"); and Monden, *Signs and Wonders*, 251–321 ("the Roman Catholic Church . . . does have a practical monopoly on what we have called 'major miracle'"). Note also the link between miracle and accreditation in Hume, *Enquiries*, 127: "No human testimony can have such force as to prove a miracle, and make it a just foundation for any such religion." On this topic, see further Daston, "Marvelous Facts."

I am, however, in a tight spot here. Once one lets in a couple of monsters, others crowd at the door, baying to enter also. Schamoni can cite firsthand accounts from canonization records of the multiplication of food,[251] and Keener can quote contemporary accounts of people walking on water.[252] So how open-minded should we be? How absurd is this theater in which we live?

I do not have the answer. My mammalian mind remains bewildered about much. Nonetheless, my tendency is to appeal to quantity. Firsthand testimonies to walking on the water are not abundant. There are more accounts of food inexplicably proliferating, but not that many. By comparison, accounts of glowing people are numerous. (I have heard two reports from people I know.) And reports of clairvoyance and telepathy dwarf all of them put together: they are a dime a dozen.[253]

Now the different quantities of testimony do not enable me to draw a firm line between what sometimes really happens and what never does. Yet they help orient my thinking.[254] The larger the pile, the better the odds that some items reflect more than coincidence, credulity, or edifying invention; and the more common I judge a phenomenon to be, the more likely I am to be open-minded when it appears in stories about Jesus. Some impossible things are, if I may so put, less impossible than others. In principle I here agree with Hume: "Suppose . . . the fact, which the testimony endeavours to establish, partakes of the extraordinary and the marvelous; in that case, the evidence, resulting from the testimony, admits of a diminution, greater or less, in proportion as the fact is more or less unusual."[255]

Summary: Comparing Like with Like

When it comes to some of the "surprising feats" (παραδόξων ἔργων, Josephus, *Ant.* 18.63) credited to Jesus, historians are not, I have urged, stuck with

251. Schamoni, *Wunder sind Tatsachen*, 206–28. Cf. Thurston, *Physical Phenomena*, 385–95.

252. Keener, *Miracles Today*, 182–84.

253. Twelftree, "Miraculous in the New Testament," 331, observes: "While Keener is able to furnish a great number of healing stories of various kinds, he offers far fewer stories that could be taken as analogous to the nature miracles in the Gospels."

254. Cf. McComb, *Christianity and the Modern Mind*, 135–36: most of the miracles in Mark are "miracles of healing, mental and physical. These deeds of mercy are . . . the most characteristic of Christ and the most frequent in His career. They are, at the same time, most in accord with well-known analogies in modern experience."

255. Hume, *Enquiries*, 113.

choosing between traditional supernaturalism, with its consistent appeal to divine intervention, and rationalistic explanations, which shoehorn everything inside the borders of today's reductionism. We may instead think, apart from whatever religious convictions we may or may not hold, that history includes circumstances, some mind-boggling, beyond current understanding.

We should, moreover, seek to do justice to the countless parallels to the Gospel materials, parallels that sometimes have no religious sense or context. This should move us to construct analogies, to classify like with like, and to evaluate the weakly attested in the light of the more strongly attested. When we do this, the traditions about Jesus display patterns familiar to students of the so-called paranormal and the history of religion; and if one believes that those patterns are not unrelated to authentic human experience, then some of the Gospel accounts may be likewise so rooted.[256] Even if, as no doubt happened, some of the miracle stories about Jesus grew out of misperception or misinterpretation, and even if some were invented out of whole cloth for this or that theological, literary, or entertaining end, we nonetheless have reason to infer that, at least on occasion, he exhibited certain out-of-the-ordinary abilities: with him, the extraordinary sometimes occurred.

Having settled on this conclusion, I am under no illusion that the reasons I have marshaled for it will breach anyone's conceptual fortress. Some readers will, à la Hume, regard my suggestions as beyond the academic pale. They will confidently assert that learning and good judgment, which I have abandoned, preclude metanormal incursions. Others, steered by theological motives, will disclaim the proposal that many of Jesus's remarkable deeds are quite like the remarkable deeds of others, and that they do not in and of themselves necessitate a Christian interpretation.[257] I hope, however, that at least a few will assess my arguments without a firm predisposition to believe or hope me wrong.

256. Cf. Sprigge, "Could Parapsychology?," 135: "If many of the miracles reported" of founders of religions "could be interpreted as, so to speak, standard paranormal phenomena, that might make us more inclined to accept the records of lives as substantially true rather than as mere myths."

257. Contrast van der Loos, *Miracles of Jesus*, 203: "Jesus' special knowledge must not be interpreted as an accidental human gift, as extrasensory perception, but as forming part of the essence of the man Jesus as the Son of God."

EXCURSUS

THEOLOGICAL MUSINGS

To this point my argument has been historical, not theological. I have nowhere appealed to God in arguing that Jesus likely did some things beyond ordinary expectation and current understanding. Nonetheless, making the historical case with theology out of the picture does not mean that theology must remain forever out of the picture, that it cannot, once the case is made, add its own reflections.

Gerd Theissen and Annette Merz, after coming to the historical conclusion that Jesus was a successful healer and exorcist, revert to theological language. One can, according to them, interpret Jesus's miracles, or at least some of them,

> in terms of the theology of creation, which is neither supernaturalistic [n]or naturalistic: the charisma to perform miracles is a power which emerges spontaneously and which is present in the creation. . . . Here leeway seems to open up in "nature" which is not determined by natural laws in the usual sense. Such a miraculous charisma appears among many people. . . . Because it appears spontaneously . . . it is natural to interpret it in religious terms. Jesus had such "paranormal" gifts to an extraordinary degree.[1]

These words, while undeveloped and indeed a bit cryptic, are nonetheless suggestive. They seem to say that, if any of Jesus's acts were genuinely metanormal, they were nonetheless possibilities inherent in creation, possibilities that have been realized in other human beings, possibilities that are often understood in religious terms since they are beyond ordinary beck and call.

This proposal makes sense of the circumstance that others, both within and without the Scriptural pages, have reportedly performed extraordinary deeds. It certainly makes more sense than the notion that Jesus's miracles somehow establish his divinity.[2] Indeed, if we compare Jesus with

1. Theissen and Merz, *Historical Jesus*, 312.

2. Note Melito of Sardis frag. 7 ("the deeds Christ performed after his baptism, especially his miracles, conclusively prove to the world that beneath his flesh was hidden the divinity"), and Liddon, *Divinity of Our Lord*, 160 (Jesus's miracles "force"

Moses, one might hazard that the latter has the upper hand when it comes to the spectacularly inexplicable. Moses, to be sure, nowhere raises the dead (although in 1–2 Kings both Elijah and Elisha do so). The Bible, however, does depict the lawgiver commanding plagues and parting the Red Sea. These flabbergasting feats outdo almost everything Jesus does in the New Testament. Yet Christians have not been moved to deify Moses.

Nor do we fret that, while Jesus was a wise and remarkable teacher, other human beings have been wise and remarkable teachers. Nor are we bothered that, while Jesus was a prophet, prophetic gifts are not his exclusive property. We should be equally untroubled by the thought that, in general, Jesus's metanormal abilities do not make him one of a kind, that they rather make him—to quote Karl Barth—only "relatively extraordinary."[3] Perhaps John 14:12 is to the point: "The one who believes in me will do the works that I do and will do greater works than these." These words concede that Jesus is not, with regard to signs and wonders, the sole member of his species.

This take on things lines up with the Christology of Sergius Bulgakov, the Russian Orthodox theologian.[4] The popular notion that Jesus's divine nature worked miracles is, for him, a heresy. It is a form of Eutychianism. It entails, he thinks, that Christ's divine nature dissolved his human nature. Rejecting this, Bulgakov proposes that Jesus's miracles were the product of a humanity brought to its telos by the divine nature. Miracles "must be judged to be natural, not supernatural and especially not unnatural"; they are "powers and possibilities of the world."[5] "Christ is the

---

the "conviction of the Divinity of the worker"). Much more sensible is Woolston, *Discourse on the Miracles*, 12: "The Power of doing Miracles is no certain, nor rational Seal of the Commission and Authority of a divine Lawgiver." Arguing from Scripture, he appeals to Pharaoh's magicians; Matt 7:21–23 (those who prophesy and cast out demons yet flunk the final judgment); 2 Thess 2:9 (the signs and wonders of "the lawless one"); and additional texts in which God is not the agent of a marvelous deed.

3. The phrase is from Barth, *Church Dogmatics*, 4.2:213. But after acknowledging that "extraordinary" and "extremely strange" things are well attested, Barth effectively nullifies the point for theology: "'The credibility we may create for them [the acts of Jesus] by means of this interpretation has nothing whatsoever to do with the faith which the New Testament means to demand and waken when it recounts them."

4. For what follows see Bulgakov, *Relics and Miracles*, 45–103.

5. Bulgakov, *Relics and Miracles*, 52. For related sentiments see Newnham, *Alresford*, 157 ("Jesus of Nazareth worked miracles in virtue of His perfect humanity, and not in virtue of His Godhead"); Tyndale, *Fragments of Science*, 31–32 ("What

Son of Man, and his acts—and in particular his miracles—are human works."[6] In other words, the miraculous powers that remain latent in humanity, or are manifested in most of us only rarely, appear in greater measure in Christ because his humanity, via the incarnation, recovered and manifested its true nature. Christ's "miracles were worked humanly, through the disclosure and actualization of human possibilities."[7] "They do not surpass the measure of man in his original state and calling."[8] Put mythologically, Jesus worked so many wonders because, as the second Adam, he recovered the miraculous potential that human beings had before the fall.

All this is, I freely grant, highly speculative, and I do not argue for its truth. I introduce Bulgakov's point of view only because (1) it shows that my approach to Jesus's miracles need not land one in a theological dead end and (2) it has the virtue of provoking thought.

---

is the . . . logical ground for concluding that the miracles of the New Testament illustrate Divine Power? May they not be the result of expanded human power?"; Jesus, "it may be contended, antedated the humanity of the future; as a mighty tidal wave leaves high upon the beach a mark which by-and-by becomes the general level of the ocean"); Otto, *Life and Ministry of Jesus*, 33 ("perhaps Christ's gift of healing which seems so mysterious to us, was 'only' a development of capabilities slumbering in human nature in general"); and Henriksen and Sandnes, *Jesus as Healer*, esp. 211–53; cf. p. 5: "Contemporary christological reflection cannot and . . . should not immediately assume that it can attribute everything that is not easy to explain in Jesus' ministry to his divine nature, which traditional dogmatic Christology has seen as conjoined with the human person Jesus of Nazareth" (italics deleted). Note also Athanasius, *Vit. Ant.* 34: "If we ever have a desire to foresee the future, let us be pure in mind. For I believe that when a soul is perfectly pure and established in its natural state [κατὰ φύσιν ἑστῶσα], it is able, being clear-sighted, to see more and further than the demons."

6. Bulgakov, *Relics and Miracles*, 58.

7. Bulgakov, *Relics and Miracles*, 62.

8. Bulgakov, *Relics and Miracles*, 80. Cf. the speculation of Van Inwagen, *Problem of Evil*, 85: the first human beings "possessed what theologians used to call preternatural powers—something like what people who believe in them today call 'paranormal abilities.'"

4

Behaving

Women with Men with Jesus

Where women are not mentioned explicitly, they should nevertheless be *imagined* as present.

—Jane Dewar Schaberg[1]

The one wishing to gain a realistic picture of the significance of women in Jesus' ministry must not remain confined to the surface of the text.

—Hildegard Gollinger[2]

Both Jesus and the evangelists are often silent just where we would like to know more.

—Gerd Theissen[3]

Were there, among Jesus's admirers, women who followed him from place to place and overnighted with him? Most who have addressed this question of late believe there were. Some indeed label the women who kept up

1. Schaberg, *Death and Resurrection*, 56.
2. Gollinger, "Frauen auf der Suche nach Jesus," 337.
3. Theissen, "Peril of Modernising," 274.

with Jesus "disciples,"[4] even though the canonical Gospels reserve the honorific μαθητής—it occurs over 230 times in the canonical Gospels—for men.[5]

Not all, however, are so persuaded. Most prominent among the contrary voices is A.-J. Levine, who has vigorously dissented from the standard line.[6] Her view is that critical scholarship has not made a compelling case for female itinerants before Easter. We cannot, in her judgment, be confident that some of the women who supported Jesus were ever away from home for days at a time or overnighting with him.

Levine has persuaded me that the evidence for the standard position is less robust than widely imagined. She has not, however, quite won me to her side. Although I do not have the confidence I once had, I still think it more likely than not that there were at least some female itinerants. The first part of this chapter explains why. After that, I will offer some suggestions as to how awareness of women in Jesus's mobile circle might affect interpretation of several Synoptic texts.

I begin, however, neither with Levine's work nor with my proposals but rather with John Meier's discussion of our subject. I do this not only because he speaks for so many but because Levine has recently unfolded her arguments by directly countering his case.

Meier's Work

Meier opens his discussion[7] of our subject by arguing that Jesus had disciples, that is, dedicated adherents who (1) were summoned at his initiative, (2) left their families, homes, and livelihoods, and thereby (3) risked danger and hostility.[8] Inquiring whether these dedicated peripatetics included women, he first considers three passages in Mark and their parallels in Matthew and Luke:

4. So, e.g., Schürmann, *Lukasevangelium*, 1:446–47; Fander, *Stellung der Frau*, 320–22; Aynard, *Bible au féminin*, 204–10; Schüssler Fiorenza, *In Memory of Her*; Ricci, *Mary Magdalene*; Melzer-Keller, *Jesus und die Frauen*, 331–39; Gollinger, "Frauen auf der Suche nach Jesus," 345; Pagola, *Jesus*, 224–27; Casey, *Jesus of Nazareth*, 195–96; Puig i Tàrrech, *Jesus*, 247–52; Ravin-Anderson, "They Had Followed Him"; C. Zimmermann, "Women in Jesus' Entourage," 325; and Carey, *Women Who Do*. For early Christian sources that designate some of the women around Jesus as "disciples" see n. 139 below.

5. I am indebted to A.-J. Levine for her critical comments on this chapter and on an ancient precursor of it.

6. Levine, "Second Temple Judaism"; Levine, "Women Itinerants"; and Levine, "Women's Itineracy."

7. For what follows see esp. Meier, *Marginal Jew*, 3:73–80.

8. In this connection he appeals primarily to Mark 8:34–35; 10:28–30; Matt 10:34–39 // Luke 12:51–53; 14:26–27; 17:33 (Q); and John 12:25.

- Mark 15:40–41 (the crucifixion): "There were also women looking on from a distance; among them were Mary Magdalene, and Mary the mother of James the younger and of Joses, and Salome. These used to follow him and provided for him when he was in Galilee; and there were many other women who had come up with him to Jerusalem" (cf. Matt 27:55–56; Luke 23:49).
- Mark 15:47 (the burial): "Mary Magdalene and Mary the mother of Joses saw where the body was laid" (cf. Matt 27:61; Luke 23:55–56).
- Mark 16:1–8 (the empty tomb): "When the Sabbath was over, Mary Magdalene, and Mary the mother of James, and Salome bought spices, so that they might go and anoint him" (cf. Matt 28:1–8; Luke 24:1–12).

According to these sentences, several women who witnessed Jesus's crucifixion and burial had earlier followed him in Galilee: ἐν τῇ Γαλιλαίᾳ ἠκολούθουν αὐτῷ (Mark 15:41). Meier finds it "surprising" that these individuals "appear so suddenly in Mark's Gospel, without any real preparation in the previous narrative (contrast Luke 8:1–3)."[9] This enhances the odds, he insists, that Mark here retains genuine memory. So too the circumstance that John's Gospel, which Meier takes to be independent of the Synoptics, also places women at the crucifixion (19:25) and has Mary the Magdalene at the empty tomb (20:1–18). This fulfills, for Meier, the criterion of multiple attestation.

Meier next turns to Luke 8:1–3. This uniquely Lukan passage offers details about some of the women who traveled with Jesus, among them Mary the Magdalene, who had been cured of evil spirits (cf. Ps.-Mark 16:9). Appealing to the criteria of embarrassment, Meier contends that Jesus, as a matter of historical fact, exorcised demons from Mary,[10] and further that, while the vocabulary in 8:1–3 is redactional, the content is traditional and independent of Mark. In addition,

9. Meier, *Marginal Jew*, 3:75.

10. Meier here refers to his earlier comments in *Marginal Jew*, 2:657–59: "It seems unlikely that the early Christian tradition would have gone out of its way to cast doubt on the reliability of such a pivotal figure"—Mary witnesses Jesus's crucifixion, burial, and the empty tomb—"by recasting her—for no apparent reason—as a former demoniac. What purpose would have been served by such an invention? The vulnerability of a female witness who was a former demoniac was not lost on male critics of the Gospels, from Celsus in the 2d century to Ernest Renan in the 19th." He also argues from coherence: "An exorcism by Jesus, freeing Magdalene from a severe disorder, would explain perfectly her intense dedication to him, even to the point of following him to his crucifixion, death, and entombment." Contrast R. M. Price, "Mary Magdalene," 73–74. For Price, the claim that Mary was a former demoniac was the product of "orthodox polemic"; it derived from opponents who denied her apostleship. Cf. Lupieri, "Earliest Magdalene," 14 n. 13: the "slander" in Luke 8:2 may reflect the evangelist's "desire to downplay the figure and the role of the Magdalene."

> granted Luke's desire to present Christianity as a "respectable" religion that does not threaten the Roman order, it hardly seems likely that he [Luke] would have created the potentially shocking picture of women, some married, traveling around Galilee with Jesus and his twelve male disciples without benefit of husbands. Nor is it likely that the picture in 8:1–3 was created by Luke simply to have a parallel in his Gospel to the various women in Acts who act as patrons or hostesses for apostles and missionaries. In Acts, Luke . . . does not shock the reader's sensibilities by portraying unchaperoned women traveling around with Peter or Paul.[11]

As it is further the case that the picture of "unchaperoned women sharing the preaching tours of a celibate male teacher is discontinuous with both the Judaism of the time and with what Luke presents—and with what we know—of the first-generation of Christian mission," it follows that "certain devoted women followers accompanied Jesus on his journeys around Galilee and finally up to Jerusalem and actually supported him and his entourage with their own money, food, or property."[12] Meier concurs with those who hold that we may fittingly refer to the women who followed Jesus as "disciples."

Having come to this judgment, Meier must confront the question: Why then are the women in the canonical Gospels never called "disciples"?[13] He forwards two possibilities. One is that the evangelists shied from dubbing any woman such because they had, through chance or androcentric bias, no stories in which Jesus calls a woman to follow him, nothing like Mark 1:16–20 (the callings of Peter, Andrew, James, and John) or 2:15 (the calling of Levi). The term, for them, required such a story. The other possibility is that Jesus's native language stood in the way. The Hebrew and Aramaic words for "disciple"—תלמיד and תלמידא respectively—had only masculine forms, so even if Jesus had loyal female followers, there was no noun to indicate the fact.

Following defense of his major conclusion, Meier goes on to underline that "the sight of a group of women—apparently, at least in some cases, without benefit of husbands accompanying them—traveling around the Galilean countryside with an unmarried male who exorcised, healed, and taught them as he taught his male disciples could not help but raise pious eyebrows and provoke impious comments." Again: "A traveling entourage of husbandless female supporters, some of whom were former demoniacs who were now

11. Meier, *Marginal Jew*, 3:76.
12. Meier, *Marginal Jew*, 3:76.
13. For what follows see Meier, *Marginal Jew*, 3:76–79.

giving Jesus money or food, would only have heightened the suspicion and scandal Jesus already faced in a traditional peasant society."[14]

Levine's Response

Levine is unpersuaded. On her view, "the evidence for women's participation in an itinerant system is," when critically scrutinized, "at best *non liquet*." In fact, "it seems more likely that women primarily formed a house-based support system of patronage";[15] and "to serve as a patron is not the same thing as to travel with the beneficiaries from Capernaum to Bethsaida . . . back to Capernaum and on to Nazareth. Following Jesus from a home to the seashore does not make one an itinerant."[16]

Unlike Meier, Levine doubts that John is independent of the Synoptics. For her, then, multiple attestation does not uphold the historical presence of women at the crucifixion. Levine nonetheless inclines to credit Mark 15:40–41, at least in part: "Jesus had women followers and some may well have witnessed his death." Yet she insists that "we cannot extrapolate from their presence at the cross to their presence in a Galilean itineracy."[17] Mark, to be sure, plainly says that the women "followed Jesus when he was in the Galilee." But the wording, Levine believes, harbors a redactional intent: "Mark depicts them as following Jesus in the Galilee in order to secure their witness that the body that died on the cross was Jesus's body, and that the same body was put into the tomb."[18] She suggests further that the named women who fail to anoint Jesus and flee from the tomb (16:8) serve "a coherent narrative purpose": they "match" the named Galilean itinerants who fall asleep in Gethsemane (14:32–42) and flee at the arrest (14:50). Over against these male and female itinerants are the nonitinerant, unnamed woman who anoints Jesus (14:8) and the unnamed centurion who

14. Meier, *Marginal Jew*, 3:79–80. Cf. Dunn, *Jesus Remembered*, 537 ("the prominence of women among Jesus' followers and his closeness to several . . . must have raised a few eyebrows in 'polite society' at the time"); Schenk, *Crispina and Her Sisters*, 9 ("Jesus' behavior would have been shocking to elite Greco-Roman and Jewish sensibilities"); and S. Douglas, "Jesus' Impact," 158 ("men were scandalised by the presence of these women").

15. Levine, "Women's Itineracy," 90.

16. Levine, "Women's Itineracy," 96. Cf. R. M. Price, *Widow Traditions*, 135: "Perhaps the radius of Jesus' travels was not great and . . . the women came from their homes to meet him each day, rather, I should imagine, like well-wishers stationed with cups of lemonade for the runners in a marathon."

17. Levine, "Women's Itineracy," 97.

18. Levine, "Women's Itineracy," 98.

confesses him to be God's Son (15:39). So while there may have been women at the cross, Levine doubts that they participated in an itinerant mission. "If we locate the women 'followers' as home-based, then we can read their presence at the cross as not indicative of a one- or three-year journey outside of their homes but as a one-time trip to Jerusalem, at Passover, when many others also were making the journey, and women could easily travel in groups."[19]

If multiple attestation fails to confirm Meier's view, and if Mark 15:40–41 is not a firm foundation, what about the criterion of dissimilarity? For Meier, the circumstance of "unchaperoned women sharing the preaching tours of a celibate male teacher is discontinuous with . . . the Judaism of the time." Levine, to the contrary, denies that publicly shadowing Jesus would have been scandalous: "Women and children could move independently, without chaperones and therefore without shame."[20] In making this point, she observes that Josephus refers more than once to the public participation of women in popular religious and revolutionary movements.[21]

Levine next notes that the verb ἀκολουθέω, used of the women in Mark 15:41, does not necessitate itineracy. The crowds that follow Jesus throughout the Synoptics are not peripatetics (Matt 4:25; 8:1; 14:13; Mark 3:7; Luke 23:27; etc.). They arrive only to depart, attending to Jesus but for a while. Furthermore, in John 8:12; 10:27; 12:26, as perhaps already in Mark 8:34 and 9:38, "following" Jesus can be metaphorical and amount to the same thing as believing in him. As for the use of διακονέω in Mark 15:41 ("they served him"), this hardly requires being on the road. In Mark 1:31, Peter's mother-in-law, who has just risen from her sickbed and so must be at home, "serves" (διηκόνει αὐτοῖς) Jesus and others. Similarly, in Luke 10:38–42, Martha welcomes Jesus into her house and "serves" (διακονεῖν) him. So women could have "served" and "followed" Jesus without spending nights away from home.[22]

What then of Luke 8:1–3, which Meier takes to substantiate the existence of female itinerants? For Levine, the Greek does not clearly indicate that Mary the

19. Levine, "Women's Itineracy," 107.

20. Levine, "Women's Itineracy," 102.

21. E.g., Josephus, *Vita* 210 ("on my appearance, the whole crowd of Galileans, which included women and children, flung themselves on their faces and with tears implored me not to abandon them to their enemies"); *Bell.* 4.505 (women followers of Simon son of Gioras); and 6.283–87 (a mixed multitude of women and children in the outer court of the temple). One may add that Matt 21:31–32 assumes that John the Baptist's audience included women as well as men; so too the Jewish gospel quoted by Jerome, *Pelag.* 3.2: "The mother of the Lord and his brothers said to him: 'John the Baptist baptizes unto the remission of sins; let us go and be baptized by him.'"

22. Meier, *Marginal Jew*, 3:80–82, also recognizes this. Cf. Acts 12:12, where the mother of John Mark is host.

Magdalene, Joanna, Susanna, and "many others" trekked hither and yon with Jesus. The Twelve alone are here mobile: "The verse can be read as indicating that the men traveled, and the women provided the support needed for their travels. . . . Luke is depicting the women in the customary role of patron."[23]

As for Meier's claim that the criterion of embarrassment establishes that Mary the Magdalene must have been possessed and so offers support for memory in Luke 8:1–3, Levine counters that, had Mary's former state made Luke uneasy, he would have left it unremarked. Furthermore, had female followers occasioned scandal during the ministry, Jesus would have been "accused of associating with prostitutes, for that is how scandalous women following a man would have been coded."[24] Yet the Synoptics seldom refer to sex workers, and nowhere do they suggest that anyone censured Jesus for mingling with women. Matthew 21:31–32 does refer to "toll collectors and prostitutes," but in connection with John the Baptist—they "believed him"—not Jesus; and Luke 15:30 belongs to a parable: the prodigal son spends money on prostitutes (see further below, pp. 276–78).

Finally, Levine observes that her hypothesis neatly explains why women are never called "disciples." It is because they were in fact not "disciples": "Jesus called men away from their wives but not wives from their husbands. Men took to the road; women stayed home. . . . The call is gender specific."[25] So while women were patrons and hosts and among the crowds that listened to Jesus, none were overnighting with him.

Levine is, to my mind, convincing in several particulars. Meier's appeals to dissimilarity and multiple attestation do not establish his conclusions. More generally, the textual evidence he adduces for his main conclusion is sparse, while his explanation for why no woman is ever called a "disciple" is *ad hoc*. And Levine's contention that the women named in the Gospels could have been stay-at-home patrons and hosts is not without force. Not only do we have illustrations of female patronage in stories about Elijah (1 Kgs 17:10–24), Elisha (2 Kgs 4:8–37), and the Pharisees (Josephus, *Ant.* 17.42–43), but all four canonical Gospels depict women supporting or serving Jesus through their domestic hospitality.[26] Levine's scenario is, thus, historically reasonable. It explains with ease, moreover, what for Meier and so many others is a trouble-

23. Levine, "Women's Itineracy," 104–5.

24. Levine, "Women's Itineracy," 106.

25. Levine, "Women's Itineracy," 111.

26. Matt 8:14–15 // Mark 1:29–31 // Luke 4:38–39 (Peter's mother-in-law "serves them"); Luke 10:38–42 (Mary and Martha host Jesus); and John 11:1–12:8 (Mary, Martha, and Lazarus host Jesus). Note also Acts 12:12–17 (Mary the mother of John Mark hosts "many") and 16:11–15, 40 (Lydia hosts Paul and his company).

some fact. Why are the women never called "disciples"? Because, quite simply, they were not.

Some Equivocal Arguments

Despite agreeing with much of Levine's assessment of Meier, I have a different take on the matter of female itinerants. But before going another way and urging that the evidence nudges us from *non liquet* to *probabilis*, I first wish to observe that three arguments sometimes marshaled to show that Jesus's entourage included females do not amount to much.

(1) One of the women in Luke 8:1–3 is Joanna, wife of a certain Chuza, Herod's "steward" (ἐπίτροπος). Beyond this passage and Luke 23:49[27] we know nothing of either Chuza or Joanna.[28] Nor do we know precisely what office ἐπίτροπος designates.[29] Yet Chuza, presuming his historicity and Luke's accuracy,[30] must have been a significant person in Herod's court or inner circle, perhaps manager of his property or head of his estate.[31] If so, he and his wife likely lived in or very near Tiberias, the capital of Antipas's kingdom. We have no evidence, however, that Jesus ever visited Tiberias.[32] The tradition, furthermore, remembers Jesus keeping his distance from Herod Antipas[33]—a likely circumstance given that the ruler had ordered the execution of the Baptist. So if, the argument runs, Jesus and the wife of one of Herod's administrators ever

27. This verse implies that Joanna went with Jesus to Jerusalem: "But all his acquaintances, including the women who had followed him from Galilee [cf. Luke 8:1–3, which names Joanna], stood at a distance, watching these things."

28. For intriguing attempts to fill in the frustrating silence see Sawicki, *Crossing Galilee*, 133–53; Sawicki, "Magdalenes and Tiberiennes"; Bauckham, *Gospel Women*, 109–202; Spencer, *Salty Wives*, 71–94; and McGrath, *What Jesus Learned from Women*, 245–73.

29. For detailed discussion of the options see Bauckham, *Gospel Women*, 135–61.

30. One might wonder whether Luke has enhanced Chuza's status.

31. Cf. BDAG, s.v., ἐπίτροπος.

32. For the possibility that Jesus deliberately avoided Tiberias see Freyne, *Galilee and Gospel*, 183–207; Bauckham, *Gospel Women*, 147–50; and Dunn, *Jesus Remembered*, 320–21. On the relationship of Jesus and cities in general see esp. Tiwald, "Rural Roots." Jesus's message was seemingly not crafted for the commercialized urban world or for those who had (to quote Tiwald) "succeeded in harmonizing Jewish and Hellenistic life."

33. Mark 3:6 ("the Herodians" plotted to destroy Jesus); 8:15 ("beware of the yeast of Herod"); 12:13 ("Herodians" seek to entrap Jesus); Luke 9:7–9 (Herod sought to see Jesus, implying that he failed to do so); 13:31–33 ("get away from here, for Herod wants to kill you"); 23:11 (Herod treats Jesus with contempt). See further Theissen, *Gospels in Context*, 25–59.

met face to face, it seems more likely that it was outside her residence and away from Tiberias. This implies she was traveling.

The argument falls short because it makes three assumptions that cannot, given the paucity of relevant evidence, be established. First, it assumes that Jesus never visited Tiberias. That, however, rests on an argument from silence: since the Gospels say nothing about Jesus being there, he never was. Yet he must have been in many places that go unnamed, and how can we be confident that Tiberias was not among them? David Fiensy, in fact, turns the argument around. Given Joanna's likely residence in Tiberias, we should, he believes, "keep an open mind" regarding the possibility that Jesus met her there or in the vicinity.[34]

Second, the argument from Luke 8:3 assumes that Joanna and her husband Chuza resided in a single place, Tiberias. If, however, Chuza was wealthy, the couple may have had a secondary residence in addition to their primary residence. So perhaps Jesus met Joanna there.

Third, maybe Joanna was a widow by the time she met Jesus. Maybe Chuza had died and she no longer resided in Tiberias, so that she encountered Jesus elsewhere. We of course have no evidence for this scenario. But then we equally have no evidence for any other scenario. We are in the dark, which is no place to build an argument.

(2) "Mary the Magdalene" (Μαρία ἡ Μαγδαληνή) appears in all four canonical Gospels (Matt 27:56, 61; 28:1; Mark 15:40, 47; 16:1; Luke 8:2; 24:10; John 19:25; 20:1, 18). Her name is usually taken to refer to her place of origin or residence: "Mary from Magdala."[35] If that is correct—some are doubtful[36]—it implies, according to Marianne Sawicki, that she "must have travelled, for no one calls you 'Magdalene' in Magdala."[37] One recalls in this connection "Joseph of Arimathea." The man obviously bore that name not in his village

34. Fiensy, *Christian Origins*, 32.

35. For the reasons see Bauckham, *Magdala of Galilee*, 358–61. The Jesus tradition refers to the other Marys by reference to male relatives: Matt 27:56; Mark 15:40, 47; John 19:25; cf. Acts 12:12. But for women identified by place of origin see Bauckham, *Magdala of Galilee*, 350. For the usual equation of Magdala with Taricheae see Strange, *Excavating the Land of Jesus*, 37–50.

36. See Schrader and Taylor, "Meaning of 'Magdalene.'" Schrader and Taylor doubt that ἡ Μαγδαληνή refers to a place or that Magdala was an alternate name for Taricheae. The Greek, they suggest, represents an Aramaic word meaning "the magnified one" or the "tower-ess." See also Rigato, "Maria la Maddalena," and J. Taylor, "Missing Magdala."

37. Sawicki, "Magdalenes and Tiberiennes," 125. Cf. Fander, *Stellung der Frau*, 320 (ἡ Μαγδαληνή indicates "that Mary of Magdala no longer lives in Magdala"); Melzer-Keller, *Jesus und die Frauen*, 435 (ἡ Μαγδαληνή "makes sense only outside the named place and so can only have been attached to Mary at a distance" from Magdala); and Cohick, *Women*, 316.

of origin—that would have made no sense—but only after he moved away.[38] In like manner, should we not presume that Μαρία ἡ Μαγδαληνή was Mary's name outside Magdala, that it was what some called her when she was away from the place? That we have no story of Jesus meeting Mary in Magdala is consistent with such an inference.[39]

Although this may well be the truth, showing it to be the truth is another matter. If—this is purely hypothetical—Mary had once or twice hosted Jesus and his company in Magdala, they might thereafter, given the ubiquity, in their time and place, of the name "Mary," have referred to her as "Mary the Magdalene." The same holds if she was their economic patron. By this they would have meant: "Our supporter who lives in Magdala." In other words, Mary could have gained the name she has in the Gospels without, until the last Passover, overnighting with Jesus and his disciples. "Lazarus of Bethany" (Λάζαρος ἀπὸ Βηθανίας) in John 11:1 would then be a parallel. The name does not suggest that Lazarus was an itinerant companion of Jesus. On the contrary, the man dies when Jesus is elsewhere. The argument from Μαρία ἡ Μαγδαληνή misses the mark.

(3) Luke's remark that women "provided for" (διηκόνουν) Jesus and his disciples ἐκ τῶν ὑπαρχόντων αὐταῖς (Luke 8:3) is sometimes understood to be another sign of itinerancy.[40] According to David Sim, the action in 8:3 "occurs in the open spaces as Jesus and those with him travel from village to village. Here serving at table or anything similar is quite out of place."[41]

The plural participial form of ὑπάρχω here means "material possessions" or "property" or (as the NRSVue has it) "resources."[42] So while διηκόνουν might, standing alone, signify supplying food and perhaps sleeping quarters, the scope of the women's contributions is broader: it likely includes some

38. Recall also "Simon of Cyrene" in Matt 27:32; Mark 15:21; Luke 23:26.

39. In Josephus, *Ant.* 18.4, "Judas the Galilean" (so *Bell.* 2.118, 433; *Ant.* 18.23; 20:102; cf. Acts 5:37) is "Judas the Gaulanite." The man was likely known as "Judas the Gaulanite" initially, when active only in the north, then later became "Judas the Galilean" after leaving Gaulanitis and becoming active in the south. That is, he was "Judas the Galilean" only outside Galilee. Cf. Theissen, "Jesus as an Itinerant Teacher," 108–9.

40. I take the subject of the clause "who provided for them out of their means" to be not "many others" but "many others" plus Mary, Joanna, and Susanna. It may be, however, that the "many others" serve the Twelve and the named women; so De Boer, "Lukan Mary Magdalene," 144–46.

41. Sim, "Women Followers," 57. Sim notes that in Mark 6:30–44; 8:1–9; and John 4:7–42 the disciples and Jesus are responsible for the food; and while one may query the amount of history in these passages, "they constitute the totality of our evidence on this subject."

42. Cf. LXX of Gen 12:5; 13:6; 24:59 (the possessions of Rebekah); Deut 21:16; also 1 En. 97:8; T. Ab. 4:11; T. Job 4:5; Luke 11:21; 12:15, 33, 44; Acts 4:32; etc.

sort of pecuniary support, that is, patronage.[43] Yet how Luke envisaged that support being obtained and handed over goes unsaid.[44] We can imagine that some women exchanged possessions for money in order to aid Jesus as they traveled with him.[45] Or we can imagine—as do those exegetes who appeal to John 12:6 and 13:29 and speak of a money box entrusted to Judas—that two or three women carried money with them and, as need arose, put it into a common purse.[46] (Finding hospitality was probably hit and miss; cf. Matt 10:8–16; Mark 6:8–11; Luke 9:2–5.) But we can equally imagine women—this is Levine's scenario—giving Jesus money without leaving home for days or nights at a time. The problem is that we have nothing but conjectures. Luke 8:3 allows multiple scenarios. For this reason, then, Luke 8:3 does not, in and of itself, detract from Levine's case against Meier.

Mark 15:40–41

That some arguments for female itinerants are anemic does not mean that all arguments for them are, and I think that we have sufficient cause to posit that

43. Cf. Rom 15:25: "I go to Jerusalem in service [διακονῶν] to the saints." This refers to Paul's collecting money for Jerusalem. Note further 15:26–27; 1 Cor 16:1–4; and the use of διακονία in 2 Cor 9:1, 12, 13. See further Bauckham, *Gospel Women*, 161–65.

44. The same is true of Mark's use of διηκόνουν in 15:41. Whether Mark and Luke understood the verb in exactly the same way is an open question; see Hentschel, *Diakonia*, 228–35.

45. Cf. Tob 4:7 ("from your possessions [ἐκ τῶν ὑπαρχόντων] give alms to all who do righteousness"); Matt 19:21 ("sell your possessions [τὰ ὑπάρχοντα] and give to the poor"); Luke 12:33 ("sell your possessions [τὰ ὑπάρχοντα] and give alms"); and Acts 2:45 ("they sold their goods and possessions [ὑπάρξεις] and distributed them to all, as any had need").

46. Inscriptions memorialize women who funded synagogues; see Brooten, *Women Leaders*, 141–44, 157–65. On women of independent means in the Greco-Roman world see further Bauckham, *Gospel Women*, 121–35, and Melzer-Keller, *Jesus und die Frauen*, 206–12. For women as patrons see Cohick, *Women*, 285–309, and Hylen, *Women*, 100–112. The New Testament itself otherwise envisages women with their own funds: Matt 25:1–10; Mark 5:26; 12:42; Acts 16:14–15. Whether any of Jesus's female supporters were well-to-do or poor or both is debated. Whereas Casey, *Jesus of Nazareth*, 193, asserts that Mary Magdalene was "relatively wealthy," Sim, "Women Followers," 53, doubts that any of the women were prosperous. His reasons are (1) the male disciples were from "the lower socio-economic strata" and (2) discipleship required renouncing possessions. But, aside from the possibility that some women of means sold all or most to follow Jesus, had Jesus asked all householders to give up everything, he would not have been welcomed anywhere. Further, we should doubt that Jesus indiscriminately laid the same uncompromising demands upon all; see Allison, *Resurrecting Jesus*, 27–55.

a few women were, at least on occasion, and before the final trip to Jerusalem, members of Jesus's peripatetic band.

(1) According to Mark 15:40–41, there were, at Jesus's crucifixion, "women looking on from a distance; among them were Mary called Magdalene, and Mary the mother of James the younger and of Joses, and Salome. These used to follow him and provided for him when he was in Galilee; and there were many other women who had come up with him to Jerusalem" (ἦσαν δὲ καὶ γυναῖκες ἀπὸ μακρόθεν θεωροῦσαι, ἐν αἷς καὶ Μαρία ἡ Μαγδαληνὴ καὶ Μαρία ἡ Ἰακώβου τοῦ μικροῦ καὶ Ἰωσῆτος μήτηρ καὶ Σαλώμη, αἳ ὅτε ἦν ἐν τῇ Γαλιλαίᾳ ἠκολούθουν αὐτῷ καὶ διηκόνουν αὐτῷ, καὶ ἄλλαι πολλαὶ αἱ συναναβᾶσαι αὐτῷ εἰς Ἱεροσόλυμα).

I know of no commentator who here takes ἠκολούθουν in the metaphorical sense of allegiance. The verb is, for this verse at least, consistently understood in the literal sense: these people followed Jesus as he moved from here to there.[47] The imperfects ἠκολούθουν and διηκόνουν are generalizations about an extended period in Galilee.

If I understand her aright, Levine admits this but confines the picture to the redactional level, to an editorial strategy. She does not deny that women may have been fellow pilgrims with Jesus as he went to Jerusalem for Passover; but she doubts that Mark 15:40–41 is good evidence for female itineracy in Galilee. The evangelist depicts the women as following Jesus "in order to secure their witness": they guarantee that the crucified and entombed body is that of Jesus of Galilee. Beyond that, the itinerant women who flee from the tomb match the itinerant men who flee at the arrest; and over against these two groups are the woman who anoints Jesus and the centurion who recognizes his identity, two nonitinerants who think and act rightly.[48]

One problem for me is that, if Mark values the women as witnesses, he seemingly, on Levine's reading, discredits them through association with the fleeing, cowardly disciples. Another difficulty is that I fail to see why, for Mark, the women need to have been itinerants in order to serve as witnesses. Mobility does not add to their powers of perception. If they knew Jesus and where he was buried, then they knew Jesus and where he was buried, whether they had been itinerants or not.

47. Mark employs ἀκολουθέω + ἐν only one other time, in 10:52, where literal movement is indicated, even if discipleship is also symbolized: "He followed him on the road" (ἠκολούθει αὐτῷ ἐν τῇ ὁδῷ). Cf. T. Job 23:11: "He followed her along the road" (ἠκολούθει αὐτῇ ἐν τῇ ὁδῷ).

48. Kelhoffer, "Two Markan Characterizations," also associates the women who flee in Mark 16 with the men who flee in Mark 14 and contrasts them with the woman who anoints Jesus in Mark 14. The issue of itinerancy vs. nonitinerancy is not, however, part of his analysis.

More importantly, why would agreement with Levine's interpretation of Mark's literary artistry demand or even imply the absence of historical memory? Although she groups the itinerant women with the itinerant men, this does not move her to deny that there were itinerant men. If the scheme does not suggest there were no itinerant men, it need not suggest that there were no itinerant women. The presence of a literary stratagem does not demand the absence of historical memory.

One last point about Mark 15:40–41. After characterizing Mary Magdalene, Mary the mother of James the younger and Joses, and Salome as having followed Jesus and provided for him when he was in Galilee, Mark refers to "many other women who had come up with him to Jerusalem." Here we may have two groups of women. One—the named individuals—followed Jesus when he was in Galilee and provided for him. The other—the unnamed individuals—went up with him to Jerusalem. Perhaps the text implies a distinction between those women who usually attended Jesus and the "many other" (ἄλλαι πολλαί) female partisans who stayed at home, at least until they joined Jesus for the journey to Jerusalem for Passover.

Luke 8:1–3

(2) "The women in Luke 8:1–3 can be seen," according to Levine, "as aligned with Mary and Martha as well as with the numerous women in Acts: secondary or second-circle adherents, home-based, with resources expended for Jesus and his needs. These 'sedentary supporters' appear to be the right category for the women in the movement, epitomized by Mary and Martha and eventually imitated by women directing what have come to be called 'house churches.'"[49] This is the Greek:

> [1]Καὶ ἐγένετο ἐν τῷ καθεξῆς καὶ αὐτὸς διώδευεν κατὰ πόλιν καὶ κώμην κηρύσσων καὶ εὐαγγελιζόμενος τὴν βασιλείαν τοῦ θεοῦ καὶ οἱ δώδεκα σὺν αὐτῷ, [2]καὶ γυναῖκές τινες αἳ ἦσαν τεθεραπευμέναι ἀπὸ πνευμάτων πονηρῶν καὶ ἀσθενειῶν, Μαρία ἡ καλουμένη Μαγδαληνή, ἀφ᾽ ἧς δαιμόνια ἑπτὰ ἐξεληλύθει, [3]καὶ Ἰωάννα γυνὴ Χουζᾶ ἐπιτρόπου Ἡρῴδου καὶ Σουσάννα καὶ ἕτεραι πολλαί, αἵτινες διηκόνουν αὐτοῖς[50] ἐκ τῶν ὑπαρχόντων αὐταῖς.

49. Levine, "Women's Itineracy," 109.

50. Whether the original was αὐτοῖς ("them") or αὐτῷ ("him") is hard to decide. Ricci, *Mary Magdalene*, 156–58, argues for the latter. For the former see Bieberstein, *Verschwiegene Jüngerinnen*, 32–35, and Hentschel, *Diakonia*, 225.

The NRSVue renders this into English as:

> [1]Soon afterward he went on through one town and village after another, proclaiming and bringing the good news of the kingdom of God. The twelve were with him, [2]as well as some women who had been cured of evil spirits and infirmities: Mary, called Magdalene, from whom seven demons had gone out, [3]and Joanna, the wife of Herod's steward Chuza, and Susanna, and many others, who ministered to them out of their own resources.[51]

Here is Levine's translation of the relevant lines:

> And it was when he himself was passing through city and village, proclaiming and bringing the good news of the kingdom of God, and the Twelve with him. And some women who had been cured of evil spirits and infirmities . . . these were providing for them out of their resources.[52]

The imperfect διώδευεν ("he went on through") signifies that Jesus passed through several cities and villages. Καὶ οἱ δώδεκα σὺν αὐτῷ adds that "the Twelve were with him" in his travels. A second καί ("and") then introduces the women. Nothing demands that Luke is moving from itinerants to non-itinerants, or that the women, unlike the men, did not accompany Jesus in his travels. Indeed, the simple, unqualified καί naturally, or so it seems to me, signals continuance: when Jesus went through cities and villages, the Twelve were with him, as were also some women. The NRSVue takes "with him" (σὺν αὐτῷ) to extend to the women, as appears from its "as well as some women."[53] The women do what the men do.

Aside from grammar, why does Luke introduce the women precisely at this point? Since they appear in a pericope that opens with "soon afterward he went on through one town and village after another," one sensible answer

51. That there might be an allusion to the three matriarchs—cf. Rigato, "Maria la Maddalena," 727—seems doubtful to me.

52. Levine, "Women Itinerants," 54.

53. See further Melzer-Keller, *Jesus und die Frauen*, 203–4, who presents the Greek this way:

> Καὶ ἐγένετο ἐν τῷ καθεξῆς
> καὶ αὐτὸς διώδευεν κατὰ πόλιν καὶ κώμην
>   κηρύσσων καὶ εὐαγγελιζόμενος . . .
> καὶ οἱ δώδεκα σὺν αὐτῷ
> καὶ γυναῖκές τινες αἳ . . .

is this: they are named here because they, like the disciples, accompanied Jesus as "he went on through one town and village after another."

Possible support for the NRSVue's reading comes from Luke 24:6–8, where angels tell the women at the empty tomb: "Remember how he told you, while he was still in Galilee, that the Son of Man must be handed over to the hands of sinners and be crucified and on the third day rise again. Then they remembered his words." This refers back to and paraphrases the predictions of death and resurrection in Luke 9:22 and perhaps 18:31–33.[54] It follows, if Luke's narrative is consistent with itself,[55] that the women were present on one or both of those occasions.[56] It further follows, since neither prediction was spoken in a house,[57] that they were outside at the time. In 9:27, furthermore, they are not part of a crowd, because the pericope to which that verse belongs commences with Jesus praying alone and then asking: "Who do the crowds say that I am?" I acknowledge, however, that Levine could counter by arguing that 24:6–8 adverts only to 18:31–33, which occurs during the pilgrimage to Jerusalem.

But then there is Acts 1:14: "All these were constantly devoting themselves to prayer, together with certain women [σὺν γυναιξίν], including Mary the mother of Jesus, as well as his brothers." Although Luke identifies none save Jesus's mother, the vast majority of commentators are understandably put in mind of the women who go to Jerusalem with Jesus (Luke 23:49 par.) or those

54. Luke 9:22: "The Son of Man must undergo great suffering, and be rejected by the elders, chief priests, and scribes, and be killed, and on the third day be raised." Luke 18:31–33: "See, we are going up to Jerusalem, and everything that is written about the Son of Man by the prophets will be accomplished. For he will be handed over to the Gentiles; and he will be mocked and insulted and spat upon. After they have flogged him, they will kill him, and on the third day he will rise again." See Maria-Luisa Rigato, "Remember" (although it is unclear to me that 18:31–33 is set in Galilee, as she thinks; see n. 57).

55. But perhaps it is not; cf. Schweizer, *Luke*, 366: the "you" with reference to the women is "inappropriate." According to Marshall, *Luke*, 886, "the women are assumed to have been with the disciples when Jesus made his prophecy, or to have heard from the disciples." But there is no exegetical justification for the disjunction "or to have heard, etc." Luke 24:6 is clear: ἐλάλησεν ὑμῖν ("he told you").

56. See further Karris, "Women and Discipleship," 10, 14–15; Rigato, "Remember"; and Bieberstein, *Verschwiegene Jüngerinnen*, 246–48. Note also 24:22, which refers to some women "of our company" (ἐξ ἡμῶν, D *l* 844 *pc* omit). This too may include women among those who regularly followed Jesus; cf. Bieberstein, *Verschwiegene Jüngerinnen*, 263–65.

57. Jesus utters the prophecy in Luke 9:22 soon after feeding the five thousand, when he is praying alone with his disciples nearby. The prophecy in 18:31–33 has no specified location; it occurs when Jesus, on his way to Jerusalem, "takes the disciples aside [παραλαβών]."

introduced in 8:1–3.[58] If one agrees, it is notable that they are not in Galilee, where they once were. They have instead stayed in Jerusalem after Pentecost, as though they have no Galilean homes to return to. And maybe, whatever the historical truth, that is what Luke thought: they had no homes to return to since they had left them long ago to follow Jesus.

The history of interpretation buoys the common reading of Luke 8:2–3. All the commentaries on the Greek text that I consulted take the women to be itinerants, not sedentary supporters. Here are five representative comments, all penned long before modern Christian feminism:

- Theophylact: "Women also followed him, so that we might learn that not even the woman is prevented by weakness from following Christ" (*Comm Lk.* 8 ad loc).
- Cornelius à Lapide: "These women followed Christ . . . for safety, lest if they were away from their physician, they might again be attacked by devils."[59]
- Matthew Poole: "Christ went every where about preaching, and the twelve were with him, sometimes hearing (as his disciples), sometimes preaching; some women also were with him. . . . They were not ashamed to be seen following of Christ, though doubtless they met with scoffs enough."[60]
- John Trapp: "These good women [testified to their thankfulness] by following Christ; when they might have staid [*sic*] at home with more ease to themselves, and more thank of their friends."[61]
- J. A. Bengel: "It was the custom among Jews . . . that women, especially widows, aided teachers from their family property, and therefore accompanied them on their journeys."[62]

The Latin tradition, beginning with Tertullian, shows the same uniformity.[63]

58. So, e.g., Poole, *Annotations*, 3:386; Alford, *Greek Testament*, 2:245 ("the women, viz. those spoken of by Luke himself, Luke viii.2, 3—where, besides those named, he mentions ἕτεραι πολλαί"); Knowling, "Acts of the Apostles," 61; Jervell, *Apostelgeschichte*, 118; Pesch, *Apostelgeschichte*, 81; Holladay, *Acts*, 78; and Marguerat, *Apostelgeschichte*, 74. But Lake and Cadbury, *Acts of the Apostles*, 11, raise the possibility that the women are the wives of the apostles; note Acts 1:14 D: ταῖς γυναιξὶ καὶ τέκνοις ("with women and children"). Cf. Thiele, "Bemerkung."

59. Lapide, *Great Commentary*, 3:405.

60. Poole, *Annotations*, 3:219. The remark about "scoffs enough" foreshadows Meier's view.

61. Trapp, *Commentary on the New Testament*, 5:318.

62. Bengel, *Gnomon Novi Testamenti*, 1:279. Bengel supplies no documentations for this alleged custom.

63. Cf. Tertullian, *Marc.* 4.19.1 (the women were disciples as well as assistants and help-

For multiple reasons, then, while I do not dispute Levine's cautious "can be seen," I prefer the NRSVue's translation. This accords with my estimate of the source-critical situation. Luke knew Mark. This means he knew Mark 15:40–41, and the latter clearly says that some women followed Jesus when he was in Galilee: ἦσαν δὲ καὶ γυναῖκες . . . αἳ ὅτε ἦν ἐν τῇ Γαλιλαίᾳ ἠκολούθουν αὐτῷ. So, although Luke 8:1–3 preserves information that does not derive from Mark,[64] it may yet be that the apparent notice of female itinerants comes from Mark.[65] This is consistent with the similarities in their Greek:

LUKE 8:2–3	**MARK 15:40–41**
γυναῖκές τινες αἳ ἦσαν	ἦσαν δὲ καὶ γυναῖκες . . . αἳ
ἕτεραι πολλαί	ἄλλαι πολλαί
διηκόνουν αὐτοῖς (v.l.: αὐτῷ)	διηκόνουν αὐτῷ

The resemblances matter because, while Luke was quite capable of revising Mark for his own agenda, nothing in Luke 8:2–3 signals disagreement with Mark 15:40–41. This enhances the odds that Luke 8:1–3 envisions female itinerants.

---

ers: *discipulas, operarias, ministras*); Augustine, *Op. monach.* 5.6 ("if anyone does not believe that wherever they preached the gospel the apostles brought women of holy life with them, so that these women might minister the necessities of life to them from their abundance, let him hear the Gospel and realize that the apostles did this by the example of our Lord himself"; Augustine goes on to quote Luke 8:1–3); and Bonaventure, *Luke*, 1:654 (certain women "were journeying with him. . . . They were accompanying him as their savior and physician, according to the counsel of the wise person in Sirach 38:11–12: 'Make a place for the physician . . . and let him not depart from you'"). At the same time, as all the commentators on Luke 8:1–3 were also familiar with Mark 15:40–41, I concede that Levine could, if so disposed, respond that this has steered them away from the right reading. She could also argue that, even if I am right about Luke, that does not determine the historical truth about Jesus. For Stegemann and Stegemann, *Jesus Movement*, 378, Luke's paragraph tells us more about Luke's agenda than the historical Jesus.

64. So, e.g., Hengel, "Maria Magdalena," 247: Luke 8:2–3 and Mark 15:40 are both "old" traditions that are "of wholly different origins." Cf. Jeremias, *Sprache des Lukasevangeliums*, 178 (while Luke 8:1–3 is "word for word Lukan," at the same time "the names were certainly given to Luke"); Bieberstein, *Verschwiegene Jüngerinnen*, 30–32; and Casey, *Jesus of Nazareth*, 195 (8:1–3 is "completely independent" of Mark). Schürmann, *Lukasevangelium*, 1:447–48, suggests that 8:2–3 belonged to a source that included 7:11–17, 36–50. So too Krämer, *Entstehungsgeschichte*, 62, who attributes 8:1–3 and portions of Luke 1–2 to the same "woman's source."

65. According to Merz, "Genderforschung," 613, Luke's ἐκ τῶν ὑπαρχόντων αὐταῖς ("from their property") is "a Lukan redactional correction"; Luke added it to Mark 15:41's διηκόνουν αὐτῷ ("they served him") in order to mitigate for "Hellenistic-Roman readers an offensive violation of gender norms."

Two Groups of Women?

(3) The tradition, as Levine stresses, depicts women welcoming Jesus into their homes (Luke 10:38–42; John 11:1–12:8). These individuals evidently did not pack their bags to follow him. Yet the tradition likewise has some men doing the same thing, that is, welcoming Jesus into their homes—Zacchaeus (Luke 19:1–10), Lazarus (John 12:1–2), Simon the leper (Mark 14:3).[66] There were, then, at least two sorts of men who were sympathetic to Jesus's cause. Some traveled with him. Some did not.[67] Why might there not have been two sorts of female sympathizers? One cannot claim that women were generally not allowed to be out and about. The evidence, as Levine observes, fails to support that stereotype.[68] In Laura Lieber's words: "Seclusion does not seem to have been a universal ideal, let alone a reality, even among the Jewish elites."[69] Over and beyond that, the women named in Luke 8:2–3—Mary the Magdalene, Joanna, Susanna—are nowhere explicitly remembered as being with Jesus in their houses. This invites us to contemplate the possibility of two different sorts of female partisans matching the two different types of male

66. Note also Mark 5:18–19 ("go home to your friends") and 8:26 (Jesus "sent him away to his home").

67. In Mark, however, Peter follows Jesus yet can host him in his home (1:29–31). Likewise, in the First Gospel, the apostle Matthew follows Jesus yet has a house to which he welcomes Jesus (9:9–13; 10:3).

68. Cf. Levine, "Women in the Q Communit(ies)," 157: "In antiquity, women traveled for various reasons: trade, pilgrimages, visiting relatives, even engaging in political protest." See further Archer, *Her Price Is Beyond Rubies*, 239–50; Kraemer, "Jewish Women," 60–62; Sawicki, *Crossing Galilee*, 126–28; Baker, *Rebuilding the House of Israel*, 77–144; Hezser, *Jewish Travel*, 389–408; E. S. Alexander, "Ancient Jewish Gender," 191–96; and Brasier, "Women on the Move." Women are not confined to their homes in the Hebrew Bible; recall Gen 38 (Tamar), Judg 5 (Deborah), 2 Sam 14 (the woman of Tekoa), and Prov 31 (the capable wife). Around the turn of the era, some Jews apparently did profess that women, or at least young unmarried women, should stay at home; cf. 2 Macc 3:19; 3 Macc 1:18; 4 Macc 18:7; Sir 9:9; 42:11–12; Philo, *Spec.* 3.169–71; *Contempl.* 69; *Flacc.* 89; *Leg.* 3.98; T. Reu. 6:1–2; Ps.-Phoc. 215–16; 'Abot R. Nat. A 2. Yet customs likely varied from place to place and maybe even family to family (cf. t. Soṭah 5:9); and questions beset the traditional drawing of clear distinctions between a private sphere for women and a public sphere for men; see Baker, "Imagined Households," and Hylen, "Public and Private Space." Furthermore, and as many have remarked, economic and class variables must have played a role in this matter. Perhaps only a few of the prosperous could afford to keep wives or virgins mostly sequestered or at home; cf. Spencer, *Salty Wives*, 74–75, and note already Jeremias, *Jerusalem in the Time of Jesus*, 362.

69. Lieber, "Jewish Women," 338.

partisans. One group interacted with Jesus in and around their homes. The other itinerated and overnighted with him.[70] The existence of the former, presumably larger group would not exclude the existence of the latter, presumably smaller group.

Matthew 27:55–56

(4) Matthew 27:55–56 reports that the witnesses to the crucifixion included many women "who had followed Jesus *from* Galilee, ministering to him" (αἵτινες ἠκολούθησαν τῷ Ἰησοῦ ἀπὸ τῆς Γαλιλαίας διακονοῦσαι αὐτῷ). This differs from Mark 15:41, which instead states that certain women followed Jesus and provided for him while he was *in* Galilee (αἳ ὅτε ἦν ἐν τῇ Γαλιλαίᾳ ἠκολούθουν αὐτῷ καὶ διηκόνουν αὐτῷ). Matthew's sentence says no more than that women provided for Jesus on the trip from Galilee to Jerusalem.[71] It does not affirm that, before that occasion, they had journeyed with him. This, over against Mark, seemingly reduces their presence and demotes their significance.[72] One recalls 1 Cor 15:3–8, which bypasses both the tradition of Jesus appearing to Mary Magdalene (Matt 28:9–10; John 20:14–18) and the story of women discovering the empty tomb (Mark 16:1–8).[73] Matthew altogether lacks the image, preserved in Mark 15:41 and Luke 8:1–3, of women accompanying Jesus and his disciples in their travels.[74] In the First Gospel, the women in 27:55–56 have no ascertainable role during the public ministry.

Matthew's redactional work is a warning, and when we observe additional signs of the contraction of women's presence in the tradition,[75] a hermeneutic of suspicion is inevitable. Our earliest sources enshrine a strong androcentric bias, and if a few women were itinerants beside Jesus, they were almost cer-

70. Cf. I. Tan, "In the Footsteps of Jesus," 125, and V. Phillips, "Full Disclosure," 19.

71. John 19:25, which names three women who were present at the crucifixion, also fails to state that they moved around Galilee with Jesus. So too Luke 23:49: "The women who had followed him from [συνακολουθοῦσαι αὐτῷ ἀπό] Galilee stood at a distance."

72. Contrast Parambi, *Discipleship of the Women*, 131–32: Matt 27:55 "probably" refers to the women's "continued physical following of Jesus from the origin of Jesus' ministry"; "they followed Jesus continuously." This reads Mark into Matthew.

73. These were not, in my judgment, post-Pauline inventions; see Allison, *Resurrection of Jesus*, 46–53, 116–66.

74. The mother of James and John is traveling with Jesus in Matt 20:20–23, but this is while they are on their way to Jerusalem (20:17), in harmony with 27:55.

75. Instructive here is Dewey, "From Storytelling to Written Text."

tainly more significant than the record indicates.[76] Indeed, as Carla Ricci puts it, Mark 15:40–41 and Luke 8:1–3 call attention to "a reality that has been wiped out" almost completely.[77] It is not so surprising that, before the male disciples exit the stage, the Synoptics recount no conversations with itinerant women or stories about them. To quote Ricci again: "The absence of women from the texts comes to an end at the point where the absence of the [male] disciples from the events begins"; the presence of men "acts as an obstacle to women being taken into account."[78] When it comes to the women around Jesus, our sources are frustratingly emaciated.

Gendered Couplets

(5) Several sayings attributed to Jesus pair the activity or circumstances of women with the activity or circumstances of men:[79]

TEXT	MEN'S CIRCUMSTANCES	WOMEN'S CIRCUMSTANCES
Matt 6:26–28 // Luke 12:24–28	sowing and reaping	spinning
Matt 10:34–36 // Luke 12:51–53	son and father in conflict	mother against daughter and mother-in-law against daughter-in-law
Matt 11:16–17 // Luke 7:32(?)	boys dance	girls playing flutes[80]
Matt 12:41–42 // Luke 11:31–32	the men of Nineveh arise	the queen of the South arises
Matt 13:31–33 // Luke 13:18–21	a man sows a seed in his garden	a woman leavens flour

76. Helpful here is Merz, "Genderforschung," 601–3.

77. Ricci, *Mary Magdalene*, 27.

78. Ricci, *Mary Magdalene*, 28.

79. There is now a substantial literature on these pairs; see esp. Melzer-Keller, *Jesus und die Frauen*, 331–46; Arnal, "Gendered Couplets"; Fricker, *Quand Jésus*; Harb, *Eschatologische Rede*, 194–225; and Parks, *Gender*.

80. This is the interpretation of Jeremias, *Parables*, 161; cf. Parks, *Gender*, 96. An allusion to gender is implicit at best, however, and the vast majority of exegetes have failed to discern it. Fricker, *Quand Jésus*, 41, is undecided.

TEXT	MEN'S CIRCUMSTANCES	WOMEN'S CIRCUMSTANCES
Matt 24:40–41 // Luke 17:34–35	two men in a field (Matthew) or couch (Luke)[81]	two women grinding at a mill
Mark 12:25; cf. Luke 17:27	marrying	being given in marriage
Luke 4:25–27	Naaman the Syrian	the widow of Zarephath
Luke 12:45 (contrast Matt 24:49)	the beating of menservants	the beating of maidservants
Luke 15:4–10	shepherd taking care of sheep	woman sweeps to find a coin[82]

Many of these units adopt stereotypes.[83] Women spin, bake, and sweep. Men sow, reap, and tend flocks.[84] In this respect there is nothing new, much less radical, over against Jesus's world. Furthermore, it scarcely astonishes when men and women are, for rhetorical purposes, paired. Such pairing naturally appears in literature far and wide.[85] Nonetheless, the number of gen-

81. Some take Luke's "two in one couch" to envisage a husband and wife. But the construction in 17:34 is masculine (ὁ εἷς . . . ὁ ἕτερος), that in 17:35 feminine (ἡ μία . . . ἡ ἕτερα). The first picture is of two men on a dining couch, the second of two women; cf. Fitzmyer, *Luke*, 2:1172, and see esp. Miroshnikov and Somov, "Two Men on a Dining Couch."

82. One might also observe that, although they are not paired in Luke, the parable of the importunate friend at midnight (11:5–8) and the parable of the persistent widow (18:1–8) mirror each other in multiple respects, and that while the former is about a man's request, the latter concerns the pleas of a woman. Jeremias, *Parables*, 157, regards 11:5–8 as "almost a doublet" of 18:1–8. Cf. Theissen, *Jesus als historische Gestalt*, 96.

83. Stereotypes do not, it is worth noting, always correspond to reality; cf. I. Tan, "Jewish Women's Life," 229: "The rabbis . . . portray women as selling merchandise in the marketplace (m. Ḥallah 2:7), on their doorsteps (t. Bava Kamma 11:7), or in a shop (m. Ketub. 9:4), or even participating in grain harvest or olive-picking (m. Yevamot 16:2); women are shown assisting their husbands in the field (a baraita in b. Bava Metzi'a 12a) or raising livestock, mostly poultry (m. Bava Qamma 10:9; t. Bava Metzi'a 4:24–25)." See further Peskowitz, *Spinning Fantasies*.

84. Cf. Schottroff, *Lydia's Impatient Sisters*, 80–84, and Harb, *Eschatologische Rede*, 224.

85. Cf. Ps 109:14 ("may the iniquity of his fathers be remembered before the LORD, and let not the sin of his mother be blotted out"); Prov 1:8 ("hear your father's instruction, and reject not your mother's teaching"); Isa 49:23 ("kings will be your foster fathers, and their queens your nursing mothers"); Joel 2:28–29 ("your sons and your daughters will prophesy"; "even on the male and female slaves, in those days, I will pour out my spirit"); Acts 13:50 ("the devout women of high standing and the leading men of the city"); Apoc. Zeph. 2:1–4 (two men on a road; two women at a mill; a man and a woman in bed); m. Neg. 2:4 (in-

dered couplets in the Synoptics is unusual and so garners attention.[86] Taken together these couplets forcefully suggest that women constituted a significant segment of Jesus's audiences,[87] and further that sometimes he consciously formulated teaching accordingly. Moreover, Sara Park's study of Q's gendered pairs seemingly establishes their distinctive nature over against other extant sources, Jewish and otherwise, as well as Jesus's likely responsibility for that distinctiveness.[88] "When compared to previous texts from Hellenistic and early-Jewish antiquity, the gender pairs stand out as innovative for their overt and repeated use of matching masculine and feminine examples to teach an identical lesson—not separate lessons for men and women, but the same lesson for both."[89] Denis Fricker's research issues in the same result: the rhetoric of "two sentences of varying length that repeat the same idea using a male then a female figure or vice versa" is "original and remarkable"; "the phenomenon is practically nonexistent in Greco-Roman rhetoric and rare and dispersed in the writings of Judaism contemporary with Jesus."[90]

Directly relevant for our subject is one particular couplet, that in Matt 6:25–34 // Luke 12:22–32 (Q). This poetic unit implies that women were among those who followed Jesus from place to place. Luke's version in the NRSVue reads in part:

> [22]He said to his disciples, "Therefore I tell you, do not worry about your life, what you will eat, or about your body, what you will wear. [23]For life is

spection of men for the signs of leprosy; inspection of women for the signs of leprosy); etc. See further I. Tan, "Women of the Q Community," 196–200.

86. The parallels in the previous note are scattered and drawn from a wide range of sources. I know of no close parallel to the concentration in the sayings assigned to Jesus, especially in Q.

87. See further Melzer-Keller, *Jesus und die Frauen*, 331–46, and Parks, *Gender*, 77–102. Cf. Luke 10:38–42, where Jesus defends a woman for listening to his teaching. But for dissent from this inference see Harb, *Eschatologische Rede*, 194–225.

88. Parks, *Gender*.

89. Parks, *Gender*, 5. On 117 she observes: "At no point prior to Q do *two parallel parables or sayings* occur in the Hebrew Bible (nor, for that matter, in the apocrypha and Pseudepigrapha), where an identical lesson is clearly geared toward both male and female audience members." For Parks, Q's "complete" gender pairs "(a) are a set of two short parables that (b) teach the same lesson (c) in a verbally parallel manner (d) wherein one parable highlights masculinity and the other femininity" (79).

90. Fricker, *Quand Jésus*, 380. One should not overlook, however, that Luke's Gospel as a whole, that is, beyond sayings attributed to Jesus, features gendered pairs; see Awad, "Women Discipleship." This may be a case where the tradition helped shape a Lukan compositional habit.

> more than food and the body more than clothing. [24]Consider the ravens: they neither sow nor reap, they have neither storehouse nor barn, and yet God feeds them. Of how much more value are you than the birds! [25]And which of you by worrying can add a single hour to your span of life? [26]If then you are not able to do so small a thing as that, why do you worry about the rest? [27]Consider the lilies, how they grow: they neither toil nor spin, yet I tell you, even Solomon in all his glory was not clothed like one of these. [28]But if God so clothes the grass of the field, which is alive today and tomorrow is thrown into the oven, how much more will he clothe you, you of little faith!"[91]

The ravens neither sow nor reap. That is stereotypically men's work. The lilies do not toil at spinning. That is stereotypically woman's work.[92] The substance of both illustrations—which are very different from the exhortations to work in Proverbs[93]—is that Jesus's followers need not be anxious about what they will eat or what they will wear, for God will take care of them.[94]

The reassurance in Matt 6:25–34 and Luke 12:22–32 is not plausibly construed as all-purpose religious wisdom, as though Jesus encouraged the general Galilean populace not to fret about making ends meet. Ulrich Luz asks: "What can it mean for the 'poor farmer who *has* to sow and reap' that the ravens do not do that? And how does it help the 'poor farmer's wife' that the lilies in the field do not spin when she '*must* spin'?"[95] It makes far more sense to suppose, in accord with the introduction in Luke 12:22—"And he said to his disciples"—that the illustrations from nature originally addressed people who, like those called away from work in Mark 1:16–20, had set aside accustomed ways of gaining food and clothing.[96] This is the implication of "they neither sow nor reap" and

91. The differences from Matthew are inconsequential for my purposes here.

92. See further L. A. Johnson and Tannehill, "Lilies Do Not Spin," and Hylen, *Women*, 51–54.

93. Cf. Prov 6:6–11 ("go to the ant, you lazybones"); 10:4 ("a slack hand causes poverty, but the hand of the diligent makes rich"); 24:33–34 ("a little sleep, a little slumber, a little folding of the hands to rest, and poverty will come upon you like a robber, and want, like an armed warrior"); and 28:19 ("anyone who tills the land will have plenty of bread").

94. Cf. the paraphrase of Jeremias, *New Testament Theology*, 236. "Have you ever seen Mr Raven sowing, harnessing up the plough, reaping and taking the crop into the barn? Or Mrs Anemone picking up the spindle and then sitting down at the loom? You have so little faith!"

95. Luz, *Matthew*, 1:343 n. 45. Cf. Rau, "Arm und Reich," 260: "Would it not be cynical to assume that poor people like Lazarus are being admonished not to worry about food and clothing?"

96. Cf. Catchpole, "Question of Q," 40 (the text implies "abandonment of life-sustaining

"they neither toil nor spin." In Gerd Theissen's words: "What this saying is talking about is the whole rigor of the life led by the wandering charismatics, outlawed, without any home and without protection, people who made their way through the countryside without any possessions and without any work."[97] One recalls the words on mission, where Jesus sends disciples forth without bag or bread or money (cf. Matt 10:9–10; Mark 6:8; Luke 9:3).[98] Matthew 6:25–34 // Luke 12:22–32 would match their situation.[99] The passage would also speak directly to any who had, even if only for a short time, forsaken their settled lives to follow Jesus and so were without their usual sources of support.[100]

Luz, in commenting on Matt 6:25–34, poses the question: "Why does Jesus say that birds do not do the work of men, and that lilies do not do the work of women?" Luz answers: "This makes sense only if it is applied to men and women who have left their ordinary work for the sake of the kingdom of God."[101] I concur.[102] Those kin to the birds are men engaged in something other than

---

work"), and Theissen, *Jesus als historische Gestalt*, 99–100. Contrast Fricker, *Quand Jésus*, 374–76, 380: he rather thinks of economic changes that had brought hardship to Jesus's hearers.

97. Theissen, *Social Reality*, 40.

98. Contrast m. Qidd. 4:14, where R. Simeon b. Eleazor says: "Have you ever seen a wild animal or a bird that practices a craft? And yet they have their sustenance without care, and were they not created for nothing than to serve me? But I was created to serve my maker. How much more then ought I to have my sustenance without care? But I have done evil, and I forfeited my [right to] sustenance [without care]." Here human beings are, because of their evil deeds, not sustained as are the animals.

99. Cf. Jeremias, *New Testament Theology*, 236; D. Zeller, *Weisheitlichen Mahnsprüche*, 92–93; Theissen, *Sociology*, 13–14; Schürmann, "Zeugnis der Redenquelle," 158; and Parks, *Gender*, 99. For Kloppenborg, *Formation of Q*, 239, Q 12:22b–28 is among those texts that "may have had their *Sitz im Leben* in the instructions given to and carried by wandering charismatic preachers." L. A. Johnson and Tannehill, "Lilies Do Not Spin," 479, suggest three possible audiences: (1) those who had left home, (2) those whose livelihood was jeopardized by ostracism, and (3) those whose charity had depleted resources. But these categories need not denote distinct groups. All three were likely relevant to some in Jesus's itinerant band.

100. On a personal note, every sermon I have heard on Matt 6:25–34 or its parallel has seemed strained, the cause always being the palpable fact that the audience works for a living.

101. Luz, *Matthew in History*, 29. Cf. Luz, *Matthew*, 1:343: "If the image is actually to be relevant, then women are addressed here who also 'do not soil and spin.'" He adds in n47: "If my overall interpretation of the text is correct, it supports the view that women also followed Jesus."

102. Cf. also Melzer-Keller, *Jesus und die Frauen*, 33–35, 344–46; Bieberstein, *Verschwiegene Jüngerinnen*, 156–57; Theissen and Merz, *Historical Jesus*, 223; and Ebner, *Jesus von Nazaret*, 168–69.

the ordinary labor that issues in food. And those kin to the lilies are women engaged in something other than the ordinary labor that produces clothing. They certainly cannot be patrons or hosts. They, like the men, are itinerants. Were they rather at home, the poetic parallelism would be defective. They would not be like the lilies that grow without toiling or spinning. They would still be about their customary tasks and presumably less worried about what to wear or eat.

Intrafamilial Conflict

(6) The saying in Matt 10:34–36 // Luke 12:51–53 (Q) may reflect the same social circumstance. After declaring that he has come not to bring peace but a "sword" (Matthew) or "division" (Luke), Jesus illustrates by rewriting Mic 7:6:

MATT 10:35–36	**LUKE 12:53**	**MIC 7:6 (MT)**[103]
For I have come to set a man against his father, and a daughter against her mother, and a daughter-in-law against her mother-in-law; and one's foes will be members of one's own household.	They will be divided: father against son and son against father, mother against daughter and daughter against mother, mother-in-law against her daughter-in-law	For the son treats the father with contempt, the daughter rises up against her mother, the daughter-in-law against her mother-in-law; a man's enemies are the men of his own house.
	and daughter-in-law against mother-in-law.	

Although Luke's chiastic formulations do not appear in the parallels, all three texts feature the same antagonistic pairs:

- man or son over against his father
- daughter over against her mother
- daughter-in-law against her mother-in-law

These three pairs exhaust the familial possibilities, for father-in-law and son-in-law did not, in Jesus's time and place, live in the same house. Each was rather head of his own household.[104]

103. The LXX closely follows the Hebrew here.
104. Cf. Bieberstein, *Verschwiegene Jüngerinnen*, 121.

Because the Gospels are close to Micah, we should perhaps refrain from seeking to correlate the three opposing parties with circumstances in Jesus's ministry. Yet the words are not introduced as a formal quotation, and the sources for Jesus often rewrite biblical intertexts for their immediate purposes. In the present instance, it would have been easy enough to drop the clauses about daughters and daughters-in-law if they had nothing to do with the speaker's situation. Just such excision has taken place in Gos. Thom. 16: "Men think, perhaps, that it is peace that I have come to cast upon the world. They do not know that it is dissension that I have come to cast upon the earth: fire, sword, and war. For there will be five in a house: three will be against two, and two against three, the father against the son, and the son against the father. And they will stand solitary." All the female characters have been deleted.

What if we seek to situate Matt 10:35–36 // Luke 12:53, with its references to mothers, daughters, mothers-in-law, and daughters-in-law, in a pre-Easter context? The conflict in the verses is generational, young versus old.[105] This coheres with other Synoptic traditions. In Mark 1:19–20, James and John leave their father behind in a boat. In Matt 8:21–22 // Luke 9:59–60 (Q), a man is rebuked for desiring to bury his father before following Jesus. In Matt 10:37 // Luke 14:26 (Q), Jesus turns "honor your father and mother" into "hate your father and mother."[106] And in Luke 9:61, Jesus's answer to a man who wishes to bid farewell to family alludes to Elisha's request to kiss father and mother goodbye (1 Kgs 19:19–21).[107]

Given all this, Matt 10:34–36 // Luke 12:51–53 would have spoken directly to young males who had left their families. But what of the words about daughter and daughter-in-law? They are consistent with Jesus's band including itinerant females. For any woman who found herself in the saying's "daughter" or "daughter-in-law" was unlikely to have been hosting Jesus or supporting him financially. Decisions about hospitality and money were typically made not by daughters or daughters-in-law but by those in charge of a household. Matthew 10:34–36 // Luke 12:51–53 seems then to be of a piece with the other evidence that some women were among Jesus's traveling companions.

105. See further Destro and Pesce, "Fathers and Householders," and Destro and Pesce, *Encounters with Jesus*, 110–16. That Peter and his companions belonged not to the older generation but to the intermediate generation not only fits the New Testament data but what we otherwise know about new religious movements; see Van Os, *Psychological Analyses*. The younger one is, the fewer bridges one has to burn.

106. On this, see Allison, *Intertextual Jesus*, 62–64.

107. See Allison, *Intertextual Jesus*, 142–44.

Post-Easter Pairs

(7) There were, after Easter, missionary couples, such as Prisca and Aquila.[108] Andronicus and Junia (Rom 16:7) may also have been among their number.[109] It is further possible that some women preachers traveled without male partners.[110] But whatever the truth about that, significant for our purposes is 1 Cor 9:6, according to which the "brothers of the Lord and Cephas" were accompanied in their journeys by a "believing wife." These individuals knew Jesus, and at least Peter had been an itinerant before Easter. Now perhaps there was no continuity in this particular between what happened before and after the crucifixion. Perhaps women left their homes to join in the missionary task only after Easter. Yet given that a few of the same individuals were involved, some continuity is a reasonable surmise,[111] and all the more as "the brothers of the Lord" appear to have lived out their lives in Israel.[112] That these relatives of Jesus moved about Israel with their wives while on mission after Pentecost lifts the odds that, before Pentecost, Jesus's itinerant associates included women.[113]

108. See Acts 18:1–3; Rom 16:3–4; 1 Cor 16:19; 2 Tim 4:19; also Murphy-O'Connor, "Prisca and Aquila"; Müller, "Priska und Aquila"; and Stenschke, "Married Women." According to Clement of Alexandria, *Strom.* 3.53, "the apostles, in conformity with their ministry, concentrated on undistracted preaching and took their wives around as Christian sisters rather than spouses, to be their fellow-ministers in relation to housewives, through whom the Lord's teaching reached into the women's quarters without scandal."

109. On Junia, a woman who appears to have been an apostle, see Epp, *Junia*, and Lin, "Junia." Some identify her with the Joanna of Luke 8:3; so, e.g., Bauckham, *Gospel Women*, 165–86; Witherington, "Joanna"; and Cohick, *Women*, 314–16 (tentatively).

110. See D'Angelo, "Women Partners." Tryphaena and Tryphosa—the names are feminine; perhaps they were sisters—are, in Rom 16:12, "workers in the Lord." That Paul knows them despite never having been in Rome implies they had not always been there. In Phil 4:1–3, Paul says that Euodia and Syntyche—again the names are feminine—"struggled beside me in the work of the gospel."

111. So too Merz, "Genderforschung," 613.

112. See Bauckham, *Jude and the Relatives*, 45–133.

113. Crossan in *Birth of Christianity*, 334–35, and "Jesus and the Kingdom," 39–40, proposes that the "two by two" of Mark 6:7 and the "in pairs" of Luke 10:1 reflect the circumstance that, before Easter, women itinerants sometimes accompanied male itinerants to whom they were not married. I am not convinced; but see J. Taylor, "Two by Two"; J. Taylor, "Male-Female Missionary Pairings"; and Ramelli, "Colleagues of Apostles." J. Taylor, "Two by Two," 65, raises an interesting issue: "If [in Mark 6] it is only men that go out, leaving Jesus behind, then Mark seems in danger of presenting an image of Jesus remaining on the road with a rather large group of women who are only concerned with serving him" (cf. 15:40–41). Note the picture in Did. apost. 15 (3:5): "The teacher himself, when he sent us,

General Reflections

(8) Mark 1:38–39 claims that Jesus "went throughout Galilee," and Luke 9:6 has him preaching and healing "everywhere" (πανταχοῦ).[114] The tradition remembers him as having been in more than a dozen named places.[115] Our sources also have him asking others to "follow" him, that is, not to remain where they are.[116] And they have him say that he has "nowhere to lay his head" (Matt 8:20 // Luke 9:58 [Q]; Gos. Thom. 86) and "I must be on my way today, tomorrow, and the next day" (Luke 13:33).[117] They further depict him sending forth others for mission, so that they too, like him, walk from place to place (Matt 10:5–15, 23; Mark 6:7–11; Luke 9:2–5; 10:1–12; Gos. Thom. 14).

Jesus, unlike John the Baptist, was an itinerant of some sort, and that by design.[118] Presumably he had a message that required, in his mind, moving

---

the Twelve, to instruct the people and the nations did not send with us the women disciples who were with us, Mary Magdalene and Mary the daughter of James and Salome, to instruct or save the world." Presumably, however, the Twelve were not the only men trailing Jesus. Other scholars envisage women traveling with husbands; so, e.g., Bauckham, *Gospel Women*, 203–23; Tiwald, *Wanderradikalismus*, 211–14; Tiwald, *Logienquelle*, 178–79; Phipps, "Itinerating Wives"; and Cohick, *Women*, 310. So too Ebner, *Jesus von Nazaret*, 149–53: Jesus called married couples to follow him; cf. Rom 16:3–4, 7; 1 Cor 9:5; and (the likely reading of) the *Did. apost.* for Luke 23:49 par.: αἱ γυναῖκες τῶν συνακολουθησάντων αὐτῷ ἀπὸ τῆς Γαλιλαίας ("the wives of those who followed him from Galilee"). Contrast Puig i Tàrrech, *Jesus*, 250: the disciples' wives "stayed home and looked after the children."

114. Cf. Mark 6:6; 9:30; Matt 4:12–17; Luke 4:44; 8:1; 13:22; 23:5; John 7:1; and Acts 10:38 ("he went about doing good").

115. E.g., Bethany and Bethphage (Mark 11:1, 11–12; 14:3; John 12:1); Bethany beyond the Jordan (John 1:28–29; 10:40); Bethsaida (Matt 11:21 // Luke 10:13 [Q]; Mark 6:45; 8:22); "beyond the Jordan" (Mark 10:1; John 10:40); Caesarea Philippi (Mark 8:27); Cana (John 2:1–11); Capernaum (Matt 4:13; Matt 11:23 // Luke 10:15 [Q]; Mark 1:21; 2:1; 9:33; John 2:12; 6:17, 24, 59); Chorazin (Matt 11:21 // Luke 10:13 [Q]); the Decapolis (Mark 5:20; 7:31); Ephraim (John 11:54); Gennesaret (Mark 6:53); Gerasa (Mark 5:1; Gadara or Gergesa in Matt 8:28); Jericho (Mark 10:46); Judea and Jerusalem (Mark 10:1; 11:1, 11, 15, 27; John 2:13, 23; 5:1; 10:22–23; 12:12); Nain (Luke 7:11); Nazareth (Mark 1:9; 6:1); Samaria (Luke 9:52); Sychar (John 4:4–5); Tyre (Mark 7:24; v.l.: "and Sidon"). Many stories are not set in a particular named place and we can only guess where they occurred (e.g., Mark 1:9–11, 40–45; 2:23–28; 3:13–19; 9:2–8; 10:1–12; etc.).

116. E.g., Matt 8:18–22 // Luke 9:57–60 (Q); Mark 1:16–20; 2:14; 10:21; Luke 9:61–62; John 1:35–39, 43; cf. Mark 10:28–30 ("we have left everything and followed you").

117. Mark 6:4—"prophets are not without honor, except in their hometown"—entails that Jesus was known beyond Nazareth; cf. Luke 4:24; John 4:44; Gos. Thom. 31. For the argument that Mark 6:4 par. was a sort of "guiding principle" for Jesus see Michaels, "Itinerant Jesus."

118. See esp. Theissen, "Jesus as an Itinerant Teacher." "The Jesus tradition," he observes,

about in order to reach more people.[119] Mark 1:38 likely catches his sense of mission: "Let us go on to the neighboring towns, so that I may proclaim the message there also, for that is what I came out to do."[120] My view is that Jesus's eschatological expectation bred missionary urgency (see above, p. 74 n. 293), and that the post-Easter Jesus movement was oriented to mission from the start in large measure because Jesus himself had been a missionary. His vocation was inherited.

Beyond this, however, I am left with many questions. Did Jesus have a well-conceived strategy as to where to go and when? How often were he and his sometime peripatetic band away from Capernaum and other places where they had relatives and friends they could count on for support? What was the usual size of that band beyond the Twelve? Or did it vary greatly from time to time?[121] One has trouble imagining "a great multitude" (πολὺ πλῆθος, Mark 3:7) or "a great crowd" (ὄχλος πολύς, 5:24; cf. 6:33; John 6:2) descending on a small village, much less a single house, in hope of hospitality. Again, how often did Jesus and his followers venture beyond day trips and go to villages further away, uncertain of the reception that lay ahead?[122] How often were they out in the

"relates only two prophets from the history of Israel closely to Jesus: Jonah and Elijah. Both of them were wandering prophets" (108). But for the possibility that economic hardship contributed to the decision to abandon work and "seek out alternative options available for survival" see Crossley and Myles, *Jesus*, 130–39 at 133.

119. But traveling may have been a habit he learned before his public ministry; builders and carpenters were commonly itinerants. See Oakman, *Jesus and the Economic Questions*, 175–98; Fiensy, *Christian Origins*, 26–29, 34–55; and Frenschkowski, "Itinerant Charismatics." The latter writes: "The one group best documented for its mobility all over the empire are the τέκτονες and similar professions, particularly the masons" (206).

120. Cf. Ryan, *Role of the Synagogue*, 145: "Jesus' travels in Galilee and in Judea are integral to the tradition. He did, after all, die in Jerusalem, not Capernaum. If we accept that Jesus was an itinerant, then it is hard to deny that carrying his message to various locales *was* his intent."

121. Matthew seemingly and Luke certainly (cf. Luke 6:13, 17; 10:1; 19:37; Acts 1:12–26) envisage "the disciples" as a group larger than the Twelve. Whether Mark did also is unclear; see Meye, *Jesus and the Twelve*. John 6:66 speaks of "many (of the) disciples" (πολλοί [ἐκ] τῶν μαθητῶν). This is part of a notice that these "many" no longer "went about" (περιεπάτουν) with Jesus; thereafter Jesus immediately addresses the Twelve (6:67), from which point on, a reader might think, they alone unfailingly follow him.

122. Many have cited Kloppenborg, *Excavating Q*, 211: "The region of the Lower Galilee is tiny; the towns in the area along the western and northwestern shores of the Kinneret are all within a day's walk of one another. Strange calculates that a traveler starting in Sepphoris could reach any of forty villages in a short day's travel. . . . 'Itinerancy' should not in any case be imagined on a very grand scale; it would have looked more like daylong excursions." Presumably the crowds who are said to have "followed" Jesus did not travel too

open at night?[123] How often were food and drink real issues?[124] Did everyone always stay together in the evenings or did they typically split up—perhaps staying in or near more than one hospitable house—and gather again in the morning? Did they ever use a traveler's inn, that is, a caravansary or khan?[125]

While such questions remain forever open, general considerations favor the supposition that Jesus's roving band regularly included a few female supporters. Jesus was, in the eyes of sympathizers, a remarkable healer, a charismatic teacher, and some sort of messianic figure. A few were so taken by him that they left everything to follow him from place to place. Now we have no reason to imagine that only men were so moved, that while some males felt compelled, in the thrall of his presence and cause, to forsake home and family for days or weeks at a time, no females were ever moved in a similar way.[126] Why would each and every woman, as opposed to multiple male admirers, have not left families, especially when Jesus taught that the current, quotidian circumstances were passing away? Did Jesus not insist that "one thing is needed"[127] and warn that those who continued as always to eat, drink, marry, buy, sell, plant, and build ran the risk of undergoing judgment (see

far from home (Mark 3:7; 5:24; etc.). Yet Theissen, "Sayings Source Q," 97, is right: "With a return on the same day, a radius of action extending more than 30 km would be unlikely—already 30 km demand a march of 60 km per day. This takes at least twelve hours. Without overnight stay Jesus and his disciples could not even reach all places in Galilee, and certainly not the territories beyond Galilee: Tyre and Sidon, Caesarea Philippi or the Decapolis. Even Sepphoris and Nazareth in Galilee were too far away from Capernaum so as to return on the same day." Theissen further argues plausibly that being "received" (δέχεσθαι) in Mark 6:11 and Luke 10:8–10 means being welcomed for the night.

123. The saying about foxes and birds (Matt 8:20 // Luke 9:58) implies nights without shelter. Luke 21:37 ("every day he was teaching in the temple, and at night he would go out and spend the night on the Mount of Olives, as it was called") may imply sleeping outside a dwelling; cf. perhaps John 7:53–8:1.

124. That they were issues at least occasionally appears from Matt 6:11 // Luke 11:3 (prayer for daily bread); Matt 6:25–34 // Luke 12:22–32 (anxiety about food and drink); Mark 6:11 (inhospitable reception of the Twelve); and the missionary discourses, where rejection is possible: Matt 10:14; Mark 6:11; Luke 9:5; 10:10. Hospitality was not guaranteed.

125. Luke 10:34 refers to a public lodge; cf. perhaps Jer 41:17 and Luke 2:7 and on the subject see Benoit, "Non erat eis locus." Synagogues at a later date could serve as inns of a sort. Did some of the smaller synagogues of earlier times ever fulfill the same function for travelers?

126. Evidently not all who followed Jesus had a formal call to do so; cf. Matt 8:19 // Luke 9:57 (Q); John 1:35–42, 43–51, and see Strotmann, *Historische Jesus*, 138–39.

127. The quoted words are from Luke 10:42, where Jesus commends a woman for leaving her usual duties.

Matt 24:37–39 // Luke 17:26–30)?[128] To take him seriously was to contemplate dramatic personal change, risk social dislocation, and embrace new commitments: "Let the dead bury their own dead" (Matt 8:22 // Luke 9:60 [Q]). And if, for some men, such commitments and change involved at times hiking in and around Galilee, what would have thwarted women from acting likewise? There was certainly, as the Gospels themselves attest, no ban on them being out and about.[129] Our sources have Jesus encountering women not just in homes (e.g., Mark 1:29–31; 7:24–30; 14:3; Luke 10:38–42) but also outside homes (e.g., Mark 3:31–32; 5:24–34; Luke 7:11–15; 11:27; 23:27; John 4:1–42), in the wilderness (e.g., Matt 14:13–21; 15:32–38), in synagogue (Luke 13:10–17; cf. Acts 18:26), and in the temple (Mark 12:41–44).[130]

That women were welcome in Jesus's itinerant circle is consistent with his eschatological orientation, for millenarian movements sometimes grope toward egalitarian ideas.[131] It also coheres with the circumstance that the tradition nowhere has Jesus composing the sort of derogatory comments one finds elsewhere. He never says that "women are not worthy of life" or that a woman "is in every respect of less worth than a man" or that "women are evil."[132]

128. Schottroff, "Itinerant Prophetesses," 349, may be right: "the issue" in this Q text "lies not in the inapprehensive attitude of Noah's generation, but in the culpable persistence of living on as before."

129. See further above, n. 68, and Kraemer, "Jewish Women and Christian Origins," 41–42.

130. Cf. Mark 15:40–41, 47; 16:1; Luke 2:22–51; John 20:1–18; also Luke 23:2 MarcE (Jesus is guilty of "misleading the women and the children") and 23:5 c e (Jesus "turned our children and wives away from us").

131. For details, see Allison, *Jesus of Nazareth*, 86, 108–10; also Wilcox, "Gender Roles," and Crossley, *Jesus and the Chaos of History*, 141–47 (on "gender and revolution"). I am aware of the problems surrounding the use of "egalitarian" in this connection. Despite this, I believe that Jesus's eschatological expectations, which anticipated God turning the present upside down, relativized elements of the status quo, and that we may perhaps speak of quasi- or proto-egalitarian features in some of his teaching and practice. See further Beavis, "Christian Origins," and Merz, "Genderforschung," 614–19. One should, however, keep in mind two of Levine's important essays—"Second Temple Judaism" and "Lilies of the Field." She is obviously correct to insist that "if Jesus and/or his earliest followers are seen as offering a liberating worldview for women, then this view should be regarded as representing 'the critical feminist impulse' already present in Judaism" ("Second Temple Judaism," 307, quoting Schussler Fiorenza, *In Memory of Her*, 107). So too Theissen, *Jesus als historische Gestalt*, 95, 98. For further discussion see Crossley and Myles, *Jesus*, 135–53; they see both "subversive" and "unsubversive" elements in the tradition.

132. The first quotation is attributed to Peter in Gos. Thom. 114. The second comes from Josephus, *C. Ap.* 2.201; it expresses a sentiment that appears to have been common; cf. Aristotle, *Pol.* 1254b ("the male is by nature superior and the female inferior, the male ruler

While we have no cause to imagine that such noxious quotations accurately represent the Judaism Jesus knew—Judith, the Testament of Job, Philo's account of the Therapeutae, Joseph and Aseneth, and the Liber Antiquitatum Biblicarum, for instance, happily offer views less odious to the modern temper[133]—we know that at least some in his time and place did hold related sentiments. That he seemingly did not do so may have made him more attractive for some who wished to follow him—although that can only have been one reason among others. (As with male acolytes, the sources of their attraction must have differed from individual to individual and must have been multiple and complex. In line with this, and as Levine writes, "some Jewish women may have joined the Jesus movement without primary regard for their position as women *per se*. They may have been attracted to the message (whatever it was) for the same reasons (whatever they were) that motivated their fathers, brothers, husbands, and sons."[134] Eschatological excitement, dissatisfaction with the status quo, a sense of belonging, fascination with a charismatic healer, and identification with what Jesus had to say were not gendered qualities.)

I hurry to add, as an aside, that we should be wary of reading present sensibilities or theological inclinations into Jesus's ministry. Nothing said so far entails that there were no distinctions in status or role between his male and female followers.[135] Perhaps we have no stories of Jesus calling women because

---

and the female subject") and *Rhet.* 1367a ("men are by nature more excellent than women"). The third quotation is from T. Reu. 5:1.

133. On women in the Testament of Job see the review of literature in Klancher, "Male Soul in Drag." On the Therapeutae and Philo's romantic account of them in his *Contemplative Life* (which is not pure fiction) see J. Taylor, *Jewish Women Philosophers*, and Taylor and Hay, *Philo of Alexandria*. On women in Joseph and Aseneth see Standhartinger, *Frauenbild im Judentum*, and Humphrey, *Joseph and Aseneth*, 64–78. On Pseudo-Philo and women see Halpern-Amaru, "Portraits of Women"; C. A. Brown, *No Longer Be Silent*; and Tervanotko, *Denying Her Voice*, 249–61. Brown concludes, perhaps rightly, that Pseudo-Philo comes from "a community in which women knew and taught Scripture; communicated freely God's messages of comfort, hope, reproof, and exhortation; led in worship and singing of hymns; and interceded before God in the community" (218).

134. Levine, "Second Temple Judaism," 308.

135. Puig i Tàrrech, *Jesus*, 251–52, urges that, although there were women itinerants, their job description was different: they "looked after the logistics of the group of disciples and traveled around with Jesus, though not by his side. They accompanied him through Galilee, ensuring the basic living conditions for the Master and his disciples and, naturally, taking advantage of the opportunity to hear him and witness all he did. They travelled with Jesus, but not physically. They followed him, as he had given them specific tasks that allowed them to be close to the Master, though they could not always be by his side." Although speculative, this is an intriguing proposal. I note, however, that many exegetes identify the ἀγγέλους of

he formally summoned only men to follow him. And perhaps Jesus nowhere commissions women to proclaim the nearness of the kingdom of God or to cast out demons or to heal because those tasks were, for him, outside their purview.[136] And maybe no woman is called a "disciple" because, as Levine suggests, he consciously attached that label to but a few males. (As a symbolic group, the Twelve were naturally male because the twelve patriarchs were male.)

Nothing I have argued, nor any textual evidence known to me, excludes these possibilities, however much one may wish it were otherwise. To claim that "Jesus practiced an unprecedented social openness that challenged the patriarchal societal structures of his culture by allowing a number of women to be part of his ministry"[137] outruns the evidence. To contend, as I have, that sometimes Jesus had a mixed-gender group of camp followers is scarcely the same as claiming that he opposed patriarchy on principle, or that his female devotees must have missionized just like the men did, or that his attitude toward women was a profound *novum* within his Jewish world.

Extracanonical Traditions

(9) A few extracanonical voices affirm that Jesus had a fixed group of female followers. Whether these later voices belong exclusively to the inventive reception history of the canonical Gospels or reflect in part an independent social memory I do not pretend to know. It may, in any event, be worth noting that in 1 Apoc. Jas. 38.16–17—which may come from the late second century[138]—Jesus is asked: "Who are the seven women who have been your disciples [ⲙⲁⲑⲏⲧⲏⲥ]?"[139] Unfortunately, the text is damaged, so the follow-

Luke 9:52 with James and John (9:54), and those who go ahead and make arrangements for Jesus in Mark 11:1–3 and 14:12–16 are male disciples.

136. Cf. Levine, "Women Itinerants," 58: if "the Gospels depict women as recipients of Jesus's healings," and if "they similarly depict the male disciples as commissioned to heal and perform exorcisms, the New Testament depicts no women as healers. Is this absence of such detail indicative of a restriction of women's roles in the Jesus movement, with the men assuming the healing functions?"

137. Awwad, "Women Discipleship," 11. Cf. Pagola, *Jesus*, 209–30.

138. See Marjanen, *Woman Jesus Loved*, 125–29.

139. This text is not alone in designating one or more women as "disciples"; note, e.g., Gospel of Peter 12:50 (μαθήτρια of Mary Magdalene); Gos. Thom. 61 (ⲙⲁⲑⲏⲧⲏⲥ of Salome); Tertullian, *Marc.* 4.19.1 (*discipulas* of the women of Luke 8:1–3); Wis. Jes. Chr. (NHC III 4) 90.16–18 (= BG 3 77.10–14) (ⲙⲁⲑⲏⲧⲉⲩⲉ of a group of seven women); Did. apost. 3.6.2

ing dialogue is full of gaps. But 40.24–26 names four of the women: Salome, Mariam, Martha, and Arisnoe.[140] A group of seven female followers likewise appears in Wis. Jes. Chr. (NHC III 4) 90.16–18 (= BG 3 77.10–14): "After he rose from the dead, his twelve male disciples and seven female disciples continued to be his followers."[141] This was likely composed in the early second century,[142] and it appears to be independent of 1 Apoc. Jas. 38.16–17.[143]

The hebtade in 1 Apoc. Jas. 18.16–17 is clearly the female counterpart of the twelve male disciples, for the question about the seven women directly follows a discussion regarding the typological meaning of the twelve disciples. The same holds for Wis. Jes. Chr. (NHC III 4) 90.16–18 (= BG 3 77.10–14), which lumps together "seven women" and "his twelve disciples" as Jesus's followers or pupils. So both sources imagine Jesus's past much like Mark 15:40–41 and the dominant reading of Luke 8:1–3: his roving band included women.

It is the same in the Gospel of Philip, although here the group of women is smaller:[144] "There were three who kept company with the Lord at all times [ⲟⲩⲟⲉⲓϣ]: Mary his mother, her [his?] sister, and Magdalene, who is called his companion [ⲧⲉϥⲕⲟⲓⲛⲱⲛⲟⲥ]. For Mary was his sister and his mother and his companion" (59.6–9)—that is, they were all named Mary. This line entails that these three women left their homes to follow Jesus.[145]

The Gospel of Thomas, while it drops no hint about a group of women, implies that at least Mary—likely the Magdalene, but this is unsaid—kept Jesus's company outside her house. In Gos. Thom. 114, Peter says: "Let Mary go away

(*discipulae* of "Mary Magdalene and Mary the daughter of James and the other Mary"); Chrysostom, *Hom. Jo.* 65 *ad* 12:1–2 (μαθήτρια for Mary of Bethany); 72 *ad* 13:28 (αἱ μαθήτριαι for the women of Luke 8:2–3).

140. For reconstruction of the Coptic see Marjanen, *Woman Jesus Loved*, 132–35.

141. Parrott, *Nag Hammadi Codices*, 37, translates the Coptic: "After he rose from the dead, his twelve disciples and seven women continued to be his followers." But the text refers to "seven female disciples": ⲥⲁϣϥⲉ ⲛ̄ⲥϩⲓⲙⲉ ⲙⲁⲑⲏⲧⲉⲩⲉ.

142. For Parrott, *Nag Hammadi Codices*, 6, a first-century date is possible. Marjanen, *Woman Jesus Loved*, 60, prefers "the early part of the second century."

143. So Marjanen, *Woman Jesus Loved*, 71–72.

144. The Gospel of Philip comes from the second or third century; it is not, however, a unified work but a collection of materials of disparate origin; see M. Turner, *Gospel according to Philip*.

145. Three females are also named in Matt 27:56 (Mary Magdalene, Mary the mother of James and of Joseph, the mother of the sons of Zebedee); Mark 15:40; 16:1 (Mary Magdalene, Mary the mother of James the younger and of Joses, Salome); Luke 8:1–3 (Mary Magdalene, Joanna, Susanna); and the Ethiopic Epistle of the Apostles 9.3 (Sarah, Martha, Mary Magdalene).

[ⲉⲓ ⲉⲃⲟⲗ] from us, for women are not worthy of life." The insult requires that Mary has been keeping company with the disciples. Peter's request can hardly mean: "Let Mary go away from us here in her own home." The text assumes that she has been following Jesus and his disciples.

We can put no trust in the numbers in the Gospel of Philip, the Wisdom of Jesus Christ, or the First Apocalypse of James. Yet the shared idea, that Jesus's full-time followers included women along with men, accords with what we can otherwise infer from the Synoptics and Gos. Thom. 114. And there is, to my knowledge, no competing tradition, that is, no source stating that only men were in Jesus's entourage. My wager, then, is that Mark 15:40–41 is not fiction: at least a few women used to accompany Jesus in his travels. Even if most of Jesus's female fans went out to see him for only a few hours at a time, at least a small number were like the Twelve: they kept his company even when he left their neighborhood to take to the road.

Unlike the apocryphal texts, I hazard no number. Mark names three women who followed Jesus when he was in Galilee: Mary Magdalene, Mary the mother of James the younger and of Joses, and Salome (15:40–41). Whether the evangelist's ensuing reference to "many other women" (ἄλλαι πολλαί) means that they too regularly followed him around or only "came up with him to Jerusalem" is unclear. By contrast, Luke 8:1–3, on the interpretation I have defended, affirms that, in addition to Mary Magdalene, Joanna, and Susanna, "many other" women (ἕτεραι πολλαί) were "with" (σύν) Jesus as he traveled through (διώδευεν) villages and cities preaching the kingdom of God. Perhaps this is not just Luke's hyperbolic flourish but the historical truth.[146] Yet even if it is, the imprecise πολλαί—how many are "many"?—regrettably leaves us guessing at their number, which surely fluctuated over time in any case.

Looking with Lust

I turn now to several Synoptic texts to consider how they might be related to the inferences made so far.[147]

Jesus, according to Matt 5:27–28, said this: "You have heard that it was said: 'You will not commit adultery' [cf. Exod 20:14; Deut 5:18]. But I say to you that

146. So Casey, *Jesus of Nazareth*, 197: "numerous" women followed Jesus.

147. In an earlier book, *Jesus of Nazareth*, 175–216, I examined these texts in making a case that Jesus was a (mild) millenarian ascetic. Here the focus is rather on how they might have functioned within the mixed company that attended Jesus.

everyone who looks at a woman with lust has already committed adultery with her in his heart." These words, which address males,[148] set a fence around the Torah: without lust in the heart, adultery will not occur. As Augustine wrote: "The man who does not commit adultery in the heart much more easily guards against committing adultery in actual fact. Hence he who gave the later precept confirmed the earlier" (*Serm. Dom.* 1.12.33).

The warning in Matt 5:27–28, which has extrabiblical parallels,[149] probably has to do specifically with a man lusting after another man's wife.[150] The Greek word translated above as "woman" (γυναῖκα) often means "wife," and the subject of the citation from the Decalogue is adultery. It remains true, however, that γυναῖκα is unqualified. This has allowed commentators to widen the scope of the admonition.[151] The possibility for such broadening was there from the beginning, for intercourse outside marriage was not a venial sin in Jesus's world.[152] Certainly Matt 5:27–28 does not imply that, while lusting after

148. Cf. Chrysostom, *Hom. Matt.* 17.3: "Why does he not discourse with them [women] also?"

149. See, e.g., T. Iss. 7:2 ("I have not had intercourse with any woman other than my wife, nor was I promiscuous by lustful look"); b. Ber. 61a ("if a man counts out money from his hand into the hand of a woman so as to have the opportunity of gazing at her, even if he can vie in Torah and good deeds with Moses our teacher, he will not escape the punishment of Gehenna"); b. ʿAbod. Zar. 20a ("one should not look intently at a beautiful woman even if she is unmarried, or at a married woman even if she is ugly"); b. B. Bat. 16a ("Dust should be put in Job's mouth; he refrained from looking at other men's wives. Abraham did not even look at his own"); Mek. R. Shim. on Exod 20:13 (ed. Hoffmann, 111: "Do not commit adultery with the hand or the foot or the eye or the heart"); Lev. Rab. 23:12 ("if he commits adultery with his eyes he is also called an adulterer"; cf. Pesiq. Rab. 24:2); Kallah 11 ("whoever gazes intentionally at a woman is as though he had intercourse with her"); Arrian, *Epict. diss.* 2.18.15 ("Today when I saw a handsome lad or a handsome woman I did not say to myself, Would that a man might sleep with her. . . . I do not even picture to myself the next scene—the woman herself in my presence, disrobing and lying down by my side"); CIL 4:7698b ("remove lustful expressions and flirtatious, tender eyes from another man's wife"). See further Büchler, *Jewish-Palestinian Piety*, 42–55, and below, pp. 267–68.

150. So Betz, *Sermon on the Mount*, 233; France, *Matthew*, 204; and Konradt, *Matthew*, 85.

151. Note, e.g., Lapide, *Great Commentary*, 2:259 ("lust for a woman who is not your wife is forbidden by this law"); Bruce, "Synoptic Gospels," 108 ("γυναῖκα: married or unmarried"); and Hagner, *Matthew*, 1:120 ("γυναῖκα is probably to be understood more broadly to mean any 'woman' and not simply the wife of another"; "if a more restrictive understanding were in view, one might expect the noun to be modified, e.g., τοῦ πλησίου [σου], 'your neighbor's'").

152. See Loader, *Making Sense of Sex*, 45–47. Cf. Philo, *Ios.* 42–43: "With us a courtesan is not even permitted to live, and death is the penalty appointed for women who ply this trade.

another man's wife is sinful, lusting after an unmarried woman is just fine. The latter case is naturally, by implication, also censored.[153]

Matthew's construction (πρὸς τὸ ἐπιθυμῆσαι αὐτήν)—which alludes to the commandment against coveting[154] and may assume that covetousness is the sin behind all other sins[155]—condemns seemingly not the arrival of a thought but what one does with it: one can hear a knock without opening the door.[156] We might translate: "Everyone looking on a woman *in order to* lust after her."[157] This is quite different from saying: "Do not look at a woman." The issue is not vision but intention, not what wanders into one's line of sight but what one chooses to gaze at with indecorous thoughts. The imagination must guard itself. It should will to abstain, not indulge. Sexual thoughts are, in Matt 5:27–28, perilous. They must not be attended to. That way lies adultery.

I forgo an attempt to pin down the pre-Matthean form of Matt 5:27–28 or to establish with full conviction that Jesus was its author. Those tasks are far more arduous than many imagine.[158] I at least do not know how to accomplish

---

Before the lawful union we know no mating with other women, but come as virgin men to virgin maidens." While the words about the death penalty are presumably overblown, one finds the same sentiment in Josephus; see Mayer-Schärtel, *Frauenbild des Josephus*, 254–56. Many decried intercourse for any purpose other than procreation; see below, n. 218.

153. Cf. Alford, *Greek Testament*, 1:48, and Culpepper, *Matthew*, 110.

154. Exod 20:17 // Deut 5:21: "Do not covet [LXX: ἐπιθυμῆσαι] your neighbor's wife." Prov 6:25 MT already merges the commandments not to commit adultery and not to covet: "Do not covet [אל־תחמד] her beauty [the beauty of the adulteress] in your heart" borrows from Exod 20:17 // Deut 5:21: "Do not covet [לא תחמד] your neighbor's wife." Rabbinic sources also associate the two prohibitions; see Ruzer, *Mapping the New Testament*, 23–26. Clement of Alexandria, *Strom.* 2.14 and 3.2, and sundry exegetes of Matthew forge the same intertextual link.

155. For this thought see Philo, *Spec.* 4.84 (covetousness is "the fountain of all evils"); *Decal.* 142, 173; *QG* 1.47; LAE Gk. 19:3 ("covetousness is the origin of every sin"); Apoc. Abr. 24:9 ("desire" is "the fount of every kind of lawlessness"); Jas 1:14–15.

156. Cf. Jerome, *Comm. Matt.* 5.28; Augustine, *Serm. Dom.* 1.12.33–34; Gregory of Nyssa, *Beat.* 2 ("he says not that one is condemned when desire happens to arise but when one is wittingly drawn to passion"); and Evagrius Ponticus, *Praktikos* 6 ("it is not in our power to determine whether we are disturbed by these [evil] thoughts, but it is up to us to decide if they are to linger within us or not and whether or not they stir up our passions").

157. Cf. the construction in Sus 8 (LXX: ἰδόντες γυναῖκα . . . ἐπιθυμήσαντες αὐτῆς; Theodotion: ἐθεώρουν αὐτήν . . . ἐπιθυμίᾳ αὐτῆς) and the use of the πρός + articular infinitive in Matt 6:1; 13:30; 23:5; and see further the extensive discussion in Tholuck, *Sermon on the Mount*, 206–11. The sense is not, as occasionally suggested: "Looks at a woman in such a way as to cause her to feel desire." See Betz, *Sermon on the Mount*, 233–34.

158. But for an attempt to authenticate the saying see Becker, *Jesus of Nazareth*, 288–89. Contrast Gundry, *Matthew*, 87: "The evidence for composition by Matthew is overwhelming."

them. I content myself with the claim that it takes only a bit of imagination to envisage a setting for Matt 5:27–28 in the pre-Easter period. I propose that we keep in mind the following:

- Some of the men who followed Jesus were, at least for short periods of time, away from home and perhaps (if they were married) from their wives.[159]
- The circle that followed Jesus included, at least now and then, a few women.
- Some of the women were, for at least short periods of time, away from home and perhaps (if they were married) husbands; and some may have been unmarried.[160]
- Jesus, in accord with his religious tradition and his ascetical tendencies,[161] viewed sexual relations outside of marriage as sinful.[162]
- Jesus's most ardent and intense admirers, enthusiastic in their common cause, would likely have bonded emotionally with each other.

159. Cf. Holland, "Celibacy in the Early Church," 66–67: "Presumably the disciples' travels with Jesus imposed at least a temporary celibacy on them, although they were not otherwise ascetic." The New Testament reports that Peter was married (Mark 1:29–31; cf. 1 Cor 9:5), and Mark 10:29–30 refers to those who have left house and relatives to follow Jesus. The parallel in Luke 18:28–30 speaks of a disciple leaving a wife. While this is probably a redactional addition (so Strotmann, *Historische Jesus*, 140–41; cf. Luke 14:20 and Matt 10:37 diff. Luke 14:26), it may, if "house" (οἰκίαν) in that verse includes "wife," correctly interpret Mark 10:29; cf. Levine, "Women Itinerants," 57. But for the proposal that some of Jesus's disciples traveled with wives see n. 113.

160. See esp. Sim, "Women Followers," 53–55. Unmarried women and widows, he notes, could have had some economic resources and independence, and he urges that "the majority" of women who followed Jesus were single. We do not alas have enough evidence to adjudicate the matter. No husband is named for Mary the Magdalene (Mark 15:40, etc.; the tradition that she married John the Evangelist at the wedding of Cana is later legend), Salome (Mark 15:40), or Susanna (Luke 8:3), and we have no evidence that Joanna (Luke 8:3) or Mary the mother of James the younger and of Joses (Mark 15:40) or the mother of the sons of Zebedee (Matt 20:20; 27:56; Mark 15:40?) traveled with their husbands. Indeed, regarding Joanna, it is hard to imagine Luke neglecting her husband's activity if he knew of it. Cf. Schaberg, *Death and Resurrection*, 173: "A significant number of women are mentioned without reference to husbands or sons, a fact that may indicate that these relationships did not define the women who were without these relationships."

161. On this subject see Allison, *Jesus of Nazareth*, 172–216, and Joseph, "Ascetic Jesus."

162. Sexual relations with another's wife is condemned categorically in the Decalogue (Exod 20:14; Deut 5:18; cf. Lev 18:20). On intercourse between the unmarried see above, n. 152. Like many and perhaps most Jews of his time—but certainly not all—and despite biblical examples of polygamy, Jesus seemingly regarded monogamy as the norm; cf. CD IV, 20–5:2; 11QTemple LVII, 15–19; Mark 10:2–9. This was in accord with the dominant Greco-Roman ethos and certainly the norm for the movement he started; cf. 1 Tim 3:2, 12; Tit 1:6.

These circumstances suggest a specific, pre-Easter function for Matt 5:27–28 as opposed to the bare possibility that the warning against carnal cogitation was, if Jesus uttered it, global counsel aimed at everyone, applicable to all without discrimination. When people met Jesus, they also met each other; and women and men, in the joint promotion of a religious cause deemed supremely important, may on occasion have experienced feelings of sexual attraction for one another. People are typically most drawn to like-minded others ("birds of a feather"). Such pull would have been the more forceful if, as multiple texts imply, some were alienated from family members, from relatives who were not so enthusiastic about Jesus. We should, moreover, keep in mind that most of Jesus's male followers were not old men with diminished sexual drive,[163] and further that we have no cause to imagine that all the women were seniors without libidos.[164]

Such a situation was potentially charged, and within it a warning against a man looking lustfully at a woman—male proximity to women is assumed[165]—would have had two concrete functions, one occasioned by Jesus's piety, the other by anxiety over public perception. He would have been sincerely concerned that his friends, for their own sakes, not fall into fornication or adultery. And he would have wanted to avert any semblance of impropriety and avoid abetting the disapproval of detractors.

On this interpretation, Jesus, if he authored something like Matt 5:27–28, was speaking not vaguely, theoretically, or proverbially. He was rather directly addressing men in the mixed company immediately around him.[166] In ad-

163. Destro and Pesce, "In and Out of the House," 302, observe: "A peculiarity of this voluntary aggregation [of Jesus's followers] consists in the fact that no male members of the older generation (the disciples' fathers) were part of it."

164. According to Van Os, *Psychological Analyses*, 49–50, the women who followed Jesus were probably "past a certain age. Their position may have been like that of the noble women in Acts 13.50 and 17.4. Typically, these were older women, often widows (about half the women above age 40 were widowed) who were financially independent when their husbands had died (the difference between bride and bridegroom could be up to 50 years)." I note that if the author of the Protevangelium of James identified the Salome present at Jesus's birth with the Salome of Mark 15:40 and 16:1, then he took her to be older rather than younger when Jesus died. Still, Matt 10:35–36 // Luke 12:53 refers to daughters and daughters-in-law, and nothing in the tradition hints that only older women found Jesus compelling.

165. Despite this, the Jesus tradition nowhere reverts to the stereotype of women as temptresses; contrast Prov 6:24–25; T. Reu. 5:1–6; T. Jud. 10:3–5; T. Jos. 2–9; Ps. Sol. 16:7, etc.

166. Cf. Jeremias, *New Testament Theology*, 227: "Jesus accepts women into the group of disciples because he expects them to control their desires." Here Luther, *Sermon on the Mount*, 85, is on the right track: "Christ is not forbidding us to live together, to eat and drink,

monishing male disciples not to look lustfully on women, he would have been warning followers about a potential or perhaps real problem. He would have been counseling imaginations, forewarning men from nurturing thoughts that might eventuate in unwelcome consequences, in sexual waywardness and scandal. Like Paul in 1 Cor 7 and so many of the Greco-Roman moralists and the church fathers, he presumed that one need not be the passive prey of the sexual impulse: self-control is possible.[167] One should be able, as m. ʾAbot 4:1 has it, to restrain or conquer one's desire or passions (יצר).[168]

Divorce and Remarriage

Paul, Mark, and (for those of us who posit its existence) Q concur that Jesus prohibited divorce and remarriage (1 Cor 7:10–11; Mark 10:2–9 par.; Matt 5:31–32; Luke 16:18). We have no good reason to doubt their joint testimony. Few do.[169] Most recent discussions of this tradition debate not the origin of the injunction but its tradition history. Can we posit an Ur-text from which all the variants derive?[170] Is the lengthy, supporting argument in Mark 10:2–9 secondary or original?[171] Did Jesus envisage the possibility of a woman divorcing

and even to laugh and have fun. That is all innocuous, provided this one thing is absent, 'to look at her lustfully.'" Contrast the pessimistic, hyperbolic warning attributed to R. ʾAḥa in b. Ned. 20a: "He who gazes at a woman eventually comes to sin, and he who looks even at a woman's heel will beget degenerate children."

167. Cf. Betz, *Sermon on the Mount*, 239 ("restraint, even asceticism, is the best way to fulfill the divine commandment"), and W. T. Wilson, *Matthew*, 1:172 ("the language . . . projects a positive view of human agency, the assumption being that individuals possess the capacity both to identify and to eliminate the sources of sin without themselves"). Contrast the advice in b. Ḥag. 16a and b. Moʿed Qaṭ. 17a: "R. Elai the elder said: 'If a man sees this his [evil] inclination is prevailing on him, let him go to a place where he is not known, and put on black garments, and let him do what his heart desires [sleep with women]; but let him not profane the Name of heaven publicly.'"

168. Cf. 1 Thess 4:3–5 ("this is the will of God . . . that you abstain from fornication; that each one of you know how to control your own body [*or* wife] in holiness and honor, not with lustful passion"); Tg. Ps 50:23 ("he who sacrifices the evil יצרא" will be reckoned as having made a "thank offering" glorifying God); and b. ʿAbod. Zar. 19a ("blessed is he who masters his יצר like a man").

169. For the usual arguments see Meier, *Marginal Jew*, 4:74–181.

170. On the complexity of the textual tradition see Parker, *Living Text of the Gospels*, 75–94.

171. For the case that the long form is original see Sanders and Davies, *Synoptic Gospels*, 328. Niederwimmer, *Askese und Mysterium*, 44–53, and R. F. Collins, *Divorce*, 214–29, take the opposite view.

a man, or was that added later?[172] What elements in Matt 5:32 and Luke 16:18 are from Q?[173] What is the meaning of the exception clause in Matt 5:32 and 19:9, and what does it intimate about Matthew's context?[174]

Scholars expend less effort explaining why Jesus felt moved to address the subject in the first place. Doubtless something concrete summoned his opinion. If no one in his world had divorced and remarried or was entertaining doing so, the subject would not have arisen. Jesus did not stroll about Galilee broadcasting halakhic opinions without occasion.

Some propose that the formulation in Mark 10:12, which forbids a woman from divorcing her husband to marry another, was a response to Herodias marrying Herod Antipas, the half-brother of her husband.[175] According to Mark 6:17–19, John the Baptist censured their union. Maybe Jesus followed his example. More common is the idea that Jesus tendered his judgment simply because, as Mark has it, some bade him to do so.[176] In other words, Jesus complied when asked for his verdict on a disputed issue of the day. The Markan setting, where Pharisees ask him, "Is it lawful for a man to divorce his wife?," suggests as much.

Yet even if that is the truth, it remains to ask: How did the prohibition function for Jesus's immediate followers? Was his ruling just an exegetical or halakic curiosity without close-to-home meaning? Or was there something in it to take to heart and remember, something potentially pertinent to those who sought to heed his teaching?

When Jesus, in Mark 10:11–12, responds to the Pharisees' question, he does not confine himself to the subject of divorce, which is all they have asked

172. The prevailing verdict has been that Mark 10, which envisages the possibility of a woman initiating divorce, reflects Roman law, and that in Judea men alone were the agents of divorce. This is, however, unclear, especially in view of Papyrus Ṣe'lim 13 (probably from Nahal Hever), in which a woman seems to initiate divorce; cf. also Josephus, *Ant.* 20.143, 147. For the issues see I. Tan, "Newly Published Divorce Bill"; J. J. Collins, "Marriage, Divorce," 119–21; Schremer, "Divorce in Papyrus Ṣe'lim"; Instone-Brewer, "Jewish Women"; Instone-Brewer, *Divorce and Remarriage*, 85–90; and Kazen, *Scripture*, 259–64.

173. Robinson, Hoffmann, and Kloppenborg, *Critical Edition of Q*, 470, propose this reconstruction: "Everyone who divorces his wife [[and marries another]] commits adultery, and the one who marries a divorcée commits adultery."

174. See, in addition to the commentaries, Instone-Brewer, *Divorce and Remarriage*, 152–59, and Kazen, *Scripture*, 271–76.

175. So Burkitt, *Gospel History*, 98–101; Hoehner, *Herod Antipas*, 139; R. F. Collins, *Divorce*, 221–22; Loader, "Sexuality and the Historical Jesus," 44–45; Kazen, *Scripture*, 277–80; and Crossley and Myles, *Jesus*, 165–66.

176. See Mark 10:2–9. Commentators routinely explain that the schools of Hillel and Shammai disagreed over what constituted legitimate cause for divorce.

about. He speaks not about divorce but about divorce and remarriage.[177] The same holds for all versions of the saying in the Synoptics and Paul: each proscribes remarriage. This is a crucial clue.

If, as Matt 5:27–28 may reveal, Jesus felt compelled to address his circle about the issue of sexual temptation, then it may have been equally incumbent for him to address the topic of divorce and remarriage.[178] While the canonical Gospels tell us next to nothing about the women around Jesus, they were there; and general human experience strongly suggests that their sometime presence with men, some of whom were alienated from their families or were now and then away from home, would have occasioned certain feelings and thoughts, especially as they were caught up together in a supremely important cause. But such thoughts and feelings would have been problematic for Jesus, who regarded intercourse outside marriage as illicit. His injunction against divorce and remarriage was, then, likely as germane to his most dedicated followers as the warning (if it rightly represents him) about sexual desire in Matt 5:27–28. If any of his married followers were strongly attracted to someone other than a spouse, the situation—which might give rise to scandal[179]—could not be remedied through the expediency of divorce and remarriage.

This proposal is, to be sure, hypothetical. It is not, however, ungrounded. If intercourse beyond wedlock was out of bounds, then forbidding divorce and remarriage would have canceled, for married followers, any possibility of turning illicit attraction into licit union. Jesus would have been vetoing the option Akiba reportedly permitted: a man may divorce his wife if he finds "another fairer than she" (see m. Giṭ. 9:10; b. Soṭah 90a).

177. Cf. Ps.-Phoc. 205 ("you should not add marriage to marriage") and Philo, *Spec.* 2.135 (this condemns those who seek a second wife because they are driven by pleasure). The Old Testament forbids priests from marrying divorced women: Lev 21:7, 13–14; cf. Ezek 44:22.

178. Cf. Jacobson, "Divided Families," 371 (the prohibition—which is focused on remarriage—addresses those who had sundered family ties to follow Jesus; it "stigmatizes" anyone wishing to divorce in order to marry a member of the in-group; Jacobson is writing about "the Q group"); Levine, "Word Becomes Flesh," 74 ("where husbands and wives are following Jesus, the last thing he and his movement need are charges of, or temptations to, adultery"); Tiwald, *Wanderradikalismus*, 218–19; Ebner, *Jesus von Nazaret*, 151 ("If a man wants to join Jesus, he must do so together with his wife. Even when the wife does not come along, the husband remains bound. This may be important apropos 'dismissed' wives who join Jesus. Inside the group [of itinerants], new liaisons could [in theory] be initiated. Jesus puts a halt to that possibility"); and Junker, *Scheidungslogion*, 256 (the saying directly addressed the mixed company of Q itinerants).

179. Cf. Levine, "Women in the Q Communit(ies)," 160: "The forbidding of remarriage may have . . . been intended to decrease negative reaction from outsiders: divorce and remarriage . . . then, as now, can easily create scandal." See further below, pp. 276–81.

Eunuchs Because of the Kingdom

In Matt 19:10, the disciples react to Jesus's teaching on divorce and remarriage with the words, "if such is the case of a man with his wife, it is better not to marry." Their teacher responds with a declaration about eunuchs (19:11–12).[180]

The connection with the previous paragraph (19:3–9), which is Matthew's revision of Mark 10:2–12, is inelegant,[181] and I share Luz's judgment that Matt 19:10–11 is a redactional stitch: it sews the traditional saying in 19:12 onto Mark's unit.[182] As to the origin of the declaration about eunuchs, many ascribe it to Jesus, often with the proposal that it was his rejoinder to the polemical jeer that he was a eunuch.[183] This is an attractive hypothesis for which I have argued elsewhere.[184] Jesus, a bit like Paul in 2 Corinthians, seems not to have ignored polemic or insults. He rather energetically rewrote slander and threw it back at opponents. "How can Satan cast out Satan?" (Mark 3:23). "John came neither eating nor drinking, and they say: 'He has a demon'; the Son of Man came eating and drinking, and they say: 'Behold a glutton and a drunkard'" (Matt 11:18–19; cf. Luke 7:33–34 [Q]). "Those who are sick have no need of a physician, but those who are sick. I came not to call the righteous but sinners" (Mark 2:17).[185]

180. Against Blinzler, "Justinus Apol. i 15,4." I doubt that Justin, *1 Apol.* 15.4, preserves an independent version of this saying.

181. This is why exegetes disagree as to whether "the word" (τὸν λόγον, Matt 19:11) refers back (1) to the ruling on divorce and remarriage (19:3–9 or 19:9), (2) to the disciples' verdict in 19:10 (it is better not to marry), or (3) forward to the saying about eunuchs in 19:12.

182. Luz, *Matthew*, 3:488.

183. So originally Blinzler, "Εἰσὶν εὐνοῦχοι" (attributing the slur to the Pharisees or scribes); cf. Dupont, *Mariage et divorce*, 199–200; Adinolfi, "Celibato"; Tannehill, *Sword of His Mouth*, 137–38; Meier, *Marginal Jew* 1:344; Moloney, *Hard Saying*, 47–51; Moxnes, *Putting Jesus in His Place*, 75, 88–89; and R. F. Collins, *Believing Wife*, 102–5. The backdrop would have been the common idea that reproduction was a religious duty; cf. Gen 1:27–28; 2:21–24; Deut 7:14; Ps.-Phoc. 175–76 ("Remain not unmarried, lest you die nameless. Give nature her due; beget in your turn as you were begotten"; on this, see the commentary by van der Horst, *Sentences of Pseudo Phocylides*, 225–27); m. Yeb. 6:6 ("No man may abstain from keeping the law: 'Be fruitful and multiply' [Gen 1:28], unless he already has children"); and b. Yeb. 63b ("R. Eliezer stated: 'He who does not engage in propagation of the race is as though he sheds blood'"). For additional rabbinic texts of similar import see McArthur, "Celibacy in Judaism," 164–68.

184. Allison, *Jesus of Nazareth*, 183–85. Jewish sources prohibit castration and often look askance at eunuchs and regard emasculation as a punishment; cf. Lev 21:20 (exclusion from the priesthood); 22:24; Deut 23:1 (exclusion from the covenant community); 2 Kgs 20:18; T. Jud. 23:3–5; Ps.-Phoc. 187; Philo, *Migr.* 69; *Spec.* 3.40–42; *Hypoth.* 7.7; Gal 5:12; Josephus, *Ant.* 4.290–91; b. Šabb. 110b; Sipra Lev. 224. Exceptions appear in Isa 56:3–4 and Wis 3:14. (Against some, I detect no allusion to Isa 56:3–4 in Matt 19:12.)

185. Note also Mark 2:7, 18, 24; 7:5; 14:64; and John 8:48 ("are we not right in saying that you are a Samaritan and have a demon?").

The declaration in Matt 19:12 envisages three types of eunuch: those so from the womb, those made so by others, and those who have, on account of the kingdom, made themselves eunuchs. The first two types were, as recent commentaries recurrently observe, conventional.[186] Rabbinic sources know of the "eunuch of the sun" (סריס חמה). This designates a man congenitally incapable of reproducing, a eunuch from the first seeing of the sun, that is, from birth.[187] Jewish sources also refer to the "eunuch of man" (סריס אדם), a man who has been sexually mutilated by another (cf. m. Zab. 2:1; m. Yeb. 8:4; t. Ber. 5:14; t. Yeb. 10:6; y. Yeb. 8:4 [9d]; b. Yeb. 75a, 79b, 80a). These two conventional entities, either occasioned by nature or imposed by others, serve to introduce a third, unconventional type of eunuch, one who wills himself into existence for the sake of the kingdom.[188]

In its triadic structure, Matt 19:12 adopts a conventional form: two self-evident, taken-for-granted facts introduce an analogous, climactic third item from the moral or religious sphere:[189]

Prov 20:15

a. "There is gold,
b. and abundance of costly stones;
c. but the lips informed by knowledge are a precious jewel."

Prov 25:3

a. "Like the heavens for height,
b. like the earth for depth,
c. so the mind of kings is unsearchable."

Prov 27:3

a. "A stone is heavy,
b. and sand is weighty,
c. but a fool's provocation is heavier than both."

186. This is different from affirming that they are both literal: that is true only of the second eunuch. The first, that "from the mother's womb," is a metaphor; it represents congenital conditions that precluded reproduction; see next note and Bradford, "Born Eunuch." (Bradford suggests that Matt 19:12 is relevant for contemporary discussions of intersexuals.)

187. This would include being born without testicles or with only one testicle or in an indeterminate state; cf. t. Ber. 5:14–16 ("eunuchs castrated by man or born without testicles or one whose testicles are crushed"; this goes on to refer to "a person with undeveloped genitals" and "a person who exhibits traits of both sexes"); t. Yeb. 10:3 (the man born with only one testicle is "a eunuch of the sun"). Note also Eusebius, *Hist. eccl.* 7.32.3: εὐνοῦχος οὕτω πεφυκὼς ἐξ αὐτῆς γενέσεως.

188. Cf. the distinction in Jerome, *Ep.* 22.19: "Some may be eunuchs from necessity. I am one of free will."

189. On the form see Yaron, "Climactic Tricolon."

Prov 30:33
a. "For as pressing milk produces curds,
b. and pressing the nose produces blood,
c. so pressing anger produces strife."

Ahiqar 21 (trans. Lindenberger)
a. "How can logs strive with fire,
b. meat with a knife,
c. (or) a man with a king?"[190]

This triadic structure also appears in aphorisms in the Jesus tradition:

Matt 8:20 // Luke 9:58 (Q) (cf. Gos. Thom. 86)
a. "Foxes have holes,
b. and birds of the air have nests;
c. but the Son of Man has nowhere to lay his head."

Matt 7:9–11
a. "What man among you, when his son asks for bread, will instead give him a stone?
b. Or again, if he asks for a fish, will give him a snake?
c. If you, then, being evil, know how to give good gifts to your children, how much more will your Father in heaven give good gifts to those who ask him."[191]

Luke 12:54–55
a. "When you see a cloud rising in the west, you immediately say: 'It is going to rain'; and so it happens.
b. And when you see the south wind blowing, you say: 'There will be scorching heat'; and it happens.
c. You hypocrites! You know how to interpret the appearance of earth and sky, but why do you not know how to interpret the present time?"[192]

190. Note also Prov 6:27–28 and 10:26.

191. The parallel Luke 11:11–13 (Q), although a bit different, has the same structure: "(a) Is there anyone among you who, if your child asks for a fish, will give a snake instead of a fish? (b) Or if the child asks for an egg, will give a scorpion? (c) If you then, who are evil, know how to give good gifts to your children, how much more will the heavenly Father give the Holy Spirit to those who ask him!"

192. Matthew's version (16:2–3) is slightly different, but it too is triadic: "(a) When it is evening, you say: 'It will be fair weather, for the sky is red.' (b) And in the morning: 'It

Mark 3:24–26

a. "If a kingdom is divided against itself, that kingdom cannot stand.
b. And if a house is divided against itself, that house will not be able to stand.
c. And if Satan has risen up against himself and is divided, he cannot stand, but his end has come."

Matt 19:12 offers one more example of the traditional structure:

a. "There are eunuchs who have been so from birth,
b. and there are eunuchs who have been made eunuchs by others,
c. and there are eunuchs who have made themselves eunuchs because of the kingdom of heaven."[193]

How might Matt 19:12, if dominical, have functioned for Jesus's hearers? If it was a riposte to the sneer that he was a eunuch,[194] it was a word of self-defense, apologetics of a sort: Jesus had no wife[195] because the kingdom, presumed to be at hand, demanded the kind of full-time commitment impossible for those entangled in run-of-the-mill affairs.[196] His goal lay "beyond the tasks posed

will be stormy today, for the sky is red and threatening.' (c) You know how to interpret the appearance of the sky, but you cannot interpret the signs of the times."

193. I take the διά in διὰ τὴν βασιλείαν to signify cause: "because of the kingdom of heaven." Celibacy is not a means to the kingdom but a calling or duty the kingdom imposes on some.

194. Cf. the depreciating stereotyping in Philo, *Somn.* 2.184 ("a vagrant from the men's quarters, an exile from the women's, a thing neither male nor female . . . base counterfeit of the human coin"); Herodotus, *Hist.* 8.106 (a eunuch says to the man who castrated him: "you made me to be nothing instead of a man"); Xenophon, *Cyr.* 7.5.61 ("eunuchs are objects of contempt to the rest of human beings"); Heraclitus, *Ep.* 9 ("a dog does not castrate another dog"); Tertullian, *Mon.* 9 ("because eunuchs and the barren used to be regarded as ignominious"); Babrius, *Fab.* 54 ("when I look into your face you seem not even to be a man"); Philostratus, *Vit. soph.* 1.541 ("making fun of him for being like a eunuch"); Apuleius, *Metam.* 7.23–28; Lucian, *Eunuchus*; and b. Šabb. 152a (the exchange of insults between a bald rabbi and a eunuch includes this: "O eunuch . . . the glory of a face is its beard; the rejoicing of one's heart is a wife; the heritage of the Lord is children. Blessed be the Omnipresent, who has denied you all three").

195. That Jesus was unmarried is not certain but likely; see Meier, *Marginal Jew*, 1:332–45, and Le Donne, *Wife of Jesus*.

196. Tertullian, *Mon.* 3, already puts Jesus within the scope of Matt 19:12; cf. Moxnes, *Jesus in His Place*, 84–86. I here need not engage the issue of Jesus's own sexuality, which has been an arena of lively debate of late; see Martin, *Sex and the Single Savior*, 91–102, and the brief overview with references to the secondary literature in King, "Jesus," 421.

by natural factors."[197] He had a calling—I would characterize it as an ascetical calling[198]—that excluded taking a wife, begetting children, and being a traditional paterfamilias.[199] He was, as Simon Joseph puts it, "'married' to God."[200]

197. So Schneider, "Εὐνοῦχος, εὐνουχίζω," 768.

198. According to Sand, *Reich Gottes*, 58, Matt 19:12 exhibits a "stark asketischer Tendenz." Cf. Luz, *Matthew*, 2:502: Jesus likely "came out of an ascetically inclined branch of Judaism to which John the Baptist also belonged."

199. Cf. the words of the celibate Shim'on ben 'Azzai in t. Yeb. 8:7: "What should I do? My soul thirsts after Torah. Let other people keep the world going." Like Matt 19:12, this appeals to a religious reason for being single. Cf. Jer 16:1–4, where God's command that Jeremiah be celibate is a prophetic sign, and the discussion of this in Adinolfi, "Celibato," 148–51. I take the language in Matthew's third strophe to be figurative, not literal; see Blinzler, "Εἰσὶν εὐνοῦχοι," 259–61, and cf. Clement of Alexandria, *Strom.* 3.7.59 ("to make himself a eunuch from all desire"; cf. Basilides according to 3.1); *Paed.* 3.4.26 ("the true eunuch is not he who cannot find pleasure but he who does not will to do so"); Origen, *Comm. Matt.* frag. 386 (ed. Klostermann, 165: the eunuch "rules his own passion"); Tertullian, *Idol.* 7; and Methodius, *Symp.* 1.1. Further patristic references in W. Bauer, "Matth. 19,12." Schmidt, "βασιλεύς κτλ.," 588, and Hester, "Eunuchs," endorse a literal reading. Moxnes, *Jesus in His Place*, 86–89—who urges that interpreters ancient and modern seek to guard Jesus's masculinity—and J. S. Alexander, "Self-Made Eunuchs," 105, are undecided. According to Hester, Jesus called "his followers to perform ritual castration as a sign of religious devotion and commitment" (31). While it is true that self-castration is attested in early Christianity, his analysis does not win my assent. (a) It would seem to make Jesus an antinomian, because the Torah was understood to forbid self-emasculation: Deut 23:1; Ps.-Phoc. 187 ("do not cut the male procreative nature of a youth"); Philo, *Ebr.* 211–13; *Somn.* 2.184; *Migr.* 69; *Spec.* 3.40–42; *Hypoth.* 7.7 (a man "must not make abortive the generative power of men by gelding nor that of women by sterilizing drugs and other devices"); Josephus, *Ant.* 4.290–91 ("you will not castrate man or beast," interpreting Deut 23:1). (b) If we set Matt 19:12 aside, nothing hints that Jesus or any of his disciples were literal castrates or rumored to be such. (c) The call for amputation in Mark 9:43–48 par. is roundly recognized to be figurative; see below, pp. 263–72. (d) Hester recognizes that, for the evangelist Matthew, "the eunuch is a figure of sexual renunciation, a figure that stands in contrast to procreativity and marriage. To make oneself a eunuch 'on account of the kingdom of heaven' was to make a certain choice that related to marriage, family and kin" (25–26). But is it sensible, unless compelled otherwise, to urge that Matthew's use of the saying was incongruent with its use before him? If Matt 19:12 had come to the evangelist with literal sense, would he not either have ignored the word—as Paul did in 1 Corinthians if he knew it—or made the metaphorical sense clearer? I also reject the suggestion of A. E. Harvey, *Eunuchs*, 9–17, that Matt 19:12 might originally have referred to three literal types of eunuch, including devotees of Cybele and Attis, and that "for the sake of the kingdom of heaven" might be a gloss. This fails, among other things, to take into account the traditional form, in which the climactic last line moves from one realm to another; cf. Dupont, *Mariage et divorce*, 191–93, and contrast Moxnes, *Jesus in His Place*, 87–88.

200. Joseph, *Jesus, the Essenes*, 112.

His thoughts may have been similar to Paul's in 1 Cor 7:7–40.[201] There the apostle recommends celibacy to those who can receive the gift or χάρισμα (7:7),[202] and his counsel is grounded in eschatology: "the appointed time has grown very short" (7:29) and "the form of this world is passing away" (7:31). Indeed, the distress that is "present" (ἐνεστῶσαν ἀνάγκην, 7:26) signals that the eschatological birth pangs have arrived[203] (a conviction Jesus shared). It is, then, best to be rid of "worldly troubles" (7:28), to be free from "anxieties" about "worldly affairs" (7:32–34), best to preoccupy oneself instead with "the affairs of the Lord" (7:32) and to secure "undivided devotion to the Lord" (7:35). Paul, one might say, made himself or remained a figurative eunuch because the end was near.

Matthew 19:12 does not implicitly isolate Jesus or defend him alone. It rather speaks of a group: the plural "eunuchs" indicates that, if Jesus is a eunuch because of the kingdom, he is not one of a kind.[204] One could, to be sure, dismiss the plural as nothing save rhetoric, an artifact of the formal parallelism. If the first example is plural—eunuchs from birth—and if the second example is plural—eunuchs emasculated by others—then it is fitting that the third example is also plural: εὐνοῦχοι . . . εὐνοῦχοι . . . εὐνοῦχοι. And yet, in Matt 8:20 // Luke 9:58, a comparable triadic utterance employs two plurals ("foxes," "birds") followed by a singular ("the Son of Man"). Matthew 19:12 could have been formulated in like manner, with Jesus as the single member of the third category: "And I am a eunuch who has made himself one because of the kingdom of heaven." But the saying is not so formulated. The plural, one infers, has real content.

Who, then, beyond Jesus, might be among "the eunuchs because of the kingdom of heaven"? One could identify them with famous or revered men. John the Baptist was presumably unmarried,[205] and tradition held that Moses—who served Jesus as a model in important ways (see ch. 2 herein)—

201. Cf. Windisch, *Paulus und Christus*, 129–31, and C. Wolff, "Niedrigkeit und Verzicht," 186–88. Clement of Alexandria, *Strom.* 3.6, already associates the two passages.

202. Paul's words "each has his own special gift from God" (1 Cor 7:7) are, as the history of reception recognizes, conceptually close to the qualifications in Matthew: "not all," "those to whom it is given," "he who is able."

203. Cf. Fitzmyer, *First Corinthians*, 315, and see further Froitzheim, *Christologie und Eschatologie*, 18–28.

204. One may again compare Paul, who in 1 Cor 7 wants others to be celibates; cf. 7:7: "I wish that all were as I myself am."

205. So Tertullian, *Mon.* 17.1, and Christian tradition thereafter. According to C. Wolff, "Niedrigkeit und Verzicht," 188, the plural "most likely refers to John the Baptist and Jesus." Cf. Schneider, "Εὐνοῦχος, εὐνουχίζω," 768 (Jesus is, in Matt 19:12, "thinking primarily of

renounced intercourse in order "to hold himself always in readiness to receive oracular messages."[206] Furthermore, Jeremiah was called not to take a wife or beget sons or daughters (Jer 16:1–2; cf. 11:19), and Daniel was remembered as a literal eunuch,[207] while Gen. Rab. 35:1 reports that Noah refrained from marital relations not only during the flood (cf. b. Sanh. 108b) but also after leaving the ark.[208] Yet given that, in Matt 19:12, those who have made themselves eunuchs have done so precisely because of the kingdom, and further that, elsewhere in the Synoptics, the kingdom is consistently entwined with Jesus's ministry,[209] it makes more sense to look at individuals around him, at his male followers.[210]

Once we do that, several possibilities appear. The saying about religious eunuchry could envision men who (1) are, like Jesus, unmarried and who plan on never being married due to their religious commitment; or (2) have left wives for the greater cause and have determined not to return to them;[211] or (3) are married but, like those praised in the Acts of Paul and Thecla, practice sexual continence.[212]

I know of little reason to import the later idea of "spiritual marriage" back into Jesus's time and place.[213] We also, in my judgment, lack clear evidence that Jesus asked men to abandon wives on a permanent as opposed to temporary basis. The most famous disciple, Peter, did not do so (cf. Mark 1:29–31; 1 Cor 9:5; see further n. 159 above). My preference, then, is for possibility 1: Je-

---

Himself, and perhaps of the Baptist"); Casey, *Jesus of Nazareth*, 298; and R. F. Collins, *Believing Wife*, 104–5.

206. So Philo, *Mos.* 2.68–69. Cf. Tg. Onq. and Tg. Ps.-J. Num 12:1–2; Sipre Num. 99–100; ʾAbot R. Nat. A 2; b. Šabb. 87a; Deut. Rab. 11:10; Exod. Rab. 46:3; and Cant. Rab. 4:4.

207. Josephus, *Ant.* 10.186; Liv. Pro. Dan 2; b. Sanh. 93b. The likely source of this tradition was Dan 1:1–4, read in the light of 2 Kgs 20:18.

208. On this tradition see Koltun-Fromm, "Aphrahat and the Rabbis."

209. E.g., Matt 12:28 // Luke 11:20 (Q): Jesus's exorcisms mark the arrival of the kingdom of God. Cf. Luke 16:16: "The law and the prophets were until John; since then the kingdom of God is preached." Jesus speaks about the kingdom as present and future, not past.

210. Cf. Blinzler, "Εἰσὶν εὐνοῦχοι," 261–64, and Theissen, *Jesus als historische Gestalt*, 102. So already Tertullian, *Monogamy* 8.

211. Some take Matt 19:12 in its redactional context to demand singleness after separation from a spouse; cf. Quesnell, "'Made Themselves Eunuchs.'"

212. See Acts of Paul and Thecla 5–12. One might add a fourth possibility: men who give up their wives for a time; cf. the provisional abstinence laid upon Noah and his family while in the ark in b. Sanh. 108b. One could also compare the temporary celibacy required for holy war; cf. 1 Sam 21:5; 2 Sam 11:11–12; 1QM VII, 3–6. But "eunuch" seems too strong a word for this alternative.

213. J. Taylor, "'Two by Two,'" however, disagrees: male and female celibate pairings may go back to Paul's time and before. See further above, n. 113.

sus was not the only single male in his immediate circle, not the only one who had given up marriage because of their common cause.[214] He was not alone in eschewing the role of paterfamilias, not alone in disowning, in Anthony Le Donne's words, "a first-century view of civic masculinity."[215]

Yet whomever exactly we count among the eunuchs because of the kingdom, Matt 19:12 breathes the same ethos as the censure of the lustful look and the prohibition of divorce and remarriage. For even if, "before the second century C.E., eunuchs did not evoke the simple image of sexual asceticism claimed by so many modern commentators,"[216] they were firmly associated with the inability to reproduce;[217] and Matt 19:12 comes from a world in which,

214. Who precisely these were we do not know. Presumably most of the disciples were, like Peter, married, in accord with social expectation. The tradition that the apostle John was unmarried cannot be confirmed; see R. F. Collins, *Believing Wife*, 106–9.

215. Le Donne, *Wife of Jesus*, 124. Cf. Bernabé, "Of Eunuchs and Predators"; Moxnes, *Jesus in His Place*, 87–90, 104–7 (Jesus left "male space" and "the existing order"); Moxnes, "Contextualizing"; and Conway, *Behold the Man*, 123. I agree with Anderson and Moore, "Matthew and Masculinity," 90: Matt 19:12 is "countercultural," if by that one means it "cuts against the grain of the hegemonic Greco-Roman conception of 'full' masculinity that required a man to engage in the generation of heirs and rule over a household consisting of a wife, offspring, and, if possible, slaves." Comparable perhaps is the injunction to become as a child: Matt 18:3; Mark 10:15; Luke 18:17. One understands why many have asserted that Jesus countered the conventional patriarchal household; note, e.g., Schüssler Fiorenza, *In Memory of Her*, 145–47, and Crossan, *Historical Jesus*, 299–302. But Jesus's opposition was, or so it seems to me, relative to circumstance, not programmatic. Although he believed that traditional social structures were passing away, he decried them not in general but only when and precisely because they came into conflict with his cause. The critical words about families reflect occasions when Jesus's call to follow him was rejected (cf. Mark 10:17–22) or effected familial strife (cf. Matt 10:35–36 // Luke 12:51–53). Cf. Jacobson, "Divided Families," 374 (with reference to Q: "There is scant evidence that the patriarchal household was rejected because it was patriarchal; rather, it appears that the patriarchal household was simply eclipsed by more urgent matters"); Dunn, *Jesus Remembered*, 592–99; Casey, *Jesus of Nazareth*, 298 (Jesus's words "in some degree" relativize "family relationships in face of the will of God for the redemption of Israel" but are not "permanently disruptive of normal human relationships"); and Spencer, *Salty Wives*, 93–94. For extensive discussion see esp. Oporto, "Kingdom and Family."

216. So Talbott, "Matthean Eunuch," 41. On the sexual activity of eunuchs see further Hester, "Eunuchs." If, however, eunuchs were as sexually notorious as Hester implies, one wonders why kings left them in charge of harems; cf. Esth 2:14; Philostratus, *Vit. soph.* 2.593. The author of T. Jud. 23:5, in prophesying that Gentiles will "castrate some of you as eunuchs for their wives," is obviously not thinking of sexually active eunuchs. Note that the first definition of εὐνοῦχος in LSJ is "castrated person, eunuch, employed to take charge of the women and act as chamberlain (whence the name, ὁ τὴν εὐνὴν ἔχων)."

217. This is not to say that some were not married. The rabbis know, at least theoreti-

it appears, reproduction was for many or most the purpose of sex.[218] So being eunuchlike because of the kingdom would have entailed celibacy.[219] One may compare Philo, *Leg.* 3.236, which associates the eunuch with sexual restraint: "To become a eunuch would be a very good thing if by doing so our soul would be able to escape wickedness and unlearn passion [τὸ πάθος]." The same association recurs in *Det.* 176: "It is better to be made a eunuch than to be mad after illicit unions." Of similar import is Justin's account of a Christian asking a doctor to remove his testicles: this is presented as evidence that believers shun "promiscuous intercourse" (ἀνέδην μίξις, *1 Apol.* 29.2–3). Here becoming a literal eunuch is the opposite of being sexually active. The same logic holds for Matt 19:12.

Disciples who found Matt 19:12 directly relevant would have taken themselves to be, like Jesus, eunuchs because of the kingdom. For them, his word would have underscored the association between their celibacy and commitment to the approaching kingdom, making their choice all the more commendable. The kingdom is a hard task, a radical challenge, a totalizing claim.[220] And if they found themselves sexually attracted to others in Jesus's company, Matt 19:12 would have been a call to combat the impulse and, in Theophylact's words, "to exercise self-control" (ἐγκρατευόμενοι).[221]

---

cally, of married eunuchs and make halakhic judgments about them; see m. Yeb. 8:2, 4, 5; m. Soṭah 4:4; y. Yeb. 8:4 (9d); b. Yeb. 75a. Note also Aristotle, *Pol.* 1311b.

218. Cf. Philo, *Ios.* 43 ("the end we seek in wedlock is not pleasure but the begetting of lawful children"); *Mos.* 1:28; *Virt.* 207; Josephus, *C. Ap.* 2.202 ("Essenes [or rather one group of them] have no intercourse with them [women] during pregnancy, thus showing that their motive in marrying is not self-indulgence but the procreation of children"); T. Iss. 2:3 (God "perceived that she [Rachel] wanted to lie with Jacob for the sake of children and not for sexual gratification"); T. Benj. 8:2 ("the person who is pure with love does not look on a woman for the purpose of having sexual relations"); Ps.-Phoc. 186 ("do not lay your hand on your wife when she is pregnant"); Hist. Rech. 11:6–8 (the Rechabites couple only once in their lives); y. Yeb. 8:5 (9d) (sexual relations with a man unable to beget children has the character of fornication). See further Allison, "Divorce, Celibacy."

219. Contrast Mayordomo, "Eunuchen im Horizont." For Mayordomo, the metaphor of the eunuch connotes slavery and a lack of manhood and represents those who, because of the kingdom, stigmatize themselves socially.

220. Cf. Tannehill, *Sword of His Mouth*, 138–39. How one deals with desire, however, goes unsaid; cf. Loader, *New Testament on Sexuality*, 443: Matt 19:12 does not in itself address the issues of what eunuchs because of the kingdom "do with the sexual desire which neither literal castration nor the option of celibacy would have removed because that is not its purpose. The answers would be governed by the common understanding of right and wrong in relation to sexual behavior."

221. Theophylact, *Comm. Matt.* ad loc. Matthew's "the one who is able to receive it"

Jesus's triadic aphorism would also have been relevant, if in a different way—indirectly as opposed to directly—for those who, because married, could not reckon themselves to be eunuchs because of the kingdom. Matthew 19:12 esteems those who abjure procreation for the right reason: διὰ τὴν βασιλείαν. Such esteem has practical consequences for all, for even if one is married, it is still possible, indeed incumbent, to be motivated by the kingdom. In addition, given that some, including Jesus, have given up married life altogether, it should be possible for others to curb or govern the sexual impulse, albeit it in a less extraordinary way—by refraining from the erotic gaze (Matt 5:27–28), for instance, or by not divorcing one's spouse in order to marry someone more appealing. Put otherwise, Matt 19:12 would have discouraged everyone in Jesus's inner circle—including women[222]—from taking a sexual interest in other followers to whom they were not married.[223]

---

underlines the difficulty of the task. Cf. Lapide, *Great Commentary*, 2:241: "Continence is a difficult thing." Greek ideas of self-control had certainly entered Judaism by Jesus's time, as the use of ἐγκράτεια, ἐγκρατής, and ἐγκρατεύομαι in Jewish sources attests: Sir 18:29 (heading); 26:15; 4 Macc 5:34; T. Iss. 2:1; T. Naph. 8:8; Let. Aris. 278; Ps.-Phoc. 145; Philo, *Ios.* 54; Gal 5:23; 1 Cor 7:9; 9:25; Josephus, *Bell.* 2.120, 138; *Ant.* 8.235. See further Stowers, *Rereading of Romans*, 56–65, and Keener, "Paul's Positive Madness."

222. Female celibacy as a religious vocation—attested in 1 Cor 7:25–35 ("the unmarried woman and the virgin are anxious about the affairs of the Lord, so that they may be holy in body and spirit"); Acts 21:9 ("four daughters, virgins, who had the gift of prophecy"); 1 Tim 4:3 ("they forbid marriage"); and Ign. *Smyrn.* 13.1 ("virgins who are called widows")—may have had a home already in Jesus's circle. Talbott, "Matthean Eunuch," is right to ask how women would have received Jesus's saying.

223. Cf. Witherington, *Women in the Ministry of Jesus*, 31–32: "Possibly, it was Jesus' teaching on eunuchs for the Kingdom that allowed women to be present among the traveling company of disciples (Lk. 8.1–3), and to remain single and serve the community of faith (Ac. 21.9)." The preceding paragraphs take a more or less conventional view of Matt 19:12. I am not won over by Llewelyn, Wearne, and Sanderson, "Guarding Entry." They urge that the third eunuch is the disciple who is "given authority to judiciously grant admission to the Kingdom (cf. Mt. 16.19, 18.15–18)" (245). This stresses the eunuch's reputation as a "trusted and loyal official" (233) and his service of guarding or controlling access (238). But the reference to "eunuchs who have been so from birth" does not send thoughts in this direction. Moreover, Llewelyn, Wearne, and Sanderson take χωρέω to mean "to move" and then speculate that an original Aramaic ל was misleadingly translated διά, with the result that the pristine sense of the final clause was: "There are eunuchs who have made themselves eunuchs. Into the kingdom of Heaven let the one who can enter, enter" (241). I decline to posit mistranslation when Matt 19:12 makes good sense as it is.

Hand, Eye, Foot

Mark 9:43–48 warns against sins of the hand, foot, and eye:

> If your hand causes you to stumble, cut it off;
> it is better for you to enter life maimed
> than to have two hands and to go to Gehenna, to the unquenchable fire.
> And if your foot causes you to stumble, cut it off;
> it is better for you to enter life lame
> than to have two feet and to be thrown into hell.
> And if your eye causes you to stumble, tear it out;
> it is better for you to enter the kingdom of God with one eye
> than to have two eyes and to be thrown into hell
> where their worm never dies, and the fire is never quenched.[224]

Commentators often find in these sentences little more than graphic illustrations of the principle of self-denial. According to Charles Cranfield: "The general point of the verses is that it is worth making the most costly sacrifices for the sake of not losing eternal life."[225] Matthew Poole similarly remarked, with reference to the parallel in Matt 5:29–30: "The sum of these two verses is, that the salvation of our immortal souls is to be preferred before all things, be they ever so dear and precious to us."[226] These generalities, however, miss much.

The Sermon on the Mount contains this paragraph:

> You have heard that it was said: "You shall not commit adultery." But I say to you that everyone who looks at a woman with lust has already committed adultery with her in his heart. If your right eye causes you to sin, tear it out and throw it away; it is better for you to lose one of your members than for your whole body to be thrown into Gehenna. And if your right hand causes

224. With modern critical editions, I regard Mark 9:44 and 9:46 as scribal additions. Yet there is perhaps room for doubt; see Chilton, *Galilean Rabbi*, 102–6.

225. Cranfield, *Mark*, 314.

226. Poole, *Annotations*, 24. Cf. Dibelius, *Sermon on the Mount*, 58: the word refers to "every kind of sacrifice which must be necessary for a disciple of Jesus. If anything prevents entrance into the coming Kingdom, those who want to become citizens of the Kingdom must renounce it."

> you to sin, cut it off and throw it away; it is better for you to lose one of your members than for your whole body to go into Gehenna. (Matt 5:27–30)

The last two sentences are very close to Mark 9:43–48. Perhaps Matthew drew upon those lines here, as later in 18:8–9. Or perhaps he had access to a related non-Markan tradition. In either case, the Matthean context for the sayings is illicit sexual desire.[227] Near to hand is the inference that, at least in Matt 5:29–30, to pluck out eye and to cut off hand is to shun sexual sin.[228] It is the same in Justin Martyr, where a variant of Matt 5:29 is included among teachings on σωφροσύνης ("temperance").[229]

Was this already the case for Jesus? That is, did he, if he uttered something like Mark 9:43–48, have sexual transgressions in mind?[230] We cannot, since the originating context is lost, answer with full conviction. Yet given the ferocity of the warnings—they are, in Robert Gundry's words, "horrifying"[231]—it is hardly credible that he was contemplating nothing in particular, only indistinctly cautioning about misdeeds in general.

Rabbinic sources come to our aid here. According to a ruling in m. Nid. 2:1, "the hand that oftentimes makes examination [of the private parts] is, among women, praiseworthy [because it is necessary to determine menstrual uncleanness]; but among men—let it be cut off!" The commentary in b. Nid. 13b on this judgment includes the following:

227. Cf. Ps.-Clem. Rec. 7.37. The subject of the doublet in Matt 18:8–9 may not be sexual sin; yet see Loader, *New Testament on Sexuality*, 124–27.

228. So also Lapide, *Great Commentary*, 1:262; Witherington, *Women in the Ministry of Jesus*, 20–21; Betz, *Sermon on the Mount*, 239; Nolland, *Matthew*, 238; and Konradt, *Matthew*, 86–87. Contrast T. W. Manson, *Sayings of Jesus*, 157: "There is no real connexion" between Matt 5:27–28 and 5:29–30.

229. Justin, *1 Apol.* 15.1–2: "Concerning temperance, then, he [Jesus] said this: 'Whoever looks at a woman to desire her has already committed adultery with her in his heart before God.' And: 'If your right eye causes you to stumble, pluck it out, for it is better for you to enter the kingdom of heaven with one eye than with two eyes to be sent to eternal fire.'" This shares elements of Matt 5:28–29 (adultery in the heart); 18:9 ("eternal fire"); and Mark 9:47 ("enter the kingdom").

230. So Niederwimmer, *Askese und Mysterium*, 30–31; R. F. Collins, *Sexual Ethics*, 62–72; Loader, *Sexuality and the Jesus Tradition*, 20–36; and Angel, "God Talk." For Gundry, *Mark*, 524–25, this is a possibility ("may"). For rejection of this view see Filannino, "Making Oneself Last," 391–92.

231. So Gundry, *Mark*, 514. Against Angel, "God Talk," 107, I find no humor in Matt 5:27–30 or its parallels.

> Have we here learned a [literal] law as in the case where R. Huna [really] cut off someone's hand [see b. Sanh. 58b]? Or is it merely a curse? Come and hear what was taught: R. Tarfon said: "If his hand touched the membrum let his hand be cut off on his belly." "But," they said to him, "would not his belly be split?" He said: "It is preferable that his belly shall be split rather than that he should go down into the pit of destruction."

This resembles Mark 9:43 in multiple respects.[232] (a) Both Rabbi Tarfon and Jesus affirm that the offending hand should be cut off. (b) Amputation is, in both texts, preferable to going to the place of eschatological judgment—the pit of destruction in b. Nid. 13b, Gehenna in Mark 9:43–48.[233] (c) The concluding evaluation in both passages takes the form of a "better . . . than" statement (κάλον . . . ἤ; מוטב . . . ו).[234] (d) Whereas hand, foot, and eye offend in Mark 9:43–48, in b. Nid. 13b, a few lines before the portion just quoted, R. Ishmael says: "You will not commit adultery [תנאף] with either hand or with foot." Furthermore, R. Ishmael's exhortation resembles an imperative in Mek. R. Shim. on Exod 20:13 (ed. Hoffmann, 111): "Do not commit adultery with the hand or the foot or the eye or the heart."[235] Aside from the addition of "heart" at the end, this matches Mark's order: hand, foot, eye.

What should we make of all this? Coincidences occur. Further, we do not know when the rabbinic lines originated.[236] It might, then, be prudent to leave it at that. For me, however, the similarities are sufficient to bespeak a connec-

232. In addition to what follows see esp. Deming, "Mark 9.42–10.12." There are also non-Jewish parallels; see Hommel, *Sebasmata*, 2:54–58, 63–73, and Schattenmann, "Jesus und Pythagoras." These appear to me to be of much lesser significance; so too Gundry, *Mark*, 525.

233. For the equation of Gehenna with "pit of destruction" see m. ʾAbot 5:19 ("inherit Gehenna and go down to the pit of destruction"); Tg. Ps 37:20 ("destroyed in the smoke of Gehenna"); b. ʿErub. 19a ("Destruction" is one of the names of Gehenna); and cf. Matt 10:28 ("destroy soul and body in Gehenna"). Elsewhere fate in Gehenna or the netherworld is the recompense for sexual sins: Prov 5:5; 7:27; 9:18; 1 En. 10:11–15; 4Q184; 1 Cor 6:9; Apoc. Pet. (Ethiopic) 7; Acts Thom. 55–56; m. ʾAbot 1:5; t. Ḥag. 1:7; b. Soṭah 4b; etc.

234. On this form see Snyder, "*Tobspruch*." Deming, "Mark 9.42–10.12," 136, notes that Matt 5:29–30 is even closer to the formulation in the Talmud: συμφέρει . . . ἤ μή = מוטב . . . ואל. Cf. also the formulation in Tg. Ps.-J. Gen 38:25: "It is better [טב] for me to be ashamed in this world, which is a passing world, and not [ואל] to be ashamed in the presence of my fathers, the righteous ones, in the world to come. It is better [טב] for me to be burned in this life in extinguishable fire and not [ואל] to burn in the world to come in inextinguishable fire."

235. On the textual problem here see Deming, "Mark 9.42–10.12," 140 n. 26.

236. But Deming, "Mark 9.42–10.12," 135–36, musters a few reasons for supposing that the basic discussion goes back to the middle of the first century.

tion. I have the sense that they are, as George Foot Moore put it, "not fortuitous."[237] I am all the more assured of this because, if Matt 5:29–30, which some take to be independent of Mark 9:43–48,[238] unfolds Jesus's reading of the commandment against adultery (5:27), the words from b. Nid. 13b quoted above belong to a discussion of what "you will not commit adultery" implies.

Should we then imagine that b. Nid. 13b and the Mekilta of Rabbi Shimon bar Yoḥai are somehow indebted, directly or indirectly, to the Gospels?[239] If that were so, the rabbinic applications to sexual matters would suggest that some Jews in antiquity understood Jesus's words about amputation to concern carnal sin.

I am, however, much more inclined to suppose that the rabbinic texts and Mark 9:43–48 are so close because they independently preserve variants of an old tradition.[240] In this case, the common references to sexual behavior derive ultimately from that tradition. The situation would be similar to other Synoptic sayings that have pronounced rabbinic parallels. In some instances, such as the maxims about speck and log and the sun rising on the good and the bad, a rabbinic line resembles a sentence in the Gospels not because a rabbi borrowed from Jesus but because the two independently drew teaching from the same well of tradition.[241]

If, with Matt 5:29–30, Justin, *1 Apol.* 15.1–2, and the rabbinic parallels in mind, one associates Mark 9:43–48 with sexual temptation, the references to eye, hand, and foot and the injunction to toss them aside make sense.

237. G. F. Moore, *Judaism in the First Centuries*, 2:268.

238. So Niederwimmer, *Askese und Mysterium*, 31; Deming, "Mark 9.42–10.12," 137; and Angel, "God Talk." According to Luz, *Matthew*, 1:242. Matt 5:29–30 derives from Q or QMt. So too Pesch, *Markusevangelium*, 2:115. Many, however, regard 5:29–30 as an adaptation of Mark 9:43–48.

239. Basser, "Meaning of 'Shtuth,'" argues that at least Gen. Rab. 11:6 ("blind your eye and cut off your hands") shows knowledge of the Synoptic saying.

240. So too Deming, "Mark 9.42–10.12"; Gundry, *Mark*, 524 ("may"); and Yarbro Collins, *Mark*, 449–50.

241. For the speck and log (Matt 7:3–5; Luke 6:41–42) see b. B. Bat. 15b ("If the judge said to a man: 'Take the splinter from between your teeth,' he would retort: 'Take the beam from between your eyes'") and b. 'Arak. 16b (R. Tarfon said, "I wonder whether there is any one in this generation who accepts reproof, for if one says to him: 'Remove the speck from between your eyes,' he would answer: 'Remove the beam from between your eyes'"). For the sun rising on the good and the bad (Matt 5:45; cf. Luke 6:35) see b. Yoma 23a ("Has it not been taught, concerning those who are insulted but do not [on account of revenge] insult others and who hear themselves reproached without replying and who [do good] work out of love of the Lord and rejoice in their sufferings, the Scripture says this: 'But they that love him are as the sun when he goes forth in his might' [Judg 5:31]?"). Cf. also b. Šabb. 88b and b. Giṭ. 36b.

In Num 15:39 LXX, the Lord through Moses commands Israel: "You will not turn aside after your thoughts and after your eyes, in the things after which you whore [ἐκπορνεύετε]." In Job 31:1, Job avows: "I have made a covenant with my eyes; how then could I look on a virgin?"[242] Jubilees 20:4 (alluding to Num 15:39) denounces those who "commit sexual offenses by following their eyes and their hearts." Sirach 9:8 admonishes: "Turn away your eyes from a shapely woman, and do not look intently at beauty belonging to another; many have been misled by a woman's beauty, and by it passion is kindled like a fire."[243] 1QS V, 3 condemns the individual who goes astray by following "his eyes and the thoughts of his *yeṣer*." The Testament of Issachar says that "the spirits of evil have no power over him [the righteous man], since he does not include feminine beauty in the scope of his vision, lest by allowing distraction he might corrupt his mind" (4:4; cf. 7:2; T. Reu. 2:4–6; 3:10; 4:1, 8; 6:1; T. Jud. 17:1; T. Benj. 8:2). According to b. Ned. 20a, R. ʾAḥa of the school of R. Josiah said: "He who gazes at a woman eventually comes to sin, and he who looks even at a woman's heel will beget degenerate children."[244] And b. Soṭah 8a recites the tradition that "the evil impulse only holds sway over what a person's eyes see."

Everybody knew the story of David and Bathsheba, which commenced when the king "*saw* from the roof a woman bathing" (2 Sam 11:2).[245] Everyone also knew the tale of the sons of God who went astray after they "*saw* that the daughters of humanity were fair" (Gen 6:1–4)—an event with catastrophic results.[246] The literature unsurprisingly contains expressions such as "lecher-

242. ʾAbot R. Nat. A 2 comments on this verse: "This teaches that Job was particularly strict with himself and would not look even on a maiden. Now, is there not an inference to be drawn here? If even in regard to a maiden—whom if he so desired he might wed himself, or give to his son to wed, or to his brother, or to a relation—Job was particularly strict with himself and would not look on her, all the more in regard to another man's wife! And why was Job so strict with himself that he would not look even on a maiden? For Job said: 'If I should look on her today and on the morrow another man comes and weds her, it will turn out that I have been looking on another man's wife.'"

243. Cf. Sir 23:4–6: "O Lord, Father and God of my life, do not give me haughty eyes, and remove evil desire from me. Let neither gluttony nor lust overcome me, and do not give me over to shameless passion."

244. Cf. Tanḥ. Buber Huggat suppl. 6a: "Whoever does not look at another woman will not have the evil inclination prevailing against him."

245. Cf. Jdt 12:16 ("from the first day he" saw Judith, Holofernes "had been waiting for an opportunity to seduce her"); Sus 8 ("every day the two elders used to see her [Susanna] . . . and they began to lust for her"); LAB 43:5 (Samson was "led astray by his eye" in desiring Delilah); and T. Reu. 3:11 ("if I [Reuben] had not seen Bilhah bathing in a sheltered place, I would not have fallen into this great lawless act").

246. See esp. 1 En. 1–36 and Jub. 5. Gen 6:2 is cited or alluded to in 1 En. 6:2; Jub. 5:1;

ous eyes" (1QS I, 6; CD II, 16), "eye brimming with adultery" (2 Pet 2:14), and "the desire of the eyes" (1 John 2:16).[247] Ephraem, *Comm. Diat.* 6.8, could say simply: "The eye is lust." If, then, Jesus ever enjoined his followers to pluck out their eyes, he was almost certainly demanding that they trammel their passions, that they mortify concupiscence.

As for the hand, the Talmud more than once shows serious concern regarding the issue of a man touching his sex organ, even when only urinating (e.g., b. Šabb. 41a, 43a; b. Nid. 13a); and (as observed already) in m. Nid. 2:1 and b. Nid. 13b, the hand that touches the male member is cut off.[248] Also germane is Philo's allegorical interpretation of Deut 25:11–12: "If men get into a fight with one another, and the wife of one intervenes to rescue her husband from the grip of his opponents by reaching out and seizing his genitals, you shall cut off her hand; show no pity" (*Somn.* 2.68). Philo does not restrict the application of this law to women, and his reading makes amputation of the hand a figurative expression of self-discipline and abstinence from ordinary concerns: "O soul . . . you must cut off your hand, your power, when it begins to lay hold of the genitals, whether they be the created world or the cares and aims of humanity."[249]

We find an even fuller explanation, which Philo attributes to "highly gifted men," in *Spec.* 3.178–79:

> The female clings to all that is born and perishes; it stretches out its faculties like a hand to catch blindly at what comes in its way, and gives the clasp of friendship to the world of created things with all its numberless changes and transmutations, instead of to the divine order, the immutable,

T. Reu. 5:6; LAB 3:1; 2 En. 18:4 J; etc. Note t. Soṭah 3:9, which quotes Gen 6:2: "R. Jose b. Durmasqit says: 'The men of the flood took pride only on account of the eyeball.'" Cf. Gen 3:6, where Eve sees that the tree of life is "a delight to the eyes" then desires the fruit and eats it, again with catastrophic results.

247. Note also Ps. Sol. 4:4 (the sinner's "eyes are on every woman indiscriminately") and 1QpHab V, 6–7 ("'Your eyes are too pure to look at evil.' Its interpretation is: they have not been a harlot following their eyes in the age of wickedness").

248. b. Nid. 13b construes Isa 1:15 ("your hands are full of blood") to refer to "those that commit masturbation with their hands." The story of the Lord's displeasure with Onan in Gen 38:9–10 was cited by rabbis—not, to the extent of my reading, by the church fathers—in arguments against masturbation; cf. b. Nid. 13a. On the widespread disapproval of masturbation in old Jewish sources see Feldman, *Marital Relations*, 109–31, 144–68. One should perhaps note that Mark 12:19 par. alludes to the story of Onan.

249. But in *Spec.* 3.175–77, he expounds the literal sense; cf. Sipre Deut. 292 and m. B. Qam. 8:1.

> the blessed, the thrice happy. Naturally therefore we are commanded in a symbol to cut off the hand that has taken hold of the "pair," not meaning that the body should be mutilated by the loss of a most essential member, but to bid us exscind from the soul the godless thoughts that take for their basis all that comes into being through birth; for the "pair" are a symbol of seed-sowing and birth.

While the scope in Mark 9:43 is, on the sexual interpretation, narrower, it shares with Philo's tradition a nonliteral sense of excising the hand.[250]

Regarding the foot, a few take this to be a euphemism for the male sex organ.[251] On this reading, the demand to cut off the "hand" would conjure the image of self-castration. This would make Mark 9:45 kin to Matt 19:12, which commends those who make themselves eunuchs. Yet the upshot of cutting off one's foot is entering eschatological life "lame" (χωλόν; so too Matt 18:8). So the image is of a foot, not a penis.[252] It is best, then, to suppose that "foot" and "feet" are used of sexual sins because feet tread the "paths of licentiousness" (CD VIII, 5; XIX, 17) and "hurry to run to evil" (Prov 6:18).[253]

I have, in the previous paragraphs, urged that the exhortations in Mark 9:43–48 are hyperbolic and figurative: they do not mandate literal amputation but are in effect parables.[254] One may object that the excision of body parts was known to Jewish law,[255] that castrated priests served the cult

250. See further below, pp. 270–72. Although "hand" is sometimes a euphemism for "penis" (Isa 57:8; Cant 5:4–5; 1QS VII, 13; 11Q5 XXI, 17; 11QTemple XLVI, 13), that seems unlikely here, even though one might then find a parallel with the metaphorical self-castration in Matt 19:12. Loader, *New Testament on Sexuality*, 128, observes, regarding the "right hand" of Matt 5:30: "'Left' or 'right' is inapplicable in an allusion to the penis."

251. As in Exod 4:25; Deut 28:57; Judg 3:24; 2 Sam 11:8; 2 Kgs 18:27 Qere ("water of their feet"); Ruth 3:4, 7, 8, 14; Isa 6:2; 7:20; Ezek 16:25; b. Yeb. 103a; and Euripides, *Med.* 679–80. See Deming, "Mark 9.42–10.12," 134.

252. Cf. Gundry, *Mark*, 524–25.

253. Cf. the use of "feet" or "foot" in Prov: 5:5 ("her feet go down to death; her steps follow the path to Sheol"—of a "loose woman"); 6:28 ("can one walk on hot coals without scorching the feet?"; the context is prostitution); 7:11 ("her feet do not stay at home"—of a prostitute); Sib. Or. 5:264–65 ("no longer will the unclean foot of Greeks revel around your land"); and Syr. Men. 2:45 ("as for an adulterous woman, her feet are not firm"; does this mean she does not stay in one place?).

254. But for literal interpretations see Stählin, "Κοπετός κτλ.," 859–60, and Gundry, *Mark*, 514.

255. See, e.g., Lev 24:19–20; Deut 25:11–12; Judg 16:21; Philo, *Spec.* 3.175, Josephus, *Vita* 171–73, 177; *Bell.* 2.642–44; b. Pesaḥ. 57b.

of Cybele and Attis,[256] that Christian castrates are attested in the second century,[257] that Jesus was not a fundamentalist about Torah,[258] and that rabbinic literature tells the tale of a righteous man literally destroying his eyes in order to defeat his evil inclination.[259] Yet the figurative loss of bodily parts in ethical discourse is well attested. Seneca the Younger advises: "If any vice rends your heart, cast it away from you; and if you cannot be rid of it in any other way, pluck out your heart also" (*Ep.* 51.13). The speaker of Ps 137:5 exclaims: "If I forget you, O Jerusalem, let my right hand wither." Proverbs 10:31 envisions the tongue of the wicked being cut off. Joel 2:13 summons repentance with the phrase "rend your heart" (cf. 4Q266 11 = 4Q270 7 I, 18–19; 4 Bar 2:5; m. Taʿan. 2:1; etc.). In 1 Cor 9:27, Paul writes of giving his body a black eye (ὑπωπιάζω) and of leading it into slavery (δουλαγωγέω)—both dramatic, vivid metaphors for self-restraint. Colossians 3:5 directs hearers to "put to death [νεκρώσατε] (your) members on the earth." These words preface a list of sexual sins: "immorality, impurity, passion, evil desire." (If, as some think, Col 3:5 alludes to the tradition behind Mark 9:43–48,[260] it becomes one more witness to the sexual interpretation.)

Mark 9:43–48, with its "distinct ascetic tinge,"[261] belongs with the texts in the previous paragraph.[262] It is rhetorical hyperbole aimed at curbing, or rather eradicating, improper sexual desire. It no more commends physical mutilation than it seriously posits maimed resurrected bodies.[263] Chrysostom was on

256. See Catullus, *Attis*; Lucian, *De Syria dea*.

257. Cf. Justin, *1 Apol.* 29; Acts John 53–54; Eusebius, *Hist. eccl.* 6.8; and Epiphanius, *Pan.* 2.1. See further Stevenson, "Eunuchs and Early Christianity."

258. Cf. Gundry, *Mark*, 514, who complains that some commentators are here timid.

259. Tanḥ. Buber Huggat suppl. 6a: "He [Satan] became like a beautiful woman. . . . When he [Matthew ben Heresh] saw her, he turned his face away. Again Satan went opposite his face. He turned his face to another side, but Satan was opposite his face. When he saw that she was turning to [face him on] all sides, he said in his heart: 'I am afraid that the evil inclination may prevail against me.' So what did the righteous man do? He called one of his students to attend him. He said to him: 'Go, my son, and get me fire and pins.' When he had brought them, he heated [the pins] in the fire and stuck them in his eyes." This act beats Satan. God then sends Raphael to heal Matthew.

260. So, e.g., Davies, *Paul and Rabbinic Judaism*, 139, and Wenham, *Paul*, 274–75.

261. Montefiore, *Synoptic Gospels*, 2:507.

262. Luz, *Matthew*, 1:247: "In the history of interpretation the literal explanation was for all practical purposes unanimously rejected." Cf. Sextus, *Sent.* 12–14 (likely a rewriting of Matt 5:29–30); Tertullian, *Idol.* 7; Ps.-Clem. Rec. 7.37; Origen, *Comm. Matt.* 15.1; *Hom. Num.* 15.3; *Hom. Josh.* 7.6; Lapide, *Great Commentary*, 1:261–62; etc.

263. The lines about entering life maimed or lame or blind are likely ironic hyperbole. In b. Sanh. 91b, Simon ben Laqish affirms—with reference to Jer 31:8: "I am going to bring

target in his comments on Matt 5:29–30: "It is not the eye that sees, but the mind and the thought. . . . Had he been speaking of members of the body, he would not have said it of one eye, nor of the right eye only [as in Matt 5:29], but of both. For he who is offended by his right eye, most evidently will incur the same evil by his left also."[264]

There is, however, one more objection to a metaphorical interpretation. R. Tarfon, in b. Nid. 13b, upholds the literal implementation of the Mishnah's ruling—"it ought to be cut off"—and he does so precisely using material that, I argue, is related to Mark 9:43–48 par. Does this not favor a literal interpretation of the Synoptic text?

I do not think so. Rabbi Tarfon's opinion is recorded as a response to the question: "Have we here learned [in m. Nid. 2:1] a [literal] law or merely a curse?" So the meaning of "it ought to be cut off" was not self-evident. Some took the imperative to be not a literal law but a figure of speech, a malediction, as in b. Šabb. 108b–9a: "If the hand be put to the eye, let it be cut off; the hand to the nose, let it be cut off; the hand to the ear, let it be cut off; the hand to the vein [opened for bloodletting], let it be cut off; the hand to the membrum, let it be cut off; the hand to the anus, let it be cut off; the hand to the vat [for wine], let it be cut off. [Because] the [unwashed] hand causes blindness, deafness, and morbid growth on the nose." When one adds that Jesus is otherwise remembered as favoring hyperbole in moral exhortations,[265] and further that we have

---

them from the land of the north and gather them from the farthest parts of the earth, among them the blind and the lame"—that "they [the dead] will rise with their defects." He goes on, however, to add that "they will be healed." Cf. 2 Macc 7:10–12 (a martyr expects to regain his severed hands and tongue in the world to come); 14:46; and Tanḥ. Buber Wayyiggash 11:9 (the blind, the lame, and those unable to hear will be healed in the world to come; so too Gen. Rab. 95.1; Eccles. Rab. 1:4:2–3). Recall also the radical transformation of bodies in 1 Cor 15 and 2 Bar. 51. Contrast Gundry, *Mark*, 514, who thinks Jesus genuinely envisages "a mutilated body in God's kingdom."

264. Chrysostom, *Hom. Matt.* 17.3. Cf. Arrian, *Epict. diss.* 2.20.19 ("those who cut off their bodily organs are unable to cut off the really important thing—their sexual desire"); and Carter, *Matthew and the Margins*, 147 ("Literally? Probably not, since Jesus' emphasis is on the origin of adultery in the heart. Tearing out the eye will not change this").

265. Recall, e.g., Mark 10:25 ("it is easier for a camel to go through the eye of a needle"); 11:23 (faith can move a mountain); Matt 5:22 ("if you say: 'You fool!,' you will be liable to the Gehenna of fire"); 6:3 ("do not let the left hand know what the right hand is doing"); 7:4–5 ("the log in your own eye"); 23:24 (the gnat and the camel); Luke 14:26 (hate father and mother), 27 ("whoever does not carry the cross cannot be my disciple").

no hint that any of his supporters had mutilated themselves, it seems best to regard Mark 9:43–48 as an example of graphic exaggeration for emphasis.[266]

If Mark 9:43–48 comes from Jesus,[267] it likely reveals that he was occupied with the problem of unwelcome sexual passion; and if one seeks for a concrete pre-Easter setting, one need look no further than the group of men and women who spent prolonged time with him: he demanded that they govern their impulses. This is surely more plausible than the supposition that Jesus offered, without a definite problem in view, advice for everyone within earshot on the delicate topic of sexual lust. In my view, Mark 9:43–48, with its fearsome eschatological threat, was not designed for broadcast to the world at large. It was not like the announcement that "the kingdom of God has come near" (Matt 10:7 // Luke 10:9 [Q]). It was rather akin to Matt 10:9–10 // Luke 10:4 (Q), the counsel not to take purse, bag, or sandal. It was, that is, composed for a very particular group in a very particular situation, that being the mixed company attending him.[268]

266. A figurative use of eye, hand, and foot also occurs in Gos. Thom. 22: "Jesus saw infants being suckled. He said to his disciples: 'These infants being suckled are like those who enter the kingdom.' They said to him: 'Shall we then, as children, enter the kingdom?' Jesus said to them: 'When you make the two one, and when you make the inside like the outside and the outside like the inside, and the above like the below, and when you make the male and the female one and the same, so that the male not be male nor the female female; and when you fashion eyes in the place of an eye, and a hand in place of a hand, and a foot in place of a foot, and a likeness in place of a likeness; then will you enter the kingdom.'" Whatever the relationship of this to Mark 9:43–48 par., it seemingly commends encratic behavior and celibacy; see DeConick, *Original Gospel of Thomas*, 115–16, and Loader, *New Testament on Sexuality*, 467–76.

267. For an attempt to show this see Zager, *Gottesherrschaft und Endgericht*, 210–23. For an argument that Matt 5:27–30 fairly represents Jesus, see Angel, "God Talk," 108–12.

268. Responding to Deming, Marcus, *Mark*, 2:696–97, declines to see Mark 9:43–48 in sexual terms. His reasons are these: (1) 9:42 warns against setting "a stumbling block before one of these little ones who believes in me." Given the qualification, "who believes in me," and the Christian identity of those in the preceding 9:41 ("you bear the name of Christ"), a reference to pederasty, which Deming urges, seems unlikely. (2) The order, "hand . . . foot . . . eye," makes it doubtful that foot = penis, for the latter would be the most serious sin, yet it is in neither first nor last place. (3) Although Deming interprets "hand" literally, it can, like foot, be a euphemism for penis. (4) In the Mekilta of Rabbi Shimon bar Yoḥai (ed. Hoffmann, 111), "foot" and "hand" are meant literally; and Deming's interpretation of "adultery by hand" and "adultery by foot" as meaning masturbation and penile intercourse respectively has no support from Rashi or the Tosaphot. (5) "Hand" and "foot" by themselves do not have sexual content unless the context indicates such. (6) "Most problematic for the X-rated interpretation, Mark 9:43 does not say that the person who amputates his foot will enter eternal life as a eunuch but as a lame person, and it implies that if he abstains from offenses of the foot, he will be able to enter it with both feet—an interesting picture to contemplate if 'foot' means penis." Points 2–4 and 6 are problems for Deming but not

Angels and Wombs

In his debate with the Sadducees over the resurrection in Mark 12:18–27, Jesus's rebuttal includes the avowal that resurrected saints will not marry or be given in marriage. They will instead "be like the angels in heaven."[269] The argument, unfortunately, is laconic, the logic cryptic.[270] Is the likeness restricted to the single trait of not being married? Or—this is my judgment—does Jesus assume that the saints will become like angels in multiple respects, among them the absence of a need to reproduce, for "where there is death, both marriage and children are necessary, but where there is immortality, there is need neither of wedlock or offspring"?[271] In the latter case, the argument moves

---

for me. I take neither "hand" nor "foot" to be a euphemism for the penis. As for point 1, perhaps the sin is not, for Mark, against children in general but children who believe, that is, Christian children. Or maybe "who believes in me" is an infelicitous Markan gloss. But unlike Deming—as well as R. F. Collins, *Sexual Ethics*, 65–67, and Loader, *Sexuality and the Jesus Tradition*, 20–27—I am doubtful of a link with pederasty (even though b. Ned. 13b condemns that behavior in close connection with its parallel to Mark 9:43–48). On my view, Mark 9:42–50 is not thematically united. It is rather a collection constructed via catchwords. Verses 43 + 45 + 47–48 were the original unit. It featured the threefold use of σκανδαλίζω (a word with sexual sense in Sir 9:5 and Ps. Sol. 16:7). The saying in Mark 9:42 was added later because it also featured σκανδαλίζω, not because its subject matter was the same. Similarly, at the end, after 9:48, the use of "fire" (πῦρ) attracted the enigmatic saying in 9:49 about being salted with fire (πυρὶ ἁλισθήσεται), which in turn attracted 9:50, another saying about salt (ἅλας). The upshot of all this is that the sense of 9:42 no more helps us with the meaning of 9:43–48 than the meaning of 9:43–48 helps us with the sense of 9:49–50. That holds both for Mark and any predecessors. As for point 5, while "hand" and "foot" do not, standing by themselves, intimate sexual sin, ὁ ὀφθαλμός σου σκανδαλίζῃ σε might well do this; see above, p. 267, and cf. Matt 5:29–30, where words on the lustful look introduce Matthew's parallel to Mark 9:47. To all this I would add that Marcus nowhere accounts for the nearness of Mark 9:43–48 to the rabbinic texts. Is it only happenstance?

269. Readers interested in the standard arguments for positing a historical encounter behind the passage may consult Schwankl, *Sadduzäerfrage*, 466–587; Meier, "Debate on the Resurrection"; and Meier, *Marginal Jew*, 3:411–44.

270. The debate over how to construe the likeness to angels goes back to exegetical beginnings; see Lehtipuu, "No Sex in Heaven."

271. Origen, *Fr. Luc.* 39.2; cf. Origen, *Comm. Matt.* 17.30. For discussion see Sullivan, *Wrestling with Angels*, 131–39, and Litwa, *Posthuman Transformation*, 94–114. For saints becoming angels or being like them see 4Q511 35; Philo, *Sacr.* 5; 2 Bar. 51:1–10; Mart. Ascen. Isa. 8:15; Herm. Sim. 9.27.2 (104.3); etc. One common interpretation of Gen 6:2 holds that the "sons of God" were wicked angels who had sexual relations with human females; the good angels by contrast "restrained themselves" (2 Bar. 56:14); cf. 1 En. 6–7; 19:1; 86:1–6; 106:13–17; Jub. 4:15, 22; 5:1–11; 1QapGen II, 1, 16; Jude 6–7; Tg. Ps.-J. Gen 6:1–4; etc. For partial Jewish

from the general—people will be like angels—to the particular—people will not reproduce.

Whichever explanation one favors, Mark 12:18–27 says, in effect, that all the saints will be, in the end, eunuchs in the kingdom. From this point of view, one could indeed construe Matt 19:12 as a bit of realized eschatology: the chaste already anticipate their eschatological condition.[272] While all will be eunuchs after the resurrection, some are so even now. The main point here, however, is that Mark 12:18–27 fits snugly with those Synoptic texts in which passion requires sober management. Sexual intercourse is, in Mark 12, temporal.[273] Like earthly treasures consumed by moth and rust, it will not survive the transition from this world to the next. It cannot, then, be of enduring value. One implicit lesson is obvious: to let a temporal circumstance divert one from the narrow road that leads to life would be folly.

The same message is to hand in Luke 23:28–31, where Jesus exclaims: "Daughters of Jerusalem, do not weep for me, but weep for yourselves and for your children. For the days are surely coming when they will say: 'Blessed are the barren, and the wombs that never bore, and the breasts that never nursed.' Then they will begin to say to the mountains: 'Fall on us,' and to the hills: 'Cover us.' For if they do this when the wood is green, what will happen when it is dry?"[274]

I do not know whether these words rest directly on something Jesus said. But if they do, he was likely evoking, as Brant Pitre has urged, the eschatological tribulation.[275] Luke 23:28–31 is reminiscent of Mark 13:17–19, which is in the middle of a discourse about the latter days: "Woe to those who are pregnant

parallels to the idea of celibacy in the messianic age or world to come see Loader, *Sexuality and Gender*, 145–65.

272. Cf. the present tense of Luke 20:35–36: "Those who are considered worthy of a place in that age and in the resurrection from the dead neither marry nor are given in marriage. Indeed they cannot die any more, because they are like angels and are children of God, being children of the resurrection." For discussion of Luke's wording see Seim, *Double Message*, 208–29, and Somov, *Representations of the Afterlife*, 181–85, 219–21. Later Christians associated celibacy with the recovery of paradise; see T. M. Shaw, *Burden of the Flesh*, 181–219.

273. The appeal to Adam and Eve in Mark 10:6–9 may presuppose the tradition that Adam and Eve did not have sexual intercourse until after the fall. For texts and discussion see G. Anderson, "Celibacy or Consummation."

274. There is a variant in Gos. Thom. 79: "For there will be days when you will say: 'Blessed are the womb that has not conceived and the breasts that have not given milk.'" For the possibility that this is independent of Luke see Soards, "Tradition, Composition," 233–36. For the case against this see Goodacre, *Thomas and the Gospels*, 97–108.

275. Pitre, "Blessing the Barren." He argues for an origin with Jesus.

and to those who are nursing infants in those days! Pray that it may not be in winter. For in those days there will be suffering, such as has not been from the beginning of the creation that God created until now, no, and never will be." Being without child in the end times will not be shameful. It will not signal divine disfavor. It will rather—and ironically, given the divine imperative to "be fruitful and multiply" (Gen 1:28)—be a blessing.[276]

What would Luke 23:28–31 have implied for Jesus's followers? It is the opposite of a recipe for what a modern might consider healthy sexual activity. If it is blessed for a woman to be barren, it would make sense for a man to be a eunuch for the sake of the kingdom.[277] And if it is blessed not to give birth, it would make sense for a man not to look at a woman in order to lust after her. And if is blessed not to nurse,[278] it would make sense not to marry or be given in marriage as well as not to divorce in order to marry another.

Closing Remarks

We know very little about the women who admired and sponsored Jesus, far less than we know about some of the men who followed him, such as Peter, James, and John; and about the latter we know little enough. We are, then, often reduced to practicing, to borrow from Carla Ricci, "an exegesis of silence."[279] That should leave us chastened and wary of claiming too much. Still, some reconstructions seem more probable than others, and some conjectures more plausible than others. As to the probable in this chapter: Jesus was sometimes followed from village to village by women as well as men. As to the plausible: the mixed company around him was the chief context in which he rebuked the erotic gaze, warned of sexual sins, commended the unmarried state, and spoke against divorce and remarriage.

276. Cf. 1 Cor 7:26; 1 En. 99:5; Jub. 23:25; Apoc. El. 2:38; Sib. Or. 2:154–59, 190–92. Contrast Ps 37:26, where children are a blessing.

277. Cf. Pitre, "Blessing the Barren," 60: Luke 23:28–31 is "an injunction against procreation."

278. Cf. Luke 11:27–28 ("While he was saying this, a woman in the crowd raised her voice and said to him: 'Blessed is the womb that bore you and the breasts that nursed you!' But he said: 'Blessed rather are those who hear the word of God and obey it!'") and Gos. Thom. 79 ("A woman from the crowd said to him: 'Blessed are the womb that bore you and the breasts that nourished you.' He said to her: 'Blessed are those who have heard the word of the Father and have truly kept it'").

279. Ricci, *Mary Magdalene*, 19.

EXCURSUS

THE ISSUE OF SCANDAL

For John Meier, the sight of women without husbands traveling around Galilee with an unmarried Jesus must have raised "pious eyebrows," provoked "impious comments," and created "scandal."[1] A.-J. Levine disagrees. She denies that it would have been shameful for women to move about without familial chaperones.[2] They could have appeared unescorted without giving offense. Furthermore, had Jesus's mingling with women occasioned aspersion, opponents would likely have accused him of mixing with prostitutes. Yet the textual evidence for that is meager.[3]

Is it, however, nonexistent? Mark 2:15–16; Matt 11:19 // Luke 7:34 (Q); and Luke 15:1 employ the phrase "toll collectors and sinners" (τελῶναι καὶ ἁμαρτωλοί). In Mark, the context is a meal: Jesus is in a house, many "toll collectors and sinners" are sitting with him, and scribes ask the disciples: "Why does he eat with toll collectors and sinners?" The accusation in Matt 11:19 and Luke 7:34 is also tied to food and drink: "The Son of Man came eating and drinking, and they say: 'Behold, a glutton and drunkard, a friend of toll collectors and sinners.'" The same association holds for Luke 15:1, where once more the insult concerns what Jesus does at table: "All the toll collectors and sinners were coming to listen to him. And the Pharisees and the scribes were grumbling and saying: 'This fellow welcomes sinners and eats with them.'"

The repeated association of "toll collectors and sinners" with Jesus eating and drinking is suggestive because, as Kathleen E. Corley has observed, "courtesans, flute girls and the like were part and parcel" of "the banquet scene," and "tax collectors, as a stereotype of despicable people, were rhetorically connected in Greco-Roman literature with those who trafficked in prostitution, particularly the 'brothel-keepers' (*pornoboskoi*)."[4] She contends that, while we have little evidence that any of the

1. Meier, *Marginal Jew*, 3:79–80.

2. Levine, "Women's Itineracy," 102.

3. Levine, "Women's Itineracy," 106–7. So too Casey, *Jesus of Nazareth*, 197.

4. Corley, "Prostitute," 643. See further Corley's other writings: "Were the Women"; *Private Women*; *Women and the Historical Jesus*, 83–100; and *Maranatha*, 69–73. Note also Theissen, *Gospels in Context*, 91 ("when women are mentioned at men's banquets, the idea of sexual contact is always present"); Loader, *New Testament*

women near Jesus were reformed prostitutes,[5] it is reasonable to infer that some of his adversaries slandered them as prostitutes with the polemical phrase "toll collectors and sinners."[6]

Is Corley right? The expression "toll collectors and sinners" occurs nine times in the Synoptics (Matt 9:10, 11; 11:19; Mark 2:15, 16 [bis], Luke 5:30; 7:34; 15:1). Twice, however, Matthew uses a similar phrase: "toll collectors and prostitutes" (οἱ τελῶναι καὶ αἱ πόρναι, 21:31–32). The setting is a discussion of John the Baptist: "The toll collectors and the prostitutes are going in the kingdom of God ahead of you. For John came to you in the way of righteousness and . . . the toll collectors and the prostitutes believed him." Now "toll collectors and prostitutes" may be a variant or near synonym of "toll collectors and sinners."[7] So even if 21:31–32 concerns not Jesus but John, the more precise "toll collectors and prostitutes" in 21:31–32 may reveal the First Evangelist's understanding of "toll collectors and sinners" in earlier passages, in Matt 9:10–11 and 11:19.[8]

Corley's proposal is additionally credible because the verbal barb that Jesus is "the friend of toll collectors and sinners" directly trails, in Matt 11:19 and Luke 7:34, the charge that he is "a glutton and a drunkard." The first three accusations—Jesus eats too much, he drinks too much, he befriends toll collectors—are not generalities. They rather denote very particular acts. If "sinners" is, by contrast, a catchall for immoral behavior or wickedness, it is of a different character. But if the word intimates inappropriate conduct with women at meals, it follows neatly as the last of four concrete allegations.[9]

---

on Sexuality, 346–49; and Merz, "Genderforschung," 612. Levine is familiar with Corley's work but unconvinced by it; see "Women's Itineracy," 106 n. 39.

5. So also Le Donne, "Sex Workers." Contrast Schüssler Fiorenza, *In Memory of Her*, 126–30; Sim, "Women Followers," 55 ("it is quite conceivable that some of the women disciples of Jesus were former prostitutes"); and M. A. Powell, "Jesus and the Pathetic Wicked," 202–6.

6. So too Stegemann and Stegemann, *Jesus Movement*, 383–96.

7. Cf. Carter, *Matthew and the Margins*, 219–20, 425; Freyne, *Galilee and Gospel*, 281–82; and France, *Matthew*, 863 (the formulation in 21:31–32 is a "starker form" of the earlier phrase "toll collectors and sinners"). Contrast Le Donne, "Sex Workers," 150.

8. For the argument that Matt 21:28–31 is related to the tradition in Luke 7:29–30 see Catchpole, *Jesus People*, 222–23; cf. Parks, *Gender*, 94–95.

9. Contrast Levine, "Women Itinerants," 49: "One could bundle prostitutes into the 'sinner' category and so see them as dining with Jesus, but since the tradition tends to make explicit particular forms of social sin, such as tax collecting, the silence on the presence of prostitutes can be read as indicating absence."

Then there is Luke 7:37. This introduces a woman with the laconic note, representing the narrator's point of view, that she was a "sinner in the city" (ἐν τῇ πόλει ἁμαρτωλός).[10] Given her public reputation ("in the city") and her possession of expensive perfume (cf. Prov 7:17; Jdt 10:3; 16:7), exegetes commonly suppose that the twice repeated ἁμαρτωλός (7:37, 39) refers to notorious sexual sin.[11] One may compare Amos 7:17: "Your wife will be a prostitute *in the city* [LXX: ἐν τῇ πόλει]."[12] This evaluation is all the more likely in the light of Luke 7:39, where a Pharisee remarks on Jesus not knowing "what kind of woman" (ποταπὴ ἡ γυνή) she is. This singles her out as being more than a run-of-the-mill failure, as more than a member of the "aren't we all sinners, after all?" category.[13] In Luke 7:37, then, "sinner" most likely means "sexual sinner."[14] This buoys the possibility that

10. I take ἐν τῇ πόλει to qualify ἁμαρτωλός; cf. Nolland, *Luke*, 1:353: "It is best to connect ἐν τῇ πόλει (lit., 'in the city') with 'sinner' and to give it in accord with Semitic idiom a sense like 'publicly' or 'well-known.'" The phrase just might, however, refer back to 7:11: "In the city (of Nain) there was a woman, a sinner."

11. Cf. Lapide, *Great Commentary*, 3:381–82 (citing in support Ambrose, Jerome, Augustine, Chrysostom, Gregory the Great, Bede); Bruce, "Synoptic Gospels," 515 (Luke's "expressive silence" represents her as a "harlot"); H. Leroy, "Vergebung und Gemeinde," 92; Corley, *Private Women*, 124; Bovon, *Luke*, 1:293; and Nolland, *Luke*, 1:353 ("the dramatic impact of the woman's actions appears most strikingly if 'sinner' is understood as a euphemism for 'prostitute' or 'courtesan'"). Contrast Reid, "Do You See This Woman?" and Reid, *Choosing the Better Part?*, 107–23; see further Hornsby, "Woman Is a Sinner," 32. I leave aside here the theological and hermeneutical (as opposed to historical) issues that, for contemporary sensibilities, attend Luke's characterization; on this see Carey, *Sinners*, 1–15.

12. Note also Deut 22:23 ("if there is a betrothed virgin, and a man meets her in the city and lies with her"); Isa 23:16 ("go about the city, O forgotten harlot"); Sir 9:6–8 ("do not give yourself to prostitutes . . . do not look around in the streets of a city"); and 4Q184 1 12 ("in squares of the city she veils herself"). Cf. Aramaic נפקת ברא (= "she who goes out"), which designates a prostitute, as in Tg. Ps.-J. Deut 23:18.

13. So it will not do to object that, in Luke, all are "sinners" (cf. 5:8; 11:4, 13; 19:7).

14. And "even if she is not a professional provider of erotic or sexual services, her actions, including loosening her hair in public, touching, kissing and perfuming Jesus' feet, likely have erotic, certainly intimate connotations"; so Bertschmann, "Hosting Jesus," 36. "Sin" and "sinner" often designate sexual sins specifically; cf. Gen 39:9 (Joseph sleeping with Potiphar's wife would be "sin against God"); Ps 50:16–18 LXX (the "sinner" keeps company with adulterers); Ps. Sol. 16:7–8 ("restrain me, O God, from sordid sin, and from every woman who seduces the foolish"); Wis 3:13 ("sinful union"); Mark 8:38 ("this adulterous and sinful generation"); John 8:11 (Jesus discharges an adulteress with "go and sin no more"); 1 Cor 6:18 ("the fornicator sins against the body itself"); 2 Pet 2:14 ("eyes full of adultery, insatiable for sin"); T. Ab. (long rec.) 10:8, 13 ("all those living in sin" includes adulterers); Tg. Neof. I

the same is true elsewhere in Luke, in 5:30; 7:34; and 15:1. Indeed, as the story about the sinful woman in 7:36–50 directly follows the remark that Jesus's opponents deride him as a "friend of toll collectors and sinners" (7:34), it is natural to give ἁμαρτωλός in 7:34 the same sense that it has in the nearby 7:37: the story illustrates or dramatizes the accusation.

With that, however, the evidence is exhausted, which means Levine is right: there is not much there.[15] Certainly we find nothing in the Synoptics like the accusation in Acts Phil. 125, that Mariamme, a woman who travels with Philip and Bartholomew, "goes about with these magicians and doubtless commits adultery with them." Nor do the canonical texts relate the kind of polemic Origen found in Celsus: the women who followed Jesus into the wilderness ignored "propriety."[16] All we have is a Lukan Pharisee accusing Jesus of letting a likely sex worker touch him (Luke 7:39) and the decent possibility—it is no more than that—that the polemical charge of consorting with "sinners" in the phrase "toll collectors and sinners" adverts to women of ill repute.

What then might we infer? One possibility is that Jesus's opponents did not take offense, or seldom took offense, at his interactions with women. Perhaps his behavior in this area was, to everyone's satisfaction, above board and so occasioned no criticism. Perhaps, when Jesus was at meals with women, nothing untoward happened, and everyone knew it; and maybe, when Jesus's band settled down for the night, the sexes were segregated, nothing untoward happened, and everyone knew it. Alternatively, if enemies derided his celibacy by jeering him as a "eunuch," that might have closed off the clashing accusation of licentiousness. In short, maybe nobody complained, or maybe only a few complained only a little.

But there is another possibility. Scandal is relative, polemic opportunistic. There was nothing indecent about being a carpenter, yet Jesus's detractors seemingly turned his vocation into an insult.[17] There was likewise nothing reprehensible in being an exorcist vanquishing evil spirits is a kindness—yet opponents imputed Jesus's successes to Beelzebul: he

Exod. 20:14 and on Deut 5:18 ("the sins of the adulterer"); y. Ta'an. 1:4 (64b) ("do not sin" = "do not commit adultery"); etc. It goes without saying that "other, complementary meanings" can be present at the same time; cf. Crossley, *Jesus and the Chaos of History*, 106 (who, on pp. 96–106, stresses the frequent link with wealth).

15. See further Levine, "Women Itinerants," 48–49.

16. Origen, *Cels.* 3.10: "Such was the charm of Jesus's words that not only were men willing to follow him into the wilderness but also women, disregarding their feminine weakness and propriety, followed their teacher into the desert."

17. See Mark 6:3 with the remarks of Yarbro Collins, *Mark*, 290.

cast out demons by the prince of demons (Matt 9:32–34; 10:25; 12:22–30; Mark 3:22–27; Luke 11:14–23; John 7:20; 8:48–52; 10:20–21). John the Baptist, it appears, was similarly accused of having a demon (Matt 11:18 // Luke 7:33 [Q]). This was not, one imagines, a good faith estimate. One does not give opponents the benefit of the doubt. Adversaries instead uncharitably hunt for reasons to complain; and they can usually espy cause for complaint whether one exists or not.

Did this happen with Jesus? Might he not have suffered insults because his table fellowship included women, or because women sometimes accompanied him on his missionary outings?[18] Yet why, if this was the case, are our sources quiescent or close to quiescent on the matter? Maybe the solution is as simple as this: the Gospels are not chronicles of all that happened. They are instead fundamentally truncated witnesses. Their memories are skeletal, and they cannot possibly preserve every gripe lodged against Jesus. Certainly neither the evangelists nor the tradents before them were interested in collecting slander for its own sake. Rather, when they recorded some calumny, it was usually because Jesus had crafted a memorable riposte, such as: "If I cast out demons by the prince of demons, by whom do your sons cast them our?" Perhaps, then, he never got around to composing an unambiguous, pithy rejoinder to what some said about the women around him. Or maybe he did respond but his retort was unmemorable or rhetorically flat, so that it never occurred to anyone to make it the heart of a chreia.

According to Mark 15:40–41, many women went up to Jerusalem with Jesus. Let us assume, for the sake of discussion, that this really happened, and further that Jesus, the Twelve, and supportive women began their trek somewhere in Galilee near Capernaum (cf. 9:33). If so, they had at least ninety miles or so to walk whatever route they took. That clearly would have entailed overnighting. And yet we read nothing about people taking offense. Nor do we read of any complaining about arrangements, whatever they were, once the group got to Jerusalem and spent evenings there. Is this because nobody took offense? Levine offers this explanation:

18. For modern illustrations involving accusations of sexual deviancy among religious minorities see Davis, "Some Themes." Sources outside the canon recognize the potential scandal inherent in Jesus and his disciples being accompanied by women; see, e.g., Gos. Phil. 63–64 (Jesus used to kiss Mary Magdalene on the mouth) and the Book of the Resurrection of Jesus Christ by Bartholomew the Apostle fol. 5b (Salome is "the temptress").

> Women from Galilee may have accompanied Jesus on that final trip to Jerusalem, but we do not know if they went only with him, went with others and met him there, or were already in Jerusalem when he arrived. If we locate the women "followers" as home-based, then we can read their presence at the cross as not indicative of a one- or three-year journey outside of their homes but as a one-time trip to Jerusalem, at Passover, when many others were also making the journey, and women could easily travel together in groups.[19]

This is one possibility. There is, however, another. Maybe a few did grumble, but the tradition did not take note because it could not put the circumstance to good use. We do not know one way or the other. The unrecorded is the unrecoverable.

19. Levine, "Women Itinerants," 54–55.

5

I Remember It Well, or Not

A Thought Experiment

> If, the day after a battle, we were to collect the narratives of eyewitnesses, we should find the action described in twenty different ways while identical details would be related from the most diverse points of view with the same amount of sincerity. . . . The sentiments and impressions of . . . [a] narrator and the camp to which he belongs, all affect his account, which is neither wholly false nor yet wholly in accordance with truth. Every man will relate his own legend.
>
> —H. Delehaye[1]

> If our research can generate probable conclusions, all the better, but often it cannot. History does not expect its practitioners to *believe* things. Doubt, especially of one's own too-easy constructions, is the highest and most necessary value in our field.
>
> —Steve Mason[2]

> One moment I have recalled so frequently that not one detail will have survived undistorted.
>
> —Raymond Tallis[3]

1. Delehaye, *Legends of the Saints*, 12–13.

2. Mason, "Response," 284. Mason continues: "Not a purely destructive doubt, to be sure, but one that clears away the fog of misunderstanding so that we may imagine new possibilities, which might take us closer to the truth of the ancient past."

3. Tallis, *Logos*, xi.

My title, "I Remember It Well, or Not," alludes to a song from the 1958 musical comedy "Gigi." In the film, an older couple—Maurice Chevalier and Hermione Gingold—remember their first date. He recollects that they met at nine while she recalls it was eight. He claims he was on time but she is sure he was late. He knows that they dined with friends while she remembers that they ate alone. He says there was a dazzling April moon but she counters that there was no moon, and it was June. And on it goes, each firmly persuaded in his or her own mind yet disagreeing with the other over nearly everything in their common past.

This is comedy. It works because viewers can identify. We all know from experience that memories of the same event often diverge. Eyewitnesses do not always see eye to eye. Their recall, even when vivid and seemingly self-authenticating, can clash. Some memories, it inexorably follows, must deceive their owners.

Historians of the Gospels have, of late, much discussed this unhappy fact. Some—Bart Ehrman for instance—stress how unreliable and misleading memories can be, especially as they travel from one individual to another.[4] Others—Richard Bauckham for one—emphasize that personal memories can be, in certain circumstances, quite accurate, and all the more so when a remembering community reinforces them.[5]

Below I will share some of my own thoughts about the reliability of memory.[6] The subject, unfortunately, is disturbingly convoluted, involving as it

4. Ehrman, *Jesus before the Gospels*. Cf. DeConick, "Human Memory," 179 ("To trust the eyewitnesses because testimony asks to be trusted is nonsense. Whatever memories are preserved in the Gospels, they are reconstructed and highly interpreted memories"), and the pessimism of Crook, "Collective Memory Distortion," 76: "Memory theory does not . . . give us cause for optimism concerning the historicity of the Gospels. On the contrary, memory theory ought to leave us feeling deeply troubled about what we can actually know about the past."

5. Bauckham, *Jesus and the Eyewitnesses*, 319–57. See also McIver, *Memory*, and Keener, *Christobiography*, 365–400.

6. The first chapter of one of my earlier books, *Constructing Jesus*, opens with remarks on the sins of memory (pp. 1–14) and follows this with a discussion of historical method (pp. 14–30). Most responses to the book, to my great dismay, have focused on its first few pages, which are for me the least important and least interesting part: they are mere preface. Moreover, no reviewer, to the best of my recall, has urged that the book's main conclusions about Jesus are wide of the mark precisely because I hold faulty ideas about memory or have adopted a defective method. Beyond this, I am surprised to find myself lumped in with those who advocate a "memory approach" to the sources; so, e.g., Havukainen, *Quest*, 209–30. This does a disservice to other scholars, such as Sandra Huebenthal, Chris Keith, Werner Kelber, Alan Kirk, Anthony Le Donne, Rafael Rodríguez, Jens Schröter, and Tom Thatcher,

does neuroscience, psychology, and the interface between oral memory and written texts. My chief purpose in this chapter, however, is to ask a series of questions about the Gospel of Mark, questions that constitute a thought experiment. My goal is to see what is involved in the recurrent endeavor to associate the Jesus tradition with reliable eyewitness testimony.

Mark and Peter

The dominant Christian tradition holds that the John Mark of Acts, a companion of both Peter and Paul, wrote the Second Gospel.[7] Many modern historians and exegetes think otherwise.[8] Were I to bet, I would put my money on the tradition.[9] My wager, however, would be with fingers crossed: I would not be robustly confident of winning. Joel Marcus, after surveying the issues, arrives at this conclusion: "not proven."[10] He decides that "our Gospel probably was written by someone named Mark," yet as to that Mark's identity, Marcus could muster only this: "The possibility cannot be excluded that this Mark was the John Mark of Acts and the Pauline correspondence."[11] A possibility not excluded is not a firm foundation on which to build, and I reluctantly concede that Clifton Black is right: "We cannot know" who wrote Mark.[12]

I could stop there, with the observation that, if we do not know who wrote Mark, we know nothing about his possible contacts with eyewitnesses. Given,

---

who (unlike me) have truly immersed themselves in the literature on individual and social memory. I am but a dabbler. Perhaps, in light of all this, I should have avoided returning to the vexed subject of memory. But I have succumbed to temptation.

7. For this individual see Acts 12:12, 25; 13:5, 13; 15:37–39; Col 4:10; 2 Tim 4:11; Phlm 24; 1 Pet 5:13. It is likely—but not demonstrable—that these texts refer to the same individual.

8. Note, e.g., Niederwimmer, "Johannes Markus"; Vielhauer, *Geschichte der urchristlichen Literatur*, 259–61; and Kok, *Gospel on the Margins*. For the view that Mark the author of the Second Gospel was identified with the John Mark of Acts and Paul's epistles only at a secondary stage see Furlong, *John Also Called Mark*.

9. For defenses of the tradition see Hengel, "Entstehungszeit"; Hengel, *Studies in the Gospel of Mark*, 45–53; Hengel, *Saint Peter*, 36–48; Gundry, *Mark*, 1026–45; Bauckham, *Jesus and the Eyewitnesses*, 155–80, 202–39; Bauckham, "Gospel of Mark"; and Bernier, *Quest for the Historical Jesus*, 126–42. Note also Bond, "Peter." She supports a possible connection to Peter without addressing the author's identity. Kok, *Gospel on the Margins*, offers an excellent review of recent debate. For the case that the name "Mark" was associated with the Second Gospel from the beginning see Gathercole, "Alleged Anonymity."

10. Marcus, *Mark*, 1:24. Cf. Black, *Mark*, 198: "We must render a verdict of *non olet sed non liquet*: it may not smell fishy, but it can't be proven."

11. Marcus, *Mark*, 1:24. He finds the evidence for a link with Peter inadequate.

12. Black, *Mark*, 27–28.

however, that I am disposed, if guardedly, to accept the tradition assigning Mark's Gospel to John Mark, questions arise.[13]

Questions about Mark and Peter

If the author of the Second Gospel knew Simon Peter,[14] what exactly was their relationship?[15] Many give credence to the well-known testimony of Papias, who wrote in the first half of the second century (in my view probably closer to its beginning than its middle):[16]

> The elder used to say this: "Mark, having become Peter's interpreter, wrote down accurately everything he remembered, though not in order, of the things either said or done by Christ." For he neither heard the Lord nor followed him, but afterward, as I said, followed Peter, who adapted his teachings toward the needs of his audience[17] but had no intention of giving an ordered account of the Lord's sayings. Mark consequently did nothing wrong in writing down some things as he remembered them, for he made it his one concern not to omit anything that he heard or to make any false statement in them. (Eusebius, *Hist. eccl.* 3.39.15–16)

Let us assume, for the sake of argument, that these words, despite their obviously apologetical slant, and despite our inability to sort out exactly what is from "the elder" and what from Papias, tell us how things were.[18] We still know far less than we would like to know. If Mark was Peter's ἑρμηνευτής, what

13. I beg the reader's indulgence for the inordinate barrage of questions in this and subsequent sections. But their surfeit is deliberate: they reflect my inability, on issue after issue, to pass beyond the interrogative mode.

14. In Acts 12:6–19, Peter goes to the house of John Mark's mother, and 1 Pet 5:13 has this: "Your sister church in Babylon, chosen together with you, sends you greetings; and so does my son Mark." Even if 1 Peter is, as seems likely, a post-70 pseudepigraphon, 5:13 could rightly remember a link between Peter and Mark.

15. For Theissen, *New Testament*, 38–39, the author of Mark may have been not Peter's associate but rather someone familiar with "a stream of tradition" going back to Peter.

16. For an early date see Yarbrough, "Date of Papias," and Gundry, *Mark*, 1027–29.

17. I prefer this translation of πρὸς τὰς χρείας. Some instead take the expression to refer to the rhetorical category *chreia*; so, e.g., Kürzinger, "Aussage des Papias," and Bauckham, *Jesus and the Eyewitnesses*, 214–17. Against this see Standaert, *Marc*, 451–54.

18. Yet we should not forget that, in the words of Eve, *Behind the Gospels*, 147, we cannot confirm "that Eusebius has accurately recorded the precise wording of what Papias wrote, that in later life Papias accurately remembered and recorded precisely what he gleaned

does ἑρμηνευτής mean?[19] Was Mark a translator, turning Peter's Aramaic sentences into Greek?[20] If so, should we envisage an oral setting or rather imagine Peter and Mark sitting down to record in writing what the apostle was wont to teach?[21] And was Mark a trustworthy translator or did he make mistakes?[22] And did the evangelist tend to the literal, or was he more like the targumist known as Pseudo-Jonathan, whose Aramaic paraphrase of the Pentateuch is full of colorful midrashic expansions?[23] Or does ἑρμηνευτής perhaps indicate instead that Mark served as Peter's "private secretary and aide-de-camp,"[24] or even that Peter authorized him to transmit Petrine traditions?[25] Or might the word convey that the Gospel in its entirety is Mark's interpretation, explanation, or mediation of Peter's teaching?[26]

Beyond the basic and unresolved problem of the sense of ἑρμηνευτής, how long, assuming Papias to have the facts, were Mark and Peter closely associated? Years? Months? Weeks?[27] And where did they find themselves together,

---

from John the Elder in his youth, and that John the Elder's account of the relation of Peter's preaching to Mark's writing was precisely accurate."

19. A perhaps rival tradition, I note, held that a certain Glaucias, the teacher of Basilides, was Peter's "interpreter" (ἑρμηνέα); so Clement of Alexandria, *Strom.* 7.17.

20. So Bauckham, *Jesus and the Eyewitnesses*, 205–10, and Witherington, "Christianity in the Making," 222–23. Cf. Gen 42:23 LXX; 1 Cor 14:28 v.l.

21. For the latter see Bauckham, *Jesus and the Eyewitnesses*, 206–7.

22. Casey, *Jesus of Nazareth*, 110, espies several translation errors in Mark.

23. Translation is never uncomplicated. Recall the prologue to Sirach: "Be indulgent in cases where, despite our diligent labor in translating, we may seem to have rendered some phrases imperfectly. For what was originally expressed in Hebrew does not have exactly the same sense when translated into another language. Not only this book, but even the Law itself, the Prophecies, and the rest of the books differ not a little when read in the original." Bauckham, *Jesus and the Eyewitnesses*, 209–10, observes that Josephus could claim, in his *Antiquities*, to be doing nothing but putting "the books of the Hebrews into the Greek tongue" (10:218). Informed readers know better.

24. So T. W. Manson, *Teaching of Jesus*, 23 n. 1.

25. Cf. Yadin-Israel, "For Mark was Peter's *Tanna*," 346–48.

26. So Kürzinger, "Aussage des Papias," 249–50. Cf. Zahn, *Introduction to the New Testament*, 2:440, 443–44.

27. While Eusebius quotes Papias as saying that Mark "followed" (παρηκολούθησεν) Peter, the length of time is unspecified. Clement of Alexandria *apud* Eusebius, *Hist. eccl.* 6.14.6–7, asserts that Mark had followed Peter for some time. Zahn, *Introduction to the New Testament*, 427, conjectures that Mark "was converted through Peter, and possibly also baptized by him." He further urges, on the basis of Acts 12:12, that Mark knew Peter in Jerusalem from an early time, and that they reunited later in Rome in the 60s (427–33, 440). Contrast Casey, *Jesus of Nazareth*, 68–69: "It is probable that Marcus heard Peter preach, but

and when?[28] And how many times did Mark hear Peter tell the same story, so that he could reliably lay it up in his memory? Or did he take written notes rather than keep everything in his head?[29] And how much time passed between Mark hearing Peter and the appearance of a Gospel?[30]

The candid answer to all these questions is: We do not know. The secondary literature, to be sure, gives it a go (as my footnotes reveal), returning replies to every query, sometimes by appeal to patristic sources. Yet while some answers may be better than others, we are, in the end, stuck with suppositions, possibilities, and fragile inferences.

If, notwithstanding all the open questions, we closely associate Mark's Gospel with Peter, how much in the book derives directly from the apostle? The greater part? Half?[31] Less than half?[32] The Gospel is unlikely to be one hundred percent Petrine, to be nothing but the "Memoirs of Peter,"[33] because the author has his own theological agenda and a consistent point of view.[34] So we can ask: if there was a pre-Markan passion narrative,[35] did Mark get it from Peter? Or did he supplement a traditional, widely known narrative with some Petrine reminiscences?[36] Again, did the evangelist hear the story of Jesus's

---

it is most improbable that he heard him often, and out of question that he knew him well." For the meaning of παρακολουθέω see Moessner, *Luke the Historian*, 68–107.

28. According to the anti-Marcionite prologue, Mark composed his Gospel in Italy, after Peter's death. Cf. Irenaeus, *Haer.* 3.1.2: Mark wrote after Peter died. I see no way to gauge the truth of these or other claims made after Papias, claims perhaps made in (partial?) dependence on him.

29. So Kennedy, "Classical and Christian Source Criticism."

30. Zahn, *Introduction to the New Testament*, 433, speculates that it may have been a period of three years.

31. For T. W. Manson, "The Gospel of Mark," in *Studies in the Gospels*, 28–45, almost half derives from Peter.

32. According to V. Taylor, *Mark*, 7–8: "The external evidence is far from suggesting that Peter was Mark's sole source of information, but, as is not surprising, the tendency was to emphasize this connexion and make it more direct." According to Casey, *Jesus*, 67–69: "While Mark may well have heard Peter teach, and this may have been the source of some of his perfectly accurate material, the *whole* of his Gospel cannot possibly have been derived from this source." Cf. Dschulnigg, *Markusevangelium*, 53.

33. The phrase (ἀπομνημονεύμασιν αὐτοῦ, sc. Πέτρου) is from Justin, *Dial.* 106, with likely reference to Mark's Gospel. Does this represent a reading of Papias? According to Moss, "Fashioning Mark," readers of Papias would have understood Mark to be a servile scribe who took dictation.

34. Cf. N. R. Petersen, "Point of View."

35. See Theissen, *Gospels in Context*, 166–99, and Allison, *Constructing Jesus*, 392–423.

36. So V. Taylor, *Mark*, 130: Mark "expanded a short Roman account of the Passion by the aid of Petrine reminiscences" (cf. 653–64).

transfiguration from a firsthand witness, or did he know it well before becoming Peter's ἑρμηνευτής? Further, did Peter ever tell stories about Jesus that he learned from others? Did he resolutely refuse to recount anything he himself had not witnessed? Or did he happily welcome stories when they buoyed his convictions?[37] For some Markan episodes—the baptism, the execution of the Baptist, the trial before Pilate, the crucifixion, the burial, the discovery of the empty tomb—Peter is elsewhere.

According to Mark 6:6–13, Jesus sent his disciples out on their own. If so, when Peter returned, did he believe the stories of what had happened in his absence?[38] Although Josephus was the eyewitness of many events in the *Jewish War* (see 1.2–3, 18), much in it he learned from others, at second- or thirdhand. He did not just stubbornly narrate only events of which he was an eyewitness. Was Peter different?[39]

Question follows question without informed answer. Some, to be sure, argue that Mark must have learned about Peter's denial from Peter himself. So too the day in Capernaum—when Peter's mother-in-law is healed (Mark 1:21–39)—as well as episodes featuring Peter, James, and John (Mark 5:35–43; 9:2–9).[40] Yet even if they are right, as they well might be, this hardly accounts for most of Mark. Indeed, it is possible to read Papias's claim, that Mark wrote down "some things" (ἔνια), to mean that much in Mark does not come from Peter.[41] While Samuel Byrskog finds truth in Papias's testimony, he nonetheless concedes that "only a minority of the Markan chreiai actually go back directly to Peter" and that "a search through the Markan narrative . . . brings rather meagre results. It is impossible to verify any large amount of Petrine chreia."[42]

Even though the tradition was anxious to tie our Gospel to an authoritative eyewitness, it concedes that the book is not a transcript of Peter's speech, for the title is "The Gospel according to Mark," not "The Gospel according to Peter."

37. For relevant considerations in this matter see A. Kirk, *Memory and the Jesus Tradition*, 84–87.

38. Or was there nothing to tell because Jesus took a break from his usual activities while his friends were away?

39. Theissen, *Gospels in Context*, 99–103, persuades me that some miracle stories in Mark show signs of having been recounted by storytellers who did not follow Jesus. This counts against an undiluted origin with Peter.

40. Note, e.g., V. Taylor, *Mark*, 170–71, 572.

41. So Zahn, *Introduction to the New Testament*, 440–43.

42. Byrskog, *Story as History*, 291, 297.

Peter's Memory

Even if we assume, what we cannot confirm, that much or most of Mark comes from Peter and that the Gospel embodies, to great extent, eyewitness testimony, it is unclear what follows. Finding an eyewitness does not slay doubt. This is why the eyewitness testimonies at the front of the Book of Mormon do not establish the nature of Mormonism. There remains room for discussion.

How good, we might wonder, was Peter's memory? As with everything else human, mnemonic capacities span a continuum. Some people have eidetic memory and are able to recall images accurately after seeing them only once. A handful have hyperthymesia and remember accurately almost everything that has ever happened to them. At the other end of the spectrum are those suffering from mild cognitive impairment or advancing toward dementia. How was it with Peter? Was he, like Rabbi Eliezer ben Hyrcanus, a cemented cistern who did not lose a drop (m. ʾAbot 2:8)? Or was he proficient at misremembering? How could we ever find out?[43]

I might add, in this connection, that if, as many urge, Mark was with Peter in Rome in the 60s, then Peter, if born around the same time as Jesus, may have been in his 60s. Memory does not get better with age. The older we become, the more we play charades with our recall. As the past recedes, many memories flicker, recollection fades.[44] One can, of course, simply assume that Peter's memory was—whenever Mark heard him—close to average and so good enough. This is, however, an assumption, not an established fact.

Yet even if Peter's memory was decent, how good is human memory? Several years ago I set out to learn what I could from modern studies of this subject.[45] I did not covet a specific answer. I did not wish to confirm that memory is usually reliable or to establish that it is often unreliable. Learning was my only agenda. Soon, however, the books and articles that stressed the failures of memory caught most of my attention, undoubtedly because so many were so unexpectedly sobering; and it remains hard for me to fathom how anyone who

43. Cf. Eve, *Behind the Gospels*, 143: we have "no way of knowing how reliable an eyewitness Peter may actually have been."

44. Helpful here is McIver, *Memory*, 21–40. Cf. Clement of Alexandria, *Strom.* 1: his στρωματεῖς are notes "stored up for old age, a remedy for forgetfulness." One can, I acknowledge, counter by appealing to the common experience that things memorized while young may be better remembered than things later learned or experienced; cf. Quintilian, *Inst.* 11.2.6; and Irenaeus *apud* Eusebius, *Hist. eccl.* 5.20.

45. I focus here on individual human memory, recognizing that it always operates with cultural elements and structures; see A. Kirk, *Memory and the Jesus Tradition*, 71–80.

undertakes review of the relevant literature with an open mind can come away not feeling humbled. Modern study does, in the words of John Dominic Crossan, "mitigate the serene complacency of common sense about memory."[46]

The relevant literature demonstrates, among other things, that memories are reconstructive as well as reproductive and so involve imagination;[47] that they are a function of self-interest; that narrative conventions inescapably sculpt them; that they are subject to sequential displacement; that we favor rehearsing pleasant memories over unpleasant ones, which may lead to the latter disappearing through disuse; that even slight suggestions can alter memory in significant ways, including the recall of individuals with first-class recall; that we are apt to project current circumstances and biases onto our former experiences, assimilating the past to the present; and that memories are not set in stone: we chisel them a bit every time we recall them.[48]

My reading led me to conclude that the shortcomings of memory should unsettle historians of Jesus. There is no reason to presume that those who remembered him were immune to the usual deficiencies of recall.[49] Some have complained that I am too cynical about memory, that I have become a sort of skeptic.[50] Alan Kirk characterizes my view as "gloomy."[51] For Rafael Rodríguez, my take on memory is "sober to the point of melancholy."[52] One critic even complains that, if eyewitness testimony is what I make it out to be,

46. Crossan, *Birth of Christianity*, 67.

47. One proof of this is that we often recall autobiographical memories from a third-person perspective, from the outside, not from the inside through our one-time eyes; see Rice and Rubin, "Remembering from Any Angle," and McCarroll and Sutton, "Memory and Perspective."

48. For all of this see Allison, *Constructing Jesus*, 2–8; also Fried, *Schleier der Erinnerung*; Gallo, *Associative Illusions of Memory*; Harris, Paterson, and Kemp, "Collaborative Recall"; Frenda, Nichols, and Loftus, "Current Issues"; Patihis et al., "False Memories"; J. Shaw, *Memory Illusion*; and Genova, *Remember*.

49. See further the overview of the discussion in Huebenthal, *Reading Mark's Gospel*, 66–74, 529–40.

50. Note esp. Bauckham, "General and the Particular." Cf. Bauckham, "Psychology of Memory," 137: Allison is among those who believe in "the pervasive unreliability of memory" (145): he holds that "'personal event memories' are comprehensively unreliable."

51. A. Kirk, *Memory and the Jesus Tradition*, 56.

52. Rodríguez, "Jesus as His Friends Remembered Him," 228. This is partially my fault. Although I explicitly eschewed "hyperskepticism" and claimed to be taking a "middle way" in *Constructing Jesus*, I did so in a footnote (9 n. 47). This has sometimes left the wrong impression—although Havukainen, *Quest*, 210–11, and Keener, *Christobiography*, 393 n. 157, get me right. At the same time, the opening few pages about memory are followed by a very long book full of conclusions about Jesus, not skepticism about historical knowledge.

then "the entire modern judicial system must be overhauled."[53] This mischaracterizes me (although our judicial system has, in fact, often been naïve about eyewitness testimony).[54] To acknowledge the sins of memory is not to claim that memory does nothing but sin. That it sometimes or often disappoints does not mean it always disappoints. Its successes are the norm in everyday life, and memories can be, as Richard Bauckham rightly and repeatedly stresses, especially accurate when they rehearse distinctive, significant events in which individuals were emotionally involved.[55] Natural selection has seen to it that human memory is sufficiently reliable to facilitate our survival. Nonetheless, I unabashedly insist that mnemonic failures are more than once-in-a-blue-moon exceptions. As the literature documents, we go astray much more often than we like to think.[56] People keep diaries for good reason.

As I was reviewing the literature on memory, I also began to pay more attention to occasions on which I disagree with someone else about the past. I soon became keenly aware of the obvious, that this happens all the time, that the undeliberate warping of recall is common enough. My wife and I often—"often" is not exaggeration—disagree over what happened twenty years ago and what happened twenty hours ago. It is a fascinating, sometimes disheartening phenomenon. Each time we disagree, at least one of us must be wrong, but whoever it is always thinks it is the other. When my children concur with my wife, so that there are two or three witnesses against me, I am defeated: my memory is wrong. Sometimes, however, I am right, and my wife's recall is off the mark.

But my children's younger minds also misremember. A while back one of my sons shared with me a memory of waking up long ago in the middle of the night, looking out into our backyard through his bedroom window, and seeing a troop of "little people" dancing around a tree. That is his vivid recall. As we spoke about it, however, he decided that it did not happen, because I reminded him that, when he was little, I read to him a passage from the autobiography of William Allen White, the once-famed Kansas journalist. In that passage

53. Lamerson, Review of *Constructing Jesus*, 839.

54. US courts have, in recent years, and partly in response to new knowledge, happily taken a more cautious approach to eyewitness testimony; cf. Schacter and Loftus, "Memory and Law." Schacter and Loftus observe that eyewitness testimony has been a factor in the majority of convictions that DNA evidence has overturned. See further the Committee on Scientific Approaches, *Identifying the Culprit*.

55. For a convenient summary of Bauckham's views on this see his "Psychology of Memory," 141–45.

56. For a famous illustration that appears again and again in the literature see Neisser, *Memory Observed*, 139–59 (a comparison of John Dean's Watergate testimony with tape recordings later discovered). In general, we frequently have more confidence in our memories than we should; cf. Kornell, "Failing to Predict Future Changes."

White tells the bizarre story of waking up one night, looking out his window, and seeing what he could only call fairies dancing around a tree. My son had moved the story from White's backyard to our backyard, and he had turned White into himself, and so for years he had carried around the memory of a graphic, haunting event that never happened, at least to him.[57]

Another anecdote. At dinner one evening, my wife and I and our youngest son were reminiscing about a startling, memorable event—we all three "remembered" it—having to do with my late mother-in-law. According to my memory, an orangutan, in the zoo in Wichita, Kansas, ran and threw itself against a glass wall that my startled mother-in-law was standing against. According to my wife, it was a chimpanzee in the zoo in Oklahoma City. According to my son, it was a capuchin in the zoo in Pittsburgh. Now we all had the gist or general idea down—a monkey or an ape in a zoo threw itself against a glass window and frightened my mother-in-law; but more than one of us had moved the event to the wrong place and recalled the wrong animal; and, in at least two cases, fictional details had displaced historical facts. It is a pity that I cannot ask my mother-in-law about her memory. She might relate a fourth version. In any case, as I have repeatedly taken note of this sort of seemingly unconscious alteration of recall, I am less sanguine than many about human memory.[58] That includes Peter's memory, which we cannot evaluate.

We need, moreover, to wonder not only about the apostle's recall but that of Mark, for Papias claims that the Second Gospel is Mark's memory of Peter's memory: "Mark . . . did nothing wrong in writing down some things as he remembered them." The key phrase is "as he [Mark] remembered them."[59] Perhaps, as Papias affirms, Mark did nothing wrong (although that is clearly an apologetical claim). We have no reason to posit that Mark was in any way cognitively impaired. We equally have no reason to imagine that his memory was better than average. Some things will be forever unknown. This includes, incidentally, whether he sought to memorize verbatim things Peter said or was satisfied with his own elaboration of the gist of the apostle's speech.

There is also the matter of forgetting. What did Peter and Mark forget? Forgetting can be, just like remembering, goal-directed and strategic.[60] This holds

57. My son's memory belongs to a category: memories that people come to disbelieve; see Mazzoni and Scoboria, "Non-Believed Memories."

58. I was also much affected when I learned that one of my most vivid, seemingly "flashbulb" memories—of an emergency medical procedure performed on me while awake—turned out to be radically inaccurate because impossible.

59. The Greek is ὡς ἀπεμνημόνευσεν. It is possible, I recognize, that the subject of this is Peter: "As he [Peter] remembered." See L. Alexander, "Memory and Tradition," 118.

60. See Harris, Sutton, and Barnier, "Autobiographical Forgetting," and the lit. cited there.

for groups as well as individuals. As a rule, human beings "try to forget—with varying degrees of success—memories of experiences that undermine the current self, contradict . . . beliefs, plans, and goals, and increase anxiety or other negative emotions."[61] No one has good cause to imagine that early followers of Jesus were, in this particular, different from the rest of us.

Storytelling

If, despite my questions and caution, one yet holds that John Mark wrote Mark, that he was associated with Peter, that much or most of the gospel goes back to the apostle, and that both Peter and Mark had hale and hearty memories, is that enough to instill the firm and abiding conviction that the Second Gospel is, on the whole, and perhaps down to details, historically trustworthy?

To respond in the affirmative presupposes that, when Peter taught and when Mark wrote, they were doing little more than calling to mind the past. That would be naïve. They must have been employing the past in order to speak to their religious present. So the questions come quickly. Did they consistently refrain from exaggerating or embellishing for this or that constructive end? Was either a storyteller with "a reputation for adding wondrous elements to a tale, which increased its entertainment value?"[62] Did they mingle nothing of their own with the speech of their hero? Were both allergic to tales that were tall but edifying, or to haggadic narratives that were unhistorical yet self-serving? Did they understand "truth in a freer and richer way than the recounting of facts, events, and propositions"?[63] Were they wholly unlike all the later historians who have looked down the well of the past and seen their own reflected faces?

They certainly cannot have been free of observer bias or confirmation bias, because nobody has ever been such.[64] Nor could they have shared Herodotus's

61. Harris, Sutton, and Barnier, "Autobiographical Forgetting," 255–56.

62. Litwa, *How the Gospels Became History*, 14.

63. The words are from Nickelsburg, *Ancient Judaism*, 27. Cf. 26: "When it came to narrative, Jews were quite broad-minded in their understanding of what was true. Storytellers could elaborate a biblical episode or create a whole new episode on the basis of a nonnarrative element in the text or in another text, or because they thought that their situation called for such an embellishment."

64. Cf. McIver, *Memory*, 185: "The crucial and disturbing events of Easter" would have introduced "a strong element of hindsight bias." The classic study on observer bias is Hastorf and Cantril, "They Saw a Game." The paper documents very different responses of Dartmouth and Princeton students to a contentious football game. Hastorf and Cantril conclude: "The 'same' sensory impingements emanating from the football field, transmitted through the visual mechanism to the brain . . . gave rise to different experiences in different

professed detachment: "Though it be my business to set down that which is told me, to believe it is none at all of my business; let that saying hold good for the whole of my history" (7:152).[65] On the contrary, we can be sure that the development of Christology, soteriological reflections, and changing eschatological expectations updated how they called to mind, interpreted, and retold their memoires, as well as what memories they bothered to retrieve. John 14:26, in having Jesus prophesy that the Holy Spirit will teach his followers everything and remind them of all he has said, confirms that post-Easter perceptions and pre-Easter assessments were not identical.[66]

I for one would like to ask Peter and Mark about Matthew's Gospel, whose author, in Ulrich Luz's words, "created various kinds of historical fictions consciously and with a clear knowledge of what he did."[67] I would also like to ask them about John's Gospel, which engulfs the sayings of Jesus with the speech of the evangelist. Would Mark and Peter have been taken aback by a work that is free of exorcisms and says next to nothing about the kingdom of God, or would they have regarded John's work as trustworthy biography and congratulated the author on his poetic license and a job well done?

Similarly, how do we know that Peter was utterly unlike the author of the Temple Scroll, who could put words into God's mouth, or that Mark was utterly unlike the author of 2 Peter, who could put words into Peter's mouth, or that neither was like whoever inserted some of the foreign nation oracles into Jeremiah's prophecies? Was one or the other like the Pythagoreans, whose custom was to attribute words to Pythagoras, words that, while composed by others, were thought to accord with his teaching?[68]

---

people. The significances assumed by different happenings for different people depend in large part on the purposes people bring to the occasion and assumptions they have of the purposes and probable behavior of other people involved. . . . There is no such 'thing' as a 'game' existing 'out there' in its own right which people merely 'observe.' The 'game' 'exists' for a person and is experienced by him only in so far as certain happenings have significance in terms of his purpose" (132–33).

65. Cf. Josephus, *Ant.* 2.348: "On these matters everyone is welcome to his own opinion." For further examples of ancient biographers and historians exhibiting critical distance see Keener, *Christobiography*, 219–20.

66. Additional verses in John observe the distinction between pre- and post-Easter ideas: 2:22; 12:16; 20:9.

67. Luz, "Matthew's Interpretive 'Tendencies,'" 581. Cf. 583: Matthew saw "no contradiction between truth, in the sense of the reliability of his Jesus story, and innovations, rearrangements, and additions of fictive texts."

68. See Iamblichus, *Vit. Pyth.* 29.158; 31.198. For the same habit among Epicureans see Seneca, *Ep.* 33.4.

Again, did they have anything in common with Plato, who freely put his own ideas into the mouth of Socrates, his teacher?[69] Were they more or less conscientious than Josephus, who was, in Steve Mason's words, a "creative writer"?[70] Josephus's histories, which sometimes contradict each other, can be tendentious, despite the author's claim to tell the truth, and he was wont "not to tell the truth for the truth's sake but to make a point."[71] If Greco-Roman historians and biographers had various ideas about how accurate they needed to be—Xenophon was not Suetonius—and if Cicero could affirm that "the privilege is conceded to rhetoricians to distort history in order to give more point to their narrative,"[72] how do we know what Peter and Mark thought of the matter, or whether they gave it much or any thought at all?

We moreover do not know how judicious or credulous Peter and his purported interpreter were regarding the so-called supernatural. Both presumably deemed the Hebrew Bible, which is full of astounding miracles, to record the past. Were they eager to espy divine agency where others might not? Would Seneca the Younger have lumped them in with those historians he took to be "too credulous" (*Nat.* 7.16.1–2)? Mark, who nowhere says "possibly this will

69. One might object that Plato wrote dialogues, not a biography, so any comparison with Mark is misleading. But the objection does not work for Peter: he did not write a biography.

70. Mason, "Contradiction or Counterpoint," 148.

71. Mason, *Life of Josephus*, xxxvii–xxxviii. In *Ant.* 20.157, Josephus claims to "target the truth." Yet Thackeray, *Josephus*, 2:xxvi, could observe that there are "unaccountable discrepancies" between the *War* and the *Life*, "and the autobiographical notices of the historian must be pronounced the least trustworthy portion of his writings"; they imply "either gross carelessness or actual fraud." Cf. p. xxiv: "Josephus lacks the sober impartiality of Thucydides and, with all his boasted zeal for truth, shows on occasions, when his statements are subject to control, a lax sense of the meaning of that word." For a helpful overview of research on the problems see Henderson, "Comparison of Josephus' Life and Jewish War."

72. Cicero, *Brut.* 42. The continuation in 43 is worth quoting: "Like your [Cicero's] story of Coriolanus's death, Clitarchus and Stratocles both have invented an account of the death of Themistocles. But Thucydides, a native Athenian of high birth and distinction, and only a little later in time, merely says that he died a natural death and was buried secretly in Attic soil, adding that rumor said he had taken his own life by poison. The others say that on sacrificing a bullock, he drank a bowl of its blood and from that draught fell dead. That's a kind of death that gave them the chance for rhetorical and tragic treatment; the ordinary natural death gave them no such opportunity. So then, since it squares with your taste to make everything the same in the careers of Themistocles and Coriolanus, take the bowl too with my leave—I will even provide a sacrificial victim—in order to make of Coriolanus a second Themistocles." For helpful discussion of how much flexibility, imprecision, and creativity ancient historians and biographies typically allowed themselves see Keener, *Christobiography*, esp. 259–327.

seem like a fable" (Plutarch, *Cam.* 5.5), reports that a number of demons once jumped from a man into a herd of pigs, which straightway threw themselves into the sea. It is a memorable story. One need not, however, be an atheist to wonder what lies behind it. Marcus judges that "several features in the story . . . suggest that it is not an original unity but has grown by a process of accretion," and further that "it is even possible that the story, or parts of it, originally had nothing to do with Jesus."[73] Perhaps he is right. Perhaps this is a story that has lost itself through its own exaggeration. I know no way to find out.

My questions need to be asked even if we cannot summon answers, or at least robustly supported answers. Autobiography, or autobiography once removed, does not annul the need for interrogation.[74] We all know some so gifted at storytelling that we inevitably wonder how tightly they are tethered to the past.

Human beings enjoy attention and, to that end, can be moved to make a good story better.[75] They like to persuade and, in order to be more persuasive, can trim or bend or embellish the facts, consciously and unconsciously. They may even, if the cause is important enough, prevaricate and, for the greater good, opt for fiction over fact. As Hume observed: "A religionist may . . . know his narrative to be false, and yet persevere in it, with the best intention in the world, for the sake of promoting so holy a cause."[76] While I wish it were not so, it is.

I regard the content of the previous paragraph as self-evident to anyone who has not sleepwalked through life. When people narrate the past, they typically do more than narrate the past. This is why, although Socrates taught both Plato and Xenophon, his students' dialogues do far more than remember

73. Marcus, *Mark*, 1:347.

74. Relevant here is Lyons, *Pauline Autobiography*, 65. "Persuasion, not truth," he contends, was the "overriding concern" of autobiographical literature in antiquity: "The emphasis upon ethical characterization and idealization permitted exaggeration and/or suppression of certain aspects of the real life as legitimate autobiographical devices. Protests of truthfulness often were made precisely at the point where truth was most seriously compromised."

75. Deliberate distortion is, at least in our world, rampant; see Marsh and Tversky, "Spinning the Stories." Summarizing their study of college students, Marsh and Tversky write: "As for spin, by their own judgments, people's retellings of what happened differed from what they believed happened. When asked to directly evaluate accuracy, participants called a large proportion (42%) of their retellings inaccurate. However, even more provocative is the discrepancy between people's direct reports of inaccuracy and their reports of distortions. When asked if they exaggerated or minimized or added or omitted information, participants labeled 61% of their retellings as distorted in one or more ways. Thus, one third of the retellings self-reported as accurate in fact contained distortions as judged by the same participants" (500).

76. Hume, *Enquiries*, 117–18.

their beloved teacher and, further, contradict each other in important ways.[77] It is why the autobiographical statements of Houdini and his wife Bess often fail to harmonize with what we otherwise know.[78] And it is why all but the most credulous will, when reading Paramahansa Yogananda's *Autobiography of a Yogi*, inevitably ask, on multiple occasions, Did that really happen?

In the prologue to his *Life of Antony*, Athanasius—writing perhaps within a year of the monk's death—avowed: "I hasten to write . . . from what I myself know (for I often saw him), and from what I was able to learn from one who followed him for not a brief time. . . . Throughout I have been mindful about the truth."[79] Tomas Hägg nonetheless opines that "what the historical Athanasius was really like, we shall never know."[80] And Anthony Kaldellis says that "the concerns of the hagiographer . . . were more important in shaping the text than the saint's life."[81]

One understands their skepticism. In the *Vita*, Antony is a model of Athanasian orthodoxy: the monk's theological agenda lines up seamlessly with Athanasius's theological agenda. Their Christologies are the same, as are their ideas about deification and their objections to the Melitians.[82] How can this not raise an eyebrow? So too the characterization of the solitary as wanting "every cleric to be held in higher regard than himself" and being happy "to bow the head to the bishops and priests" (Athanasius, *Vit. Ant.* 67). This is remarkably convenient given that the author was a bishop. Again, what does one make of the following story?

> Someone stood at the door [of Antony] and pulled the plait on which he was working, for he used to weave baskets and gave them to those who came, in return for items they brought him. Standing up he saw a beast like a man to the thighs yet with legs and feet like those of an ass. And Antony only crossed himself and said: "I am Christ's servant. If you are sent against me, behold I am here." But the beast, together with demons, fled, so that, through his speed, he fell and died. The death of the beast was the downfall of the demons. (Athanasius, *Vit. Ant.* 53)

77. For a concise statement of the differences and contradictions that constitute "the Socratic problem," see Dorion, "Xenophon's Socrates." For the differing portraits of Socrates within Plato's own writings see Vlastos, *Socrates*.

78. See Posnanski, *Life and Afterlife of Harry Houdini*.

79. While Athanasius was probably the author of the *Vita*, much of it likely derives from a source or sources he employed; see Barnes, *Early Christian Hagiography*, 160–70.

80. Hägg, "Life of St Antony," 28.

81. Kaldellis, "Hagiography of Doubt and Scepticism," 456.

82. Harmless, *Desert Christians*, 85–104.

Although this was penned by someone who knew Antony face to face and professed to be "mindful about the truth," I confess to wondering about the literal sense of this account. Did a humanoid with donkeylike limbs really once interfere with Antony's basket weaving?[83]

How, to return to Peter and Mark, was it with them and their memories of Jesus? It would be a fallacy to argue: (a) memory is generally reliable; (b) Mark is eyewitness memory of Peter's eyewitness memory; thus (c) Mark is generally reliable.[84] The problem, despite my earlier caveats, is less (a)—memory is generally reliable—than (b)—Mark is eyewitness memory of Peter's eyewitness memory. The gospel is not merely someone's unelaborated recall of someone's unelaborated recall. As the critical literature since William Wrede and the form critics has rightly reiterated, the tradents of the Jesus tradition and the authors of the Gospels were, whatever else they may have been, not impartial chroniclers serenely striving, for good or ill, to reconstruct the past as it truly was. This is one reason the canonical and noncanonical Gospels display theological and other differences, many far from insubstantial.[85] According to Mark, Jesus declared all foods clean (7:19b). This can be understood as an "explicit revocation of the OT kosher laws."[86] According to Matthew—who omits Mark 7:19b—Jesus did not come to abolish the Torah, not an iota of it (5:17–20).[87]

Some modern historians may profess to aspire to be inexorably impartial, to give "an accurate account of the past, even if it means" abandoning "favored and often self-serving narratives"; but the authors of our Gospels and their sources were not so disposed.[88] They rather utilized their first- or second- or

83. Questions also follow from comparing the *Life of Antony* with letters the monk evidently wrote; see Rubenson, *Letters of St. Antony*. For an exposé of Athanasius's misrepresentations of his own career see Barnes, *Athanasius and Constantine*.

84. Cf. McIver, *Memory*, 186: "Eyewitness memory is generally reliable, and the eyewitness memories that lie behind the Gospel accounts should therefore be approached with an attitude that expects them to be a generally reliable record of Jesus' sayings and doings."

85. Instructive here is Kloppenborg, "Memory, Performance." He shows how the measure-for-measure aphorism is deployed differently in different sources, and how the meaning varies even as the wording stays mostly the same.

86. Marcus, *Mark*, 1:458.

87. If the First Evangelist believed that Peter was behind Mark, he was still able to edit the Second Gospel in multiple, significant ways; and if Matthew could do that, perhaps Mark could, too.

88. The quoted words are from Wertsch and Roediger, "Collective Memory," 320. Cf. Lucian, *Hist.* 47: the historian should "listen to those who tell the more impartial story, those whom one would suppose least likely to subtract from the facts or add to them out of favor or malice."

thirdhand memories for persuasion, edification, and exhortation, and all of that in religiously charged public gatherings.[89] They were not indifferent but committed, not vessels of multiple perspectives—how often do we read "some say this while others say that"?[90]—but devotees of one hallowed view. Within the larger social context, moreover, their religious convictions were controversial and sometimes even the object of attack (cf. Gal 1:13). Given this, it is no surprise that the Gospels are so ideologically loaded, so apologetically obliging, so intertextually fertile, so theologically resonant, so symbolically rich. The traditions about Jesus were formulated and reformulated to be rhetorical, apologetical, and theological resources; and the Gospels that take them up are a mix of life, art, and theology. This, among other reasons, is why they contain much more than eyewitness recall.[91]

To suppose otherwise is implicitly to contend that the quest for the historical Jesus has been needless, that the whole enterprise has been a grand error. But the ideologically charged nature of our partisan sources and their frequent differences from one another—differences so memorably displayed and dissected by David Friedrich Strauss[92]—demand, if our goal is history, the modern quest. That is, the sources themselves—which, as Origen candidly observed, "do not agree at many points" and contain "things that, from the eye of history, occurred otherwise"[93]—impel us to ask critical questions.

89. Cf. Bond, "Peter," 52: "Peter would have shared his memories with the gathered Christians, and this group context would have exerted a powerful pull on the way those memories were presented and heard." That the canonical Gospels reflect rhetorical strategies for persuasion is clear; see Byrskog, "Eyewitnesses as Interpreters," 161–66.

90. Contrast Plutarch, *Rom.* 27.4: "Some say that he [Scipio Africanus] passed away naturally . . . some that he died of poison administered by his own hand, and some that his enemies broke into his house at night and smothered him." What Dibelius, *Studies in the Acts of the Apostles*, 151, wrote of the speeches in Acts holds equally for the canonical evangelists and their predecessors: "It was obviously not Luke's intention to prepare the way for a final decision by first quoting the two sides of a controversy, or to encourage the reader himself to make an independent judgment of the case. . . . The author does not wish to be impartial, indeed he wants to plead his cause."

91. Relevant here are parts of Crook, "Collective Memory Distortion"; also Kloppenborg, "Memory, Performance."

92. Strauss, *Life of Jesus*.

93. Origen, *Comm. Jo.* 10.2, 4. He also wrote that the evangelists could "speak of something that happened in one place as if it had happened in another, or of what happened at a certain time as if it had happened at another time," and that they introduced "into what was spoken in a certain way some changes of their own," so that "the spiritual truth was often preserved, one might say, in the material falsehood" (10.4).

Social Context

One might reject the drift of the previous pages by asserting that those who recited sayings of Jesus and told stories about him were typically surrounded by others whose presence functioned to curb fictions: coreligionists would not have let anyone stray too far from what was already known and believed.[94] Invention, that is, would have been unpersuasive if it did not harmonize with already-established convictions. As Barry Schwartz has written: "The earliest construction of an historical object limits the range of things subsequent generations can say about it," so that there is a social constraint on memory.[95] Collective identity depends on collaborative recall, on people hearing and rehearsing the same stories.

I do not dispute this.[96] Augustine relates that, when a new translation for the "gourd" of Jonah 4:6 was read in church, a translation different from "that which had been of old familiar to the senses and memory of all the worshipers, and had been chanted for so many generations in the church," there arose a "tumult." People in the congregation—not the priests and teachers but the laity—corrected and denounced what had been read (*Ep.* 75.21–22; cf. 82.35).

It nonetheless remains true that groups in all times and places have believed misleading rumors, distorted anecdotes, and fictitious stories.[97] Communal memories, like individual memories, can be false as well as genuine. Legends about important individuals often arise within groups venerating them.

94. So, e.g., Bockmuehl, *Seeing the Word*, 174–76; Eddy and Boyd, *Jesus Legend*, 262–64; Keener, "Before Biographies," 347–48; and Blomberg, *Jesus the Purifier*, 170–71. Cf. Schwartz, "Where There's Smoke." Schwartz generalizes: "Reality counts more than bias in the remembering of most events most of the time" (21, italics deleted). Note Seneca the Elder, *Suas.* 6.15: "Eyewitnesses of his [Pollio's] speech for Lamia assert that he did not say these things, not being prepared to lie when the triumvirs could show him up, but composed them (only) later." For the other side see Ehrman, *Jesus before the Gospels*, 75–78. There is a large literature on the relationship between individual and collective or social memory. For helpful orientations see A. Kirk, *Memory and the Jesus Tradition*; the articles in *Memory* 16.3 (2008); and Dudai and Edelson, "Personal Memory." There is also now a significant literature on social memory theory and early Christianity. For an introduction to this subject with reference to the Jesus tradition see Keith, "Social Memory Theory"; Eve, *Writing the Gospels*, 103–24; and Huebenthal, *Reading Mark's Gospel*.

95. Schwartz, "Social Change," 232.

96. For my own thoughts along these lines see Allison, *Constructing Jesus*, 160–64.

97. See Hobsbawm and Ranger, *Invention of Tradition*. For illustrations see Kloppenborg, "Memory, Performance," and cf. Hengel, "Eye-witness Memory," 88–89: "The investigation of 'oral history' has shown that oral tradition based upon memory can often be flawed even for eye-witnesses."

Gershom Scholem observed regarding Sabbatai Ṣevi: "The transition from history to legend took place with extraordinary rapidity in what are practically eyewitness accounts."[98]

Nascent Christianity was not miraculously insulated from legends. Had it been, there would be no talking cross in the Gospel of Peter. Or the conflicting accounts of Judas's suicide.[99] Or a Jewish crowd calling out: "His blood be on us and on our children!" (Matt 27:25). Or the resurrection of many saints in Matt 27:51–53.[100] Or the fiction of the guard at Jesus's tomb in Matt 27.[101] Or Matthew's triumphant conclusion, wherein the just-risen Jesus inaugurates the Gentile mission and uses a Trinitarian formula (28:16–20). These episodes cast the shadow of legend over the canonical Gospels, over writings which must embody "a complex symbiosis" of "fiction and reality."[102]

The situation in the first century was unlike that in the churches Augustine wrote about, churches whose members protested the new translation of Jonah 4:6. If the earlier situation had been like the latter, the story of the risen Jesus meeting Peter in John 21 could not have mutated into the call story in Luke 5:1–11 or (the other possibility) vice versa.[103] Nor could John's

98. Scholem, *Sabbatai Ṣevi*, 215. Cf. 252 (Sabbatai soon became more of "a slogan or image rather than a living personality") and 265 (even before his death, "the realm of imaginative legend . . . dominated the mental climate" of Sabbatai's followers in Palestine). A tale about Sabbatai's empty tomb circulated within a few years of his death; see Halperin, *Sabbatai Zevi*, 88–89. Halperin's book bulldozes the idea that legends take time to develop. For conflicting traditions about the Baal Shem Tov, see Ehrman, *Jesus before the Gospels*, 95–100. For the legendary growth of stories surrounding missionary John Hogg—the center of Ken Bailey's case study on oral transmission (n. 105)—see Eve, *Behind the Gospels*, 66–85. The story that Luther was the product of sexual relations between his mother and the devil circulated within two decades of his death.

99. See Matt 27:3–10; Acts 1:16–20; and Papias frag. 18 (*Catenae graecorum partum in Novum Testamentum*, ed. J. A. Cramer, 3:12–13).

100. Nothing hints that Matthew took this to be purely symbolic or as any less historical than the traditions that surround it; see Allison, *Resurrection of Jesus*, 167–82.

101. Already Alford, *Greek Testament*, 1:300, observed that the "historical accuracy" of the story of the guard had been "very generally given up by even the best of the German Commentators (Olshausen, Meyer; also De Wette, Hase, and others)." Cf. Schmiedel, "Resurrection- and Ascension-Narratives," 4065: Matthew's story "is now very generally given up even by those scholars who still hold by the resurrection narratives as a whole." This remains a fair generalization, despite some apologetically motivated scholarship. See Paul, *"Untypische" Texte*, 103–17, 221–33, and Kankaanniemi, *Guards of the Tomb*.

102. The words are from Matthews, review of *Story as History*, 177.

103. On the relationship between these two stories, see Allison, *Resurrection of Jesus*, 68–72.

Gospel have gotten away with expressly denying, what the Synoptics affirm, that Jesus did not carry his own cross (Matt 27:32; Mark 15:21; Luke 23:26; John 19:17). Nor could John 12:27, in opposition to the story of Gethsemane, avow that Jesus did not pray to God: "Save me from this hour." Nor could the canonical accounts of Jesus's resurrection display what Markus Bockmuehl calls their "narrative mayhem."[104] The textual facts seemingly imply that the sort of oral transmission that Ken Bailey proposed as a parallel to early transmission of the Jesus tradition may be less helpful than sometimes supposed.[105] Indeed, the tradition was sufficiently malleable that it could attract fictional add-ons.[106]

Exactly how fictions entered the world of Christ groups we can only conjecture, just as we can only conjecture what those who first fashioned them thought they were doing.[107] Part of the answer, I believe, is that some—perhaps a bit like the author of 1–2 Chronicles—could opt for what we deem to be a fiction because they thought, on theological grounds, that something must have been so, even if they had no tradition or memory to that effect.[108] Whatever the truth about that, the tales are there. This means that we cannot make a convincing case for the overall trustworthiness of the Jesus tradition solely through appeal to the conservative nature of communal memory.

Imagine that a certain Nicanor and his Christian friends in Rome were familiar with the parable of the sower yet then heard a newly arrived Peter recite a markedly different version. How would they have reacted? Can we be confident that they would have interrupted in protest? Again, what would they have done if, after hearing Peter once recount the story of Jesus healing a blind man, they later heard the apostle again tell the same story, this time with noticeable embellishments? Although I do not know, I can imagine a context in which the social pressure was such that they would let it go. They might have been reluctant to query a famed apostle.

104. Bockmuehl, "Resurrection," 111.

105. Bailey, "Informal Controlled Oral Tradition"; Bailey, "Middle Eastern Oral Tradition." For a valuable survey of the debate surrounding Bailey's work see Derico, *Oral Tradition*, 63–116. Also helpful is Eve, *Behind the Gospels*, 66–85.

106. See further Catchpole, "On Proving Too Much." Heffernan, *Sacred Biography*, 32, asserts, with reference to both the canonical Gospels and later lives of the saints, that "the persistence of textual contradictions suggests the lack of a dominant consolidating tradition."

107. On the vexed problem of intentional fiction in the canonical Gospels see Allison, *Constructing Jesus*, 435–59.

108. See further Marcus, "Did Matthew Believe His Myths?," and Marcus, "History and Theology in Matthew." Perhaps there is an analogy with historians and biographers turning their inferences into narratives; on this see Keener, *Christobiography*, 320.

Again, how would John of Zebedee have reacted if, while standing beside Peter in public, he heard his friend recall an event quite differently than he recalled it, or one he did not recall at all? Would he, with confident, introspective discrimination, have challenged the speaker, or would he have held his peace? Or, given that accurate memories can mutate in response to the erroneous recall of others—cognitive scientists call this "memory conformity"[109]—might John have revised his own recollection?[110] Once more, I have no answer. Nor do I know how anyone else could have one. For what it is worth, I have heard others tell stories they first heard from me, stories that, when repeated in my presence, strayed surprisingly far from what I had recounted, and yet I have kept quiet, sometimes out of politeness, sometimes out of respect, sometimes out of anticipated awkwardness.

One may further wonder how any particular memory of an event first came to speech. Suppose that Jesus happened on a young woman who, according to mourners, had just expired. And suppose further that Jesus laid hands on her, after which, before he moved on—and whatever the explanation—the woman climbed back to the land of the living. Surely Jesus's disciples would have excitedly conversed with each other—and maybe with Jesus himself—over what had just happened.[111] One or more might have conjectured that the woman had not really died while others protested to the contrary. Someone might have called attention to a detail with its parallel in the tale of Elijah raising a widow's son (1 Kgs 17:17–24) whereas another might have suggested associating the event with Elisha bringing back the dead (2 Kgs 4:32–37). Yet another might have hazarded association with the prophecies of resurrection in Isaiah (26:19) or Daniel (12:1–3) and thought this evidence that the end was at hand.

My point is that, even before stories were told, even before events became narratives, they were likely the subject of communal conversation and deliberation. It is, moreover, precisely just such a circumstance that judicial authorities, in our time and place, seek to forestall when they ask for the segregation of witnesses and order them not to discuss a case until it is finished.[112] The

109. See, e.g., Meade and Roediger, "Explorations in the Social Contagion"; Horry et al., "Memory Conformity"; and Gabbert et al., "Memory Conformity." But for caution on the matter see Harris et al., "Collaborative Remembering."

110. False memories can be implanted surprisingly easily; cf. Scoboria et al., "Mega-Analysis of Memory."

111. Cf. Mark 9:10: "So they kept the matter to themselves, questioning what this rising from the dead could mean."

112. For the problem of memory contamination in modern legal contexts see Wixted et al., "Initial Eyewitness Confidence."

testimony of one, they fear, might affect the testimony of another. Hearing others can modify memories. Two or three witnesses reliably establish a charge only if they have not been speaking with each other. Yet from the beginning Jesus's followers must have been talking with one another continually as they formed, recalled, and verbalized their memories of his time among them.

Even if, then, the story of the woman's resurrection was, from 33 CE on, forever repeated word-for-word, without any change at all, we would have access, not to an unmediated event or "immaculate perception"[113] but rather to an *ex eventu* formulation produced by memories affected in nonincidental ways by social interaction, religious commitments, and cultural and biblical scripts.[114] A scribal opponent who had been on the scene would, we can be sure, have remembered and narrated the event very differently.[115] Memories—which always involve selection, abstraction, elucidation, and integration[116]—are inescapably formed, recalled, and narrated by interpreting minds.[117] Being an eyewitness does nothing to change that.[118]

113. The phrase is from Malina, "Social-Scientific Approaches," 759.

114. Note the criticism of Bauckham by Redman, "How Accurate Are Eyewitnesses?," 192–93: "Bauckham fails to take into consideration . . . that inaccuracies can, and almost inevitably will, arise in eyewitness testimony before it *becomes* valuable community tradition that is seen to be in need of preservation. . . . The changes described in psychological research occur within hours, days, or weeks of the event," and "the importance of most 'Jesus events' as community tradition" would have been established only later. Cf. Genova, *Remember*, 100: "Nascent memories are highly susceptible to influence and creative editing, especially during the period—hours, days, and longer—when these memories are being consolidated, before they're committed to long-term memory."

115. Note already Origen, *Fg. Luc.* 1.4: "For if seeing Jesus' body made one an eyewitness of God's word [cf. Luke 1:2], then Pilate, who condemned him, was an eyewitness of God's word, as was Judas the betrayer, and all those saying: 'Crucify him, crucify him.'" Cf. 3.3: "Not everyone who saw him was able to lay eyes on him."

116. For this analysis see Alba and Hasher, "Is Memory Schematic?"

117. This is why Luz, "Matthew's Interpretive 'Tendencies,'" 583, could write: "*Res factae* and *res fictae* cannot be separated in the Aristotelian way, because history is only living as narrated history. No narration is possible without fictions and without creative imagination." See further below, pp. 368–75.

118. Cf. Bauckham, "In Response to My Respondents," 229: "Reports were interpreted and 'rhetorised' from the beginning," and "fact and interpretation coinhere in all history." Useful here is Byrskog, *Story as History*, 145–98, 301–3 (although we differ on other matters), and esp. Le Donne, *Historical Jesus*, and R. Zimmermann, "Augenzeugenschaft." I should add that, even if all perception involves interpretation, and even if all remembrance involves interpretation, and even if all articulation of memories involves interpretation, not all interpretations are equal: some represent the past better than others.

Memories Ancient and Modern

The previous pages have, at times, moved from studies of the memories of our contemporaries to the early Christian world. Perhaps this is a blunder. Maybe Jesus's followers had better memories than most of us today.[119]

Culture and education can improve mnemonic talent, and culture and education can inhibit it. Memory is like a muscle. It increases with use and decreases with disuse. Having moved from a typewriter to a computer screen, I find it harder to recall many things. My built-in spell checker has made my spelling worse, and my electronic thesaurus has reduced my ability to conjure synonyms. By contrast, in the old Greek and Roman worlds, "exercise of mental gymnastics practiced at every level of education aimed at strengthening the student's natural capacity for retention to levels unheard of in the modern world . . . the ancients' experience of . . . memory-images [employed in education] was much more vivid and intense than our own."[120]

Jesus's followers lived in a predominantly oral culture, so perhaps their memories were, on the whole, better than ours—especially if any had some education; for Jewish education, like Greco-Roman education, revolved around memorization. Paul, trained as a Pharisee, seemingly carried much or most of Jewish Scripture in his memory.[121] If so, he was more capable mnemonically than most of us. The same may have been true for some of Jesus's Galilean followers. Perhaps they were less like us and more like the rabbis, who held so many texts and traditions in their heads.[122] Maybe we err when we project conclusions about memory derived from modern studies onto those who initially passed on the Jesus tradition.[123]

I do not disallow the possibility that the ability of Peter or Mark to recall the past was, compared with most of us, superior, or even vastly superior. The catch is that ability is not execution. The capability to do something does not dictate one does it. Having prodigious memories prevented rabbis neither from recounting fictions—such as the legends about Ḥoni the Circle Drawer and Ḥanina ben Dosa[124]—nor from attributing to one authority something

119. In addition to what follows see Allison, *Constructing Jesus*, 27–28.

120. Cribiore, *Gymnastics of the Mind*, 166.

121. Cf. Sanders, *Paul*, 71–75, 170–71.

122. See Elman, "Orality and the Redaction." Gerhardsson's *Memory and Manuscript* and *Tradition and Transmission* are the classic works urging that what we know about the transmission of rabbinic tradition sheds light on how early Christians handled their traditions.

123. Cf. Keener, *Christobiography*, 420–32, 469–73, and Blomberg, *Jesus the Purifier*, 167.

124. On these see Eve, *Jewish Context*, 273–95.

said by another authority.[125] Nor did it guarantee that rabbis present at the same event would agree on what happened. According to t. Mak. 1:3: "A writ dated on the Sabbath or on the tenth of Tishre [the Day of Atonement] is, according to R. Judah, valid, but R. Yose declares it invalid. R. Judah said to him: 'Such a case came before you in Sepphoris and you declared the deed valid.' R. Yose said to him: 'I never declared such a writ to be valid. But if I did declare it valid, I declared it valid.'"

My judgment is that the differences between the infancy stories and genealogies in Matthew and Luke;[126] between the parable of the marriage feast in Matt 22:1–14 and the parable of the great banquet in Luke 14:16–24;[127] between the parable of the talents in Matt 25:14–30 and the parable of the pounds in Luke 19:11–27;[128] between the story of the centurion in Matt 8:5–13 // Luke 7:1–10 and its variant in John 4:46–54;[129] between the differing accounts of the Lord's Supper in Matthew (26:26–29), Mark (14:22–25), Luke (22:15–20), and Paul (1 Cor 11:23–26); between the narrative of Jesus's disturbance in the temple in Mark 11 and its counterpart in John 2;[130] between the conflicting versions of what happened on the first Easter Sunday and immediately thereafter;[131] and

125. See Neusner, *Peripatetic Saying*; also the overview in Bregman, "Pseudepigraphy in Rabbinic Literature." Bregman writes: "A number of detailed studies have shown that particularly in the Babylonian Talmud there are statements which are incorrectly and probably even falsely attributed, fictitious baraitot (i.e. tannaitic statements not found in the Mishnah) and stories about sages that seem more legend than history"; "there has been a shift in the last generation or so of scholarship toward viewing rabbinic texts less as historical reportage and more as literature" (34–35, 37).

126. The differences proved to be problematic from the beginning; see Julius Africanus's attempt at harmonization in Eusebius, *Quaest. Steph.* 4 and 16.

127. The commentary tradition often thinks of two different parables; cf. Trench, *Parables*, 171, and Alford, *Greek Testament*, 1:218.

128. While the "substance [of the two parables] is the same"—so Poole, *Annotations*, 3:260—many nonetheless think them "altogether distinct, and uttered on a different occasion"; so Alford, *Greek Testament*, 1:251.

129. While one could, in theory, urge that the difference between Matt 22:1–14 and Luke 14:16–24 and between Matt 25:14–30 and Luke 19:11–27 derive from different versions of the parables that Jesus himself uttered, it is highly unlikely that the accounts in Matt 8:5–13 // Luke 7:1–10 and John 4:46–54 descend from more than one event; see Wegner, *Hauptmann von Kafarnaum*, 18–74.

130. Origen, *Comm. Jo.* 10.15, already recognized the truth: it is "impossible for those who admit nothing more than history in their interpretation to show that these discrepant statements are in harmony with each other."

131. The observations of Strauss, *Life of Jesus*, 709–28, are, despite their polemical character, still profitably consulted.

between the Synoptics and the Fourth Gospel as a whole—all these establish that Jesus's followers not only did not undertake word-for-word memorization but did not fret, at least consistently, about synchronizing differing memories or traditions.[132] In theory they could have done so. In fact they did not. Although there was a tradition,[133] it was not deliberately memorized word for word.[134] The Lord's Prayer and the accounts of the Last Supper settle the issue. The tradition was malleable, and further not immune to apocryphal extensions. Memories appear to have been acquired largely through passive means; that is, they were the upshot of hearing something enough to make the main elements familiar. The canonical Gospels do not, as Jens Schröter has written, "support the idea of a verbatim preservation of Jesus's teaching in its original contexts"; they instead support "the impression of new interpretation, adaptations to new situations, and free shaping of their verbal presentation."[135]

132. Here I may not be too far from Keener, *Christobiography*, given the allowance he makes for flexibility and adaptation within the Jesus tradition and his emphasis upon gist rather than details (e.g., 325, 385–88). He observes: "Hardly anyone, including the scholars most often accused of it, claims that the memories of Jesus's teachings in the Gospels are verbatim recollections" (385).

133. In this respect I agree with Gerhardsson, *Memory and Manuscript*: the Jesus tradition had an integrity or identity of its own. It was a collection of sayings and stories that was thought to be of and about Jesus. See Allison, "Pauline Epistles." This should not surprise. Jesus was, as the tradition everywhere attests, a teacher, and he had "disciples" (μαθηταί); and he was remembered as dispensing "wisdom" and being a "wise man" or σοφός (Mark 6:2; Luke 2:52; Gos. Thom. 13; Josephus, *Ant.* 18.63). These are not incidental facts; cf. Keener, *Christobiography*, 401–48. Still useful for thinking about this subject is Culpepper, *Johannine School*, 215–46, on "the school of Jesus." But for another view see Schröter, "Remarks." Schröter contends that the sayings of the Jesus, scriptural texts, and early Christian parenesis were often intermingled and then not distinguished.

134. Worth pondering here is Graieg, *Resurrection Remembered*. He develops the idea of a "formal" yet "uncontrolled" tradition.

135. Schröter, "Remembered Jesus," 113. Cf. Kelber, *Imprints*, 377 ("It is well understood that folkloric and anthropological studies have shown that rote memorization is a fact, and can be an important fact, in oral tradition. But the likelihood for the phenomenon to have existed in the early Jesus tradition seems to me to be a meager one"), and Keener, "Before Biographies," 333 ("repeatedly telling the stories about Jesus would likely produce patterns of recitation over time, but no one expected verbatim preservation of wording. . . . Even in elite rhetorical training, paraphrase was a standard practice"). See further Mournet, "Jesus Tradition"; Schröter, "Memory and Memories"; and Tripp, "Eyewitnesses." One should add, however, that while comments such as these are often directed at Gerhardsson, his view is more nuanced than sometimes implied; note, e.g., Gerhardsson, *Reliability*, 63: "The Jesus tradition lies before us in an edited form. Jesus' followers have influenced his words in various ways, by interpreting them, explicating them, or undertaking certain alterations of their

Some Closing Generalizations

(1) The issues I have broached about Peter and Mark can also be raised about the other canonical evangelists and whatever sources they might have drawn on. If one were to undertake the exercise, the results would be equally frustrating: we would recurrently find ourselves awash in ignorance. This is true whether or not we identify the First Evangelist with the apostle Matthew[136] or take the claim about eyewitnesses in Luke 1:1–4 at face value[137] or suppose that the Fourth Gospel was penned by someone who knew Jesus.[138]

(2) If one were to consider the other canonical Gospels and their possible sources, one could not take for granted but would rather have to argue at length that Luke 1:1–4 (which refers to "eyewitnesses") and the claims to firsthand testimony in John (1:14; 19:35; 21:24) merit assent.[139] The account of the transfiguration in 2 Pet 1:16–18 features the first person—"we had been eyewitnesses of his majesty," "we ourselves heard this voice," "we were with

---

wording—omissions, additions, and reformulations—and above all when they themselves shaped or reshaped certain narrative traditions. Certain parts—especially the prologues (prehistories, the stories of the baptism and temptation)—seem to be relatively free creations. There is probably also reason to ask whether certain 'disciple-works'—logia and parables formulated in the spirit and style of Jesus (cf. Matt 13:51–52)—did not in good faith become a part of the Jesus tradition."

136. I more than doubt that we should. I do, however, remain attracted to the possibility that the First Gospel incorporates a source that was attributed to Matthew, the disciple of Jesus; see Allison, *Jesus Tradition in Q*, 62–66; cf. T. W. Manson, *Studies in the Gospels*, 68–104; Koester, *Ancient Christian Gospels*, 166–67; and Casey, *Jesus*, 87–88. On this view, the First Gospel would be a bit like Isaiah. Although the original oracles of the prophet were intermingled with much else, so that in the end far more is from others than from Isaiah, his name nonetheless stands over the whole.

137. For the argument that we should do so see Bauckham, *Jesus and the Eyewitnesses*, 116–24; Hengel, "Lukan Prologue"; and Peter, "Luke's Source Claims."

138. We should, in my view, identify the Beloved Disciple with John of Zebedee and regard him as a major source behind, but not the author of, the Gospel. This, however, scarcely settles the question of John and history. Others identify the Beloved Disciple with someone else who knew Jesus; note, e.g., Charlesworth, *Beloved Disciple* (he was Thomas) and Bauckham, *Jesus and the Eyewitnesses*, 412–68 (he was John the Elder; cf. Papias *apud* Eusebius, *Hist. eccl.* 3.39.3–4). Still others regard the Beloved Disciple as an ideal, fictitious figure; so, e.g., Kügler, *Jünger*.

139. According to Patterson, "Can You Trust a Gospel?," 198, Luke 1:2 is "a mere literary contrivance." Bauckham, *Jesus and the Eyewitnesses*, urges that Mark, through an *inclusio* involving Peter, also signals dependence on an eyewitness. For criticism see Jerome Murphy-O'Connor, review of *Jesus and the Eyewitnesses*; Patterson, "Can You Trust a Gospel?"; and Eve, *Behind the Gospels*, 143–47.

him on the holy mountain"—and yet Peter was not the author.[140] The surviving portions of the Gospel of Peter (a second-century pseudepigraphon) likewise revert to the first person.[141] The first person also appears in the Protevangelium of James, the Apocalypse of Peter, the Epistle of the Apostles, the Infancy Gospel of Thomas, and many later Gospels (e.g., the Narrative of Joseph of Arimathea and the Revelation of the Magi).[142] Some tendentious Greek histories sought to validate themselves by affirming the author's status as an eyewitness (e.g., Dictys, *Diary of the Trojan War*) or by purporting to incorporate eyewitness sources (e.g., Antonius Digenes, *Wonders beyond Thule*; Philostratus, *Life of Apollonius*).[143] There were, in short, bogus claims to eyewitness testimony as well as true claims, so each needs to be evaluated in light of the larger work within which it occurs. Luke 1:1–4 is not, in and of itself, evidence for Luke's historical reliability. Rather, one's estimate of Luke 1:1–4 will depend on one's estimate of the rest of Luke-Acts.[144]

(3) Eyewitnesses were undoubtedly active at the beginning of the tradition and surely played a role in its promulgation. To hold that the Gospels tell us important things regarding Jesus requires that some who knew or met him talked about him, and that people listened to them.[145] Indeed, everything depends on this: any real memory in the Gospels necessarily derives ultimately from individuals who heard and saw Jesus. Furthermore, Papias's interest in eyewitnesses cannot have been idiosyncratic. From the beginning it would have been natural for people to want to learn about Jesus from those who had known him.

Nonetheless, the fictions in the tradition entail either that some eyewitnesses were, like so many later hagiographers, not averse to fashioning pious fictions, or that not everything derives with fidelity from eyewitnesses. We cannot, additionally, know how far any particular story, if it does stem from an eyewitness, is

140. Bauckham, *Jude, 2 Peter*, 158–62.

141. "I was grieving with my friends" (26); "we fasted because of all these things" (27); "we, the twelve disciples of the Lord, were weeping and grieving" (58); "my brother Andrew and I, Simon Peter, took our fishing nets and went out to the sea" (60).

142. See further Syreeni, "Eyewitness Testimony." For later Christian examples see Van Pelt, "Hagiographer as Holy Fool?"

143. See on all this Litwa, "Literary Eyewitnesses," and Litwa, *How the Gospels Became History*, 194–208. The phenomenon continues in later Christian hagiography; see Hinterberger, "Byzantine Hagiographer," 214.

144. Moreover, even if Luke 1:1–4 does not mislead, it fails to specify what exactly in Luke comes from eyewitnesses and what does not.

145. The references to eyewitness in Luke 1:1–4; John 21:24; Papias frags. 4, 15; and Irenaeus, *Epistle to Florinus*, *apud* Eusebius, *Hist. eccl.* 5.20.5–7, reflect an interest that cannot have been foreign to an earlier time.

removed from that eyewitness. Even if the pigs ran over the cliff, no one knows whether the author of Mark got the story from Peter directly rather than from D, who got it from C, who got it from B, who got it from A, who was there. Nor, if there was a chain of tradition, can we determine how or when the story first came to speech or detect how it later grew or morphed, if it did.

While scholars have reconstructed genealogies for all the stories in the Gospels, the result is disconcerting discord. While I sometimes find this or that tradition history persuasive, more than a frail *ex post facto ad hoc*, genuine knowledge is much more often than not impossible. Regarding any particular story in the Gospels, we do not know who first narrated it, nor do we know how informed, reliable, or credulous that narrator was. Nor do we know how close the written accounts we possess are to a firsthand version. Regrettably T. M. Derico is right regarding whatever oral traditions or written sources or aids to memory there may have been:[146] "We do not know how those traditions were composed, preserved, or transmitted."[147]

(4) My time in the literature on memory has left me, on the whole, not more confident but more cautious. Moreover, and as I have observed, parts of the tradition about Jesus are late and misleading, the recollection behind some of them close to homeopathic proportions. So the tradition contains more than faithful memory, whether individual or collective. It contains some large distortions—in the pejorative sense of the term[148]—and later inventions. If I may so put it, Christ followers came to remember some things that had never taken place. Their communal memory was not allergic to the unhistorical. Any reconstruction of the tradition that cannot account for this, for the distance between some of the stories and Jesus's history, is deficient.

(5) Even if one is more optimistic about autobiographical memory than am I, no one can claim that it is always accurate or deny that it is often imperfect, usually in small ways, sometimes in large ways. Beginning with the initial recall of an event, eyewitnesses are piloted by expectation and subject to suggestibility and social influence. They further project the present onto the past, elide the inconvenient, and downplay, alter, or add items to make

146. For the possibility of written aids for memory see B. J. Wright, *Communal Reading*.

147. Derico, *Oral Tradition*, 10. It may indeed be, in the words of Eve, *Behind the Gospel*, xiv, "a mistake to assume that the same model of oral tradition applies equally well to all phases of the transmission of the Jesus material" (cf. 45).

148. Within memory studies, "distortion" often refers to the necessary processes for encoding and remembrance that enable us to achieve decent approximations of the past. Given the usual pejorative connotations of the word, Le Donne, *Historiographical Jesus*, 50–52, prefers "refraction."

a better story.[149] Just realizing that multiple factors influence the accuracy of recall should be enough, it seems to me, to give one pause. Memories are neither camera nor video recorder.[150] Nor are they hermetically sealed. They are partly porous—things can exit and enter—and so they resemble the past more or less. Thucydides remarked on the obvious: "Different eyewitnesses give different accounts of the same events, speaking out of partiality for one side or the other or else from imperfect memories" (1.22).[151]

Discussion of the virtues or vices of individual memory, its accomplishments and sins, does not enable us to divine which sayings come close to sentences Jesus uttered, which passages are fair representations or decent approximations of events that happened, and which repeating themes and motifs faithfully reflect his activities. Human memory can, in the right circumstances, be highly accurate. Bauckham, McIver, and others are right about that.[152] It

149. This may be true even of so-called flashbulb memories; cf. Talarico and Rubin, "Flashbulb Memories." Evidence suggests that such memories form through "a consolidation-like process: Some details learned later are incorporated into the initial memory, and many others are discarded. After this process, memories stabilize. Therefore, the best predictor of flashbulb memories at long intervals is not the memory as initially reported but memories reported a week or more after the event." So Weaver and Krug, "Consolidation-like Effects," 517.

150. This fact is now admitted on all sides; cf. Bauckham, *Jesus and the Eyewitnesses*, 325–30, and Keener, *Christobiography*, 373–74.

151. Conflicting versions from eyewitnesses throughout history are innumerable. For two striking illustrations see Force, *American Archives*, 2:490–503 (divergent accounts of "the shot heard around the world"), and Fitchett, *Tale of the Great Mutiny*, 359–63 (different memories of a battle; Fitchett remarks at one point: "It illustrates the unreliability of human testimony to notice how . . . both actors in the tragedy flatly contradict each other"). There is also, of course, the well-known phenomenon of people contradicting themselves. For an arresting example involving the well-known Bible translator, J. B. Phillips, see "Apparition of C. S. Lewis" (https://europaranormal.com/life-after-death/the-apparition-of-c-s-lewis/).

152. See Wixted et al., "Initial Eyewitness Confidence"; Schmidt, *Extraordinary Memories*; and Baddeley, "Study of Memory." According to McIver, *Memory*, human memory "is generally trustworthy, but the level of accuracy varies from individual to individual" (20), and it "provides first-order faithfulness to the past" and is particularly good at retaining the "gist" of an event (15). Baum (*Mündliche Faktor* and "Zwischen Abschreibeverhältnis") contends that Synoptic verbal agreements are best explained by trained memories: the hypothesis of literary dependence is unnecessary. While I think otherwise—cf. Derico, *Oral Tradition*, 142–71—his larger point, that human memory can be capacious, even in details, is correct. Those of us who know by heart multiple long poems or the lyrics of hundreds if not thousands of popular songs know this aside from scientific and anthropological studies. But for confirmation from the latter see Lord, *Singer of Tales*, and Parry, *Making of Homeric Verse*; also the overview in Keener, *Christobiography*, 420–32.

also, however, can fail us in nontrivial ways and often does. Zeba Crook and others are right about that.[153] So if one peruses the literature on memory looking for reasons to believe that memory is inaccurate, one can find them. And if one reads that literature seeking reasons to believe that it is trustworthy, one can find them, too. General reflections on memory do not, then, enable us to solve or circumvent the historical questions we have always had.[154]

(6) According to McIver, "personal event memories" are "intense memories of a very short period, full of sensory information." They regularly include "irrelevant details," often have no "further narrative context," and are unanchored "to a specific point in time and space." McIver then suggests that a story in the Gospels may be "based on some form of eyewitness recollection" if it (a) consists of narratives of events, places, and people; (b) is imprecise concerning time and place; (c) lacks much narrative context; (d) covers a short period of time; and (e) is full of "sensory information" and "irrelevant details."[155] Although there is no value to (a)—the generalization is so vast that it encompasses all stories whose protagonists are not animals or aliens—there is a point to the rest of the list. One might expect stories deriving from eyewitnesses to enshrine such features, and many stories in the Gospels do. The stumbling block is that fiction imitates life. This is why so many unhistorical tales also exhibit (b), (c), and (d). This includes Talmudic anecdotes about rabbis and worldwide folktales. So McIver can urge no more than what we see in much of the Gospels is "consistent with what would be expected of material that derives from eyewitness accounts."[156]

Similarly restricted in force is Bauckham's proposal that certain events in the Synoptics are "highly distinctive" and, on that account, encourage supposing that they reflect "the sort of exceptional events that are exceptionally well remembered precisely because of their distinctiveness."[157] Yet fictional epi-

153. Crook, "Collective Memory Distortion." J. Shaw, *Memory Illusion*, begins her last chapter with this: "If I have done my job, your memory should now seem hopelessly fragile, impossibly inaccurate. To bring you to an acceptance that all of us have critically flawed memories is the reason I wrote this book" (242).

154. Cf. A. Kirk, *Memory and the Jesus Tradition*, 229: "The question of the historical referentiality of the tradition is not really a question of its relationship to individual eyewitness recollection." Note also Ehrman, *Jesus before the Gospels*, 100: memories "are not necessarily reliable. And, of course, they are not necessarily unreliable either! All of them have to be examined historically to see whether and how far they preserve accurate memories of Jesus and distorted memories."

155. McIver, *Memory*, 124.

156. McIver, *Memory*, 130.

157. Bauckham, "General and the Particular," 35. Cf. Bauckham, *Jesus and the Eye-*

sodes, including Peter walking on the water (Matt 14:28–31), Pilate washing his hands (27:24–25), and saints exiting tombs and visiting Jerusalem (27:51–53), can also be highly distinctive and so memorable.[158] Remember Lot's wife.[159]

Reflections on social-memory theory also do not help us here.[160] Oral traditions are, in general, indebted to the past and present, and they regularly display a mixture of stability and change. But the degree to which any particular tradition in the Gospels has been stable or subject to revision cannot be inferred from the study of oral transmission in general.

(7) My qualms about memory, my caveats about Peter and Mark, and my recognition of fictions in the canonical sources are not intended to promote cynicism about the quest for the historical Jesus. As my previous publications and other chapters in this book reveal, one can be critical without being skeptical, and I remain, vis-à-vis the German scholarship into which I was baptized in my academic youth, rather optimistic about the quest. I am not a minimalist. I do not share what T. W. Manson dubbed "the disseminated incredulity" of Bultmann's *History of the Synoptic Tradition*.[161] Nor, unlike Robyn Faith Walsh, do I think that Gospels "reveal little about the beginnings they profess to relate."[162] I rather believe that Jesus said and did memorable things and so

---

witnesses, 346: "The memories of eyewitnesses of the history of Jesus score highly by the criteria for likely reliability that have been established by the psychological study of recollective memory."

158. According to Keener, *Christobiography*, while the evangelists and their predecessors could treat the tradition with great flexibility, it is unlikely that stories were fabricated wholesale. I do not know whether he would defend the historicity of Matt 14:28–31; 27:24–25; and 27:51–53 or instead characterize these passages as Christian haggadah or deem them to be creative expansions of already existing stories that fall within the usual practice of Greco-Roman biography. In any case, I hesitate to let decisions about genre inform estimates of historicity. As L. Alexander, *Acts in Its Ancient Literary Context*, 156, observes: "'Fact' and 'fiction' are not generic categories at all, and in ancient literature it is clear that the conventional markers of factuality (in any genre) were easily—and regularly—subverted."

159. Luke 17:32. See further Harrison, "Synoptic Gospels."

160. Cf. Keith, "Social Memory Theory," 536–41.

161. T. W. Manson, "The Quest of the Historical Jesus—Continued," in *Studies in the Gospels*, 6. Cf. Bultmann, *Jesus and the Word*, 8: "I do indeed think that we can now know almost nothing concerning the life and personality of Jesus, since the early Christian sources show no interest in either, are moreover fragmentary and often legendary; and other sources about Jesus do not exist."

162. R. Walsh, *Early Christian Literature*, 5. She continues: "The gospels reveal more about the *writers* who created them." I prefer a different formulation: the Gospels tell us much about Jesus and much about their authors.

was, naturally enough, remembered.[163] My work, like that of so many others, occupies the space between skepticism and trust.[164]

This chapter has aimed only to be cautionary, to suggest that appealing to eyewitness testimony in order to undergird the reliability of the Jesus tradition has less utility than might at first appear. It requires a leap of faith, or rather several leaps of faith. There are other and, to my mind, better ways to conduct business. But that is the subject of the next chapter.

163. Words as well as deeds can be memorable; cf. Allison, *Constructing Jesus*, 24, and Keener, *Christobiography*, 389–90. Recall Josephus's ability to quote Jesus son of Ananias: "A voice from the east, a voice from the west, a voice from the four winds; a voice against Jerusalem and the sanctuary, a voice against the bridegroom and the bride, a voice against all the people" (*Bell.* 6.301). The parallelism, the structure—φωνὴ ἀπό ("a voice from") repeated three times, φωνὴ ἐπί ("a voice against") repeated three times—and the echo of Jeremiah (7:34; 16:9; 25:10) make the prophecy easy to remember.

164. For this formulation I am indebted to Theissen, "Zwischen Skepsis und Zuversicht." Cf. Becker, "Jesus' Specific Profile," 89: there is "a middle path between historical skepticism and an excessive confidence in the historical reliability of the gospels."

EXCURSUS

MIRACLES AND EYEWITNESS

In an earlier chapter I registered my agreement with Craig Keener that miracle stories are not always legendary, that they are not always friend-of-a-friend tales: eyewitnesses can relate them. I also disclosed my open-mindedness regarding many metanormal claims. I feel bound, however, to add here that the world's books are filled with firsthand testimonies that are very hard to credit, even for the open-minded. Those who seek to buttress the historicity of the Gospels via appeal to eyewitnesses should not neglect this fact, which has contributed greatly to skepticism about many biblical stories. If trusting eyewitness testimony is a sensible strategy when assessing the Synoptics and John, why does it not work elsewhere, beyond the biblical borders?

Maximus the Hutburner (thirteenth–fourteenth centuries) was an ascetic and anchorite of Mount Athos. He got his name because he liked to be by himself and would burn his hut and move on when too many people found where he was. We find the following in a biography written by a certain Theophanes, a metropolitan in western Thrace:

> As God is my witness, I will not conceal what I myself saw with regard to the holy one. I myself regularly used to spend time in conversation with him, and so one day, when I came from Vatopedi monastery with another monk, I did not find the holy one in his cell. After looking all around his cell I still did not find him. . . . I went up a short distance behind his cell in order to see in the direction of the path to Kyr Isaiah, and I looked very carefully to catch sight of the man I sought. And lo and behold, I saw him at the sheep trough that brings water down there, at a distance of about two thousand paces from where I was standing and looking; and the intervening space is rough and rocky, and the path is not straight but twisting and full of potholes. As God is my witness, I saw him raised up and flying like a winged eagle above the forest and the huge rocks and coming toward me. When I saw him like this, I trembled with fear and was astounded at the miracle and cried out: "You are great, O Lord." I recoiled a bit out of fear, and in a moment the holy one appeared at the spot where I was standing, chanting something that I did not understand in my wonder. As I fell

> at his feet, the holy one kept asking me: "How long have you been in this place?" Then he took me by the hand and led me to his cell; after much teaching and instruction, he said to me: "See that you do not tell anyone what you have seen as long as I'm alive."[1]

Later on in the same life of Maximus, Theophanes notes in passing: "I myself . . . saw the holy man flying above the earth."[2] This is, whatever one makes of it, a firsthand account from a pious man who swears he is telling the truth: "as God is my witness" (ἐπὶ θεῷ μάρτυρι). Moreover, and to recall McIver and Bauckham, it covers a short period of time, is full of "sensory information," features "irrelevant details," and is "highly distinctive"; and if it occurred it would likely be "well remembered."

Such astounding stories, told by eyewitnesses, fill Christian literature. In the early seventh century, John Moschos wrote *The Spiritual Meadow*, a work that collects stories he heard firsthand from monks in Egypt, Jerusalem, Cyprus, and elsewhere. Among the stories are these two:

> (1) There were three of us [the speaker is Abba Gerontios, the prior of a monastery] who were grazers living beyond the Red Sea, over towards Besimon. Once when we were walking around on the mountainside another grazer was walking along the shore of the sea, down below us. It happened that he met with some Saracens passing through the area. As they passed by him, one of the Saracens turned back and struck off the head of the anchorite. We saw all this from a distance as we were on the mountain. While we were grieving for the anchorite, suddenly a bird came over the Saracen, seized him and carried him up into the air. It then let him drop to the ground, where he was turned into carrion.[3]

> (2) A blind man recalled: "When I was young, I thoroughly detested work; so I became a prodigal. When it came to the point where I had nothing to eat, I resorted to theft. One day, after I had accomplished many deeds of wickedness, I was standing in the marketplace and I saw a richly decked-out corpse being taken for burial. I followed the cortège to see where they were going to bury the body. They went behind Saint John's Church and placed it in a sepulchre; then they

1. Greenfield and Talbot, *Holy Men of Mount Athos*, 539. Another account of this event, in essentials the same, appears in another biography of Maximus; see *Men of Mount Athos*, 429–31.

2. Greenfield and Talbot, *Men of Mount Athos*, 563.

3. Moschos, *Spiritual Meadow*, 15.

> went their way. When I saw that everyone had gone, I went into the sepulchre and stripped the corpse of all its clothes—except for a single shroud. As I was leaving the sepulchre (taking a considerable amount of booty with me) my evil habits said to me: 'Take the shroud too; it's worth the trouble.' So, wretch that I am, I turned back and removed the shroud from the corpse, leaving it naked. At which point the dead man sat up before me and stretched out his hands towards me. With his fingers he clawed my face and plucked out both my eyes. I cravenly left all behind and fled from the sepulchre, badly hurt and chilled with horror. Now I have told you how I came to be blind."[4]

I hazard no guess as to what lies behind these two tales. All that matters here is that they purport to be from participants in the events.

The ascetical nun Christina the Astonishing (of Brustem) died in 1224. Thomas of Cantimpré wrote her biography eight years later. It tells us that, in her early thirties, Christina grew sick and died. When, however, her lifeless body was laid out in church and the Requiem Mass was being said, she came to life and ascended like a bird to the ceiling, where she stayed for some time.[5] The biography goes on to relate that she walked on the water, lived for nine weeks on milk from her virginal breasts, and that scalding water left her unharmed.[6] Where did Thomas of Cantimpré get his stories? From, he avows, reliable, firsthand witnesses:

> I am quite certain of the account that has been reported to me. I do not say "certain" without cause, for I have as many witnesses to most of the events I have described as there were rational persons living at that time in the town of Sint-Truiden. These things were not done in narrow corners but openly among the people. Nor has so much time elapsed that oblivion has swallowed up and buried these occurrences, for I wrote this Life not more than eight years after her death. I personally heard other things that no one could have known except Christina herself from people who swore they learned them from her own mouth. Whoever reads these things should bear in mind that I have believed them on the testimony of witnesses who would by no means deviate from the truth even at the risk of losing their heads.[7]

4. Moschos, *Spiritual Meadow*, 60.
5. B. Newman, *Thomas of Cantimpré*, 130.
6. B. Newman, *Thomas of Cantimpré*, 132–34.
7. B. Newman, *Thomas of Cantimpré*, 128.

Although this seems to me to claim more than Luke 1:1–4, it does not quell my doubts.

Astounding eyewitness reports do not cluster exclusively around later Christian saints. On my library shelves is a book containing stories about Tibetan Buddhist adepts.[8] The author is Khenpo Karthar Rinpoche, a revered lama who died in 2019. In the foreword he declares: "Most of the events recounted here occurred during my lifetime, and were either witnessed by me or told to me at the time; these accounts are therefore trustworthy. My nephew, Lama Karma Drodhul, wrote these stories down with the best of intentions."[9] The volume is the product of an illustrious old timer recounting his memories while another wrote them down—a bit reminiscent of the conventional scenario regarding Peter and Mark. The volume is, in any case, overflowing with astounding stories: a monk whose body, upon death, shrinks to the length of a cubit; a renunciate whose corpse floats an inch above the mat on which it is laid out; a monk who expires and whose body dissipates, leaving behind only hair, nails, and clothing; a prodigious faster who lives for three years on a single sheep's liver; a monk who correctly answers all questions before they are asked; a yogini who cures blind humans and animals by her breath alone; a monk who remembers what he did the day after his birth; a retreat master who walks through walls; a boy who leaves footprints in hard rock; and a bag of vermilion supplying enough paint to cover a temple with eighty columns.[10] Again, all this is prefaced by this statement: "Most of the events recounted here occurred during my lifetime, and were either witnessed by me or told to me at the time; these accounts are therefore trustworthy."

Another example. I once chanced upon the following in an old work on the Cheyenne:

> Some Shoshones and Arapahos came over from Fort Washakie to visit the Cheyenne agency, and when they got to the Cheyenne camp they

8. Drodhul, *Siddhas of Ga*.

9. Drodhul, *Siddhas of Ga*, vii.

10. The parallel with Mark 6:30–44, the feeding of the five thousand, is noteworthy: the Siddah of Kojo promises to supply the pigment for painting a temple; he hands the monastery's custodian a kidskin bag of vermilion; the custodian responds: "If you had told us that this is all the pigment you have, we could have made arrangements to find more elsewhere. How will this be enough for such a large temple?" The Siddah says: "Not only will this suffice for the painting of the entire temple; you will have enough left over to fill cracks in the columns"; and so it comes to pass. See Drodhul, *Siddhas of Ga*, 70.

> reported that while travelling along on the prairie they had met with a party of Indians who had been dead thirty or forty years, and who had been resurrected by the Messiah. Since their resurrection, the formerly dead Indians, so the visitors said, had been going about just like the other Indians who had never died.[11]

I have no explanation for this story, which most would reject out of hand. It nonetheless comes from an eyewitness reporting what he learned from eyewitnesses—just like Mark's Gospel, if that is somebody's account of Peter's memories.

The situation is similar with the *Shri Sai Satcharita*, written by Govind Raghunath Dabholkar.[12] The subject of this is the Indian saint Sāī Bābā of Śirḍī, who died in 1918. Dabholkar knew Sāī Bābā, received his blessing to compose a biography, conversed with eyewitnesses, and started writing before the saint died. Chapters began to be serialized in 1923, and the whole work was published in 1929. It is teeming with miracles and extraordinary claims. Here are two that pass my boggle threshold:

> Without anybody's knowledge, he [Bābā] would go to some secluded spot, take a bath and then bring out his intestines (through the mouth), which he would then wash and hang up to dry. . . . On one occasion, when he was sitting down to his bath, he hurriedly brought out his intestines and began washing them at that place. . . . He then spread them out on the guava tree, to the consternation of the people around. Even now, there are people alive in Shirdi who have seen Bābā in this condition with their own eyes, who say that he was a unique saint.
>
> Sometimes he would practice Khanda-yoga, separating hands, legs, etc., from the trunk. And these parts of his body could be seen fallen off at different places in the mosque. And when the people, in large numbers, came running to see the shocking spectacle of his body thus severed into parts, what they always saw was Bābā, whole and in one piece. Once a spectator was terrified in seeing such a scene and thought that some wicked person must have killed Bābā and committed such an atrocity.[13]

I refrain from adding further illustrations, although not for lack of material: I could go on. The eyewitness reports of astonishing events are

11. Grinnell, "Account of the Northern Cheyennes," 61.
12. For what follows see Rigopoulos, "Sāī Bābā."
13. As quoted in Rigopoulos, "Sāī Bābā," 396.

countless. Now, as I confessed in an earlier chapter, I do not incant Hume's name every time I run across a miracle. So far from disbelieving in the metanormal in principle, the world is, to my mind, exceedingly peculiar, and I accept the testimony to some extraordinary claims, including claims outside my religious tradition. My sole point here, however, is this. If we contend that the canonical Gospels, miracles and all, merit our trust in large part because eyewitnesses inform them, then why not be even-handed and lend similar credence to eyewitness claims outside the Bible? It would be, from a historical point of view, parochial and inconsistent to deploy the argument from eyewitness testimony when defending the Gospels and their miracles but to refrain from doing so by adopting, in effect, a secular logic when contemplating other sources.

6

Cogitations on Method

Multiple versus Recurrent Attestation

> The grammarians have not handed down to us a criterion for true history, so that we might determine when it is true and when false.
>
> —Sextus Empiricus[1]

> I think differently of the whole type, taken collectively, from the way in which I may think of the single instance.
>
> —William James[2]

> Criteria are notoriously difficult to apply.
>
> —W. D. Davies[3]

Throughout this book I have sought to muster warrant for my assertions about the historical Jesus. Yet I have nowhere undertaken to demonstrate either that Jesus uttered any particular saying or that any particular event occurred as narrated. This may strike some as peculiar. Books and articles on Jesus commonly validate their conclusions by seeking to establish, via the so-called criteria of authenticity, which stories actually happened and which sayings Jesus really authored.[4] For some time, however, I have been disillu-

1. Sextus Empiricus, *Against the Mathematicians* 266.

2. James, "Final Impressions of a Psychical Researcher," 321.

3. Davies, "A Quest to Be Resumed in New Testament Studies," in *Christian Origins and Judaism*, 14.

4. For convenient presentations of the criteria see Meier, *Marginal Jew*, 1:166–95, and Holmén, "Authenticity Criteria." For the history of the criteria within critical scholarship see Theissen and Winter, *Quest for the Plausible Jesus*.

sioned with the usual criteria and their all-too-often facile deployment. In previous publications I have explained why. I have also pursued an alternative approach.[5] But the discussion moves on, and this volume allows me to revisit the subject, clarify some issues, respond to critics, and add a few more reflections.

Here at the outset of this chapter I wish to stress that little about the matter of method is easy or obvious, and I may, I freely admit, be wrong about any number of things. I do not dwell in the land of unwavering conviction. I regularly wonder what I have missed and whether better thoughts are to be had. This chapter, then, promulgates no dogmata. While I favor certain ideas, I am not welded to them, and I hope, even after all my years in the field, to learn more tomorrow.

The Problem of Independent Sources

The criterion of multiple attestation has been a staple of our discipline for decades. Its logic is this: a tradition attested in two or more independent sources has a better chance of being historical than a tradition attested but once.[6] Practitioners concede that the principle is limited. According to John Meier, it should not be "used mechanically and in isolation," and "the mere fact that a saying occurs only in one source is no proof that it was not spoken by Jesus." Furthermore, "it is not a priori impossible that a saying invented early on by a Christian community or prophet met the needs of the Church so perfectly that it rapidly entered into a number of different strands of tradition."[7] Despite such qualifications, Meier and others have built much on this criterion, as though it were a firm foundation.

5. Allison, *Jesus of Nazareth*, 1–77; *Constructing Jesus*, 1–30; "How to Marginalize the Criteria"; and "It Don't Come Easy." For rejoinders to two of my critics see "Response to Rafael Rodríguez" and "Memory, Methodology."

6. Cf. Meier, *Marginal Jew*, 1:174: multiple attestation "focuses on those sayings or deeds of Jesus that are attested in more than one independent literary source (e.g., Mark, Q, Paul, John)." He continues: "And/or in more than one literary form or genre (e.g. parable, dispute story, miracle story, prophecy, aphorism). The force of this criterion is increased if a given motif or theme is found in both different literary sources and different literary forms." Meier here conflates, as do many others, what are for my purposes two very different things: individual sayings or deeds on the one hand and broadly attested themes and motifs on the other. The distinction—which Holmén, "Authenticating Criteria," 47, and others recognize—is central to my argument throughout this chapter.

7. Meier, *Marginal Jew*, 1:175.

Their judgment, that truly independent sources are to hand, is far-flung. Nils Dahl wrote: "It is of great advantage that the most important groups of New Testament writings are independent of each other; Paul, the Synoptics, John, the Epistle to the Hebrews, et cetera, cannot be arranged into one straight line of development."[8] John Dominic Crossan has operated with the same presupposition: we have several independent sources, among them (in his view) the Gospel of Thomas.[9]

But is the premise true? That is, do we know, or have good reason to believe, that some of our primary sources are truly independent of one another?

A Thought Experiment

I invite readers to imagine, for the sake of discussion, that ecclesiastical tradition is correct about the authorship of both Mark and Luke-Acts. That is, the John Mark known from Acts (12:12, 25; 13:5, 13; 15:37–40), who is a coworker of Paul in Col 4:10; 2 Tim 4:11; and Phlm 24, wrote the Second Gospel; and the Luke mentioned in Col 4:14; 2 Tim 4:11; and Phlm 24 composed Luke and Acts, including the latter's "we sections." On this hypothetical scenario, three New Testament authors knew one another fairly well.

What would follow were this true, if the authors of Mark and Luke and the apostle Paul all knew one another face to face? The consequences for our work on the historical Jesus would, I submit, be substantial.

Consider the tradition of the Last Supper and the words of institution. Those words appear in Matt 26:26–29; Mark 14:22–25; Luke 22:17–20; and 1 Cor 11:24–25. Common wisdom has it that we have here two or three independent sources. Matthew's version is usually presumed to depend on Mark, from which it differs only slightly. Mark and Paul are regularly thought to represent two different streams of tradition. As for Luke 22:17–20, with its notorious text-critical puzzles, it is routinely reckoned to depend on Mark and a source closely allied to 1 Cor 11:24–25, or perhaps both. The task, then, is to figure out which of the three accounts, if any, better preserves what Jesus likely said. Many opt for Mark. Some favor Paul. A few pick Luke.[10] What-

8. Dahl, *Crucified Messiah*, 68.

9. Crossan, *Historical Jesus*. Cf. also Sanders and Davies, *Synoptic Gospels*, 323: "When Paul cites a saying by the Lord, he provides the greatest possible independent attestation of it."

10. For the issues see Pesch, *Abendmahl*; Marshall, "Last Supper"; and Winninge, "Lord's Supper."

ever one's answer, multiple attestation allegedly enables us to go behind the surviving sources.

Robert Webb exemplifies the usual procedure. For him, 1 Cor 11:24–25 was written two decades before Mark, and we have "no evidence that Mark is dependent on Paul's letter. Thus for at least a core of elements within this tradition there is multiple attestation." We may, accordingly, judge those elements "as having a greater probability of historicity."[11]

What if, however, the authors of Mark and Luke were onetime coworkers of Paul? They must, in that case, have jointly participated in cultic gatherings, so they would have been with the apostle when the words of institution were cited, for celebration of the Eucharist was a significant Pauline practice (cf. 1 Cor 11:17–34). In what sense, then, could Mark 14:22–25 and Luke 22:17–20 be independent of 1 Cor 11:24–25?[12] If Paul and the authors of Mark 14 and Luke 22 celebrated the Lord's Supper while together, how could one ever escape the suspicion that, with regard to the points of agreement, everything goes back to the single ritual conducted in the Pauline churches?[13]

Entering my thought experiment might indeed move one to entertain the hypothesis, upheld by Hyam Maccoby and Francis Watson, that Paul himself received the words of institution in a vision or revelation from the risen Lord;[14] for the standard counter to this—appeal to multiple independent attestation—would fall to the ground. Henry Alford, long before Maccoby and Watson, remarked: "The similarity between this account of the Institution [1 Cor 11:24–25] and that in Luke's Gospel, is only what might be expected on the supposition of a special revelation made to Paul, of which that Evangelist, being Paul's companion, availed himself."[15]

11. Webb, "Historical Enterprise," 62. (Webb holds that Luke 22:17–20 depends exclusively on Mark.) Cf. Sanders, *Historical Figure of Jesus*, 263: "The passage in general has the strongest possible support, putting it on a par with the saying on divorce in terms of certainty: there are two slightly different forms, which have reached us through two independent channels, the synoptic tradition and the letters of Paul."

12. Cf. Hengel, "Lukan Prologue," 556 n. 94: "Paul cannot be excluded as a mediator of several traditions [in Luke]. See the account of the Last Supper in Lk 22:19f., which combines Mark 14:22–24 and Paul's Last Supper tradition."

13. Cf. the judgment of some that the Pauline version has priority over the versions in both Mark and Luke; so, e.g., Schweizer, *Mark*, 300–302, and D. A. Smith, "More Original Form."

14. Cf. 1 Cor 11:23 ("for I received from the Lord") and see Maccoby, "Paul and the Eucharist," and Watson, "I Received from the Lord." Note also Eisenman, *James the Brother of Jesus*, 733.

15. Alford, *Greek Testament*, 2:572. Many older commentators understand 1 Cor 11:23 to

One might counter all this by urging that at least John 6:53 ("unless you eat the flesh of the Son of Man and drink his blood, you have no life in you") reflects independent knowledge of the words of institution. Yet, apart from the real possibility that John has been influenced, directly or indirectly, by one or more of the Synoptics—a view that I have slowly and reluctantly come to adopt[16]—the final edition of John is usually thought to have appeared at least two or three decades after Paul's death, so on chronological grounds alone one wonders whether John can be altogether unaffected by Paul.[17] This is all the more so if one credits the patristic tradition that John's Gospel first appeared in Ephesus.[18] Acts reports, and Paul's letters confirm, that the apostle spent much time there.[19] Why presume that celebration of the Lord's Supper in a city where Paul conducted a prolonged ministry was free of Pauline influence, especially as John 6:51–58 shows points of contact with the eucharistic traditions in Paul?[20]

Similar problems would, if Mark, Luke, and Paul were associates, beset widespread presumption regarding Jesus's prohibition of divorce. The usual line is that we have three independent witnesses to this: Mark 10:10–12; Luke 16:18 (Q) (cf. Matt 5:31–32); and 1 Cor 7:10–11. Yet again, what if the authors of Mark, Luke, and 1 Corinthians were on occasion in contact with one another? How could we simply posit, without further ado, that all three re-

mean that Paul received the words of institution in an immediate revelation; cf., e.g., Godet, *First Epistle to the Corinthians*, 2:147–49, and Wesley, *Explanatory Notes*, 620.

16. See my article "Reflections on Matthew." See further North, *What John Knew*, and Becker, Bond, and Williams, *John's Transformation of Mark*.

17. According to Bultmann, *Theology of the New Testament*, 2:9, "John is not of the Pauline school and is not influenced by Paul; he is, instead, a figure with his own originality and stands in an atmosphere of theological thinking different from that of Paul." Dodd, *Interpretation of the Fourth Gospel*, 5, was more measured: "That the evangelist has not escaped the powerful influence of the first great Christian theologian whose works are extant, is probable enough. But the actual range of Pauline influence upon Johannine thought has been exaggerated." Although work since Bultmann and Dodd has not much dissented from them on this issue, the subject is in my view ripe for reconsideration, and the sort of investigation undertaken in Barnett, *Paul Becomes a Literary Influence*, needs to be carried forward with updated tools and methods.

18. The most important passages are Irenaeus, *Haer.* 3.1.1, 4; Clement of Alexandria, *Quis. div.* 42; Polycrates *apud* Eusebius, *Hist. eccl.* 5.24.3–4; and Dionysius *apud* Eusebius, *Hist. eccl.* 7.25.16. Cf. the second-century Acts of John, which relates multiple tales about John of Zebedee in Ephesus.

19. Acts 18–20; 1 Cor 15:32; 16:8; also 1 Tim 1:3; 2 Tim 1:18; 4:12. Paul wrote 1 Corinthians and perhaps Philippians and Philemon while in Ephesus.

20. See Borgen, *Gospel of John*, 128–32.

ceived, remembered, and revised the same injunction without ever speaking about it with one another?

As a further illustration of what my thought experiment leads to, consider 1 Cor 10:27: "If one of the unbelievers invites you to dinner and you are disposed to go, eat whatever is set before you [πᾶν τὸ παρατιθέμενον ὑμῖν ἐσθίετε] without raising any question on the ground of conscience." Luke 10:8 has this: "Whenever you enter a town and they receive you, eat what is set before you [ἐσθίετε τὰ παρατιθέμενα ὑμῖν]." Luke's line has no parallel in Mark or Matthew. Scholars debate whether we should assign it to Q, Q^{lk}, L, or Lukan redaction. Whatever one's view on that, the nearness to 1 Cor 10:27 is remarkable. How should we explain it? One could contend that Paul's advice depends on a saying that Luke found independently in his tradition. If, however, the evangelist knew Paul, one could equally urge that the apostle inspired the evangelist, who turned a word of Paul into a word of Jesus.[21]

Mark and the Sayings Source (Q)

Because Paul's letters interact with the Jesus tradition so infrequently, the criterion of multiple attestation is appealed to more commonly with reference to the canonical Gospels and their sources. Perhaps most important are the overlaps between Mark and—for those who think its existence likely—Q.[22] To illustrate: on the assumption that these are two independent sources, Benedict Viviano has insisted that the traditions they share are the sure footing on which the quest for Jesus should erect its work:[23] "If Q and Mark are indeed *independent* of each other, the cases where they echo the same saying or phenomenon take on high significance as the most solidly grounded early sources available."[24]

21. For this possibility (without the hypothesis that the author of Luke-Acts knew Paul) see Tuckett, "Paul and the Synoptic Mission Discourse," 378.

22. Those who infer rather that Luke used Matthew or that Matthew used Luke can and usually do dispense with Q altogether. This also drastically shrinks the scope of multiple attestation. Cf. Porter, *Criteria for Authenticity*, 87–89, and Snodgrass, *Stories with Intent*, 576 ("if Matthew knew Mark and Luke knew both there is no multiple attestation of anything"). Note further Eve, "Meier, Miracle," 31: "It is always possible that what is seen as multiple attestation could simply be an accident of survival. . . . If an older, common source had survived, sources now taken to be independent might no longer appear so." See further Goodacre, "Criticizing the Criterion."

23. Viviano, "Historical Jesus" (reprinted in *Trinity—Kingdom—Church*, 21–63). For a similar approach from an earlier time see Burkitt, *Gospel History*, 147–68.

24. Viviano, "Historical Jesus," 367. On 408–9, Viviano speaks of "the increased historical

Yet, once more, what if the authors of Mark and Luke were the figures named together in Phlm 23–24, where we find this: "Epaphras . . . sends greetings to you, as do also Mark, Aristarchus, Demas, and Luke, my fellow workers" (cf. Col 4:10; 2 Tim 4:11)? What if the man behind Mark's Gospel was an occasional colleague of the author of Luke and so an associate of one who, on a common theory of Synoptic sources—Q, Mark, M, L—knew and made extensive use of the Sayings Source? If the two coworkers were so interested in the Jesus tradition that they wrote Gospels, it is hard to imagine they never spoke with one other about what ended up in their writings. It seems to follow that the strict independence of Mark over against Q would be imperiled. If Luke and Mark were together in the 60s, as would be the case if (as often argued) Paul penned Philemon from Rome, and if, beyond that, Luke already knew Q,[25] would it not be peculiar if Mark knew nothing of it?

In this connection, and aside from who wrote Mark or Luke, one should recall that a few have posited the Second Gospel's knowledge of the Sayings Source.[26] Their thesis has the advantage of explaining why Mark, at least by comparison with the other canonical Gospels and Thomas, preserves far fewer sayings of Jesus: the evangelist took his task to be something other than the duplication of Q. B. H. Streeter once wrote: "Mark wrote expressly not to supersede Q, but, since Q contained practically nothing but discourse, to supplement Q with the biographical narrative for which a demand had arisen. Accordingly Mark quotes Q as little as he conveniently can without omitting features which no biography of our Lord could well do without."[27]

---

certitude which accompanies the method of listening carefully to two independent and early witnesses."

25. According to Kloppenborg, *Excavating Q*, 80–87, "a date [for Q] in the late 50s or very early 60s is certainly possible," although he tentatively posits a later date for the final form. For an argument for a much earlier date—possibly in the 40s—see my *Jesus Tradition in Q*, 54–60.

26. See, e.g., Fleddermann, *Mark and Q*; Fleddermann, *Q*, 180–83; Becker, "Mark with and against Q"; Van Dore, "Evidence for a Relationship"; and the scholars listed in MacDonald and Van Dore, *From the Earliest Gospel*, 277–82.

27. Streeter, "St. Mark's Knowledge," 165. Streeter later changed his mind on the matter. Alternatively, if one believed in proto-Luke—a theory that, in my judgment, has undeservedly fallen on hard times—one could perhaps imagine that Mark knew proto-Luke and desired to highlight largely different materials. In any case, it is hard to disagree with Luz, "Looking at Q," 587: "We would certainly like to know why the Gospel of Mark did not convey more of Jesus' teaching. Given the value accorded it by Mark, it is probable that he knew more than he actually records." I think it is more than probable; cf. E. Meyer, *Ursprung und Anfänge*, 124: "Mark by no means recorded everything available to him; for many of the sayings and stories in Q and elsewhere that he lacks must by then and for a long time have been available and widespread. Rather, as the ever-bourgeoning remains of

The view that Mark knew some form of Q remains, to be sure, that of a minority.[28] Nonetheless, on a very common theory of Synoptic relationships, there are somewhere around thirty significant overlaps between Mark and Q,[29] and Mark's acquaintance with someone having a copy of Q would help explain this circumstance.[30]

From Thought Experiment to History

Of what value is my thought experiment? Despite the pose I have adopted until now, I here confess that, for me, it is not purely hypothetical. The ecclesiastical traditions about Mark and Luke still have learned defenders, and they could, in my judgment, be correct. I do not claim to know that they are correct, only that they are not obviously wrong. Joseph Fitzmyer made a reasonable case for the Lukan authorship of Luke-Acts, and Claus-Jürgen Thornton has forwarded his own arguments for coming to the same verdict.[31] As for Mark, Joel Marcus's verdict is that it "probably was written by someone named Mark," and we cannot exclude the possibility "that this Mark was the John Mark of Acts and the Pauline correspondence."[32] Since I agree, I cannot dismiss as indubitably false the premise of my imagined scenario, namely, that Paul, John Mark, and Luke all knew each other.

My thought experiment is also relevant because, at present, some who employ the criterion of multiple attestation hold that John Mark wrote the Second Gospel, and further that the Luke of Colossians and Philemon wrote the Third Gospel.[33] But how can the criterion work if Mark and Luke knew not only each other but also Paul? The criteria of authenticity were first deployed

other λόγια, ἄγραφα, and ἀντιλεγόμενα show, all the Gospels give only a selection out of the mass of circulating traditions."

28. For arguments for the literary independence of Mark and Q see Laufen, *Doppelüberlieferungen*, and Tuckett, "Mark and Q."

29. For an overview of the data see Viviano, "Historical Jesus."

30. If one objects that, where they overlap, Mark sometimes seems more primitive than a Lukan parallel from Q, one can retort that this is no different from what we find in Matthew and Luke: neither consistently preserves the earlier form of likely Q sayings; see Laufen, *Doppelüberlieferungen*.

31. Fitzmyer, *Luke*, 1:35–59; Fitzmyer, *Luke the Theologian*, 1–26; Thornton, *Zeuge des Zeugen*. Cf. Casey, *Jesus*, 96–104, and Keener, *Acts*, 1:402–22; 3:2350–74. For the standard arguments to the contrary see Radl, *Lukas*, 1:4–7.

32. Marcus, *Mark*, 1:24.

33. See, e.g., Licona, "Is the Sky Falling?," and Blomberg, *Jesus the Purifier*, 156–66.

and later refined by scholars who discarded the ecclesiastical traditions about the canonical Gospels. If one instead accepts those traditions, why does the criterion of multiple attestation not fade away?

For those who judge that Mark's Gospel is, as Papias thought, partly or largely indebted to Peter (*apud* Eusebius, *Hist. eccl.* 3.39.15–16; see above, p. 285), another concern obtrudes. Paul, we know from Galatians, spoke with Peter face to face (Gal 1:18; 2:6–14; cf. Acts 15:1–11). Should this not cast a shadow over the confident assumption that Paul and the evangelist Mark, if he really did channel Petrine material, are truly independent sources? Could not Mark and Paul, where they overlap, be indebted to the same witness?[34] This might qualify as multiple independent attestation for Peter, but in what way would it qualify as multiple independent attestation for Jesus?

There is, perhaps I should add, yet one more possible glitch. What if one holds, as some still do, that John the son of Zebedee wrote the Gospel of John or was a major source of its traditions?[35] Acts, over several chapters, has this man in constant contact with Peter. If one accepts this as the historical truth and further associates Peter with the Second Gospel, then major figures informing the two texts would be close post-Easter companions. The implications would be similar to holding that John, whoever wrote it, shows signs of knowing Mark, whoever wrote it. A modern court hopes, when looking for ideal testimony, to find two or more eyewitnesses who, after seeing the same thing, went their separate ways, never speaking to one another about it. John and Peter would flunk that requirement.

Signs of Pauline Contact

To make my main points, however, I need not insist that Mark wrote Mark and that Luke wrote Luke. Even when one sets aside old traditions about authorship, treating Paul and the Synoptics as independent witnesses is not free

34. According to Tomson, *Jew and Christians*, 409–10, Peter was Paul's chief source for the Jesus tradition. Others have thought this; cf. Dodd, *Apostolic Preaching*, 16–17.

35. The identity of the Beloved Disciple with John of Zebedee continues to have sponsors; note, e.g., Barrett, *John*, 100–134; J. A. T. Robinson, *Priority of John*, 93–122; Schmithals, *Johannesevangelium*, 242–49; L. T. Johnson, *Writings of the New Testament*, 525 ("it is not unreasonable to identify the beloved disciple with John the son of Zebedee"); Keener, *John*, 1:83–104; P. N. Anderson, *Christology of the Fourth Gospel*, 274–77; and Hagner, *New Testament*, 266–68.

of difficulty.[36] Luke the Evangelist was, to note the obvious, not outside the Pauline orbit.[37] Even if he was never Paul's coworker, and even if he did not know Paul's epistles, he was, beyond cavil, quite well acquainted with a very large number of "traditions and memories of Paul and his mission."[38]

The situation with Mark is more controversial. Nonetheless, a number of scholars have drawn our attention to strong parallels between Mark and Paul, arguing that the sole explanation is not likely to be general Christian tradition.[39] There are significant overlaps between Paul's letters and Mark's Gospel in both terminology and ideas, and it is (at least for me) hard to shake the sense of a direct connection between Rom 14:14 and Mark 7:14–23:[40]

ROM 14:14, 20	**MARK 7:14–23**
I know and am persuaded in the Lord Jesus that nothing is unclean [κοινόν] in itself; but it is unclean [κοινόν] for anyone who thinks it unclean [κοινόν]. . . . Do not, for the sake of food [βρώματος], destroy the work of God. All things are pure [πάντα μὲν καθαρά].	There is nothing outside a person that by going in can defile [κοινῶσαι] him. . . . Whatever goes into a person from outside cannot defile [κοινῶσαι]. . . . thereby purifying all foods [καθαρίζων πάντα τὰ βρώματα].

This is Marcus's general judgment on the relationship between Mark and Paul:

36. There is also, in theory, the possibility that the tradition about Luke is correct and that about Mark incorrect, or vice versa. It is likewise possible that both traditions are fiction and that Paul nonetheless knew the author of Mark or the author of Luke or both.

37. See Radl, *Paulus und Jesus*.

38. Barrett, *Acts*, 2:xxx. Those who date Acts to the second century—I remain unpersuaded—can infer that our author knew the Pauline letters; so, e.g., Pervo, *Acts*, 12–14.

39. E.g., Romaniuk, "Problème des Paulinismes"; Bird, "Mark"; Marcus, "Mark"; Theissen, "Evangelium"; Diaz, *Marc*; Mitchell, "Mark"; Mader, *Markus und Paulus*; Mader, "Narratives Gestalten"; and Ferguson, "Paul's Possible Influence." For dissent see Kok, "Does Mark Narrate?"; Kok, *Gospel on the Margins*, 89–104. Crossley, "Mark, Paul," is also critical, yet he ends his essay with this: "It seems reasonable enough to suggest that one [Paul or Mark] was at least aware of the other, perhaps one (or both) even taking a precise idea here and there from the other." For the novel hypothesis that Mark used 1 Corinthians see Nelligan, *Quest for Mark's Gospel*. For a helpful overview of the recent discussion see Telford, "Resurgence."

40. Cf. Thompson, *Clothed with Christ*, 185–99; Jewett, *Romans*, 859; and Bird, "Mark," 49–51. For me the decisive work on this is now Mader, *Markus und Paulus*, 141–52. Her case for the dependence of Mark 7:14–23 on Paul compels.

> Mark writes in the Pauline sphere of activity and shows some sort of Pauline influence on his thought, although he is not a member of a Pauline "school" in the same sense that the authors of Colossians-Ephesians and the Pastorals are; unlike them, he has not studied, internalized, and imitated Paul's letters. But neither is he hermetically sealed off from the influence of Paul.[41]

This is a sensible verdict.

Even aside, then, from the issue of who authored the Synoptics, my hypothetical state of affairs may still to some degree match the historical situation. This in turn would, as we have seen, unsettle confidence in the criterion of multiple attestation when Paul is one of the relevant sources.[42]

The Larger Context

The judgment that our sources may not be unrelated to each other fits with what we otherwise know of Christian origins. Acts paints a picture of itinerant leaders traveling around the Mediterranean world, leaders who know about and interact with one another. We should not, to be sure, equate Acts with history, but on this matter the book clearly enshrines the historical truth, because Paul offers confirmation. His letters verify that he was in direct touch with James ("the Lord's brother"), Peter (Cephas),[43] and John (presumably John son of Zebedee; cf. Gal 1:18–19; 2:9), and that he attended an important assembly in Jerusalem (Gal 2:1–10; cf. Acts 15). His writings also place him

41. Marcus, *Mark*, 1:75.

42. How many early sources are wholly independent of Paul is unclear. James, Jude, Revelation, and the Didache (or its basic building blocks) are candidates. Yet three of these—Matthew, James, and Revelation—arguably contain anti-Pauline elements, which entails acquaintance or familiarity with the apostle. For Matthew see Sim, *Matthew and Christian Judaism*, 188–211; Sim, "Matthew's Anti-Paulinism"; Sim, "Matthew 7.21–23"; Sim, "Jew against Jew"; and Theissen, "Kritik an Paulus." For James see my article "Jas 2:14–26." For Revelation see Frankfurter, "Jews or Not?"; Pagels, *Revelations*, 53–72; and Barr, "Jezebel and the Teachings of Balaam." For criticism of Sim see Willitts, "Paul and Matthew"; Foster, "Paul and Matthew"; and Strotmann and Tiwald, "Matthäusevangelium." Against seeing Revelation as anti-Pauline see Willitts, "John of Patmos." My inclination regarding Matthew (which marks a change of opinion) is to side with Sim, in part because I deem it unlikely that, if Matthew appeared in 80–95, its author and first audiences were unfamiliar with controversies surrounding Paul.

43. Despite occasional doubt, Cephas should be identified with Peter; see Allison, "Peter and Cephas."

in Syria, Asia Minor, and Greece and show his desire to go to Italy and even Spain. They further reveal that he had numerous friends and acquaintances in all parts of the Roman Empire, even in places he had not visited (cf. esp. Rom. 16:1–16), and also that some among his coworkers, such as Aquila and Prisca, worked as did he in multiple locations far and wide. Beyond all this, Paul's epistles show us that believers in one place knew much about what was going on with believers in other places.[44]

Paul was, in short, known "from Jerusalem to Rome and in all points in between."[45] To invoke the jargon of social network theory, he had "high degree centrality," that is, he was linked face-to-face and through his letters to many others. Paul also had "high betweenness centrality," that is, he was a bridge between otherwise unconnected network clusters, such as the communities he founded and those in Jerusalem, Antioch, and elsewhere. He had, moreover, "closeness centrality," that is, there were relatively few degrees of separation between him and most others in the early Christian network.[46]

As similar remarks could be made about others, such as Peter, Aquila, and Priscilla,[47] my view is that, during the first few decades after the crucifixion—when the total number of Christ adherents may have been no more than 1,500[48]—most or all the prominent leaders likely knew each other or, at the very least, knew about each other.[49]

When it first appeared, I read Richard Bauckham's well-known essay "For Whom Were the Gospels Written?" with its argument that "the early Christian movement" was "a network of communities with constant, close communication among themselves."[50] I also read, in the same volume that featured Bauckham's piece, Michael Thompson's "The Holy Internet: Communication between Churches in the First Christian Generation." I recall finding the latter

44. Note Rom 1:8; 15:26; 16:19; 1 Cor 16:1, 8–9, 19–20; 2 Cor 8:1–5; 9:2–4; Gal 2:11–14; Phil 1:12–14; 2:25–26; 4:15–16, 22; Col 4:7–9, 16; 1 Thess 1:6–10; 2:14–16.

45. Sim, "Jew against Jew," 114.

46. For an introduction to social network theory see Liu et al., "Social Network Theory." On Paul's social network see further Duling, "Paul's Aegean Network"; D. A. Smith, "Paul's 'Friends'"; and D. A. Smith, *Epistles for All Christians*, esp. 108–18.

47. See further Trebilco, "Early Jewish Communities," 217–19. Trebilco notes that John the Revelator had information regarding seven different churches and that 2–3 John refer to traveling teachers, and further that Polycrates, in the second century, claimed to have "conversed with the brothers and sisters from all parts of the world" (Eusebius, *Hist. eccl.* 5.24.7).

48. Ehrman, *Triumph of Christianity*, 170–73, 286–94.

49. On the opportunities for travel in the first century see Hezser, "Travel and Mobility."

50. Bauckham, "For Whom Were the Gospels Written?," esp. 30–44.

persuasive and important.[51] I failed, however, to consider the apparent implications for my work on the Gospels.

This was partly due no doubt to long-engrained habits of thought. The books and articles I read as a young scholar tended to put the accent on the independence and diversity of early Jesus loyalists. I entered the guild at a time when it was common to speak about the Markan community, the Lukan community, the Matthean community, and the Johannine community. Each was often envisaged as though it were a group in its own locale that had its own history, traditions, leaders, and distinctive or even sectarian version of the new faith.

This way of thinking was carried forward by work on Q in the 1970s, 1980s, and 1990s, in publications that sought to reconstruct the beliefs and history of what came to be called the "Q community."[52] Quite a few placed this community in Galilee and highlighted its theological distance from Mark, John, Acts, and Paul.[53]

All this was part of a larger movement in the study of early Christianity, one much indebted to Walter Bauer's influential study of orthodoxy and heresy in the early church.[54] In reaction to an ecclesiastical tradition that saw all "heresy" as secondary, that did its best to iron out differences between canonical books—to show, for instance, that Matthew and Paul do not contradict each other in the matter of Torah, or that James and Paul are truly at one when it comes to faith and works, or that Luke's Christology is really the same as John's—scholarship came to appreciate the various emphases and even contradictory ideas in early Christian texts, including canonical texts. Indeed, redaction criticism, scholarship on the Nag Hammadi library, literary readings of the New Testament, and renewed interest in so-called Jewish Christianity—admittedly a term with different meanings and functions for different

51. Thompson's "Holy Internet." Also helpful is Epp, "New Testament Papyrus Manuscripts." Epp documents the reach and speed of the transmission of "intellectual commerce" in early Christian times.

52. Influential, representative works include Tödt, *Son of Man*, and Kloppenborg, *Formation of Q*.

53. Note, e.g., Mack, *Lost Gospel*. According to Mack's reconstruction, the Q group "did not think of Jesus as a messiah or the Christ. They did not take his teachings as an indictment of Judaism. They did not regard his death as a divine, tragic, or saving event. And they did not imagine that he had been raised from the dead to rule over a transformed world" (4). For a more evenhanded evaluation of Q's witness to early Christian diversity see Kloppenborg, *Excavating Q*, 345–79.

54. W. Bauer, *Orthodoxy and Heresy*.

scholars[55]—seemed to annul altogether any notion of the theological unity of early Christianity.[56]

The developments just catalogued are, in general, an effective antidote to the unhistorical harmonization that ruled most of exegetical history. If we are playing the role of historian, we should interpret a text in the first place according to what it says, not according to what other early Christian sources and later theologians say. Yet ideological diversity should not be confused with the issue of historical connection. Diversity of thought can exist because two individuals or groups have developed their ideas without knowing one another. But, to state the obvious, individuals and groups who know each other or each other's writings can also hold dissimilar and conflicting opinions. Friends can disagree with each other, and enemies can meet face to face.[57]

Matthew's author belonged to a group that heard Mark's Gospel. Yet Matthew's understanding of the Torah is seemingly at odds with what we find in Mark.[58] Again, the Epistle of James does not speak about faith and works the way Paul does; yet this is not because James and Paul represent two different early Christian streams that never crossed. On the contrary, it is—at least in my judgment—due precisely to their crossing, and the result was antagonism.[59] All of which is to say: even though multiple groups held diverse theological views during the first decades of the Christian movement, this scarcely entails that those groups did not exist side by side or that their leaders conducted business without knowing what was going on elsewhere. Differences do not entail ignorance.[60]

55. While I recognize the problems with this term as well as (with reference to the first century) "Christianity," I am at a loss for replacements. For discussion, see Jackson-McCabe, *Jewish Christianity*; and Joseph, *Social History of Christian Origins*, 9–12. The logomachy over our traditional terms belongs, I note, to a moment of wider critique: the list of analytical concepts that some urge we abandon—these include history, culture, religion, art, science, politics, the law, gender, race, society, word, economy, anthropology—is long; see Josephson Storm, *Metamodernism*, 49–84, 303–6.

56. See Dunn, *Unity and Diversity*; Hultgren, *Rise of Normative Christianity*; and King, "Factions."

57. Cf. Trebilco, "Early Jewish Communities," 219: "The evidence for conflict and disagreement suggests, not enclaves of isolated churches, but teachers and leaders promoting different things in different places and an intense interest in conflicts happening elsewhere. This speaks of trans-local inter-connectedness."

58. Sim, *Matthew and Christian Judaism*, 123–39.

59. Allison, "Jas 2:14–26."

60. Helpful here are Hurtado, "Interactive Diversity," and Horrell, "Letters for All."

More Hypotheticals

In order to enlarge my argument, I now wish to turn it on its head. What would follow if I am wrong and we do, after all, have multiple independent sources? What if, contrary to what I have urged, Paul, Q, Mark, and John have no literary relationship and represent disparate bodies of tradition? The payoff, I contend, is far less than often imagined.

Consider several scenarios. In the first, four individuals—A, B, C, D—hear Jesus utter X. A later repeats X to E, who in turn reports it to Paul. Eyewitness B independently recalls the saying while in the presence of F, a friend of the author of Q, who later adds X to the Sayings Source. Then witness C quotes the logion to G, who relates it to the author of Mark, while the fourth witness, D, tells H, who in turn speaks with the author of John's Gospel. In such a case, and on the assumption that A, B, C, and D and E, F, G, and H never spoke with one another on the matter, we would have four truly independent witnesses. Pictorially:

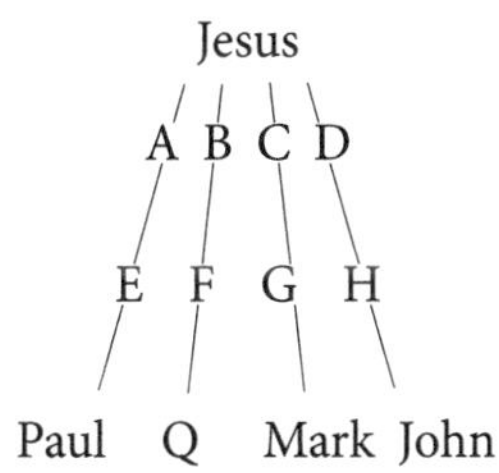

In the second scenario, A, B, C, and D again hear Jesus utter X. Thereafter, however, they discuss the matter with each other at length, debating what Jesus meant and even exactly what he said. When, down the road, they in turn relate X to the sources for Paul, Q, Mark, and John, their accounts are not unconnected. Independence in this case is qualified and far from ideal:

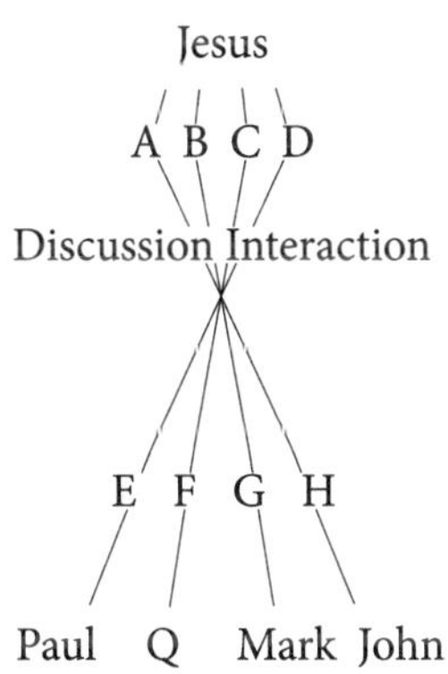

Imagine yet a third scenario. In this Jesus utters X and a single disciple, A, hears him. A then reports X to four others—R, S, T, and U—who subsequently relate the saying to Paul and the authors of Q, Mark, and John. In this hypothetical, our independent sources would derive from a single testimony, and the evidence of R, S, T, and U would, in the lingo of our legal system, be hearsay. Despite the literary independence of the extant sources, we would in truth have only a single witness—A—to what Jesus said:

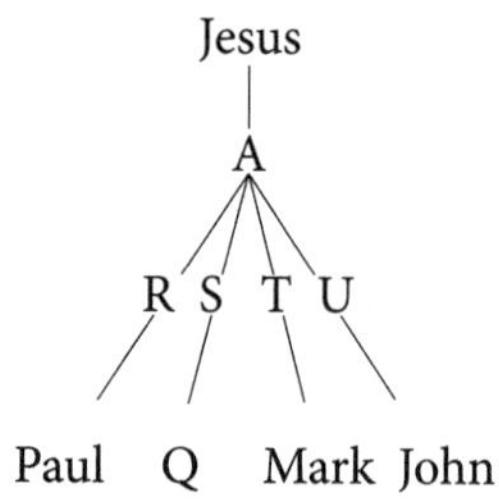

The fourth scenario has two witnesses. A and B hear Jesus utter X. They never speak to each other about it. Afterward, A quotes Jesus to E who informs both Paul and a contributor to Q. B then reports what he heard to F. The latter speaks with G, who informs the author of Mark, as well as with H, who informs the author of John. In this case, the literary independence of four sources would go back to two independent witnesses:

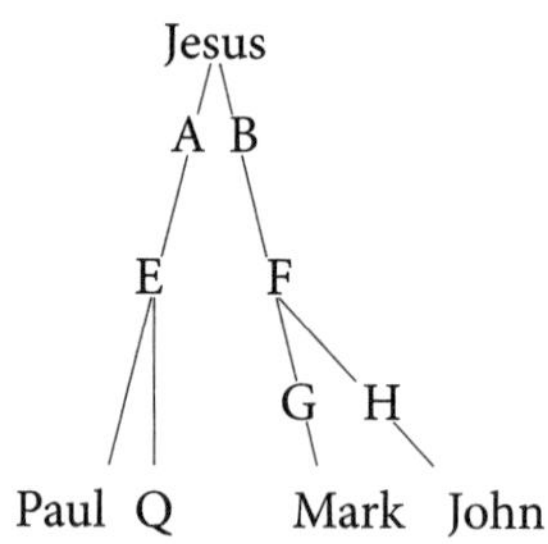

I refrain from excogitating further hypotheticals. They could fill a book, especially if, as must have been the case, Jesus said the same thing more than once. The point is this. Even when one grants the literary independence of Paul, Q, Mark, and John, this hardly guarantees the independence of those who originated a given tradition, if indeed more than one individual did so.[61]

61. Cf. Theissen and Winter, *Quest for the Plausible Jesus*, 14: "In the Gospels we can

Nor does it enlighten us as to how a tradition was passed on. While a saying or story could, if there is no literary relationship between Paul, Q, Mark, and John, go back to witnesses strictly independent, it could also stem from a single eyewitness just as it could derive from individuals who, being in constant dialogue, forged their memories together. We lack sufficient knowledge to reconstruct how any particular story was first formulated, subsequently altered (or not altered), and later conveyed to one of our authors. We cannot investigate a particular tradition and determine whether its history resembled one of my four scenarios or some other. Run-of-the-mill appeals to multiple attestation keep our vast ignorance out of sight.

This obdurate circumstance should perturb us all, no matter our preferred procedure. So also should the fact, too little appreciated, that our canonical sources, which are our chief sources, are not only ideologically close in important respects[62] but uniformly promote Jesus and his cause. We have nothing from eyewitnesses who disliked Jesus or opposed him or were indifferent. As Tom Holmén remarks: "The sources are not 'independent' in the sense that they might cherish different, maybe even conflicting interests, etc. All the sources we utilize have too much in common regarding their interests and views to be characterized as 'independent' in this sense."[63] This is one more reason for epistemic modesty.

John Meier, the Criteria, and Jesus's Parables

The preceding pages record some misgivings about one criterion, multiple attestation. It is, in my judgment, "compromised,"[64] maybe fatally compromised. I now wish to stand back and contemplate what we are doing when we apply the several criteria to individual sayings and events. For this I turn to the work of the late John Meier.

The first volume of Meier's *Marginal Jew* appeared in 1991. The most recent (and regrettably final) installment, volume five, appeared in 2016. So we have here a quarter century's worth of work. The project, which by my count runs to 3,481 pages, is unparalleled in scope. No critical scholar has written as much

never be certain whether the variant traditions originated through independent access to the same historical event or go back to a single tradition that has secondarily branched out into two different directions."

62. On this see Gathercole, *Gospel and the Gospels*.

63. Cf. Holmén, "Authenticating Criteria," 49.

64. So Levine, "Christian Faith," 98: "Multiple attestation is compromised."

about his subject as has Meier. Happily, the volumes are exceedingly useful. They constitute a treasure trove of information about modern scholarship and are magnificent repositories of arguments regarding all sorts of matters. There is nothing like them.

Despite my admiration of and indebtedness to Meier's work, I differ with him regarding basic method. His project is, from first to last, from volume one to volume five, married to the criteria of authenticity. In fact, in his final tome, Meier reiterates, without modification, the views articulated in his first tome.[65] Although he is aware of recent criticisms and proposed revisions of the standard criteria, he is unimpressed and so unmoved: he sees no need to reconsider their utility or amend them in any way.

The most remarked upon feature of volume five, which is dedicated to the narrative parables in Matthew, Mark, and Luke, is its major conclusion. According to Meier, of the more than thirty narrative parables in the Synoptics, a critical sifting establishes only four as likely coming from Jesus: the mustard seed (Mark and Q), the evil tenants in the vineyard (Mark), the great supper (M and L), the talents/minas (M and L). In his words:

> Stripped of their unearned presumption of historicity, most of the parables cannot mount convincing arguments in favor of their authenticity. Creation by the early church or by the evangelists seems a likely explanation not only for the Wheat and the Weeds and the Ten Virgins but also, in my view, for most if not all of the L parables. Less clear cases—in other words, most of the remaining parables—are rightly assigned to the limbo of *non liquet*: no strong arguments tip the scales in either direction.[66]

The criterion of multiple attestation plays a key role in this general verdict. Of the four parables Meier confidently attributes to Jesus, three of them enjoy, in his judgment, such attestation. Aside from those three, all the other parables derive solely from one primary source.[67] And only one of them—the evil tenants in the vineyard—belongs to "the happy few" that originated with Jesus.

Meier nowhere asserts that we should assign a parable to the church solely because it lacks multiple attestation, and I have already quoted him as avowing that "the mere fact that a saying occurs only in one source is no proof that it was not spoken by Jesus." So even though he affirms that "the criterion of mul-

65. See also Meier's article "Basic Methodology."

66. Meier, *Marginal Jew*, 5:210.

67. Meier does not regard the Gospel of Thomas as an independent witness.

tiple attestation of independent sources will prove to be the most important of the criteria when it comes to evaluating the historicity of any given parable,"[68] additional factors must be driving his skepticism.

As I read him, there are at least four. First, some parables not only lack multiple attestation but "other criteria like discontinuity or embarrassment do not apply."[69] Second, "the remarkable increase in the number of parables found only in Matthew or in Luke (as compared with Mark or Q)" makes him "leery":[70]

> In the first Christian generation, both Q and Mark are notable for the relatively small number of narrative parables they contain (by one count, as few as four each). In the second Christian generation, the number of parables proper to a given Gospel jumps to nine (or possibly eleven) in Matthew. The inflation of parables found only in a Gospel's special sources continues in Luke (composed possibly as late as the beginning of the third Christian generation), which contains at least thirteen and possibly sixteen L parables. . . . The increasing number of unique parables in chronologically later Gospels should at least give one pause before presuming that any and every Synoptic parable is to be attributed to the historical Jesus unless serious objections intervene.[71]

Third, "a good number of the M parables evince what one might call a strong Matthean redactional tone, coloration, or theology."[72] This prevents

68. Meier, *Marginal Jew*, 5:56. Cf. 6 ("the vast majority of Synoptic parables lack any positive argument for their authenticity because they cannot satisfy even one criterion of historicity, especially the criterion of multiple attestation of independent sources"), 192 ("do any of these narrative parables give a preliminary indication of satisfying one or more of the criteria of historicity—notably, the criterion of multiple attestation of independent sources—thus escaping the judgment of either 'inauthentic' or *non liquet*?"), 367 ("what all too often lacks the support of multiple attestation or any other criterion of historicity—is that Jesus taught this or that particular parable"), 369 ("given the small number of parables that our inventory listed in more than one source, we immediately got the sinking feeling that the number of parables that would prove viable candidates for the accolade of coming from the historical Jesus would be few and far between"). Such remarks have led some to complain that, in Meier's fifth volume, the criterion of multiple attestation has taken pride of place and become an instrument of exclusion; cf. Blomberg, review of *A Marginal Jew*, 861.

69. Meier, *Marginal Jew*, 5:195.

70. Meier, *Marginal Jew*, 5:210.

71. Meier, *Marginal Jew*, 5:197–98.

72. Meier, *Marginal Jew*, 5:196. Cf. 197: signs of "Matthew's redactional hand" in the parables from M make it "more arduous" to show that they derive from Jesus.

easy attribution to Jesus. Fourth, "the L parables, besides lacking multiple attestation, strongly reflect the redactional theology of the Gospel in which they are found"; "they are steeped in and give voice to" Luke's "redactional concerns."[73] As illustration of this last contention, Meier dedicates ten pages to arguing that the parable of the good Samaritan is "a pure product of Luke the evangelist."[74]

I raise no objections in principle to Meier's second, third, and fourth points. Although I suspect that most of the parables in L derive not from Lukan redaction but from a special source,[75] and while I am slower than is Meier to move from conspicuous redactional features to unalloyed redactional invention,[76]

73. Meier, *Marginal Jew*, 5:198.

74. Meier, *Marginal Jew*, 5:199–209 at 209. Contrast his earlier statement in *Marginal Jew*, 3:546: "I consider it more likely that, while the parable of the good Samaritan shows the redactional style and theology of Luke in its final form and placement, it is not simply a creation of Luke but goes back to his special L tradition. . . . The introductory dialogue between a lawyer and Jesus on the two commandments of love (Luke 10:25–29) seems to be Luke's recycling of a tradition also found in Mark 12:28–34 // Matt 22:34–40. . . . Luke's need to refashion an older tradition to make it a suitable introduction to the parable of the good Samaritan and the fact that nevertheless the introduction does not perfectly fit what it is supposed to introduce probably indicate that the parable itself is an earlier tradition taken over by Luke and reworked for his larger theological and literary plan. Whether the parable goes back to the historical Jesus is more difficult to say."

75. Here I can appeal to Strong, *Fables of Jesus*, 479–522.

76. I recall in this connection Matt 28:16–20. Although it is a compendium of Matthean themes and full of redactional traits, the passage nonetheless depends on a commissioning story that also lies behind Luke 24:36–49 and John 20:19–23; see Hubbard, *Matthean Redaction*, and Allison, *Resurrection of Jesus*, 60–64. I likewise think of Matt 26:36–46, Jesus in Gethsemane. Had we only Matthew's version of this story, many would surely consider it to be a redactional innovation. (1) Jesus's words mirror the Lord's Prayer in Matt 6 (πάτερ, εἰς πειρασμόν, γενηθήτω τὸ θέλημα σου). (Van Tilborg, "Form-Criticism," urges that the Our Father was spun out of Gethsemane. One could, without Mark to hand, just as readily urge that Gethsemane was spun out of the Our Father.) (2) If Jesus prays three times, triadic structures frequent Matthew. (3) Matt 26:42 repeats much of 26:39 while 26:44 repeats parts of 26:42, and parallelism is a prominent feature of the First Gospel. (4) Peter, to whom Jesus speaks directly, is conspicuous elsewhere in Matthew. (5) Whereas the content of the first and second prayers is given, the third is summarized ("saying the same words"). This abbreviating technique recurs in 20:1–16: the instructions to the laborers hired early and at the third hour are related, but of those hired at the sixth and ninth hours we read only that "he did the same." Similarly, 27:39–44 quotes the taunting words of one group, then the taunting words of a second group, but of a third relates only: they "taunted him the same way." (6) The possible allusion to Abraham and Isaac in 26:36 coheres with a Matthean interest; see Huizenga, *New Isaac*, 250–60. In sum, had Mark vanished, some doubtless would wrongly ascribe Matt 26:36–46 to Matthean invention.

and even though I believe that post-Easter frameworks and creations can incorporate and preserve memories of Jesus,[77] Meier offers defensible reasons for his skepticism. My problem lies elsewhere, with the limited outcomes his method begets.

After Meier decides which parables likely go back to Jesus and which do not, many remain unaccounted for. With them Meier does nothing. They fall into the unserviceable bin of "who knows?":

> What all too often lacks the support of multiple attestation—or any other criterion of historicity—is that Jesus taught this or that particular parable. Let me be clear on this point: I do not claim that I can prove in most cases that Jesus did *not* speak this or that parable. Proving a negative in ancient history is usually nigh impossible. Rather, my contention is that many of the parables necessarily lie in the literary limbo of *non liquet*. . . . When multiple attestation, embarrassment, or discontinuity work in only a small number of cases, and the other criteria are totally inapplicable in many other cases, *non liquet* is the only honest though frustrating conclusion that a serious researcher can reach.[78]

Many have been taken aback by this outcome, which they deem excessively skeptical. But I am not surprised. I have long shared Origen's conviction that "the endeavor to show, with regard to almost any history, however true, that it actually occurred . . . is one of the most difficult undertakings that can be attempted, and is in some instances an impossibility."[79] Meier has, to my mind, recognized the truth when he concedes that, when scrupulously applied, "multiple attestation, embarrassment, or discontinuity work in only a small number of cases."

The criteria do not leave a lot standing in their wake. Applied to small, isolated units, they become a trapdoor through which most of the tradition drops into desuetude. Indeed, their conscientious application leaves us, in my judgment, without a secure verdict not only for most of the parables but, more generally, a majority of the sayings and stories in the canonical Gospels.[80]

77. Helpful here is Le Donne, *Historiographical Jesus*, 52–59. He shows how "typological narrativization is often a means of remembering itself and not necessarily a literary device employed in a far removed context."

78. Meier, *Marginal Jew*, 5:367.

79. Origen, *Cels.* 1.42. I wish, however, that he had written "many" rather than "some" (ἐνίοις).

80. Cf. Casey, *Jesus of Nazareth*, 141 ("the criteria of multiple attestation and embar-

An Alternative

Meier authenticates four parables, decides that several others probably stem from the church, informs us that "Not Proven" stands over the rest, then walks away from the large pile of materials of indeterminate origin. The latter become the silent majority that tell us nothing about Jesus.

Fortunately there is another way to do business. Meier's method, with its diminishing returns, is not our only option.

In parts of this volume, as in previous publications, I have focused first of all—not exclusively but first of all—on patterns across the sources rather than isolated sayings and events. That is, I have urged that, rather than constructing the historical Jesus from the bottom up, with individual bricks authenticated one by one, it is more sensible and more profitable to commence with themes and motifs recurring throughout the early sources.[81] In one book, for example, I began to sketch a profile of Jesus by offering the following generalizations:

- He taught about "the kingdom of God."
- He promised future reward.
- He warned of future judgment.
- He foresaw suffering and persecution for the saints.
- He proclaimed God's victory over evil powers.
- He had a sense that something new was here or at hand.
- He thought highly of John the Baptist.
- He used the idiom "the Son of Man."
- He spoke of God as "Father."
- He emphasized loving, serving, and forgiving others.
- He showed and encouraged special regard for the unfortunate.
- He stressed the importance of intention.
- He displayed hostility to wealth.
- He made extraordinary requests and difficult demands.
- He came into conflict with religious authorities.
- He had disciples who were both students and helpers.
- He thought of himself as a miracle worker, as did others.

---

rassment are . . . of some value, though they are of limited application"); Snodgrass, "Are the Parables?," 136 ("I do not find them useless, even if the gains are relatively small"); and R. Zimmermann, "Memory and Jesus' Parables," 160 ("the criteria approach to the historical Jesus can only achieve minimalist results").

81. Cf. Horsley, "Study of the Historical Jesus." He too seeks a more holistic method, one that is oriented to the Gospels as wholes and to their discourses as wholes rather than isolated sayings.

My justification in each case was a long list of texts from Q, Mark, Matthew, Luke, John, and the Gospel of Thomas.

I inferred from my list, as a working hypothesis, that Jesus was an eschatological prophet who expected God's kingdom in short order, that he was a moral rigorist who was nonetheless perceived at times to be compassionate, and that he was a well-known teacher whose miracles prompted many to pay him heed. All this was, of course, nothing but a very preliminary sketch. The details remained to be filled out. This is why the volume continued after chapter 1. But my claim was that, without seeking to establish the origin of any particular saying or event, I had secured some sensible starting points. I also offered that, if my inferences were off the mark, then our sources are such poor guides to the past that we will never find our way.[82]

I further observed that certain formal features or rhetorical strategies recur often enough to suggest strongly that they characterized Jesus's speech:[83]

- parables
- antithetical parallelism
- rhetorical questions
- prefatory "amen"
- the divine passive
- exaggeration/hyperbole
- aphoristic formulation
- the unexpected or seemingly paradoxical

Most of the individual traditions I cited to support my large generalizations would flunk Meier's assiduous analysis. I am confident in my conclusions nonetheless.[84]

In a later volume, and more controversially, I listed the numerous Synoptic texts that look into the future and see Jesus front and center. I observed that Jesus's

> starring role in the eschatological drama appears in all the Synoptic strata, in logia attributed to him and in words assigned to others, and in stories as well as in sayings; and in this matter the Synoptics are at one with John,

82. Cf. Wedderburn, *Jesus and the Historians*, 171: "It would at any rate be hard to believe that so many different witnesses should be similarly mistaken. And, if we dispute these motifs or themes that are best attested, can we know anything at all about Jesus or say anything about him?"

83. Here my approach has forerunners in T. W. Manson, *Teaching of Jesus*, 50–81, and Jeremias, *New Testament Theology*, 8–37. Note also Pokorný, "Lexikalische."

84. Allison, *Jesus of Nazareth*, 46–50.

> Acts, Paul, and other early Christian sources. . . . The pattern, I submit, is sufficiently early and prevalent to intimate a pre-Easter genesis, and indeed to establish such a genesis if . . . additional facts fall in line.[85]

This proposal was then followed by a long argument that, apart from the title on the cross ("The King of the Jews"), nowhere labored to establish the authenticity of any particular detail. My case that Jesus thought of himself in messianic terms and had an exalted self-conception moved forward via arguments concerning a large pattern, not arguments about individual units of the tradition.

Meier's Objections

Meier has objected to all this. In order not to misrepresent him, I quote him at length:

> If we remain skeptical about every individual saying and deed of Jesus (allowing therefore that any and indeed all of them might be inventions of the early church and/or the evangelists), it is difficult to see how a number of these highly dubious sayings and deeds, when taken together, create a pattern, overarching theme, or persistent image that is not also highly dubious. In reconstructing a historical Jesus, the whole *is* the sum of its parts selected for analysis. If each item that makes up the whole is viewed with skepticism, the whole must be viewed in the same way. Put bluntly: seeking broad outlines, recurring patterns, or overall pictures without making any decisions about the probable historicity of the individual sayings or deeds that form these patterns strikes me as a kind of exegetical sleight of hand or artful dodging that in the end goes nowhere. In the last analysis, if one remains deeply skeptical about any and all criteria as well as about the authenticity of any given individual saying or deed of Jesus, then logic demands that one should be equally skeptical about constructing any probable portrait of the historical Jesus. The whole project should simply be abandoned.[86]

85. Allison, *Constructing Jesus*, 231.

86. Meier, *Marginal Jew*, 5:27 n. 28. The quoted words are in a footnote that follows these sentences: "Some critics find themselves increasingly skeptical about criteria in general. While some of these skeptics prefer to 'muddle through' as best they can with their scholarly instinct [Meier here names Geza Vermes], others appeal to modern studies of phenomena

These words perplex me. At points in his five volumes, Meier reaches conclusions solely on the basis of recurrent attestation. In his initial volume, for instance, he writes:

> One reason that critics so readily affirm that Jesus did speak in some sense of the kingdom of God (or kingdom of heaven) is that the phrase is found in Mark, Q, special Matthean tradition, special Lucan tradition, and John, with echoes in Paul, despite the fact that "kingdom of God" is not Paul's preferred way of speaking. At the same time, the phrase is found in various literary genres (e.g., parable, beatitude, prayer, aphorism, miracle story). Granted this wide sweep of witnesses in different sources and genres, coming largely from the first Christian generation, it becomes extremely difficult to claim that such material is simply the creation of the Church.[87]

The logic here is the same that I have employed: Meier makes his move without bothering to authenticate any particular unit of tradition. How does this comport with his claim that one cannot draw conclusions about the whole without judging any particulars?

One finds the same tactic in his second volume: "The abundance of parables in the Synoptic tradition, distributed among all the sources, plus the absence of equally deft, artistic parables elsewhere in the NT, argues well for the origin of many—though not all—of the Gospel parables in Jesus' teaching."[88] Meier says much the same about the miracle stories, too. Before he turns to evaluate the individual accounts, he raises "the global question of historicity" and asserts: "Even before we get to the application of the criteria of historicity, the sheer massiveness of the miracle traditions in the Four Gospels makes sweeping them under a respectable modern carpet unacceptable."[89] After a quick overview of the data, he goes on:

> The mere recitation of this catalogue is not meant to be a proof that all of the items listed here are historical. The summary accounts of Jesus' wonder-working activity and various references to his more-than-human knowledge no doubt come from the evangelists, and certain full-length stories

like communal memory, the oral transmission of traditions in particular ethnic groups, and the broad patterns preserved in such memories and oral traditions."

87. Meir, *Marginal Jew*, 1:174–75.

88. Meier, *Marginal Jew*, 2:145.

89. Meier, *Marginal Jew*, 2:617–18.

> may indeed be Christian creations. But the enormous amount of data does serve to give one an initial, healthy skepticism of any attempt to dismiss or play down such a large . . . corpus of material with an airy wave of the existentialist hand. At first glance, the material seems simply too mammoth and omnipresent in the various strata of the Gospel tradition to be purely the creation of the early church.[90]

To be sure, Meier adds that, by itself, this argument leads to "mere general impressions,"[91] and that to learn more we need to apply his criteria to isolated items. While I dissent on these points, here I note only that his main conclusion about Jesus's miracles derives solely from a large, repeating pattern and comes prior to running any of the relevant items through the gauntlet of his criteria. Meier may be unhappy with my preference for marginalizing the criteria, but his own work communicates that patterns across the sources point us in the right direction.[92]

It is the same in his most recent volume, where Meier states: "Even if we invoked no criterion beyond multiple attestation, that would be a sufficient argument for the basic thesis that the historical Jesus used parables in his teaching and was well known for doing so."[93]

Maybe the chief difference between us is this. Whereas Meier believes that, in order to gain more than "mere general impressions," we must move from repeated themes and motifs to appraisal of each individual piece, I believe we can, without deciding on the authenticity of the individual items, do much more than gain "mere general impressions."

90. Meier, *Marginal Jew*, 2:618–19.

91. Cf. Holmén, "Authenticity Criteria," 47 ("The recurrently attested motifs tend to be rather general ones. Consequently, the knowledge yielded by the criterion will usually remain on quite a general level. The composite picture of Jesus based solely on such knowledge, again, will turn out nonspecific and cursory"), and Fowl, "Gospels," 109 (Allison's approach "yields a very generalized picture that might fit numerous characters in the first century without giving much specific information about Jesus"). *Constructing Jesus* is my rejoinder to such objections, and I am gratified that Hägerland, "Future of Criteria," 53, deems it convincing: "What Allison attempts to demonstrate in his final [*sic*] book on Jesus—and I think he is successful here—is that by constantly attending to the recurrent patterns in the Gospels, all the while refraining from the endeavour to authenticate individual items in the tradition, a picture of Jesus can be painted which is not sketchy or blurred but remarkably colourful and rich in detail." I hope the present volume fortifies this appraisal.

92. See further Meier, *Marginal Jew*, 3:498–500: multiple traditions, taken together, show us that Jesus accepted the temple of his day.

93. Meier, *Marginal Jew*, 5:49. Note also 2:41–47, where Meier argues, without authenticating any single saying or episode, that Jesus had disciples.

It is unfortunate that Meier offers no example of a recurrent theme or motif he deems to be unhistorical because no one can authenticate any of the pieces. It is also unfortunate that he nowhere indicates which of my conclusions concerning Jesus are wrong precisely because I have adopted a faulty tactic. His objections remain, at least with reference to my work, theoretical and unillustrated.

There is another cause for confusion. Meier understands multiple attestation to cover two sorts of materials. The criterion is first of all applicable to individual sayings, such as that on divorce. It also, however, works for "a given motif or theme [that] is found in both different literary sources and different literary forms."[94] I, by contrast, draw a firm distinction between these two cases, between attempts to authenticate a particular saying or event that appears in two or more purportedly independent sources and to validate a theme or motif that recurs across multiple traditions. For me, multiple attestation of individual items is crucially different from recurrent attestation of a theme or motif. But the immediate point here is that multiple attestation according to Meier includes the strategy I adopt, so his staunch opposition leaves me nonplussed. He clearly thinks that what I call multiple recurrence can do far less than I do, but that is a difference in judgment about scope, not a disagreement over legitimacy.

Recurrent Attestation as an Academic Convention

I am far from being the only member of the guild to think that generalizations drawn from aggregates of material can, when supplemented by the right arguments, profit greatly. Indeed, many have drawn significant conclusions about Jesus by making inferences from patterns, or from what I call "recurrent attestation." In this connection I have done nothing exceptional. My approach is a variation on and extension of what others have done before me.[95]

Friedrich Loofs is an early example of someone insisting on the historicity of a pattern while being uncertain of its pieces. In *What Is the Truth about Jesus Christ?* (1913), he set himself against that species of "liberal German Jesus re-

94. Meier, *Marginal Jew*, 1:174.

95. According to Bauckham, "General and the Particular," 29, I offer "a new solution" as to how the quest should proceed. I have never claimed such. I have rather confessed my indebtedness to Dodd's *History and the Gospel*, 92–110, and observed that my line of reasoning appears in the work of numerous scholars (see *Constructing Jesus*, 15–20). According to Brown and Evans, *History of the Quest for Jesus*, 2:578, whereas "Allison used general summaries as the basis for his construct of Jesus," Dodd "used them as reservoirs of tradition." I fail to understand the distinction being drawn.

search" that denied that Jesus had an exalted self-conception.[96] In making his argument, Loofs conceded that "in no single case" can we "disprove the assertion that the belief of the later community altered" or created a saying of Jesus. That is, in no instance can we guarantee authenticity. So "it is impossible" to reach a conclusion by "any single saying." On the contrary, "only the general impression of the words of Jesus can be used." That is, "what the single words cannot achieve, that is achieved by their whole." Loofs, despite his self-proclaimed "skeptical attitude" about particulars, nonetheless believed that he could arrive at large and important conclusions. If a number of sayings have "essentially" the same import and occur "in all the sources," we may trust their combined testimony.[97]

Twenty-five years after Loofs, C. H. Dodd wrote *History and the Gospel* (1938). This was largely a response to the skepticism of early form criticism. Dodd thought that "the chief value of the method" is that "it enables us to study our material in fresh groupings, which point to distinct strains of tradition, preserved from various motives, and in some measure through different channels, and to compare these strains of tradition."[98] As illustration, he put these items together:[99]

1. the call of Levi (Mark 2:14)
2. the feast with publicans and sinners (Mark 2:15–17)
3. the story of Zacchaeus (Luke 19:2–10)
4. the story of the sinful woman in Simon's house (Luke 7:36–48)
5. the story of the woman taken in adultery (John 7:53–8:11)
6. the parable of the lost sheep (Luke 15:4–7; Matt 18:12–13)
7. the parable of the Pharisee and the publican (Luke 18:10–14)
8. the parable of the children in the marketplace (Matt 11:16–19; Luke 7:31–35)
9. the saying "the publicans and harlots enter the kingdom of God before you" (Matt 21:31)

These passages are from Mark (1, 2), Q (6, 8), M (9), L (3, 4, 7), and John (5). They also display "a great variety of traditional 'forms'—aphorisms, parables, poetical sayings, dialogues, stories of various kinds."[100] What holds them together? In each Jesus shows a "friendly attitude to the outcasts of society."[101]

96. Loofs nowhere appears in Theissen and Winter's *Quest for the Plausible Jesus*, which surveys the history of method in critical work on Jesus.

97. Loofs, *What Is the Truth?*, 129, 137–38, 144.

98. Dodd, *History and the Gospel*, 91.

99. Dodd, *History and the Gospel*, 92–94.

100. Dodd, *History and the Gospel*, 93. Dodd's criterion has been called the criterion of "multiple forms"; so, e.g., C. A. Evans, "Authenticity Criteria," 10.

101. Dodd, *History and the Gospel*, 94.

For Dodd, the shared motif or theme from multiple sources in a variety of forms tells us something noteworthy about Jesus: "On strictly critical grounds . . . we have here a well-attested fact." Furthermore, "this fact stands independently of the historical status of the several stories in detail."[102] Dodd went on to evaluate additional groupings, with these results:

- "Jesus was, with His followers, an exile from home and family."
- "The New Age had dawned, the age of miracle, the age in which the arm of the Lord is laid bare for the salvation of men and the discomfiture of the powers of evil."
- "The old order" is giving way to "the new."
- "The time is fulfilled."
- Rejection of Jesus is "a sign of divine judgment, the Last Judgment of which prophecy and apocalypse spoke."[103]

To my mind all this takes us beyond mere general impressions.

As Dodd was reacting to German form criticism, it is perhaps ironic that a semblance of his method appears in the works of the two most prominent form critics, Rudolf Bultmann and Martin Dibelius. Bultmann wrote: "Though one may admit the fact that for no single word of Jesus is it possible to produce positive evidence of its authenticity, still one may point to a whole series of words found in the oldest stratum of tradition which do give us a consistent representation of the historical message of Jesus."[104] Dibelius expressed himself similarly: "Discussion as to whether a particular saying is 'genuine' is often idle because on neither side are the arguments decisive. In general the historian will do well to look at the tradition as a whole, and not build too much upon an individual saying if it is at variance with the rest of the tradition."[105]

A quarter century after Dodd, Nils Dahl addressed "The Problem of the Historical Jesus" (1962).[106] He urged that, despite legitimate skepticism, it is yet possible to say much about Jesus. This is because

102. Dodd, *History and the Gospel*, 94.

103. Dodd, *History and the Gospel*, 96, 98, 99, 100, 101.

104. Bultmann in Bultmann and Kundsin, *Form Criticism*, 61. Cf. Bultmann, *History of the Synoptic Tradition*, 50: "In face of the entire content of the Tradition it can hardly be doubted that Jesus did teach as a Rabbi, gather disciples and engage in disputations. The individual controversy dialogues may not be historical reports of particular incidents in the life of Jesus, but the general character of his life is rightly portrayed in them."

105. Dibelius, *Jesus*, 28.

106. Dahl, "Problem of the Historical Jesus." The essay originally appeared in Braaten and Harrisville, *Kerygma and History* (1962).

> cross sections of the tradition bring to the fore what was characteristic, e.g., of his proclamation of the kingdom of God, of his position toward the law, or of his attitude toward various groups. . . . Words and reports of differing form and genre, transmitted within various layers of the tradition, mutually illumine each other and yield a total picture in which there appears something that is characteristic of Jesus. Whether the historicity of individual words or episodes remains uncertain is consequently of lesser importance.[107]

Although Dahl did not cite him, this sounds very much like Dodd.

Norman Perrin, in his influential *Rediscovering the Teaching of Jesus* (1967), urged that what he called "the criterion of multiple attestation" has "a usefulness in terms of establishing the authenticity of motifs from the ministry of Jesus . . . and particularly when we think in terms of strands and forms of tradition rather than in terms of synoptic gospel sources." In other words, "a motif which can be detected in a multiplicity of strands of tradition and in various forms (pronouncement stories, parables, sayings, etc.) will have a high claim to authenticity, always provided that it is not characteristic of an activity, interest or emphasis of the earliest Church."[108] Perrin took Jesus's "special concern for 'tax collectors and sinners'" to be sufficiently attested in multiple forms and traditions so as to establish its historicity. He also decided that the tradition remembered accurately when it used the phrase "your faith has made you well" or equivalents in the stories about the paralytic's friends (Mark 2:5), the woman with a flow of blood (5:34), blind Bartimaeus (10:52), the woman who was a sinner (Luke 7:50), and the Samaritan with a skin disease (17:19). For "although we are not prepared to argue for the authenticity of any of the narratives concerned, we are arguing for the authenticity of such an element in the historical ministry of Jesus: he did help those who confronted him in their need in a way his contemporaries regarded as remarkable, and he did link this with the 'faith' of the people concerned."[109]

Shortly after Perrin, Harvey McArthur, who was "dubious about the possibility of demonstrating the authenticity of single, isolated sayings,"[110] addressed "The Burden of Proof in Historical Jesus Research" (1971). His main point was that "when three or four of the synoptic sources"—for him Mark, Q, M, and L—"concur in providing evidence for a given motif in the ministry of

107. Dahl, *Crucified Messiah*, 67.
108. Perrin, *Rediscovering*, 46.
109. Perrin, *Rediscovering*, 137.
110. McArthur, "Burden of Proof," 117.

Jesus then the burden of proof should be regarded as having shifted to those who deny the historicity of that motif."[111] Again, "the convergence of evidence from three or four of these sources indicates a relatively early date for the motif in question and justifies the assumption of historicity unless contrary evidence is forthcoming." To illustrate his proposal, McArthur listed items that satisfy his criterion:

- proclamation of the kingdom of God
- the presence of disciples
- healing miracles
- a link with John the Baptist
- the use of parables
- concern for outcasts, especially "tax collectors and sinners"
- a radical ethic
- the love commandment
- the demand that the disciples practice forgiveness
- clashes with his contemporaries over Sabbath observance
- the Son of Man
- introductory "amen"

This resembles my own initial sketch of Jesus, introduced above.

Peter Carnley is not a New Testament scholar but rather an Australian Anglican bishop. Yet he is also a well-informed author who, in 1987, published a noteworthy volume on the resurrection of Jesus.[112] His project required that he make historical decisions about the Jesus tradition. In justifying his judgments, he wrote:

> Though we do not know with certainty that Jesus said or did any particular thing, we do know with a high degree of confidence that he said and did a certain kind of thing. In other words, Jesus is remembered to have been "the kind of person he was," and if we cannot be certain that he spoke particular words, we can be sure that he was the kind of person who could have spoken them. Or again, though we cannot feel absolute confidence in the original authenticity of specific separate words or acts of Jesus merely as such, he is remembered to have been a specific kind of person. . . . Though particular

111. McArthur, "Burden of Proof." This extends the argument of his earlier article: "Survey of Recent Gospel Research."

112. Carnley, *Resurrection Belief.*

> incidents and episodes in the Jesus story may be open to question on the grounds of dubious historicity, the story itself may be said to be true in so far as it has the ability to communicate with accuracy the kind of person Jesus was, the general disposition of his character.[113]

Returning to the guild, David Aune, in an article published in 1991, examined the aphorisms attributed to Jesus. He concluded that "the interplay between oral and written transmission of the Jesus tradition was an extraordinarily complex phenomenon which will probably never be satisfactory unraveled." Despite this (in his words) "pessimistic judgment," he went on to assert that this does not disallow us from making a large generalization: "While it may be difficult to argue that this or that particular saying is 'historical' or 'authentic' . . . the sheer number of such aphorisms together with their persistent attribution to Jesus makes it certain that Jesus regarded himself and was regarded by his followers and later Christian generations as a Jewish sage and teacher of wisdom."[114] Again, "the tenacity with which aphorisms cling" to Jesus tells us something about him.[115]

In their standard textbook *The Historical Jesus* (1998), Gerd Theissen and Annette Merz write: "There is no reason to deny that Jesus preached judgment. The tradition of this is too broad."[116] This is a straightforward appeal to recurrent attestation without any claim about the authenticity of specific sayings. In another jointly written volume, *The Quest for the Plausible Jesus* (2002), Theissen and Winter defend what they dub "the coherence of sources."[117] This lays "hold of the elements" in independent sources "that recur repeatedly and thus may represent the effect of the historical Jesus." Such "elements" include "formal motifs and structures in different streams of tradition." Invoking this criterion, they are "certain that Jesus really did speak in parables." They also (like Dodd) think in terms of themes and motifs that appear in different forms and genres:

113. Carnley, *Resurrection Belief*, 289–90.

114. Aune, "Oral Tradition," 240–41.

115. Aune, "Oral Tradition," 241. He adds: "Even in the case of sayings of the historical Jesus judged to be 'authentic' by critical scholarship, what is preserved accurately is the *ipsissima structura* of such aphorisms, not the *ipsissima verba*."

116. Theissen and Merz, *Historical Jesus*, 269. Cf. Merz, "How a Woman," 73: that Jesus promised persons of low social status a place in the kingdom "is supported by so many texts that it may count as certain, irrespective of the question of the authenticity of individual traditions."

117. Theissen and Winter, *Quest for the Plausible Jesus*, 177–78. See also Theissen and Merz, "Delay of the Parousia."

> The motif of "seeking the lost" is found not only in the famous parables of the lost (Luke 15:1–32), but also in apophthegms, when Jesus turns to publicans and sinners (Mark 2:15–17), or in sayings in which he speaks of the lost sheep of the house of Israel to whom he is sent (Matt 15:24). The motif is so well documented and present in such different genres that nothing speaks against its attribution to the historical Jesus.[118]

I call a halt there, although not for lack of material.[119] My point is made. My focus on repeated themes and motifs, and my conviction that they can take us beyond "mere general impressions," are not novelties. They do not mark a

118. Theissen and Winter, *Quest for the Plausible Jesus*, 178. See further Theissen, "Zwischen Skepsis und Zuversicht."

119. Note also Riches, *Jesus and the Transformation of Judaism*, 53 ("what one is looking for is a *group* of sayings sufficiently distinctive that, although one cannot be sure of the authenticity of any one of them, one can say with some confidence that, taken as a group they present characteristic features of Jesus' teaching"); Stein, "'Criteria' for Authenticity"; Vermes, *Jesus and the World of Judaism*, 22 ("the fact that Jesus' love and kindness towards the outcasts of Jewish society appears in stories, sayings, parables etc., is a safe indication of valid historical evidence"); N. T. Wright, *Victory of God*, 533 ("this argument advances across the swamp of historical scepticism not by means of the tightrope of isolated sayings, but on the broad and well-built causeway formed out of praxis, stories and sayings taken together as a whole"); Dunn, *Jesus Remembered*, 332–35; Dunn, *Oral Gospel Tradition*, 285–88; Forbes, "Historical Jesus," 240 ("the 'multiple attestation' criterion works far better when it is used for ideas, not just sayings or stories"); Meggitt, "Historical Jesus and Healing," 21 ("It is impossible to say anything for certain historically about any *specific* healing or exorcism. That is not the same as saying that they were not thought to have occurred in ways that resemble the accounts found in the gospels, but we really do not have sufficient grounds to say that any particular miracle tradition is based on a particular historical incident"); Eve, *Behind the Gospels*, 114–15, 181–83; Hooker, "Foreword," xv ("if we concentrate on the whole rather than the details . . . we shall find that we know quite a bit about Jesus, even though we may not be able to reconstruct with certainty any of his sayings or actions"); Crossley, *Jesus and the Chaos of History*, 35–48 (although Crossley often prefers to speak about "the earliest tradition" rather than Jesus); Frayer-Griggs, *Saved through Fire*, 24, 197–98; Keener, "Before Biographies," 333; Barber, "Did Jesus Anticipate Suffering?"; and Barber, *Historical Jesus*, 30–41. Also comparable is the approach of Horsley, *Prophet Jesus*: he focuses not on individual stories and sayings but on the portrays of Jesus in "whole texts." Cf. L. T. Johnson, *Acts of the Apostles*, 4, on the history in Acts: "Whatever historical basis there is to his [Luke's] account must be found at the level of substance and pattern rather than at the level of detail or specific incident." I recall what James, "Final Impressions," 320–21, had to say about investigating unusual claims: "I am . . . constantly baffled as to what to think of this or that particular story, for the sources of error in any one observation are seldom fully knowable. But weak sticks make strong bundles; and when the stories fall into consistent sorts that point each in a definite direction, one gets a sense of being in the presence

departure from convention. They rather belong to an academic tradition. And my contention is that so many have done the same thing because it makes good, indeed obvious sense, to do so.

Logic

Meier, as we have seen, avows that the whole is the sum of its parts, and that if one is undecided or skeptical about each individual sayings and deed, "it is difficult to see how a number of these highly dubious sayings and deeds, when taken together, create a pattern, overarching theme, or persistent image that is not also highly dubious." It follows, he contends, that "seeking broad outlines, recurring patterns, or overall pictures without making any decisions about the probable historicity of the individual sayings or deeds that form these patterns strikes me as a kind of exegetical sleight of hand or artful dodging that in the end goes nowhere."

It is true that adding zeroes amounts to nothing, no matter how many zeroes there are. The sum of 0 + 0 + 0 + 0 + 0 + 0 is the same as 0 + 0. In the abstract, then, it seems sensible for Meier to assert that we cannot rely on a pattern without further investigation. The irony is that I concur. To be sure, some things are so abundantly attested that we cannot doubt them without doubting everything. That Jesus was a teacher, that he spoke of the kingdom of God, that he was a healer, and that he was crucified all come to mind. But once we leave such uncontroversial items behind, argument becomes necessary. We cannot just parade a pattern and say, "Voilà! That must be Jesus." "Holism alone"[120] is not enough. It is rather incumbent on us to stack arguments for attributing something to the influence of Jesus himself. This is precisely what I have done in chapters 1, 2, and 3 of this book. In these I supply, beyond an observed pattern, reasons to infer that Jesus likely had a contingent eschatology, that he held a Mosaic self-conception, and that he exhibited some metanormal talents. In making my arguments, I do not screen individual traditions with the criteria of authenticity. All I need is the tried and true axiom that "the best hypothesis is that which accounts for the largest number of relevant known facts"[121]—in this case narrative facts. Put otherwise, I seek to envisage a past that the evidence, taken as a whole, implies.

---

of genuinely natural types of phenomena. . . . I think differently of the whole type, taken collectively, from the way in which I may think of the single instance."

120. The phrase is from Licona, "Is the Sky Falling?," 358.

121. So Dodd, "The Mind of Paul II," in *New Testament Studies*, 107. See further N. T.

As Loofs argued and as I have sought to show in this book and elsewhere, we can establish the likely genesis of a theme or motif without claiming to know precisely which of its individual pieces derive from Jesus. The proof is in the doing, and I think I have done the trick. If others agree, that is all there is to it.

Yet what about the objection that adding zeroes to zeroes amounts to nothing, that we might be working with materials produced exclusively by the church? The protest falls flat. Once we establish that a pattern preserves memories, it follows that we are not adding zeroes. We are rather assured that some of the items constituting the pattern go back to Jesus or are at least congruent with things he said and did, even when we cannot demonstrate which ones.

A Note on Skepticism

As already observed, Meier asserts that "if one remains deeply skeptical about any and all criteria as well as about the authenticity of any given individual saying or deed of Jesus, then logic demands that one should be equally skeptical about constructing any probable portrait of the historical Jesus."[122] This mingles two sorts of skepticism—that regarding "all the criteria" and that regarding the authenticity of items in the tradition. These, however, are scarcely the same. Skepticism about the utility of the criteria is not the same as skepticism about the historicity of the tradition. Some—Richard Bauckham comes to mind[123]—find much history in the Gospels yet have negligible faith in the usual criteria.

My own case is complicated. We have, in my judgment, several reasons for holding that the Synoptics tell us much about Jesus.[124] My goal, then, has never been to find the few kernels of dominical wheat scattered on the mountain of apocryphal chaff. My skepticism is of a different sort. It concerns our

---

Wright, *People of God*, 98–100, and Allison, *Constructing Jesus*, 20–22. That this always involves contextual plausibility within first-century Judaism should go without saying; cf. Theissen and Winter, *Quest for the Plausible Jesus*, 204–7, and Pitre, *Last Supper*, 34–36.

122. Meier, *Marginal Jew*, 5:27 n. 28.

123. Cf. Bauckham, "Eyewitnesses and Healing Miracles," 353: rejecting the usual criteria of authenticity, which he associates with form criticism, he urges that "the way to assess the historical reliability of the Gospels is to do what historians normally do with literary sources: they assess the general reliability of a source, a source being a literary work such as the Gospel of Mark. This may well involve assessing the reliability of some contents of the source where other sources allow it to be verified, but it is never possible to assess the reliability of this or that report contained within a literary source."

124. For some of these reasons see Allison, *Constructing Jesus*, 23–26, 159–64.

limitations as historians. Not always, but more often than not, the arguments a scholar has assembled to show that a particular event or single saying should be judged authentic or inauthentic leave me with doubts.

This has certainly been my experience with Meier. For him, the standard criteria—whose application, he tellingly acknowledges, is "more art than science"[125]—establish that Jesus composed the parable of the evil tenants in the vineyard in Mark 12:1–12 and forbade divorce, but they reveal that Jesus did not utter the golden rule or the prophecy of a near end in Mark 9:1. Some of his points regarding divorce are convincing and I share his conclusion. Yet I remain, despite his reasoning, uncertain about the origin of Mark 12:1–12, and I disagree about Mark 9:1 and the golden rule: he has not persuaded me that Jesus likely did not author them (which is not to say anyone has established the contrary). The reasons for my dissent do not matter here, only the discouraging, stubborn fact that, even after following Meier's meticulous enquiries, I can disagree with him or fail to lay hold of a firm conclusion.[126]

Because my experience with Meier is not atypical, because arguments utilizing the criteria with reference to particular traditions have often failed to win my assent, I have lost my affection for them. Even though those criteria, despite all their problems, occasionally assist us in evaluating some individual items—more on this below—the number of these last is constricted. Meier is the proof. In his work on the parables, *non liquet* is the prevailing verdict. Too often the criteria leave us where we were before we summoned their aid.

Skepticism of the criteria, however, is not skepticism of the tradition as a whole. Nor is doubt about our ability to establish the origin and history of a discrete tradition the same as holding that it does not go back to Jesus. One can remain, as so often happens with me, suspended in an open-minded indecision.[127] Nor is such hesitancy the same as general disbelief in the Syn-

125. Meier, *Marginal Jew*, 5:19.

126. Meier can also disagree with Meier; see n. 74.

127. Keener, "Before Biographies," opens his discussion by contrasting those who think that the canonical Gospels are "historically reliable" with "those who dismiss [the historicity of] the Jesus tradition." But of course (as Keener recognizes) there is a spectrum of opinion here. Trust and doubt do not exhaust the possibilities—see below, pp. 368–75—and I for one cannot answer the question, "Are the Gospels reliable?," with a simple yes or no. The question is too large. Each Gospel is, in crucial respects, its own world, so each should be evaluated by itself. Yet others disagree and argue, in part from their genre, that the four canonical Gospels or the Synoptics are likely to be, in general, historically reliable; so, e.g., Keener, *Christobiography*, and Zolondek, *Quest for a Historical Jesus Methodology*. "Reliable," however, is a slippery term, especially in connection with "gist memory," "general impressions," "substantial core," "essential content," "overall picture," "basic substance," and

optic record. I have more faith in the whole, in the impressions made by the Synoptic narratives, than in anyone's ability to authenticate most of the details with precision.[128]

Joel Marcus has written, concerning the Last Supper, that "categorical pronouncements about historicity are out of place, but so are categorical pronouncements about fictitiousness."[129] Similarly, Arland Hultgren has remarked, concerning the parable of the unjust judge (Luke 18:2–5), that while the emphasis on prayer and the "outlandish form of argument from the behavior of an unjust judge to an assertion about God" do not "prove its authenticity, there is nothing to preclude its authenticity either."[130] For me, cautious, even-handed generalizations such as these cover large swaths of the tradition.

Meier's Leftovers

Once Meier has determined that four parables are authentic, it remains for him to interpret them within the context of what he otherwise believes about Jesus and his context. But working with recurrent attestation of themes and motifs opens additional options, especially as some of the parables whose origin Meier cannot establish surely go back to Jesus. (It would be peculiar indeed to imagine—Meier does not commit this sin—a one-to-one correlation between what Jesus said and what we can, with our crude tools, confidently assign to him.)[131]

Meier himself urges that the large number of parables in Q, Mark, M, and L is of itself sufficient evidence Jesus taught in parables. But it is not just parables that recur: themes, motifs, and structures recur within the parables them-

so on. Was Josephus a reliable historian or not? In some ways yes, in other ways no. The answer depends on the qualifiers. Moreover, what is reliable to one is unreliable to another. Whereas Licona, *Why Are There Differences?*, thinks that his understanding of the canonical Gospels is consistent with their historical reliability, McGrew, *Mirror or the Mask*, believes that Licona's ideas render the evangelists unreliable.

128. Cf. A. E. Harvey, *Jesus and the Constraints of History*, 5: "What impresses you is the fact that there is so much information which all points in the same direction and allows you to infer a character of consistency and integrity. . . . Attention has moved away from establishing the truth or falsity of any particular report about Jesus, and is now directed more towards the impression made by the narrative as a whole."

129. Marcus, *Mark*, 2:963.

130. Hultgren, *Parables*, 258.

131. This is all the more likely as the narrative *meshalim* fail to thematize, in clear ways, Jesus's activity in Israel or his crucifixion or resurrection; cf. Gerhardsson, "Earthly Jesus."

selves; and if we can infer one thing from the parables as a collective without deciding which precisely Jesus authored, perhaps there are other conclusions to draw or entertain from them.

A large percentage of parables depict loss or warn of judgment:

- Mark 12:1–12 (cf. Gos. Thom. 65–66): the owner of a vineyard will destroy the wicked tenants.
- Mark 13:33–37: one should watch lest the master of the house comes and finds one sleeping.
- Luke 6:47–49 // Matt 7:24–27 (Q): those not heeding Jesus's words will be like a destroyed house.
- Luke 12:42–46 // Matt 24:45–51 (Q): the master will punish the unfaithful steward.
- Luke 14:16–24 // Matt 22:1–14 (cf. Gos. Thom. 64): in Luke, the invited guests will not participate in the banquet; in Matthew, an inappropriately dressed guest is bound and cast out.
- Luke 19:12–27 // Matt 25:14–30 (Q?): the wicked servant who did not multiply the one pound/talent he was given is punished.
- Matt 13:24–30 (cf. Gos. Thom. 57): weeds are bound and burned.
- Matt 13:47–50: the bad fish will be thrown away.
- Matt 18:23–35: the unforgiving servant is delivered to the jailers or torturers.
- Matt 21:28–32: "toll collectors and harlots" enter the kingdom before others.
- Matt 25:1–12: foolish virgins are shut out of a marriage feast.
- Luke 12:16–21: a rich man who is not rich toward God dies and loses all.
- Luke 13:6–9: if the fig tree is given more time and still fails to produce fruit, it will be cut down.
- Luke 16:19–31: the rich man suffers in Hades.

The Synoptic frames for many of these parables are eschatological, and in most cases those frames do not appear to be artificial impositions against the intent of the stories themselves. So my preliminary inference from this material, taken as a whole—an inference made without endeavoring to do the impossible, to decide exactly what goes back to Jesus and what does not—is that Jesus thought of eschatological failure as a genuine possibility for some or many of his hearers. He appears not to have shared the optimistic view of m. Sanh. 10:1: "All Israel has a place in the world to come."[132] The relevant parables also seem to reveal a mind that, at least for the purposes of exhor-

132. See further Allison, "Jesus and the Covenant."

tation, was urgent and without shades of gray: right behavior is incumbent, wrong behavior imperils. These inferences are, to be sure, only preliminary, and they need to be buttressed by additional arguments that move beyond the parables. Yet it remains that the parables as a corpus suggest more than that Jesus spoke in parables.

One could also, after reviewing the parables in their entirety, infer that Jesus was fond of stories with three characters or groups, including stories featuring "an authority figure and two contrasting subordinates."[133] Or, to offer one more illustration, studying the parables as a body might move one to ask why so few feature a king, especially when Jesus proclaimed the kingdom of God and so many rabbinic parables have a king.[134] But one illustration should suffice. I find useful what Meier does not use.

Two Clarifications

(1) It may have occurred to readers that I have, over the course of this chapter, unwittingly contradicted myself. I began with criticism of the criterion of multiple attestation, questioning its foundational assumption that, for our historical purposes, we may regard our major sources as independent. We have, I urged, no assurance that those who passed on traditions about Jesus and wrote our texts did so apart from others involved in those activities. I have nonetheless gone on to defend recurrent attestation, which in a similar way appeals to the principle of repetition in multiple sources. What, one may ask, is gained by this alternative if our chief sources may not be independent of each other?

Although we cannot recover the genealogies of most of our materials, it stands to reason that, the more material we take into account, the greater the odds that at least some of it may derive from disparate sources and be genuinely independent. This is reason enough for relying, when possible, more on the recurrent attestation of a theme or motif than on multiple attestation of a single saying or event. Unlike a solitary saying or discrete episode, which has a single tradition history, a broad array of units will have had multiple points of origin and multiple histories, so whatever those units have in common must go back to the beginning or very close to it. More is better. To deny that would be to deny the obvious. Theissen and Winter are right:

133. For this see Blomberg, *Interpreting the Parables*, 171–253; quotation from 171.
134. For this see Bauckham's helpful article "Kingdom and Church."

> Multiple attestation [of an individual tradition] only permits inferences regarding the historical reality when we can explain the different references to one and the same traditional element not as variations of a single tradition, but only as two independent windows into historical reality—in other words, only if they can be traced back ultimately to two different eye witnesses. This possibility can never be excluded, but it can hardly be proven. On the other hand, in the case of materially and formally related elements in different streams of tradition and in different genres . . . it is a priori more likely that several mutually independent "contacts" are based on historical reality.[135]

(2) Reliance on aggregates of themes and motifs hardly entails that we can never arrive at reasonable verdicts about individual events or sayings. In my judgment, for instance, and as I have indeed argued in other publications, we can muster good arguments for holding that Jesus selected a group of twelve disciples, that he was crucified as "king of the Jews," that a certain Joseph of Arimathea buried him, and even that shortly thereafter his tomb was unexpectedly discovered to be empty.[136] Those are discrete events. I likewise find persuasive arguments for thinking that Jesus prohibited divorce, authored most of the sayings in Luke 6:27–42 (Q), predicted the destruction of the temple, and promised certain followers that they would sit on thrones and judge the twelve tribes.[137] Those are discrete sayings.

These are important results. The problem is that such items constitute for me—others are of course much more optimistic—a relatively small pile: I am unable to draw confident inferences about most of the sayings and stories (just as Meier is unable to pass beyond *non liquet* for most of the parables). I am in the same place as E. P. Sanders and Margaret Davies: "Some aspects of Jesus'

135. Theissen and Winter, *Quest for the Plausible Jesus*, 238–39.

136. For my reasons for these judgments see *Constructing Jesus*, 67–76, 233–40, and *Resurrection of Jesus*, 94–166.

137. For the injunction against divorce see Meier, *Marginal Jew*, 4:74–181. On Luke 6:27–42 see Allison, *Constructing Jesus*, 305–86. On the prophecy of the temple's demise (Mark 13:2; Luke 19:44; John 2:13–22; Acts 6:14; Gos. Thom. 71) see p. 190 n. 192 above. On the promise of rule (Matt 19:28 // Luke 22:28–30) see Sanders, *Jesus and Judaism*, 98–106. Yet there are almost always learned dissenters. E.g., according to Kloppenborg, "Sources, Methods," 264–66, "the fact that the expression of judgment [in Matt 19:28 // Luke 22:28–30] fits so well with Q's redactional framing ought to raise serious suspicions about the authenticity of the saying." D. Zeller, "Jesus, Q," 363–64, attributes the saying to "an early Christian prophet."

teaching and career are firmly established, some things attributed to him are disproved, and most of the material is placed somewhere in between."[138]

I have no clear and distinct idea about the origin and tradition histories of the transfiguration or the entry into Jerusalem, or of the parable of the good Samaritan or the woes in Matt 23 and Luke 11. I do not really know what to make of the stilling of the storm and the cursing of the fig tree, of the parable of the wheat and weeds (Matt 13:24–30) or the so-called *Jubelruf* in Matt 11:25–27 // Luke 10:21–22. I have nothing but conjectures or ineliminable puzzlement regarding the Gadarene demoniac (Mark 5:1–20), the strange exorcist (9:38–41), the lamentation over Jerusalem (Matt 23:37–30 // Luke 13:34–35), and the parable of the wicked tenants (Mark 12:1–12). It would not surprise me in the least to learn that every single one of these items incorporates some historical memory. But no one to my satisfaction has cogently established how much. This is not, I should add, because I hanker after certainty. I long ago put away that childish thing. Today I seek only for what seems more likely than not.[139] But even that often escapes me.

My indecision about so many particulars leads me to embrace an approach that (1) does not continually demand more from us than we can deliver and (2) makes use of as much material as possible as opposed to the relatively small portion that successfully runs Meier's methodological gauntlet. For me, attending to repeating patterns and general substance is not a retreat but a way forward.

The Logic of the Criteria versus Their Use

My criticism of the criteria is not, I need to stress, that their logic is defective.[140] They are, in the abstract, "quite reasonable and based on common-sense prin-

138. Sanders and Davies, *Synoptic Gospels*, 304.

139. Cf. Allison, *Jesus of Nazareth*, 57–58. On the benefits of uncertainty see Theissen, "Zwischen Skepsis und Zuversicht," 52–55. Keener, *Christobiography*, 380 n. 65, in contrasting my approach with that of Bauckham, thinks we "are working for different levels of certainty." For me, however, certainty is certainty: there are no levels. I rather think only in terms of different levels of probability.

140. Cf. Allison, *Jesus of Nazareth*, 2–10. Note also Keith, "Indebtedness of Authenticity," 47–48—although unlike Keith my problems with the criteria are not directly related to issues surrounding form criticism—and Ferda, *Galilean Crisis*, 12–13. According to Havukainen, *Quest*, 293, Allison employs "some principles of the criteria despite seemingly rejecting them." Cf. Hägerland, "Future of Criteria," who asks whether some of my conclusions do not, despite my criticism of the standard criteria, nonetheless rely on those criteria or principles

ciples."[141] The trouble is not a priori but a posteriori, not in theory but in application, and specifically application to individual sayings and events (and above all when they become tools, as too often, for exclusion).[142] It was only years of hard work that roused me from my criteriological slumbers and left me persuaded that, aside from a handful of cases,[143] they are, when directed at single items, broken promises: the epistemological security they pledge is unwarranted. I agree with Larry Hurtado: if their aim is "to obtain a representative and adequate body of material on the basis of which to produce a historical portrait of Jesus, then . . . the critics of the criteria are correct in judging that they do not achieve this."[144]

To take them in turn: (1) Hankering after multiple attestation for a concrete event or individual saying may make sense in the abstract, but as I urged above, it is unclear whether our primary sources really are literarily independent of

---

embedded in them. They do. In addition to what follows note, among other illustrations, Allison, *Jesus of Nazareth*, 97–101, on Jesus's prophecy about the destruction and rebuilding of the temple ("when the tradition struggles this much with a saying one is prodded to infer that it goes back to something Jesus said—something which, because so well known, generally disallowed . . . discrete silence"), and Allison, *Constructing Jesus*, 425 ("a few of the stories [in the passion narrative] likely mirror real events because they cannot be derived from the Jewish Bible and because there is no obvious motivation for Christian invention").

141. So Licona, "Is the Sky Falling?," 366.

142. In earlier works, some of my grievances about the criteria had to do with scholars authenticating discrete traditions and then, in the name of consistency, leveraging them against other traditions, even when that meant going against repeating themes and motifs. See, e.g., my discussion of Jesus and Gehenna in *Resurrecting Jesus*, 56–110; and cf. the conclusion of Rodríguez, *Structuring Christian Memory*, 224–25: "The programme of atomizing, decontextualizing and recontextualizing snippets of the gospel tradition in order to critically reconstruct the 'historical Jesus' has been exposed as culturally and historically inappropriate."

143. "A handful of items" is not a hollow qualification. Even in my most pessimistic treatment of the criteria—"How to Marginalize the Traditional Criteria of Authenticity"—I did not assert that they are altogether useless but that they should be "marginalized," moved from "the center of our discussion to the periphery" because they are "too often unworkable and so of quite limited utility" (9). "Too often" is not the same as "always," and "limited utility" is not the same as "no utility." Zolondek, *We Have Found the Messiah*, 84–85, characterizes me as holding that "the criteria should be abandoned, and that it is only by doing so that historical Jesus studies can proceed effectively." But in my attempts to find a better starting point, I have sought to demote the criteria, not liquidate the principles they embody. I have further observed that "nothing prohibits those less skeptical of the criteria of authenticity from employing them in connection with what I have called 'recurrent attestation'" (*Constructing Jesus*, 20 n. 85).

144. Hurtado, "Response," 346.

one another or what would follow even if they were. Multiple attestation may work for the crucifixion: the testimony casts out all reasonable doubt.[145] That event, however, is the exception, not a pledge of the criterion's general utility. How many other particulars can claim the sort of broad attestation Jesus's execution has?

(2) Again, one can hardly gainsay the demand for coherence, to which we all pledge allegiance in one way or another.[146] The Jesus of every book, including this volume, is self-consistent in the eyes of its author—just as the Jesus of Matt 1–28 was coherent for Matthew, the Jesus of Mark 1–16 coherent for Mark, and so on. Yet as a principle for inclusion or exclusion of individual items, coherence is often imprudent.[147] Regarding inclusion: items from different individuals can cohere nicely, especially if one person admires the other, as Jesus's devotees admired him.[148] Regarding exclusion: a sentence in which Jesus refers to Nirvana or his visits to China or his conversations with Augustus Caesar would not cohere with what we otherwise know. Nothing in our sources is as easy as that, however.

(3) Nor, as is widely recognized, is the criterion of double dissimilarity or discontinuity, despite its one-time attractiveness to so many, a faithful servant.[149] With Maurice Casey, I believe that "it has generally caused more trouble than it is worth."[150] Morna Hooker long ago protested that, even if its logic is sound, we do not know enough about either early Judaism or the early Jesus movement to apply it with assurance.[151] Despite all we have learned since then—the advances in our knowledge and methods over the past half century have been stunning—her gripe remains cogent. Arguments from dissimilarity are arguments about silence: there is no parallel. Yet we possess only a portion of the Jewish and Christian texts that must have been in circulation.[152] Do we,

145. Here I concur with Licona, "Is the Sky Falling?," 363–64.

146. Cf. Le Donne, "Criterion of Coherence," 113: "Insomuch as historians will continue to build from premises that lend support to their conclusions, coherence will continue to be a guiding principle in Jesus research."

147. See further Allison, *Jesus of Nazareth*, 2–4; J. T. Sanders, "Criterion of Coherence"; and Le Donne, "Criterion of Coherence."

148. I expounded this point at length in Allison, *Jesus of Nazareth*, 7–10.

149. On the ideological background of this criterion see Winter, "Saving the Quest."

150. Casey, *Jesus of Nazareth*, 104.

151. Hooker, "Christology and Methodology"; Hooker, "On Using the Wrong Tool." Cf. Häfner, "Ende der Kriterien?," 123, and Hengel and Schwemer, *Jesus and Judaism*, 278. Contrast Meier, *Marginal Jew*, 1:172, who is not impressed by this impediment.

152. According to Markschies, "Canon of the New Testament," 176, "we only possess 14% of the Christian literature of the 2nd century that, according to our sources, must have

moreover, have any writings from Galilean Jews who lived when Jesus did? Contemplating the question does not embolden me. Beyond that, surely many ideas in circulation in his time and place never made it into books at all. Our ignorance is substantial. We should own it.

Even were that not so, the criterion of discontinuity—which so often delivers "a decidedly minimalist Jesus"[153]—shrinks and devalues Jesus's debt to his Jewish tradition as well as the continuity between him and his followers. So many have complained about this because it is so obviously true.[154] Far fewer, however, have observed the problem that dissimilarity, like coherence, exists only in the eye of the beholder. It is not an intrinsic fact. It exists "only with respect to variable and shifting criteria of relevance."[155] As philosopher Stephen Braude has it:

> Intrinsic similarity is nonsense. . . . Things are never similar solely in virtue of static relations between them or in virtue of properties inherent in them. Things must *count* or *be taken as* similar or dissimilar relative to some context of inquiry and criteria of relevance. For example, the movements of an elephant aren't inherently similar or dissimilar to those of a flea. They might count as similar in a situation where the size of an organism isn't relevant but dissimilar in a context where size is a major concern.[156]

One can always, if A is not B, find ways in which A and B differ, which means one can always find ways in which something in the Jesus tradition differs from something in Jewish or Christian sources (just as one can always unearth parallels of one sort of another). The question is not whether we can discern differences—we can always do that—but what the differences we construct mean or how they matter. Meier finds the double commandment of love in Mark 12:28–34 sufficiently dissimilar from Jewish sources to establish authenticity.[157] I find the Jewish parallels sufficiently similar to regard Jesus's

existed." The situation cannot have been wholly dissimilar with Jewish sources around the turn of the era. Here the survey of lost books in M. R. James, *Lost Apocrypha*, remains, despite being badly dated, instructive. Likewise sobering is the large number of Qumran fragments that do not belong to books we otherwise know.

153. Bryan, review of Meier, *Marginal Jew*, 623.

154. See Holmén, "Doubts about Double Dissimilarity," 50–51.

155. Braude, *Crimes of Reason*, 9.

156. Braude, *Crimes of Reason*, 8.

157. Meier, *Marginal Jew*, 4:499–515.

teaching as conventional.[158] I further deem both his conclusion and mine to be irrelevant for the question of origin.

(4) Of more utility than dissimilarity, coherence, and multiple attestation is the so-called criterion of embarrassment. This, in Meier's words, "pinpoints Gospel material that would hardly have been invented by the early church, since such material created embarrassment or theological difficulties for the church even during the NT period—a prime example being the baptism of Jesus by John the Baptist at the beginning of the public ministry."[159]

As with individual memories, so too with social memories: groups do not always forget the potentially unedifying.[160] And some items in the Gospels are much more likely to belong to indelible memory than to be the product of free invention. For instance, given the conviction that Jesus was, for his followers, greater than the Baptist, the baptism of the former by the latter must have raised questions.[161] If the past had mattered not at all, so that fiction was free to run untrammeled, a story about Jesus dunking the Baptist would, from everything we know, have served far better. In other words, the story of John baptizing Jesus, if unalloyed legend, is unexpected. It is, then, unlikely to be unalloyed legend.

I am unsure that "embarrassment" is, despite its prevalence, quite the right term here. One can find something difficult without feeling embarrassed.[162] Perhaps it would be preferable to speak of "implausibility."[163] That is, if a tradition is in seeming tension with what its tradents believed or wanted to believe,

158. Allison, *Resurrecting Jesus*, 152–60. Cf. Sanders, *Question of Uniqueness*, 19: "The combination of Deut. 6.5 and Lev. 19.18, 34 constitutes a commonplace of Jewish teaching." Sanders's reflections throughout *Question of Uniqueness* are directly relevant to the criterion of dissimilarity, even though that is not his topic.

159. Meier, *Marginal Jew*, 5:12. Cf. 1:168.

160. See above, p. 76. Helpful here is A. Kirk, *Memory and the Jesus Tradition*, 26–30.

161. Cf. Matt 3:14: "I need to be baptized by you, and do you come to me?" Frey, *Theology and History*, 113, is clearly correct: "The overall tendency of all four canonical Gospels is to present Jesus in a category of his own, to distance him from his precursor, and to avoid any direct comparison between the two whereby the Baptizer could possibly appear superior to Jesus."

162. Meier perhaps recognizes this with his disjunction: "created embarrassment or theological difficulties."

163. But the word has been used for another criterion; cf. Hägerland, *Jesus and the Forgiveness of Sins*, 26: "The criterion of implausibility assesses as unhistorical features which contradict known facts about the conditions of first-century Palestine." There is the further catch that Theissen and Winter, *Quest for the Plausible Jesus*, speak of "the criterion of plausibility," "contextual plausibility," "plausibility of effects," and "comprehensive plausibility."

or if it was likely inconvenient for their cause or unflattering of Jesus, then we naturally suspect they did not concoct it from nothing.[164] Surely Christians did not trouble themselves needlessly. When it is hard to imagine the wholesale, pious invention of some particular, when we can tell no good story that excludes the historical Jesus, then invention unmoored from the past is implausible.

From this angle, several particulars, in addition to Jesus's baptism, seemingly commend themselves. It is implausible that Christ adherents hatched *ex nihilo* the idea that opponents took Jesus to be possessed by an unclean spirit (Mark 3:22, 30).[165] It is implausible that they concocted out of thin air the notion that some reviled him as a drunkard and glutton (Matt 11:19 // Luke 7:34; cf. Deut 21:18–21) or the friend of toll collectors and sinners (Matt 11:19 // Luke 7:34; Mark 2:15–17; Luke 7:37–39; 19:7). It is implausible that they fabricated without memory the motif that he was accused of blasphemy (Mark 2:7; 14:64).[166]

One value of such items is what they say about the Synoptics in general. Were those Gospels utterly bereft of memory, they would not preserve such material. So they must in part remember. Moreover, as no one can believe that Jesus's followers handed on only what might have discomfited them, it follows that the Synoptics contain additional memories. On this I agree wholeheartedly with Meier:

> That embarrassing material is found as late as the redaction of the Gospels reminds us that beside a creative thrust there was also a conservative force in the Gospel tradition. Indeed, so conservative was this force that a string of embarrassing events (e.g., baptism by John, betrayal by Judas, denial by Peter, crucifixion by the Romans) called forth agonized and varied theological reflection, but not, in most cases, convenient amnesia. In this sense, the criterion of embarrassment has an importance for the historian far beyond the individual data it may help verify.[167]

164. Cf. Theissen and Winter, *Quest for the Plausible Jesus*, 239–42, who discuss "the criterion of resistance to tendencies of the tradition."

165. Yet there is perhaps room for doubt even here; cf. Nicklas, "Alternatives to Form," 736: "The accusation that the miracles of Jesus were brought about by demonic power or magical means could have arisen in the context of the Christian proclamation of such mighty deeds."

166. Cf. John 10:33–36 and see further Bermejo-Rubio, "Changing Methods." He shows that multiple texts seem to betray unease over the political implications of some of Jesus's words and deeds.

167. Meier, *Marginal Jew*, 1:170. As with almost everything else, to be sure, one can find

There are, however, two major snags here, both of which Meier acknowledges. The first is (as one would expect since believers in Jesus authored our texts) that "clear-cut cases" of "embarrassment are not numerous in the Gospel tradition."[168] So the criterion fails to get us very far.

The second hitch is that it can be hard to decide what might have given early tradents second thoughts.[169] Some hold that Jesus's struggle in Gethsemane and his cry of abandonment on the cross must have been "embarrassing."[170] Yet there was an edifying Jewish tradition about the righteous who suffer.[171] Matthew, moreover, did nothing to change Mark's picture, and both Markan scenes snugly fit the Second Gospel's portrayal of Jesus as the martyr prophesied in Second Isaiah and certain Davidic psalms.[172] What, then, should we infer?[173] Again, Mark and Matthew relate that Jesus said to James and John: "To sit at my right hand or at my left is not mine to grant." This troubled many later exegetes, whose Christology had no place for subordinationism. The plain sense of Matt 20:23 // Mark 10:40 was for them a stumbling block.[174] But did

---

scholars on the other side, scholars who are unsure that John baptized Jesus or that Judas betrayed him or that Peter denied him. Their number, however, is few, and I do not find their arguments compelling.

168. Meier, *Marginal Jew*, 1:170. Cf. Hengel and Schwemer, *Jesus and Judaism*, 279: "While the 'criterion of dissimilarity' [within which they include the criterion of embarrassment] may be a point of departure for the investigative probe, on its own it yields only intermittent and therefore completely inadequate results."

169. To the point here is Rodríguez, "Embarrassing Truth about Jesus." Cf. also Porter, *Criteria for Authenticity*, 109–10; Goodacre, "Criticizing the Criterion," 165–67; and Crossley, *Jesus and the Chaos of History*, 38 ("that which is embarrassing to one need not necessarily be embarrassing to another. How do we judge what is embarrassing?"). Note also Crossley, p. 39: "If a saying or deed is embarrassing, why does it have to be Jesus who created the embarrassing moment? Why not someone else earlier in the tradition?"

170. Cf. Hilary, *Comm. Matt.* 31.2: "If he [Jesus] is sad to the point of fear, if weak to the point of pain, if anxious to the point of death, eternity will be subjected to corruption, and thus it will fall into corruption as an effect of its many weaknesses." John's Gospel already denies the gist of the episode in Gethsemane as the Synoptics relate it; see Frey, *Theology and History*, 73–76.

171. See Ruppert, *Leidende Gerechte*; Ruppert, *Leidende Gerechte und seine Feinde*; Ruppert, *Jesus als der leidende Gerechte?*; and Nickelsburg, "Genre and Function."

172. On the suffering David as a model for Jesus see N. C. Johnson, *Suffering Son of David*.

173. Cf. Meier, *Marginal Jew*, 1:170–71, and Meier, "Basic Methodology," 313–14: the criterion of embarrassment may not apply to Mark 15:34.

174. Cf. Jerome, *Comm. Matt.* 4 *ad* 26:37; Chrysostom, *Hom. Matt.* 65.3; Calvin, *Harmony of the Gospels*, 2:273; Bengel, *Gnomon Novi Testamenti*, 1:49.

Jesus's concession disturb only later Christians as opposed to Mark, Matthew, and their predecessors? I am unable to find the answer.[175]

The Challenge of the Spectrum

Before drawing this chapter to its close, I wish to make explicit something that has been implicit in the previous pages and in my criticism of the endeavor to authenticate, via the standard criteria, individual items.

Scholars have often gone about their business as though two options confront them: either Jesus said A or he did not say A; either B occurred or B did not occur. This is a stark and unimaginative dichotomy. Even when such critics confess, as they sometimes do, that they cannot make up their mind, this does nothing to eliminate the crude binary: A or not A, B or not B.

But it is not so. That Abraham Lincoln was assassinated is true. That Abraham Lincoln was the first man on the moon is false. Rarely, however, are things so straightforward.

The Letter of Aristeas tells us that Ptolemy, the king of Egypt, aspired to collect all the books in the world. At his instigation, Demetrius of Phalerum, supervisor of the great library in Alexandria, sent a letter to Eleazar, the high priest in Jerusalem, asking that six blameless elders from each tribe in Israel—seventy-two in all—come to Egypt to translate the laws of the Jews into Greek. In the event they arrived. They were then escorted to the island of Pharos, where they produced, after laboring for seventy-two days, a translation that, when publicly read to the Jews of Alexandria, was cheered. Copies were therewith demanded. That is how the Torah first appeared in Greek.

Even though it is written in the first-person, most modern scholars classify Aristeas as a historical romance. The book not only contains a number of obvious errors but relates several highly unlikely events.[176] At the same time, Aristeas does not appear to be utterly dissociated from the historical past.[177] The Old Greek Pentateuch was not translated by a Gentile or Gentiles; it was rather the work of more than one Jew. (The various books exhibit more than

175. Wallace, "Textual Criticism," is right to insist that multiple texts and stories puzzled or embarrassed Christians: the textual evidence is undeniable. The tricky part is showing, in any particular instance, that later sensibilities, such as those of Matthew, Luke, John, and later scribes, were already felt by Mark and pre-Markan tradents.

176. See B. G. Wright, "Letter of Aristeas."

177. See Honigman, *Septuagint and Homeric Scholarship*, 93–143.

one translation technique.)[178] It is, furthermore, reasonable to suppose that it initially appeared in Egypt, especially as there are a few Egyptian loanwords in the Pentateuch. And, to judge by the language, much or most of it plausibly appeared in the third century BCE, when Ptolemy II ruled. It is even plausible, according to some, that a king wanted to have a copy of Jewish religious literature in his library.[179] So while Aristeas is very far from being the truth, the whole truth, and nothing but the truth, it is not exactly lies and nothing but lies either. As Siegfried Kreuzer puts it, with reference to Aristeas: "Even a pseudonymous text can contain accurate information."[180]

Historicity is often not a matter of yes or no, true or false. Of course the extremities may be susceptible to easy, clear-cut evaluation. Jesus of Nazareth, for instance, was crucified. That is history. But there is not a tincture of truth to the tale that Jesus, as a wee lad, once molded sparrows from clay, clapped his hands, and brought them to life, whereupon they chirped and flew away. That is fiction from the Infancy Gospel of Thomas. However, most of the earlier traditions and narratives about Jesus, including most of the materials in the Synoptics, have a more complex relationship to facticity than such straightforward, uncontested examples. They display degrees of accuracy and inaccuracy, varying amounts of memory and invention, gradations of preservation and literary creativity.

Consider C. H. Dodd's analysis of John 20:26–29:

> The story of Doubting Thomas is a pendant to the "concise" narrative of the appearance to the disciples in xx.19–21. . . . It hardly forms a separable *pericopé*, for it is not fully intelligible without the connecting narrative of xx.24–5. Its theological and apologetical motives are obvious. . . . We should not be far wrong in saying that John has chosen to split up the composite traditional picture of a group some of whom recognize the Lord while others doubt, and to give contrasting pictures of the believers and the doubter, in order to make a point which is essentially theological.[181]

I agree with this sensible assessment. John 20:26–29 does not depict a historical scene. Yet this scarcely entails that the passage is memory free. Fiction need

178. See H. Kim, *Multiple Authorship of the Septuagint Pentateuch*.

179. For details see B. G. Wright, "Letter of Aristeas," 313–17 (although Wright does not go along).

180. Kreuzer, "Origins and Transmission," 12.

181. Dodd, *More New Testament Studies*, 115–16.

not be wholly fictive. Here, as so often, the customary antithesis, historical versus unhistorical, ill serves us. The past can enter even a late, redactional creation. For there was indeed, as 1 Cor 15:5 reports, a historical appearance to the Twelve (however one understands it). Furthermore, the best explanation for the motif of doubt in so many stories about the resurrection is that unexpected events soon after Good Friday left some of Jesus's disciples not knowing exactly what to think.[182] John 20:26–29 is not the work of an amnesiac. It is the creative, dramatic enlargement of a couple of memories.

Again, consider Luke 4:16–30, which narrates Jesus's inaugural sermon in a synagogue in Nazareth. Is the passage, which is programmatic for the Third Gospel, a creative, redactional enlargement of Mark 6:1–6, or does it mostly preserve a pre-Lukan, non-Markan narrative, or is it a mingling of multiple traditions?[183] As so often, disagreement reigns, and I am unsure what to think. Yet even if the scene is a mostly Lukan production, it dramatizes his image of Jesus; and since that image was largely formed by tradition, it need not be historically misleading.[184] I for one believe that it incorporates multiple memories, among them: Jesus attended synagogue;[185] he associated his ministry with Isa 61 (Luke 4:18–19);[186] he believed that eschatological hopes were coming to realization in his ministry (4:21);[187] some warmly welcomed him (4:22), others were hostile (4:23–24, 28–29);[188] some opposition came from

182. See further Hubbard, *Matthean Redaction*; Atkins, *Doubt of the Apostles*; and Allison, *Resurrection of Jesus*, 60–64, 205–6.

183. For discussion see Schürmann, "Zur Traditionsgeschichte" (Luke used a non-Markan version of the story of Jesus's rejection in Nazareth); Tannehill, "Mission of Jesus" (multiple sources); Busse, *Nazareth-Manifest* (Luke's composition); Meier, *Marginal Jew* 1:269–71 (a firm decision is impossible); Tuckett, *Q and the History*, 226–37 (Q is the main source); Ryan, *Role of the Synagogue*, 172–83 (a non-Markan source carrying "the memory of an eyewitness from the Land").

184. Especially helpful here is Rodríguez, *Structuring Christian Memory*, 138–73. Cf. Bockmuehl, *This Jesus*, 20: "Even a pericope freely composed in an evangelist's own language and theology does not . . . have to be invented out of thin air."

185. The relevant materials are cited and discussed by Ryan, *Role of the Synagogue*, 125–69. See also Dunn, "Did Jesus Attend Synagogue?"

186. See Allison, *Constructing Jesus*, 263–66. Cf. Dunn, *Jesus Remembered*, 516–17: "Even if Luke's portrayal of Jesus reading the passage [Isa 61:1–3] and explicitly claiming its fulfilment . . . is an elaboration of the briefer tradition in Mark 6.1–6a, we can still be confident that his elaboration was based on a strong remembrance of Jesus making clear allusion to the passage on more than one occasion." Whether Jesus could read, as Luke 4 has it, remains disputed; for the issues see esp. Keith, *Jesus' Literacy*.

187. See Allison, *Constructing Jesus*, 98–116.

188. The theme of mixed reception runs throughout the tradition.

members of his own village, Nazareth (4:24); and he sometimes formulated gendered couplets (4:25–27) (see above, pp. 230–32). The extent to which Luke 4:16–30 depicts a historical event I do not know. Is it "authentic" or "inauthentic"? Perhaps it is neither because it is both.[189]

Another example: in Luke 24:13–35, a certain Cleopas and his companion, shortly after the crucifixion, are discussing "all the things that have happened" (24:14). The risen Jesus interrupts their conversation, asking what they are talking about. The response includes these words: "We had hoped that he was the one about to redeem Israel" (24:21). Then, in Acts 1:6, the apostles ask the resurrected Jesus if "at this time" he is going to "restore the kingdom to Israel." Both verses purport that the disciples expected a national deliverance, and that they expected it soon.[190] Now I do not know how to unravel the tradition history of the appearance on the Emmaus road,[191] and I think that the dialogue in Acts 1:6–8 is a redactional product from beginning to end.[192] I am nonetheless convinced that Luke 24:14 and Acts 1:6 remember rightly. While the latter belongs to a fictional scene, the former to a passage whose origin cannot be ascertained, Jesus's followers did hope—because Jesus hoped—that the end was near, and they expected—because Jesus expected—that they would see the deliverance and redemption of Israel.[193]

Another example: Matt 9:32–34 relates the following short story: "After they had gone away, a demoniac who was mute was brought to him. And when the demon had been cast out, the one who had been mute spoke; and the crowds were amazed and said: 'Never has anything like this been seen in Israel.' But the Pharisees said: 'By the ruler of the demons he casts out the demons.'" The Jesus Seminar colored this passage black, indicating that it should not be included "in the primary database for determining who Jesus was," this because it "is

189. Cf. the generalization of Keith, *Jesus' Literacy*, 61: "Scholars cannot separate Jesus traditions into authentic and inauthentic bodies of tradition because all Jesus tradition (in one form or another) belongs to both categories."

190. This is manifest in Acts 1:6: ἐν τῷ χρόνῳ = "at this time." The same holds, I believe, for Luke 24:21: ὁ μέλλων λυτροῦσθαι τὸν Ἰσραήλ. The NRSVue translates: "The one to redeem Israel." This takes μέλλω in its weakened sense, as a periphrasis for the future. Yet the first meaning in BDAG, s.v., is "be about to," and Luke 19:11 ("they supposed that the kingdom of God was to appear immediately") and Acts 1:6 establish this as the likely sense for Luke 24:41. For relevant observations, see Mattill, *Luke and the Last Things*, 43–47.

191. For various options see Allison, *Resurrection of Jesus*, 66–68.

192. So too Barrett, *Acts*, 1:62; Lüdemann, *Acts of the Apostles*; and Pesch, *Apostelgeschichte*, 1:65.

193. Cf. Ryan, *Role of the Synagogue*, 137; and see further Klausner, *Jesus of Nazareth*, 398–402, and Allison, *Jesus of Nazareth*, 141–45.

largely or entirely fictive."[194] One understands their verdict. Matthew almost certainly invented the episode.[195] Leading up to the summarizing list of Jesus's activities in 11:2–4 (Jesus's reply to John the Baptist), the evangelist wanted an instance of each activity; and as one of those listed is healing the deaf and mute (κωφοί), he composed, by drawing on multiple traditions,[196] 9:32–34, in which Jesus heals a κωφός.[197] Matthew also needed a story at the end of chapter 9 in order to fill out his sequence of 3 + 3 + 3 miracle stories.[198] Strictly speaking, then, 9:32–34 is not history, by which I mean it is not the record of an actual event. Yet it is not unhistorical, for its basic elements do not mislead. The historical Jesus did (whatever the explanation) cure demoniacs. His wonders did garner him popular support. Some Pharisees did oppose him. And the charge that he casts out demons by the ruler of demons is much more likely to be memory than invention.

Another example: according to John 6:14–15, the feeding of the five thousand led people to infer that Jesus was "the prophet who is to come into the world," and when he learned that they wanted to "take him by force to make him king, he withdrew again to the mountain by himself." These verses once played a large role in reconstructions of the life of Jesus.[199] They do so no longer, in large part because of the general disinclination to find much history in the Fourth Gospel. Tucker Ferda, however, has recently argued that, even if John's story never happened, it "captures an important political dimension

194. Funk and Jesus Seminar, *Acts of Jesus*, 36–37, 187.

195. So too Meier, *Marginal Jew*, 2:657.

196. Above all the Beelzebul controversy in Matt 12:22–30 // Luke 11:14–23 (Q) and Mark 3:22–27. Sometimes Matt 9:32–34 is labeled a doublet of 12:22–24; so, e.g., Gnilka, *Matthäusevangelium*, 1:346, and W. T. Wilson, *Matthew*, 1:335.

197. "The blind see" (9:27–31). "The lame walk" (9:2–8). "Lepers are cleansed" (8:1–4). "The deaf [κωφοί] hear" (9:32–34). (Κωφός can mean "mute" or "deaf" or both; cf. BDAG, s.v.) "The dead are raised" (9:18–26). "The poor have good news preached to them" (5:3). Cf. Bultmann, *History of the Synoptic Tradition*, 218: 9:32–34 is the evangelist's own formulation "from traditional motifs" designed to illustrate the healing of κωφοί in 11:5.

198. See further Meier, *Vision of Matthew*, 68–74; Davies and Allison, *Matthew*, 1:67, 101–2; 2:3–4; Talbert, *Matthew*, 110–11; and W. T. Wilson, *Matthew*, 1:263. This is the scheme:

first triad: healing (8:1–4) + healing (8:5–13) + healing (8:14–15)
 + summary report and words of Jesus (8:16–22)
second triad: natural miracle (8:23–27) + demoniacs cured (8:28–34) + healing (9:1–8)
 + call of Levi and words of Jesus (9:9–17)
third triad: two healed (9:18–26) + two healed (9:27–31) + healing (9:32–34)
 + summary report and words of Jesus (9:35–38)

199. Note, e.g., Goguel, *Life of Jesus*, 374–77, and T. W. Manson, *Servant Messiah*, 70–71.

of Jesus's Galilean ministry and his response to 'fame' that are likely to be historical."[200] I cannot here rehearse the details of Ferda's argument, but only express my conviction that he is persuasive: Jesus not only attracted "fame and enthusiasm that had political implications" but further was "aware of this as a potential problem."[201] As the fate of the Baptist had shown, "too much attention was dangerous,"[202] and Jesus acted accordingly.[203] The upshot is that "even if Jn 6.14–15 is unhistorical in the traditional sense, memory helped create it."[204]

As a final illustration of how fiction can rightly remember, consider the account of Jesus's temptation in Matt 4:1–11 and Luke 4:1–13. This is, in my judgment, a haggadic tale. It imagines its hero recapitulating the experience of Israel in the wilderness and appropriately quoting words of Moses from Deut 6–8.[205] It is akin to a legend in the Babylonian Talmud that features a debate between Abraham and Satan wherein the two exchange scriptural phrases and sentences.[206] When Jesus is tempted by hunger and idolatry, the devil quotes Ps 91:1–12. Jesus counters with Deut 8:3; 6:16; and 6:13. None of this is history as it was.

Yet that is not the end of the matter. The story in Matthew and Luke depicts Jesus as successfully combating the devil. It associates him with the Spirit of God. It attributes to him the ability to quote Scripture. It portrays him as having great faith. It takes for granted his ability to perform miracles as well as his

200. Ferda, "Crowds, Bread, and Fame," 140. Helpful for thinking about the nature of the crowds in Jesus's life are Myles, "Crowds and Power," and Crossley and Myles, *Jesus*, 89–92.

201. Ferda, "Crowds, Bread, and Fame," 153.

202. Ferda, "Crowds, Bread, and Fame," 155.

203. Ferda, "Crowds, Bread, and Fame," 155, suggests that Jesus's itineracy may have been "motivated in part by a political reality."

204. Ferda, "Crowds, Bread, and Fame," 142.

205. See Gerhardsson, *Testing of God's Son*, and Farrer, *Triple Victory*. Contrast the verdict of Sanday, *Life of Christ*, 110: "There is nothing in the Gospels that is more authentic" than the story of Jesus's temptation. This is for me a sober reminder of how subjective and relative our confident historical judgments can be.

206. b. Sanh. 89b: "On the way Satan came toward him [Abraham] and said to him: 'If one ventures a word with you, will you be offended? . . . Behold, you have instructed many, and you have strengthened weak hands. Your words have supported the one who was stumbling, and you have strengthened the feeble knees. But now it is come to you, and you are impatient' (Job 4:2–5). He replied: 'I will walk in my integrity' (cf. Ps 26:2). 'But,' Satan said to him, 'should not your fear be your confidence?' (Job 4:6). He retorted: 'Remember, I pray, whoever perished being innocent?' (Job 4:7). Seeing that he would not listen to him, he said to him: 'Now a thing was secretly brought to me' (Job 4:12); thus have I heard behind the curtain, 'the lamb for a burnt offering but not Isaac for a burnt offering' (cf. Gen 22:8). He replied: 'It is the penalty of a liar, that even if he tell the truth, he is not listened to.'"

reluctance to do so at another's bidding. And it presupposes Jesus's messianic destiny. All this arguably matches what we otherwise know of him.[207] One may even wonder, as I did in chapter 2, whether Jesus undertook, at some point, a lengthy fast in the desert. The upshot is that, while the Synoptic episode is, strictly considered, unhistorical, more broadly considered it aligns with much we otherwise know. It rightly catches important aspects of Jesus's character and mission. It is, in short, a fair impressionist sketch.

How many stories in the Gospel are kin to the temptation story? I do not know. I am, however, confident that, in general, a mixture of memory and elaboration runs throughout the sources; and while some stories and sayings have a large purchase on history, others a very small purchase, my sense is that most of the materials, if we had enough knowledge to work out the details and track the truth, belong to the capacious spectrum in between. Much in the Gospels is neither clearly historical nor clearly unhistorical; it is rather, in Eric Eve's words, "a blend of recollection, reinterpretation, reflection, conflation, confusion and distortion that simply cannot be reverse-engineered."[208]

We must learn to set aside our instinctive desire for exactitude.[209] Memories of Jesus can inform sentences he never uttered and stories that never took place.[210] It follows that using the criteria of authenticity to detach the authentic from the inauthentic, the pre-Easter from the post-Easter, is to narrow unduly the range of inquiry and the scope of relevant materials.[211] As we have seen,

207. See further Allison, "Behind the Temptations."

208. Eve, *Behind the Gospels*, 182. He continues: "The very concepts of authentic and inauthentic material need rethinking. If 'authentic' means a literal transcription of historical fact as it might have been recorded by a video camera, then little or nothing in the Gospels will count as authentic, but such an understanding of authenticity would be quite inappropriate to the material. If, on the other hand, 'authentic' is taken to mean reflective of the sort of things Jesus typically said and did, appropriately interpreted in the light of primitive Christian experience, belief, and practice, then a great deal of the material that appears in the Gospels may be broadly authentic in this sense." For related comments see Hahn, *Historical Investigation*, 49–50; Rodríguez, "Authenticating Criteria"; Hägerland, "Future of Criteria," 62–63; and Keith, "Narratives of the Gospels."

209. Unlike Sanders, *Jesus and Judaism*, 13, I do not believe that each saying attributed to Jesus "must be tested by appropriate criteria and assigned (tentatively) to an author—either to Jesus or to an anonymous representative of some stratum in the early church."

210. Cf. Bornkamm, *Jesus of Nazareth*, 11 ("it is not apparent why a word or a story which was first formulated by the church should not in content possess historical genuineness"); Funk et al., *Five Gospels*, 36 (a vote of gray for a saying means "Jesus did not say this, but the ideas contained in it are close to his own"); and Crossan, *Historical Jesus*, 434 (some traditions represent "a dramatic historicization of something that took place over a much longer period").

211. So too Hooker, "Foreword," xv–xvi, and Rodríguez, *Structuring Christian Memory*, 179.

after Meier decides, in his volume on the parables, that Jesus did not compose a particular parable, or that its origin cannot be determined, he pays it no further heed. This implies that the secondary, the redactional, the fictional, the unconfirmable should not inform our ideas about the historical Jesus.

William Walker wrote: "If the early Church did, in fact, create traditions about Jesus (and it surely did), it would no doubt have attempted, at least for the most part, to create such traditions as would fit 'reasonably well' into the general picture of Jesus which it had received through the prior traditions."[212] This is a sensible claim, which is why so many others have said similar things.[213] And to think in these terms means that even an unhistorical episode or apocryphal saying may carry memory insofar as it is congruent with who Jesus was or what he was like. History and fiction need not repel. To the contrary: they often attract one other.

Attention to recurrent attestation, which means appraisal of themes and motifs recurring in the sources, is better equipped to handle this cloudy situation than is an atomizing method. The standard technique, whose focus is the single story or saying, demands that we establish whether Jesus said or did a particular thing or verify exactly how much memory lies within a particular saying or story. Yet too often—not always but all too often—we are not up to the task: discussion ends not in the probable but the inconclusive. Over against this, analysis of recurring elements operates at a different level and is unhindered by our inability to know what we cannot know.

Final Remarks

According to Roger Trigg, "hankering after a fixed method may be understandable, but it is the death of human creative reasoning."[214] I am not so extreme, and this chapter promotes a particular *modus operandi*: search for patterns, account for them, then interpret them. I nonetheless share Trigg's fondness for what he calls "creative reasoning." Indeed, imagination and even

212. W. Walker, "Quest for the Historical Jesus," 50.

213. Note, e.g., Dahl, *Crucified Messiah*, 67 (that a "word or occurrence found a place within the tradition about Jesus indicates that it agreed with the total picture as it existed within the circle of the disciples"); Hahn, *Historical Investigation*, 49 ("completely new creations are an exception, because what was added by the church in its tradition was closely associated with other transmitted materials, and extended them"); Rau, "Wie entstehen unechte Jesusworte?"; Dunn, *Jesus Remembered*, 333–34; and Rodríguez, *Structuring Christian Memory*, 179.

214. Trigg, *Beyond Matter*, xii.

intuition are central to the historian's task.[215] We must not only read between the lines but draw our own lines. And we must fill in the blanks. Of course imagination must be disciplined and informed, but it is imagination nonetheless.[216] In line with this, my approach, although a rational strategy, cannot be quantified. It pays no obeisance to a set of fixed formal rules.[217] And it has no place for Bayesian equations or any other sort of arithmetical calculations. It rather involves what Cardinal Newman called the "illative sense," which means the ability to consider and to weigh factors "too fine to avail separately, too subtle and circuitous to be convertible into syllogisms, too numerous and various for such conversion, even were they convertible."[218]

If I am asked, How often does a theme or motif need to be attested in order to be dubbed recurrent?,[219] I have nothing to say. If I am asked, How does one discern which texts should be colligated in order to reveal some theme?,[220] I again have no answer. And I do not regard my inability to respond as a debilitating defect. We can, in my judgment, muddle through just fine without formalizing everything we do.[221]

According to Aristotle, the treatment of a subject is adequate "if it achieves that amount of precision that belongs to its subject matter. The same exactness must not be expected in all departments of philosophy alike, any more than in all the products of the arts and crafts" (*Eth. nic.* 1094b). How much precision can we hope to obtain when it comes to evaluating the early sources for Jesus?

215. Cf. Schweitzer, *Quest of the Historical Jesus*, 7: solving the problem of the historical Jesus "must ultimately rest upon historical intuition." See further Ryan, "Jesus at the Crossroads," and Schröter, "Memory, Theories of History," 93–99.

216. Cf. von Humboldt, "On the Historian's Task," 58–59: "If the historian . . . can only reveal the truth of an event . . . by filling in and connecting the disjointed fragments of direct observation, he can do so, like the poet, only through imagination. The crucial difference, which removes all potential dangers, lies in the fact that the historian subordinates his imagination to experience and the investigation of reality. In this subordination, the imagination does not act as pure fantasy."

217. In some moods I sympathize with Vermes, *Religion of Jesus the Jew*, 7: while he follows some "guidelines," he thinks "it would be quite inappropriate . . . to attach [to them] the grandiloquent, but highly fashionable, label of *methodology*. In my opinion, research aiming to be innovative should not be bound by strict, predetermined rules. . . . Methodology, no doubt irrationally, makes me see red."

218. J. H. Newman, *Grammar of Assent*, 187.

219. Cf. Rodríguez, "Jesus as His Friends Remembered Him," 239–40.

220. Cf. Rodríguez, "Jesus as His Friends Remembered Him," 238–39.

221. Contrast Everton and Cunningham, "Quest for the Gist of Jesus," who apply semantic network analysis to the sayings of Jesus. Whether there is merit in or a future for their approach I leave to others.

Practitioners of the traditional criteria often, in my view, aspire to an exactitude we can obtain only rarely. We do better, then, to adopt a strategy that recognizes the messy nature of our materials and the difficulties that attend attempts to sort them into neat piles or clean categories.[222]

Fiction can convey facts, as in today's historical novels. In like fashion, even stories and sayings that are not, in the strict sense, historical, can preserve a decent impression of the sort of person Jesus was, his general disposition, the type of thing he was wont to do or teach. As Bultmann wrote: "Even though many of the sayings may have originated in the community, the spirit that lives in them goes back to the work of Jesus."[223] "Spirit" is of course a slippery term, yet I nonetheless agree with Bultmann. The task, then, is much more complex than uprooting the fictional weeds, binding them into bundles to be ignored, then gathering the historical wheat into our books and articles. Jesus was often remembered not in letter but in spirit.

222. Cf. Ryan, "Jesus at the Crossroads," 61: "Evidence comes in many forms, so the historian's primary task is not merely to sift traditions in order to separate 'authentic' from 'inauthentic,' but to understand the data, know what is relevant and how to apply it as evidence to the investigation and questions at hand."

223. Bultmann in Bultmann and Kundsin, *Form Criticism*, 58. The relevant German is "der Geist, der in ihnen lebendig ist." See Bultmann, *Erforschung der synoptischen Evangelien*, 31. Cf. Theissen, *New Testament*, 25: "Since Jesus himself was an itinerant preacher, the early Christian itinerant charismatics constitute a certain guarantee that his words were retained for us in his spirit [*in seinem Geist*]."

Acknowledgments

The author and publisher are grateful to E. J. Brill Publishing for kind permission to incorporate in chapter 1 portions of "Contingent Eschatology," in *The Cradle of Christianity: Judaism, Jesus, and the New Testament*, ed. Thomas B. Hatina and Stanley E. Porter (Leiden: Brill, 2024), 151–71, as well as to T&T Clark, an imprint of Bloomsbury Publishing Plc, for kind permission to incorporate in chapter 6 portions of "Did Everybody Know Everybody? The Case of Paul, Mark, and Luke," in *Cyprus within the Biblical World: Are Borders Barriers?*, ed. James H. Charlesworth and Jolyon G. Pruzinski (London: T&T Clark, 2021), 127–46.

Works Cited

Aarde, Andries van. "Jesus als Joshua, Moses en Dawidiese Messias in Matteus." *Scriptura* 84 (2003): 453–67.

Adamantius. *Der Dialog des Adamantius Peri tēs eis theon orthēs pisteōs*. Edited by W. H. van de Sande Bakhuyzen. GCS 4. Leipzig: J. C. Hinrich, 1901.

Adinolfi, Marco. "Il celibato di Gesu." *BeO* 13 (1971): 145–58.

Ådna, Jostein. *Jesu Stellung zum Tempel: Die Tempelaktion und das Tempelwort als Ausdruck seiner messianischen Sendung*. WUNT 2/119. Tübingen: Mohr Siebeck, 2000.

Akagi, Kai. "Not the Prophet Like Moses, but the One of Whom the Prophets Spoke: Deut 18:15–18 in Acts 3:22 and 7:37." *NovT* 64 (2022): 432–49.

Alba, Joseph W., and Lynn Hasher. "Is Memory Schematic?" *Psychological Bulletin* 93 (1983): 203–31.

Alexander, Elizabeth Shanks. "Ancient Jewish Gender." Pages 174–98 in *Early Judaism: New Insights and Scholarship*. Edited by Frederick E. Greenspahn. New York: New York University Press, 2018.

Alexander, Jennifer Sylvan. "Self-Made Eunuchs as Model Disciples: Matthew 19:12 in Narrative and Historical Context." Pages 89–114 in *The Theologically Formed Heart: Essays in Honor of David J. Gouwens*. Edited by Warner M. Bailey, Lee C. Barrett III, and James O. Duke. Eugene, OR: Pickwick, 2014.

Alexander, Loveday. *Acts in Its Ancient Literary Context: A Classicist Looks at the Acts of the Apostles*. LNTS 289. London: T&T Clark, 2005.

———. "Memory and Tradition in the Hellenistic Schools." Pages 113–54 in *Jesus in Memory: Traditions in Oral and Scribal Perspectives*. Edited by Werner H. Kelber and Samuel Byrskog. Waco, TX: Baylor University Press, 2009.

———. "What Is a Gospel?" Pages 13–33 in *The Cambridge Companion to the Gospels*. Edited by Stephen C. Barton. Cambridge: Cambridge University Press, 2006.

Alford, Henry. *The Greek Testament*. 4 vols. London: Rivington, 1883 (1861).

Allison, Dale C., Jr. *4 Baruch: Paraleipomena Jeremiou*. CEJL. Berlin: de Gruyter, 2019.
———. "Behind the Temptations of Jesus: Q 4:1–13 and Mark 1:12–13." Pages 195–214 in *Authenticating the Activities of Jesus*. Edited by Bruce Chilton and C. A. Evans. NTTS 28.2. Leiden: Brill, 1999.
———. *Constructing Jesus: Memory, Imagination, and History*. Grand Rapids: Baker Academic, 2010.
———. "Contingent Eschatology." Pages 151–71 in *The Cradle of Christianity: Judaism, Jesus, and the New Testament*. Edited by Thomas B. Hatina and Stanley E. Porter. Leiden: Brill, 2024.
———. "Cyprus and Early Christianity: Did Everybody Know Everybody?" Pages 127–46 in *Cyprus within the Biblical World: Are Borders Barriers?* Edited by James H. Charlesworth and Jolyon G. R. Pruszinski. Jewish and Christian Texts in Context and Related Studies 32. London: T&T Clark, 2021.
———. "Divorce, Celibacy, and Joseph (Matt. 1.18–25 and 19.1–12)." *JSNT* 49 (1993): 3–10.
———. *Encountering Mystery: Religious Experience in a Secular Age*. Grand Rapids: Eerdmans, 2022.
———. *The End of the Ages Has Come: An Early Interpretation of the Passion and Resurrection of Jesus*. Philadelphia: Fortress, 1985.
———. "How to Marginalize the Criteria of Authenticity." Pages 3–30 in vol. 1 of *The Handbook of the Study of the Historical Jesus*. Edited by Tom Holmén and Stanley E. Porter. Leiden: Brill, 2010.
———. *The Intertextual Jesus: Scripture in Q*. Harrisburg, PA: Trinity Press International, 2000.
———. "Ist die Apokalyptik die Mutter der neutestamentlichen Theologie? Eine alte Frage neu gestellt." *ZNT* 22 (2008): 46–52.
———. "It Don't Come Easy: A History of Disillusionment." Pages 173–85 in *Jesus, History, and the Demise of Authenticity: The Rise and Fall of the Search for an Authentic Jesus. Authenticity after the Third Quest*. Edited by Anthony Le Donne and Chris Keith. London: T&T Clark, 2012.
———. "Jas 2:14–26: Polemic against Paul, Apology for James." Pages 123–49 in *Ancient and New Perspectives on Paul*. Edited by Tobias Nicklas, Andreas Merkt, and Joseph Verheyden. NTOA 102. Göttingen: Vandenhoeck & Ruprecht, 2013.
———. "Jesus and the Covenant: A Response to E. P. Sanders." *JSNT* 29 (1987): 57–78.
———. "Jesus and the Victory of Apocalyptic." Pages 126–41 in *Jesus and the Resto-*

ration of Israel: A Critical Assessment of N. T. Wright's "Jesus and the Victory of God." Edited by Carey C. Newman. Downers Grove, IL: InterVarsity, 1999.

———. *Jesus of Nazareth: Millenarian Prophet*. Minneapolis: Fortress, 1998.

———. *The Jesus Tradition in Q*. Harrisburg, PA: Trinity Press International, 1997.

———. "Job in the *Testament of Abraham*." *JSP* 12 (2001): 131–47.

———. "Luke Rewriting Matthew? The Case of the Sermon on the Plain." Pages 94–122 in *Gospel Reading: Early Christian Reception and Interpretations of Jesus*. Edited by Simon Gathercole, Madison N. Pierce, and Andrew J. Byers. Oxford: Oxford University Press, 2022.

———. "Matt. 23:39 = Luke 13:35b as a Conditional Prophecy." *JSNT* 18 (1983): 75–84.

———. "Memory, Methodology, and the Historical Jesus: A Response to Richard Bauckham." *JSNT* 14 (2016): 13–27.

———. *The New Moses: A Matthean Typology*. Minneapolis: Fortress, 1993.

———. "The Paranormal Jesus." Pages 78–88 in *Super Religion*. Edited by Jeffrey J. Kripal. Farmington Hills, MI: Gale, 2016.

———. "The Pauline Epistles and the Synoptic Gospels: The Pattern of the Parallels." *NTS* 28 (1982): 1–32.

———. "Peter and Cephas: One and the Same." *JBL* 111 (1992): 489–95.

———. "Q 12.51–53 and Mk 9:11–13 and the Messianic Woes." Pages 289–310 in *Authenticating the Words of Jesus*. Edited by Bruce Chilton and C. A. Evans. NTTS 28.1. Leiden: Brill, 1998.

———. "Reflections on Matthew, John, and Jesus." Pages 47–68 in *Jesus Research: The Gospel of John and the Historical Jesus*. Edited by James H. Charlesworth and Jolyon G. R. Pruszinski. London: Bloomsbury T&T Clark, 2019.

———. "Response to Rafael Rodríguez, 'Jesus as His Friends Remembered Him: A Review of Dale Allison's *Constructing Jesus*.'" *JSNT* 12 (2015): 245–54.

———. *Resurrecting Jesus: The Earliest Christian Tradition and Its Interpreters*. London: T&T Clark, 2005.

———. *The Resurrection of Jesus: Apologetics, Polemics, History*. London: T&T Clark, 2021.

———. "Rom. 11:11–15: A Suggestion." *PRS* 12 (1985): 23–30.

———. "The Son of God as Israel: A Note on Matthean Christology." *IBS* 9 (1987): 74–81.

———. "Two Notes on a Key Text: Matt. xi.25–30." *JTS* 39 (1988): 472–80.

Allmen, Daniel von. "L'apocalyptique juive et le retard de la parousie en II Pierre 3:1–13." *RTP* 99 (1966): 255–74.

Alston, William P. "How to Think about Divine Action." Pages 51–70 in *Divine Action: Studies Inspired by the Philosophical Theology of Austin Farrer*. Edited by Brian Hebblethwaite and Edward Henderson. Edinburgh: T&T Clark, 1990.

Alvarado, Carlos S. "Observations of Luminous Phenomena around the Human Body: A Review." *Journal of the Society for Psychical Research* 54 (1987): 38–60.

Amir, Yehoshua. *Die hellenistische Gestalt des Judentums bei Philon von Alexandrien*. Forschungen zum jüdisch-christlichen Dialog 5. Neukirchen-Vluyn: Neukirchener Verlag, 1983.

Andersen, Francis I. *Habakkuk*. AB 25. New York: Doubleday, 2001.

Anderson, Gary. "Celibacy or Consummation in the Garden? Reflections on Early Jewish and Christian Interpretations of the Garden of Eden." *HTR* 82 (1989): 121–48.

Anderson, Janice Capel, and Stephen D. Moore. "Matthew and Masculinity." Pages 67–91 in *New Testament Masculinities*. Edited by Stephen D. Moore and Janice Capel Anderson. SemeiaSt 45. Atlanta: Society of Biblical Literature, 2003.

Anderson, Paul N. *The Christology of the Fourth Gospel: Its Unity and Disunity in the Light of John 6 (with a New Introduction, Outlines, and Epilogue)*. Eugene, OR: Cascade, 2010.

———. "The Having-Sent-Me Father—Aspects of Agency, Encounter, and Irony in the Johannine Father-Son Relationship." *Semeia* 85 (1999): 33–57.

Angel, Andrew W. "God Talk and Men's Talk: Jesus, Tarfon, and Ishmael in Dialogue." Pages 95–117 in *Judaism, Jewish Identities, and the Gospel Tradition: Essays in Honour of Maurice Casey*. London: Equinox, 2010.

Archer, Léonie J. *Her Price Is Beyond Rubies: The Jewish Woman in Graeco-Roman Palestine*. JSOTSup 60. Sheffield: JSOT Press, 1990.

Arnal, W. E. "Gendered Couplets in Q and Legal Formulations from Rhetoric to Social History." *JBL* 116 (1997): 75–94.

Assemani, Stefano Evodio. *Acta sanctorum martyrum orientalium et occidentalium*. 2 vols. Rome: Collini, 1748.

Asting, Ragnar. *Die Heiligkeit im Urchristentum*. FRLANT 29. Göttingen: Vandenhoeck & Ruprecht, 1930.

Atkins, J. D. *The Doubt of the Apostles and the Resurrection Faith of the Early Church*. WUNT 2/495. Tübingen: Mohr Siebeck, 2019.

Aune, David E. "Oral Tradition and the Aphorisms of Jesus." Pages 211–65 in *Jesus and the Oral Gospel Tradition*. Edited by Henry Wansbrough. JSNTSup 64. Sheffield: JSOT Press, 1991.

———. *Prophecy in Early Christianity and the Ancient Mediterranean World*. Grand Rapids: Eerdmans, 1983.

———. *Revelation 6–16*. WBC 52B. Nashville: Nelson, 1998.

Aune, David E., and Eric Stewart. "From the Idealized Past to the Imaginary Future: Eschatological Restoration in Jewish Apocalyptic Literature." Pages 147–77 in *Restoration: Old Testament, Jewish, and Christian Perspectives*. Edited by James M. Scott. JSJSup 72. Leiden: Brill, 2001.

Aus, Roger David. *Feeding the Five Thousand: Studies in the Judaic Background of Mark 6:30–44 par and John 6:1–15*. Lanham, MD: University Press of America, 2010.

———. *Matthew 1–2 and the Virginal Conception: In Light of Palestinian and Hellenistic Judaic Traditions on the Birth of Israel's First Redeemer*. Lanham, MD: University Press of America, 2004.

Awwad, Johnny B. "Traits of Women Discipleship in Luke's Gospel." *TRev* 41 (2021): 3–16.

Aynard, Laure. *La Bible au féminin: de l'ancienne tradition à un christianisme hellénisé*. LD 138. Paris: Cerf, 1990.

Backhaus, Knut, and Gerd Häfner. *Historiographie und fiktionales Erzählen: Zur Konstruktivität und Exegese*. BThSt 86. Neukirchen-Vluyn: Neukirchener, 2007.

Baddeley, Alan D. "Is the Study of Memory Unduly Preoccupied with Its Sins?" *Memory* 30.1 (2022): 55–59.

Bailey, Kenneth E. "Informal Controlled Oral Tradition and the Synoptic Gospels." *AsJT* 5 (1991): 34–54.

———. "Middle Eastern Oral Tradition and the Synoptic Gospels." *ExpTim* 106 (1995): 363–67.

Baker, Cynthia M. "Imagined Households." Pages 113–28 in *Religion and Society in Roman Palestine: Old Question, New Approaches*. Edited by Douglas R. Edwards. New York: Routledge, 2004.

———. *Rebuilding the House of Israel: Architecture of Gender in Jewish Antiquity*. Divinations: Rereading Late Ancient Religions. Stanford: Stanford University Press, 2003.

Balabanski, Vicky. *Eschatology in the Making: Mark, Matthew, and the Didache*. SNTSMS 97. Cambridge: Cambridge University Press, 1997.

Baltzer, Klaus. *Deutero Isaiah: A Commentary on Isaiah 40–55*. Hermeneia. Minneapolis: Fortress, 2001.

Barber, Michael Patrick. "Did Jesus Anticipate Suffering a Violent Death? The Implications of Memory Research and Dale C. Allison's Methodology." *JSNT* 18 (2020): 191–219.

———. *The Historical Jesus and the Temple: Memory, Methodology, and the Gospel of Matthew*. Cambridge: Cambridge University Press, 2023.

Bardy, G., ed. *Les trophées de Damas: controverse judéo-chrétienne du VIIe siècle.* PO 2/73. Turnhout: Brepols, 1973.

Barnes, Timothy D. *Athanasius and Constantine: Theology and Politics in the Constantinian Empire.* Cambridge: Harvard University Press, 1993.

———. *Early Christian Hagiography and Roman History.* 2nd ed. Tübingen: Mohr Siebeck, 2016.

Barnett, Albert E. *Paul Becomes a Literary Influence.* Chicago: University of Chicago Press, 1941.

Barnett, P. W. "The Jewish Sign Prophets—A.D. 40–70—Their Intentions and Origin." *NTS* 27 (1981): 679–97.

Barr, David L. "Jezebel and the Teachings of Balaam: Anti-Pauline Rhetoric in the Apocalypse of John." *PRS* 45 (2018): 153–65.

Barrett, C. K. "The Background of Mark 10.45." Pages 1–18 in *New Testament Essays: Studies in Memory of T. W. Manson.* Edited by A. J. B. Higgins. Manchester: Manchester University Press, 1959.

———. *A Critical and Exegetical Commentary on the Acts of the Apostles.* 2 vols. ICC. London: T&T Clark, 1994–98.

———. *The Gospel according to St. John: An Introduction with Commentary and Notes on the Greek Text.* 2nd ed. Philadelphia: Westminster, 1978.

———. *Jesus and the Gospel Tradition.* Philadelphia: Fortress, 1968.

Barrington, Mary Rose, Ian Stevenson, and Zofia Weaver. *A World in a Grain of Sand: The Clairvoyance of Stefan Ossowiecki.* Jefferson, NC: McFarland, 2005.

Barstad, Hans M. *A Way in the Wilderness: The "Second Exodus" in the Message of Second Isaiah.* JSSM 12. Manchester: University of Manchester, 1989.

Barth, Karl. *The Doctrine of Reconciliation.* Vol. 4, part 2 of *Church Dogmatics.* Translated by G. W. Bromiley. Edited by G. W. Bromiley and T. F. Torrance. Edinburgh: T&T Clark, 1958.

Bartlett, Robert. *The Natural and the Supernatural in the Middle Ages.* Cambridge: Cambridge University Press, 2008.

Bartsch, Hans Werner. *Die Auferstehungszeugnis: Sein historisches und sein theologisches Problem.* TF 41. Hamburg-Bergstedt: Reich, 1965.

Barušs, Imants, and Julia Mossbridge. *Transcendent Mind: Rethinking the Science of Consciousness.* Washington, DC: American Psychological Association, 2017.

Bashear, Suliman. "Muslim Apocalypses and the Hour: A Case-Study in Traditional Reinterpretation." *Israel Oriental Studies* 13 (1993): 75–99.

Basser, Herbert W. "The Meaning of 'Shtuth,' Gen. R. 11 in Reference to Matthew 5.29–30 and 18.8–9." *NTS* 31 (1985): 148–51.

Bauckham, Richard J. "The Delay of the Parousia." *TynBul* 31 (1980): 3–36.

———. "Eyewitnesses and Healing Miracles in the Gospel of Mark." *BibAn* 10 (2020): 341–54.
———. "For Whom Were the Gospels Written?" Pages 9–48 in *The Gospels for All Christians*. Edited by Richard Bauckham. Grand Rapids: Eerdmans, 1998.
———. "The General and the Particular in Memory: A Critique of Dale Allison's Approach to the Historical Jesus." *JSHJ* 14 (2016): 28–51.
———. "The Gospel of Mark: Origins and Eyewitnesses." Pages 145–69 in *Earliest Christian History: History, Literature, and Theology. Essays from the Tyndale Fellowship in Honor of Martin Hengel*. Edited by Michael F. Bird and Jason Maston. Tübingen: Mohr Siebeck, 2012.
———. *Gospel Women: Studies of the Named Women in the Gospels*. Grand Rapids: Eerdmans, 2002.
———. "In Response to My Respondents: Jesus and the Eyewitnesses in Review." *JSHJ* 6 (2008): 225–53.
———. "James and the Church in Jerusalem." Pages 415–80 in *The Book of Acts in Its Palestinian Setting*. Edited by Richard Bauckham. Grand Rapids: Eerdmans, 1995.
———. *Jesus and the Eyewitnesses: The Gospels as Eyewitness Testimony*. 2nd ed. Grand Rapids: Eerdmans, 2017.
———. *Jude, 2 Peter*. WBC 50. Waco, TX: Word, 1983.
———. *Jude and the Relatives of Jesus in the Early Church*. Edinburgh: T&T Clark, 1990.
———. "Kingdom and Church According to Paul and Jesus." *HBT* 18 (1996): 1–27.
———. *Magdala of Galilee: A Jewish City in the Hellenistic and Roman Period*. Waco, TX: Baylor University Press, 2018.
———. "Messianism According to the Gospel of John." Pages 34–68 in *Challenging Perspectives on the Gospel of John*. Edited by John Lierman. WUNT 2/219. Tübingen: Mohr Siebeck, 2006.
———. "The Psychology of Memory and the Study of the Gospels." *JSHJ* 16 (2018): 136–55.
———. "The Restoration of Israel in Luke-Acts." Pages 435–87 in *Restoration: Old Testament, Jewish, and Christian Perspectives*. Edited by James M. Scott. JSJSup 72. Leiden: Brill, 2001.
———. "The Two Fig Tree Parables in the Apocalypse of Peter." *JBL* 104 (1985): 269–87.
Bauer, J. B. "Drei Tage." *Bib* 39 (1958): 354–58.
Bauer, Walter. "Matth. 19,12 und die alten Christen." Pages 235–44 in *Neutestamentliche Studien: George Heinrici zu seinem 70. Geburtstag*. Leipzig: Hinrichs, 1914.

———. *Orthodoxy and Heresy in Earliest Christianity*. Philadelphia: Fortress, 1971.

Baum, Armin D. "Biographien im alttestamentlich-rabbinischen Stil: Zur Gattung der neu-testamentlichen Evangelien." *Bib* 94 (2013): 534–64.

———. "Biographies of Jesus in Old Testament and Rabbinic Style: The Genre of the New Testament Gospels." Pages 33–58 in *The Earliest Perceptions of Jesus in Context: Essays in Honour of John Nolland on His 70th Birthday*. Edited by Craig A. Evans, David Wenham, and Aaron White. LNTS 566. London: Bloomsbury, 2018.

———. *Der mündliche Faktor und seine Bedeutung für die synoptische Frage: Analogien aus der antiken Literature, der Experimentalpsychologie, der Oral Poetry-Forschung und dem rabbinischen Traditionswesen*. Tübingen: Francke, 2008.

———. "Zwischen Abschreibeverhältnis und früjüdischer Gedachtniskultur: McIvers experimentalpsychologische Kriterien zur Identifizierung eines Abschreibeverhältnisses zwischen den synoptischen Evangelien." Pages 137–72 in *Der jüdische Messias Jesus und sein jüdischer Apostel Paulus*. Edited by Armin D. Baum, Detlef Häusser, and Emmanuel L. Rehfeld. WUNT 2/425. Tübingen: Mohr Siebeck, 2016.

Beasley-Murray, G. R. *Jesus and the Kingdom of God*. Grand Rapids: Eerdmans, 1986.

Beavis, Mary Ann. "Christian Origins, Egalitarianism, and Utopia." *JFSR* 23 (2007): 27–49.

Becker, Eve-Marie. "Mark with and against Q: The Earliest Gospel Narrative as a Counter Model." Pages 151–63 in *Gospel Interpretation and the Q Hypothesis*. Edited by Mogens Müller and Heike Omerzu. LNTS 573. London: T&T Clark, 2018.

Becker, Eve-Marie, Helen K. Bond, and Catrin H. Williams, eds. *John's Transformation of Mark*. London: T&T Clark, 2021.

Becker, Jürgen. *Jesus of Nazareth*. New York: de Gruyter, 1998.

———. "The Search for Jesus' Specific Profile." Pages 57–89 in vol. 1 of *The Handbook of the Study of the Historical Jesus*. Edited by Tom Holmén and Stanley E. Porter. Leiden: Brill, 2010.

Beckwith, Roger T. *Calendar and Chronology, Jewish and Christian: Biblical, Intertestamental, and Patristic Studies*. AGJU 33. Leiden: Brill, 1996.

———. *Calendar, Chronology, and Worship: Studies in Ancient Judaism and Early Christianity*. AGJU 61. Leiden: Brill, 2005.

Bedjan, Paul. *Acta martyrum et manctorum Syriace*. 7 vols. Paris: Harrassowitz, 1890–97.

Begg, Christopher. "Josephus's Portrayal of the Disappearance of Enoch, Elijah, and Moses: Some Observations." *JBL* 109 (1990): 691–93.

Beloff, John. "Extreme Phenomena and the Problem of Credulity." Pages 328–45 in *Exploring the Paranormal: Perspectives on Belief and Practice*. Edited by G. K. Zollschan, J. F. Schumaker, and G. F. Walsh. Dorset: Prism, 1989.

Bem, D., P. Tressoldi, T. Rabeyron, and M. Duggan. "Feeling the Future: A Meta-Analysis of 90 Experiments on the Anomalous Anticipation of Random Future Events." F1000Research 4.10 (2016) 1188. https://doi.org/10.12688/f1000research.7177.2.

Ben-Amos, Dan, and Jerome R. Mintz. *In Praise of the Baal Shem Tov [Shivḥei ha-Besht]*. Bloomington: Indiana University Press, 1970.

Benedetti, Fabrizio. *Placebo Effects: Understanding the Mechanisms in Health and Disease*. 3rd ed. Oxford: Oxford University Press, 2021.

Bengel, Johann Albrecht. *Gnomon Novi Testamenti*. 2 vols. Tübingen: Ludov. Frid. Fues, 1850.

Benoit, Pierre. "'Non erat eis locus in diversorio' (Lc 2,7)." Pages 173–86 in *Mélanges bibliques en hommage au R. P. Béda Rigaux*. Edited by Albert Descamps and R. P. André Halleux. Gembloux: Duculot, 1970.

Bentzen, Aage. *King and Messiah*. London: Lutterworth, 1955.

Benz, Ernst. *Die Vision: Erfahrungsformen und Bilderwelt*. Stuttgart: Klett, 1969.

Berger, Klaus. *Formgeschichte des Neuen Testaments*. Heidelberg: Quelle & Meyer, 1984.

Bermejo-Rubio, Fernando. "Changing Methods, Disturbing Material: Should the Criterion of Embarrassment Be Dismissed in Jesus Research?" *REJ* 175 (2016): 1–15.

Bernabé, Carmen. "Of Eunuchs and Predators: Matthew 19:1–12 in a Cultural Context." *BTB* 33 (2003): 128–34.

Bernier, Jonathan. *The Quest for the Historical Jesus after the Demise of Authenticity: Toward a Critical Realist Philosophy of History in Jesus Studies*. LNTS 540. London: Bloomsbury, 2016.

Bernstein, Moshe J. "'The Employment and Interpretation of Scripture in 4QMMT: Preliminary Observations." Pages 29–51 in *Reading 4QMMT: New Perspectives on Qumran Law and History*. Edited by John Kampen and Moshe J. Bernstein. SymS 2. Atlanta: Scholars Press, 1996.

Bertschmann, Dorothea H. "Hosting Jesus: Revisiting Luke's 'Sinful Woman' (Luke 7.36–50) as a Tale of Two Hosts." *JSNT* 40 (2017): 30–50.

Bettley, F. R. "Ichthyosis and Hypnosis." *British Medical Journal* 2 (1952): 996.

Betz, Hans Dieter. *The Sermon on the Mount: A Commentary on the Sermon on the*

Mount, Including the Sermon on the Plain (Matthew 5:3–7:27 and Luke 6:20–49). Hermeneia. Minneapolis: Fortress, 1995.

Betz, Otto. "Jesus and Isaiah 53." Pages 70–87 in *Jesus and the Suffering Servant: Isaiah 53 and Christian Origins*. Edited by William H. Bellinger Jr. and William R. Farmer. Harrisburg, PA: Trinity Press International, 1998.

Bieberstein, Sabine. *Verschwiegene Jüngerinnen—vergessene Zeuginnen: Gebrochene Konzepte im Lukasevangelium*. NTOA 38. Freiburg: Universitätsverlag, 1998.

Bieler, Ludwig. *ΘΕΙΟΣ ΑΝΗΡ: Das Bild des "göttlichen Menschen" in Spätantike und Frühchristentum*. Vienna: Höfels, 1935.

Bilde, Per. *The Originality of Jesus: A Critical Discussion and a Comparative Attempt*. Studia Aarhusiana Neotestamentica 1. Göttingen: Vandenhoeck & Ruprecht, 2013.

Bird, Michael F. "Mark: Interpreter of Peter and Disciple of Paul." Pages 30–61 in *Paul and the Gospels: Christologies, Conflicts, and Convergences*. Edited by Michael F. Bird and Joel Willitts. LNTS 411. London: T&T Clark, 2011.

———. "Mission as an Apocalyptic Event: Reflections on Luke 10:8 and Mark 13:10." *EvQ* 76 (2004): 117–34.

Black, C. Clifton. *The Lord's Prayer*. Louisville: Westminster John Knox, 2018.

———. *Mark*. Abingdon New Testament Commentary. Nashville: Abingdon, 2011.

Blackburn, Barry L. "The Miracles of Jesus." Pages 353–94 in *Studying the Historical Jesus: Evaluations of the Current State of Research*. Edited by Bruce Chilton and Craig A. Evans. NTTS 19. Leiden: Brill, 1994.

Blenkinsopp, Joseph. *Isaiah 40–55*. AB 19A. New Haven: Yale University Press, 2002.

Blinzler, Josef. "Εἰσὶν εὐνοῦχοι: Zur Auslegung von Mt 19 12." *ZNW* 48 (1957): 254–70.

———. "Justinus Apol. i 15,4 und Matthäus 19,11–12." Pages 45–55 in *Mélanges bibliques en hommage au R. P. Béda Rigaux*. Edited by Albert M. Descamps and André de Halleux. Gembloux: Duculot, 1970.

Blomberg, Craig L. *Interpreting the Parables*. Downers Grove, IL: InterVarsity, 1990.

———. *Jesus the Purifier: John's Gospel and the Fourth Quest for the Historical Jesus*. Grand Rapids: Baker Academic, 2023.

———. Review of *A Marginal Jew* (volume 5), by John P. Meier. *JETS* 60 (2017): 859–62.

Bockmuehl, Markus. "Resurrection." Pages 102–20 in *The Cambridge Companion to Jesus*. Edited by Markus Bockmuehl. Cambridge: Cambridge University Press, 2001.

———. *Seeing the Word: Refocusing New Testament Study*. Grand Rapids: Baker Academic, 2006.

———. *This Jesus: Martyr, Lord, Messiah*. Downers Grove, IL: InterVarsity, 1994.

Boero, Dina. "The Context of Production of the Vatican Manuscript of the Syriac Life of Symeon the Stylite." *Hugoye: Journal of Syriac Studies* 18 (2015): 319–59.

Böhlemann, Peter. *Jesus und der Täufer: Schlüssel zur Theologie und Ethik des Lukas*. SNTSMS 99. Cambridge: Cambridge University Press, 1997.

Boissarie, P. G. *Healing at Lourdes*. Baltimore: John Murphy, 1933.

Bonaventure. *Commentary on the Gospel of Luke Chapters 1–8*. Saint Bonaventure, NY: Franciscan Institute, 2001.

Bond, Helen. "Was Peter behind Mark's Gospel?" Pages 46–61 in *Peter in Early Christianity*. Edited by Helen K. Bond and Larry W. Hurtado. Grand Rapids: Eerdmans, 2015.

Bonhoeffer, Dietrich. *The Cost of Discipleship*. Rev. ed. New York: Macmillan, 1963.

Borg, Marcus. *Conflict, Holiness, and Politics in the Teaching of Jesus*. New York: Mellen, 1984.

Borgen, Peder. *The Gospel of John: More Light from Philo, Paul, and Archaeology. The Scriptures, Tradition, Exposition, Settings, Meaning*. NovTSup 154. Leiden: Brill, 2014.

Bornkamm, Günther. "Die Verzögerung der Parusie: Exegetische Bemerkungen zu zwei synoptischen Texten." Pages 46–55 in *Geschichte und Glaube I*. Munich: Kaiser, 1968.

———. *Jesus of Nazareth*. New York: Harper & Row, 1960.

Boucher, Madeleine. *The Mysterious Parable: A Literary Study*. CBQMS 6. Washington, DC: Catholic Biblical Association of America, 1977.

Bousset, Wilhelm. *Kyrios Christos: A History of the Belief in Christ from the Beginnings of Christianity to Irenaeus*. Nashville: Abingdon, 1970.

Bovon, François. "Apocalyptic Traditions in the Lukan Special Material: Reading Luke 18:1–8." *HTR* 90 (1997): 383–91.

———. *Luke: A Commentary*. 3 vols. Hermeneia. Minneapolis: Fortress, 2002–12.

Box, G. H. *The Apocalypse of Abraham*. Translations of Early Documents. London: SPCK, 1919.

Braaten, Carl, and Roy A. Harrisville, eds. *Kerygma and History*. Nashville: Abingdon, 1962.

Bradford, Timothy P. "Born Eunuch: Recovering an Ancient Metaphor." Pages 101–21 in *The Future of Gospels and Acts Research*. Edited by Peter G. Bolt. Macquarie Centre, NSW: SCD, 2021.

Brasier, Susan. "Women on the Move with Jesus." Pages 97–109 in *Feminist Interpretations of Biblical Literature*. Edited by Lilly Nortjé-Meyer. Cambridge: Cambridge Scholars, 2022.

Braude, Stephen E. *Crimes of Reason: On Mind, Nature, and the Paranormal*. Lanham, MD: Rowman & Littlefield, 2014.

Bregman, Marc. "Pseudepigraphy in Rabbinic Literature." Pages 27–41 in *Pseudepigraphic Perspectives: The Apocrypha and Pseudepigrapha in Light of the Dead Sea Scrolls*. Edited by Esther G. Chazon, Michael Stone, and Avital Pinnick. STDJ 31. Leiden: Brill, 1999.

Brenner, Athalya, ed. *Feminist Companion to the Hebrew Bible in the New Testament*. Sheffield: Sheffield Academic, 1996.

Breytenbach, Cilliers. "The Gospel according to Mark: The Yardstick for Comparing the Gospels with Ancient Texts." Pages 179–200 in *Modern and Ancient Literary Criticism of the Gospels: Continuing the Debate on Gospel Genre(s)*. Edited by Robert Matthew Calhoun, David P. Moessner, and Tobias Nicklas. WUNT 451. Tübingen: Mohr Siebeck, 2020.

Brooten, Bernadette. *Women Leaders in the Ancient Synagogue: Inscriptional Evidence and Background Issues*. BJS 36. Chico, CA: Scholars Press, 1982.

Brown, Cheryl Anne. *No Longer Be Silent: First Century Jewish Portraits of Biblical Women*. Louisville: Westminster John Knox, 1992.

Brown, Colin, with Craig A. Evans. *A History of the Quest for Jesus*, vol. 2: *From the Post-War Era through Contemporary Debates*. Grand Rapids: Zondervan Academic, 2022.

Brown, Derren. "Miracles for Sale." April 28, 2011. YouTube video, 1:13:09. https://www.youtube.com/watch?v=iuP5uOI7Xwc.

Brown, Jonathan A. C. "Faithful Dissenters: Sunni Skepticism about the Miracles of Saints." *Journal of Sufi Studies* 1 (2012): 123–68.

Brown, Raymond E. *An Introduction to the New Testament*. New York: Doubleday, 1993.

———. *Jesus: God and Man: Modern Biblical Reflections*. New York: Macmillan, 1967.

———. "Jesus and Elisha." *Perspective* 12 (1971): 85–99.

Bruce, Alexander Balmain. "The Synoptic Gospels." Pages 3–651 in vol. 1 of *The Expositors Greek Testament*. Edited by W. Robertson Nicoll. New York: Doran, n.d.

Bruce, F. F. "The Speeches in Acts—Thirty Years Later." Pages 53–68 in *Reconciliation and Hope: New Testament Essays on Atonement and Eschatology Presented to L. L. Morris on His 60th Birthday*. Edited by Robert Banks. Grand Rapids: Eerdmans, 1974.

Bryan, Steven M. *Jesus and Israel's Traditions of Judgement and Restoration*. SNTSMS 117. Cambridge: Cambridge University Press, 2002.

———. Review of *A Marginal Jew* (volume 3), by John P. Meier. *JTS* 53 (2002): 615–23.

Büchler, Adolph. *Types of Jewish-Palestinian Piety from 70 BCE to 70 CE: The Ancient Pious Men*. London: Milford, 1922.

Bulgakov, Sergius. *Relics and Miracles: Two Theological Essays*. Grand Rapids: Eerdmans, 2011.

Bullard, Colin Blake. *Jesus and the Thoughts of Many Hearts: Implicit Christology and Jesus' Knowledge in the Gospel of Luke*. LNTS 530. London: Bloomsbury T&T Clark, 2015.

Bultmann, Rudolf. *Die Erforschung der synoptischen Evangelien*. Giessen: Töpelmann, 1925.

———. *Faith and Understanding*. New York: Harper & Row, 1969.

———. *Glauben und Verstehen: Gesammelte Aufsätze*. Vol. 1. Tübingen: Mohr Siebeck, 1961.

———. *The Gospel of John: A Commentary*. Philadelphia: Westminster, 1971.

———. *History of the Synoptic Tradition*. Rev. ed. New York: Harper & Row, 1963.

———. *Jesus and the Word*. New York: Scribner's Sons, 1934.

———. *Jesus Christ and Mythology*. New York: Scribner's Sons, 1958.

———. *Theology of the New Testament*. 2 vols. New York: Scribner's Sons, 1951–55.

Bultmann, Rudolf, and K. Kundsin. *Form Criticism: Two Essays on New Testament Research*. New York: Harper & Row, 1962.

Burkitt, F. Crawford. *Christian Beginnings: Three Lectures*. London: University of London Press, 1924.

———. *The Gospel History and Its Transmission*. Edinburgh: T&T Clark, 1911.

Burridge, Richard A. *What Are the Gospels? A Comparison with Graeco-Roman Biography*. Waco, TX: Baylor University Press, 2018.

Busse, Ulrich. *Das Nazareth-Manifest: Eine Einführung in das lukanischen Jesusbild nach Lk 4,16–30*. SBS 91. Stuttgart: Katholisches Bibelwerk, 1978.

Butler, Joseph. *The Analogy of Religion*. New York: Ungar, 1961 (1736).

Butticaz, S., and D. Marguerat. "Le figure de Moïse en Actes 7." Pages 223–47 in *Le construction de la figure de Moïse*. Edited by T. Römer. Paris: Gabalda, 2007.

Byrskog, Samuel. "The Eyewitnesses as Interpreters of the Past: Reflections on Richard Bauckham's *Jesus and the Eyewitnesses*." *JSHJ* 6 (2008): 157–68.

———. *Story as History—History as Story: The Gospel Tradition in the Context of Ancient Oral History*. WUNT 123. Tübingen: Mohr Siebeck, 2000.

Cacciari, P. T. *Della Vita, virtù, e doni sopranaturali del V. Angelo Paoli Carmelitano*. Rome: Collini, 1756.

Caciola, Nancy. *Discerning Spirits: Divine and Demonic Possession in the Middle Ages*. Ithaca, NY: Cornell University Press, 2003.

Cadbury, Henry J. *The Making of Luke-Acts*. 2nd ed. London: SPCK, 1958.
Cadoux, A. T. *Essays in Christian Thinking*. New York: Doran/Swarthmore, 1922.
Cadoux, C. J. *The Historic Mission of Jesus: A Constructive Re-Examination of the Eschatological Teaching in the Synoptic Gospels*. New York: Harper & Brothers, n.d.
Caird, George B. *The Language and Imagery of the Bible*. Philadelphia: Westminster, 1980.
Calhoun, Robert Matthew, David P. Moessner, and Tobias Nicklas, eds. *Modern and Ancient Literary Criticism of the Gospels: Continuing the Debate on Gospel Genre(s)*. WUNT 451. Tübingen: Mohr Siebeck, 2020.
Calmet, Augustin. *Commentarium literale in omnes ac singulos tum Veteris cum Novi Testamenti libros*. Vol. 7. N. P.: Augustae Vindelicorum & Graecii, 1735.
Calvin, John. *A Harmony of the Gospels Matthew, Mark, and Luke*. Vol. 2. Grand Rapids: Eerdmans, 1972.
———. *Institutes of the Christian Religion*. Translated by F. L. Battles. Edited by J. T. McNeill. 2 vols. Philadelphia: Westminster, 1960.
Canivet, Pierre. *Le Monachisme syrien selon Théodoret de Cyr*. ThH 42. Paris: Beauchesne, 1977.
Capps, Donald. *Jesus the Village Psychiatrist*. Louisville: Westminster John Knox, 2007.
Cardeña, Etzel, Steven Jay Lynn, and Stanley Krippner, eds. *The Varieties of Anomalous Experience: Examining the Scientific Evidence*. Washington, DC: American Psychological Association, 2000.
Carey, Greg. *Sinners: Jesus and His Earliest Followers*. Waco, TX: Baylor University Press, 2009.
Carey, Holly J. *Women Who Do: Female Disciples in the Gospels*. Grand Rapids: Eerdmans, 2023.
Carlebach, Elisheva. "Two Amens That Delayed the Redemption: Jewish Messianism and Popular Spirituality in the Post-Sabbatian Century." *JQR* 82 (1992): 241–61.
Carlson, David C. "Vengeance and Angelic Mediation in *Testament of Moses* 9 and 10." *JBL* 101 (1982): 85–95.
Carmignac, Jean. *Recherches sur le "Notre Père."* Paris: Letouzey & Ané, 1969.
Carnley, Peter. *The Structure of Resurrection Belief*. Oxford: Clarendon, 1987.
Carrel, Alexis. *The Voyage to Lourdes*. Fraser, MI: Real-View-Books, 1994.
Carroll, John T. *Response to the End of History: Eschatology and Situation in Luke-Acts*. SBLDS 92. Atlanta: Scholars Press, 1988.
Carroll, John W. "Laws of Nature." *Stanford Encyclopedia of Philosophy*. November 16, 2020. https://plato.stanford.edu/entries/laws-of-nature/.

Carroll, Robert P. *When Prophecy Failed: Cognitive Dissonance in the Prophetic Traditions of the Old Testament*. New York: Seabury, 1979.
Carter, Warren. *Matthew and the Margins: A Sociopolitical and Religious Reading*. Maryknoll, NY: Orbis Books, 2000.
Carver, Daniel E. "Biblical Prophecy in Its Ancient Near Eastern Context: A New Interpretation of Jeremiah 30–33." *JBL* 142 (2023): 267–87.
Caseau, Béatrice. "Syméon l' Ancien entre puanteur et parfum." *Revue des êtudes byzantines* 63 (2005): 71–96.
Casey, Maurice P. *Aramaic Sources of Mark's Gospel*. SNTSMS 102. Cambridge: Cambridge University Press, 1999.
———. *Jesus: Evidence and Argument or Mythicist Myths?* London: Bloomsbury, 2014.
———. *Jesus of Nazareth: An Independent Historian's Account of His Life and Teaching*. London: T&T Clark, 2010.
Castro, Madeleine, Roger Burrows, and Robin Wooffitt. "The Paranormal Is (Still) Normal: The Sociological Implications of a Survey of Paranormal Experiences in Great Britain." *Sociological Research Online* 19 (2014): 30–44.
Catchpole, David R. *Jesus People: The Historical Jesus and the Beginnings of Community*. Grand Rapids: Baker Academic, 2006.
———. "On Proving Too Much: Critical Hesitations about Richard Bauckham's *Jesus and the Eyewitnesses*." *JSHJ* 6 (2008): 169–81.
———. "The Question of Q." *STRev* 36 (1992): 3–44.
———. "The Son of Man's Search for Faith (Luke xviii 8b)." *NovT* 19 (1977): 81–104.
Chafer, Lewis Sperry. *The Kingdom in History and Prophecy*. New York: Revell, 1915.
Charles, R. H., ed. *Pseudepigrapha*. Vol. 2 of *The Apocrypha and Pseudepigrapha of the Old Testament in English*. Oxford: Clarendon, 1913.
Charlesworth, James H. *The Beloved Disciple: Whose Witness Validates the Gospel of John?* Valley Forge, PA: Trinity Press International, 1995.
———, ed. *The Old Testament Pseudepigrapha*. 2 vols. Garden City, NY: Doubleday, 1983–85.
Chavasse, Claude. "Jesus: Christ and Moses—I." *Theology* 54 (1951): 244–50.
Chesterton, G. K. "Miracles and Modern Civilisation." Pages 386–89 in *Heretics, Orthodoxy, the Blatchford Controversies*. Vol. 1 of *The Collected Works of G. K. Chesterton*. San Francisco: Ignatius, 1986.
———. *Orthodoxy*. Garden City, NY: Image, 1959.
Chilton, Bruce D. *A Galilean Rabbi and His Bible: Jesus' Use of the Interpreted Scripture of His Time*. Good News Studies 8. Wilmington, DE: Glazier, 1984.
———. "Jesus and the Repentance of E. P. Sanders." *TynBul* 39 (1988): 1–18.
Coats, George W. *The Moses Tradition*. JSOTSup 161. Sheffield: JSOT, 1993.

Cohick, Lynn H. *Women in the World of the Earliest Christians: Illuminating Ancient Ways of Life*. Grand Rapids: Baker Academic, 2009.

Collins, John J. *The Apocalyptic Imagination: An Introduction to Jewish Apocalyptic Literature*. 3rd ed. Grand Rapids: Eerdmans, 2016.

———. *Daniel: A Commentary on the Book of Daniel*. Hermeneia. Minneapolis: Fortress, 1993.

———. "The Expectation of the End in the Dead Sea Scrolls." Pages 74–90 in *Eschatology, Messianism, and the Dead Sea Scrolls*. Edited by Craig A. Evans and Peter W. Flint. Grand Rapids: Eerdmans, 1997.

———. "'He Shall Not Judge by What His Eyes See': Messianic Authority in the Dead Sea Scrolls." *DSD* 2 (1995): 145–64.

———. "Jesus and the Messiahs of Israel." Pages 287–302 in vol. 1 of *Geschichte—Tradition—Reflexion: Festschrift für Martin Hengel*. Edited by H. Cancik, H. Lichtenberger, and P. Schäfer. Tübingen: Mohr Siebeck, 1996.

———. "Marriage, Divorce, and Family in Second Temple Judaism." Pages 104–62 in *Families in Ancient Israel*. Edited by Leo G. Purdue. Louisville: Westminster John Knox, 1997.

———. *The Scepter and the Star: Messianism in Light of the Dead Sea Scrolls*. 2nd ed. Grand Rapids: Eerdmans, 2010.

Collins, Raymond F. *Accompanied by a Believing Wife: Ministry and Celibacy in the Earliest Christian Communities*. Collegeville, MN: Liturgical Press, 2013.

———. *Divorce in the New Testament*. Collegeville, MN: Liturgical Press, 1992.

———. *Sexual Ethics and the New Testament: Behavior and Belief*. New York: Herder & Herder, 2000.

Colwell, Ernest C. *An Approach to the Teaching of Jesus*. Nashville: Abingdon, 1947.

Committee on Scientific Approaches to Understanding and Maximizing the Validity and Reliability of Eyewitness Identification in Law Enforcement and the Courts, National Research Council of the National Academies. *Identifying the Culprit: Assessing Eyewitness Identification*. Washington, DC: National Academic Press, 2014.

Conway, Colleen. *Behold the Man: Jesus and Greco-Roman Masculinity*. Oxford: Oxford University Press, 2008.

Conzelmann, Hans. *Jesus*. Philadelphia: Fortress, 1973.

Cook, David. "The Beginnings of Islam as an Apocalyptic Movement." Pages 79–94 in *War in Heaven/Heaven on Earth: Theories of the Apocalyptic*. Edited by Stephen D. O'Leary and Glen S. McGhee. London: Equinox, 2005.

Corely, Kathleen E. *Maranatha: Women's Funerary Rituals and Christian Origins*. Minneapolis: Fortress, 2010.

———. *Private Women, Public Meals*. Peabody, MA: Hendrickson, 1993.

———. "Prostitute." Page 643 in *Dictionary of Jesus and the Gospels*. Edited by

Joel B. Green, Scot McKnight, and I. Howard Marshall. Downers Grove, IL: InterVarsity, 1992.

———. "Were the Women around Jesus Really Prostitutes? Women in the Context of Greco-Roman Meals." Pages 487–521 in *Society of Biblical Literature 1989 Seminar Papers*. Edited by David J. Lull. Atlanta: Scholars Press, 1989.

———. *Women and the Historical Jesus: Feminist Myths of Christian Origins*. Santa Rosa, CA: Polebridge, 2002.

Corliss, W. R. *Rare Halos, Mirages, Anomalous Rainbows, and Related Electromagnetic Phenomena*. Glen Arm, MD: Sourcebook Project, 1984.

Crabbe, Kylie. *Luke/Acts and the End of History*. BZNW 238. Berlin: de Gruyter, 2019.

Craffert, Pieter F. *The Life of a Galilean Shaman: Jesus of Nazareth in Anthropological-Historical Perspective*. Eugene, OR: Cascade, 2008.

Cranfield, C. E. B. *The Gospel according to St Mark*. Rev. ed. CGTC. Cambridge: Cambridge University Press, 1977.

Cribiore, Raffaella. *Gymnastics of the Mind*. Princeton: Princeton University Press, 2005.

Crook, Zeba R. "Collective Memory Distortion and the Quest for the Historical Jesus." *JSHJ* 11 (2013): 57–76.

———. "On the Treatment of Miracles in New Testament Scholarship." *SR* 40 (2011): 461–78.

Crossan, John Dominic. *The Birth of Christianity: Discovering What Happened in the Years Immediately After the Execution of Jesus*. San Francisco: HarperSanFrancisco, 1998.

———. *The Historical Jesus: The Life of a Mediterranean Jewish Peasant*. San Francisco: HarperSanFrancisco, 1991.

———. "Jesus and the Kingdom: Itinerants and Householders in Earliest Christianity." Pages 21–53 in *Jesus at 2000*. Edited by Marcus Borg. Boulder, CO: Westview, 1997.

Crossley, James G. *Jesus and the Chaos of History*. Oxford: Oxford University Press, 2015.

———. "Mark, Paul, and the Question of Influences." Pages 10–29 in *Paul and the Gospels: Christologies, Conflicts and Convergences*. Edited by Michael F. Bird and Joel Willitts. LNTS 411. London: T&T Clark, 2011.

———. "The Nature Miracles as Pure Myth." Pages 66–85 in *The Nature Miracles of Jesus: Problems, Perspectives, and Prospects*. Edited by Graham H. Twelftree. Eugene, OR: Cascade, 2017.

———. "The Semitic Background to Repentance in the Teaching of John the Baptist and Jesus." *JSHJ* 2 (2004): 138–57.

Crossley, James, and Robert J. Myles. *Jesus: A Life in Class Conflict*. Winchester, UK: Zero, 2023.

Cullmann, Oscar. "Eschatology and Missions in the New Testament." Pages 409–21 in *The Background of the New Testament and Its Eschatology: Studies in Honor of Charles Harold Dodd*. Edited by W. D. Davies and D. Daube. Cambridge: Cambridge University Press, 1954.

———. *Salvation in History*. London: SCM. 1967.

Culpepper, R. Alan. *The Johannine School: An Evaluation of the Johannine School Hypothesis Based on an Investigation of the Nature of Ancient Schools*. SBLDS 26. Missoula, MT: Scholars Press, 1974.

———. *Matthew: A Commentary*. NTL. Louisville: Westminster John Knox, 2021.

Curkpatrick, Stephen. "Dissonance in Luke 18:1–8." *JBL* 121 (2002): 107–21.

Dabeck, Paul. "'Siehe, es erscheinen Moses und Elias' (Matt 17,3)." *Bib* 23 (1942): 175–89.

Dahl, Nils Alstrup. *The Crucified Messiah and Other Essays*. Minneapolis: Augsburg, 1974.

———. *Jesus in the Memory of the Early Church*. Minneapolis: Augsburg, 1976.

Damgaard, Finn. "Propaganda against Propaganda: Revisiting Eusebius' Use of the Figure of Moses in the Life of Constantine." Pages 115–32 in *Eusebius of Caesarea: Tradition and Innovation*. Edited by Aaron Johnson and Jeremy Schott. Hellenic Studies Series 60. Washington, DC: Center for Hellenic Studies, 2013.

———. *Recasting Moses: The Memory of Moses in Biographical and Autobiographical Narratives in Ancient Judaism and 4th-Century Christianity*. Early Christianity in the Context of Antiquity 13. Frankfurt am Main: Lang, 2013.

D'Angelo, Mary Rose. "Women Partners in the New Testament." *JFSR* 6 (1990): 65–86.

Daniélou, Jean. *From Shadows to Reality: Studies in the Biblical Typology of the Fathers*. London: Burns & Oates, 1960.

Daston, Lorraine. "Marvelous Facts and Miraculous Evidence in Early Modern Europe." *Critical Inquiry* 18 (1991): 93–124.

Daube, David. "Typology in Josephus." *JJS* 31 (1980): 18–36.

Davies, Stevan L. *Jesus the Healer: Possession, Trance, and the Origins of Christianity*. New York: Continuum, 1995.

Davies, W. D. *Christian Engagements with Judaism*. Harrisburg, PA: Trinity Press International, 1999.

———. *Christian Origins and Judaism*. Philadelphia: Westminster, 1962.

———. *Paul and Rabbinic Judaism: Some Rabbinic Elements in Pauline Theology*. Rev. ed. New York: Harper & Row, 1967.

Davies, W. D., and Dale C. Allison Jr. *A Critical and Exegetical Commentary on the Gospel according to Saint Matthew*. 3 vols. ICC. Edinburgh: T&T Clark, 1988–97.

Davis, David Brion. "Some Themes of Counter-Subversion: An Analysis of Anti-

Masonic, Anti-Catholic, and Anti-Mormon Literature." *Mississippi Valley Historical Review* 47 (1960): 216–21.

Dawkins, Richard. *The Magic of Reality: How We Know What's Really There*. New York: Free Press, 2011.

De Boer, Esther A. "The Lukan Mary Magdalene and the Other Women Following Jesus." Pages 140–60 in *A Feminist Companion to Luke*. Edited by Amy-Jill Levine with Marianne Blickenstaff. London: Sheffield Academic, 2002.

DeConick, April D. "Human Memory and the Sayings of Jesus: Contemporary Experimental Exercises in the Transmission of the Jesus Tradition." Pages 135–79 in *Jesus, the Voice, and the Text*. Edited by Tom Thatcher. Waco, TX: Baylor University Press, 2008.

———. *The Original Gospel of Thomas in Translation with a Commentary and New English Translation of the Complete Gospel*. LNTS 287. London: T&T Clark, 2006.

Delehaye, Hippolyte. *The Legends of the Saints: An Introduction to Hagiography*. London: Longmans, Green, 1907.

———. *Les saints stylites*. Subsidia Hagiographica 14. Brussels/Paris: Société des Bollandistes/Picard, 1923.

———. "Saint Martin et Sulpice Sévère." *Analecta Bollandiana* 38 (1920): 5–135.

Delling, Gerhard. "Das Gleichnis vom gottlosen Richter." *ZNW* 53 (1962): 1–25.

Deming, Will. "Mark 9.42–10.12, Matthew 5.27–32, and b. Nid. 13b: A First Century Discussion of Male Sexuality." *NTS* 36 (1990): 130–41.

Derico, T. M. *Oral Tradition and Synoptic Verbal Agreement: Evaluating the Empirical Evidence for Literary Dependence*. Eugene, OR: Pickwick, 2016.

Destro, Adriano, and Mauro Pesce. *Encounters with Jesus: The Man in His Place and Time*. Minneapolis: Fortress, 2012.

———. "Fathers and Householders in the Jesus Movement: The Perspective of the Gospel of Luke." *BI* 11 (2003): 211–38.

———. "In and Out of the House: Changes in Women's Role from Jesus's Movement to the Early Churches." Pages 299–320 in *Gospels: Narrative and History*. Edited by Mercedes Navarro Puerto, Marinella Perroni, and Amy-Jill Levine. Bible and Women: New Testament 2. Atlanta: SBL Press, 2015.

Dewey, Joanna. "From Storytelling to Written Text: The Loss of Early Christian Women's Voices." *BTB* 26 (1996): 71–78.

Dewick, E. C. *Primitive Christian Eschatology*. Cambridge: Cambridge University Press, 1912.

Dexinger, Ferdinand. "Josephus Ant 18,85–87 und der samaritanische Taheb." Pages 49–59 in *Proceedings of the First International Congress of the Société d'études samaritaines, Tel-Aviv, April 11–13, 1988*. Edited by Abraham Tal and Moshe Florentin. Tel Aviv: Tel Aviv University, 1988.

———. "Reflections on the Relationship between Qumran and Samaritan Messianology." Pages 83–99 in *Qumran-Messianism: Studies on the Messianic Expectations in the Dead Sea Scrolls*. Edited by James H. Charlesworth, Hermann Lichtenberger, and Gerbern S. Oegema. Tübingen: Mohr Siebeck, 1998.

———. *Der Taheb: Ein "messianischer" Heilsbringer der Samaritaner.* Salzburg: Müller, 1986.

Dharamraj, Havilah. *A Prophet Like Moses? A Narrative-Theological Reading of the Elijah Stories*. Paternoster Biblical Monographs. Milton Keynes: Paternoster, 2011.

Díaz, Mar Pérez i. *Evangeli de Marc: Una relectura de les tradicions de Jesús a la llum de la teologia de Pau*. WUNT 2/521. Tübingen: Mohr Siebeck, 2020.

Dibelius, Martin. *Jesus*. Philadelphia: Westminster, 1949.

———. *The Sermon on the Mount*. New York: Scribner's Sons, 1940.

———. *Studies in the Acts of the Apostles*. London: SCM, 1956.

DiLella, Alexander A. "The Deuteronomistic Background of the Farewell Discourse in Tob 4:3–11." *CBQ* 41 (1979): 380–89.

Dingwall, Eric John. *Some Human Oddities—Studies in the Queer, Uncanny, and the Fanatical*. Secaucus, NJ: University Books, 1962.

Dinkler, Michal Beth. "What Is a Genre? Contemporary Genre Theory and the Gospels." Pages 77–96 in *Modern and Ancient Literary Criticism of the Gospels: Continuing the Debate on Gospel Genre(s)*. Edited by Robert Matthew Calhoun, David P. Moessner, and Tobias Nicklas. WUNT 451. Tübingen: Mohr Siebeck, 2020.

Dodd, C. H. *According to the Scriptures*. London: Fontana, 1965.

———. *The Apostolic Preaching and Its Developments*. Chicago: Willett, Clark, 1937.

———. *The Founder of Christianity*. London: Fontana, 1973.

———. *History and the Gospel*. New York: Scribner's Sons, 1938.

———. *The Interpretation of the Fourth Gospel*. Cambridge: Cambridge University Press, 1953.

———. *More New Testament Studies*. Grand Rapids: Eerdmans, 1968.

———. *New Testament Studies*. Manchester: Manchester University Press, 1953.

———. *The Parables of the Kingdom*. Rev. ed. New York: Scribner's Sons, 1961.

Dodds, E. R. "Supernormal Phenomena in Classical Antiquity." Pages 156–208 in Dodds, *The Ancient Concept of Progress and Other Essays*. Oxford: Clarendon, 1973.

Donfried, K. P. "The Allegory of the Ten Virgins (Mt 25.1–13) as a Summary of Matthean Theology." *JBL* 93 (1974): 415–28.

Doran, Robert. *The Lives of Simeon Stylites*. Cistercian Studies 112. Kalamazoo, MI: Cistercian, 1992.

Dorion, Louis-André. "Xenophon's Socrates." Pages 93–109 in *A Companion to Socrates*. Edited by Sara Ahbel-Rappe and Rachana Kamtekar. Malden, MA: Blackwell, 2006.

Douglas, John. *The Criterion; or, Rules by Which True Miracles Recorded in the New Testament Are Distinguished from the Spurious Miracles of Pagans and Papists*. New ed. London: Cadell & Davies, 1807.

Douglas, Sally. "Jesus' Impact on Understandings of Gender: Attending to First-Century Dialogue." Pages 155–78 in *The Impact of Jesus of Nazareth: Historical, Theological, and Pastoral Perspectives*, vol. 2: *Social and Pastoral Studies*. Edited by Peter G. Bolt and James R. Harrison. Macquarie Centre, NSW: SCD, 2021.

Drodhul, Karma. *Siddhas of Ga, Remembered by Khenpo Karthar Rinpoche*. Woodstock, NY: KTD, 2013.

Dschulnigg, Peter. *Das Markusevangelium*. ThKNT 2. Stuttgart: Kohlhammer, 2007.

Dudai, Yadin, and Micah G. Edelson. "Personal Memory: Is It Personal? Is It Memory?" *Memory Studies* 9 (2016): 275–83.

Duffin, Jacalyn. *Medical Miracles: Doctors, Saints, and Healing in the Modern World*. Oxford: Oxford University Press, 2009.

———. *Medical Saints: Cosmas and Damian in a Postmodern World*. Oxford: Oxford University Press, 2013.

Duling, Dennis C. "Paul's Aegean Network: The Strength of Strong Ties." *BTB* 43 (2013): 135–54.

Dumsday, Travis. *The Marian Apparitions at Zeitoun: An Evidential Inquiry*. Yonkers, NY: Saint Vladimir's Seminary Press, 2024.

Dunn, James D. G. "Did Jesus Attend Synagogue?" Pages 206–22 in *Jesus and Archaeology*. Edited by James H. Charlesworth. Grand Rapids: Eerdmans, 2006.

———. *Jesus and the Spirit: A Study of the Religious and Charismatic Experience of Jesus and the First Christians as Reflected in the New Testament*. Philadelphia: Westminster, 1975.

———. *Jesus Remembered*. Vol. 1 of *Christianity in the Making*. Grand Rapids: Eerdmans, 2003.

———. *The Oral Gospel Tradition*. Grand Rapids: Eerdmans, 2013.

———. *Unity and Diversity in the New Testament: An Inquiry into the Character of Earliest Christianity*. Philadelphia: Westminster, 1977.

Dupont, Jacques. *Mariage et divorce dans l'Evangile: Matthieu 19,3–12 et paralleles*. Abbaye de Saint-André: Desclee de Brouwer, 1959.

Dusenbury, David Lloyd. *I Judge No One: A Political Life of Jesus*. London: Hurst, 2022.

Dyson, Freeman. *The Scientist as Rebel*. New York: New York Review of Books, 2006.

Earman, John. *Hume's Abject Failure: The Argument against Miracles*. Oxford: Oxford University Press, 2000.

Eastmond, Antony. "Body vs. Column: The Cults of St Symeon Stylites." Pages 87–100 in *Desire and Denial in Byzantium: Papers from the Thirty-first Spring Symposium of Byzantine Studies, University of Sussex, Brighton, March 1997*. Edited by Liz James. Society for the Promotion of Byzantine Studies Publications 6. Aldershot: Ashgate, 1999.

Ebner, Martin. *Jesus von Nazaret in seiner Zeit: Sozialgeschichtliche Zugänge*. SBS 196. Stuttgart: Katholisches Bibelwerk, 2003.

Eddy, Paul Rhodes, and Gregory A. Boyd. *The Jesus Legend: A Case for the Historical Reliability of the Synoptic Jesus Tradition*. Grand Rapids: Baker Academic, 2007.

Ego, Beate. *Tobit*. Internationaler Exegetischer Kommentar zum Alten Testament. Stuttgart: Kohlhammer, 2021.

Ehrman, Bart. *Jesus before the Gospels: How the Earliest Christians Remembered, Changed, and Invented Their Stories of the Savior*. San Francisco: HarperOne, 2016.

———. *The Triumph of Christianity*. New York: Simon & Schuster, 2018.

Eire, Carlos M. N. "The Good, the Bad, and the Airborne: Levitation and the History of the Impossible in Early Modern Europe." Pages 307–23 in *Ideas and Cultural Margins in Early Modern Germany: Essays in Honor of H. C. Erik Midelfort*. Edited by Margorie Elizabeth Plummer and Robin Barnes. Farnham, VT: Ashgate, 2009.

———. "Incombustible Weber: How the Protestant Reformation Really Disenchanted the World." Pages 132–48 in *Faithful Narratives: Historians, Religion, and the Challenge of Objectivity*. Edited by Andrea Sterk and Nina Caputo. Ithaca, NY: Cornell University Press, 2014.

———. *They Flew: A History of the Impossible*. New Haven: Yale University Press, 2023.

Eisenman, Robert H. *James the Brother of Jesus: The Key to Unlocking the Secrets of Early Christianity and the Dead Sea Scrolls*. New York: Viking, 1997.

Eliade, Mircea. "Folklore as an Instrument of Knowledge." Pages 25–40 in *Mircea Eliade: A Critical Reader*. Edited by Bryan Rennie. London: Equinox, 2006.

Elliott, Mark Adam. *The Survivors of Israel: A Reconsideration of the Theology of Pre-Christian Judaism*. Grand Rapids: Eerdmans, 2000.

Elman, Yaakov. "Orality and the Redaction of the Babylonian Talmud." *Oral Tradition* 14 (1999): 52–99.

Emmet, C. W. "The Miracles of Sadhu Sundar Singh." *HibJ* 19 (1921): 308–18.

Epp, Eldon Jay. *Junia: The First Woman Apostle*. Minneapolis: Fortress, 2005.

———. "New Testament Papyrus Manuscripts and Letter Carrying in Greco-Roman Times." Pages 35–56 in *The Future of Early Christianity: Essays in Honor of Helmut Koester*. Edited by Birger A. Pearson. Minneapolis: Fortress, 1990.

Erikson, Erik H. *Childhood and Society*. New York: Norton, 1993.

Erlemann, Kurt. *Naherwartung und Parusieverzögerung im Neuen Testament*. TANZ 17. Tübingen: Francke, 1995.

Evans, Craig A. "Authenticity Criteria in Life of Jesus Research." *Christian Scholars Review* 19 (1989): 6–31.

———. "The Baptism of John in a Typological Context." Pages 45–71 in *Dimensions of Baptism: Biblical and Theological Studies*. Edited by Stanley E. Porter and Anthony R. Cross. JSNTSup 234. Sheffield: Sheffield Academic, 2002.

———. *Mark 8:27–16:20*. WBC 34B. Nashville: Nelson, 2001.

———. *Matthew*. New York: Cambridge University Press, 2012.

Evans, Donald. *Spirituality and Human Nature*. Albany: SUNY Press, 1993.

Eve, Eric. *Behind the Gospels: Understanding the Oral Tradition*. Minneapolis: Fortress, 2013.

———. "The Growth of the Nature Miracles." Pages 66–85 in *The Nature Miracles of Jesus: Problems, Perspectives, and Prospects*. Edited by Graham H. Twelftree. Eugene, OR: Cascade, 2017.

———. *The Jewish Context of Jesus' Miracles*. JSNTSup 231. Sheffield: Sheffield Academic, 2002.

———. "Meier, Miracle, and Multiple Attestation." *JSHJ* 3 (2005): 23–35.

———. *Relating the Gospels: Memory, Imitation, and the Farrer Hypothesis*. LNTS 592. London: T&T Clark, 2021.

———. *Writing the Gospels: Composition and Memory*. London: SPCK, 2016.

Everton, Sean F., and Daniel T. Cunningham. "The Quest for the Gist of Jesus, the Jesus Seminar, Dale Allison, and Improper Linear Methods." *JSHJ* 18 (2020): 156–89.

Fabisiak, Thomas. *The "Nocturnal Side of Science" in David Friedrich Strauss's "Life of Jesus Critically Examined."* Emory Studies in Early Christianity. Atlanta: SBL Press, 2015.

Fabry, Heinz-Josef. "Moses, der 'Gesalbte JHWHs': Messianische Aspekte der Mose-Interpretation in Qumran." Pages 129–43 in *Moses in Biblical and*

Extra-Biblical Traditions. Edited by Axel Graupner and Michael Wolter. BZAW 372. Berlin: de Gruyter, 2007.

Fales, Evan. "It Is Not Reasonable to Believe in Miracles." Pages 298–310 in *Debating Christian Theism*. Edited by J. P. Moreland, Chad Meister, and Khaldoun A. Sweis. Oxford: Oxford University Press, 2013.

———. *Reading Sacred Texts: Charity, Structure, Gospel*. Denver: Global Center for Religious Research, 2021.

Fander, Monika. *Die Stellung der Frau im Markusevangelium: Unter besonderer Berücksichtigung kultur- und religionsgeschichtlicher Hintergründe*. Münsteraner theologische Abhandlungen 8. Altenberge: Telos, 1989.

Farber, Zev. *Images of Joshua in the Bible and Their Reception*. BZAW 457. Berlin: de Gruyter, 2016.

Farrer, Austin. "Ministry in the New Testament." Pages 113–82 in *The Apostolic Ministry: Essays on the History and the Doctrine of Episcopacy*. Edited by Kenneth E. Kirk. London: Hodder & Stoughton, 1957.

———. *The Triple Victory: Christ's Temptation According to St. Matthew*. Cambridge, MA: Cowley, 1990.

Feldman, David. *Marital Relations, Birth Control, and Abortion in Jewish Law*. New York: Schocken, 1968.

Feldman, Louis H. *Josephus's Interpretation of the Bible*. Berkeley: University of California Press, 1998.

———. *Philo's Portrayal of Moses in the Context of Ancient Judaism*. Christianity and Judaism in Antiquity 15. Notre Dame: University of Notre Dame Press, 2007.

Ferda, Tucker S. "Crowds, Bread, and Fame: John 6.1–15 and History Revisited." *JSNT* 42 (2019): 139–61.

———. *Jesus, the Gospels, and the Galilean Crisis*. LNTS 601. London: T&T Clark, 2019.

———. *Jesus and His Promised Second Coming: Jewish Eschatology and Christian Origins*. Grand Rapids: Eerdmans, 2024.

———. "John the Baptist, Isaiah 40, and the Ingathering of the Exiles." *JSHJ* 10 (2012): 154–88.

Ferguson, Cameron Evan. "Paul's Possible Influence on the Synoptics." Pages 81–99 in *The Oxford Handbook of the Synoptic Gospels*. Edited by Stephen P. Ahearne-Kroll. Oxford: Oxford University Press, 2023.

Festugière, A. J. *Antioche païenne et chrètienne: Libanius, Chrysostome et les moines de Syrie*. Bibliothèque des Écoles françaises d'Athènes et de Rome 194. Paris: Boccard, 1959.

Fiedler, Peter. *Das Matthäusevangelium*. ThKNT 1. Stuttgart: Kohlhammer, 2006.

Fiensy, David A. *Christian Origins and the Ancient Economy*. Eugene, OR: Cascade, 2014.

Filannino, Francesco. "Making Oneself Last in the Community: Mark 9:43–7 in Its Context and Co-Text." *NTS* 69 (2023): 387–99.

Fiordalis, David V. "The Wondrous Display of Superhuman Power in the Vimalakīrtinirdeśa: Miracle or Marvel?" Pages 97–125 in *Yoga Powers: Extraordinary Capacities Attained through Meditation and Concentration*. Edited by Knut A. Jacobsen. Brill's Indological Library 37. Leiden: Brill, 2012.

Fisk, Bruce N. "*See My Tears*: A Lament for Jerusalem (Luke 13:31–35; 19:41–44)." Pages 147–78 in *The Word Leaps the Gap: Essays on Scripture and Theology in Honor of Richard Hays*. Edited by A. Katherine Grieb, C. Kavin Rowe, and J. Ross Wagner. Grand Rapids: Eerdmans, 2008.

Fitchett, W. H. *The Tale of the Great Mutiny*. New York: Scribner's Sons, 1901.

Fitzmyer, Joseph A. *First Corinthians*. AB 32. New Haven: Yale University Press, 2008.

———. *The Gospel according to Luke*. 2 vols. AB 28–28A. Garden City, NY: Doubleday, 1981–85.

———. *Luke the Theologian: Aspects of His Teaching*. New York: Paulist Press, 1989.

———. *Tobit*. CEJL. Berlin: de Gruyter, 2003.

Flammarion, Camille. *Death and Its Mystery*. 2 vols. New York, Century, 1922–23.

Fleddermann, Harry T. *Mark and Q: A Study of the Overlap Texts*. BETL 122. Leuven: Peeters, 1995.

———. *Q: A Reconstruction and Commentary*. BTS 1. Leuven: Peeters, 2005.

Fletcher-Louis, Crispin H. T. *All the Glory of Adam: Liturgical Anthropology in the Dead Sea Scrolls*. STDJ 42. Leiden: Brill, 2002.

Flew, Antony. "The Problem of Evidencing the Improbable, and the Impossible." Pages 313–27 in *Exploring the Paranormal: Perspectives on Belief and Practice*. Edited by G. K. Zollschan, J. F. Schumaker, and G. F. Walsh. Dorset: Prism, 1989.

Floyd, Michael H. "A Glimpse of the Emerging Synagogue in the Book of Baruch." Pages 25–42 in *Studies in Baruch: Composition, Literary Relations, and Reception*. Edited by Sean A. Adams. DCLS 23. Berlin: de Gruyter, 2016.

Flusin, B. "Syméon et les philologues, ou la mort du stylite." Pages 1–23 in *Les saints et leur sanctuaire à Byzance: Textes, images et monuments*. Edited by Catherine Jolivet-Lévy, Michel Kaplan, and Jean-Pierre Sodini. Paris: Publications de la Sorbonne, 1993.

Flusser, David. *The Sage from Galilee: Rediscovering Jesus' Genius*. Grand Rapids: Eerdmans, 2007.

Forbes, Chris. "The Historical Jesus." Pages 231–62 in *The Content and Setting of the Gospel Tradition*. Edited by Mark Harding and Alanna Nobbs. Grand Rapids: Eerdmans, 2010.

Force, Peter. *American Archives, Fourth Series: Containing a Documentary History of the English Colonies in North America, from the King's Message to Parliament, of March 7, 1774, to the Declaration of Independence by the United States*. Vol. 2. Washington: Clark & Force, 1839.

Foster, George Burman. *The Finality of the Christian Religion*. Chicago: University of Chicago Press, 1906.

Foster, Paul. "Paul and Matthew: Two Strands of the Early Jesus Movement with Little Sign of Connection." Pages 86–114 in *Paul and the Gospels: Christologies, Conflicts, and Convergences*. Edited by Michael F. Bird and Joel Willitts. LNTS 411. London: T&T Clark, 2011.

Fowden, Garth. "Pagan Versions of the Rain Miracle of A.D. 172." *Historia* 36 (1987): 83–95.

Fowl, Stephen E. "The Gospels and 'the Historical Jesus.'" Pages 91–111 in *The Cambridge Companion to the Gospels*. Edited by Stephen C. Barton and Todd Brewer. 2nd ed. Cambridge: Cambridge University Press, 2021.

Fox, Mark. *Spiritual Encounters with Unusual Light Phenomena: Lightforms*. Cardiff: University of Wales Press, 2008.

Fraassen, Bas C van. *Laws and Symmetry*. Oxford: Oxford University Press, 1989.

France, R. T. *The Gospel of Matthew*. NICNT. Grand Rapids: Eerdmans, 2007.

Frankemölle, Herbert. *Jahwe-Bund und Kirche Christi: Studien zur Form- und Traditionsgeschichte des "Evangeliums" nach Matthäus*. NTAbh 10.2. Münster: Aschendorff, 1974.

Frankfurter, David. *Elijah in Upper Egypt: The Apocalypse of Elijah and Early Egyptian Christianity*. Minneapolis: Fortress, 1993.

———. "Jews or Not? Reconstructing the Other in Rev 2:9 and 3:9." *HTR* 94 (2001): 403–25.

———. "Stylites and Phallobatēs: Pillar Religions in Late Antique Syria." *VC* 44 (1990): 168–98.

Frayer-Griggs, Daniel. *Saved through Fire: The Fiery Ordeal in New Testament Eschatology*. Eugene, OR: Pickwick, 2016.

Fredriksen, Paula. *Jesus of Nazareth: King of the Jews*. New York: Vintage, 1999.

———. *When Christians Were Jews: The First Generation*. New Haven: Yale University Press, 2018.

Freed, Edwin D. "The Parable of the Judge and the Widow (Luke 18.1–8)." *NTS* 33 (1987): 38–60.

Frenda, Steven J., Rebecca M. Nichols, and Elizabeth F. Loftus. "Current Issues and

Advances in Misinformation Research." *Current Directions in Psychological Science* 20 (2011): 20–23.

Frenschkowski, Marco. "Itinerant Charismatics and Travelling Artisans—Was Jesus' Travelling Lifestyle Induced by His Artisan Background?" Pages 191–222 in *The Q Hypothesis: Theological, Sociological, and Hermeneutical Issues behind the Sayings Source*. BWANT 225. Stuttgart: Kohlhammer, 2020.

Frey, Jörg. *Theology and History in the Fourth Gospel: Tradition and Narration*. Waco, TX: Baylor University Press, 2018.

Freyne, Sean. *Galilee and Gospel: Collected Essays*. WUNT 125. Tübingen: Mohr Siebeck, 2000.

Frickenschmidt, Dirk. *Evangelium als Biographie: Die vier Evangelien im Rahmen antiker Erzählkunst*. TANZ 22. Tübingen: Francke, 1997.

Fricker, Denis. *Quand Jésus parle au masculin-féminin: Étude contextuelle et exégétique d'une forme littéraire originale*. EBib 53. Paris: Gabalda, 2004.

Fried, Johannes. *Der Schleier der Erinnerung: Grundzüge einer historischen Memorik*. Munich: Beck, 2004.

Froitzheim, Franzjosef. *Christologie und Eschatologie bei Paulus*. FB 35. Würzburg: Echter-Seelsorge, 1978.

Fuller, Michael E. *The Restoration of Israel: Israel's Re-Gathering and the Fate of the Nations in Early Jewish Literature and Luke-Acts*. BZNW 138. Berlin: de Gruyter, 2007.

Fuller, Reginald H. *A Critical Introduction to the New Testament*. London: Duckworth, 1966.

———. *The Foundations of New Testament Christology*. London: Collins, 1965.

———. *Interpreting the Miracles*. Philadelphia: Westminster, 1963.

———. *The Mission and Achievement of Jesus*. SBT 12. London: SCM, 1954.

Funk, Robert. *Honest to Jesus: Jesus for a New Millennium*. New York: Macmillan, 1996.

Funk, Robert, Roy Hoover, and the Jesus Seminar. *The Five Gospels: The Search for the Authentic Words of Jesus*. New York: Macmillan, 1993.

Funk, Robert, and the Jesus Seminar. *The Acts of Jesus: The Search for the Authentic Deeds of Jesus*. San Francisco: HarperSanFrancisco, 1998.

Furlong, Dean. *The John Also Called Mark: Reception and Transformation in Christian Tradition*. WUNT 2/518. Tübingen: Mohr Siebeck, 2020.

Fusco, Vittorio. "'Point of View' and 'Implicit Reader' in Two Eschatological Texts: Lk 19,11–28; Acts 1,6–8." Pages 1687–91 in *The Four Gospels 1992: Festschrift Frans Neirynck*. Edited by F. Van Segbroeck, C. M. Tuckett, G. Van Belle, and J. Verheyden. 3 vols. BETL 100. Leuven: Peeters, 1992.

Gabbert, Fiona, Daniel Wright, Amina Memom, and Elin M. Skagerberg. "Memory Conformity between Eyewitnesses." *Court Review: The Journal of the American Judges Association* 48 (2012): 36–43.

Gager, John G. *Moses in Greco-Roman Paganism*. Nashville: Abingdon, 1972.

Gallo, David A. *Associative Illusions of Memory: False Memory Research in DRM and Related Tasks*. New York: Psychology Press, 2006.

Gardner, Rex. *Healing Miracles: A Doctor Investigates*. London: Darton, Longman & Todd, 1986.

Garland, David E. *Reading Matthew: A Literary and Theological Commentary on the First Gospel*. New York: Crossroad, 1993.

Gaston, Lloyd. *No Stone on Another: Studies in the Significance of the Fall of Jerusalem in the Synoptic Gospels*. NovTSup 23. Leiden: Brill, 1970.

Gathercole, Simon. "The Alleged Anonymity of the Canonical Gospels." *JTS* 69 (2018): 447–76.

———. *The Gospel and the Gospels: Christian Proclamation and Early Jesus Books*. Grand Rapids: Eerdmans, 2022.

Gemünden, Petra von. *Vegetationsmetaphorik im Neuen Testament und seiner Umwelt: Eine Bildfelduntersuchung*. NTOA 18. Göttingen: Vandenhoeck & Ruprecht, 1993.

Genova, Lisa. *Remember: The Science of Memory and the Art of Forgetting*. New York: Harmony, 2021.

Gerhardsson, Birger. "The Earthly Jesus in the Synoptic Parables." Pages 49–62 in *Christology, Controversy, and Community: New Testament Essays in Honour of David R. Catchpole*. Edited by David G. Horrell and Christopher M. Tucket. NovTSup 99. Leuven: Brill, 2000.

———. *Memory and Manuscript: Oral Tradition and Written Transmission in Rabbinic Judaism and Early Christianity*. ASNU 22. Uppsala: Gleerup, 1961.

———. *The Reliability of the Gospel Tradition*. Peabody, MA: Hendrickson, 2001.

———. *The Testing of God's Son (Matt 4:1–11 & Par.)*. ConBNT 2/1. Lund: Gleerup, 1966.

———. *Tradition and Transmission in Early Christianity*. ConBNT 20. Lund: Gleerup, 1964.

Gfrörer, A. F. *Das Jahrhundert des Heils*. Stuttgart: Schweizerbart, 1838.

Giambrone, Anthony. *A Quest for the Historical Christ: "Scientia Christi" and the Modern Study of Jesus*. Washington, DC: Catholic University Press of America, 2022.

Ginzberg, Louis. *Legends of the Jews*. 2 vols. Philadelphia: Jewish Publication Society, 2003.

Girgis, Ragy R. *On Satan, Demons, and Psychiatry: Exploring Mental Illness in the Bible*. Eugene, OR: Wipf & Stock, 2020.

Glasson, T. Francis. *Moses in the Fourth Gospel*. SBT 40. London: SCM, 1963.

———. *The Second Advent: The Origin of a New Testament Doctrine*. 3rd ed. London: Epworth, 1963.

Gnilka, Joachim. *Das Evangelium nach Markus (Mk 8,27–16,20)*. EKKNT 2/2. Neukirchen-Vluyn: Neukirchener, 1979.

———. *Das Matthäusevangelium: Kommentar zu Kap 1,1–13,58*. HThKNT 1/1. Freiburg: Herder, 1986.

Godet, Frédéric Louis. *Commentary on the Gospel of John: John 1–5*. Translated by Timothy Dwight. 3rd ed. New York: Funk & Wagnalls, 1890–93.

———. *A Commentary on the Gospel of St. Luke*. Translated by M. D. Cusin. 2 vols. Edinburgh: T&T Clark, 1889.

———. *Commentary on St. Paul's First Epistle to the Corinthians*. Translated by A. Cusin. 2 vols. Edinburgh: T&T Clark, 1886.

Goguel, Maurice. *The Life of Jesus*. New York: Macmillan, 1933.

Goldstone, Matthew. *The Dangerous Duty of Rebuke: Leviticus 19:17 in Early Jewish and Christian Interpretation*. JSJSup 185. Leiden: Brill, 2018.

———. "Rebuke, Lending, and Love: An Early Exegetical Tradition on Leviticus 19:17–18." *JBL* 136 (2017): 307–21.

Gollinger, Hildegard. "Frauen auf der Suche nach Jesus." Pages 319–47 in *Jesus von Nazaret—Spuren und Konturen*. Edited by Ludger Schenke. Stuttgart: Kohlhammer, 2004.

Goodacre, Mark. "Criticizing the Criterion of Multiple Attestation: The Historical Jesus and the Question of Sources." Pages 152–69 in *Jesus, History, and the Demise of Authenticity: The Rise and Fall of the Search for an Authentic Jesus. Authenticity after the Third Quest*. Edited by Anthony Le Donne and Chris Keith. London: T&T Clark, 2012.

———. *Thomas and the Gospels: The Making of an Apocryphal Text*. London: SPCK, 2012.

Goodwin, W. W. *Syntax of the Moods and Tenses of the Greek Verb*. New York: St. Martin's, 1965.

Gradwohl, R. "Drei Tage und der dritte Tag." *VT* 47 (1997): 373–78.

Graieg, David. *Resurrection Remembered: A Memory Approach to Jesus' Resurrection in First Corinthians*. London: Routledge, 2024.

Grasser, Eric. *Die Naherwartung Jesu*. SBS 61. Stuttgart: KBW, 1973.

———. *Der Problem der Parusieverzögerung in den synoptischen Evangelien und in der Apostelgeschichte*. BZNW 22. Berlin: Töpelmann, 1957.

Gray, John. *I and II Kings: A Commentary*. 2nd rev. ed. OTL. Philadelphia: Westminster, 1970.

Gray, Rebecca. *Prophetic Figures in Late Second Temple Jewish Palestine: The Evidence from Josephus*. Oxford: Oxford University Press, 1993.

Greeley, Andrew. *The Sociology of the Paranormal: A Reconnaissance*. London: Sage, 1975.

Green, Joel B. *The Gospel of Luke*. NIGTC. Grand Rapids: Eerdmans, 1997.

Greenfield, Richard P. H., and Alice-Mary Talbot, eds. *Holy Men of Mount Athos*. Dumbarton Oaks Medieval Library. Cambridge: Harvard University Press, 2016.

Gregg, Brian Han. *The Historical Jesus and the Final Judgment Sayings in Q*. WUNT 2/207. Tübingen: Mohr Siebeck, 2006.

Greig, J. C. G. "The Eschatological Ministry." Pages 109–16 in *The New Testament in Historical and Contemporary Perspective: Essays in Memory of G. H. C. MacGregor*. Edited by Hugh Anderson and William Barclay. Oxford: Blackwell, 1965.

Grelot, P. "La quatrième demande du 'Pater' et son arrière-plan sémitique." *NTS* 25 (1975): 299–314.

Grimm, Werner. *Jesu Einspruch Gegen das Offenbarungssystem Daniels (Matt 11,25–17; Luke 17,20–21)*. Vol. 1 of *Jesus und das Danielbuch*. ANTJ 6.1. Frankfurt am Main: Lang, 1984.

Grindheim, Sigurd. *God's Equal: What Can We Know about Jesus' Self-Understanding in the Synoptic Gospels?* LNTS 446. London: T&T Clark, 2011.

Grinnell, George Bird. "Account of the Northern Cheyennes concerning the Messiah Spiritualism." *Journal of American Folklore* 4 (1891): 61–69.

Grosso, Michael. *Frontiers of the Soul: Exploring Psychic Evolution*. Wheaton, IL: Quest, 1992.

———. *The Man Who Could Fly: St. Joseph of Copertino and the Mystery of Levitation*. Lanham, MD: Rowman & Littlefield, 2016.

Grotius, Hugo. *Operum Theologicarum*. Vol. 2, part 1. Amsterdam: Joannis Blaev, 1679.

Gruber, Margareta. "Gerichtskonsequenz oder Gnadenchance? (Der unfruchtbare Feigenbaum)—Lk 13,6–9." Pages 579–85 in *Kompendium des Gleichnisse Jesu*. Edited by Ruben Zimmermann. Gütersloh: Gütersloher, 2007.

Guelich, Robert A. *Mark 1–8:26*. WBC 34A. Waco, TX: Word, 1989.

Gundry, Robert H. *Mark: A Commentary on His Apology for the Cross*. Grand Rapids: Eerdmans, 1993.

———. *Matthew: A Commentary on His Handbook for a Mixed Church under Persecution*. 2nd ed. Grand Rapids: Eerdmans, 1994.

———. *The Use of the Old Testament in St. Matthew's Gospel, with Special Reference to the Messianic Hope*. NovTSup 18. Leiden: Brill, 1967.

Gurney, Edmund, Frederic W. H. Myers, and Frank Podmore. *Phantasms of the*

Living. Edited by Eleanor Mildred Sidgwick. New Hyde Park, NY: University Books, 1918.

Gustafsson, Daniel. *Aspects of Coherency in Luke's Composite Christology*. WUNT 2/567. Tübingen: Mohr Siebeck, 2022.

Haacker, Karl. *Die Apostelgeschichte*. ThKNT 5. Stuttgart: Kohlhammer, 2019.

———. *Was Jesus lehrte: Die Verkündigung Jesu—vom Vaterunser aus entfaltet*. Neukirchen-Vluyn: Neukirchener, 2010.

———. "'What Must I Do to Inherit Eternal Life?' Implicit Christology in Jesus' Sayings about Life and the Kingdom." Pages 140–53 in *Jesus Research: The First Princeton-Prague Symposium on Jesus Research, Prague 2005*. Edited by James H. Charlesworth with Brian Rhea and Petr Pokorný. Grand Rapids: Eerdmans, 2009.

Häfner, Gerd. "Das Ende der Kriterien? Jesusforschung angesichts der geschichtstheoretischen Diskussion." Pages 97–130 in Knut Backhaus and Gerd Häfner, *Historiographie und fiktionales Erzählen: Zur Konstruktivität und Exegese*. BThSt 86. Neukirchen-Vluyn: Neukirchener, 2007.

Hägerland, Tobias. "The Future of Criteria in Historical Jesus Research." *JSHJ* 13 (2015): 43–65.

———. *Jesus and the Forgiveness of Sins: An Aspect of His Prophetic Mission*. SNTSMS 150. Cambridge: Cambridge University Press, 2012.

———. "A Prophet like Elijah or According to Isaiah? Rethinking the Identity of Jesus." Pages 70–86 in *The Identity of Jesus: Nordic Voices*. Edited by Samuel Byrskog, Tom Holmén, and Matti Kankaanniemi. Tübingen: Mohr Siebeck, 2014.

Hägg, Tomas. "The Life of St Antony between Biography and Hagiography." Pages 17–34 in *Periods and Places*. Vol. 1 of *The Ashgate Research Companion to Byzantine Hagiography*. Edited by Stephanos Efthymiadis. Burlington, VT: Ashgate, 2011.

Hagner, Donald A. *Matthew 1–13*. WBC 33A. Dallas: Word, 1993.

———. *The New Testament: A Historical and Theological Introduction*. Grand Rapids: Baker Academic, 2012.

———. "A Response to John P. Meier's 'Did the Historical Jesus Prohibit All Oaths?'" *JSHJ* 6 (2008): 25–32.

Hahn, Ferdinand. *Bekenntnisbildung und Theologie in urchristlicher Zeit*. Vol. 2 of *Studien zum Neuen Testament*. Edited by Jörg Frey and Juliane Schlegel. Tübingen: Mohr Siebeck, 2006.

———. *Historical Investigation and New Testament Faith: Two Essays*. Philadelphia: Fortress, 1983.

Halperin, David J. *Sabbatai Zevi: Testimonies to a Fallen Messiah*. Oxford: Littman Library of Jewish Civilization, 2007.

Halpern-Amaru, Betsy. "Portraits of Women in Pseudo-Philo's *Biblical Antiquities*." Pages 83–106 in *"Women Like This": New Perspectives on Jewish Women in the Greco-Roman World*. Edited by Amy-Jill Levine. EJL 1. Atlanta: Scholars Press, 1991.

Hampel, Volker. *Menschensohn und historischer Jesus: Ein Rätselwort als Schlüssel zum messianischen Selbstverständnis Jesu*. Neukirchen-Vluyn: Neukirchener, 1990.

Hankoff, L. D. "Religious Healing in First-Century Christianity." *Journal of Psychohistory* 10 (1992): 387–408.

Hanneken, Todd R. *The Subversion of the Apocalypses in the Book of Jubilees*. EJL 34. Atlanta: Society of Biblical Literature, 2016.

Hansel, C. E. M. *ESP: A Scientific Evaluation*. New York: Scribner's Sons, 1966.

Hanson, Paul D. *The Dawn of Apocalyptic: The Historical and Sociological Roots of Apocalyptic Eschatology*. Rev. ed. Philadelphia: Fortress, 1975.

Haraldsson, E. *Modern Miracles: An Investigative Report on Psychic Phenomena Associated with Sathya Sai Baba*. New York: Fawcett Columbine, 1987.

Harb, Gertraud. *Die eschatologische Rede des Spruchevangeliums Q: Redaktions- und traditionsgeschichtliche Studien zu Q 17,23–37*. BTS 19. Leuven: Peeters, 2014.

Harmansa, H.-Konrad. *Die Zeit der Entscheidung: Lk 13,1–9 als Beispiel für das lukanischen Verständnis der Gerichtspredigt Jesu an Israel*. ETS 69. Leipzig: Benno, 1995.

Harmless, William. *Desert Christians: An Introduction to the Literature of Early Monasticism*. Oxford: Oxford University Press, 2004.

Harnack, Adolf von. *Christianity and History*. London: Black, 1896.

———. *What Is Christianity?* New York: Harper & Brothers, 1957.

Harrington, Daniel J. *The Gospel of Matthew*. SP 1. Collegeville, MN: Liturgical, 1991.

Harris, Celia B., Helen M. Paterson, and Richard I. Kemp. "Collaborative Recall and Collective Memory: What Happens When We Remember Together?" *Memory* 16 (2008): 213–30.

Harris, Celia B., Paul G. Keil, John Sutton, and Amanda J. Barnier. "Collaborative Remembering: When Can Remembering with Others Be Beneficial?" *ASCS09: Proceedings of the 9th Conference of the Australasian Society for Cognitive Science*. file:///C:/Users/DALEAL~1.PTS/AppData/Local/Temp/Collaborative_remembering_when_can_remembering_wit-1.pdf.

Harris, Celia B., John Sutton, and Amanda J. Barnier. "Autobiographical Forgetting, Social Forgetting, and Situated Forgetting." Pages 253–84 in *Forgetting*. Edited by Sergio Della Sala. Current Issues in Memory. New York: Psychology Press, 2010.

Harrison, John. "Synoptic Gospels as Evidence of Jesus Remembered by Eyewitnesses." Pages 104–21 in *Jesus and Christian Origins: Directions Toward a New Paradigm*. Edited by Ben Wiebe. Eugene, OR: Cascade, 2019.

Harvey, A. E. *Eunuchs for the Sake of the Kingdom*. London: University of London Press, 1995.

———. *Jesus and the Constraints of History*. Philadelphia: Westminster, 1982.

Harvey, S. Ashbrook. "Homily on Simeon Stylite." Pages 15–25 in *Ascetic Behavior in Greco-Roman Antiquity: A Sourcebook*. Edited by Vincent L. Wimbush. Minneapolis: Fortress, 1990.

———. "The Sense of a Stylite: Perspectives on Simeon the Elder." *VC* 42 (1988): 376–94.

———. "The Stylite's Liturgy: Ritual and Religious Identity in Late Antiquity." *JECS* 6 (1998): 523–39.

Harvey, Van A. *The Historian and the Believer: The Morality of Historical Knowledge and Christian Belief*. Urbana: University of Illinois Press, 1996.

Hastorf, Albert H., and Hadley Cantril. "They Saw a Game: A Case Study." *Journal of Abnormal and Social Psychology* 49 (1954): 129–34.

Havukainen, Tuomas. *The Quest for the Memory of Jesus: A Viable Path or a Dead End?* Leuven: Peeters, 2020.

Haynes, Renée. *Philosopher King: The Humanist Pope Benedict XIV*. London: Weidenfeld & Nicolson, 1970.

Hays, Christopher M. "The Delay of the Parousia: A Traditional and Historical-Critical Reading of Scripture: Part 2." Pages 79–107 in Christopher Hays et al., *When the Son of Man Didn't Come: A Constructive Proposal on the Delay of the Parousia*. Minneapolis: Fortress, 2016.

Hays, Christopher M., with Brandon Gallaher, Julia S. Konstantinovsky, Richard J. Ounsworth, and C. A. Strine. *When the Son of Man Didn't Come: A Constructive Proposal on the Delay of the Parousia*. Minneapolis: Fortress, 2016.

Heffernan, Thomas J. *Sacred Biography: Saints and Their Biographers in the Middle Ages*. New York: Oxford University Press, 1988.

Heininger, Bernhard. *Metaphorik, Erzählstruktur und Szenisch-dramatische Gestaltung in den Sondergutgleichnissen bei Lukas*. NTAbh 24. Münster: Aschendorff, 1991.

Henderson, John Jordan. "A Comparison of Josephus' Life and Jewish War: An Attempt at Establishing the Acceptable Outer Limits of Biographies' Historical Reliability." Pages 261–75 in *Biographies and Jesus: What Does It Mean for the Gospels to Be Biographies?* Edited by Craig S. Keener and Edward T. Wright. Lexington: Emeth, 2016.

Hengel, Martin. *Acts and the History of Earliest Christianity*. Philadelphia: Fortress, 1979.

———. *Between Jesus and Paul: Studies in Earliest Christian History*. Philadelphia: Fortress, 1983.

———. "Entstehungszeit und Situation des Markusevangeliums." Pages 1–45 in *Markus-Philologie: Historische, literargeschichtliche und stilistischen Untersuchungen zum zweiten Evangelium*. Edited by Hubert Cancik. WUNT 33. Tübingen: Mohr Siebeck, 1984.

———. "Eye-Witness Memory and the Writing of the Gospels: Form Criticism, Community Tradition, and the Authority of the Authors." Pages 70–96 in *The Written Gospel*. Edited by Markus Bockmuehl and Donald A. Hagner. Cambridge: Cambridge University Press, 2005.

———. "The Lukan Prologue and Its Eyewitnesses: The Apostles, Peter, and the Women." Pages 533–87 in *Earliest Christian History: History, Literature, and Theology. Essays from the Tyndale Fellowship in Honor of Martin Hengel*. Edited by Michael F. Bird and Jason Maston. Tübingen: Mohr Siebeck, 2012.

———. "Maria Magdalena und die Frauen als Zeugen." Pages 243–56 in *Abraham unser Vater: Juden und Christen in Gespräch über die Bibel. Festschrift für Otto Michel zum 60. Geburtstag*. Edited by Otto Betz, Martin Hengel, and Peter Schmidt. AGSU 5. Leiden: Brill, 1963.

———. *Saint Peter: The Underestimated Saint*. Grand Rapids: Eerdmans, 2010.

———. *Studies in the Gospel of Mark*. Philadelphia: Fortress, 1985.

———. *The Zealots: Investigations into the Jewish Freedom Movement in the Period from Herod I until 70 A.D.* Edinburgh: T&T Clark, 1989.

Hengel, Martin, and Anna Maria Schwemer. *Jesus and Judaism*. Waco, TX: Baylor University Press, 2019.

Henriksen, Jan-Olav, and Karl Olav Sandnes. *Jesus as Healer: A Gospel for the Body*. Grand Rapids: Eerdmans, 2016.

Henry, Matthew. *Matthew to John*. Vol. 5 of *Commentary on the Whole Bible*. Old Tappan, NJ: Revell, 1986.

Hentschel, Anni. *Diakonia im Neuen Testament: Studien zur Semantik unter besonderer Berücksichtigung der Rolle von Frauen*. WUNT 2/226. Tübingen: Mohr Siebeck, 2007.

Heschel, Abraham J. *The Prophets*. Vol. 2. New York: Harper & Row, 1971.

Hester, J. David. "Eunuchs and the Postgender Jesus: Matthew 19.12 and Transgressive Sexualities." *JSNT* 28 (2005): 13–40.

Hezser, Catherine. *Jewish Travel in Antiquity*. TSAJ 144. Tübingen: Mohr Siebeck, 2011.

———. "Travel and Mobility." Pages 210–26 in *The Oxford Handbook of Jewish Daily Life in Roman Palestine*. Edited by Catherine Hezser. Oxford: Oxford University Press, 2010.

Hibbard, J. Todd. "True and False Prophecy: Jeremiah's Revision of Deuteronomy." *JSOT* 35 (2011): 339–58.

Hiers, Richard H. *Jesus and the Future: Unresolved Questions for Understanding and Faith*. Atlanta: Knox, 1981.

Hill, David. *New Testament Prophecy*. New Foundations Theological Library. Atlanta: Knox, 1979.

Hinterberger, Martin. "The Byzantine Hagiographer and His Texts." Pages 212–46 in *Genres and Contexts*. Vol. 2 of *The Ashgate Research Companion to Byzantine Hagiography*. Edited by Stephanos Efthymiadis. Burlington, VT: Ashgate, 2014.

Hirshberg, Caryle, and Marc Ian Barasch. *Remarkable Recovery: What Extraordinary Healings Tell Us about Getting Well and Staying Well*. New York: Riverhead, 1995.

Hobbes, Thomas. *Leviathan or the Matter, Forme, and Power of a Common-Wealth Ecclesiasticall and Civill*. London: Crooke, 1651.

Hobsbawm, Eric, and Terrence Ranger, eds. *The Invention of Tradition*. Cambridge: Cambridge University Press, 1983.

Hodgson, Peter C. "Editor's Notes." Pages xv–l in David Friedrich Strauss, *The Life of Jesus Critically Examined*. Philadelphia: Fortress, 1972.

Hoehner, Harold W. *Herod Antipas: A Contemporary of Jesus Christ*. SNTSMS 17. Cambridge: Cambridge University Press, 1972.

Holladay, Carl R. *Acts: A Commentary*. NTL. Louisville: Westminster John Knox, 2016.

Holladay, William L. *Jeremiah 1*. Hermeneia. Philadelphia: Fortress, 1986.

Holland, Glenn. "Celibacy in the Early Church." Pages 65–83 in *Celibacy and Religious Tradition*. Edited by Carl Olson. Oxford: Oxford University Press, 2008.

Hollander, H. W., and M. de Jonge. *The Testaments of the Twelve Patriarchs: A Commentary*. SVTP 8. Leiden: Brill, 1985.

Holmén, Tom. "Authenticity Criteria." Pages 43–54 in *Encyclopedia of the Historical Jesus*. Edited by Craig A. Evans. New York: Routledge, 2008.

———. "Doubts about Double Dissimilarity: Restructuring the Main Criterion of Jesus-of-History Research." Pages 47–80 in *Authenticating the Words of Jesus*. Edited by Bruce Chilton and Craig A. Evans. NTTS 28.1. Leiden: Brill, 1999.

Hommel, Hildebrecht. *Sebasmata: Studien zur antiken Religionsgeschichte und zum frühen Christentum*. Vol. 2. WUNT 32. Tübingen: Mohr Siebeck, 1984.

Honigman, Sylvie. *The Septuagint and Homeric Scholarship in Alexandria: A Study in the Narrative of the Letter of Aristeas*. London: Routledge, 2003.

Hooker, Morna Dorothy. "Christology and Methodology." *NTS* 17 (1971): 480–87.

———. "Did the Use of Isaiah 53 to Interpret His Mission Begin with Jesus?" Pages 88–103 in *Jesus and the Suffering Servant: Isaiah 53 and Christian Origins*. Edited by William H. Bellinger Jr. and William R. Farmer. Harrisburg, PA: Trinity Press International, 1998.

———. "Foreword: Forty Years On." Pages xiii–xvii in *Jesus, History, and the Demise of Authenticity: The Rise and Fall of the Search for an Authentic Jesus. Authenticity after the Third Quest*. Edited by Anthony Le Donne and Chris Keith. London: T&T Clark, 2012.

———. *Jesus and the Servant: The Influence of the Servant Concept of Deutero-Isaiah in the New Testament*. London: SPCK, 1959.

———. "On Using the Wrong Tool." *Theology* 75 (1972): 570–81.

Horbury, W. "The Twelve and the Phylarchs." *NTS* 32 (1986): 503–27.

Horn, Friedrich W. "Die synoptischen Einlaßsprüche." *ZNW* 87 (1996): 187–203.

Hornby, K., L. Hornby, and S. D. Shemie. "A Systematic Review of Autoresuscitation after Cardiac Arrest." *Critical Care Medicine* 38 (2010): 1246–53.

Hornsby, Teresa J. "The Woman Is a Sinner/The Sinner Is a Woman." Pages 121–32 in *A Feminist Companion to Luke*. Edited by Amy-Jill Levine with Marianne Blickenstaff. London: Sheffield Academic, 2002.

Horrell, David G. "The Letters for All (Local) Christians: Were There 'Pauline Churches'?" Pages 15–26 in *The Making of Christian Morality: Reading Paul in Ancient and Modern Contexts*. Grand Rapids: Eerdmans, 2016.

Horry, Ruth, M. A. Palmer, M. L. Sexton, and N. Brewer. "Memory Conformity for Confidently Recognized Items: The Power of Social Influence on Memory Reports." *Journal of Experimental Social Psychology* 48 (2012): 783–86.

Horsley, Richard A. "Can Study of the Historical Jesus Escape Its Typological Captivity?" *JSHJ* 19 (2021): 265–329.

———. *Jesus and Magic: Freeing the Gospel Stories from Modern Misconceptions*. Eugene, OR: Cascade, 2014.

———. *The Prophet Jesus and the Renewal of Israel: Moving beyond a Diversionary Debate*. Grand Rapids: Eerdmans, 2012.

Horst, Pieter W. van der. *The Sentences of Pseudo-Phocylides*. SVTP 4. Leiden: Brill, 1978.

Hort, Gerta. "The Plagues of Egypt." *ZAW* 69 (1957): 84–103; 70 (1958): 48–59.

Howes, Llewellyn. *The Formative Stratum of the Sayings Gospel Q*. WUNT 2/545. Tübingen: Mohr Siebeck, 2021.

Hubbard, Benjamin J. *The Matthean Redaction of a Primitive Apostolic Commissioning: An Exegesis of Matthew 28:16–20*. SBLDS 19. Missoula, MT: Scholars Press, 1974.

Huebenthal, Sandra. *Reading Mark's Gospel as a Text from Collective Memory*. Grand Rapids: Eerdmans, 2020.

Hugenberger, G. P. "The Servant of the Lord in the 'Servant Songs' of Isaiah: A Second Moses Figure." Pages 105–39 in *The Lord's Anointed: Interpretation of Old Testament Messianic Texts*. Edited by Philip E. Satterthwaite, Richard S. Hess, and Gordon J. Wenham. Carlisle, UK: Paternoster, 1995.

Huizenga, Leroy. *The New Isaac: Tradition and Intertextuality in the Gospel of Matthew*. NovTSup 131. Leiden: Brill, 2009.

Hultgren, Arland J. *The Parables of Jesus: A Commentary*. Grand Rapids: Eerdmans, 2000.

———. *Rise of Normative Christianity*. Philadelphia: Fortress, 1994.

Humboldt, Wilhelm von. "On the Historian's Task." *History and Theory* 6 (1967): 57–71 (1821).

Hume, David. *Enquiries concerning Human Understanding and concerning the Principles of Morals*. 3rd ed. Oxford: Clarendon, 1975.

Humphrey, Edith M. *Joseph and Aseneth*. Guides to Apocrypha and Pseudepigrapha. Sheffield: Sheffield Academic, 2000.

Hurtado, Larry. "Interactive Diversity: A Proposed Model of Christian Origins." *JTS* 64 (2013): 445–62.

———. *Lord Jesus Christ: Devotion to Jesus in Earliest Christianity*. Grand Rapids: Eerdmans, 2003.

———. "A Response." Pages 341–50 in *Jesus, Skepticism, and the Problem of History: Criteria and Context in the Study of Christian Origins*. Edited by Darrell L. Bock and J. Ed Komoszewski. Grand Rapids: Zondervan Academic, 2019.

Huxley, T. H. *Science and Christian Thought: Essays*. London: Macmillan, 1894.

Hylen, Susan E. "Public and Private Space and Action in the Early Roman Period." *NTS* 66 (2020): 534–53.

———. *Women in the New Testament World*. Essentials of Biblical Studies. Oxford: Oxford University Press, 2019.

Instone-Brewer, David. *Divorce and Remarriage in the Bible: The Social and Literary Context*. Grand Rapids: Eerdmans, 2002.

———. "Jewish Women Divorcing Their Husbands in Early Judaism: The Background to Papyrus Ṣe'lim 13." *HTR* 92 (1999): 349–57.

Isaac, Hiermonk. *Saint Paisios of Mount Athos*. 7th ed. Chalkidiki: Holy Monastery Saint Arsenios the Cappadocian, 2009.

Israeli, Edna. "'Taxo' and the Origin of the *Assumption of Moses*." *JBL* 128 (2009): 735–57.

Isser, Stanley Jerome. *The Dositheans: A Samaritan Sect in Late Antiquity*. SJLA 17. Leiden: Brill, 1976.

Jackson-McCabe, Matt. *Jewish Christianity: The Making of the Christianity-Judaism Divide*. New Haven: Yale University Press, 2020.

Jacobson, Arland D. "Divided Families and Christian Origins." Pages 361–80 in *The Gospel behind the Gospels: Current Studies on Q*. Edited by Ronald A. Piper. NovTSup 75. Leiden: Brill, 1994.

James, Montague Rhodes. *The Lost Apocrypha of the Old Testament: Their Titles and Fragments*. London: SPCK, 1920.

James, William. "The Final Impressions of a Psychical Researcher." Pages 309–26 in *William James on Psychical Research*. Edited by Gardner Murphy and Robert O. Ballou. New York: Viking, 1960.

Jani, Padmanabh S. *The Jaina Path of Purification*. Berkeley: University of California Press, 1979.

Jason, Mark A. *Repentance at Qumran: The Penitential Framework of Religious Experience in the Dead Sea Scrolls*. Minneapolis: Fortress, 2015.

Jassen, Alex P. *Mediating the Divine: Prophecy and Revelation in the Dead Sea Scrolls and Second Temple Judaism*. STDJ 68. Leiden: Brill, 2007.

Jawer, Michael A., and Marc S. Micozzi. *The Spiritual Anatomy of Emotion: How Feelings Link the Brain, the Body, and the Sixth Sense*. Rochester, VT: Park Street, 2009.

Jeremias, Joachim. "Die Drei-Tage-Worte der Evangelisten." Pages 221–29 in *Tradition und Glaube: Das frühe Christentum in seiner Umwelt. Festgabe für Karl Georg Kuhn zum 65. Geburtstag*. Edited by Gert Jeremias, Heinz-Wolfgang Kuhn, and Hartmut Stegemann. Göttingen: Vandenhoeck & Ruprecht, 1971.

———. "Die Naherwartung des Endes in den Worten Jesu." Pages 139–45 in *Aspekte der Unfehlbarkeit: Kritische Untersuchungen und Interpretationen*. Edited by Franz Theunis. TF 56. Hamburg: Reich, 1975.

———. *Die Sprache des Lukasevangeliums: Redaktion und Tradition im Nicht-Markusstoff des dritten Evangeliums*. KEK 1.3. Göttingen: Vandenhoeck & Ruprecht, 1980.

———. *Jerusalem in the Time of Jesus: An Investigation into Economic and Social Conditions during the New Testament Period*. Philadelphia: Fortress, 1969.

———. *Jesus and the Message of the New Testament*. Edited by K. C. Hanson. Minneapolis: Fortress, 2002.

———. “Μωυσῆς.” *TDNT* 4:848–73.
———. *New Testament Theology: The Proclamation of Jesus*. New York: Scribner’s Sons, 1971.
———. “Νύμφη, νυμφίος.” *TDNT* 4: 1099–106.
———. *The Parables of Jesus*. 2nd rev. ed. New York: Scribner’s Sons, 1972.
———. *The Servant of God*. SBT 20. London: SCM, 1965.
Jeremias, Jörg. *Die Reue Gottes: Aspekte alttestamentlicher Gottesvorstellung*. BThSt 65. Neukirchen-Vluyn: Neukirchener, 1975.
Jervell, Jacob. *Die Apostelgeschichte*. KEK 3. Göttingen: Vandenhoeck & Ruprecht, 1998.
Jewett, Robert. *Romans: A Commentary*. Hermeneia. Minneapolis: Fortress, 2007.
Johnson, David. *Hume, Holism, and Miracles*. Ithaca, NY: Cornell University Press, 1999.
Johnson, Lee A., and Robert C. Tannehill. “Lilies Do Not Spin: A Challenge to Female Social Norms.” *NTS* 56 (2010): 475–90.
Johnson, Luke Timothy. *The Acts of the Apostles*. SP 5. Collegeville, MN: Liturgical, 1992.
———. *The Writings of the New Testament: An Interpretation*. Rev. ed. Minneapolis: Fortress, 1999.
Johnson, Nathan C. *The Suffering Son of David in Matthew’s Passion Narrative*. SNTSMS 183. Cambridge: Cambridge University Press, 2023.
Johnson, Steven R., with Michael G. Steinhauser and Ronald L. Jolliffe. *Q 13:34–35: Judgment over Jerusalem*. Documenta Q. Leuven: Peeters, 2014.
Jong, Matthijs J. de. “The Fallacy of True and False in Prophecy Illustrated by Jer 28:8–9.” *JHebS* 12 (2012): 1–29.
Joseph, Simon J. “The Ascetic Jesus.” *JSNT* 8 (2010): 146–81.
———. “‘His Wisdom Will Reach All Peoples’: 4Q534–536, Q 17:26–27, 30, and *1 En.* 65:1–67:3, 90.” *DSD* 19 (2012): 71–105.
———. *Jesus, the Essenes, and Christian Origins: New Light on Ancient Texts and Communities*. Waco, TX: Baylor University Press, 2018.
———. *A Social History of Christian Origins: The Rejected Jesus*. London: Routledge, 2023.
Josephson Storm, Jason Ananda. *Metamodernism: The Future of Theory*. Chicago: University of Chicago Press, 2021.
Junker, Lothar. *Das Scheidungslogion Q 16.18 und frühjüdische Reinheitsvorstellungen*. WUNT 2/479. Tübingen: Mohr Siebeck, 2019.
Justice, Steven. “Did the Middle Ages Believe in Their Miracles?” *Representations* 103 (2008): 1–29.
Kahl, Werner. “Jesus als Wundertäter.” Pages 137–82 in *Fragen nach Jesus*. Edited

by Marco Hofheinz and Nils Neumann. Leipzig: Evangelische Verlagsanstalt, 2022.

Kaldellis, Anthony. "The Hagiography of Doubt and Scepticism." Pages 453–77 in *Genres and Contexts*. Vol. 2 of *The Ashgate Research Companion to Byzantine Hagiography*. Edited by Stephanos Efthymiadis. Burlington, VT: Ashgate, 2014.

Kankaanniemi, Matti. *The Guards of the Tomb (Matt 27:62–66 and 28:11–15): Matthew's Apologetical Legend Revisited*. Åbo: Åbo Akademi University Press, 2010.

Karris, Robert J. "Women and Discipleship in Luke." *CBQ* 56 (1994): 1–20.

Kartzow, Marianne Bjelland. "Rewritten Stereotypes: Scripture and Cultural Echo in Luke's Parable of the Widow and the Judge." Pages 208–24 in *Luke's Literary Creativity*. Edited by Jesper Tang Nielsen and Mogens Müller. LNTS 550. London: T&T Clark, 2016.

Käsemann, Ernst. *Essays on New Testament Themes*. SBT 41. London: SCM, 1964.

Kazen, Thomas. *Scripture, Interpretation, or Authority? Motives and Arguments in Jesus' Halakic Conflicts*. WUNT 320. Tübingen: Mohr Siebeck, 2013.

Keener, Craig S. *Acts: An Exegetical Commentary*. 4 vols. Grand Rapids: Baker Academic, 2012–15.

———. "Before Biographies: Memory and Oral Tradition." Pages 329–54 in *Biographies and Jesus: What Does It Mean for the Gospels to Be Biographies?* Edited by Craig S. Keener and Edward T. Wright. Lexington: Emeth, 2016.

———. *Christobiography: Memory, History, and the Reliability of the Gospels*. Grand Rapids: Eerdmans, 2019.

———. *The Gospel of John: A Commentary*. 2 vols. Peabody, MA: Hendrickson, 2003.

———. *The Historical Jesus of the Gospels*. Grand Rapids: Eerdmans, 2009.

———. *Miracles: The Credibility of the New Testament Accounts*. 2 vols. Grand Rapids: Baker Academic, 2011.

———. *Miracles Today: The Supernatural Work of God in the Modern World*. Grand Rapids: Baker Academic, 2021.

———. "Paul's Positive Madness in Acts 26:24–25." Pages 311–19 in *Goldene Anfänge und Aufbrüche: Johann Jakob Wettstein und die Apostelgeschichte*. Edited by Manfred Lang and Joseph Verheyden. ABG 57. Leipzig: Evangelische Verlagsanstalt, 2016.

Keener, Craig S., and Edward T. Wright, eds. *Biographies and Jesus: What Does It Mean for the Gospels to Be Biographies?* Lexington: Emeth, 2016.

Keim, Theodore. *The History of Jesus of Nazara, Considered in Its Connection with the National Life of Israel*. 6 vols. London: Williams & Norgate, 1878–83.

Keith, Chris. "The Indebtedness of Authenticity in Jesus Research and Historiographical Method to Form Criticism and Recent Attempts to Rehabilitate the Search for an Authentic Jesus." Pages 125–48 in *Jesus, History, and the Demise of Authenticity: The Rise and Fall of the Search for an Authentic Jesus. Authenticity after the Third Quest*. Edited by Anthony Le Donne and Chris Keith. London: T&T Clark, 2012.

———. *Jesus' Literacy: Scribal Culture and the Teacher from Galilee*. LNTS 8. London: T&T Clark, 2011.

———. "The Narratives of the Gospels and the Historical Jesus: Current Debates, Prior Debates, and the Goal of Historical Jesus Research." *JSNT* 38 (2016): 426–55.

———. "Social Memory Theory and Gospels Research: The First Decade." *Early Christianity* 6.3 (2015): 354–76; 6.4 (2015): 517–42.

Kelber, Werner H. *Imprints, Voiceprints, and Footprints of Memory: Collected Essays of Werner H. Kelber*. Atlanta: Society of Biblical Literature, 2013.

———. "On 'Mastering the Genre.'" Pages 57–76 in *Modern and Ancient Literary Criticism of the Gospels: Continuing the Debate on Gospel Genre(s)*. Edited by Robert Matthew Calhoun, David P. Moessner, and Tobias Nicklas. WUNT 451. Tübingen: Mohr Siebeck, 2020.

Kelhoffer, James A. "A Tale of Two Markan Characterizations: The Exemplary Woman Who Anointed Jesus's Body for Burial (14:3–9) and the Silent Trio Who Fled the Empty Tomb (16:1–8)." Pages 85–98 in *Women and Gender in Ancient Religions: Interdisciplinary Approaches*. Edited by Stephen P. Ahearne-Kroll, Paul A. Holloway, and James A. Kelhoffer. WUNT 263. Tübingen: Mohr Siebeck, 2010.

Kelly, Edward, and Emily Williams Kelly with Adam Crabtree, Alan Gauld, Michael Grosso, and Bruce Greyson. *Irreducible Mind: Toward a Psychology for the 21st Century*. Lanham, MD: Rowman & Littlefield, 2007.

Kelly, Emily Williams. "Psychophysiological Influence." Pages 117–239 in Edward Kelly and Emily Williams Kelly et al., *Irreducible Mind: Toward a Psychology for the 21st Century*. Lanham, MD: Rowman & Littlefield, 2007.

Kennedy, George. "Classical and Christian Source Criticism." Pages 125–55 in *The Relationships among the Gospels: An Interdisciplinary Dialogue*. Edited by William O. Walker Jr. San Antonio: Trinity University Press, 1978.

Kertelge, Karl. *Die Wunder Jesu im Markusevangelium: Eine redaktionsgeschichtliche Untersuchung*. SANT 23. Munich: Kösel, 1970.

Kiefer, Jörn. *Exil und Diaspora: Begrifflichkeit und Deutungen im antiken Judentum und in der hebräischen Bibel*. ABG 19. Leipzig: Evangelische Verlagsanstalt, 2005.

Kiffiak, Jordash. "Zimmermann's Genre 'frühchristliche Wundergeschichte': Some Theoretical and Comparative Considerations." Pages 79–116 in *Faszination der Wunder Jesu und der Apostel: Die Debatte um die frühchristlichen Wundererzählungen geht weiter*. Edited by Ruben Zimmermann. BThSt 184. Göttingen: Vandenhoeck & Ruprecht, 2020.

Kim, Hayeon. *Multiple Authorship of the Septuagint Pentateuch: The Original Translators of the Pentateuch*. Supplements to the Textual History of the Bible 4. Leiden: Brill, 2020.

Kim, Sun Wook. *Jesus and the Missional Movement in Galilee: Markan Presentation and Its Hermeneutical Significance*. Eugene, OR: Pickwick, 2019.

King, Karen L. "Factions, Variety, Diversity, Multiplicity: Representing Early Christian Differences for the 21st Century." *MTSR* 23 (2011): 216–37.

———. "Jesus." Pages 406–27 in *The Oxford Handbook of New Testament, Gender, and Sexuality*. Edited by Benjamin H. Dunning. Oxford: Oxford University Press, 2018.

Kirk, Alan. *Jesus Tradition, Early Christian Memory, and Gospel Writing: The Long Search for the Authentic Source*. Grand Rapids: Eerdmans, 2023.

———. *Memory and the Jesus Tradition*. London: Bloomsbury T&T Clark, 2018.

Kirk, J. R. Daniel. *A Man Attested by God: The Human Jesus of the Synoptic Gospels*. Grand Rapids: Eerdmans, 2016.

Klancher, Nancy B. "The Male Soul in Drag: Women-as-Job in the Testament of Job." *JSP* 19 (2010): 225–45.

Klauck, Hans-Josef. *Vorspiel im Himmel? Erzähltechnik und Theologie im Markusprolog*. BThSt 32. Neukirchen-Vluyn: Neukirchener, 1997.

Klausner, Joseph. *Jesus of Nazareth: His Life, Times, and Teaching*. New York: Macmillan, 1925.

———. *The Messianic Idea in Israel from Its Beginning to the Completion of the Mishnah*. New York: Macmillan, 1955.

Klawans, Jonathan. "The Prohibition of Oaths and Contra-Scriptural Halakhot: A Response to John P. Meier." *JSHJ* 6 (2008): 33–48.

Klein, Ralph W. *1 Samuel*. WBC 10. Waco, TX: Word, 1983.

Kloppenborg, John S. *Excavating Q: The History and Setting of the Sayings Gospel*. Edinburgh: T&T Clark, 2000.

———. *The Formation of Q: Trajectories in Ancient Christian Wisdom Collections*. SAC. Philadelphia: Fortress, 1987.

———. "Memory, Performance, and the Sayings of Jesus." *JSHJ* 10 (2012): 97–132.

———. "Sources, Methods, and Discursive Locations in the Quest of the Historical Jesus." Pages 264–66 in vol. 1 of *The Handbook of the Study of the Historical Jesus*. Edited by Tom Holmén and Stanley E. Porter. Leiden: Brill, 2010.

———. *Synoptic Problems: Collected Essays*. WUNT 329. Tübingen: Mohr Siebeck, 2014.

Knowles, Michael P. *Jeremiah in Matthew's Gospel: The Rejected Prophet Motif in Matthean Redaction*. JSNTSup 69. Sheffield: JSOT Press, 1993.

Knowling, R. J. "The Acts of the Apostles." Pages 3–554 in vol. 2 of *The Expositors Greek Testament*. Edited by W. Robertson Nicoll. New York: Doran, 1901.

Koester, Helmut. *Ancient Christian Gospels: Their History and Development*. Philadelphia: Trinity Press International, 1990.

Koestler, Arthur. *The Roots of Coincidence: An Excursion into Parapsychology*. New York: Vintage, 1972.

Kohlmann, B. "Lk 12.35–38—ein Gleichnis der Logienquelle." *ZNW* 81 (1990): 254–61.

Kok, Michael J. "Does Mark Narrate the Pauline Kerygma of 'Christ Crucified'? Challenging an Emerging Consensus on Mark as a Pauline Gospel." *JSNT* 37 (2014): 139–60.

———. *The Gospel on the Margins: The Reception of Mark in the Second Century*. Minneapolis: Fortress, 2015.

Kollmann, Bernd. "Brot und Fisch bis zum Abwinken (Die Speisung der Fünftausend) Mk 6,30–44 (ActJoh 93)." Pages 294–303 in *Die Wunder Jesu*. Vol. 1 of *Kompendium der frühchristlichen Wundererzählungen*. Edited by Ruben Zimmermann, Detlev Dormeyer, Judith Hartenstein, Christian Münch, Enno Edzard Popkes, and Uta Poplutz. Gütersloh: Gütersloher, 2013.

Koltun-Fromm, Naomi. "Aphrahat and the Rabbis on Noah's Righteousness in Light of the Jewish-Christian Polemic." Pages 57–71 in *The Book of Genesis in Jewish and Oriental Christian Interpretation: A Collection of Essays*. Edited by Judith Frishman and Lucas Van Rompay. Traditio Exegetica Graeca 5. Leuven: Peeters, 1997.

Konradt, Matthias. *The Gospel according to Matthew: A Commentary*. Waco, TX: Baylor University Press, 2020.

———. *Israel, Church, and the Gentiles in the Gospel of Matthew*. Waco, TX: Baylor University Press, 2014.

Kornell, Nate. "Failing to Predict Future Changes in Memory: A Stability Bias Yields Long-Term Overconfidence." Pages 365–86 in *Successful Remembering and Successful Forgetting: A Festschrift in Honor of Robert A. Bjork*. Edited by A. S. Benjamin. New York: Psychology Press, 2011.

Kraemer, Ross S. "Jewish Women and Women's Judaism at the Beginning of Christianity." Pages 35–49 in *Women and Christian Origins*. Edited by Ross S. Kraemer and Mary Rose D'Angelo. New York: Oxford University Press, 1999.

Krämer, Michael. *Die Entstehungsgeschichte der synoptischen Evangelien: Das Lukasevangelium*. Würzburg: Echter, 2016.

Kreuzer, Siegfried. "The Origins and Transmission of the Septuagint." Pages 3–56 in *Introduction to the Septuagint*. Edited by Siegfried Kreuzer. Waco, TX: Baylor University Press, 2019.

Kripal, Jeffrey J. *Authors of the Impossible: The Paranormal and the Sacred*. Chicago: Chicago University Press, 2010.

———. *Comparing Religions: Coming to Terms*. Chichester: Wiley-Blackwell, 2014.

———. *The Flip: Epiphanies of Mind and the Future of Knowledge*. New York: Belleview Literary, 2019.

———. *The Superhumanities: Historical Precedents, Moral Objections, New Realities*. Chicago: University of Chicago Press, 2022.

Krueger, Derek. "Typological Figuration in Theodoret of Cyrrhus's *Religious History* and the Art of Postbiblical Narrative." *JECS* 5 (1997): 393–419.

Kugel, James L. *Traditions of the Bible: A Guide to the Bible as It Was at the Start of the Common Era*. Cambridge: Harvard University Press, 1998.

Kügler, Joachim. *Der Jünger, den Jesus liebte: Literarische, theologische und historische Untersuchungen zu einer Schlüsselgestalt johanneischer Theologie und Geschichte*. Stuttgart: Katholisches Bibelwerk, 1988.

Kugler, Robert. "Continuing Exile among the People of the Dead Sea Scrolls: Nuancing N. T. Wright's Hypothesis." Pages 163–82 in *Exile: A Conversation with N. T. Wright*. Edited by James M. Scott. Downers Grove, IL: IVP Academic, 2017.

Kümmel, Werner Georg. *Promise and Fulfilment: The Eschatological Message of Jesus*. SBT. London: SCM, 1957.

Künzi, Martin. *Das Naherwartungslogien Matthäus 10.23*. BGBE 9. Tübingen: Mohr Siebeck, 1970.

Kürzinger, Josef. "Die Aussage des Papias von Hierapolis zur literarischen Form des Markusevangeliums." *ZNW* 21 (1977): 245–64.

Kwaak, H. van der. "Die Klage über Jerusalem (Matth. xxiii 37–39)." *NovT* 8 (1966): 156–70.

Labahn, Antje. "The Delay of Salvation with Deutero-Isaiah." *JSOT* 85 (1999): 71–84.

Labahn, Michael. "Jesu Exorzismen (Q 11,19–20) und die Erkenntnis der Ägyptischen Magier (Exod 8,15)." Pages 617–33 in *The Sayings Source Q and the Historical Jesus*. Edited by A. Lindemann. BETL 158. Leuven: Peeters, 2001.

Laidlaw, James. "A Life Worth Living: Fasting to Death as Telos of a Jain Religious Life." *Economy and Society* 34 (2005): 178–99.

Lake, Kirsopp, and Henry J. Cadbury. *The Acts of the Apostles: English Translation and Commentary*. Vol. 4 of *The Beginnings of Christianity*. Edited by F. J. Foakes and Kirsopp Lake. London: Macmillan, 1933.

Lambert, David A. "Did Israel Believe That Redemption Awaited Its Repentance? The Case of *Jubilees* 1." *CBQ* 68 (2006): 631–50.

———. *How Repentance Became Biblical: Judaism, Christianity, and the Interpretation of Scripture*. Oxford: Oxford University Press, 2016.

———. "Repentance." Pages 1134–35 in *The Eerdmans Dictionary of Early Judaism*. Edited by John J. Collins and Daniel C. Harlow. Grand Rapids: Eerdmans, 2010.

Lamerson, Samuel. Review of *Constructing Jesus*, by Dale C. Allison Jr. *JETS* 54 (2011): 837–39.

Lamon, Ward Hill. *Recollections of Abraham Lincoln, 1847–1865*. Lincoln: University of Nebraska Press, 1999.

Landman, Leo. "Introduction." Pages xi–xxxv in *Messianism in the Talmudic Era*. Edited by Leo Landman. New York: Ktav, 1979.

Lane, William L. *The Gospel according to Mark: The English Text with Introduction, Exposition, and Notes*. NICNT. Grand Rapids: Eerdmans, 1974.

Lane-Fox, Robin. "The *Life of Daniel*." Pages 175–226 in *Portraits: Biographical Representation in the Greek and Latin Literature of the Roman Empire*. Edited by Mark Edwards and Simon Swain. Oxford: Clarendon, 1997.

Lapide, Cornelius à. *Commentaria in Scripturam Sacram Tomus Secundus: In Pentateuchum Mosis: Leviticus, Numeri et Deuteronomium*. Paris: Ludovicus Vivès, 1868.

———. *The Great Commentary*. 4 vols. Fitzwilliam, NH: Loreto, 2008 (1876).

Larmer, Robert. "Miracles and Criteria." Pages 76–82 in *Questions of Miracles*. Edited by Robert Larmer. Montreal: McGill-Queen's University Press, 1996.

Latourelle, René. *The Miracles of Jesus and the Theology of Miracles*. New York: Paulist Press, 1988.

Laufen, Rudolf. *Die Doppelüberlieferungen der Logienquelle und des Markusevangelium*. BBB 54. Königstein: Hanstein, 1980.

Laurentin, René. *Miracles in El Paso?* Ann Arbor, MI: Servant Books, 1982.

Le Donne, Anthony. "The Criterion of Coherence: Its Development, Inevitability, and Historiographical Limitations." Pages 95–114 in *Jesus, History, and the Demise of Authenticity: The Rise and Fall of the Search for an Authentic Jesus. Authenticity after the Third Quest*. Edited by Anthony Le Donne and Chris Keith. London: T&T Clark, 2012.

———. "Did Jesus Befriend Sex Workers?" *JSHJ* 20 (2022): 147–55.

———. *Historical Jesus: What Can We Know and How Can We Know It?* Grand Rapids: Eerdmans, 2011.

———. *The Historiographical Jesus: Memory, Typology, and the Son of David*. Waco, TX: Baylor University Press, 2009.

———. *The Wife of Jesus: Ancient Texts and Modern Scandals*. London: Oneworld, 2013.

Lear, Joseph M., Jr. "Luke's Use of the Old Testament in the Sending of the Seventy(-Two): A Compositional Study." Pages 160–82 in *Luke's Literary Creativity*. Edited by Jesper Tang Nielsen and Mogens Müller. LNTS 550. London: T&T Clark, 2016.

Lecky, W. E. H. *History of the Rise and Influence of the Spirit of Rationalism in Europe*. 2 vols. New York: Appleton, 1872.

Lehtipuu, Outi. "No Sex in Heaven—Nor on Earth? Luke 20:27–38 as a Proof-Text in Early Christian Discourses on Resurrection and Asceticism." Pages 22–39 in *Bodies, Borders, Believers: Ancient Texts and Present Conversations. Essays in Honor of Turid Karlsen Seim on Her 70th Birthday*. Edited by Anne Hege Grung, Marianne Bjelland Kartzow, and Anna Rebecca Solevåg. Eugene, OR: Pickwick, 2015.

Lent, Frederick. *The Life of Saint Simeon Stylites: A Translation of the Syriac Text in Bedjan's "Acta Martyrum et Sanctorum."* Christian Roman Empire Series 7. Merchantville, NJ: Evolution, 2009.

———. "The Life of Simeon Stylites." *JAOS* 25 (1915): 103–98.

Leroy, H. "Vergebung und Gemeinde nach Lukas 7.36–50." Pages 85–94 in *Wort Gottes in der Zeit: Festschrift Karl Hermann Schelkle zum 65. Geburtstag*. Edited by Helmut Feld and Josef Nolte. Düsseldorf: Patmos, 1973.

Leroy, O. "Le visage resplendissant de Sainte Thérèse." *Revue d'ascétique et de mystique* 35 (1959): 194–99.

Lessius, Leonardus. *A Consultation What Faith and Religion Is Best to Be Imbraced*. N. P.: St. Omar, 1621.

Leuret, François, and Henri Bon. *A Documented Account of Miracles and Medicine in the 20th Century*. New York: Farrar, Straus & Cudahy, 1957.

Levertoff, Paul. "Matthew." Pages 124–205 in vol. 3 of *A New Commentary on Holy Scripture*. Edited by Charles Gore, Henry Leighton Goudge, and Alfred Guillaume. New York: Macmillan, 1928.

Levine, Amy-Jill. "Christian Faith and the Study of the Historical Jesus: A Response to Bock, Keener, and Webb." *JSHJ* 9 (2011): 96–106.

———. "Discharging Responsibility: Matthean Jesus, Biblical Law, and Hemorrhaging Woman." Pages 379–97 in *Treasures Old and New: Contributions to Matthean Studies*. Edited by David R. Bauer and Mark Allan Powell. Atlanta: Scholars Press, 1996.

———. "Jesus, Second Temple Judaism, and Women: Yeast of Eden." Pages 302–31 in *Feminist Companion to the Hebrew Bible in the New Testament*. Edited by Athalya Brenner. Sheffield: Sheffield Academic, 1996.

———. "Lilies of the Field and Wandering Jews: Biblical Scholarship, Women's Roles, and Social Location." Pages 329–52 in *Transformative Encounters: Jesus and Women Re-viewed*. Edited by Ingrid Rosa Kitzberger. BibInt 43. Leiden: Brill, 2000.

———. "Women in the Q Communit(ies) and Traditions." Pages 150–70 in *Women and Christian Origins*. Edited by Ross S. Kraemer and Mary Rose D'Angelo. New York: Oxford University Press, 1999.

———. "Women Itinerants, Jesus of Nazareth, and Historical-Critical Approaches: Reevaluating the Consensus." Pages 45–64 in *Gender and Second-Temple Judaism*. Edited by Kathy Ehrensperger and Shayna Sheinfeld. Lanham, MD: Lexington, 2020.

———. "Women's Itineracy and the Criteria of Authenticity in John Meier's *Marginal Jew*." Pages 90–113 in *The Figure of Jesus in History and Theology: Essays in Honor of John Meier*. Edited by Vincent T. M. Skemp and Kelley Coblentz Bautch. CBQ Imprints 1. Washington, DC: Catholic Biblical Association of America, 2020.

———. "The Word Becomes Flesh: Jesus, Gender, and Sexuality." Pages 62–83 in *Jesus Two Thousand Years Later*. Edited by James H. Charlesworth and Walter P. Weaver. Harrisburg, PA: Trinity Press International, 2000.

Lewis, I. M. *Ecstatic Religion: An Anthropology of Spirit Possession*. Baltimore: Penguin, 1971.

Licht, Jacob. "Taxo, or the Apocalyptic Doctrine of Vengeance." *JJS* 12 (1961): 95–103.

Licona, Michael R. "Historians and Miracle Claims." *JSHJ* 12 (2014): 106–29.

———. "Is the Sky Falling in the World of Historical Jesus Research?" *BBR* 26 (2016): 353–67.

———. *The Resurrection of Jesus: A New Historiographical Approach*. Downers Grove, IL: IVP Academic, 2010.

———. *Why Are There Differences in the Gospels? What We Can Learn from Ancient Biography*. Oxford: Oxford University Press, 2017.

Liddon, H. P. *The Divinity of Our Lord and Saviour Jesus Christ: Eight Lectures Preached before the University of Oxford in the Year 1866*. London: Rivingtons, 1889.

Lieber, Laura S. "Jewish Women: Texts and Contexts." Pages 329–42 in *A Companion to Women in the Ancient World*. Edited by Sharon L. James and Sheila Dillon. Chichester: Wiley-Blackwell, 2015.

Lierman, John. "The Mosaic Pattern of John's Christology." Pages 210–34 in *Challenging Perspectives on the Gospel of John*. Edited by John Lierman. WUNT 2/219. Tübingen: Mohr Siebeck, 2006.

———. *The New Testament Moses*. WUNT 2/173. Tübingen: Mohr Siebeck, 2004.

Lietzmann, Hans. *Das Leben des heiligen Symeon Stylites*. TU 32.4. Leipzig: Hinrichs, 1908.

Lightfoot, John. *A Commentary on the New Testament from the Talmud and Hebraica*. 4 vols. Oxford: Oxford University Press, 1859.

Lim, Timothy M. *The Earliest Commentary on the Prophecy of Habakkuk*. Oxford: Oxford University Press, 2020.

Lin, Yii-Jan. "Junia: An Apostle before Paul." *JBL* 139 (2020): 191–209.

Lincicum, David. *Paul and the Early Jewish Encounter with Deuteronomy*. Grand Rapids: Baker Academic, 2013.

Lindars, Barnabas. "Discourse and Tradition: The Use of the Sayings of Jesus in the Discourses of the Fourth Gospel." *JSNT* 13 (1981): 83–101.

———. *The Gospel of John*. New Century Bible. London: Oliphants, Marshall, Morgan & Scott, 1977.

———. *Jesus Son of Man: A Fresh Examination of the Son of Man Sayings in the Gospels*. Grand Rapids: Eerdmans, 1983.

———. *New Testament Apologetic*. London: SCM, 1961.

Litwa, M. David. *How the Gospels Became History: Comparing Jesus and Mediterranean Myths*. New Haven: Yale University Press, 2019.

———. "Literary Eyewitnesses: The Appeal to an Eyewitness in John and Contemporaneous Literature." *NTS* 64 (2018): 343–61.

———. *Posthuman Transformation in Ancient Mediterranean Thought: Becoming Angels and Demons*. Cambridge: Cambridge University Press, 2021.

Liu, Wenlin, Anupreet Sidhu, Amanda M. Beacom, and Thomas W. Valente. "Social Network Theory." Pages 1–12 in vol. 2 of *The International Encyclopedia of Media Effects*. Edited by Patrick Rössler, Cynthia A. Hoffner, and Liesbet van Zoonen. Chichester: Wiley-Blackwell, 2017.

Llewelyn, Stephen R., Gareth J. Wearne, and Bianca L. Sanderson. "Guarding Entry to the Kingdom: The Place of Eunuchs in Mt. 19.12." *JSNT* 10 (2012): 228–46.

Loader, William. *Making Sense of Sex: Attitudes towards Sexuality in Early Jewish and Christian Literature*. Grand Rapids: Eerdmans, 2013.

———. *The New Testament on Sexuality*. Grand Rapids: Eerdmans, 2012.

———. *Sexuality and Gender: Collected Essays*. WUNT 458. Tübingen: Mohr Siebeck, 2021.

———. "Sexuality and the Historical Jesus." Pages 34–48 in *Jesus from Judaism to Christianity: Continuum Approaches to the Historical Jesus*. Edited by Tom Holmén. London: Bloomsbury, 2007.

———. *Sexuality and the Jesus Tradition*. Grand Rapids: Eerdmans, 2005.

Locke, John. *The Reasonableness of Christianity with a Discourse of Miracles and*

Part of a Third Letter concerning Toleration. Edited by I. T. Ramsey. Stanford: Stanford University Press, 1958.

Loewenstamm, Samuel E. "The Death of Moses." Pages 185–217 in *Studies on the Testament of Abraham*. Edited by G. W. E. Nickelsburg. SCS 6. Missoula, MT: Scholars Press, 1976.

Lohfink, Gerhard. *Jesus of Nazareth: What He Wanted, Who He Was*. Collegeville, MN: Liturgical, 2012.

Loofs, Friedrich. *What Is the Truth about Jesus Christ? Problems of Christology*. New York: Scribner's Sons, 1913.

Loos, Hendrik van der. *The Miracles of Jesus*. NovTSup 9. Leiden: Brill, 1966.

Lord, Albert Bates. *The Singer of Tales*. Harvard Studies in Comparative Literature 24. Cambridge: Harvard University Press, 1960.

Loughborough, John N. *The Great Second Advent Movement*. Washington, DC: Review & Herald, 1905.

Lövestam, Evald. *Jesus and "This Generation": A New Testament Study*. ConBNT 25. Stockholm: Almqvist & Wiksell, 1995.

———. *Spiritual Wakefulness in the New Testament*. LUÅ 55.3. Lund: Gleerup, 1963.

Lowis, Michael J. *The Gospel Miracles: What Really Happened? A Systematic, Open-Minded Review of the Evidence*. Eugene, OR: Resource, 2014.

Lüdemann, Gerd. *The Acts of the Apostles: What Really Happened in the Earliest Days of the Church*. Amherst, NY: Prometheus, 2005.

Luff, Rosemary Margaret. *The Impact of Jesus in First-Century Palestine: Textual and Archaeological Evidence for Long-Standing Discontent*. Cambridge: Cambridge University Press, 2019.

Lugli, Remo. *Gustavo Rol: Una vita di prodigy*. 3rd ed. Rome: Edizioni mediterranee, 2008.

Lundbom, Jack R. *Jeremiah 1–20*. AB 21A. New Haven: Yale University Press, 1999.

Lupieri, Edmondo. "The Earliest Magdalene: Varied Portrayals in Early Gospel Narratives." Pages 11–25 in *Mary Magdalene from the New Testament to the New Age and Beyond*. Edited by Edmondo F. Lupieri. Themes in Biblical Narrative 24. Leiden: Brill, 2020.

Luther, Martin. *The Sermon on the Mount (Sermons) and the Magnificat*. Edited by Jaroslav Pelikan. Luther's Works 21. Saint Louis: Concordia, 1956.

———. "The Small Catechism." Pages 143–68 in *Basic Luther*. Springfield, IL: Templegate, 1984.

Luz, Ulrich. "Looking at Q through the Eyes of Matthew." Pages 571–90 in *New Studies in the Synoptic Problem. Oxford Conference, April, 2008: Essays in Honour of Christopher M. Tuckett*. Edited by P. Foster, A. Gregory, J. S. Kloppenborg, and J. Verheyden. BETL 239. Leuven: Peeters, 2011.

———. *Matthew: A Commentary*. 3 vols. Hermeneia. Minneapolis: Fortress, 2001–7.

———. *Matthew in History: Interpretation, Influence, and Effects*. Minneapolis: Fortress, 1994.

———. "Matthew's Interpretive 'Tendencies' and the 'Historical' Jesus." Pages 577–97 in *Jesus Research: The First Princeton-Prague Symposium on Jesus Research, Prague 2005*. Edited by James H. Charlesworth with Brian Rhea and Petr Pokorný. Grand Rapids: Eerdmans, 2009.

———. "Warum zog Jesus nach Jerusalem?" Pages 409–29 in *Der historische Jesus: Tendenzen und Perspektiven der gegenwärtigen Forschungen*. Edited by Jens Schröter and Ralph Brucker. BZNW 114. Berlin: de Gruyter, 2002.

Lyons, George. *Pauline Autobiography*. SBLDS 73. Atlanta: Scholars Press, 1985.

Maccoby, Hyam. "Paul and the Eucharist." *NTS* 37 (1991): 247–67.

MacDonald, Dennis R. *Mythologizing Jesus: From Jewish Teacher to Epic Hero*. Lanham, MD: Rowman & Littlefield, 2015.

MacDonald, Dennis R., with James R. Van Dore. *From the Earliest Gospel (Q+) to the Gospel of Mark: Solving the Synoptic Problem with Mimesis Criticism*. Lanham, MD: Lexington, 2020.

MacIntyre, Alasdair C. *Difficulties in Christian Belief*. New York: Philosophical Library, 1959.

Mack, Burton. *The Lost Gospel: The Book of Q and Christian Origins*. San Francisco: Harper, 1993.

Maddox, Robert. *The Purpose of Luke-Acts*. FRLANT 126. Göttingen: Vandenhoeck & Ruprecht, 1982.

Mader, Heidrun E. *Markus und Paulus: Die beiden ältesten erhaltenen literarischen Werke und theologischen Entwürfe des Urchristentums im Vergleich*. BZ Supplement 1. Leiden: Brill, 2020.

———. "Narratives Gestalten paulinischer Theologoumena? Paulus und Markus im Vergleich." *ZNT* 47 (2021): 41–58.

Magee, Bryan. *Ultimate Questions*. Princeton: Princeton University Press, 2016.

Maldonatus, Juan. *Commentarii Quartuor Evangelista*. Vol. 1. London: Moguntiae, 1853.

———. *A Commentary on the Holy Gospels: S. Matthew's Gospel, Chapters I to XIV*. 2nd ed. London: Hodges, 1888.

Malina, Bruce. "Social-Scientific Approaches and Jesus Research." Pages 747–75 in vol. 1 of *Handbook for the Study of the Historical Jesus*. Edited by Tom Holmén and Stanley E. Porter. Leiden: Brill, 2011.

Manson, T. W. *The Sayings of Jesus as Recorded in the Gospels According to St. Matthew and St. Luke Arranged with Introduction and Commentary*. London: SCM, 1949.

———. *The Servant Messiah: A Study of the Public Ministry of Jesus*. Cambridge: Cambridge University Press, 1953.

———. *Studies in the Gospels and Epistles*. Edited by Matthew Black. Manchester: Manchester University Press, 1962.

———. *The Teaching of Jesus*. 2nd ed. Cambridge: Cambridge University Press, 1967.

Manson, William. *Jesus the Messiah: The Synoptic Tradition of the Revelation of God in Christ: With Special Reference to Form-Criticism*. London: Hodder & Stoughton, 1943.

Marcar, Katie. "Exodus in the General Letters." Pages 169–78 in *Exodus in the New Testament*. Edited by Seth M. Ehorn. LNTS 663. London: T&T Clark, 2022.

Marchi, John de. *Fatima: The Facts*. Cork, Ireland: Mercier, 1950.

Marcus, Joel. "Did Matthew Believe His Myths?" Pages 217–49 in *An Early Reader of Mark and Q*. Edited by Joseph Verheyden and Gilbert Van Belle. BTS 21. Leuven: Peeters, 2016.

———. "The Enigma of the Antitheses." *NTS* 69 (2023): 121–37.

———. "History and Theology in Matthew." Pages 47–56 in *History and Theology in the Gospels*. Edited by Tobias Nicklas, Karl-Wilhelm Niebuhr, and Mikhail Seleznev. WUNT 447. Tübingen: Mohr Siebeck, 2020.

———. "John the Baptist and Jesus." Pages 179–97 in *Christianity in the Beginning*. Vol. 1 of *When Judaism and Christianity Began: Essays in Memory of Anthony J. Saldarini*. Edited by Daniel Harrington, Alan J. Avery-Peck, and Jacob Neusner. Leiden: Brill, 2003.

———. *John the Baptist in History and Theology*. Columbia: University of South Carolina Press, 2018.

———. *Mark: A New Translation with Commentary*. 2 vols. AB 27–27A. New Haven: Yale University Press, 2000–2009.

———. "Mark—Interpreter of Paul." Pages 29–49 in *For and against Pauline Influence on Mark*. Vol. 2 of *Mark and Paul: Comparative Essays*. Edited by Eve-Marie Becker, Troels Engberg-Pedersen, and Mogens Müller. BZNW 199. Berlin: de Gruyter, 2014.

———. "Mark 9,11–13: 'As It Has Been Written.'" *ZNW* 90 (1989): 42–63.

———. "Sacred Subversion: Ironic Twists on Biblical Psalms." Pages 161–78 in *"To Recover What Has Been Lost": Essays on Eschatology, Intertextuality, and Reception History in Honor of Dale C. Allison Jr.* Edited by Tucker S. Ferda, Daniel Frayer-Griggs, and Nathan C. Johnson. NovTSup 183. Leiden: Brill, 2021.

———. *The Way of the Lord: Christological Exegesis of the Old Testament in the Gospel of Mark*. Louisville: Westminster John Knox, 1992.

Marguerat, Daniel. *Die Apostelgeschichte*. KEK 3. Göttingen: Vandenhoeck & Ruprecht, 2022.

Marjanen, Antti. *The Woman Jesus Loved: Mary Magdalene in the Nag Hammadi Library and Related Documents*. NHMS 40. Leiden: Brill, 1996.

Markschies, Christoph. "The Canon of the New Testament in Antiquity: Some New Horizons for Future Research." Pages 175–94 in *Homer, the Bible, and Beyond: Literary and Religious Canons in the Ancient World*. Edited by Margaret Finkelberg and Guy G. Stroumsa. Jerusalem Studies in Religion and Culture 2. Leiden: Brill, 2003.

Marsh, Elizabeth J., and Barbara Tversky. "Spinning the Stories of Our Lives." *Applied Cognitive Psychology* 18 (2004): 491–503.

Marshall, I. Howard. *The Gospel of Luke: A Commentary on the Greek Text*. NIGTC. Grand Rapids: Eerdmans, 1978.

———. "The Last Supper." Pages 560–75 in *Key Events in the Life of the Historical Jesus: A Collaborative Exploration of Context and Coherence*. Edited by Darrell L. Bock and Robert L. Webb. Grand Rapids: Eerdmans, 2009.

———. *The Origins of New Testament Christology*. Downers Grove, IL: InterVarsity, 1976.

Martin, Dale B. *Sex and the Single Savior: Gender and Sexuality in Biblical Interpretation*. Louisville: Westminster John Knox, 2006.

Martyn, J. Louis. *History and Theology in the Fourth Gospel*. Rev. ed. Nashville: Abingdon, 1979.

Marxsen, Willi. *Mark the Evangelist: Studies in the Redaction History of the Gospel*. Nashville: Abingdon, 1969.

März, Claus-Peter. *". . . Lasst eure Lampen Brennen!" Studien zur Q-Vorlage von Lk 12,35–14,24*. ETS 20. Leipzig: Benno, 1991.

Mason, A. A. "Case of Congenital Ichthyosiform Erythrodermia of Brocq Treated by Hypnosis." *British Medical Journal* 2 (1952): 422–23.

Mason, Steve. "Contradiction or Counterpoint? Josephus and Historical Method." *Review of Rabbinic Judaism* 6 (2003): 145–88.

———. *Life of Josephus*. Vol. 9 of *Flavius Josephus: Translation and Commentary*. Leiden: Brill, 2001.

———. "Response." Pages 277–312 in *Rethinking the Jewish War: Archaeology, Society, Traditions*. Edited by Anthony Giambrone. EBib 84. Leuven: Peeters, 2021.

Matthews, Christopher R. Review of *Story as History—History as Story*, by Samuel Byrskog. *JBL* 121 (2002): 175–77.

Mattill, A. J., Jr. *Luke and the Last Things: A Perspective for the Understanding of Lukan Thought*. Dillsboro: Western North Carolina Press, 1979.

Matusova, Ekaterina. *The Meaning of the Letter of Aristeas in Light of Biblical Interpretation and Grammatical Tradition, and with Reference to Its Historical Context*. FRLANT 260. Göttingen: Vandenhoeck & Ruprecht, 2015.

Mauser, Ulrich. *Christ in the Wilderness: The Wilderness Theme in the Second Gospel and Its Basis in the Biblical Tradition*. SBT 39. Naperville, IL: Allenson, 1963.

Mayer, Elizabeth Lloyd. *Extraordinary Knowing: Science, Skepticism, and the Inexplicable Powers of the Human Mind*. New York: Bantam, 2007.

Mayer, Wendy, and Pauline Allen. *The Churches of Syrian Antioch (300–638 CE)*. Late Antique History and Religion 1. Leuven: Peeters, 2012.

Mayer-Schärtel, Bärbel. *Das Frauenbild des Josephus: Eine sozialgeschichtliche und kulturanthropologische Untersuchung*. Stuttgart: Kohlhammer, 1995.

Mayordomo, Moisés. "Eunuchen im Horizont der Gottestherrschaft (Mt 19,12): Überlegungen zu einer kühnen Metapher." *Jahrbuch für biblische Theologie* 33 (2018): 85–106.

Mazzoni, Giuliana, and Alan Scoboria. "Non-Believed Memories." *Psychological Science* 21 (2010): 1134–40.

McArthur, Harvey K. "The Burden of Proof in Historical Jesus Research." *ExpTim* 82 (1970–71): 116–19.

———. "Celibacy in Judaism at the Time of Christian Beginnings." *AUSS* 25 (1987): 163–81.

———. "A Survey of Recent Gospel Research." *Int* 18 (1964): 39–55.

McCarroll, Christopher Jude, and John Sutton. "Memory and Perspective." Pages 113–26 in *The Routledge Handbook of Philosophy of Memory*. Edited by Sven Bernecker and Kourken Michelilan. New York: Routledge, 2017.

McClure, Kevin. *The Evidence for Marian Apparitions*. Wellingborough: Aquarian, 1984.

McComb, Samuel. *Christianity and the Modern Mind*. London: Methuen, 1910.

McGrath, James F. *What Jesus Learned from Women*. Eugene, OR: Cascade, 2021.

McGrew, Lydia. *The Mirror or the Mask: Liberating the Gospels from Literary Devices*. Tampa, FL: DeWard, 2019.

McHugh, John F. *A Critical and Exegetical Commentary on John 1–4*. Edited by Graham N. Stanton. ICC. London: T&T Clark, 2009.

McIver, Robert K. *Memory, Jesus, and the Synoptic Gospels*. RBS 59. Atlanta: Society of Biblical Literature, 2011.

McKay, J. Michael, Jr. "Is Joshua a Type of Christ in Hebrews 4.8? An Assessment of the Referent of Ἰησοῦς." *NTS* 68 (2022): 105–18.

McKnight, Scot. *Jesus and His Death: Historiography, the Historical Jesus, and Atonement Theory*. Waco, TX: Baylor University Press, 2005.

———. "Jesus and Prophetic Actions." *BBR* 10 (2000): 197–232.

———. "Jesus and the Twelve." Pages 181–214 in *Key Events in the Life of Jesus: A Collaborative Exploration of Context and Coherence*. Edited by Darrell L. Bock and Robert L. Webb. Grand Rapids: Eerdmans, 2009.

McMahon, Jean. *Harriet Tubman: The Life and Life Stories*. Madison: University of Wisconsin Press, 2003.

Meade, Michelle L., and Henry L. Roediger. "Explorations in the Social Contagion of Memory." *Memory and Cognition* 30 (2002): 995–1009.

Meeks, Wayne A. "Moses as God and King." Pages 354–71 in *Religions in Antiquity: Essays in Memory of Erwin Ramsdell Goodenough*. Edited by Jacob Neusner. Leiden: Brill, 1970.

———. *The Prophet-King: Moses Traditions and the Johannine Christology*. NovTSup 14. Leiden: Brill, 1967.

Meggitt, Justin. "The Historical Jesus and Healing: Jesus' Miracles in Psychosocial Context." Pages 17–43 in *Spiritual Healing: Scientific and Religious Perspectives*. Edited by Fraser Watts. Cambridge: Cambridge University Press, 2011.

Méheust, Bertrand. *Jésus thaumaturge: Enquête sur l'homme et ses miracles*. Paris: InterEditions, 2015.

———. *Un voyant prodigieux: Alexis Didier, 1826–1866*. Paris: Les Empêcheurs de penser en rond, 2003.

Meier, John. "Basic Methodology in the Quest for the Historical Jesus." Pages 291–331 in vol. 1 of *The Handbook of the Study of the Historical Jesus*. Edited by Tom Holmén and Stanley E. Porter. Leiden: Brill, 2010.

———. "The Circle of the Twelve: Did It Exist during Jesus' Public Ministry?" *JBL* 116 (1997): 635–72.

———. "The Debate on the Resurrection of the Dead: An Incident from the Ministry of the Historical Jesus?" *JSNT* 77 (2000): 3–24.

———. "Did the Historical Jesus Prohibit All Oaths?" *JSHJ* 5 (2007): 175–204; 6 (2008): 3–24.

———. "From Elijah-Like Prophet to Royal Davidic Messiah." Pages 45–83 in *Jesus: A Colloquium in the Holy Land*. Edited by Doris Donnelly. New York: Continuum, 2001.

———. "The Historical Jesus and Oaths: A Response to Donald A. Hagner and Jonathan Klawans." *JSHJ* 6 (2008): 49–58.

———. "Jesus, the Twelve, and the Restoration of Israel." Pages 365–404 in *Restoration: Old Testament, Jewish, and Christian Perspectives*. Edited by James M. Scott. JSJSup 72. Leiden: Brill, 2001.

———. *A Marginal Jew: Rethinking the Historical Jesus*. 5 vols. AYRL. New Haven: Yale University Press, 1991–2016.

———. *The Vision of Matthew: Christ, Church, and Morality in the First Gospel.* New York: Paulist, 1979.

Melton, J. Gordon. "Spiritualization and Reaffirmation: What Really Happens When Prophecy Fails." Pages 145–57 in *Expecting Armageddon: Essential Readings in Failed Prophecy*. Edited by Jon R. Stone. New York: Routledge, 2000.

Melzer-Keller, Helga. *Jesus und die Frauen: Eine Verhältnisbestimmung nach den synoptischen Überlieferungen*. HBS 14. Freiburg: Herder, 1997.

Merklein, Helmut. "Die Umkehrpredigt bei Johannes dem Täufer und Jesus von Nazaret." *BZ* 25 (1981): 29–46.

Merz, Annette. "How a Woman Who Fought Back and Demanded Her Rights Became an Importunate Widow: The Transformations of a Parable of Jesus." Pages 49–86 in *Jesus from Judaism to Christianity: A Continuum Approach to the Historical Jesus*. Edited by Tom Holmén. London: Bloomsbury, 2007.

———. "Wie verändert die Genderforschung die Frage nach dem historischen Jesus?" Pages 597–622 in *Jesus—Gestalt und Gestaltungen: Rezeption des Galiläers in Wissenschaft, Kirche und Gesellschaft: Festschrift für Gerd Theissen zum 70. Geburtstag*. Edited by Petra von Gemünden, David G. Horrell, and Max Küchler. NTOA/SUNT 100. Göttingen: Vandenhoeck & Ruprecht, 2013.

Meye, Robert P. *Jesus and the Twelve: Discipleship and Revelation in Mark's Gospel.* Grand Rapids: Eerdmans, 1968.

Meyer, Ben F. "Appointed Deed, Appointed Doer: Jesus and the Scriptures." Pages 155–76 in *Authenticating the Activities of Jesus*. Edited by Bruce Chilton and Craig A. Evans. NTTS 28.2. Leiden: Brill, 1999.

Meyer, Eduard. *Ursprung und Anfänge des Christentums*. Vol. 1. Darmstadt: Wissenschaftliche Buchgesellschaft, 1962.

Michaels, J. Ramsey. "The Itinerant Jesus and His Home Town." Pages 177–93 in *Authenticating the Activities of Jesus*. Edited by Bruce Chilton and C. A. Evans. NTTS 28.2. Leiden: Brill, 1999.

Mickelm, E. R. *Miracles and the New Psychology: A Study in the Healing Miracles of the New Testament*. Oxford: Oxford University Press, 1922.

Middleton, Conyers. *A Free Inquiry into the Miraculous Powers, Which Are Supposed to Have Been Fulfilled in the Christian Church, from the Earliest Ages through Several Successive Centuries*. London: Manby & Cox, 1743.

Miller, Robert J. "The Domain and Function of Epistemological Humility in Historical Jesus Studies." *JSHJ* 12 (2014): 130–42.

Miroshnikov, Ivan, and Alexey B. Somov. "Two Men on a Dining Couch: Luke 17,34 as a Meal Scene." *ETL* 99 (2023): 113–29.

Mitchell, Margaret M. "Mark, the Long-Form Pauline Εὐαγγέλιον." Pages 201–17 in *Modern and Ancient Literary Criticism of the Gospels: Continuing the Debate on Gospel Genre(s)*. Edited by Robert Matthew Calhoun, David P. Moessner, and Tobias Nicklas. WUNT 451. Tübingen: Mohr Siebeck, 2020.

Moessner, David P. *Lord of the Banquet: The Literary and Theological Significance of the Lukan Travel Narrative*. Minneapolis: Fortress, 1989.

———. *Luke the Historian of Israel's Legacy, Theologian of Israel's "Christ."* BZNW 182. Berlin: de Gruyter, 2016.

Moloney, Francis J. *"A Hard Saying": The Gospel and Culture*. Collegeville, MN: Liturgical, 2001.

Monden, Louis. *Signs and Wonders: A Study of the Miraculous Element in Religion*. New York: Desclee, 1966.

Montefiore, C. G. *The Synoptic Gospels*. 2 vols. 2nd ed. New York: Ktav, 1968 (1927).

Montefiore, Hugh. *The Miracles of Jesus*. London: SPCK, 2005.

———. "Revolt in the Desert?" *NTS* 8 (1961): 135–41.

Moo, Douglas J. *The Epistle to the Romans*. NICNT. Grand Rapids: Eerdmans, 1996.

Moore, C. J. "Can We Hasten the Parousia? An Examination of Matt 24:14 and Its Implications for Missional Practice." *Themelios* 44 (2019): 291–311.

Moore, George Foot. *Judaism in the First Centuries of the Christian Era*. 2 vols. New York: Schocken, 1971.

Morris, Leon. *The Gospel according to John: The English Text with Introduction, Exposition, and Notes*. NICNT. Grand Rapids: Eerdmans, 1971.

Moschos, John. *The Spiritual Meadow (Pratum Spirituale)*. Cistercian Studies 139. Kalamazoo, MI: Cistercian, 1992.

Moss, Candida. "Fashioning Mark: Early Christian Discussions about the Scribe and Status of the Second Gospel." *NTS* 21 (2021): 181–204.

Mosse, Martin. *The Three Gospels: New Testament Introduced by the Synoptic Problem*. Eugene, OR: Wipf & Stock, 2007.

Moule, C. F. D. "The Influence of Circumstances on the Use of Eschatological Terms." *JTS* 15 (1964): 1–15.

Mournet, Terence C. "The Jesus Tradition as Oral Tradition." Pages 39–61 in *Jesus in Memory: Traditions in Oral and Scribal Perspectives*. Edited by Werner H. Kelber and Samuel Byrskog. Waco, TX: Baylor University Press, 2009.

Mowinckel, Sigmund. *He That Cometh*. Oxford: Blackwell, 1956.

Moxnes, Halvor. "The Contextualizing of Constructing Histories of Jesus: Modern and Ancient Masculinities." Pages 93–114 in *Jesus, quo vadis? Entwicklungen und Perspektiven der aktuellen Jesusforschung*. Edited by Eckart David Schmidt. BThSt 177. Göttingen: Vandenhoeck & Ruprecht, 2018.

———. *Putting Jesus in His Place: A Radical Vision of Household and Kingdom*. Louisville: Westminster John Knox, 2003.

Müller, Christoph G. "Priska und Aquila: Der Weg eines Ehepaares und die paulinische Mission." *MTS* 54 (2003): 195–210.

Mullin, Robert Bruce. *Miracles and the Modern Imagination*. New Haven: Yale University Press, 1996.

Munck, Johannes. *Paul and the Salvation of Mankind*. Atlanta: John Knox, 1977.

Muñoa, Phillip. "John, Jesus, and Metatron: Mediators, Knowledge, and the Importance of a Neglected Interpretation." Pages 415–37 in *With Wisdom as a Robe: Qumran and Other Jewish Studies in Honour of Ida Fröhlich*. Edited by Károly Dániel Dobos and Miklós Kőszeghy. Hebrew Bible Monographs 21. Sheffield: Sheffield Phoenix Press, 2009.

Murphy, Gardner, and Robert O. Ballou. *William James and Psychical Research*. New York: Viking, 1960.

Murphy, Michael. *The Future of the Body: Explorations into the Further Evolution of Human Nature*. Los Angeles: Tarcher, 1992.

Murphy-O'Connor, Jerome. "Prisca and Aquila: Traveling Tentmakers and Church Builders." *BRev* 8.2 (1992): 40–51, 62.

———. Review of *Jesus and the Eyewitnesses*, by Richard Bauckham. *RB* 114 (2007): 621–30.

Myles, Robert J. "Crowds and Power in Early Palestinian Tradition." *JSHJ* 18 (2020): 124–40.

Naegeli-Osjord, Hans. *Possession and Exorcism*. Oregon, WI: New Frontiers Center, 1988.

Narasimhaswamiji, H. H. *Life of Sai Baba*. 2nd ed. Mylapore: All India Sai Samaj, 2004.

Neisser, Ulric. *Memory Observed: Remembering in Natural Contexts*. San Francisco: Freeman, 1982.

Nelligan, Thomas P. *The Quest for Mark's Gospel: An Exploration of the Case for Mark's Use of First Corinthians*. Eugene, OR: Pickwick, 2015.

Neusner, Jacob. *Eliezer ben Hyrcanus: The Tradition and the Man*. Vol. 1. SJLA 3. Leiden: Brill, 1973.

———. *Messiah in Context: Israel's History and Destiny in Formative Judaism*. Philadelphia: Fortress, 1984.

———. *The Peripatetic Saying: The Problem of the Thrice-Told Tale in Talmudic Literature*. BJS 89. Chico, CA: Scholars Press, 1985.

Nevin, Alfred. *Popular Expositor of the Gospels and Acts*. Philadelphia: Ziegler & McCurdy, 1872.

Newman, Barbara. *The Permeable Self: Five Medieval Relationships*. Philadelphia: University of Pennsylvania Press, 2021.

———., ed. *Thomas of Cantimpré: The Collected Saints' Lives*. Turnhout, Belgium: Brepols, 2008.

Newman, John Henry. *An Essay in Aid of a Grammar of Assent*. Edited by I. T. Kerr. Oxford: Clarendon, 1985.

———. *Two Essays on Biblical and on Ecclesiastical Miracles*. London: Longmans, Green, 1890.

Newnham, W. O. *Alresford: Essays for the Times*. London: Longmans, Green, 1891.

Nichols, Terence L. "Miracles in Science and Theology." *Zygon* 37 (2002): 703–16.

Nickell, Joe. *Looking for a Miracle: Weeping Icons, Relics, Stigmata, Visions, and Healing Cures*. Amherst, NY: Prometheus, 1993.

Nickelsburg, George W. E. *Ancient Judaism and Christian Origins*. Minneapolis: Fortress, 2003.

———. "The Genre and Function of the Markan Passion Narrative." *HTR* 73 (1980): 153–84.

———. *Jewish Literature between the Bible and the Mishnah*. 2nd ed. Minneapolis: Fortress, 2005.

———. "Torah and the Deuteronomic Scheme in the Apocrypha and Pseudepigrapha: Variations on a Theme and Some Noteworthy Examples of Its Absence." Pages 222–35 in *Das Gesetz im frühen Judentum und im Neuen Testament: Festschrift für Christoph Burchard zum 75. Geburtstag*. Edited by Dieter Sänger and Matthias Konradt. NTOA/SUNT 57. Fribourg: Vandenhoeck & Ruprecht, 2006.

Nickelsburg, George W. E., and James C. VanderKam. *1 Enoch 2: A Commentary on the Book of 1 Enoch Chapters 37–82*. Hermeneia. Minneapolis: Fortress, 2012.

Nicklas, Tobias. "Alternatives to Form and Tradition Criticism in Jesus Research." Pages 715–42 in vol. 1 of *The Handbook of the Study of the Historical Jesus*. Edited by Tom Holmén and Stanley E. Porter. Leiden: Brill, 2010.

Niederwimmer, Kurt. *Askese und Mysterium: Über Ehe, Ehescheidung und Eheverzicht in den Anfängen des christlichen Glaubens*. FRLANT 113. Göttingen: Vandenhoeck & Ruprecht, 1975.

———. "Johannes Markus und die Frage nach dem Verfasser des zweiten Evangeliums." *ZNW* 58 (1967): 172–86.

Niemand, Christoph. *Jesus und sein Weg zum Kreuz: Ein historisch-rekonstruktives und theologisches Modellbild*. Stuttgart: Kohlhammer, 2007.

Nietzsche, F. W. *The Antichrist*. New York: Knopf, 1920.

Nineham, D. E. *Saint Mark*. Westminster Pelican Commentaries. Philadelphia: Westminster, 1977 (1963).

Ninow, Friedbert. *Indicators of Typology within the Old Testament: The Exodus Motif*. Friedensauer Schriftenreihe 4. Frankfurt am Main: Lang, 2001.

Nolland, John. *The Gospel of Matthew*. NIGTC. Grand Rapids: Eerdmans, 2005.

———. *Luke*. 3 vols. WBC 35A–C. Nashville: Nelson, 1989–93.

North, Wendy E. S. *What John Knew and What John Wrote: A Study in John and the Synoptics*. Lanham, MD: Lexington, 2020.

Notley, R. Steven, and Ze'ev Safrai. *Parables of the Sages: Jewish Wisdom from Jesus to Rav Ashi*. Jerusalem: Carta, 2011.

Novenson, Matthew V. *The Grammar of Messianism: An Ancient Jewish Political Idiom and Its Uses*. Oxford: Oxford University Press, 2017.

Oakman, Douglas E. *Jesus and the Economic Questions of His Day*. Studies in the Bible and Early Christianity 8. Lewiston, NY: Mellen, 1986.

Öhler, Markus. "Die Jesusforschung und die Wundererzählungen—eine dreidimensionale Perspektive." Pages 31–58 in *Christologie zwischen Judentum und Christentum*. Edited by Christian Danz, Kathy Ehrensperger, and Walter Homolka. Dogmatik in der Moderne 30. Tübingen: Mohr Siebeck, 2020.

———. "The Expectation of Elijah and the Presence of the Kingdom of God." *JBL* 118 (1999): 461–76.

Oke, C. C. "The Rearrangement and Transmission of Mark ix.11–13." *ExpTim* 64 (1953): 187–88.

O'Neill, J. C. *Messiah: Six Lectures on the Ministry of Jesus*. Cambridge: Cochrane, 1980.

Oporto, Santiago Guijarro. "Kingdom and Family in Conflict: A Contribution to the Study of the Historical Jesus." Pages 210–38 in *Social Scientific Models for Interpreting the Bible: Essays by the Context Group in Honor of Bruce J. Malina*. Edited by John Pilch. BibInt 53. Leiden: Brill, 2000.

O'Regan, Brenda, and Caryle Hirshberg. *Spontaneous Remission: An Annotated Bibliography*. Petaluma, CA: Institute of Noetic Sciences, 1993.

Os, Bas van. *Psychological Analyses and the Historical Jesus: New Ways to Explore Christian Origins*. London: Bloomsbury, 2012.

Otto, Rudolf. *The Kingdom of God and the Son of Man*. New rev. ed. London: Lutterworth, 1943.

———. *Life and Ministry of Jesus According to the Historical and Critical Method*. Chicago: Open Court, 1908.

Ounsworth, Richard J. *Joshua Typology in the New Testament*. WUNT 2/328. Tübingen: Mohr Siebeck, 2012.

Pagels, Elaine. *Revelations: Visions, Prophecy, and Politics in the Book of Revelation*. New York: Penguin, 2012.

Pagola, José Antonio. *Jesus: An Historical Approximation*. Miami: Convivium, 2009.

Paley, William. *Evidences of Christianity*. Edited by George Fisk. Cambridge: Hall & Son, 1884.

Palmer, Jerome. *Our Lady Returns to Egypt*. San Bernardino: Culligan, 1969.

Pannenberg, Wolfhart. *Jesus—God and Man*. Philadelphia: Westminster, 1968.

———. *Systematic Theology*. Vol. 2. Grand Rapids: Eerdmans, 1994.

———. *Theology and the Philosophy of Science*. Philadelphia: Westminster, 1976.

Pao, David W., and Eckhard Schnabel. "Luke." Pages 251–414 in *Commentary on the New Testament Use of the Old Testament*. Edited by G. K. Beale and D. A. Carson. Grand Rapids: Baker Academic, 2007.

Parambi, Baby. *The Discipleship of the Women in the Gospel of Matthew: An Exegetical Study of Matt 27:51b–56, 57–61 and 28:1–10*. TGST 94. Rome: Pontifica Università Gregoriana, 2003.

Parker, D. C. *The Living Text of the Gospels*. Cambridge: Cambridge University Press, 1997.

Parks, Sara. *Gender in the Rhetoric of Jesus: Women in Q*. Lanham, MD: Lexington, 2019.

Parrott, Douglas M. *Nag Hammadi Codices iii,3–4 and v,1 with Papyrus Berolinensis 8502,3 and Oxyrhynchus Papyrus 1081: Eugnostos and the Sophia of Jesus Christ*. NHS 27. Leiden: Brill, 1991.

Parry, Milman. *The Making of Homeric Verse: The Collected Papers of Milman Parry*. Edited by Adam Parry. Oxford: Clarendon, 1971.

Parton, James. "Our Roman Catholic Brethren." *Atlantic Monthly* 21 (April 1868): 432–45.

Pastrovicchi, Angelo. *St. Joseph of Copertino*. St. Louis: Herder, 1918.

Patai, Raphael. *The Messiah Texts*. New York: Avon, 1979.

Patihis, Lawrence, Steven J. Frenda, Aurora K. R. LePort, Nicole Petersen, Rebecca M. Nichols, Craig E. L. Stark, James L. McGaugh, and Elizabeth F. Loftus. "False Memories in Highly Superior Autobiographical Memory Individuals." *Proceedings of the National Academy of Sciences* 110 (2013): 20947–52.

Patterson, Stephen J. "Can You Trust a Gospel? A Review of Richard Bauckham's *Jesus and the Eyewitnesses*." *JSHJ* 6 (2008): 194–210.

Pattison, E. Mansell, Nikolajs A. Lapins, and Hans Doerr. "Faith Healing: A Study of Personality and Function." *Journal of Nervous and Mental Disease* 157 (1973): 397–403.

Paul, Dagmar J. *"Untypische" Texte im Matthäusevangelium? Studien zu Charakter, Funktion und Bedeutung einer Textgruppe des matthäischen Sonderguts*. NTAbh 50. Münster: Aschendorff, 2005.

Paulus, H. E. G. *Das Leben Jesu als Grundlage einer reinen Geschichte des Ur-*

christentums: Dargestellt durch eine allgemeinverständliche Geschichterzählung über alle Abschnitte der vier Evangelien und eine wortgetreue durch Zwischensätze erklärte. 3 vols. Heidelberg: Winter, 1828.

Peeters, Paul. *Le tréfonds oriental de l'hagiographie Byzantine.* Orient et Byzance. Brussels: Société des Bollandistes, 1950.

Perrin, Norman. *Rediscovering the Teaching of Jesus.* New York: Harper & Row, 1967.

Pervo, Richard I. *Acts: A Commentary.* Hermeneia. Minneapolis: Augsburg Fortress, 2008.

Pesch, Rudolf. *Das Abendmahl und Jesu Todesverständnis.* QD 80. Freiburg: Herder, 1978.

———. *Das Markusevangelium.* 2 vols. HThKNT 2. Freiburg: Herder, 1976–77.

———. *Die Apostelgeschichte.* 2nd ed. EKKNT 5. Neukirchen-Vluyn: Neukirchener Theologie, 2014.

Peskowitz, Miriam. *Spinning Fantasies: Rabbis, Gender, and History.* Berkeley: University of California Press, 1997.

Peter, John J. "Luke's Source Claims in the Context of Ancient Historiography." *JSHJ* 18 (2020): 35–60.

Petersen, Norman R. "'Point of View' in Mark's Narrative." *Semeia* 12 (1978): 97–121.

Petersen, Silke. "Mutmaßungen über eine mögliche These, oder: Was erwartete Jesus in Jerusalem?" Pages 298–305 in Eckhard Rau's *Perspektiven des Lebens Jesu: Plädoyer für die Anknüpfung an eine schwierige Forschungstradition.* Edited by Silke Petersen. BWANT 203. Stuttgart: Kohlhammer, 2013.

Phelan, Edna Beyer. *Don Bosco: A Spiritual Portrait.* New York: Doubleday, 1963.

Phillips, Godfrey E. *The House of the Virgin Mary: The Miraculous Story of Its Journey from Nazareth to a Hillside in Italy.* Manchester, NH: Sophia Institute, 2017.

Phillips, Victoria. "Full Disclosure: Towards a Complete Characterization of the Women Who Followed Jesus in the Gospel according to Mark." Pages 13–32 in *Transformative Encounters. Jesus and Women Re-Viewed.* Edited by Ingrid Rosa Kitzberger. BibInt 43. Leiden: Brill, 2000.

Philonenko, Marc. *Le Notre Père: De la Prière de Jésus à la prière des disciples.* Bibliothèque des Histoires. Paris: Gallimard, 2001.

Phipps, William E. "Itinerating Wives and Mary Magdalene." *Currents in Theology and Mission* 33 (2006): 394–96.

Piotrowski, Nicholas G. "The Concept of Exile in Late Second Temple Judaism: A Review of Recent Scholarship." *CBR* 15 (2017): 214–47.

Pitre, Brant James. "Blessing the Barren and Warning the Fecund: Jesus' Message for Women concerning Pregnancy and Childbirth." *JSNT* 81 (2001): 59–80.

———. "From Reimarus to Allison: The Quest for Jesus and the Christological 'Thunderbolt' (Matt 11:25–27)//Luke 10:21–22." Pages 373–404 in *"To Recover What Has Been Lost": Essays on Eschatology, Intertextuality, and Reception History in Honor of Dale C. Allison Jr.* Edited by Tucker S. Ferda, Daniel Frayer-Griggs, and Nathan C. Johnson. NovTSup 183. Leiden: Brill, 2021.

———. "The Historical Jesus and the Apocalyptic 'Thunderbolt' (Matthew 11:25–27//Luke 10:21–22)." Pages 169–85 in *The Figure of Jesus in History and Theology: Essays in Honor of John Meier*. Edited by Vincent T. M. Skemp and Kelley Coblentz Bautch. CBQ Imprints 1. Washington, DC: Catholic Biblical Association of America, 2020.

———. "Jesus, the New Temple, and the New Priesthood." *Letter and Spirit* 2 (2006): 47–83.

———. *Jesus, the Tribulation, and the End of the Exile*. WUNT 2/204. Tübingen: Mohr Siebeck, 2005.

———. *Jesus and the Last Supper*. Grand Rapids: Eerdmans, 2015.

Poirier, John C. "Jesus as an Elijianic Figure in Luke 4:16–20." *CBQ* 71 (2009): 349–63.

Poirier, John C., and Jeffrey Peterson, eds. *Marcan Priority without Q: Explorations in the Farrer Hypothesis*. LNTS 455. London: T&T Clark, 2015.

Pokorný, Petr. "Lexikalische und rhetorische Eigentümlichkeiten der ältesten Jesustradition." Pages 393–408 in *Der historische Jesus: Tendenzen und Perspektiven der gegenwärtigen Forschungen*. Edited by Jens Schröter and Ralph Brucker. BZNW 114. Berlin: de Gruyter, 2002.

Poole, Matthew. *Annotations on the Holy Bible*. 3 vols. London: Bohn, 1846.

Porter, Stanley. *The Criteria for Authenticity in Historical-Jesus Research*. JSNTSup 191. Sheffield: Sheffield Academic, 2000.

Porter, Stanley, and Bryan R. Dyer. *Origins of New Testament Christology: An Introduction to the Traditions and Titles Applied to Jesus*. Grand Rapids: Baker Academic, 2023.

Posnanski, Joe. *The Life and Afterlife of Harry Houdini*. New York: Avid Reader, 2019.

Powell, Diane Hennacy. *The ESP Enigma: The Scientific Case for Psychic Phenomena*. New York: Walker, 2009.

Powell, Mark Allan. "Jesus and the Pathetic Wicked: Re-visiting Sanders's View of Jesus' Friendship with Sinners." *JSNT* 13 (2015): 188–208.

Price, Richard M., trans. *A History of the Monks of Syria by Theodoret of Cyrrhus*. Cistercian Studies 88. Kalamazoo, MI: Cistercian, 1988.

Price, Robert M. "Mary Magdalene: Gnostic Apostle?" *Grail* 6 (1990): 54–76.

———. *The Widow Traditions in Luke-Acts: A Feminist-Critical Scrutiny*. SBLDS 155. Atlanta: Scholars Press, 1997.

Prince, Walter. *Noted Witnesses for Psychic Occurrences*. New York: University Books, 1963.

Puig i Tàrrech, Armand. *Jesus: A Biography*. Waco, TX: Baylor University Press, 2011.

———. "Jesus and Jewish Writings." Pages 79–114 in *Authoritative Writings in Early Judaism and Early Christianity: Their Origin, Collection, and Meaning*. Edited by Tobias Nicklas and Jens Schröter. WUNT 441. Tübingen: Mohr Siebeck, 2020.

———. *La parabole des dix vierges (Mt 25,1–13)*. AnBib 102. Rome: Biblical Institute Press, 1983.

Pulos, Lee, and Gary Richman. *Miracles and Other Realities*. New York: Simon & Schuster, 2021.

Qimron, Elisha, and John Strugnell. *Qumran Cave 4.V: Miqṣat Maʿaśe Ha-Torah*. DJD 5. Oxford: Clarendon, 1994.

Quesnell, Quentin. "'Made Themselves Eunuchs for the Kingdom of Heaven' (Mt 19,12)." *CBQ* 30 (1968): 335–58.

Rabenau, Merten. *Studien zum Buch Tobit*. BZAW 220. Berlin: de Gruyter, 1994.

Rad, Gerhard von. *The Theology of Israel's Prophetic Traditions*. Vol. 2 of *Old Testament Theology*. New York: Harper & Row, 1965.

Radin, Dean. *The Conscious Universe: The Scientific Truth of Psychic Phenomena*. San Francisco: HarperSanFrancisco, 1997.

———. *Supernormal: Science, Yoga, and the Evidence for Extraordinary Psychic Abilities*. New York: Crown, 2013.

Radl, Walter. *Das Evangelium nach Lukas 1,1–9,50*. Freiburg: Herder, 2003.

———. *Paulus und Jesus im lukanischen Doppelwerk: Untersuchungen zu Parallelmotiven im Lukasevangelium und in der Apostelgeschichte*. EHS.T 49. Bern: Lang, 1975.

Rahner, Karl. *Visions and Prophecies*. New York: Herder & Herder, 1963.

Raitt, Thomas M. "The Prophetic Summons to Repentance." *ZAW* 83 (1971): 30–49.

———. *A Theology of Exile: Judgment/Deliverance in Jeremiah and Ezekiel*. Philadelphia: Fortress, 1977.

Ramelli, Ilaria L. E. "Colleagues of Apostles, Presbyters, and Bishops: Women *Syzygoi* in Ancient Christian Communities." Pages 26–58 in *Patterns of Woman's Leadership in Early Christianity*. Edited by Joan E. Taylor and Ilaria Ramelli. Oxford: Oxford University Press, 2021.

Rapp, Claudia. "Comparison, Paradigm, and the Case of Moses in Panegyric and Hagiography." Pages 277–98 in *The Propaganda of Power: The Role of Panegyric in Late Antiquity*. Edited by Mary Whitby. Mnemosyne Supplement 183. Leiden: Brill, 1998.

Rau, Eckhard. "Arm und Reich im Spiegel des Wirkens Jesu." Pages 249–68 in *Eschatologie und Ethik im frühen Christentum: Festschrift für Günter Haufe zum 75. Geburtstag*. Edited by Christfried Böttrich. Frankfurt am Main: Lang, 2006.

———. "Wie entstehen unechte Jesusworte?" Pages 159–85 in *Gemeinschaft am Evangelium: Festschrift für Wiard Popkes zum 60. Geburtstag*. Edited by Edwin Brandt, Paul S. Fiddes, and Joachim Molthagen. Leipzig: Evangelische Verlagsanstalt, 1996.

Ravin-Anderson, Angela. "They Had Followed Him from Galilee: The Female Disciples." *Priscilla Papers* 28 (2014): 5–8.

Redman, Judith C. S. "How Accurate Are Eyewitnesses? Bauckham and the Eyewitnesses in the Light of Psychological Research." *JBL* 129 (2010): 177–97.

Reid, Barbara E. *Choosing the Better Part? Women in the Gospel of Luke*. Collegeville, MN: Liturgical Press, 1996.

———. "Do You See This Woman? Luke 7:36–50 as a Paradigm for Feminist Hermeneutics." *BR* 40 (1995): 37–49.

Reimarus, Hermann Samuel. *Reimarus: Fragments*. Edited by Charles H. Talbert. Philadelphia: Fortress, 1970.

Reiser, Marius. *Jesus and Judgment: The Eschatological Proclamation in Its Jewish Context*. Minneapolis: Fortress, 1997.

Remus, Harold. *Jesus as Healer*. Cambridge: Cambridge University Press, 1997.

Rhine, J. B. *The Reach of the Mind*. New York: Sloane, 1962.

Rhine, Louisa E. *Hidden Channels of the Mind*. New York: Morrow, 1961.

Ricci, Carla. *Mary Magdalene and Many Others: Women Who Followed Jesus*. Minneapolis: Fortress, 1994.

Rice, Heather J., and David C. Rubin. "Remembering from Any Angle: The Flexibility of Visual Perspective during Retrieval." *Consciousness and Cognition* 20 (2011): 568–77.

Riches, John. *Jesus and the Transformation of Judaism*. London: Darton, Longman & Todd, 1980.

Riesner, Rainer. *Messias Jesus: Seine Geschichte, seine Botschaft und ihre Überlieferung*. Giessen: Brunnen, 2019.

Rigato, Maria-Luisa. "Maria la Maddalena: Ancora riflessioni su colei che fu chiamata 'le Resa-grande' (Lc 8,2; 24,10; Gv 20,1.10–17)." *Studia Patavina* 50 (2003): 727–52.

———. "'Remember . . . Then They Remembered': Luke 24.6–8." Pages 269–80 in *A Feminist Companion to Luke*. Edited by Amy-Jill Levine with Marianne Blickenstaff. London: Sheffield Academic, 2002.

Rigopoulos, Antonio. "Sāī Bābā of Śirḍī and Yoga Powers." Pages 381–426 in *Yoga*

Powers: Extraordinary Capacities Attained through Meditation and Concentration. Edited by Knut A. Jacobsen. Brill's Indological Library 37. Leiden: Brill, 2012.

Riniker, Christian. *Die Gerichtsverkündigung Jesu*. EHS.T 653. Bern: Lang, 1999.

Roberts, Kathryn L. "God, Prophet, and King: Eating and Drinking on the Mountain in First Kings 18:41." *CBQ* 62 (2000): 632–44.

Robinson, James M., Paul Hoffmann, and John S. Kloppenborg. *The Critical Edition of Q*. Hermeneia. Minneapolis: Fortress, 2000.

Robinson, John A. T. "Elijah, John, and Jesus: An Essay in Detection." *NTS* 4 (1958): 263–81.

———. *Jesus and His Coming*. 2nd ed. Philadelphia: Westminster, 1979.

———. *The Priority of John*. Edited by J. F. Coakley. London: SCM, 1985.

Robinson, Jonathan Rivett. *Markan Typology: Miracle, Scripture, and Christology in Mark 4:35–6:45*. LNTS 678. London: T&T Clark, 2023.

Rodríguez, Rafael. "Authenticating Criteria: The Use and Misuse of a Critical Method." *JSHJ* 7 (2009): 152–67.

———. "The Embarrassing Truth about Jesus: The Criterion of Embarrassment and the Failure of Historical Authenticity." Pages 132–51 in *Jesus, History, and the Demise of Authenticity: The Rise and Fall of the Search for an Authentic Jesus. Authenticity after the Third Quest*. Edited by Anthony Le Donne and Chris Keith. London: T&T Clark, 2012.

———. "Jesus as His Friends Remembered Him: A Review of Dale Allison's *Constructing Jesus*." *JSHJ* 12 (2014): 224–44.

———. *Structuring Christian Memory: Jesus in Tradition, Performance, and Text*. LNTS 407. London: T&T Clark, 2010.

Rogers, T. J. "Shaking the Dust off the Markan Mission Discourse." *JSNT* 27 (2004): 169–92.

Rogo, D. Scott. *Miracles: A Parascientific Inquiry into Wondrous Phenomena*. Chicago: Contemporary Books, 1983.

Romaniuk, K. "Le Problème des Paulinismes l'Évangile de Marc." *NTS* 23 (1977): 266–77.

Rose, Louis. *Faith Healing*. London: Gollancz, 1968.

Roth, Dieter T. *The Parables in Q*. LNTS 582. London: T&T Clark, 2018.

Rothschild, Claire. *Baptist Traditions and Q*. WUNT 190. Tübingen: Mohr Siebeck, 2005.

Rowlands, Jonathan. *The Metaphysics of Historical Jesus Research: A Prolegomenon to a Future Quest for the Historical Jesus*. London: Routledge, 2023.

Rubenson, Samuel. *The Letters of St. Antony: Monasticism and the Making of a Saint*. SAC. Minneapolis: Fortress, 1995.

Rubinkiewicz, Ryszard. *L'Apocalypse d'Abraham en vieux slave: Introduction, texte critique, traduction et commentaire*. Lublin: Société des Lettres et des Sciences de l'Université Catholique de Lublin, 1987.

Runesson, Anders. *Divine Wrath and Salvation in Matthew: The Narrative World of the First Gospel*. Minneapolis: Fortress, 2016.

Ruppert, Lothar. *Der leidende Gerechte*. Würzburg: Echter, 1972.

———. *Der leidende Gerechte und seine Feinde: Eine Wortfelduntersuchung*. Würzburg: Echter, 1973.

———. *Jesus als der leidende Gerechte? Der Weg Jesu im Lichte eines alt- und zwischentestamentlichen Motivs*. SBS 59. Stuttgart: Katholisches Bibelwerk, 1972.

Russell, Edward H. "Parapsychic Luminosities." *Quadrant* 8.2 (1975): 58–61.

Ruzer, Serge. "Eschatological Failure as God's Mystery: Reassessing Prophecy and Reality at Qumran and in Nascent Christianity." *DSD* 23 (2016): 347–64.

———. *Mapping the New Testament: Early Christian Writings as a Witness for Jewish Biblical Exegesis*. Jewish and Christian Perspectives 13. Leiden: Brill, 2007.

Ryan, Jordan J. "Jesus at the Crossroads of Inference and Imagination: The Relevance of R. G. Collingwood's Philosophy of History for Current Methodological Discussions in Historical Jesus Research." *JSHJ* 13 (2015): 66–89.

———. *The Role of the Synagogue in the Aims of Jesus*. Minneapolis: Fortress, 2017.

Saadia Gaon. *The Book of Beliefs and Opinions*. New Haven: Yale University Press, 1948.

Sabatier, Auguste. *Outlines of a Philosophy of Religion Based on Psychology and History*. London: Hodder & Stoughton, 1901.

Sahlin, H. "The New Exodus of Salvation." Pages 81–95 in *The Root of the Vine: Essays in Biblical Theology*. Edited by Anton Fridrichsen. Westminster: Dacre, 1953.

Saito, Tadashi. *Die Mosevorstellungen im Neuen Testament*. EHS.T 100. Bern: Lang, 1977.

Sand, Alexander. *Reich Gottes und Eheverzicht im Evangelium nach Matthäus*. SBS 109. Stuttgart: Katholisches Bibelwerk, 1983.

Sanday, William. *The Life of Christ in Recent Research*. New York: Oxford University Press, 1907.

Sanders, E. P. *Comparing Judaism and Christianity: Common Judaism, Paul, and the Inner and Outer in the Study of Religion*. Minneapolis: Fortress, 2016.

———. *The Historical Figure of Jesus*. London: Penguin, 1993.

———. *Jesus and Judaism*. Philadelphia: Fortress, 1985.

———. *Judaism: Practice and Belief 63 BCE–66 CE*. London: SCM, 1992.

———. *Paul: The Apostle's Life, Letters, and Thought*. Philadelphia: Fortress, 2015.

———. *The Question of Uniqueness in the Teaching of Jesus*. London: University of London Press, 1990.

Sanders, E. P., and Margaret Davies. *Studying the Synoptic Gospels*. London: SCM, 1989.

Sanders, Jack T. "The Criterion of Coherence and the Randomness of Charisma: Poring through Some Aporias in the Jesus Tradition." *NTS* 44 (1998): 1–25.

Santos, Franklin Santana, and Peter Fenwick. "Death, End of Life Experiences, and Their Theoretical and Clinical Implications for the Mind-Brain Relationship." Pages 165–90 in *Exploring the Frontiers of the Mind-Brain Relationship*. Edited by A. Moreira-Almeida and F. S. Santos. New York: Springer, 2012.

Sauerwein, Ruth. *Elischa: Eine redaktions- und Religionsgeschichte Studie*. BZAW 465. Berlin: de Gruyter, 2014.

Sawicki, Marianne. *Crossing Galilee: Architectures of Contact in the Occupied Land of Jesus*. Harrisburg, PA: Trinity Press International, 2000.

———. "Magdalenes and Tiberiennes: City Women in the Entourage of Jesus." Pages 181–202 in *Transformative Encounters: Jesus and Women Re-Viewed*. Edited by Ingrid Rosa Kitzberger. BibInt 43. Leiden: Brill, 2000.

Schaberg, Jane Dewar. *The Death and Resurrection of the Author and Other Feminist Essays on the Bible*. Sheffield: Sheffield Phoenix, 2012.

Schacter, Daniel L., and Elizabeth F. Loftus. "Memory and Law: What Can Cognitive Neuroscience Contribute?" *Nature Neuroscience* 16 (2013): 119–23.

Schäfer, Peter. "Die messianischen Hoffnungen des rabbinischen Judentums zwischen Naherwartung und religiösem Pragmatismus." Pages 214–43 in Schäfer's *Studien zur Geschichte und Theologie des rabbinischen Judentums*. AGJU 15. Leiden: Brill, 1978.

Schamoni, Wilhelm. *Parallelen zum Neuen Testament aus Heiligsprechungsakten übersetz*. Abensberg: Kral, 1971.

———. *Wunder sind Tatsachen: Eine Dokumentation aus Heiligsprechungsakten*. 3rd ed. Würzburg: Naumann, 1976.

Schamoni, Wilhelm, and Karl Besler. *Charismatische Heilige: Besondere Gnadengaben bei Heiligen nach Zeugenaussagen aus heiligsprechungsakten*. Stein am Rhein: Christiana, 1989.

Schattenmann, Johannes. "Jesus und Pythagoras." *Kairos* 21 (1979): 215–20.

Schenk, Christine. *Crispina and Her Sisters: Women and Authority in Early Christianity*. Minneapolis: Fortress, 2017.

Schiffner, Kerstin. *Lukas liest Exodus: Eine Untersuchung zur Aufnahme ersttestamentlicher Befreiungsgeschichte im lukanischen Werk als Schrift-Lektüre*. BWANT 172. Stuttgart: Kohlhammer, 2008.

Schleiermacher, Friedrich. *The Life of Jesus*. Edited by Jack C. Verheyden. Translated by S. MacLean Gilmour. Philadelphia: Fortress, 1975 (1832).

Schlosser, Jacques. *Le règne de Dieu dans les dits de Jésus*. Vol. 1. EBib 1. Paris: Gabalda, 1980.

Schmidt, Karl Ludwig. "Βασιλεύς κτλ." *TDNT* 1:574–93.

Schmidt, Stephen R. *Extraordinary Memories for Exceptional Events*. New York: Psychology Press, 2012.

Schmiedel, Paul Wilhelm. "Gospels." Pages 1761–898 in vol. 2 of *Encyclopaedia Biblica*. Edited by T. K. Cheyne and J. Sutherland Black. New York: Macmillan, 1901.

———. "Resurrection- and Ascension-Narratives." Pages 4039–87 in vol. 4 of *Encyclopaedia Biblica*. Edited by T. K. Cheyne and J. Sutherland Black. New York: Macmillan, 1903.

Schmithals, Walter. *The Apocalyptic Movement: Introduction and Interpretation*. Nashville: Abingdon, 1975.

———. *Johannesevangelium und Johannesbriefe: Forschungsgeshichte und Analyse*. BZNW 64. Berlin: de Gruyter, 1992.

Schneider, Johannes. "Εὐνοῦχος, εὐνουχίζω." *TDNT* 2:765–68.

Schnelle, Udo. *Theology of the New Testament*. Grand Rapids: Baker Academic, 2009.

Schoeps, Hans Joachim. *Theologie und Geschichte des Judenchristentums*. Tübingen: Siebeck, 1949.

Scholem, Gershom. *The Messianic Idea in Judaism and Other Essays on Jewish Spirituality*. New York: Schocken, 1971.

———. *Sabbatai Ṣevi: The Mystical Messiah*. Bollingen Series 93. Princeton: Princeton University Press, 1973.

Schöttler, Heinz-Günther. "'. . . Uns zum Heil' (Jes 53,5): Die Frage nach 'Mose'—ein soteriologische Frage." Pages 77–105 in *Exodus: Interpretation durch Rezeption*. Edited by Matthias Ederer and Barbara Schmitz. Stuttgart: Katholisches Bibelwerk, 2017.

Schottroff, Luise. "Conceptions of the History of Early Christianity in Feminist-Theological Perspective." Pages 201–11 in *Feminist Interpretation: The Bible in Women's Perspective*. Edited by Luise Schottroff, Silvia Schroer, and Marie-Theres Wacker. Minneapolis: Fortress, 1998.

———. "Itinerant Prophetesses: A Feminist Analysis of the Sayings Source Q." Pages 347–60 in *The Gospel behind the Gospels: Current Studies on Q*. Edited by Ronald A. Piper. NovTSup 75. Leuven: Brill, 1994.

———. *Lydia's Impatient Sisters: A Feminist Social History of Early Christianity*. Louisville: Westminster John Knox, 1995.

Schrader, Elizabeth, and Joan E. Taylor. "The Meaning of 'Magdalene': A Review of the Literary Evidence." *JBL* 140 (2021): 751–73.

Schremer, Adiel. "Divorce in Papyrus Ṣe'lim Again: A Reply to Tal Ilan." *HTR* 91 (1998): 193–202.

Schröter, Jens. "Memory, Theories of History, and the Reception of Jesus." *JSHJ* 16 (2018): 85–107.

———. "Memory and Memories in Early Christianity: The Remembered Jesus as a Test Case." Pages 79–96 in *Memory and Memories in Early Christianity*. Edited by Simon Butticaz and Enrico Norelli. WUNT 398. Tübingen: Mohr Siebeck, 2018.

———. "Remarks on James D. G. Dunn's Approach to Jesus Research." Pages 129–43 in *Memories of Jesus: A Critical Appraisal of James D. G. Dunn's "Jesus Remembered."* Edited by Robert B. Stewart and Gary R. Habermas. Nashville: B&H Academic, 2010.

———. "The 'Remembered Jesus': Memory as a Historiographical-Hermeneutical Paradigm of Research on Jesus." Pages 108–20 in *The Jesus Handbook*. Edited by Jens Schröter and Christine Jacobi. Grand Rapids: Eerdmans, 2022.

Schulz, Siegfried. *Q: Spruchquelle der Evangelisten*. Zurich: Theologischer Verlag, 1972.

Schürmann, Heinz. *Das Lukasevangelium*. 2 vols. HtKNT 3.1–2. Freiburg: Herder, 1969–94.

———. "Das Zeugnis der Redenquelle fur die Basileia-Verkündigung Jesu." Pages 121–200 in *Logia: Les Paroles de Jésus—The Sayings of Jesus*. Edited by Joël Delobel. BETL 59. Leuven: Peeters, 1982.

———. *Traditionsgeshichtliche Untersuchungen zu den synoptischen Evangelien*. Düsseldorf: Patmos, 1968.

———. "Zur Traditionsgeschichte der Nazareth-Perikope Lk 4,16–30." Pages 187–205 in *Mélanges bibliques en homage au R. P. Béda Rigaux*. Edited by Albert Descamps and André de Halleux. Gembloux: Duculot, 1970.

Schüssler Fiorenza, Elisabeth. *In Memory of Her: A Feminist Theological Reconstruction of Christian Origins*. 10th anniversary ed. New York: Crossroad, 1994.

Schwankl, Otto. *Die Sadduzäerfrage (Mk 12,18–27): Eine exegetische-theologische Studie zur Auferstehungserwartung*. BBB 66. Frankfurt am Main: Athenäum, 1987.

Schwarz, Barry. "Social Change and Collective Memory: The Democratization of George Washington." *American Sociological Review* 56 (1991): 221–35.

———. "Where There's Smoke, There's Fire: Memory and History." Pages 7–39 in *Memory and Identity in Ancient Judaism and Early Christianity: A Conver-*

sation with Barry Schwartz. Edited by Tom Thatcher. SemeiaSt 78. Atlanta: SBL Press, 2014.

Schweitzer, Albert. "La Métapsychique au Gabon." *Revue Métapsychique* 16 (1951): 162–68.

———. *The Mystery of the Kingdom of God: The Secret of Jesus' Messiahship and Passion*. New York: Schocken, 1964 (1914).

———. *The Mysticism of Paul the Apostle*. New York: Seabury, 1931.

———. *The Quest of the Historical Jesus*. Edited by John Bowden. Minneapolis: Fortress, 2001 (1913).

Schweizer, Eduard. *The Good News according to Luke*. Atlanta: Knox, 1984.

———. *The Good News according to Mark*. Atlanta: Knox, 1976.

Schwenke, Heiner. *Transcendente Begegnungen: Phänomenologie und Metakritik*. Schwabe Mystica 1. Basel: Schwabe, 2014.

Scoboria, Alan, Kimberley A. Wade, D. Stephen Lindsay, Tanjeem Azad, Deryn Strange, James Ost, and Ira E. Hyman. "A Mega-Analysis of Memory Reports from Eight Peer-Reviewed False Memory Implantation Studies." *Memory* 25.2 (2017): 146–63.

Seim, Turid Karlsen. *The Double Message: Patterns of Gender in Luke-Acts*. Edinburgh: T&T Clark, 1994.

Sernett, Milton C. *Harriet Tubman*. Durham, NC: Duke University Press, 2007.

Shaffir, William. "When Prophecy Is Not Validated: Explaining the Unexpected in a Messianic Campaign." *Jewish Journal of Sociology* 37 (1995): 119–36.

Shaw, Frances. *Discernment of Revelation in the Gospel of Matthew*. New York: Lang, 2007.

Shaw, Julia. *The Memory Illusion: Remembering, Forgetting, and the Science of False Memory*. London: Random, 2016.

Shaw, Teresa M. *The Burden of the Flesh: Fasting and Sexuality in Early Christianity*. Minneapolis: Fortress, 1998.

Sheehan, D. P., D. J. Mallin, J. T. Garamella, and W. F. Sheehan. "Experimental Test of a Thermodynamic Paradox." *Foundations of Physics* 44 (2014): 235–47.

Shively, Elizabeth. "A Critique of Richard Burridge's Genre Theory: From a One-Dimensional to a Multi-Dimensional Approach to Gospel Genre." Pages 97–144 in *Modern and Ancient Literary Criticism of the Gospels: Continuing the Debate on Gospel Genre(s)*. Edited by Robert Matthew Calhoun, David P. Moessner, and Tobias Nicklas. WUNT 451. Tübingen: Mohr Siebeck, 2020.

Silverio de Santa Teresa, P. *Obras de Sta. Teresa de Jesus*. Biblioteca Mistica Carmelitana 1. Burgos: El Monte Carmelo, 1915.

Sim, David C. *The Gospel of Matthew and Christian Judaism: The History and Social Setting of the Matthean Community*. STNW. Edinburgh: T&T Clark, 1998.

———. “Jew against Jew: The Reception of Paul in Matthew’s Christian-Jewish Community.” Pages 107–19 in *The Early Reception of Paul the Second Temple Jew: Text, Narrative, and Reception History*. Edited by Isaac W. Oliver and Gabriele Boccaccini. London: T&T Clark, 2018.

———. “Matthew 7.21–23: Further Evidence of Its Anti-Pauline Perspective.” *NTS* 53 (2007): 325–43.

———. “Matthew’s Anti-Paulinism: A Neglected Feature of Matthean Studies.” *HTS* 58 (2002): 767–83.

———. “The Women Followers of Jesus: The Implications of Luke 8:1–3.” *HeyJ* 30 (1989): 51–62.

Simon-Shoshan, Moshe. “‘On That Day’: The Deeds of the 72 (m. Yadayim 3:5–4:4) as Foundational Narrative for Rabbinic Judaism.” *JSQ* (2022): 109–34.

Smith, Barry D. *Jesus’ Twofold Teaching about the Kingdom of God*. NTM 24. Sheffield: Sheffield Phoenix, 2009.

———. “The More Original Form of the Words of Institution.” *ZNW* 83 (1992): 166–86.

Smith, David A. *The Epistles for All Christians: Epistolary Literature, Circulation, and “The Gospel for All Christians.”* BibInt 186. Leiden: Brill, 2020.

———. “Paul’s ‘Friends’: Rethinking Paul in Light of His Social Network.” *Stone-Campbell Journal* 22 (2019): 77–87.

Smith, D. Moody. *John among the Gospels*. 2nd ed. Columbia: University of South Carolina Press, 2001.

Smith, Morton. *Jesus the Magician*. San Francisco: Harper & Row, 1978.

Smith, Robert D. *Comparative Miracles*. St. Louis: Herder, 1965.

Snodgrass, Klyne R. “Are the Parables Still the Bedrock of the Jesus Tradition?” *JSHJ* 15 (2017): 131–46.

———. *Stories with Intent: A Comprehensive Guide to the Parables of Jesus*. 2nd ed. Grand Rapids: Eerdmans, 2018.

Snyder, G. F. “The *Tobspruch* in the New Testament.” *NTS* 23 (1976): 117–20.

Soards, Marion L. “Tradition, Composition, and Theology in Jesus’ Speech to the ‘Daughters of Jerusalem’ (Luke 23,26–32).” *Bib* 68 (1987): 221–44.

Sommer, Andreas. “Geisterglaube, Aufklärung und Wissenschaft—Historiographische Skizzen zu einem westlichen Fundamentaltabu.” Pages 183–216 in *Jenseits des Vertrauten: Facetten transzendenter Erfahrungen*. Edited by Heiner Schwenke. Transzendente Erfahrungen—Phänomene und Deutungen 2. Freiburg: Alber, 2019.

Somov, Alexey. *Representations of the Afterlife in Luke-Acts*. LNTS 556. London: Bloomsbury T&T Clark, 2017.

Spencer, F. Scott. *Salty Wives, Spirited Mothers, and Savvy Widows: Capable Women of Purpose and Persistence in Luke's Gospel*. Grand Rapids: Eerdmans, 2012.

Spinoza, Benedict de. *A Theologico-Political Treatise and a Political Treatise*. Translated by R. H. M. Elwes. New York: Dover, 1951.

Sprigge, Timothy. "Could Parapsychology Have Any Bearing on Religion?" Pages 127–45 in *Parapsychology, Philosophy, and the Mind*. Edited by Fiona Steinkamp. Jefferson, NC: McFarland, 2002.

Sprinkle, Preston M. *Paul and Judaism Revisited: A Study of Divine and Human Agency in Salvation*. Downers Grove, IL: IVP Academic, 2013.

Stählin, Gustav. "Κοπετός κτλ." *TDNT* 3:830–60.

Stancliffe, Clare. *St. Martin and His Hagiographer: History and Miracle in Sulpicius Severus*. Oxford: Clarendon, 1983.

Standaert, Benoît. *L'évangile selon Marc: Composition et genre litteraire*. Nijmegen: Stichting Studentenpers Nijmegen, 1978.

Standhartinger, Angelia. *Das Frauenbild im Judentum der hellenistischen Zeit: Ein Beitrag anhand von "Joseph und Aseneth."* AGJU 26. Leiden: Brill, 1995.

Stang, Charles M. "Digging Holes and Building Pillars: Simeon Stylites and the 'Geometry' of Ascetic Practice." *HTR* 103 (2010): 447–70.

Stanton, Graham N. "Jesus of Nazareth: A Magician and a False Prophet Who Deceived God's People?" Pages 164–80 in *Jesus of Nazareth: Lord and Christ. Essays on the Historical Jesus and New Testament Christology*. Edited by Joel B. Green and Max Turner. Grand Rapids: Eerdmans, 1994.

Staples, Jason Andrew. "Reconstructing Israel: Restoration Eschatology in Early Judaism and Paul's Gentile Mission." PhD diss., University of North Carolina at Chapel Hill, 2016.

Stec, David M. *The Genizah Psalms: A Study of MS 798 of the Antonin Collection*. Cambridge Genizah Studies Series 5. Leiden: Brill, 2013.

Steck, Odil Hannes. *Israel und das gewaltsame Geschick der Propheten: Untersuchungen zur Überlieferung des deuteronomistischen Geschichtsbildes im Alten Testament, Spätjudentum und Urchristentum*. WUNT 23. Neukirchen-Vluyn: Neukirchener, 1967.

Stegemann, Ekkehard W., and Wolfgang Stegemann. *The Jesus Movement: A Social History of the First Century*. Minneapolis: Fortress, 1999.

Stegner, William Richard. *Narrative Theology in Early Jewish Christianity*. Louisville: Westminster John Knox, 1989.

Stein, Robert H. "The 'Criteria' for Authenticity." Pages 225–63 in vol. 1 of *Gospel Perspectives: Studies of History and Tradition in the Four Gospels*. Edited by R. T. France and David Wenham. Sheffield: JSOT, 1980.

———. *Jesus, the Temple, and the Coming Son of Man*. Downers Grove, IL: IVP Academic, 2014.

Stenschke, Christoph. "Married Women and the Spread of Early Christianity." *Neot* 43 (2009): 145–94.

Stephen, James Fitzjames. "Remarks on the Proof of Miracles." Pages 328–44 in vol. 1 of *The Papers of the Metaphysical Society, 1869–1880: A Critical Edition*. Edited by Catherine Marshall, Bernard Lightman, and Richard England. Oxford: Oxford University Press, 2015.

Stephenson, Ian. "Precognition of Disaster." *Journal of the American Society for Psychical Research* 64 (1971): 187–210.

Sterk, Andrea. *Renouncing the World Yet Leading the Church*. Cambridge: Harvard University Press, 2004.

Steudel, Annette. "אחרית הימים in the Texts from Qumran." *RevQ* 16 (1993): 225–46.

Stevenson, Walter. "Eunuchs and Early Christianity." Pages 123–42 in *Eunuchs in Antiquity and Beyond*. Edited by Shaun Tougher. London: Duckworth, 2002.

Stone, Jon R., ed. *Expecting Armageddon: Essential Readings in Failed Prophecy*. New York: Routledge, 2000.

Stowers, Stanley K. *A Rereading of Romans*. New Haven: Yale University Press, 1994.

Strack, Hermann L., and Paul Billerbeck. *Kommentar zum Neuen Testament aus Talmud und Midrasch*. 6 vols. Munich: Beck, 1922–61.

Strange, James Riley. *Excavating the Land of Jesus: How Archaeologists Study the People of the Gospels*. Grand Rapids: Eerdmans, 2023.

Strauss, David Friedrich. *Das Leben Jesu kritisch bearbeitet*. Vol. 2. 3rd ed. Tübingen: Osiander, 1839.

———. *The Life of Jesus Critically Examined*. Translated by G. Eliott. Philadelphia: Fortress, 1972.

———. *A New Life of Jesus*. Vol. 1. London: Williams & Norgate, 1865.

Streeter, B. H. "St. Mark's Knowledge and Use of Q." Pages 165–83 in *Studies in the Synoptic Problem*. Edited by W. Sanday. Oxford: Clarendon, 1911.

Strobel, August. "Der Berg der Offenbarung (Mt 28,16, Apg 1,12): Erwägungen zu einem urchristliche Erwartungstopos." Pages 133–46 in *Verborum Veritas: Festschrift für Gustav Stählin zum 70. Geburtstag*. Edited by Otto Böcher and Klaus Haacer. Wuppertal: Brockhaus, 1970.

———. *Untersuchungen zum eschatologischen Verzögerungsproblem auf Grund der spätjüdisch-urchristlichen Geschichte von Habakuk 2,2ff.* NovTSup 2. Leiden: Brill, 1961.

Strong, Justin David. *The Fables of Jesus in the Gospel of Luke: A New Foundation for the Study of Parables*. Leiden: Brill, 2021.

Strotmann, Angelika. *Der historische Jesus: Eine Einführung*. 3rd ed. Paderborn: Schöningh, 2012.

Strotmann, Angelika, and Markus Tiwald. "Das Matthäusevangelium—eine Paulus-Polemik? Überlieferungen zum Toraverständnis des ersten Evangelisten." Pages 64–106 in *Kontroverse Stimmen im Kanon*. Edited by Martin Ebner, Gerd Häfner, and Konrad Huber. QD 279. Freiburg im Breisgau: Herder, 2016.

Stuhlmacher, Peter. *Biblical Theology of the New Testament*. Grand Rapids: Eerdmans, 2018.

Stuhlmann, Rainer. *Das eschatologische Mass im Neuen Testament*. FRLANT 132. Göttingen: Vandenhoeck & Ruprecht, 1983.

Stuhlmueller, Carroll. *Creative Redemption in Deutero-Isaiah*. AnBib 43. Rome: Biblical Institute, 1970.

Subramanian, J. Samuel. *The Synoptic Gospels and the Psalms as Prophecy*. LNTS 351. London: T&T Clark, 2007.

Sullivan, Kevin P. *Wrestling with Angels: A Study of the Relationship between Angels and Humans in Ancient Jewish Literature and the New Testament*. AGJU 55. Leiden: Brill, 2004.

Sundkler, Bengt. "Jesus et les païens." *RHPR* 16 (1936): 462–99.

Swartley, Willard M. *Israel's Scripture Traditions and the Synoptic Gospels*. Peabody, MA: Hendrickson, 1994.

Swete, H. B. *The Gospel according to St. Mark: The Greek Text with Introduction, Notes, and Indices*. 3rd ed. London: Macmillan, 1913.

Syreeni, Kari. "Eyewitness Testimony, First-Person Narration, and Authorial Presence as Means of Legitimation in Early Gospel Literature." Pages 89–110 in *Social Memory and Social Identity in the Study of Early Judaism and Early Christianity*. Edited by Samuel Byrskog, Raimo Hakola, and Jutta Maria Jokiranta. NTOA/SUNT 116. Göttingen: Vandenhoeck & Ruprecht, 2016.

———. "From John's Ministry to the Mission of Jesus: The Question of Continuity and Change in a Psychological Perspective." Pages 77–91 in *The Mission of Jesus*. Edited by Samuel Byrskog and Tobias Hägerland. WUNT 2/391. Tübingen: Mohr Siebeck, 2015.

Talarico, Jennifer M., and David C. Rubin. "Flashbulb Memories Are Special after All; In Phenomenology, Not Accuracy." *Applied Cognitive Psychology* 21 (2007): 557–78.

Talbert, Charles H. *Matthew*. Paideia: Commentaries on the New Testament. Grand Rapids: Baker Academic, 2010.

———. *Reading Acts: A Literary and Theological Commentary on the Acts of the Apostles*. Rev. ed. Macon, GA: Smyth & Helwys, 2005.

Talbot, Elizabeth. "Rest, Eschatology, and Sabbath in Matthew 11:28–30: An Investigation of Jesus' Offer of Rest in the Light of the Septuagint's Use of *Anapausis*." Pages 57–69 in *The Synoptic Gospels*. Vol. 1 of *"What Does the Scripture Say?": Studies in the Function of Scripture in Early Judaism and Christianity*. Edited by Craig A. Evans and H. Daniel Zacharias. London: T&T Clark, 2012.

Talbot, Michel. *"Heureux les doux, car ils hériteront le terre" (Mt 4,4[5])*. EBib 46. Paris: Gabalda, 2002.

Talbott, Rick. "Imagining the Matthean Eunuch Community: Kyriarchy on the Chopping Block." *JFSR* 22 (2006): 21–43.

Tallis, Raymond. *Logos: The Mystery of How We Make Sense of the World*. Newcastle upon Tyne: Agenda, 2018.

Tan, Ilan. "In the Footsteps of Jesus: Jewish Women in a Jewish Movement." Pages 115–36 in *Transformative Encounters: Jesus and Women Re-viewed*. Edited by Ingrid Rosa Kitzberger. BibInt 43. Leiden: Brill, 2000.

———. "Jewish Women's Life and Practice in the World of the New Testament." Pages 220–37 in *The Oxford Handbook of New Testament, Gender, and Sexuality*. Edited by Benjamin H. Dunning. Oxford: Oxford University Press, 2019.

———. "On a Newly Published Divorce Bill from the Judaean Desert." *HTR* 89 (1996): 195–202.

———. "The Women of the Q Community within Early Judaism." Pages 195–212 in *Social Setting and Archeological Background of the Sayings Source*. Vol. 2 of *Q in Context*. Edited by Markus Tiwald. BBB 173. Göttingen: V&R Unipress, 2015.

Tan, Kim Huat. *The Zion Traditions and the Aims of Jesus*. SNTSMS 91. Cambridge: Cambridge University Press, 1997.

Tannehill, Robert C. *Luke*. Nashville: Abingdon, 1996.

———. "The Mission of Jesus according to Luke iv 16–30." Pages 51–75 in *Jesus in Nazareth*. Edited by W. Eltester. BZNW 40. Berlin: de Gruyter, 1972.

———. *The Sword of His Mouth*. SemeiaSup 1. Missoula, MT: Society of Biblical Literature, 1975.

Targ, Elizabeth, Marilyn Schlitz, and Harvey J. Irwin. "Psi-Related Experiences." Pages 219–52 in *The Varieties of Anomalous Experience: Examining the Scientific Evidence*. Edited by Etzel Cardeña, Steven Jay Lynn, and Stanley Krippner. Washington, DC: American Psychological Association, 2000.

Taves, Ann. *Fits, Trances, and Visions: Experiencing Religion and Explaining Experience from Wesley to James*. Princeton: Princeton University Press, 1999.

Taylor, Joan E. *The Immerser: John the Baptist within Second Temple Judaism*. Grand Rapids: Eerdmans, 1997.

———. *Jewish Women Philosophers of First Century Alexandria: Philo's Therapeutae Reconsidered*. London: Oxford University Press, 2004.

———. "Male-Female Missionary Pairings among Jesus' Disciples: Some Further Considerations." Pages 11–25 in *Patterns of Woman's Leadership in Early Christianity*. Edited by Joan E. Taylor and Ilaria Ramelli. Oxford: Oxford University Press, 2021.

———. "Missing Magdala and the Name of Mary 'Magdalene.'" *PEQ* 146 (2014): 205–23.

———. "'Two by Two': The Ark-etypal Language of Mark's Apostolic Pairings." Pages 58–82 in *The Body in Biblical, Christian, and Jewish Texts*. Edited by Joan E. Taylor. London: Bloomsbury T&T Clark, 2014.

Taylor, Joan E., and David M. Hay. *Philo of Alexandria: On the Contemplative Life. Introduction, Translation, and Commentary*. Philo of Alexandria Commentary Series 7. Leiden: Brill, 2022.

Taylor, Vincent. *The Gospel according to St. Mark*. 2nd ed. New York: St. Martin's, 1966.

———. *Jesus and His Sacrifice: A Study of the Passion-Sayings in the Gospels*. London: Macmillan, 1965.

Teeple, Howard M. *The Mosaic Eschatological Prophet*. SBLMS 10. Philadelphia: Society of Biblical Literature, 1957.

Telford, William R. "The Resurgence of the Paul/Mark Nexus: A History of Scholarship from Volkmar to Crossley." Pages 183–201 in *Treasures Old and New: Essays in Honor of Donald A. Hagner*. Edited by Carl S. Sweatman and Clifford B. Kvidahl. Wilmore, KY: GlossaHouse, 2017.

Tervanotko, Hanna. *Denying Her Voice: The Figure of Miriam in Ancient Jewish Literature*. Göttingen: Vandenhoeck & Ruprecht, 2016.

Thackeray, H. St. John. *Josephus: The Jewish War, Books I–III*. LCL. Cambridge: Harvard University Press, 1926.

Theissen, Gerd. "'Evangelium' im Markusevangelium: Zum traditionsgeschichtlichen Ort des ältesten Evangelium." Pages 63–86 in *For and against Pauline Influence on Mark*. Vol. 2 of *Mark and Paul: Comparative Essays*. Edited by Eve-Marie Becker, Troels Engberg-Pedersen, and Mogens Müller. BZNW 199. Berlin: de Gruyter, 2014.

———. *The Gospels in Context: Social and Political History in the Synoptic Tradition*. London: T&T Clark, 1992.

———. *Jesus als historische Gestalt: Beiträge zur Jesusforschung*. Edited by Annette Merz. FRLANT 202. Göttingen: Vandenhoeck & Ruprecht, 2003.

———. "Jesus and His Followers as Healers: Symbolic Healing in Early Christianity." Pages 56–77 in *The Problem of Ritual Efficacy*. Edited by William S. Sax, Johannes Quack, and Jan Weinhold. Oxford: Oxford University Press, 2010.

———. "Jesus as an Itinerant Teacher: Reflections from Social History on Jesus' Roles." Pages 98–122 in *Jesus Research: An International Perspective. The First Princeton-Prague Symposium on Jesus Research, Prague 2005*. Edited by James H. Charlesworth with Petr Pokorný. Grand Rapids: Eerdmans, 2009.

———. "Kritik an Paulus im Matthäusevangelium? Von der Kunst verdeckter Polemik im Urchristentum." Pages 465–90 in *Polemik in der frühchristlichen Literature: Texte und Kontextere*. Edited by Oda Wischmeyer and Lorenzo Scornaienchi. BZNW 170. Berlin: de Gruyter, 2011.

———. *The Miracle Stories of the Early Christian Tradition*. Philadelphia: Fortress, 1983.

———. *The New Testament: A Literary History*. Minneapolis: Fortress, 2012.

———. "The Peril of Modernising and De-modernising Jesus." Pages 273–93 in *"To Recover What Has Been Lost": Essays on Eschatology, Intertextuality, and Reception History in Honor of Dale C. Allison Jr.* Edited by Tucker S. Ferda, Daniel Frayer-Griggs, and Nathan C. Johnson. NovTSup 183. Leiden: Brill, 2021.

———. "The Sayings Source Q and Itinerant Radicalism." Pages 93–110 in *Social Setting and Archeological Background of the Sayings Source*. Vol. 2 of *Q in Context*. Edited by Markus Tiwald. BBB 173. Göttingen: V&R unipress, 2015.

———. *Social Reality and the Early Christians: Theology, Ethics, and the World of the New Testament*. Minneapolis: Fortress, 1992.

———. *The Sociology of Early Palestinian Christianity*. Philadelphia: Fortress, 1978.

———. "Wunder Jesu und urchristliche Wundergeschichten: Historische, psychologische und theologische Aspekte." Pages 68–86 in *Hermeneutik der frühchristlichen Wundererzählung: Geschichtliche, literarische und rezeptionsorientierte Perspektiven*. Edited by Bernd Kollmann and Ruben Zimmermann. WUNT 339. Tübingen: Mohr Siebeck, 2014.

———. "Zwischen Skepsis und Zuversicht: Über die Instabilität der Jesusforschung." Pages 15–60 in *Jesus, quo vadis? Entwicklungen und Perspektiven der aktuellen Jesusforschung*. Edited by Eckart David Schmidt. BThSt 177. Göttingen: Vandenhoeck & Ruprecht, 2018.

Theissen, Gerd, and Annette Merz. "Das Zeichen Jona: Von der Menschenfreundlichkeit Gottes (Lk 11,29–32 parr)." Pages 182–93 in *Der Freund des Menschen: Festschrift für Georg Christian Macholz zur Vollendung des 70. Lebensjahres*. Edited by Arndt Meinhold and Angelika Berlegung. Neukirchen-Vluyn: Neukirchener, 2003.

———. "The Delay of the Parousia as a Test Case for the Criterion of Coherence." *Louvain Studies* 32 (2007): 49–65.

———. "From the Historical Jesus to the Kerygmatic Son of God: How Role Analysis Contributes to the Understanding of New Testament Christology." Pages 235–60 in *Jesus Research: New Methodologies and Perceptions*. Edited by James H. Charlesworth with Brian Rhea. Grand Rapids: Eerdmans, 2014.

———. "Gerichtsverzögerung und Heilsverkündigung bei Johannes dem Täufer und Jesus." Pages 228–53 in *Jesus als historische Gestalt: Beiträge zur Jesusforschung*. Edited by Annette Merz. Göttingen: Vandenhoeck & Ruprecht, 2003.

———. *The Historical Jesus: A Comprehensive Guide*. Minneapolis: Fortress, 1998.

Theissen, Gerd, and Dagmar Winter. *The Quest for the Plausible Jesus: The Question of Criteria*. Louisville: Westminster John Knox, 2002.

Theodoret of Cyrrus. *Histoire des moines de Syrie*. 2 vols. Edited by Pierre Canivet and Alice Leroy-Molinghen. SC 234, 257. Paris: Cerf, 1977, 1979.

Theophilos, Michael P. *Jesus as New Moses in Matthew 8–9: Jewish Typology in First Century Greek Literature*. Piscataway, NJ: Georgias, 2011.

Thiele, Walter. "Eine Bemerkung zu Acts 1 14." *ZNW* 53 (1962): 110–11.

Tholuck, A. *On the Sermon on the Mount*. Philadelphia: Smith, English, 1860.

Thompson, Michael. *Clothed with Christ: The Example and Teaching of Jesus in Romans 12:1–15:13*. JSNTSup 59. Sheffield: JSOT Press 1991.

———. "The Holy Internet: Communication between Churches in the First Christian Generation." Pages 49–70 in *The Gospels for All Christians*. Edited by Richard Bauckham. Grand Rapids: Eerdmans, 1998.

Thornton, Claus-Jürgen. *Der Zeuge des Zeugen: Lukas als Historiker der Paulusreisen*. WUNT 56. Tübingen: Mohr Siebeck, 1991.

Thurston, Herbert. *The Physical Phenomena of Mysticism*. Chicago: Regnery, 1952.

Tiemeyer, Lena-Sofia. "Prophecy as a Way of Cancelling Prophecy—The Strategic Uses of Foreknowledge." *ZAW* 117 (2005): 329–50.

Tiwald, Markus. *Die Logienquelle: Text, Kontext, Theologie*. Stuttgart: Kohlhammer, 2016.

———. "Hat Gott sein Haus verlassen (vgl. 13,35)? Das Verhältnis der Logienquelle zum Frühjudentum." Pages 63–88 in *Kein Jota wird vergehen: Das Gesetzesverständnis der Logienquelle vor dem Hintergrund frühjüdischer Theologie*. Edited by Markus Tiwald. BWANT 200. Stuttgart: Kohlhammer, 2013.

———. "The Rural Roots of the Jesus Movement and the 'Galilean' Silence." Pages 149–75 in *Early Christian Encounters with Town and Countryside: Essays on the Urban and Rural Worlds of Early Christianity*. Edited by Markus Tiwald and Jürgen K. Zangenberg. NTOA/SUNT 126. Göttingen: Vandenhoeck & Ruprecht, 2021.

———. *The Sayings Source: A Commentary on Q*. Stuttgart: Kohlhammer, 2020.

———. *Wanderradikalismus: Jesu erste Jünger—ein Anfang und was davon bleibt*. ÖBS 20. Frankfurt am Main: Lang, 2002.

Tödt, H. E. *The Son of Man in the Synoptic Tradition*. NTL. London: SCM, 1965.

Tomson, Peter. *Studies on Jew and Christians in the First and Second Centuries*. WUNT 418. Tübingen: Mohr Siebeck, 2019.

Trapp, John. *A Commentary on the New Testament*. Vol. 5. London: Dickinson, 1865 (1656).

Treblico, Paul R. "Early Jewish Communities in Asia Minor and the Early Christian Movement." Pages 213–31 in *Social Setting and Archeological Background of the Sayings Source*. Vol. 2 of *Q in Context*. Edited by Markus Tiwald. BBB 173. Göttingen: V&R unipress, 2015.

———. *Jewish Communities in Asia Minor*. SNTSMS 69. Cambridge: Cambridge University Press, 1991.

Treece, Patricia. *The Sanctified Body*. New York: Doubleday, 1989.

Trench, Richard Chenevix. *Notes on the Parables of Our Lord*. New York: Appleton, 1853.

Trigg, Roger. *Beyond Matter: Why Science Needs Metaphysics*. West Conshohocken, PA: Templeton, 2015.

Trilling, Wolfgang. *Studien zur Jesusüberlieferung*. SBAB 1. Stuttgart: Katholisches Bibelwerk, 1988.

Tripp, Jeffrey. "The Eyewitnesses in Their Own Words: Testing Richard Bauckham's Model Using Verifiable Quotations." *JSNT* 44 (2022): 411–34.

———. "Jesus' Special Knowledge in the Gospel of John." *NovT* 61 (2019): 269–88.

Troeltsch, Ernst. *The Absoluteness of Christianity and the History of Religions*. Richmond, VA: Knox, 1971.

———. *Christian Thought: Its History and Application*. Westport, CT: Hyperion, 1979.

———. *Zur religiösen Lage, Religionsphilosophie und Ethik*. Vol. 2 of *Gesammelte Schriften*. Tübingen: Mohr, 1913.

Tromp, Johannes. *The Assumption of Moses: A Critical Edition with Commentary*. SVTP 10. Leiden: Brill, 1993.

Trumbower, Jeffrey A. "The Role of Malachi in the Career of John the Baptist." Pages 28–41 in *The Gospels and the Scriptures of Israel*. Edited by Craig A. Evans and W. Richard Stegner. JSNTSup 104. Sheffield: Sheffield Academic, 1994.

Tuckett, Christopher M. "Mark and Q." Pages 149–75 in *The Synoptic Gospels:*

Source Criticism and the New Literary Criticism. Edited by Camille Focant. BETL 110. Leuven: Peeters, 1993.
———. "Paul and the Synoptic Mission Discourse." *ETL* 60 (1984): 376–81.
———. *Q and the History of Early Christianity: Studies on Q*. London: T&T Clark, 1996.
Tumminia, Diana G. *When Prophecy Never Fails: Myth and Reality in a Flying Saucer Group*. Oxford: Oxford University Press, 2005.
Turner, David L. *Israel's Last Prophet: Jesus and the Jewish Leaders in Matthew*. Minneapolis: Fortress, 2015.
Turner, Martha Lee. *The Gospel according to Philip: The Sources and Coherence of an Early Christian Collection*. NHMS 38. Leiden: Brill, 1996.
Twain, Mark. "Mental Telegraphy: A Manuscript with a History." *Harper's New Monthly Magazine* 84 (December 1891): 95–104. http://www.nitrosyncretic.com/rah/telepath.html.
Twelftree, Graham H. *Jesus the Miracle Worker: A Historical and Theological Study*. Downers Grove, IL: InterVarsity, 1999.
———. "The Miraculous in the New Testament: Current Research and Issues." *CBR* 12 (2014): 321–52.
Tyndale, John. *Fragments of Science: A Series of Detached Essays, Addresses, and Reviews*. Vol. 2. New York: Appleton, 1898.
Unterman, Jeremiah. *From Repentance to Redemption: Jeremiah's Thought in Transition*. JSOTSup 54. Sheffield: Sheffield Academic, 1987.
———. *Justice for All: How the Jewish Bible Revolutionized Ethics*. Philadelphia: Jewish Publication Society, 2017.
Urbach, Ephraim E. "Redemption and Repentance in Talmudic Judaism." Pages 190–206 in *Types of Redemption: Contributions to the Theme of the Study-Conference Held at Jerusalem 14th to 19th July 1968*. Edited by R. J. Zwi Weblowsky and C. Louco Bleeker. SHR 18. Leiden: Brill, 1970.
———. *The Sages: Their Concepts and Beliefs*. 2 vols. Jerusalem: Magnes, 1979.
Vallançon, Henri. *Le développement des traditions sur Élie et l'histoire de la formation de la Bible*. EBib 80. Paris: Peeters, 2019.
VanderKam, James C. *Jubilees*. 2 vols. Hermeneia. Minneapolis: Fortress, 2018.
———. "Recent Scholarship on the Book of Jubilees." *CBR* 6 (2008): 405–31.
Van Dore, James. "Evidence for a Relationship between Mark and Q." Pages 45–69 in *Greco-Roman and Jewish Tributaries to the New Testament: Festschrift in Honor of Gregory J. Riley*. Edited by Christopher S. Crawford. Claremont, CA: Claremont Press, 2019.
Van Inwagen, Peter. *The Problem of Evil: The Gifford Lectures Delivered in the University of St. Andrews in 2003*. Oxford: Clarendon, 2006.

Van Pelt, Julie. "The Hagiographer as Holy Fool? Fictionality in Saints' Lives." Pages 73–78 in *The Hagiographical Experiment: Developing Discourses of Sainthood*. Edited by Christa Gray and James Corke-Webste. VCSup 158. Leiden: Brill, 2020.

Van Tilborg, S. "A Form-Criticism of the Lord's Prayer." *NovT* 14 (1972): 94–105.

Vecoli, Frabrizio. *Lo spirito soffia nel deserto: Carismi, discernimento e autorità nel monachesimo egiziano antico*. Brescia: Morcelliana, 2006.

Vélez, Karin. *The Miraculous Flying House of Loreto: Spreading Catholicism in the Early Modern World*. Princeton: Princeton University Press, 2019.

Verellen, Franciscus. "'Evidential Miracles in Support of Taoism': The Inversion of a Buddhist Apologetic Tradition in Late Tang China." *T'oung Pao* 78 (1992): 217–63.

Verheyden, Jozef. "Persecution and Eschatology: Mk 13,9–13." Pages 1141–60 in *The Four Gospels 1992: Festschrift Frans Neirynck*. Edited by F. Van Segbroeck, C. M. Tuckett, G. Van Belle, and J. Verheyden. 3 vols. BETL 100. Leuven: Peeters, 1992.

Vermes, Geza. *Jesus and the World of Judaism*. Philadelphia: Fortress, 1984.

———. *Jesus the Jew: A Historian's Reading of the Gospels*. Philadelphia: Fortress, 1981.

———. *The Religion of Jesus the Jew*. Minneapolis: Fortress, 1993.

Vidal, Fernando. "Modernizing the Miraculous Body in Prospero Lambertini's *De servorum Dei*." Pages 151–74 in *Benedict XIV and the Enlightenment: Art, Science, and Spirituality*. Edited by Rebecca Messbarger, Christopher M. S. Johns, and Philip Gavitt. Toronto: University of Toronto Press, 2017.

Vielhauer, Philipp. *Geschichte der urchristlichen Literatur: Einleitung in das Neue Testament, die Apokryphen und die Apostolischen Väter*. Berlin: de Gruyter, 1975.

Vivian, Tim, Kim Vivian, and Jeffrey Burton Russell. *The Life of the Jura Fathers: The Life and Rule of the Holy Fathers Romanus, Lupicinus, and Eugendus, Abbots of the Monasteries in the Jura Mountains*. Cistercian Studies 178. Kalamazoo, MI: Cistercian, 1999.

Viviano, Benedict Thomas. "The Historical Jesus in the Doubly Attested Sayings: An Experiment." *RB* 103 (1996): 367–410.

——— *Trinity—Kingdom—Church: Essays in Biblical Theology*. NTOA 48. Freiburg: Universitätsverlag, 2001.

Vlastos, Gregory. *Socrates: Ironist and Moral Philosopher*. Ithaca: Cornell University Press, 1991.

Vööbus, Arthur. "Discovery of New Manuscript Sources for the Biography of Simeon the Stylite." Pages 479–84 in *After Chalcedon: Studies in Theology and Church History Offered to Professor Albert Van Roey for His Seventieth Birthday*. Edited by C. Laga, J. A. Munitiz, and L. Van Rompay. OLA 18. Leuven: Peeters, 1985.

———. *Early Monasticism in Mesopotamia and Syria*. Vol. 2 of *History of Asceticism in the Syrian Orient: A Contribution to the History of Culture in the Near East*. CSCO 197. Louvain: Secrétariat du CorpusSCO, 1960.

Vos, Cornelius de. "Josua und Jesus im Neuen Testament." Pages 523–40 in *The Book of Joshua*. Edited by Ed. Noort. BETL 250. Leuven: Leuven University Press, 2010.

Wacholder, Ben Zion. *The Dawn of Qumran: The Sectarian Torah and the Teacher of Righteousness*. Cincinnati: Hebrew Union College, 1983.

Wacker, Marie-Theres. *Baruch and the Letter of Jeremiah*. Wisdom Commentary 31. Collegeville, MN: Liturgical, 2016.

Wailes, Stephen L. *Medieval Allegories of Jesus' Parables*. Berkeley: University of California Press, 1987.

Walker, D. P. "The Cessation of Miracles." Pages 111–24 in *Hermeticism and the Renaissance: Intellectual History and the Occult in Early Modern Europe*. Edited by Ingrid Merkel and Allen G. Debus. London: Associated University Presses, 1988.

Walker, William. "The Quest for the Historical Jesus: A Discussion of Methodology." *ATR* 51 (1969): 38–56.

Wall, Robert W. "'The Finger of God': Deuteronomy 9.10 and Luke 11.20." *NTS* 33 (1987): 144–50.

Wallace, Daniel B. "Textual Criticism and the Criterion of Embarrassment." Pages 93–124 in *Jesus, Skepticism, and the Problem of History: Criteria and Context in the Study of Christian Origins*. Edited by Darrell L. Bock and J. Ed Komoszewski. Grand Rapids: Zondervan Academic, 2019.

Wallis, Ian G. *The Galilean Wonderworker: Reassessing Jesus' Reputation for Healing and Exorcism*. Eugene, OR: Cascade, 2020.

Walsh, Jerome T. *1 Kings*. Berit Olam. Collegeville, MN: Liturgical, 1996.

Walsh, Robyn Faith. *The Origins of Early Christian Literature: Contextualizing the New Testament within Greco-Roman Literary Culture*. Cambridge: Cambridge University Press, 2021.

Ward, Benedicta. *Miracles and the Medieval Mind: Theory, Record, and Event, 1000–1215*. Philadelphia: University of Pennsylvania Press, 1987.

Watson, Francis. "'I Received from the Lord . . .': Paul, Jesus, and the Last Supper." Pages 103–24 in *Jesus and Paul Reconsidered: Fresh Pathways into an Old Debate*. Edited by Todd D. Still. Grand Rapids: Eerdmans, 2007.

Watts, Rikki E. *Isaiah's New Exodus and Mark*. WUNT 2/88. Tübingen: Mohr Siebeck, 1997.

Weaver, Charles A., and Kevin S. Krug. "Consolidation-Like Effects in Flashbulb Memories: Evidence from September 11, 2001." *American Journal of Psychology* 117 (2004): 517–30.

Webb, Robert L. "The Historical Enterprise and Historical Jesus Research." Pages 9–93 in *Key Events in the Life of the Historical Jesus: A Collaborative Exploration of Context and Coherence*. Edited by Darrell L. Bock and Robert L. Webb. Grand Rapids: Eerdmans, 2009.

———. *John the Baptizer and Prophet: A Socio-Historical Study*. JSNTSup 62. Sheffield: JSOT, 1991.

———. "The Rules of the Game: History and Historical Method in the Context of Faith: The Via Media of Methodological Naturalism." *JSHJ* 9 (2011): 59–84.

Weber, Max. *The Sociology of Religion*. Boston: Beacon, 1993.

Wedderburn, Alexander J. M. *Jesus and the Historians*. WUNT 269. Tübingen: Mohr Siebeck, 2010.

Weddle, David L. *Miracles: Wonder and Meaning in World Religions*. New York: New York University Press, 2010.

Weder, Hans. *Die Gleichnisse Jesu als Metaphern: Traditions- und redaktionsgeschichtliche Analysen und Interpretation*. 3rd ed. FRLANT 120. Göttingen: Vandenhoeck & Ruprecht, 1984.

Wegner, Uwe. *Der Hauptmann von Kafarnaum (Mt 7,28a; 8,5–10,13 par Lk 7,1–10): Ein Beitrag zur Q-Forschung*. WUNT 2/14. Tübingen: Mohr Siebeck, 1985.

Weiser, Alfons. *Die Knechtsgleichnisse der synoptischen Evangelien*. SANT 29. Munich: Kösel, 1971.

Weiss, Johannes. *Jesus' Proclamation of the Kingdom of God*. Philadelphia: Fortress, 1971 (1892).

Weissenberg, Hanne von. *4QMMT: Reevaluating the Text, the Function, and the Meaning of the Epilogue*. STDJ 82. Leiden: Brill, 2009.

Wells, Kyle B. *Grace and Agency in Paul and Second Temple Judaism: Interpreting the Transformation of the Heart*. NovTSup 157. Leiden: Brill, 2015.

Wenell, Karen J. *Jesus and Land: Sacred and Social Space in Second Temple Judaism*. LNTS 334. London: T&T Clark, 2007.

Wenham, David. *The Parables of Jesus*. Downers Grove, IL: InterVarsity, 1989.

———. *Paul: Follower of Jesus or Founder of Christianity?* Grand Rapids: Eerdmans, 1995.

Wertsch, James V., and Henry L. Roediger III. "Collective Memory: Conceptual Foundations and Theoretical Approaches." *Memory* 16 (2008): 318–26.

Wesley, John. *Explanatory Notes on the New Testament*. London: Epworth, 1950.

Westcott, B. F. *The Gospel according to St. John: The Greek Text with Introduction and Notes*. London: Murray, 1908.

Wettstein, Johann Jakob. *Novum Testamentum Graecum*. 2 vols. Amsterdam: Ex officina Dommeriana, 1751–52.

Wiese, C. H. R., U. E. Bartels, S. Orso, and B. M. Graf. "Lazarus-Phänomen: Spontane Kreislauffunktion nach beendeten Reanimationsbassnahmen." *Der Anaesthesist* 59 (2010): 333–41.

Wilcox, Melissa M. "Gender Roles, Sexuality, and Children in Millennial Movements." Pages 171–90 in *The Oxford Handbook of Millennialism*. Edited by Catherin Wessinge. Oxford: Oxford University Press, 2011.

Wilder, Amos Niven. *Eschatology and Ethics in the Teaching of Jesus*. London: Harper & Brothers, 1939.

Willey, Patricia Tull. *Remember the Former Things: The Recollection of Previous Texts in Second Isaiah*. SBLDS 161. Atlanta: Scholars Press, 1997.

Willitts, Joel. "Jesus, the Kingdom and the Promised Land: Engaging N. T. Wright on the Question of Kingdom and Land." *JSHJ* 13 (2015): 347–72.

———. "John of Patmos and the Apostle Paul: Antinomy or Affinity?" Pages 131–48 in *The Early Reception of Paul in the Second Temple Jew: Text, Narrative, and Reception History*. Edited by Isaac W. Oliver and Gabriele Boccaccini. London: T&T Clark, 2018.

———. "Paul and Matthew: A Descriptive Approach from a Post–New Perspective Interpretative Framework." Pages 62–85 in *Paul and the Gospels: Christologies, Conflicts, and Convergences*. Edited by Michael F. Bird and Joel Willitts. LNTS 411. London: T&T Clark, 2011.

Wilson, Anna. "Biographical Models: The Constantinian Period and Beyond." Pages 107–35 in *Constantine: Historiography and Legend*. Edited by Samuel N. C. Lieu and Dominic Montserrat. London: Routledge, 1998.

Wilson, S. G. *The Gentiles and the Gentile Mission in Luke-Acts*. SNTSMS 23. Cambridge: Cambridge University Press, 1973.

Wilson, Walter T. *The Gospel of Matthew*. 2 vols. Grand Rapids: Eerdmans, 2022.

Windisch, Hans. "Die Sprüche vom Eingehen in das Reich Gottes." *ZNW* 27 (1928): 163–92.

———. *Paulus und Christus: Ein biblisch-religionsgeschichtlicher Vergleich*. Leipzig: Hinrichs, 1934.

Winninge, Mikael. "The Lord's Supper in 1 Cor 11 and Luke 22: Traditions and Development." Pages 579–602 in *Old Testament, Early Judaism, New Testament*. Vol. 1 of *The Eucharist—Its Origins and Contexts: Sacred Meal, Communal Meal, Table Fellowship in Late Antiquity, Early Judaism, and Early Christian-*

ity. Edited by David Hellholm and Dieter Sänger. WUNT 376. Tübingen: Mohr Siebeck, 2017.

Winter, Dagmar. "Saving the Quest for Authenticity from the Criterion of Dissimilarity: History and Plausibility." Pages 115–31 in *Jesus, History, and the Demise of Authenticity: The Rise and Fall of the Search for an Authentic Jesus. Authenticity after the Third Quest*. Edited by Anthony Le Donne and Chris Keith. London: T&T Clark, 2012.

Witherington, Ben, III. "'Christianity in the Making': Oral Mystery or Eyewitness History?" Pages 197–26 in *Memories of Jesus: A Critical Appraisal of James D. G. Dunn's "Jesus Remembered."* Edited by Robert B. Stewart and Gary R. Habermas. Nashville: B&H Academic, 2010.

———. *Jesus the Seer: The Progress of Prophecy*. Minneapolis: Fortress, 2014.

———. "Joanna: Apostle of the Lord—or Jailbait?" *BRev* 21 (2005): 12–14, 46–47.

———. *Women in the Ministry of Jesus: A Study of Jesus' Attitudes to Women and Their Roles as Reflected in His Earthly Life*. SNTSMS 51. Cambridge: Cambridge University Press, 1984.

Witmer, Amanda. *Jesus, the Galilean Exorcist: His Exorcisms in Social and Religious Context*. LNTS 459. London: T&T Clark, 2012.

Wixted, John T., Laura Mickes, Steven E. Clark, Scott D. Gronlund, and Henry L. Roediger III. "Initial Eyewitness Confidence Reliably Predicts Eyewitness Identification Accuracy." *American Psychologist* 70 (2015): 515–26.

Wojcik, Daniel. "Avertive Apocalypticism." Pages 66–88 in *The Oxford Handbook of Millennialism*. Edited by Catherin Wessinger. Oxford: Oxford University Press, 2011.

Wolff, Christian. "Niedrigkeit und Verzicht in Wort und Weg Jesu und in der apostolischen Existenz des Paulus." *NTS* 34 (1988): 183–96.

Wolff, Hans Walter. "The Kerygma of the Deuteronomistic Historical Work." Pages 94–122 in *Reconsidering Israel and Judah: Recent Studies on the Deuteronomistic History*. Edited by G. N. Knoppers and J. G. McConville. Winona Lake, IN: Eisenbrauns, 2000.

———. *Studien zum Jonabuch*. Biblische Studien 47. Neukirchen-Vluyn: Neukirchener Verlag, 1965.

Wolter, Michael. "'Gericht' und 'Heil' bei Jesus von Nazareth und Johannes dem Täufer: Semantische und pragmatische Beobachtungen." Pages 355–92 in *Der historische Jesus: Tendenzen und Perspektiven der gegenwärtigen Forschungen*. Edited by Jens Schröter and Ralph Brucker. BZNW 114. Berlin: de Gruyter, 2002.

Woods, Edward J. *The "Finger of God" and Pneumatology in Luke-Acts*. JSNTSup 205. Sheffield: Sheffield Academic, 2001.

Woods, G. F. "The Evidential Value of Miracles." Pages 19–32 in *Miracles: Cambridge Studies in Their Philosophy and History*. London: Mowbray, 1965.

Woolston, Thomas. *A Discourse on the Miracles of Our Saviour, in View of the Present Controversy between Infidels and Apostates*. 3rd ed. London: n.p., 1727.

Wright, Benjamin G. "The Letter of Aristeas and the Question of Septuagint Origins Redux." *JAJ* 2 (2011): 303–25.

Wright, Brian J. *Communal Reading in the Time of Jesus: A Window into Early Christian Reading Practices*. Minneapolis: Fortress, 2017.

Wright, C. J. *Miracle in History and in Modern Thought or Miracle and Christian Apologetic*. New York: Holt, 1930.

Wright, G. R. H. "The Heritage of the Stylites." *Australian Journal of Biblical Archaeology* 1/3 (1970): 82–107.

———. "Simeon's Ancestors (or the Skeleton in the Closet)." *Australian Journal of Biblical Archaeology* 1.1 (1968): 41–49.

Wright, N. T. "Hope Deferred? Against the Dogma of Delay." *EC* 9 (2018): 37–82.

———. *Jesus and the Victory of God*. Vol. 2 of *Christian Origins and the People of God*. Minneapolis: Fortress, 1996.

———. *The New Testament and the People of God*. Vol. 1 of *Christian Origins and the Question of God*. Minneapolis: Fortress, 1992.

———. *Paul and the Faithfulness of God*, Vol. 4.1 of *Christian Origins and the Question of God*. Minneapolis: Fortress, 2013.

Wright, T. H. "Miracles." Pages 186–91 in vol. 2 of *A Dictionary of Christ and the Gospels*. Edited by James Hastings. Edinburgh: T&T Clark, 1908.

Xeravits, Géza G. *King, Priest, Prophet: Positive Eschatological Protagonists of the Qumran Library*. STDJ 47. Leiden: Brill, 2003.

Yadin-Israel, Azzan. "'For Mark Was Peter's *Tanna*': Tradition and Transmission in Papias and the Early Rabbis." *JECS* 23 (2015): 337–62.

Yarbro Collins, Adela. *Mark: A Commentary*. Hermeneia. Minneapolis: Fortress, 2007.

Yarbrough, Robert W. "The Date of Papias: A Reassessment." *JETS* 26 (1983): 181–91.

Yaron, Reuven. "The Climactic Tricolon." *JJS* 37 (1986): 153–59.

Yeung, Maureen W. *Faith in Jesus and Paul: A Comparison with Special Reference to "Faith That Can Remove Mountains" and "Your Faith Has Healed/Saved You."* WUNT 2/147. Tübingen: Mohr Siebeck, 2002.

Young, David E., and Jean-Guy Goulet. *Being Changed by Cross-Cultural Encounters: The Anthropology of Extraordinary Experience*. Peterborough: Broadview, 1994.

Zager, Werner. *Gottesherrschaft und Endgericht in der Verkündigung Jesu: Eine*

Untersuchung zur markinischen Jesusüberlieferung einschließlich der Q-Parallelen. BZNW 82. Berlin: de Gruyter, 1996.

Zahn, Theodor. *Introduction to the New Testament*. New York: Scribner's Sons, 1909.

Zaki, Pearl. *Our Lord's Mother Visits Egypt in 1968 and 1969*. Cairo: Dar El Alam El Arabi, 1977.

Zehnle, Richard F. *Peter's Pentecost Discourse: Tradition and Lukan Reinterpretation in Peter's Speeches of Acts 2 and 3*. SBLMS 15. Nashville: Abingdon, 1971.

Zeller, Dieter. "Bedeutung und religionsgeschichtlicher Hintergrund der Verwandlung Jesu (Markus 9:2–8)." Pages 303–21 in *Authenticating the Activities of Jesus*. Edited by Bruce Chilton and Craig A. Evans. NTTS 28.2. Leiden: Brill, 1999.

———. *Die weisheitlichen Mahnsprüche bei den Synoptikern*. FB 17. Würzburg: Echter, 1977.

———. "Jesus, Q und die Zukunft Israels." Pages 351–69 in *The Sayings Source Q and the Historical Jesus*. Edited by A. Lindemann. BETL 158. Leuven: Peeters, 2001.

Zeller, E. "Die Tübinger historische Schule." *Historisches Zeitschrift* 4 (1860): 90–173.

Zimmermann, Christine. "Women in Jesus' Entourage." Pages 323–30 in *The Jesus Handbook*. Edited by Jens Schröter and Christine Jacobi. Grand Rapids: Eerdmans, 2022.

Zimmermann, Ruben. "'Augenzeugenschaft' als historisches und hermeneutisches Konzept—nicht nur im Johannesevangelium." Pages 209–51 in *Wie Geschichten Geschichte Schreiben: Frühchristliche Literatur zwischen Faktualität und Fiktionalität*. Edited by Susanne Luther, Jörg Röder, and Eckart D. Schmidt. WUNT 2/395. Tübingen: Mohr Siebeck, 2015.

———. "Frühchristlichen Wundererzählungen—Eine Einführung." Pages 5–67 in vol. 1 of *Kompendium der frühchristlichen Wundererzählungen*. Edited by Ruben Zimmermann. Gütersloh: Gütersloher Verlagshaus, 2013–17.

———, ed. *Kompendium der frühchristlichen Wundererzählungen*. 2 vols. Gütersloh: Gütersloher, 2013–17.

———, ed. *Kompendium des Gleichnisse Jesu*. 2 vols. Gütersloh: Gütersloher, 2013–17.

———. "Memory and Jesus' Parables: J. P. Meier's Explosion and the Restoration of the 'Bedrock' of Jesus' Speech." *JSHJ* 16 (2018): 156–72.

———. *Puzzling the Parables of Jesus: Methods and Interpretation*. Minneapolis: Fortress, 2015.

Zmijewski, Josef. *Die Apostelgeschichte*. Regensburg: Pustet, 1994.

Zolondek, Michael Vicko. *The Quest for a Historical Jesus Methodology: Graeco-*

Roman Biographies, the Gospels, and the Practice of History. Eugene, OR: Pickwick, 2023.

———. *We Have Found the Messiah: How the Disciples Help Us Answer the Davidic Messianic Question*. Eugene, OR: Pickwick, 2016.

Zwiep, Arie W. "Haggadic Motifs in Acts 1–3." Pages 307–33 in *Haggadah in Early Judaism and the New Testament*. Edited by Roger David Aus. WUNT 461. Tübingen: Mohr Siebeck, 2021.

Index of Authors

Index of Subjects

Index of Scripture and Other Ancient Sources

Old Testament

Genesis

Exodus

Dead Sea Scrolls and Related Texts

Ancient Jewish Writers

Mishnah, Talmud, and Related Literature

Mishnah

Greco-Roman Literature